Autograph® '99

American Automobile Association

1000 AAA Drive, Heathrow, FL 32746-5063
ISBN 1-56251-281-1 • Stock No. 2295

Autograph®

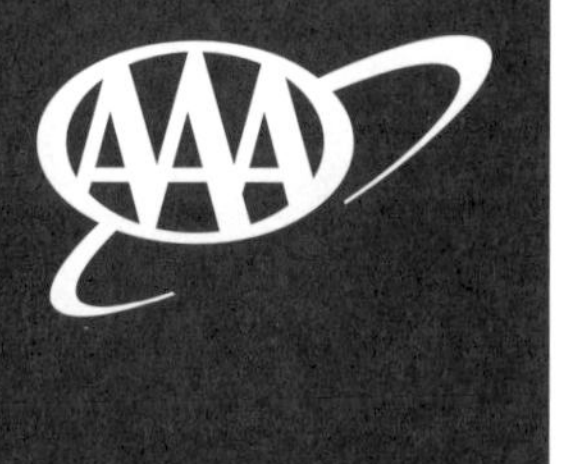

table of CONTENTS

Our Staff

All the vehicles in this book have been driven and evaluated by AAA's David Van Sickle. As a consultant to AAA, Eric LeFrançois, respected automototive journalist, has provided updating, editing and additional information to complete the evaluations.

David G. Van Sickle

Presently employed by the AAA as Director of Automotive and Consumer Information in the Washington, D.C. office. Responsible for providing information about automotive issues to the media. Writes and edits several AAA automotive publications.

Most recently held position of Director of Automotive Engineering at AAA's National Headquarters in Heathrow, Florida. Administered programs for automotive technical training, diagnostic testing, repair facility certification, and other automotive activities.

Prior to joining AAA, was employed by General Motors in a wide variety of positions, including engineering, manufacturing, assembly, and facility construction.

Holds Bachelor of Science Degree in Electrical Engineering, Member Society of Automotive Engineers, Vice President Washington Automotive

Press Association, Director National Institute of Automotive Service Excellence (ASE)

Éric LeFrançois

Éric LeFrançois heads an orginial and avant garde project: Cars on CD; the automobile section of Touring magazine, writes the editorial contents of the official magazine of the Montreal International Auto Show; produces a publication on winter driving, and contributes to several Canadian magazines.

Prior to journalism, he devoted his efforts to managing the Public Affairs activities of CAA-Québec in Montreal.

Holds a Bachelor in Specialized Communication.

Editor in Chief
Dave Van Sickle
AAA Automotive and Consumer Information

Managing Editor
Alan Borne

Technical Editor and Editorial Coordinator
Éric LeFrançois
AAA Cars on CD

Art Director
Chantal Messier

Photographers
Tony Glese
Eric LeFrançois
Dave Van Sickle

Contributing Writers
Marc Lachapelle
Tim Lindsay

Publisher
AAA

Project Management
SAJY PUBLISHERS Inc.

Data in Autograph™ were current when it went to press, and all information is complete to the best of our knowledge. Due to last-minute changes by automobile manufacturers in vehicle design, performance, and specifications, some data may change during the current model year. All recommendations are made without guarantees on the part of the publisher, and AAA disclaims all liability in connection with the use of this information.

Auto**graph**®

a word

FROM THE PRESIDENT

Welcome to AAA's AutoGraph '99

It's my pleasure to introduce you to AAA's AutoGraph '99. A new reader-friendly format, inclusion of the AAA Top Car Awards for 1999, and helpful new features make the point right away: This installment of AAA's indispensable review and rating of new cars, pickup trucks, sport-utility vehicles, and minivans is our best yet.

Since the first edition in 1990, AutoGraph has been an example of AAA's commitment to the motoring public. All vehicle makes and models appearing on these pages are carefully road-tested according to stringent AAA standards. Our reviews give special consideration to such crucial automotive safety features as air bags, antilock brakes, traction control, and keyless entry systems. AutoGraph exemplifies AAA's long-standing mission of public service and education with regard to auto-related issues.

AAA is committed to its role as an advocate on behalf of all motorists — not just our 41 million members. AAA is also a leader in safety as exemplified by our service programs: School's Open - Drive Carefully, the School Safety Patrol Lifesaving Award, as well as the development of driver improvement and child passenger safety seat training programs.

AutoGraph '99 will give you up-to-date information on vehicle insurance, the buy vs. lease decision, choosing the proper child safety seat (they're required in every state), and tips on how to be a savvy safety shopper. There's even a look at how to avoid the disturbing phenomenon of road rage.

I'm sure you'll find the 1999 edition a valuable addition to your personal bookshelf. For help with any other motoring or travel needs, visit the AAA club nearest you.

Safe Driving!

Robert L. Darbelnet
AAA President and CEO

Choosing the right vehicle

Smart shopping for your next new car begins with analyzing the car you have now. What do you like most about it? What do you like least? Before you visit a dealership, list your expectations for the new car as specifically as possible in order of priority.

In a family car, the primary driver should set the standards, but everyone should have a say—especially part-time drivers. Consider the factors below when you assess your needs.

Size & Body Style

How many people will ride in the car regularly? Compact, two-door coupes do well for singles, small families, and lone commuters. These cars can be economical and easy to park, but they usually offer little room in the back seat or trunk. If you're considering a coupe and plan to carry three children regularly in the back seat, check the number of safety belts; some two-door coupes have no belt for the center-rear position.

Convertibles offer the unique pleasure of open-air driving on nice days, but you have to live, with their impracticalities in all kinds of weather. Soft tops require more upkeep, invite theft and let in a lot of noise. Plastic rear windows scratch and discolor with age or abuse and hamper visibility. Folding tops take up trunk space, too. (See list on p. 9)

Four-door sedans carry five to six people, with easy access to the back seat. A four-door version of a car often costs less to insure than a two-door version of the same car. Also, if ride quality matters to you, consider the car's wheelbase. Generally, the shorter the wheelbase, the more you'll feel bumps and rough spots on the road.

Station wagons may be making a comeback. Also, are hatchbacks really larger than sedans, or is the back just more convenient to reach?

Perhaps record: Families with children might consider a vihicle with more room or easier access to the back. Station wagons and hatchbacks offer such advantages. (see lists, p.9).

Minivans combine car-like ride and handling with some van-like roominess and versatility. They typically offer seating for up to seven people and have removable or folding seats for carrying cargo. Larger minivans offer even more interior room, but their longer wheelbases compromise the handling and maneuverability of a true minivan. Truck-based and full-size vans are quite roomy and, properly equipped, can tow large trailers. However, because such vehicles are built on a truck chassis, their ride, handling maneuverability may not be as smooth as in a passenger car or minivan.

Sport-utility vehicles (SUVs) have been called "the station wagons of the '90s." With four-wheel drive and high ground clearance, these truck-based vehicles can go on snowy or muddy roads, or no roads at all. Their go-anywhere versatility, combined with rugged looks and roominess, appeals to hunters, sports enthusiasts, and families who like back-country camping. As everyday transportation, however, SUVs can't match the ride, cornering ability, or overall agility of a car. Their high ground clearance makes entry and exit difficult. A few insurance companies are increasing the liability rates for larger vehicles like SUVs, which may mean higher insurance bills. And, if you're considering four-wheel drive, weigh its benefits and drawbacks (see below). Most SUVs are available in two-wheel-drive versions, which are less expensive to buy and own.

Drivetrains

Front-, rear-, or four-wheel drive? Different drivetrains make a big difference.

■ Front-wheel drive, the most common design on today's cars, permits a roomier interior by eliminating the transmission hump in the center and allowing carmakers to mount the engine sideways, which reduces the

size of the engine compartment. Front-wheel drive also improves starting traction in snow. The design's disadvantages show up in more difficult steering and handling, however; front-wheel-drive cars are more prone to front-wheel skids in which the driver loses steering control. Many also suffer from "torque steer"—the tendency to pull to one side during sudden, hard acceleration.

■ Rear-wheel-drive cars steer much more easily than those with front-wheel drive, because one set of wheels guides the car while the other set powers it. Good snow tires or a traction control system can offset rear-wheel drive's disadvantages in snow.

■ Four-wheel drive (4WD), a common option on most trucks and minivans and on a few passenger cars, sends power to all four wheels. Part-time 4WD, the least expensive design, can be used only on surfaces that allow some wheel slippage. It has no center differential to allow the front and rear axles to turn at different rates, so the slippage must occur at the tires. Using part-time 4WD on roads with good traction will damage the system and wear the tires rapidly.

Full-time 4WD incorporates a center differential, so it can be used at will or not at all. Some vehicles switch from 2WD to 4WD either manually (when you decide) or automatically (when sensors detect wheel slippage). Automatic 4WD works much like a traction control system, giving you traction when you need it but minimizing gas consumption and wear and tear on the system.

All-wheel drive (AWD), the system used in passenger cars, is permanent, full-time 4WD; you cannot disengage it to run in 2WD. Some AWD trucks have an additional two-speed transmission with extra-low gearing for going up and down steep hills off-road. Such a transmission is standard with full- and part-time 4WD.

Although 4WD and AWD improve traction for driving on slippery surfaces, they don't improve stopping. Also, the added weight and complexity of these systems make these vehicles more expensive to buy and to own. Consider a traction control system or a good set of snow tires as a more cost-effective way to improve traction on snowy roads.

Equipment

Choosing from the list of available equipment on your car will depend on your priorities and budget. Here are some general guidelines:

■ **Engine.** Smaller-displacement engines get better gas mileage, but they're generally noisier. Larger engines are more expensive in initial cost and usually in fuel consumption, but provide more power for acceleration, climbing inclines, towing, and hauling passengers and cargo.

■ **Transmission.** Avoid three-speed automatic transmissions; they increase engine noise and highway gas consumption. With four and five-speed automatic transmissions, engines run more quietly and use less gas. When used properly, manual transmissions are the most economical and give the driver more control, but they demand constant attention to shifting in city and suburban driving. The fuel efficiency of automatic transmissions has improved so much that most people have no reason to consider a manual, except in a sports car or small economy car, where shifting manually helps extract the engine's power.

■ **Suspension.** Up-to-date cars have four-wheel independent suspension for a smoother, more comfortable ride. Sport suspension (usually offered as an option) gives a stiffer, less comfortable ride, but improves a car's handling by reducing body lean in turns and emergency lane changes. Some cars offer adjustable suspension, which lets you choose the ride and handling characteristics.

■ **Brakes.** Disc brakes on all four wheels perform better than front-disc/rear-drum combinations. Four-wheel antilock brakes enhance safety by allowing the driver to maintain steering control during sudden, hard stops.

■ **Safety/Security.** Insist on a rear-window defroster and a side mirror on the passenger's door. (This basic equipment improves visibility but is still an option on some economy models.) Some upscale cars have run-flat tires (which can be driven for limited distances with no air pressure) or limp-home cooling systems (which allow the engine to run on limited power without overheating even after losing all its coolant). Many cars now offer global positioning and on-board navigation systems (electronic mapping displays that guide you to your destination); some even use satellite communications to pinpoint the location of your car and send help in an emergency breakdown or collision.

If you have a young child, be sure the car you choose can accommodate a safety seat. (The next chapter, "Shopping for Safety," discusses child restraints in more detail.)

■ **Amenities.** Air conditioning is now expected everywhere. Without it, your car's resale value will be lower. Other extras to consider are antitheft systems, high-quality audio systems, and power seats, windows, and locks.

Fuel Economy

By law, every new car must carry a window sticker with gas mileage estimates from the Environmental Protection Agency (EPA). The label spells out projected fuel economy for city and highway driving, annual fuel costs (based on driving 15,000 miles a year and paying $1.20 per gallon for regular or $1.40 per gallon for premium), and the average fuel economy for similar cars.

Note: The EPA ratings are only estimates to help you compare models. The exact gas mileage will depend on your driving habits and upkeep.

Was It Made in the USA?

The federal government requires all new cars and light trucks to carry a content label specifying where that particular vehicle was assembled and where its engine and transmission were made. The label also shows the percentage of parts from U.S./Canadian suppliers and from suppliers in other countries. In interpreting this information, keep in mind that the label includes only the value of parts—not assembly labor or sales, marketing, and transportation. Furthermore, the label shows the average parts content for that vehicle line—not the particular car to which the label is attached.

Finally, in some cases a mathematical formula—not the actual cost—may have been used to determine the value of a part, depending on whether it came from a wholly owned subsidiary of a U.S./Canadian carmaker.

Warranties

The basic, or bumper-to-bumper, warranty covers the whole vehicle, sometimes even the tires. The powertrain warranty covers the engine, transmission, and driveline. The corrosion warranty covers rust-through—visible holes in the body panels. With any warranty, carefully compare the length of coverage (in mileage or time), deductibles, and exclusions. To keep your coverage valid you must maintain the vehicle as specified in the owner's manual. Scheduled preventive maintenance is your cost; keep detailed records and receipts.

The federal government mandates an emissions control warranty for every car and light truck to protect systems that affect air quality. The basic warranty covers repair of all emissions-control and related parts for 2 years/ 24,000 miles. Major components such as the catalytic converter and the electronic units that store and process emissions-related information are covered for 8 years/80,000 miles.

An extended warranty, or service contract, is actually car repair insurance. Unlike insurance, however, it usually can't be canceled for a refund of the unused premium. With most new-car warranties, you probably don't need it. If you want to consider the additional protection, first, compare the extended warranty side by side with the manufacturer's basic warranty. Make sure you understand precisely who backs the service contract: the car's manufacturer, the dealer, or an independent company? Also ask where repairs will be performed and whether deductibles apply.

Extended warranties from dealers can add $1,000 to the price of a new car. You can probably either negotiate a lower price with the dealer or consult your local AAA club or insurance carrier for a better bargain.

Where to find

Shopping | for safety

Carmakers know that safety sells. According to recent surveys, two out of every three shoppers consider safety a primary factor in choosing a new vehicle. Recognizing such overwhelming consumer demand—and responding to stronger government regulations—automakers have continually improved not only the crashworthiness of their cars, but also features to help drivers avoid crashes in the first place.

Thanks to federal mandates all passenger cars now have improved door reinforcements to better withstand side impact. All '99 passenger cars have air bags for both the driver and front-seat passenger; all light trucks, including minivans and sport-utility vehicles, must have dual air bags by next year.

Consumer demand also has made cars safer. High-tech features such as antilock brakes—once confined to expensive luxury cars—are now available on cars in every price range, although they may be considered an option.

Avoiding a Crash

The best way to survive an accident is not to have one. That's why quick acceleration, stable handling, and precise, responsive steering are essential safety attributes they help you control the vehicle in an emergency.

■ Antilock brakes won't improve a car's stopping distance, but they will help you maintain steering control during sudden, hard braking, especially on slippery roads. With an antilock brake system (ABS), you don't need to pump the brakes. By keeping a steady, firm pressure on the pedal with your toes, you activate an automatic system that "pumps" the brakes for you when necessary—a slight pulsation when you press the pedal tells you the system is working.

Some safety experts recently have questioned the benefit of antilock brakes; statistics on the frequency and severity of collisions fail to show a significant difference between cars with antilock brakes and cars without them. (In fact, some studies show a higher incidence of single-vehicle, run-off-the-road incidents for ABS-equipped cars.) Other experts, however, claim that such statistics are misleading. Many drivers are still unfamiliar with antilock technology, and they haven't yet changed their old habits; they still pump the brakes in a panic stop, which effectively shuts off the antilock system.

Some pickup trucks still have an antilock system on the rear wheels only, which doesn't provide the steering control of four-wheel ABS. AAA strongly suggests that you settle for nothing less than full, four-wheel antilock brakes on any new vehicle.

■ Traction control, offered on many new models, prevents the drive wheels from spinning on slippery surfaces by applying the brakes, reducing the engine power, or both. Traction control is particularly useful for starting on slick surfaces or maintaining control on wet or icy roads.

■ Stability control takes traction control a step further to help drivers regain control in a skid. The system senses lateral movement in a turn and applies a single wheel's brake as necessary to maintain stability. Although this won't allow you to take turns faster, it does help you recover from a mistake in a front or rear-wheel skid. It's available this year on several upscale models.

■ Daytime running lights (DRLs) operate a car's front lights whenever the engine is on. Research shows that making a car more conspicuous to other drivers significantly reduces head-on and front-corner collisions. They have been required for years on cars in Canada and certain Scandinavian countries, and many carmakers include them as standard equipment on cars sold in the U.S. Usually, DRLs operate the headlights at 80 percent power to conserve bulb life; switching on your headlights boosts them to full power at night.

Other lights (rear fog lights, directional signals on the front fenders, and cornering lights on the side) also can make a car more visible and less likely to be hit by inattentive drivers.

Surviving a Crash

Several factors improve the chances of you and your passengers surviving a collision.

■ Size matters. Generally, bigger cars have much lower fatality and injury rates than smaller cars.

■ Lap-and-shoulder belts are still the single best protection available—but only if they're used. Two innovations make safety belts more comfortable and effective. First, adjustable-height shoulder-belt anchors (available on some cars) allow you get a correct, comfortable fit regardless of your size. Second, automatic pretensioners (also available on more and more cars) spool up slack in a split-second after a crash; an electronic system senses crash forces and instantly tightens the belt for a snug fit and better protection.

■ Air bags, when used with safety belts, dramatically improve your chances of surviving a frontal crash. The National Highway Traffic Administration (NHTSA) credits air bags with saving about 2,000 lives over the past decade. Many models in all price ranges now offer door-, pillar-, or roof-mounted air bags for better protection in side-impact crashes.

Nevertheless, many people doubt the safety of air bags, particularly for short adults. Fueling those doubts have been reports that scores of children and adults have died in minor or moderately severe crashes in which the air bag deployed. Only a few of the adults were wearing lap-and-shoulder belts, but most of the victims who were properly restrained were shorter than average. Safety experts emphasize that suspected air bag-related fatalities are extremely rare; they say that the statistics reinforce the importance of wearing safety belts, driving in a proper position (at least 12 inches away from the steering wheel), and placing all children age 12 and under in the back seat.

To allay consumer concerns, the government has permitted carmakers to reduce the deployment force of air bags by 20 to 35 percent. Some '99 models have these so-called "second-generation," "next-generation," or "depowered" air bags. However, federal regulations do not provide guidelines for labeling cars equipped with reduced-force air bags.

NHTSA crash-test rating

	Frontal		Side	
	Driver	Front passenger	Driver	Rear passenger
Acura Integra	★★★★	★★★	NT	NT
Acura SLX	★★★	★★★	NT	NT
Acura 3.2 TL	★★★★	★★★★	NT	NT
Audi A4 S	★★★★	★★★★★	NT	NT
Audi A8 4.2 Quattro	★★★★★	★★★★★	NT	NT
BMW 318Ti	★★★★	★★★★	NT	NT
Buick Century	NT	NT	★★★	★★★
Buick Le Sabre	★★★★	★★★★	★★★	★★★
Buick Park Avenue	★★★★★	★★★	NT	NT
Buick Regal	NT	NT	★★★	★★★
Cadillac De Ville	★★★★	★★★★	★★★★	★★★★
Cadillac Eldorado	★★★★	★★★★	NT	NT
Cadillac Seville	★★★★	★★★★	NT	NT
Chevrolet Astro	★★★	★★★	NT	NT
Chevrolet Blazer	★★★★	★★★★	NT	NT
Chevrolet Camaro	★★★★	★★★★★	★★★	★★★★
Chevrolet Cavalier	★★★★	★★★★	★	★★★
Chevrolet Lumina	★★★★	★★★★★	★★★★	★★★
Chevrolet Malibu	★★★★	★★★★	★	★★★
Chevrolet Metro	★★★★	★★★★	NT	NT
Chevrolet Monte Carlo	★★★★	★★★★	NT	NT
Chevrolet Prizm	★★★★	★★★★	★★★	★★★
Chevrolet S10	★★★★	★★★★	NT	NT
Chevrolet Suburban	★★★★	★★★★	NT	NT
Chevrolet Tahoe	★★★★	★★★★	NT	NT
Chevrolet Venture	★★★★	★★★	NT	NT
Chrysler Cirrus	★★★	★★★★	★★★	★★
Chrysler Sebring	★★★★★	★★★★★	NT	NT
Chrysler Town-Country	★★★	★★★	NT	NT
Chrysler Sebring Cabriolet	★★★★	★★★★	NT	NT
Chrysler Concorde	★★★★	★★★★	NT	NT
Dodge Avenger	★★★★★	★★★★★	NT	NT
Dodge Dakota	★★★★	★★★★	NT	NT
Dodge Durango	★★	★★★	NT	NT
Dodge Caravan	★★★★	★★★★	NT	NT
Dodge Intrepid	★★★★	★★★★	NT	NT
Dodge Neon	★★★	★★★★	★★	★★★
Dodge RAM 1500	★★★★	★★★★	NT	NT
Dodge Ram Wagon	★★★	★★★★	NT	NT
Dodge Stratus	★★★	★★★★	★★★	★★
Ford Contour	★★★★★	★★★★	★★★	★★★★
Ford Crown Victoria	★★★★★	★★★★★	★★★★	★★★★
Ford Econoline	★★★	★★★★	NT	NT
Ford Escort	★★★	★★★	★★★	★★★
Ford Expedition	★★★★	★★★★	NT	NT
Ford Explorer	★★★★	★★★★	NT	NT
Ford F150	★★★★★	★★★★	NT	NT
Ford Mustang	★★★★★	★★★★	★★★	★★★
Ford Ranger	★★★★	★★★★	NT	NT
Ford Taurus	★★★★	★★★★	★★★	★★★
Ford Windstar	★★★★★	★★★★★	NT	NT
GMC Sierra Classic & 1500	★★★★	★★★	NT	NT
Hondo Civic 3 doors	★★★★	★★★★	★★	★★★
Honda Accord	★★★★	★★★★	★★★★	★★★★
Hondo CR-V	★★★★	★★★★★	NT	NT
Honda Passport	★★★	★★★★	NT	NT
Hyundai Accent	★★★	★★★★	NT	NT
Hyundai Elantra	★★★	★★★	NT	NT
Hyundai Sonata	★★★	★★★★	NT	NT
Infiniti I30	★★★★	★★★★	★★★★	★★★
Infiniti QX4	★★★	★★★	NT	NT
Isuzu Hombre SpaceCab	★★★★	★★★★	NT	NT
Isuzu Rodeo	★★★	★★★★	NT	NT
Isuzu Trooper	★★★	★★★	NT	NT
Jeep Cherokee 2 doors	★★★	★★★	NT	NT
Jeep Grand Cherokee	★★★	★★★	NT	NT
Jeep Wrangler	★★★★	★★★★★	NT	NT
Kia Sephia	★★★	★★★	NT	NT
Kia sportage	★★★	★★★	NT	NT
Land RoverDiscovery	★★★	★★★	NT	NT
Lexus ES300	★★★★	★★★★	★★★★★	★★★★
Lincoln Navigator	★★★★	★★★★	NT	NT
Lincoln Town Car	★★★★★	NT	NT	NT
Mazda 626	★★★★	★★★★★	★★★	★★★
Mazda SERIE B	★★★★	★★★★	NT	NT
Mazda Millenia	★★★★	★★★★★	NT	NT
Mercedes C280	★★★★	★★★★	★★★	★★★★
Mercedes E430 E300DT E320	★★★★	★★★★	NT	NT
Mercedes ML320	★★★★	★★★★★	NT	NT
Mercury GrandMarquis	★★★★★	★★★★★	★★★★	★★★★
Mercury Mountainer	★★★★	★★★★	NT	NT
Mercury Mystique	★★★★★	★★★★	★★★	★★★★
Mercury Sable	★★★★★	★★★★★	★★★	★★★
Mitsubishi Eclipse	★★★★	★★★★	NT	NT
Mitsubishi Montero sport	★★★	★★★	NT	NT
Nissan Altima	★★★	★★	★★★	★★★
Nissan Frontier 4x2	★★★	★★★★	NT	NT
Nissan Maxima	★★★★	★★★★	★★★★	★★★
Nissan Pathfinder	★★★	★★★	NT	NT
Nissan Sentra	★★★	★★★★	★★★	★★★
Oldsmobile Aurora	★★★	★★★	NT	NT
Oldsmobile Bravada	★★★★	★★★★	NT	NT
Oldsmobile Intrigue	★★★★	★★★	★★★	★
Oldsmobile Silhouette	★★★★	★★★	NT	NT
Plymouth Breeze	★★★	★★★★	★★★	★★
Plymouth Voyager	★★★★	★★★★	NT	NT
Pontiac Bonneville	★★★★★	★★★	★★★	★★
Pontiac Firebird	★★★★	★★★★★	★★★	★★★★
Pontiac Grand Prix	★★★★	★★★★	NT	NT
Pontiac Sunfire	★★★	★★★★	★	★★
Pontiac Trans Sport	★★★★	★★★	NT	NT
Saab 9-3	★★★★	★★★★	NT	NT
Saturn SC1 SL SW	★★★★★	★★★★	★★★	★★★
Subaru Impreza	★★★★	★★★★	NT	NT
Subaru Legacy	★★★★	★★★★	★★★	NT
Suzuki Swift	★★★★	★★★★	NT	NT
Toyota Runner	★★★	★★★	NT	NT
Toyota Avalon	★★★★	★★★★★	★★★★★	★★★★
Toyota Camry	★★★★	★★★★★	★★★	★★★
Toyota Corolla	★★★★	★★★★	★★★	★★★
Toyota Sienna	★★★★★	★★★★★	NT	NT
Toyota Tacoma Xtracab	★★★★	★★★	NT	NT
Volkswagen Golf 5 doors	★★★	★★★	NT	NT
Volkswagen Jetta	★★★	★★★	★★★	★★
Volvo C70	★★★★★	★★★★★	★★★★	NT

NT: Not tested

Star system

NHTSA uses a "star system" to rate vehicles' crashworthiness as measured in front- and side-impact tests. The stars represent the level of crash protection in various seating positions—the more stars, the better the protection relative to other vehicles of similar weight.

Some manufacturers plan to use a sticker to identify them.

Safety experts stress that disconnecting an air bag is not only unwise, but also illegal.

■ Child safety seats are required for young children in every state. In many cars and minivans, the rear seat conceals an integrated child safety seat that can be opened and used as necessary. Integrated safety seats solve an important safety problem facing parents: getting a store-bought safety seat to fit properly in the car. To protect the child fully, a safety seat must be installed so that it doesn't move when you tug it firmly side to side or forward and back. It should seem embedded in the car's seat. Studies show that 80 percent or more of all child safety seats are installed incorrectly, putting children at risk unnecessarily in a crash. Always follow the manufacturer's instructions when installing a safety seat.

Never put a rear-facing infant seat (for babies less than a year old and under 20 pounds) in the front seat of a car with passenger air bag; the air bag could gravely injure the infant when it deploys in a crash. Two-seaters and pickups, where children in rear-facing safety seats must ride in the front, may have a switch to deactivate the air bag.

All children 12 years of age and under, especially those in safety seats, should ride in the rear whenever possible. But in some cars, safety seats don't fit there: the car's seat cushion may be too deeply contoured, or the distance between the lap belt anchors is too narrow. In other cars, you may need additional hardware or supplemental belts, depending on the design of the safety belts.

Be sure the car you choose can accommodate a safety seat if your child needs one. Take the seat with you on the test drive and try to install it according to the safety seat manufacturer's directions and the instructions in the car's owner's manual.

Getting a **good deal**

Getting the right car at the right price isn't an impossible dream. With research, patience, and persistence, you can get the deal you want. Before you begin your search, know the exact model and options you want and follow these handy tips.

Alternatives to Haggling

If you hate to negotiate the price of a new car, there are other ways to buy.

■ **One-price dealers.** About 2,000 U.S. dealerships have adopted "one-price" selling. They discount the manufacturer's list price, post the discounted price, and don't negotiate. Because of this practice, they're sometimes called "no-dicker-sticker" dealers.

■ **Buying services.** If you specify the make, model, and equipment, a buying service or professional shopper will acquire a car for you. These services may negotiate on your behalf, or buy the car at a contracted discount, or give you a certificate to exchange at a dealer. Some services require you to pay a fee; others get a commission from the dealer. Most AAA clubs offer car-buying help or can refer you to a service.

■ **On-line buying.** The World Wide Web and the major commercial on-line services offer what are essentially buying services in cyberspace. You can order a car at a discount and pick it up at a participating dealer. Some of these services charge a fee.

Pricing

The manufacturer's suggested retail price (MSRP), or the "sticker price" posted on the window, includes a markup between 7 and 20 percent on the base price of the car. The sticker prices of factory-installed options include markups as high as 25 percent; dealer-installed options may carry even higher markups. Carmakers usually group some options in "packages," offering the group at a lower price than you would pay if you bought each item separately. Although the option package discount is often substantial, it still includes a sizable dealer profit; furthermore, you might be forced to get equipment you don't want or need as part of the package. Some dealers even add a second sticker to the car, specifying extras such as rustproofing, which add on dealer profit.

Smart shoppers never settle for the sticker price (except at a one-price dealer); they research the invoice price—what the dealer paid for the car and the options. You can find the invoice price by consulting a pricing guide (available at your bank or the reference desk of most public libraries) or by using a pricing service. For a fee, a pricing service will give you the most up-to-date invoice prices for the car, factory-installed options, and option packages. Check with your AAA club for a pricing service.

Next, calculate the value of your trade-in. Again, your bank or public library can provide used-car pricing guides, your local AAA club may offer a used-car pricing service, or you can have the car appraised.

Financing

Walking into a dealership with pre-approved financing gives you a negotiating advantage.

Know your limits: the down payment you can make and the monthly payment that fits your budget. Monthly payments are determined not only by the principal (the amount you borrow) but also by the term (the length of the loan) and the interest rate. The longer the term, the lower the monthly payment, but the higher the total cost of the loan. Choosing the shortest possible term with a monthly payment you can afford will reduce the total cost of the loan.

Shop around for the best interest rate. Your bank, credit union, or local AAA club are good sources.

1999 Automotive Twins

Automotive "twins" are vehicles that have different nameplates but share a drivetrain and chassis. They may even come off the same assembly line. One twin may offer different equipment or a better deal in the marketplace than the other.

Small cars

■ Dodge Neon – Plymouth Neon
■ Ford Escort – Ford ZX2 – Mercury Tracer
■ Chevrolet Metro – Suzuki Swift
■ Chevrolet Prizm – Toyota Corolla
■ Saturn SC – Saturn SL – Saturn SW
■ Volkswagen Golf – Volkswagen Jetta – Volkswagen New Beetle

Mid-size cars

■ Acura CL – Honda Accord
■ Acura Integra – Honda Civic
■ Chevrolet Cavalier – Pontiac Sunfire
■ Chevrolet Malibu – Oldsmobile Cutlass
■ Pontiac Grand AM – Oldsmobile Alero
■ Chrysler Cirrus – Dodge Stratus – Plymouth Breeze
■ Ford Contour – Mercury Mystique – Mercury Cougar
■ Hyundai Elantra – Hyundai Tiburon
■ Infiniti I30 – Nissan Maxima –
■ Toyota Camry – Toyota Camry Solara
■ Chrysler Sebring – Dodge Avenger

Large cars

■ Chrysler 300M – Chrysler LHS
■ Buick Century – Buick Regal – Oldsmobile Intrigue – Pontiac Grand Prix
■ Buick LeSabre – Pontiac Bonneville
■ Chevrolet Lumina – Chevrolet Monte Carlo
■ Chrysler Concorde – Dodge Intrepid
■ Ford Crown Victoria – Mercury Grand Marquis
■ Ford Taurus – Mercury Sable
■ Oldsmobile Aurora – Buick Park Avenue – Cadillac Seville
■ Jaguar Type S – Lincoln LS

Sporty cars

■ Chevrolet Camaro – Pontiac Firebird
■ Chrysler Sebring – Dodge Avenger

Vans and Minivans

■ Chevrolet Astro – GMC Safari
■ Chevrolet Express – GMC Savana
■ Chevrolet Venture – Oldsmobile Silhouette – Pontiac Montana
■ Chrysler Town & Country LX – Dodge Grand Caravan – Plymouth Grand Voyager
■ Chrysler Town & Country SX – Dodge Caravan – Plymouth Voyager
■ Mercury Villager – Nissan Quest

Trucks and Sport-Utility vehicles

■ Acura SLX – Isuzu Trooper
■ Chevrolet Blazer – GMC Jimmy – Oldsmobile Bravada
■ Chevrolet Silverado – GMC Sierra Pickups
■ Chevrolet S10 – GMC Sonoma – Isuzu Hombre
■ Chevrolet Suburban – GMC Suburban
■ Chevrolet Tahoe – GMC Yukon
■ Chevrolet Tracker – Suzuki Vitara
■ Ford Expedition – Lincoln Navigator
■ Ford Explorer – Mercury Mountaineer
■ Ford Ranger – Mazda B-series Pickup
■ Honda Passport – Isuzu Rodeo
■ Infiniti QX4 – Nissan Pathfinder
■ Lexus LX 470 – Toyota Land Cruiser

Staying within your budget

Negotiating

When you know the invoice price of the car and its options, the value of your trade-in and the best available financing rates, you're ready to deal.

■ **Visit more than one dealer.** Shop around for the best deal, and consider a "twin". Consult the list of "Automotive Twins" (at left) to see whether the car you want is offered under another name. You may find better safety equipment, a better combination of standard equipment and available options and—more important—a better deal.

■ **Use the invoice price, not the sticker, as the basis for negotiating.** You can expect to add a reasonable dealer profit to the invoice price. How much is "reasonable"? That depends on the demand for the car and the local market. The more popular the car, the greater the demand—and the higher the price a dealer can demand.

■ **Focus on one item at a time.** Salespeople sometimes jump back and forth from trade-in to financing to price until the whole negotiation blurs in your mind. Take your time, consider each part of the deal separately and know precisely how the figures compare with your research.

■ **Know the power of "No."** A salesperson never wants a serious prospect to walk out without buying a car, because that prospect may not come back. The word "no" is your strongest negotiating tool.

■ **Keep your cool.** In making any deal, the party who best controls his or her emotions usually controls the negotiation. You may be left waiting for long periods while the salesperson gets the sales manager to approve a proposed deal. Recognize the tactic for what it is: a way to make you anxious. Whenever you feel frustrated, pressured or angry, take a walk and regain your composure.

■ **Double check the contract before you sign.** Be sure the figures are the ones you've agreed to. Check the vehicle identification number (VIN) to be sure the car you want is the one specified on the contract. Before you take delivery, take time to inspect the vehicle carefully in good light to be sure the color and equipment are what you ordered.

For easy reference, the chart below groups the models reviewed in Autograph by price. On each review, a price range at the upper right of the page indicates the approximate extent of the prices within that model line.

Under 12,500	
Chevrolet Metro	62
Daewoo Lanos	70
Hyundai Accent	100
Hyndai Elantra	101
Kia Sephia	118
Saturn SL/SW	185
Suzuki Swift	192

$12,500 - $15,000	
Chevrolet Cavalier	47
Chevrolet S10	55
Daewoo Nubira	70
Dodge Neon	76
Ford Escort	83
Ford Ranger	88
GMC Sonoma	93
Honda Civic	95
Hyundai Tiburon	103
Isuzu Hombre	109
Mazda B-Series	133
Mazda Protegé	137
Mitsubishi Mirage	157
Nissan Frontier	161
Nissan Sentra	165
Pontiac Sunfire	178
Saturn SC	184
Suzuki Esteem	189
Toyota Corolla	197
Toyota Tacoma	203
Volkswagen Golf	205

$15,000 - $20,000	
Buick Century	35
Chevrolet Astro	44
Chevrolet C/K Pickup	56
Chevrolet Camaro	46
Chevrolet Lumina	50
Chevrolet Malibu	51
Chevrolet Monte Carlo	53
Chevrolet Prizm	54
Chevrolet Silverado	56
Chevrolet Tracker	60
Daewoo Leganza	70
Dodge Avenger	71
Dodge Dakota	72
Dodge Ram	77
Dodge Stratus	79
Ford Contour	80
Ford F-Series	86
Ford Mustang	87
Ford Taurus	89
GMC Sierra	91
Honda Accord	94
Honda CR-V	96
Hyundai Sonata	102
Isuzu Rodeo	110
Jeep Cherokee	115
Jeep Wrangler	117
Kia Sportage	119
Mazda 626	132
Mercury Cougar	146
Mercury Mystique	150
Mitsubishi Eclipse	155
Mitsubishi Galant	156
Mitsubishi Montero Sport	159
Nissan Altima	160
Oldsmobile Alero	166
Plymouth Breeze	171
Plymouth Voyager	173
Pontiac Grand Am	176
Subaru Impreza	187
Subaru Legacy	188
Suzuki Grand Vitara	190
Toyota Camry	195
Toyota Prius	199
Toyota Rav 4	200
Volkswagen New Beetle	208
Volkswagen Jetta	206

$20,000 - $25,000	
Acura CL	20
Acura Integra	21
BMW 3 Series	30
Buick Le Sabre	36
Buick Regal	38
Chevrolet Blazer	45
Chevrolet Express	49
Chevrolet Venture	61
Chrysler Cirrus	65
Chrysler Concorde	66
Dodge Grand Caravan	74
Dodge Intrepid	75
Dodge Ram Wagon	78
Ford Econoline	82
Ford Crown Victoria	81
Ford Explorer	85
Ford Windstar	90
GMC Jimmy	92
GMC Safari	92
GMC Savana	92
Honda Passport	98
Honda Prelude	99
Mazda Miata	134
Mercury Grand Marquis	148
Mercury Sable	151
Mercury Villager	152
Nissan Maxima	162
Nissan Quest	164
Oldsmobile Intrigue	169
Oldsmobile Silhouette	170
Pontiac Bonneville	174
Pontiac Firebird	175
Pontiac Grand Prix	177
Pontiac Montana	179
Subaru Forester	186
Toyota 4 Runner	193
Toyota Solara	202
Toyota Celica	196
Toyota Sienna	201
Wolkswagen Passat	207

$25,000 - $30,000	
Acura TL	24
Audi A4	26
Chevrolet Suburban	58
Chevrolet Tahoe	59
Chrysler Sebring	67
Chrysler Town & Country	69
Chrysler Sebring Cab.	68
Dodge Durango	73
Infiniti G20	104
Isuzu Trooper	111
Jeep Grand Cherokee	116
Mazda Millenia	136
Mercury Mountaineer	149
Mitsubishi 3000GT	153
Mitsubishi Diamante	154
Nissan Pathfinder	163
Saab 9-3	182
Toyota Avalon	194
Volvo V70	212

$30,000 - $35,000	
Audi TT	29
BMW Z3	34
Buick Park Avenue	37
Cadillac Catera	39
Chrysler 300M	62
Chrysler LHS	64
Ford Expedition	84
GMC Yukon	93
Infiniti I30	106
Lexus ES 300	122
Lexus RX300	126
Mercedes-Benz C-Class	138
Oldsmobile Bravada	168
Volkswagen Eurovan	204

$35,000 - $40,000	
Acura SLX	23
Audi A6	27
Cadillac De Ville	40
Cadillac Eldorado	41
Infiniti QX4	108
Land Rover Discovery	120
Lexus GS	123
Mercedes-Benz M-Class	142
Mitsubishi Montero	158
Oldsmobile Aurora	167
Plymouth Prowler	172
Saab 9-5 Wagon	183

$40,000 - $50,000	
Acura RL	22
BMW 5-Series	33
Cadillac Escalade	42
Cadillac Seville	43
Chevrolet Corvette	48
Infiniti Q45	107
Lexus SC	127
Lincoln Continental	129
Lincoln Navigator	130
Lincoln Town Car	131
Mercedes-Benz CLK	140
Mercedes-Benz E-Class	141
Mercedes-Benz SLK	145
Porsche Boxster	181
Toyota Land Cruiser	198
Volvo C70	211
Volvo S80	210

Over $50,000	
Acura NSX	214
Aston Martin DB7	215
Audi A8	28
BMW 7-Series	33
Dodge Viper	216
Ferrari 550 Maranello	218
Ferrari F355	217
Ferrari F456M	219
Jaguar XK8	114
Jaguar XJ	113
Lamborghini Diablo	220
Lexus LS 400	124
Lexus LX 470	125
Lotus Esprit	221
Mercedes C43	139
Mercedes S Class	143
Mercedes-Benz SL	144
Porsche 911	180
Land Rover Range Rover	121

Negotiating a lease

Just a few years ago, many consumers discovered leasing as a way to drive status symbol cars for little money up front and relatively low monthly payments.

Before you consider leasing, ask yourself two questions: First, do you expect to keep the car for more than three years? Second, do you drive more than 15,000 miles a year? If you answered "yes" to one or both of those questions, you're probably better off buying. Although agreements can include purchase options, you're not building equity and the car's ultimate price is determined when you sign the lease, either by negotiation or by predetermined tables. (Most leases also include penalties for early termination.) And nearly all leases charge 15 cents or more for each mile over an annual allowance (usually, 12,000 to 15,000 miles) and require you to pay for "excessive wear." If you don't want to drive a new car every three years, if you put more miles on a car than average, or if you're harder on a car than average, a lease isn't for you.

A lease can have distinct advantages. It requires little or no down payment, and monthly lease payments are usually lower than loan payments would be on the same car because you're not paying off principal or building equity.

But leasing is merely another form of renting. At the end of the lease, you return the car to the lessor (although some leases give you the option to buy). During the lease, you must pay for gas, oil, upkeep and all repairs not covered by a warranty. The lease agreement should spell out who provides insurance coverage; check with your insurer to be sure you're covered for the value of the car.

Getting a Good Deal

Wherever you shop for a lease, the "sell price" of the vehicle—the negotiated price upon which the lease is based—is critical. Even though you're not buying the car, you should negotiate the sell price. Accepting the manufacturer's suggested retail price (MSRP) can be as expensive a mistake in leasing as it can be in buying. Research the invoice price of the vehicle you want and negotiate from there. Your AAA club may be able to help you with a lease. (See "Getting a Good Deal," pp. 12-.13) Although a number of factors determine a good sell price (for example, the competition among local dealers or the availability of the model you want), a sell price 2 to 4 percent above dealer invoice is generally regarded as fair, with the higher end of that range reserved for luxury cars. Be sure to ask about discounts, either from the factory or the dealer.

The higher the residual value (see sidebar, below) of the vehicle, the lower your monthly lease payments. When you compare quotes from various dealers, compare the residual values upon which the quotes are based.

Heading Off Headaches

Government consumer agencies have noted a big increase in the number of consumer complaints about auto leases. Among the most frequent complaints are misunderstandings about substantial penalties for ending the lease early, high charges for excessive wear and tear at the end of the lease and "disappearing trade-ins" (the lessor promises a high trade-in value for the consumer's old car, but it does not appear on the written agreement).To head off these and other problems, read the leasing agreement carefully, and get all promises in writing. Pay particular attention to the following:

- **High fees** for the lessor preparing your car for sale at the end of the lease (called "disposition charges").
- **Low mileage limits** of less than 12,000 to 15,000 miles per year.
- **Vague definitions of "excessive wear."** You might have to pay for stains and tears in the interior or dings and scratches on the finish. Make sure the contract spells out the requirements in detail and save all your repair and maintenance receipts.
- **The addition of credit insurance** or other kinds of insurance without your explicit consent.
- **Any charge** to include an option for you to purchase the car at the end of the lease.
- **High down payments or security deposits.** Many leases require a security deposit, which should be slightly more than one monthly payment.

Under new federal rules, dealers must provide consumers with a document clearly spelling out the basis for calculating monthly payments, the total payments, the penalties for ending the lease early and other revelant information.

Common Leasing Terms

Closed-end lease: One in which you return the vehicle at the end of the leasing period. Also called a "walk-away" lease. Although you owe nothing unless the vehicle is badly damaged, the monthly payments are usually higher on a closed-end lease because you "walk away" without purchasing. Compare with "open-end" lease.

Open-end lease: One in which you and the lessor, at the beginning of the lease, estimate what the vehicle will be worth at the end of the lease. If it's worth less than the estimate (due to excessive mileage or damage), you owe the difference. Because you assume some risk, an open-end lease generally offers lower monthly payments than a closed-end lease.

Capitalized cost: The negotiated price of the vehicle, plus the acquisition fee and extras, minus a down payment. Sometimes called the"cap cost." Acquisition fee: An up-front fee you pay to the lessor to cover administrative costs, similar to points on a loan. Capitalized cost reduction: Down payment (either as cash or trade-in). Residual value: What the car will be worth when the lease is up. Dealers either use charts to determine this amount or negotiate it with you at the beginning of the lease.

Depreciation: How much a vehicle's value declines over time. This is calculated by subtracting the residual value from the capitalization cost. You pay for it every month as a "depreciation payment," which is the total depreciation divided by the number of months in the lease.

Lease charge: Interest you pay on both the cap cost and the residual value.

Coping with **the aggressive driver**

One unfortunate byproduct of our nation's vast highway network and the sheer number of vehicles sharing the streets is a higher level of driver aggression, a phenomenon popularly referred to as"road rage". Although they erupt sporadically, incidents of road rage have made national news headlines in the last decade. What accounts for this disturbing behavior? A recent report prepared by the AAA Foundation for Traffic Safety-a not-for-profit, publicly supported charitable research and educational organization dedicated to saving lives by preventing traffic accidents offers some significant findings.

Studies commissioned by AAA indicate that more than 1,500 men, women, and children in the United States are injured or killed each year as a result of "aggressive driving". The term is defined as an incident in which an angry or impatient motorist or passenger intentionally injures or kills another motorist, passenger, or pedestrian or attempts to injure or kill another motorist, passenger, or pedestrian in response to a traffic dispute, altercation, or grievance. In the 1990s alone, thousands of people have been killed or injured in tens of thousands of aggressive-driving incidents.

In its broadest sense, road rage can refer to any display of aggression on a driver's part. However, the term is often used to define extreme acts of aggression, such as a physical assault, that occur as a direct result of a disagreement between drivers. In some cases, the cause of these incidents appears to be a simple misunderstanding. One driver may make a momentary error of judgment, for example, but the perception of another is that he or she is driving aggressively.

The causes behind road rage likely take into account factors other than the incident at hand. An individual may have had a bad day at work or be experiencing troubles at home. Sometimes it may be difficult to pinpoint the cause of the frustration. Although they may be ignited by seemingly trivial events "stealing" someone's parking space, for instance, or being cut off in traffic violent traffic disputes are often the cumulative result of a series of stressful events in a motorist's life. An altercation that leads to violence, verbal or physical, may be the so-called "straw that broke the camel's back."

How can you avoid becoming the victim of an aggressive-driving incident? The No. 1 rule of thumb is to keep your cool in traffic. Exhibit patience and courtesy yourself, and work to correct unsafe driving habits that are likely to endanger, infuriate, or antagonize other motorists. Be aware of those behaviors that have sparked violence:

■ **Lane blocking.** Never block the passing lane. Stay out of the far left lane unless you intend to pass, and yield to the right for any driver who wants to pass you. If another driver signals or otherwise demands to pass you, allow him or her to do so.

■ **Tailgating.** Maintain a safe distance from the vehicle ahead of you. Many deadly traffic altercations stem from one driver tailgating another.

■ **Signal use.** Don't switch lanes without first signaling your intentions; this is not only common courtesy but a lawfully recognized rule of the road. Avoid cutting someone off when you change lanes.

■ **Gestures.** Needless to say, refrain from using obscene finger gestures. They have gotten people shot, stabbed, and beaten in every state.

■ **Horn use.** Use your horn sparingly in any non-emergency situation. If a stressed-out motorist is on edge, this jarring noise may be enough to trigger rage.

■ **Failure to turn.** In most areas, right-hand turns are allowed after a complete stop at a red light. Avoid being in the right-hand lane if you're not planning to turn right.

■ **Parking.** Don't take up more than one parking space, and don't allow your door to strike an adjacent parked vehicle.

■ **Headlight use.** Keep your headlights on low beam, except where unlighted conditions warrant the use of high beams.

■ **Merging.** When traffic permits, move out of the right-hand acceleration lane of a freeway to allow vehicles to enter from the on-ramp.

■ **Blocking traffic.** Never block traffic behind you if you've momentarily stopped to talk or give directions to a pedestrian on the sidewalk.

■ **Car phone use.** Don't let a car phone become a distraction; research shows that aggressive drivers were especially angered by fender-benders with motorists who were talking on the phone.

■ **Alarms.** If you have an antitheft alarm on your vehicle, be sure you know how to turn it off.

■ **Displays.** Refrain from showing any type of bumper sticker, license plate message, or slogan that could be considered offensive.

■ **Eye contact.** If a hostile motorist tries to pick a fight, do not make eye contact. Instead, get out of the way without acknowledging the other driver.

■ **You also can reduce your own stress level.** Making a few simple changes in how you approach the daily driving routine will not only benefit your health but also defuse potential traffic confrontations.

■ **Altering your schedule** to avoid the worst congestion on routes you normally drive.

■ **Improve the comfort** of your vehicle.

■ **Stays alert** but relaxed while in traffic.

■ **Don't drive when you are angry**, upset, or fatigued.

■ **Adjust your attitude** and give the other driver the benefit of the doubt. Assume that other drivers'mistakes are neither intentional nor personal. Remain polite and courteous, even if the other driver doesn't; it's far better to err on the side of caution.

General ratings

Model	Rating
Mercedes-Benz S-Class	174
BMW 7-Series	173
Lexus GS	172
Mercedes-Benz E-Class	171
BMW 5-Series	168
Volvo S80	168
BMW 3-Series	166
Lexus LS	166
Infiniti Q45	165
Lexus ES300	165
Saab 9-5 Wagon	165
Volvo V70	165
Buick Park Avenue	163
Oldsmobile Aurora	163
Acura RL	162
Acura TL	162
Cadillac DeVille	162
Chrysler 300M	162
Lincoln Town Car	162
Mercedes-Benz C-Class	162
Oldsmobile Intrigue	162
Audi A6	161
Cadillac Seville	161
Dodge Intrepid	161
Mercedes-Benz C-43	161
Toyota Avalon	161
Volkswagen Passat	161
Audi TT	160
Cadillac Catera	160
Jaguar XJ	160
Saab 9-3	160
Audi A4	159
Buick LeSabre	159
Chevrolet Malibu	159
Lincoln Continental	159
Mazda 626	159
Mercedes-Benz SL	159
Porsche Boxster	159
Chevrolet Silverado	158
Chrysler LHS	158
Chrysler Concorde	158
Mercedes-Benz M-Class	158
Volvo C70	158
Audi A8	157
Honda Odyssey	157
Lexus RX 300	157
Lexus SC	157
Oldsmobile Alero	157
Pontiac Bonneville	157
Pontiac Grand Am	157
Ford Crown Victoria	156
GMC Sierra	156
Mercury Grand Marquis	156
Pontiac Grand Prix	156
Toyota Camry	155
Toyota Corolla	155
Volkswagen Golf	155
Volkswagen Jetta	155
Cadillac Eldorado	154
Chevrolet Prizm	154
Chrysler Town & Country	154
Mercedes-Benz CLK	154
Oldsmobile Bravada	154
Buick Regal	153
Mazda Millenia	153
Oldsmobile Silhouette	153
Pontiac Montana	153
Chevrolet Blazer	152
Chevrolet Corvette	152
Chevrolet Venture	152
GMC Jimmy	152
Jeep Grand Cherokee	152
Toyota Solara	152
Buick Century	151
Honda Civic	151
Mercury Sable	151
Toyota Sienna	151
Chevrolet Tahoe	150
Ford Windstar	150
GMC Yukon	150
Honda Accord	150
Infiniti 130	150
Jaguar XK8	150
Lexus LX 470	150
Porsche 911	150
Toyota Land Cruiser	150
BMW Z3	149
Mazda Protege	149
Mercedes-Benz SLK	149
Nissan Altima	149
Volkswagen New Beetle	149
Acura CL	148
Acura Integra	148
Cadillac Escalade	148
Chevrolet Cavalier	148
Ford Taurus	148
Hyundai Sonata	148
Isuzu Trooper	148
Mazda Miata	148
Mitsubishi Diamante	148
Nissan Maxima	148
Plymouth Voyager	148
Subaru Forester	148
Subaru Legacy	148
Chrysler Cirrus	147
Dodge Neon	147
Infiniti G20	147
Land Rover Range Rover	147
Mitsubishi Galant	147
Subaru Impreza	147
Chevrolet Tracker	146
Dodge Durango	146
Acura SLX	145
Chrysler Sebring	145
Dodge Avenger	145
Ford Mustang	145
Mercury Mystique	145
Mercury Villager	145
Nissan Quest	145
Saturn SL/SW	145
Toyota Celica	145
Chevrolet Suburban	144
Suzuki Grand Vitara	144
Chevrolet Lumina	143
Dodge Grand Caravan	143
Nissan Pathfinder	143
Saturn SC	143
Chevrolet Camaro	142
Chevrolet Monte Carlo	142
Chrysler Sebring Cab	142
Dodge Ram	142
Dodge Stratus	142
Ford Escort	142
Infiniti QX4	142
Isuzu Rodeo	142
Mitsubishi Montero	142
Ford Contour	141
Ford F-Series	141
Land Rover Discovery	141
Pontiac Firebird	141
Pontiac Sunfire	141
Suzuki Esteem	141
Hyundai Tiburon	140
Mercury Cougar	140
Mitsubishi Montero Sport	140
Ford Explorer	139
Honda Passport	139
Honda Prelude	139
Mercury Mountaineer	139
Toyota Prius	139
Toyota Tacoma	138
Kia Sportage	137
Plymouth Breeze	137
Chevrolet S10	136
Ford Expedition	136
GMC Sonoma	136
Hyundai Elantra	136
Jeep Cherokee	136
Mitsubishi 3000GT	136
Mitsubishi Eclipse	136
Mitsubishi Mirage	136
Ford Ranger	135
Hyundai Accent	135
Plymouth Prowler	135
Toyota 4Runner	135
Dodge Dakota	134
Lincoln Navigator	134
Mazda B-Series	134
Volkswagen Eurovan	133
Honda CR-V	132
Toyota RAV4	132
Nissan Sentra	131
Kia Sephia	130
Nissan Frontier	130
Dodge Ram Wagon	128
Isuzu Hombre	128
Chevrolet Express	127
Chevrolet Metro	127
GMC Savana	127
Chevrolet Astro	126
GMC Safari	126
Suzuki Swift	123
Ford Econoline	119
Jeep Wrangler	115
Chevrolet C/K	NR
Daewoo Lanos	NR
Daewoo Leganza	NR
Daewoo Nubira	NR
Jaguar Type S	NR
Lincoln LS	NR

NR: Not Rated

1999 AAA TOP CARS

Toyota Corolla 155

Chevrolet Malibu 159

Oldsmobile Intrigue 162

Acura 3.2TL 162

BMW 328i 166

Saab 9-5 Wagon 165

Lexus GS400 172

Mercedes S500 174

1999 AAA TOP MINIVAN

Ford Windstar 150

1999 AAA TOP SPORT UTILITY VEHICLE

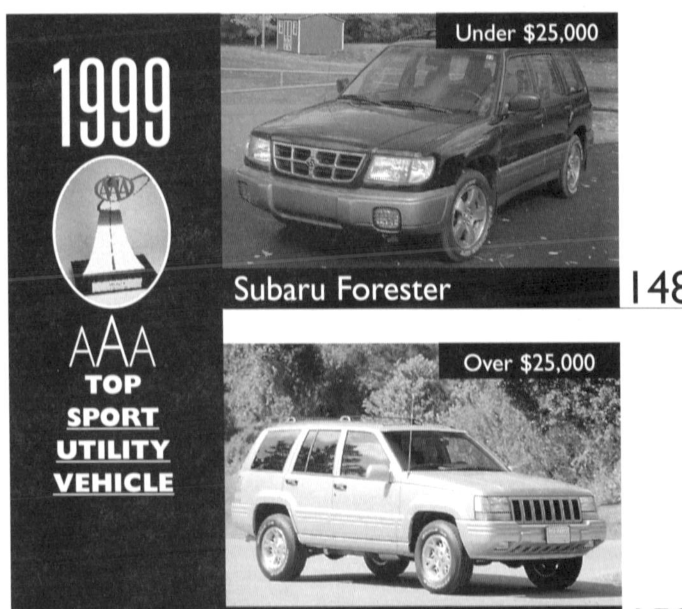

Subaru Forester 148

Jeep Grand Cherokee 152

How we test and rate vehicles

To compile Autograph reviews, AAA automotive experts test the vehicles in a variety of everyday driving situations. We rate the vehicles in each of 20 categories, using a 10-point scale:

In theory, a "perfect" vehicle would earn 200 points, or 10 points in all 20 categories. We constantly monitor the ratings and periodically revise them to better distinguish cars' performances and to keep up with evolving automotive technology.

Manufacturers provide all of our test vehicles. Some reviews are based on '98 models, because the '99 model had no major changes.

Ratings

We assign numerical ratings for the characteristics explained below.

■ Over-the-Road ratings evaluate how the car behaves on different road surfaces under a variety of conditions. "Acceleration" rates 0- to 60-mph times; cars must take 10.9 seconds or less to earn a 6.

We also grade the transmission (smoothness, performance, and harmony with the engine), braking (control, pedal feel, and performance: cars that earn a 6 must stop from 60 mph in 127 feet or less), steering (effort and precision at various speeds), ride (comfort and control), handling (control and maneuverability), and driveability (on-the-road behavior).

"Fuel economy" includes EPA estimates as well as actual mileage from our test drives. A car must average 24 mpg or better to earn a score of 6 or above.

■ Passenger Environment ratings consider the safety and creature comforts of the car's interior. "Comfort/ convenience" considers seat design, safety belt design, climate control system, interior lighting, and other amenities.

We also grade interior room (leg, head, and hip room in all seats), driving position (adjustability of the driver's seat and steering wheel), instrumentation (completeness and day or night legibility), controls (ease of use and quality of operation), visibility (to front, rear, and sides while driving and parking), entry/exit ease, quietness (wind, engine, road, and tire noise under various conditions), and cargo space/liftover (the dimensions of the trunk or cargo area and the distance from the ground to the lower opening of the trunk).

■ Workmanship considers the exterior assembly quality (body panels, trim, and paint) and interior quality (materials, fit, finish, and integrity).

■ Value considers the vehicle's strengths, weaknesses, and price compared with its competitors.

How we rate

10	points	ideal
9	points	excellent, but not necessarily the best
8	points	
7	points	
6	points	average, but not bad
5	points	average, with room for improvement
4	points	
3	points	
2	points	below average
1	point	among the worst
Ratings		
TOTAL		

What's New

In each review, the section headlined "New for '99" highlights major changes in equipment availability, warranty coverage, and/or styling since the previous model year. It will help you compare a '99 model with leftover '98 models and used cars.

Prices

We list the manufacturer's suggested retail price (MSRP) for each trim level. The prices quoted were accurate as this edition went to press; NA indicates prices that were not available. The price range each review indicates the approximate extent of prices within that model line, including extra-cost options. The exact price you pay may vary greatly, depending on a number of factors (see "Getting a Good Deal," pp. 12-13).

Equipment

In this section we list the significant standard equipment for each trim level and significant options, as space permits. To help you compare different makes and models, we use standard terms rather than manufacturers' trade names. For example, we translate Chrysler's AutoStick transmission and Porsche's Tiptronic as "semi-automatic transmissions", because both can be shifted either manually without a clutch or automatically. Some of these terms are defined in the glossary at the back of this book.

When reading sales literature to compare makes and models, you may find some manufacturers' equipment names to be confusing, inflated, or perhaps even misleading. Some of the worst examples of inflated names that we've found include "access portals" (otherwise known as "doors"), "argent wheels" (silver-painted wheels), "simulated leather" (vinyl), "keyless locking" (old-fashioned slam-locking the doors, not a remote keyless entry system), "contoured bench seat" (a bench that seats two people instead of three), and a "radio accommodation package" (wiring for a radio, but no radio).

Specifications

Finally, we list the specifications of the vehicle that we tested, including its exterior and interior dimensions, engine data, performance measurements, and warranty information. Under "interior dimensions," head and leg room is listed in inches for the front (F) and rear (R) seats. For vans and minivans, the second- and third-row seats are identified as R1 and R2, respectively.

Autograph®

PERFORMANCE

SPECIFICATIONS

PASSENGER COMFORT

NEW FOR 99

PROS AND CONS

EQUIPMENT

ENGINE

RATINGS

ACURA
AUDI
BMW
BUICK
CADILLAC
CHEVROLET
CHRYSLER
DAEWOO
DODGE
FORD
GMC
HONDA
HYUNDAI
INFINITI
ISUZU
JAGUAR
JEEP
KIA
LAND ROVER
LEXUS
LINCOLN
MAZDA
MERCEDES-BENZ
MERCURY
MITSUBISHI
NISSAN
OLDSMOBILE
PLYMOUTH
PONTIAC
PORSCHE
SAAB
SATURN
SUBARU
SUZUKI
TOYOTA
VOLKSWAGEN
VOLVO

Acura

CL

New for 99

Cargo net in the trunk
Alloy wheel rims (3.0 only)

Pros

Styling
Standard equipment
Comfort

Cons

Rear-seat room
Transmission
Standard engine

Equipment

Major Standard Equipment: 2.3-liter I-4, manual transmission, 4-wheel antilock brakes, rear defroster, variable-intermittent wipers, automatic air conditioning, tilt steering wheel, cruise control, power windows, power mirrors, power locks, remote keyless entry, power moonroof, remote-control decklid release, AM/FM/CD stereo, steering-wheel stereo controls, aluminum wheels. **3.0 adds:** 3-liter V-6, automatic transmission, heated mirrors, power driver's seat.
Major Options: Automatic transmission, leather upholstery, heated seats.

PRICES
$22,000
$27,000
2.3 coupe $22,310
3.0 coupe $25,310

WARRANTY (years/miles)
Bumper-to-bumper 4/50,000
Powertrain 4/50,000
Rust-through 5/unlimited

OTHER TO CONSIDER
Chrysler Sebring
Toyota Camry Solara

Just looking...

After dropping the Legend coupe, Honda developed the front-wheel-drive Acura CL, a fully U.S.-designed and -built sporty coupe that's about the same size as the Legend was. It's similar to Acura's TL 4-door sedans, but the CL has smaller engines and costs a bit less.

The CL has the same wheelbase and track dimensions as the Honda Accord and shares many of the latter's drivetrain components, but the similarity ends there.

The CL certainly looks sporty. The two versions — 2.3CL and 3.0CL — differ mainly in their engines. The former has the Accord's 2.3-liter, 150-horsepower 4-cylinder; the latter has a 3-liter, 200-horsepower V-6. A manual transmission is offered only with the 2.3.

The CL's soft, comfortable interior boasts leather upholstery, wood trim, and a clean, wraparound instrument panel. Large cushions position the driver and front passenger for good visibility. The rear seats are comfortable for two, but a little short on leg room. As in most coupes, the shoulder belts are not adjustable for height.

Also typical of coupes, entry and exit are easy in the front but not so easy in the rear. Interior storage space is limited to the center console and a little compartment in the dash. The average-size trunk has a pass-through to the rear seat to extend versatility. The liftover is at bumper height, but the wide tail lights pinch the trunk opening.

Although the CL clearly doesn't drive as well as its rear-wheel-drive competition, it's still fun. It handles more like a luxury car than a sports car, allowing moderate body roll in hard turns. A supple ride over rough pavement surprised us, considering the low-aspect ratio tires. The steering is accurate and precise, but would be better with real variable-assist for more highway feel. The brakes were well above average.

The engine you choose will determine your level of satisfaction with the CL. The little 2.3-liter engine takes 9.1 seconds to reach 60 mph, but it feels slower because it has to work so hard and makes so much noise. The automatic transmission makes matters worse with harsh, ill-timed shifts. The V-6 solves many of these problems. It improves acceleration to 60 mph to 8.1 seconds. The V-6 is also more refined and civilized than the standard engine; it runs smoothly from idle and all the way up to full speed. It better communicates Acura luxury. The automatic transmission is still a little rough, even with the smooth V-6.

The fit and finish on our test car were well above average, as we have come to expect from Acura.

The styling of the 2.3CL catches your attention, but its modest horsepower belies its looks. Go for the V-6, if you can afford it. **D.V.S.**

Specifications of Test Vehicle

Model: 3.0CL

Exterior Dimensions	
Wheelbase	106.9 in.
Overall length	190 in.
Overall width	70.1 in.
Overall height	54.7 in.
Curb weight	3,050 lb.
Interior Dimensions	
Seating capacity	5
Head room	F:37.4/R:35.9 in.
Leg room	F:42.9/R:31 in.
Cargo volume	12 cu. ft.
Engine	
Displacement	V-6, 3 L.
Horsepower	200 @ 5,000 rpm
Torque, lb-ft.	196 @ 4,800 rpm
Performance	
0-60 mph, acceleration	8.1 sec.
60-0 mph, braking	120 ft.
Turning circle	39 ft.
EPA city/highway	20/28 mpg
Test mileage	25 mpg
Fuel tank capacity	17.2 gal.

Ratings

Group	Category	Rating
Over The Road	Acceleration	8
	Transmission	6
	Braking	7
	Steering	8
	Ride	8
	Handling	7
	Drivability	9
	Fuel Economy	7
Passenger Environment	Comfort/Conven.	8
	Interior Room	7
	Driving Position	8
	Instrumentation	8
	Controls	7
	Visibility	7
	Entry/Exit	7
	Quietness	7
	Cargo Space	6
Workmanship	Interior	9
	Exterior	8
	Value	6

Ratings 148

Acura

Integra

New for 99

No changes

Pros

Model exclusivity
Astounding performance
Devilish power

Cons

Aging chassis
Loss of motor functions
Dull interior

Equipment

Major Standard Equipment: 1.8-liter I-4, manual transmission, variable-assist power steering, 4-wheel disc brakes, power mirrors, tilt steering column, power windows, AM/FM/CD stereo. **LS adds:** 4-wheel antilock brakes, air conditioning, power locks, power moonroof. **GS adds:** leather upholstery, larger tires. **GS-R adds:** more powerful 1.8-liter. **Type R adds:** even more powerful 1.8-liter, limited-slip differential, and deletes: Air conditioning, power moonroof.

Devilish energy

Now that Acura no longer depends exclusively on the Integra to compete with Mazda and Toyota in the subcompact market. The Integra is now in a position to receive and embrace just about every fantasy cherished by the engineers assigned to its development. Their first fantasy: the GS-R. Today they're pushing their flight of fancy a bit further with the Type R. Fasten your seat belts!

As the Integra proves, even the most attentive care can't completely reverse the effects of aging. Take, for example, the not-very-sticky stickers used to identify the controls for the air conditioning system, the rear seatback that folds down in one piece, the lack of a mechanism to automatically swing down bucket seats to provide easier access to the rear of the vehicle, the dashboard's so-so look, and I could go on. However, age has nothing to do with this model's poor rear visibility (even without the spoiler that perches on top of the Type R's trunk lid and the fact that there is no wiper for the rear windshield). And it has nothing to do with the high trunk sill, which requires an extra effort when loading and unloading heavy items, or the minimal room available for rear-seat passengers. In contrast, those lucky enough to travel in the front bucket seats will be delighted by their good support. And the driver will like the small leather-wrapped steering wheel and the easy access to main controls.

What strikes the imagination onboard the Type R Integra is the tachometer, or more specifically its red zone, which begins at 8,500 rpm! To get there, Honda's magicians (the cylinder head cover bears the developer's signature) introduced several changes (valves, camshaft, crankshaft, nothing escaped the process) so that such an rpm range would have no negative effect on the reliability or durability of this car which has a solid reputation in both areas. This technological feat, however, shouldn't turn attention away from this engine's congenital problem, namely its poor ability to handle actual road conditions. To capitalize on its full potential, you have to make it scream (and believe me, the sound isn't very pleasant) up to 6,200 rpm before its horsepower agrees to gallop at a reasonable speed. And of course, the engine is combined with a sportier chassis which can have a hard time dealing with all the power under its hood, to the point that there is a loss of motor functions when cornering.

Lively and agile, the Integra Type R leads you to believe that you can test yourself against Jeff Gordon. Luckily, its braking system has the power to slow down your enthusiasm. **E.L.**

Specifications of Test Vehicle

Model: Integra Type R

Exterior Dimensions	
Wheelbase	101.2 in.
Overall length	172.4 in.
Overall width	67.3 in.
Overall height	52.6 in.
Curb weight	2,650 lb.
Interior Dimensions	
Seating capacity	4
Head room	F:38.6/R:35 in.
Leg room	F:42.7/R:28.1 in.
Cargo volume	13.3 cu. ft.
Engine	
Displacement	I-4 1.8 L.
Horsepower	195 @ 8,000 rpm
Torque, lb-ft.	130 @ 7,500 rpm
Performance	
0-60 mph, acceleration	6.9 sec.
60-0 mph, braking	118 ft.
Turning circle	34.8 ft.
EPA city/highway	25/31 mpg
Test mileage	21 mpg
Fuel tank capacity	13.2 gal.

Prices

$19,000
$34,000

RS hatchback $16,200
LS hatchback $19,200
LS sedan $20,000
GS hatchback $20,850
GS sedan $21,400
GS-R hatchback $21,300
GS-R sedan $21,600
Type R $24,000 (est.)

Warranty
(years/miles)

Bumper-to-bumper 4/50,000
Powertrain 4/50,000
Rust-through 5/unlimited

Other to Consider

Subaru 2.5 Rs

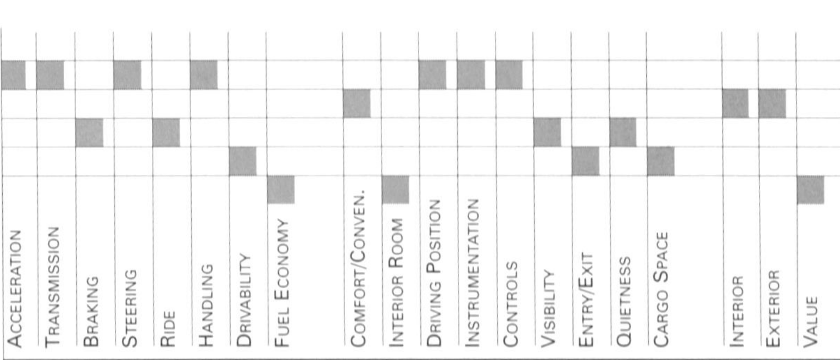

10
9
8
7
6
5
4
3
2
1

Ratings
148

Acura RL

New for 99

Side air bags
Sturdier chassis
Revamped design

Pros

Braking
Ride comfort
Conservative design

Cons

Fuel economy
Cargo space

Equipment

Major Standard Equipment: 3.5-liter V-6, automatic transmission, variable-assist power steering, automatic air conditioning, cabin air filter, speed-sensitive variable-intermittent wipers, automatic headlights, power heated mirrors, power windows, power locks, remote keyless entry, cruise control, power moonroof, rear defroster, leather upholstery, power tilt and telescoping steering wheel, power seats, driver's memory system, remote-control decklid release, AM/FM/CD/cassette stereo, theft alarm system, aluminum wheels. **Major Options:** Traction control, heated seats, navigation system.

PRICES
$41,000
$46,000
3.5 4-door sedan
$41,200

WARRANTY
(years/miles)
Bumper-to-bumper
4/50,000
Powertrain
4/50,000
Rust-through
5/unlimited

OTHER TO CONSIDER
BMW 528 i
Mercedes E 320

Reason over passion

The sales pitch for the Acura 3.5RL focuses on mark-up and fuel consumption, two topics the competition prefers to ignore. Acura's rational argument seems to be designed to get people to reflect on the price they're paying and the real advantages they're getting from the technology bidding war in which all manufacturers in this niche are engaged.

With the 3.5RL, Acura is betting on technical solutions that are diametrically opposed to those of the competition, without sacrificing an ounce of luxury, comfort, or sophistication. For 1999, designers have been unconvincing in their revision of the RL's body work and engineers have added side air bags and made the model's structure more rigid.

Acura makes its intentions clear with the luxury appointments inside this model. Leather abounds on the seats and door panels, with (fake) woodwork added for warmth. The dashboard instruments are housed in three cylinders of different sizes, which is reminiscent of the Japanese cars of the 1970s. The ignition is also in the dash, crammed in between the steering column and the bulge in the central console. The main controls are easily accessed by the driver, and only the traction control and cruise control switches are hidden by the steering wheel rim. Four adults can sit comfortably in this car, but some models from the competition offer more room, and unfortunately for Acura, more cargo space as well.

On this level, the 3.5RL is more of a disappointment. Perhaps it should be judged more on efficiency, in which case its performance is staggering. This engine is so quiet, you'd think it was napping, but hit the pedal and it really kicks up its heels. The car accelerates well and has energetic pick-up (despite a bit of a hole between third and fourth). Basically, the 3.5RL zips along without showing the slightest sign of fatigue. The suspension absorbs bumps nicely, provided the road surface isn't too badly deteriorated, in which case it loses face. Braking is reassuringly stable, and the steering, while a little light, is careful not to reveal which wheels are driving this car. In short, the 3.5RL is astonishingly agile (despite significant roll on tight corners) and its turning radius is ideal.

One small tip: go for the TL, which is more fun, more exciting, and much less expensive. **E.L.**

Category	Rating
Over The Road	
Acceleration	8
Transmission	8
Braking	6
Steering	9
Ride	9
Handling	8
Drivability	8
Fuel Economy	4
Passenger Environment	
Comfort/Conven.	9
Interior Room	8
Driving Position	8
Instrumentation	9
Controls	9
Visibility	9
Entry/Exit	9
Quietness	9
Cargo Space	7
Workmanship	
Interior	9
Exterior	9
Value	7

Ratings
162

Specifications of Test Vehicle

Model: 3.5RL

Exterior Dimensions	
Wheelbase	114.6 in.
Overall length	195.1 in.
Overall width	71.3 in.
Overall height	54.5 in.
Curb weight	3,650 lb.
Interior Dimensions	
Seating capacity	5
Head room	F:38.8:/R:36.8 in.
Leg room	F:42.1:/R:35.4 in.
Cargo volume	14 cu. ft.
Engine	
Displacement	V-6 3.5 L.
Horsepower	210 @ 5,200 rpm
Torque, lb-ft.	224 @ 2,800 rpm
Performance	
0-60 mph, acceleration	8.1 sec.
60-0 mph, braking	125 ft.
Turning circle	36.1 ft.
EPA city/highway	19/25 mpg
Test mileage	19 mpg
Fuel tank capacity	18 gal.

Acura

SLX

New for 99
Carry over

Pros
Interior room
Ride comfort
Standard features

Cons
Non-Honda pedigree
Entry/exit
Handling

Equipment

Major Standard Equipment: 3.5-liter V-6, automatic transmission, automatic 4-wheel drive, 4-wheel antilock disc brakes, variable-assist power steering, air conditioning, rear defroster, variable-intermittent wipers, rear defroster, rear washer and wiper, tilt steering column, cruise control, leather upholstery, power heated seats, split-folding rear seat, power heated mirrors, power locks, remote keyless entry, AM/FM/ CD/cassette stereo, theft-deterrent system, power moonroof, aluminum wheels.
Major Options: None.

An Isuzu in disguise

Meet the Acura that's not an Acura. This one isn't even a Honda. The Acura SLX is really an Isuzu. That's not bad, unless you think you're buying a pedigree with your sport-utility vehicle.

Isuzu makes the Trooper and sells it to Honda, which in turn sells it to consumers as the SLX for its upscale Acura line. As an Acura, the SLX comes loaded with everything that's optional on the Trooper. However, Isuzu offers a better warranty on the Trooper than Acura does on the SLX.

The SLX comes only as a 4-door truck wagon. It stands as tall as some full-sized SUVs. Its track width (the lateral spacing between wheels) is quite narrow, though, especially for its height.

Like the Trooper, the SLX has an Isuzu engine — 215-horsepower, 3.5-liter V-6. Acura has also dropped the deceptive rear-wheel-only antilock brakes system in favor of 4-wheel antilock brakes.

With the 3.5-liter V-6, we reached 60 mph from a standing start in a touch under 11 seconds. That's not particularly zippy response. The SLX weighs a half-ton more than the Acura RL, but its engine produces the same power and torque. The "no-brainer" automatic 4-wheel-drive system senses wheel slippage and decides when 4WD traction is needed. A winter mode on the automatic transmission allows third-gear starts on very slick surfaces. Combined with 4WD, it insulates you from heavy-footed pedal action on slick surfaces. We averaged a distinctly unimpressive 16 mpg.

The most luxurious attribute of the SLX is its plush ride. It's almost like a big American sedan. Yes, the SLX can go off-road — real back-country off-roading, not just off-pavement. Beware of body lean in turns taken only slightly fast. Tall for its width, the SLX doesn't like quick steering maneuvers. The variable-assist power steering communicates good road feel overall.

The SLX's high stance and short doors make getting in trickier than it is in other SUVs. The cabin is roomy and comfy once you're in, however. The firm, comfortable front seats are chair-like, if that's your preference. There's good head room, front and rear; however, the standard moonroof takes a valuable 2 inches of head room in the back seat. Visibility is good to the sides and front. Privacy glass and a full-size spare tire mounted outside restrict vision to the rear. Twin cargo doors of different widths replace a more traditional SUV liftgate.

A little sleight-of-hand transforms a Trooper into an SLX. If you want a real Acura, buy the TL sedan. If you want real value in this SUV, ignore the nameplates and buy a Trooper. **D.V.S.**

Prices
$36,000
$37,000
4-door truck wagon
$36,300

Warranty
(years/miles)

Bumper-to-bumper
4/50,000

Powertrain
4/50,000

Rust-through
5/unlimited

Other to consider
Isuzu Trooper

Mitsubishi Montero

Specifications of Test Vehicle

Model: SLX

Exterior Dimensions	
Wheelbase	108.7 in.
Overall length	187.8 in.
Overall width	69.5 in.
Overall height	72.2 in.
Curb weight	4,600 lb.

Interior Dimensions	
Seating capacity	5
Head room	F:39.8/R:37.8 in.
Leg room	F:40.8/R:39 in.
Cargo volume	43.7 cu. ft.

Engine	
Displacement	V-6 3.5 L.
Horsepower	215 @ 5,400 rpm
Torque, lb-ft.	230 @ 3,000 rpm

Performance	
0-60 mph, acceleration	11.3 sec.
60-0 mph, braking	135 ft.
Turning circle	38.1 ft.
EPA city/highway	15/19 mpg
Test mileage	16 mpg
Fuel tank capacity	22.5 gal.

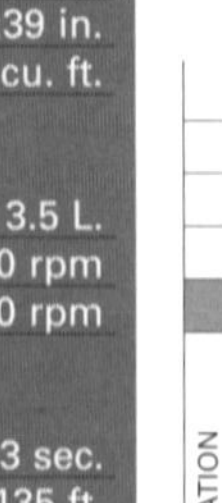

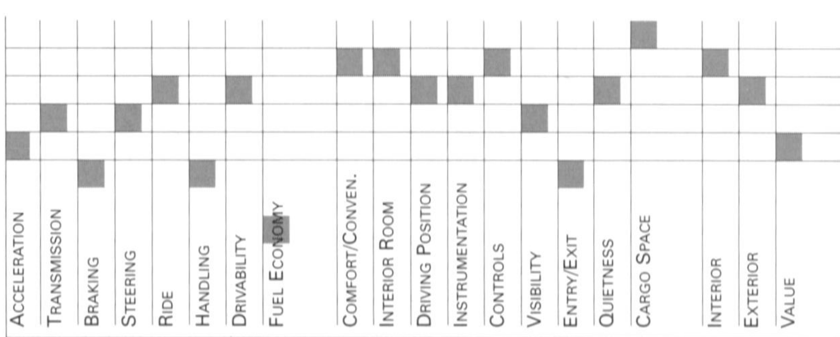

Ratings
145

Acura TL

new MODEL

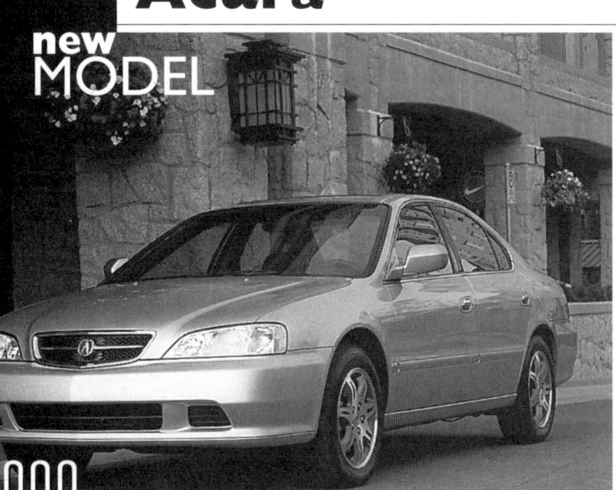

1999

AAA TOP CAR

New For 99

Restyled body and interior
Powertrain
Suspension components.

Pros

Powertrain
Comfort/convenience
Value

Cons

Climate control display

Equipment

Major Standard Equipment: 3.2L V-6 engine, 4-speed SportShift transmission, traction control, 4-wheel antilock disc brakes, HID headlights, leather interior, heated power front seats, automatic climate control, tile wheel, Bose AM/FM/cassette/CD audio system, speed-sensing wipers, keyless entry, power moonroof, automatic headlights, security system.
Major Options: Navigation System

A pleasant surprise

The new Acura 3.2 TL has been reengineered from bumper to bumper to offer new levels of performance, refinement, handling, comfort, and value. It competes in the near-luxury segment with the Lexus ES300, Mercedes-Benz C-Class, BMW 3 Series, Audi A4, and Infinity I30.

The TL is available in just one trim level with a full list of standard features. Luxury touches like heated leather seats and a moonroof are standard. The only option is a navigation system. For '99, a single powertrain drives the 3.2 TL. A new 3.2-liter VTEC-equipped engine delivers 225 hp to a 4-speed transmission that can operate as a full automatic or shifted manually. The engine is now mounted transversely for better packaging and styling.

The interior looks upscale, but is not overdone. The gray instrument panel is trimmed conservatively with wood grain. The optional navigation system has a new 6-inch screen located above the center console. It has a split-screen display that can show a moving map, as well as instructions. Destinations can be programmed by entering a phone number. The screen doubles as the control for the ventilation system by switching to a touch-sensitive display of icons. It works adequately, but requires the driver to divert too much attention from the road. Audio controls are located low on the center console, offering

yet another distraction for the driver.

Seat bottoms are a little on the short side, but are still comfortable and supportive. Front seats offer plenty of head and leg room — rear seats are surprisingly generous as well. Trunk space is ample and the liftover is low. A sloping hood and deck, combined with large side-view mirrors make visibility good in all directions. Entry and exit for both front and rear is near-luxury easy.

On the road is where the 3.2 TL really shines. The engine is refined and responsive at any speed. Honda's VTEC hardware ensures good torque over a broad engine speed range. Gear changes are almost imperceptible and the "grade logic" feature helps the transmission decide which gear is best in hilly terrain. For those who still like to shift, the shift lever can be moved to the left to engage what Acura calls SportShift. Moving the lever back and forth manually changes gears up and down for better control in heavy traffic or on twisty roads.

Acceleration from a stop to cruising speed is silky-smooth and linear, yet pleasantly quick. The ride is exceptional. Rough country roads, and the broken pavement of city streets are handled without discomfort. The good ride compromises handling slightly, but only during the most aggressive cornering. The 4-wheel disc brakes have good pedal feel and accomplished a panic stop test for us in a better-than-average distance for a car this size. Expect fuel economy in the low 20s with premium fuel.

Acura lovers should be pleased with this new-generation TL. It's sleek, fast, comfortable, and luxurious. And the best news is the price — about $5,000 less for a much better car than last year's model. **D.V.S.**

Specifications of Test Vehicle

Model: 3.2TL

Exterior Dimensions	
Wheelbase	108.1 in.
Overall Length	192.9 In.
Overall Width	70.3 In.
Overall Height	55.7 In.
Curb Weight	3461 lbs.
Interior Dimensions	
Seating Capacity	5
Head Room	F: 39.9/R: 36.8 in.
Leg Room	F: 42.4/R: 35.0 in.
Cargo Room	14.3 cu.ft.
Engine	
Displacement	3.2L V-6
Horsepower	225@5500 rpm
Torque, lb-ft.	216@5000 rpm
Performance	
0-60 mph, acceleration	7.7 sec.
60-0 mph, braking	127 ft.
Turning Circle	36.8 ft.
EPA City/Highway	19/27 mpg.
Test Mileage	24.0
Fuel Tank Capacity	17.2 gal.

Counterpoint

If you believe that a successful past is the best guarantee of a successful future, the situation certainly didn't augur very well when Acura announced that for 1999 it was bringing us the second-generation TL. By all indications, despite the fact that it features the Accord's latest platform — modified, of course — that it comes with an accessory list as long as your arm, and that it sells for less than its predecessor, consumers expected the situation to remain as is. Wrong!

A new platform spells a new size and in this regard, note that the new TL's interior is roomier than the former model's. What statistics don't show: leg room is a bit limited in the front given the design chosen for the dashboard, which is positioned low for optimal visibility; door pockets are not deep enough; bucket seats offer minimal lumbar support. Other drawbacks: an emergency brake that's foot-operated (, and the lack of side air bags, a feature that is very common in this market segment.

The "new" 3.2-liter is an extrapolation of the Accord's 3.0-liter V-6. More modern, lighter, and more compact than the engine it replaces, this 3.2-liter is also more powerful and it delivers more torque. To translate potential power into actual power the TL uses an efficient, smooth cooperative semiautomatic transmission.

The TL also offers a precise and linear steering system, a smooth suspension, and a personality that leans toward understeering and a relatively useless traction control system since it works only when the vehicle is traveling at low speeds.

The most disappointing factor is a braking system that faded to almost nothing during our test drive. After a few of the make's representatives denied that any such problem existed, Acura then sent us a note mentioning that it "is aware of the situation on preproduction models — standard production models will be perfect." Consumers expect nothing less than perfection.

E.L.

PRICES

$28,000
$30,000

3.2 TL 4-door sedan
$28,385

WARRANTY
(years/miles)

Bumper-to-Bumper
4/50,000

Power Train
4/50,000

Rust-through
5/Unlimited

OTHER TO CONSIDER

Audi A 4S

Infiniti I30

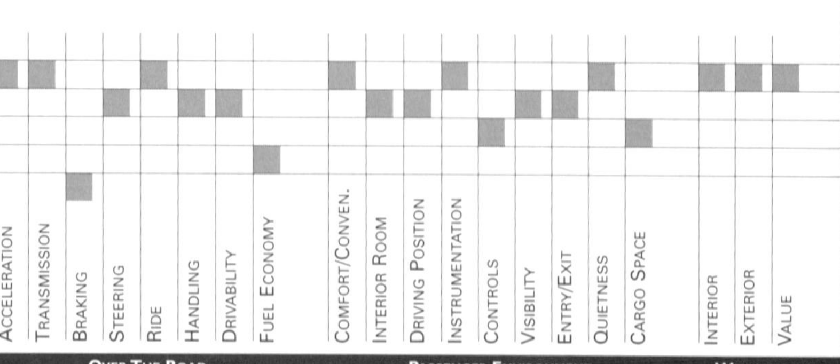

Ratings

162

Audi

A4

New for 99

Bigger right-hand side-view mirror
Steering-mounted semi-automatic transmission controls
Dual turbo V-6 available

Pros

The safety of all-wheel drive
Extremely high-quality finish
Modern design concept

Cons

Limited room
Confused semi-automatic transmission
Pumping phenomenon

Equipment

Major Standard Equipment: 1.8-liter I-4, manual transmission, 4-wheel antilock disc brakes, automatic air conditioning, cabin air filter, variable-intermittent wipers, rear defroster, headlamp washer, rear foglight, power heated mirrors, powerlocks, AM/FM cassette stereo, split-folding rear seat, tilt and telescoping steering column, cruise control, theft alarm system, aluminum wheels. **2.8 adds:** 2.8-liter V-6, traction control, power driver's seat, 205/55 HR16.
Major Options: 5-speed manual automatic transmission, all-wheel drive, leather upholstery, heated seats, driver's door lock, remote keyless entry, power moonroof.

All is well

PRICES
$24,000
$34,000

1.8 T sedan
$24,290

2.8 sedan
$28,890

2.8 wagon
$31,540

WARRANTY
(years/miles)

Bumper-to-bumper
3/50,000

Powertrain
3/50,000

Rust-through
10/unlimited

OTHER TO CONSIDER

Acura 3.2TL
BMW 323i

The A4 in a nutshell: automotive industry critics are jubilant, consumers' hearts are aflutter, and Audi is grinning ear-to-ear after years of frustration, doubt, and disappointments.

The corporation that uses four interlocking circles as its symbol is running on its second wind this year, offering steering-mounted controls for the semi-automatic transmission, a new tint for the model's leather, and a bigger right-hand side-view mirror.

You should wash an A4 by hand to appreciate how sturdy its coachwork is and to get a feel for its quality construction. This car is as solid on the inside as it is on the outside. Doors open wide to provide easy access to very-well-designed seats. Dials and switches are well laid-out on the instrument panel while the driver's hands grip a very comfortable steering wheel that shows no signs of housing an air-bag. While front-seat passengers have all the room they need, their rear-seat counterparts are a bit more cramped and have less space at their disposal than they would have in similar models. The same holds true for the trunk, which has a hard time holding all the paraphernalia most people take with them on vacation. Audi fans will tell you that the A4 is superior to the 90, its predecessor, but there's still a lot more to be done.

Motorists usually expect a form of magic from the supercharged turbo engine and the 1.8-liter can't deliver it. The four-cylinder may feel more powerful than the 24-valve, 2.8 version that powered last year's A4, but the numbers don't lie. To this Audi's credit, we should point out that the computer system that links the engine to the five-speed automatic transmission (optional) is up and ready as soon as the turbocharger makes its presence felt. All in all, it may be wise to opt for the manual transmission even if the gear shift is on the hesitant side. The choice is harder to make on the 2.8, available with a five-speed Tiptronic transmission at extra cost (thank you, Porsche!). But whether manual or automatic, the A4 reaches new heights with the new 30-valve V-6, especially if you check the sport performance box (lower suspension, high-performance springs and shocks, all the usual hardware!) thus eliminating roll and sway even during hard braking. As for the rest of the car, there's nothing to complain about. Ride is good, the steering system is responsive, and braking is powerful.

Sold at a competitive price, the A4 has the advantages of youth and the quality associated with its country of origin. Too bad the package is so small.
E.L.

Specifications of Test Vehicle

Model: A4 2.8

Exterior Dimensions	
Wheelbase	103 in.
Overall length	178 in.
Overall width	68.2 in.
Overall height	55.8 in.
Curb weight	3,100 lb.
Interior Dimensions	
Seating capacity	5
Head room	F:38.1/R:36.8 in.
Leg room	F:41.3/R:33.4 in.
Cargo volume	13.7 cu. ft.
Engine	
Displacement	V-6 2.8 L.
Horsepower	190 @ 6,000 rpm
Torque, lb-ft.	207 @ 3,200 rpm
Performance	
0-60 mph, acceleration	8.6 sec.
60-0 mph, braking	118 ft.
Turning circle	36.4 ft.
EPA city/highway	20/29 mpg
Test mileage	23 mpg
Fuel tank capacity	16.4 gal.

Ratings

Group	Category	Rating (1–10)
Over The Road	Acceleration	8
	Transmission	9
	Braking	7
	Steering	9
	Ride	8
	Handling	9
	Drivability	8
	Fuel Economy	5
Passenger Environment	Comfort/Conven.	8
	Interior Room	7
	Driving Position	9
	Instrumentation	8
	Controls	7
	Visibility	8
	Entry/Exit	8
	Quietness	9
	Cargo Space	6
Workmanship	Interior	9
	Exterior	9
	Value	8

Ratings
159

Audi

A6

New for 99

Manual transmission available
Sport suspension available
Bigger right-hand side-view mirror
A6 Avant (wagon)

Pros

Competitive price
AWD (Quattro) advantages
Virtually perfect interior

Cons

Marginal engine performance
Overly smooth suspension
Some clumsy controls

Equipment

Major Standard Equipment: 2.8-liter V-6, 5-speed semiautomatic transmission, traction control, 4-wheel antilock brakes, dual-temperature air conditioning, power windows, power locks, remote keyless entry, tilt and telescope steering wheel, cruise control, power heated mirrors, power driver's seat, trip computer, theft alarm system, AM/FM/cassette stereo, aluminum wheels.
Major Options: All-wheel drive, driver's memory system, automatic-dimming mirrors, high-intensity headlights, heated steering wheel, heated seats, vinyl upholstery, leather upholstery, AM/FM/CD stereo, power rear sunshade, 205/55R16

To boldly go...

Audi made automotive industry observers and consumers very happy by reviewing its intermediate product line, developed more than 10 years ago. Their major transformation came at a time when several new faces, all equally promising, were barreling onto the scene in the market segment. Regardless, A6 has no trouble attracting the spotlight to its corner: in fact, it has qualities that are too rare for it to go unnoticed by consumers.

"Should a sedan look like a sedan?" That is the question addressed by Audi stylists, who looked for an answer by giving a variety of forms and colors to the new A6. Whether it shocks, astonishes, or pleases onlookers is immaterial. And the A6 has the advantage of backing away from the shy styling prominent on the competition's models, even throwing in low wind resistance.

Luckily, the bold approach adopted by Audi stylists has had no negative effects from the standpoint of practicality, as is all too often the case with other builders. As proof, the head room is slightly superior to what it was on the previous generation, already one of the roomiest in its category.

Let's look inside: it's bright, huge, and superbly finished. As usual, attention to detail is obvious; you can feel and see it aboard this Audi. Better still, at no extra cost buyers can dress the passenger compartment "to suit their style and needs."

So much for praise, now comes the criticism. Audi may have repositioned certain controls, formerly aligned like piano keys, but they forgot to review those dedicated to the air conditioning system and the radio, which are still too small and needlessly complicated.

You may hate winter with a passion, yet you have to recognize that when you drive an Audi Quattro you'll eventually start to look forward to snow-covered roads. The excellent motor functions that the Quattro system provides give the A6 a definite advantage over its rear-wheel drive rivals, too often clumsy on slippery roads.

While it may be true that the A6 shares many of the A4's mechanical components, it still has its own distinctive personality. Take the engine, for instance. At first glance it looks like the same 2.8-liter V-6 as the little A4, except that the A6's has an output of 200 horses versus the A4's 190. Torque is identical on both models, though, and the 10 extra horses are not many, not enough, even if the five-speed Tiptronic automatic transmission does excellent work and never seems confused or rough. The better to optimize mechanical capabilities, buyers should consider the five-speed manual transmission, available exclusively on the Quattro version, although it does tend to be a bit rubbery.

The steering system is so responsive and so precise you can measure your trajectory to the nearest and smallest of fractions of an inch and cornering is totally problem-free. Other than small engine problems, the only other criticism goes to an overly smooth suspension that hurts the car's sporty handling; at the very least, a bit more firmness would contain roll. **E.L.**

Specifications of Test Vehicle

Model: A6

Exterior Dimensions	
Wheelbase	108.7 in.
Overall length	192 in.
Overall width	71.3 in.
Overall height	57.2 in.
Curb weight	3,450 lb.
Interior Dimensions	
Seating capacity	5
Head room	F:39.3/R:37.9 in.
Leg room	F:41.3/R:37.3 in.
Cargo room	17.2 cu. ft.
Engine	
Displacement	V-6 2.8 L.
Horsepower	200 @ 6,000 rpm
Torque, lb-ft.	207 @ 3,200 rpm
Performance	
0-60 mph, acceleration	9.5 sec.
60-0 mph, braking	120 ft.
Turning circle	38.3 ft.
EPA city/highway	17/28 mpg
Test mileage	NA
Fuel tank capacity	18.5 gal.

Prices

$34,000
$44,000

Sedan
$34,250

Warranty

(years/miles)

Bumper-to-bumper
3/50,000

Powertrain
3/50,000

Rust-through
10/unlimited

Other to Consider

BMW 528 i
Saab 9-5

Ratings

Category	Rating
Over The Road	
Acceleration	7
Transmission	9
Braking	7
Steering	9
Ride	7
Handling	9
Drivability	9
Fuel Economy	5
Passenger Environment	
Comfort/Conven.	8
Interior Room	7
Driving Position	9
Instrumentation	8
Controls	8
Visibility	8
Entry/Exit	8
Quietness	9
Cargo Space	8
Workmanship	
Interior	9
Exterior	9
Value	8

Audi

A8

New for 99

Bigger right-hand sideview mirror
17-inch wheels available
Changes to the accessory list

Pros

Distinctive personality
Ride comfort
Innovations

Cons

Base-engine power
Large engine availability
Unproven construction

Equipement

Major Standard Equipment:
3.7-liter V-8, 5-speed manual automatic transmission, front and rear side air bags, traction control, variable-assist power steering, four-wheel antilock disc brakes, dual-temperature automatic air conditioning, cabin air filter, rear defroster, rear fog light, variable-intermittent wipers, headlight washers, heated windshield washers, automatic dimming rear-view mirror, power seats, leather upholstery, cruise control, power tilt and telescope steering column, power windows, power heated mirrors, power locks, remote keyless entry, power decklid release, power moonroof, trip computer, theft alarm system, AM/FM/cassette stereo, aluminum wheels. 4.2 Quattro adds: 4.2-liter V-8, all-wheel drive.

Avant-garde

PRICES
$57,000
$68,000
3.7 4-door sedan
$57,900
4.2 Quattro 4-door sedan
$65,500

WARRANTY
(years/miles)
Bumper-to-bumper
3/50,000
Powertrain
3/50,000
Rust-through
10/unlimited

OTHER TO CONSIDER
BMW 740 il
Mercedes Classe S

Audi's A8 dares to be different. In building this flagship for its upscale line, Volkswagen employs potentially revolutionary engineering.

Technophiles will find a lot to like about the A8. To begin, it has six air bags: two for frontal crashes, and four for side impacts. The A8's structure, too, piques interest. Using a lot of aluminum, Volkswagen has adapted aircraft construction techniques in which all pieces contribute to the strength of the vehicle. For example, the fenders are no longer decorative splash guards but structural components. This new concept in automaking decreases weight, thereby improving fuel economy, and could be applied to all cars, large and small, in the future.

Serious luxury calls for a V-8 engine. The base A8 has a 235-horsepower, 3.7-liter V-8. There's also a 4.2-liter engine with 300 horsepower — but only with all-wheel-drive. The big engine would make the front-wheel drive version too difficult to drive. As in other high-powered front-wheel-drive cars (Mitsubishi's 3000GT, for example), AWD becomes a crutch.

The smaller engine isn't tuned as aggressively, so it produces about 30 horsepower less than it should, based on its size relative to the 4.2. Considering the A8's pretensions, acceleration is modest: 8.3 seconds to from 0 to 60 mph. The 5-speed automatic, still a rarity, does an excellent job, picking the gear that the driver would if shifting manually. Push-buttons on the steering wheel allow you to do just that. Of course, both engines need high-octane gas; you can expect overall mileage of about 20 mpg.

The sumptuous interior contradicts Audi's traditional austerity. Good seats, like good mattresses, feel hard at first but hold their comfort over a long time; these are good seats. The main driving controls are close at hand. secondary controls on the stereo and air conditioning have many small, similarly shaped buttons. Combined, they present an overwhelming array of 40 buttons and 3 knobs. The rear-seat head restraints restrict the view out of the back window; with those obstacles, you use the side mirrors a lot. The A8 has a bigger trunk than the Mercedes S-Class, one indication of luxury detailing.

Behind the wheel, the A8 shows its German heritage. Like the lowly VW Golfs or the lofty BMWs, this A8 goes where it's pointed without fuss. The ride is stiff but compliant.

Manufacturers run risks with new technology, and buyers bear some of that risk financially when they purchase unique, new products. At the very, very worst, the A8 will give you a lot to talk about at the next neighborhood get-together. **D.V.S.**

Ratings

Group	Category	Rating (1–10)
Over The Road	Acceleration	8
	Transmission	9
	Braking	5
	Steering	8
	Ride	9
	Handling	8
	Drivability	9
	Fuel Economy	5
Passenger Environment	Comfort/Conven.	8
	Interior Room	7
	Driving Position	8
	Instrumentation	9
	Controls	6
	Visibility	8
	Entry/Exit	8
	Quietness	8
	Cargo Space	8
Workmanship	Interior	9
	Exterior	9
	Value	8

Specifications of Test Vehicle

Model: A8 3.7

Exterior Dimensions	
Wheelbase	113 in.
Overall length	198.2 in.
Overall width	74 in.
Overall height	56.7 in.
Curb weight	3,700 lb.
Interior Dimensions	
Seating capacity	5
Head room	F:37.1/R:37.9 in.
Leg room	F:41.3/R:38.4 in.
Cargo volume	18 cu. ft.
Engine	
Displacement	V-8 3.7 L.
Horsepower	230 @ 5,500 rpm
Torque, lb-ft.	235 @ 2,700 rpm
Performance	
0-60 mph, acceleration	8.3 sec.
60-0 mph, braking	130 ft.
Turning circle	40.2 ft.
EPA city/highway	17/26 mpg
Test mileage	21 mpg
Fuel tank capacity	23.7 gal.

Audi

TT

New for 99

New model

Pros

Incredible road grip
Original styling
Well appointed

Cons

Very low step-in height
Difficult to unload cargo area
Tight interior

Equipment

Major Standard Equipment: Anti-lock braking system, AM/FM stereo/cassette, climate control, telescoping steering, power windows, heated mirrors.
Major options: Semi-automatic transmission (late availability), heated seats, leather seats, larger tires, trip computer.

Nostalgia

When Audi unveiled the TT concept car back in 1995 at the Frankfurt Auto Show, it was greeted with a great deal of enthusiasm. Within months, a team was put together to put Audi's California Design Center creation into production. Now in production in Györ, Hungary, the TT pays homage to the Tourist Trophy, a motorsport legend that began in 1905 as a car and motorcycle race on the Isle of Man. To blend technology and driving pleasure, Audi adopted the "form follows function" philosophy that kept the TT design pure both inside and out.

Under the rear hatch is a useable 10 cu ft of space which can be expanded to 19 cu ft when the 50/50 split rear seats are folded flat. Yes, rear seats! This coupe does in fact have them, but their use is restricted to people on the small side — adults will not be happy campers.

Up front, the cockpit boasts a design of simplicity and functionality. Circular and aluminum are two themes that run rampant throughout the TT design. In short, the driver's seat is an interesting place to be. One gripe, however, is that the padding on those supports needs to be increased. When cornering becomes enthusiastic, bracing a leg against them becomes painful.

Under that clamshell hood is Audi's 1.8 liter, turbocharged 4-cylinder engine. Unlike other Audi models, the motor is mounted transversely to fit the tight confines of the engine compartment. While this powerplant is used in the Turbo to produce 150-hp, in the TT it generates 180 at 5500 rpm and a whopping 235 lb.-ft. of torque from 1950 to 5000 rpm. Because the car only weighs 2,904 lbs, these figures are good for a 0-60 mph acceleration time of 7.4 seconds. The 50-70 mph passing maneuver takes about six. Mated to this engine is a five-speed manual transmission with incredibly short throws and fairly narrow gates. We found it could use a stronger self-centering action to improve shifts from second to third. A Tiptronic-style automatic is still in development, so manually is the only way to shift gears for the time being. An up-level version of the TT with a 225-hp variant of the same engine will have a six-speed box.

Spring tuning is relatively firm, as a sports car should be, but even so it provides a comfortable ride at the same time as it is contributing to outstanding handling.

Braking power for the TT is provided by four-wheel discs. Anti-lock braking is standard of course, plus an electronic differential lock on the front axle which uses ABS to control wheelspin and redirect the power to the other wheel. Electronic brake-pressure distribution (EBD) is also standard. Put simply, they work very well.

Pricing for the TT coupe is expected to be below $35,000 in the United States. Incidentally, the coupe isn't the only TT in the family — a convertible TT roadster will be coming too. Audi has done a bang-up job with the TT. It looks great, handles and rides very well, and is sensibly appointed. **T.L.**

Specifications of Test Vehicle

Model: TT Coupe 1.8 T

Exterior Dimensions	
Wheelbase	95.4 in.
Overall lenght	159.1 in.
Overall widht	73.1 in.
Overall height	53 in.
Curb weight	2740 lb.
Interior dimensions	
Seating capacity	2+2
Head room	F: 37.5/R: 32 in.
Leg room	F:43.5/ R: na in.
Cargo room	10.5 cu. ft.
Engine	
Displacement	I-4 1.8
Horsepower	180 @ 5.500
Torque, lb-ft	173 @ 1 950
Performance	
0-60 mph, acceleration	7.4
60-0 mph, braking	121 ft
Turning circle	34.2 ft
EPA city/highway	na
Test mileage	22 mpg (est.)
Fuel tank capacity	14.5 gal.

PRICES
$32,000
(est.)

WARRANTY
(years/miles)

Bumper-to-bumper
3/50,000

Powertrain
3/50,000

Rust-through
10/unlimited

OTHER TO CONSIDER

BMW Z23

Mercedes SLK

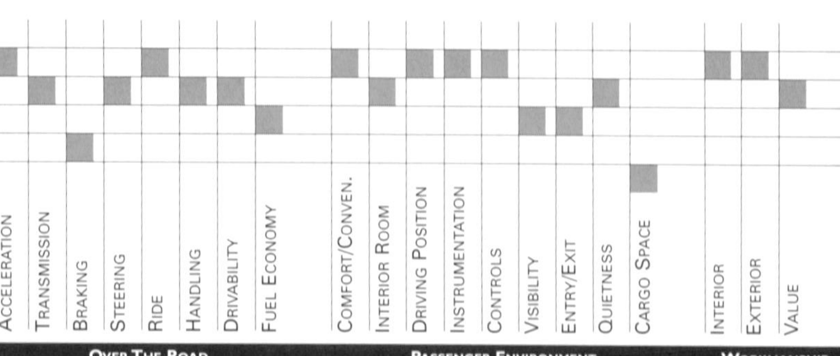

Ratings
160

BMW 3-Series

new MODEL

1999

AAA TOP CAR

New for 99

3-Series sedans are essentially all new. All others are carryover. (coupe - cabriolet)

Pros

Powertrain performance
Ride/steering/handling
Fit & finish

Cons

Fuel economy
Cargo space

Equipment

Major Standard Equipment: 3.5 liter I-6 engine, 5-speed manual transmission, cornering brake control, traction control, antilock brakes, keyless entry/security, leather tilt/telescope wheel, automatic climate control, power windows and locks, AM/FM/cassette audio system, front seat head protection system, **328i Adds:** 2.8 liter I-6 engine, trip computer, fingertip cruise, audio and phone controls, power memory seats. **Major Options:** 5-speed automatic transmission, alloy wheels, Xenon headlights, park distance control, on-board navigation system, leather seats, moonroof, CD player, split folding rear seats, rear side-impact air bags.

The best in the class

The BMW 3-Series has been a hugh success. If all of the variations are included, threes account for about half of BMW sales. Inside BMW, redesigning the 3-Series sedan was not taken lightly. The mandate was to retain the look, feel, and size of the current model, while improving refinement, safety, and passenger room. It looks like BMW has succeeded in doing just that.

Maintaining a distinction between the 3-5-series is a priority at BMW. When redesigning the new 3-Series sedans, BMW resisted the temptation to make them larger. Size is not what the 3-Series is all about. BMW customers want performance, so that's what BMW delivers. The major difference between the 323i and the 328i is the engine. The 323i gets a 2.5-liter in line six good for 170 hp. The better-equipped 328i comes with a 2.8-liter six, capable of 193 hp.

From the driver's seat, the surroundings are pleasant and down to earth. Both the steering column and driver's seat are fully adjustable. Seats are firm, but fully supportive. Rear-seat passengers have to endure a lack of leg room — entry and exit for the rear seat requires a little bending. The optional folding rear seat provides additional cargo space. The steering wheel is small, but contains controls for the cruise and the audio system. All instruments are large and readable, featuring BMW's trademark red glow at night. Audio and vent controls are properly located high on the instrument panel, but a proliferation of small, difficult to interpret buttons can distract the driver. Visibility is good in all directions, thanks to a sloping hood and decklid, and large side-view mirrors.

On the highway is where the 328i really shows its worth. The ride is nothing short of superb. Handling is just as

good. BMW has found the perfect formula for a smooth ride and great handling. Low-friction components in the suspension system allow it to absorb the worst of potholes, while staying level and linear in the most outrageous cornering maneuvers. This is one great car to drive on twisty mountain roads, and invites the driving enthusiast to take the long way home from work. Steering is precise, with excellent on-center feel. The brake pedal is sensitive to the lightest touch for instant response and better than average stopping distance.

The powertrain performs flawlessly, whether with the manual or automatic transmission. Variable valve timing delivers the right amount of torque at the right time, so a run from 0 to 60 mph can take as little as 6.7 seconds. Delivery of power is smooth and quiet. When pushed hard, the exhaust has a muscular throaty sound — another BMW trademark.

The current 3-Series BMW has been with us for almost eight years and has evolved slowly during that time. This is the first major change. Those thinking of buying a new 3-Series sedan will be happy that this new design only improves the breed. They just keep getting better. **D.V.S.**

Specifications of Test Vehicle

Model: 328i

Exterior Dimensions	
Wheelbase	107.3 in.
Overall Length	176.1 In.
Overall Width	68.5 In.
Overall Height	55.7 In.
Curb Weight	3197 lbs.
Interior Dimensions	
Seating Capacity	5
Head Room	F: 38.4/R: 37.5 in.
Leg Room	F: 41.4/R: 34.6 in.
Cargo Room	10.7 cu.ft.
Engine	
Displacement	2.8L I-6
Horsepower	193@5500 rpm
Torque, lb-ft.	206@3500 rpm
Performance	
0-60 mph, acceleration	6.7 sec.
60-0 mph, braking	120 ft.
Turning Circle	34.4 ft.
EPA City/Highway	20/29 mpg.
Test Mileage	26.1
Fuel Tank Capacity	16.6 gal.

Counterpoint

For the time being, it continues to tout the previous generation coupe and convertible, available at the same price as they were last year.

The new 3-Series proves that BMW has listened to and addressed the frequently criticized failings of the previous generation. The list of these shortcomings is surprising when you consider the halo of prestige surrounding this particular car builder. Weaknesses include access to rear seats, a cramped passenger compartment with minimal room in all directions, and worst of all, a finishing whose quality is dubious in some instances. Then there's the lifeless design, with no resemblance to — let's say — the legendary joviality of Bavarians when Oktoberfest comes around. We might comment (one last time) on the endless and expensive list of optional accessories (BMW still isn't giving everything it could to buyers!), often crucial to hoist the 3-Series to an acceptable standard of comfort and luxury.

The "added value" of the in-line 2.8-liter six-cylinder is obvious instantly. Responsive and powerful, this powertrain lets you capitalize on a chassis as finely tuned as the 3-Series' chassis. As for the 2.5-liter model, obviously not as strong, it's every bit as smooth and every bit as capable (barely one second separates the acceleration times recorded for the two engines). But let's get back to the question of performance. Handling is well balanced and reassuring and the responsive steering system adds to the pleasure of being behind the wheel. In fact, driving these models is tricky only on wet or snowy roads, even if they do feature the ASC+T traction control system.

Faithful BMW fans may consider it a bit harsh, but we think the tough love concept applies perfectly to the current 3-Series.

E.L.

Category	Rating
Over The Road	
Acceleration	10
Transmission	9
Braking	7
Steering	9
Ride	7
Handling	9
Drivability	9
Fuel Economy	6
Passenger Environment	
Comfort/Conven.	9
Interior Room	8
Driving Position	9
Instrumentation	9
Controls	8
Visibility	8
Entry/Exit	8
Quietness	9
Cargo Space	5
Workmanship	
Interior	9
Exterior	10
Value	9

BMW

PRICES

$23,000
$48,000

318ti 2-door hatchback $21,390

318i 4-door sedan $26,150

323is 2-door coupe $29,840

323i 2-door convertible $35,840

328i 4-door sedan $33,100

328is 2-door coupe $34,340

328i 2-door convertible $42,640

M3 2-door coupe $40,840

M3 4-door sedan $39,700

WARRANTY (years/miles)

Bumper-to-Bumper 4/50,000

Power Train 4/50,000

Rust-through 6/Unlimited

OTHER TO CONSIDER

Acura 3.2 TL

Mercedes C-Class

Ratings

166

BMW 5-Series

New for 99

Steptronic transmission
M version
Touring (wagon) version

Pros

Exquisite road stability
High-performance mechanics
Reasonable prices

Cons

Unexciting styling
Ridiculously small trunk
Minimal rear room

Equipment

Major Standard Equipment: 2.8-liter I-6, 4-wheel antilock disc brakes, side air bags, head protection system, variable-intermittent wipers, rear defroster, dual-temperature automatic air conditioning, cabin air filter, AM/FM/cassette stereo, power heated mirrors, power tilt and telescoping steering column, power seats, driver's memory system, power windows, remote keyless entry, power locks, theft-alarm system, **540i adds:** 4.4-liter V-8, 5-speed automatic transmission, traction control, automatic stability control, automatic dimming rear-view mirror, leather upholstery, power moonroof, automatic ventilation system, larger tires.

A winning number

PRICES
$40,000
$62,000
528i sedan $40,040
540i sedan $42,240

WARRANTY (years/miles)
Bumper-to-bumper 4/50,000
Powertrain 4/50,000
Rust-through 6/unlimited

OTHER TO CONSIDER
Mercedes E-Class
Lexus GS

Imagine an autopsy room where pathologists play with screwdrivers, hammers, and electric saws. Brrrr! This, however, is pretty much what you can expect to find behind the closed doors of car manufacturers' R&D centers, as they try to dissect the secrets of their rivals' models. And with the passage of time, there must have been many bloodied 5-Series carcasses on the tables of these labs, because the Munich firm clearly holds the winning ticket. This year the 528 has more power and the 540 has a five-speed semiautomatic transmission (the Steptronic). Oh, yes! I was forgetting: an M5 is on its way, along with a wagon (Touring) version.

Is the 5-Series comfier? Certainly more than the prior generation, but still not as much as an E-Class Mercedes or even an Audi A6. As is often the case, the fifth seat (equipped with a headrest) requires the occupant to sit tight, hunch shoulders, and spread legs around the transmission housing, while tilting the head (the central armrest is slightly elevated). In the trunk, baggage and other items had better be compact because the 5-Series has about the same kind of trunk volume as a Neon. The dashboard should look familiar to BMW customers, although two-toned plastics make the design less austere. On the other hand, this Bavarian goes overboard with accessories and the dash and steering wheel are chock full of similar, hard-to-identify controls.

The 5-Series is disconcertingly easy to drive. It turns without excessive roll and is always predictable. Such behavior is neither exciting nor entertaining, but obviously affords great safety. In fact, only on a slick road does the car show the slightest hesitation – but the standard traction control system keeps everything under control. The 5-Series is equipped with a modern, diabolically efficient rear multiple-control-arm suspension. It is firm but smooth and undoubtedly the best there is! Still, whatever model you may select, steering is imprecise at the center, a typical BMW failing. The 528i's rack-and-pinion system is firmer than the 540i's recirculating ball system.

Smooth and capable of high performance levels, the in-line six-cylinder is simply brilliant. Those concerned about feeling smothered in a 5-Series will quickly change their minds. Furthermore, these six cylinders work hand-in-hand with the five-speed manual transmission (the 540i has six), the gear ratio is good, shifting is problem-free, and clutching is progressive. Positive comments all around! With the 540i's 4.4-liter V-8 engine, acceleration rates drop by one or two seconds (depending on the transmission) compared with the 528i, but both reach the same peak speeds, electronically governed to 123.6 mph.

The vitality of the 5-Series has made it a smashing success. And into the bargain, they offer enviable reliability. **E.L.**

Specifications of Test Vehicle

Model: 540i

Exterior Dimensions	
Wheelbase	111.4 in.
Overall length	188 in.
Overall width	70.9 in.
Overall height	56.5 in.
Curb weight	3,750 lb.
Interior Dimensions	
Seating capacity	5
Head room	F:37.4/R:37.2 in.
Leg room	F:41.7/R:34.2 in.
Cargo volume	11.1 cu. ft.
Engine	
Displacement	V-8 4.4 L.
Horsepower	282 @ 5,700 rpm
Torque, lb-ft.	310 @ 3,900 rpm
Performance	
0-60 mph, acceleration	6.1 sec.
60-0 mph, braking	127 ft.
Turning circle	37.4 ft.
EPA city/highway	15/24 mpg
Test mileage	18 mpg
Fuel tank capacity	18.5 gal.

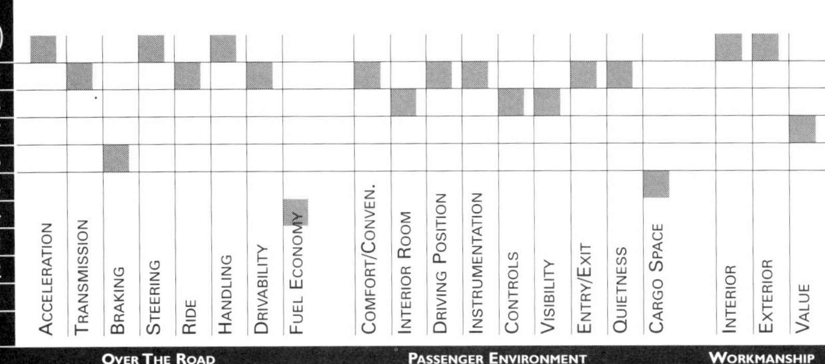

Ratings
168

BMW

7-Series

New for 99

No changes

Pros

Luxury features
Performance
Interior design

Cons

Trunk space
Fuel economy

Equipment

Major Standard Equipment: 4.4-liter V-8, 4-wheel antilock disc brakes, dual-temperature automatic air conditioning, cabin air filter, automatic ventilation system, power tilt and telescoping steering column, theft-alarm system, windshield wiper de-icer, power moonroof, remote keyless entry, AM/FM/WB/cassette stereo. **750iL adds:** 5.4-liter V-12, longer wheelbase, automatic stability control, high-intensity headlamps, headlamp washers, automatic leveling suspension, automatic shock absorber control, parking assist system, AM/FM/WB/CD/cassette stereo, heated steering wheel, heated front and rear seats, power rear seats, power rear sunshade.

Muscular and refined

The BMW 7-Series costs $10,000 more than its only real competitor, the Mercedes S-Class sedan. The big BMW has lower sales but a sportier edge.

The 7-Series comes only as a 4-door sedan in two wheelbase lengths, 115.5 or 121 inches. You can choose between two engines: a 4.4-liter V-8 and an optional 5.4-liter V-12, both with a 5-speed automatic transmission. Some people may see the Lexus LS 400 as a 7-Series rival, but the BMW is much larger, as are the long-wheelbase versions of the Mercedes S-Class and the Jaguar Vanden Plas.

As the BMW flagship sedan, the 7-Series offers safety features that other luxury cars don't have. Optional side air bags give added protection in the rear seat. Front air bags deploy with more force if occupants are wearing safety belts and with less force if they are not. Also, inflatable tubular bags protect the front seat occupants' heads from hitting the window or roof rail in a side crash.

The 750iL is quick; it gets to 60 mph in less than 7 seconds. From a standstill, the car seems to move lethargically until the engine speed climbs about half-way to the red line. The V-12 has plenty of passing power, and it uses high-octane gas. The 7-Series is almost as nimble and fun to drive as the less expensive 5-Series fitted with the V-8 engine and automatic transmission.

With handling unmatched by most sports cars, the 2-ton 750iL is built for the long-distance cruising at speeds not permitted in the U.S. In fact, in the 7-Series, you have to use the cruise control constantly lest you find yourself doing twice the legal limit.

Around town, the 750iL feels quiet and relaxed, but with the subdued power of a thoroughbred. This BMW really has two personalities: soft enough for trips around town, but tough enough for entertaining mountain roads. But even pottering along, it never loses its sporty edge or its composure.

The driving position is nearly perfect, with all controls in logical spots. A fat-rimmed steering wheel, white-on-black analog gauges lit red at night, a dashboard covered in two-tone leather separated by wood trim, and a center console with black-on-black controls—all say BMW loud and clear.

Entry and exit are easy to the front and rear seats. Head room is not as generous as that in other luxury cars. Otherwise, front-seat occupants are comfortable. Back-seat passengers have just as much head and leg room as front-seat ones, emphasizing a fundamental luxury concept: comfort for all. The trunk has a low liftover height for easy loading, but it's small for a luxury touring car's.

The BMW 750iL is a fine example of the balance between muscular sportiness and refined luxury. **D.V.S.**

Specifications of Test Vehicle

Model: 750iL

Exterior Dimensions	
Wheelbase	120.9 in.
Overall length	201.7 in.
Overall width	73.3 in.
Overall height	56.1 in.
Curb weight	4,300 lb.
Interior Dimensions	
Seating capacity	5
Head room	F:37.5/R:38.1 in.
Leg room	F:41.9/R:41.9 in.
Cargo volume	13 cu. ft.
Engine	
Displacement	V-12 5.4 L.
Horsepower	328 @ 5,000 rpm
Torque, lb-ft.	361 @ 3,900 rpm
Performance	
0-60 mph, acceleration	6.9 sec.
60-0 mph, braking	118 ft.
Turning circle	40 ft.
EPA city/highway	15/20 mpg
Test mileage	16 mpg
Fuel tank capacity	22.5 gal

Prices

$62,000
$95,000

740i sedan $63,540

740iL sedan $67,540

750iL sedan $93,240

Warranty

(years/miles)

Bumper-to-bumper 4/50,000

Powertrain 4/50,000

Rust-through 6/unlimited

Other to Consider

Jaguar Vanden Plas

Mercedes S-Class

Ratings

Group	Category	Rating (1–10)
Over The Road	Acceleration	10
	Transmission	10
	Braking	7
	Steering	9
	Ride	9
	Handling	9
	Drivability	9
	Fuel Economy	3
Passenger Environment	Comfort/Conven.	9
	Interior Room	10
	Driving Position	10
	Instrumentation	9
	Controls	8
	Visibility	8
	Entry/Exit	9
	Quietness	10
	Cargo Space	6
Workmanship	Interior	10
	Exterior	10
	Value	8

Ratings 173

BMW Z3

New for 99
Four-cylinder engine withdrawn

Pros
New six-cylinder
Sporty handling
Competitive price

Cons
Short touring range
No-tilt steering wheel
Inconsistent finishing

Equipment
Major Standard Equipment: 2.5 liter I-6, manual transmission, variable-assist power steering, 4-wheel antilock disc brakes, air conditioning, intermittent wipers, power mirrors, cruise control, power seats, vinyl upholstery, power windows, power locks, theft-alarm system, aluminum wheels. **2.8 adds:** 2.8-liter I-6, limited-slip differential, leather upholstery.
Major Options: Automatic transmission, leather upholstery, heated seats, heated mirrors, trip computer, power top.

Revenge

PRICES
$29,000
$40,000
1.9 2-door convertible $29,425
2.8 2-door convertible $35,900

WARRANTY (years/miles)
Bumper-to-bumper 4/50,000
Powertrain 4/50,000
Rust-through 6/unlimited

OTHER TO CONSIDER
Chevrolet Corvette Cabriolet
Porsche Boxster

With the Z3, BMW got its revenge for the failure of its 507 roadster, withdrawn in 1959 after finding only 252 takers in four years, the most famous of which was "the King" himself. The Z3 is an entirely different story and the Carolina assembly plant is running full steam to keep up with an insatiable clientele. Confident that it has found the right formula, the Munich builder is pushing its luck and a short while ago introduced a Mcoupe — akin to the fun-loving Volvo P1800 and other MGBs — and its diabolical M version. But the big news this year is the elimination of the 1.9-litre four-cylinder in favor of a 170-hp 2.5-litre six-cylinder. At long last, Z3 fans won't have to suffer the humiliation of staring into the tail lights of the Miata whenever both models happen to be traveling the same roads.

Despite a small cockpit, there are a number of practical storage spaces. Although the trunk is small, it provides an adequate amount of space for baggage. The top is easy to put down, but rear pillars are thick and they hinder visibility. Luckily, the Z3 has generously sized side-view mirrors to compensate. Are there any oversights to report? The steering column is still not height adjustable, seatbacks don't mold to the body very well, and the quality of finishing needs improvement. In addition, seat belts are anchored very high and saw into your collarbone, and the plastic rear windshield has no defroster.

As we told you once before, the 1.9-liter four-cylinder engine was much too tame to make the most of the chassis, even though it did its level best to convince you that it could. But never mind all that, now the 2.5-liter six-cylinder lets you have fun without breaking the bank. But hold your horses, the in-line 2.8-liter has wings (80% of the torque is available at 1500 rpm) and it really makes driving the Z3 an awful lot of fun. From the original Z3, the 2.8 has kept only a trace of its tendency to understeer and the rear end stays solidly anchored to the road surface. The only small criticism it deserves is for its slight instability on rough roads and a limited touring range when you drive over a fair distance with your foot solidly pressed down on the gas pedal.

Compared to the Boxster and SLK, the Z3 is the most respectful of the roadster spirit, the very spirit that has you digging out your white silk scarf, goggles, and leather helmet to fill your lungs with fresh air. **E.L.**

Specifications of Test Vehicle
Model: Z3 2.8

Exterior Dimensions	
Wheelbase	96.3 in.
Overall length	158.5 in.
Overall width	66.6 in.
Overall height	50.7 in.
Curb weight	1,290 lb.
Interior Dimensions	
Seating capacity	2
Head room	F:37.6 in.
Leg room	41.8 in.
Cargo volume	5 cu. ft.
Engine	
Displacement	I-6 2.8 L.
Horsepower	193 @ 5,800 rpm
Torque, lb-ft.	203 @ 3,950 rpm
Performance	
0-60 mph, acceleration	7,2 sec.
60-0 mph, braking	120 ft.
Turning circle	32.8 ft.
EPA city/highway	NA
Test mileage	NA
Fuel tank capacity	13.5 gal.

Ratings 149

Group	Category	Rating
Over The Road	Acceleration	10
	Transmission	9
	Braking	7
	Steering	9
	Ride	8
	Handling	9
	Drivability	8
	Fuel Economy	6
Passenger Environment	Comfort/Conven.	7
	Interior Room	6
	Driving Position	8
	Instrumentation	9
	Controls	9
	Visibility	6
	Entry/Exit	7
	Quietness	7
	Cargo Space	2
Workmanship	Interior	8
	Exterior	8
	Value	6

Buick Century

New for 99

Custom version with more equipment
Revised ABS system
Better traction control

Pros

Appealing lines
Proven mechanical system
Roomy interior

Cons

Virtually no driving pleasure
Outdated mechanics
Marshmallow suspension

Equipment

Major Standard Equipment: 3.1-liter V-6, automatic transmission, 4-wheel antilock brakes, tilt steering wheel, air conditioning, cabin air filter, rear defroster, power windows, power locks, remote keyless entry, AM/FM stereo, theft-deterrent system, stainless-steel exhaust system. **Limited adds:** Dual temperature controls, variable-assist steering, power heated mirrors. **Major Options:** Satellite communications system, integrated child safety seat, power moonroof, automatic dimming rear-view mirror, steering wheel stereo controls, AM/FM/cassette stereo, leather upholstery, power seats, dual temperature controls.

A model in waiting

Yes, the Buick Century is a model that uses the W platform. So it has the same drag coefficient as the Regal (0.31), the same weight distribution (64/36), the same turning radius (39.2 feet), the same instrument panel, etc. Are there any differences? Of course, a lot! The first is a 160-hp, 3.1-liter V-6, the only drivetrain available on Custom and Limited versions. Then come rear drum brakes, rack and pinion power steering (at least on the Custom, which according to Buick should be the most popular version), and suspension calibration that favors comfort over road stability. Result: a car that shows much less inspiration than the Regal.

The Century's interior design is disappointing from a number of standpoints and is decidedly dull. On the up side, the passenger compartment is roomy and bright, even if contrary to Buick's claims that the front bench seat (in a 55/45 configuration) makes it impossible to accommodate six passengers (especially given that, for safety, young children should always be seated in the rear of the vehicle). Having said that, the seats are comfortable whether you happen to be in the front or the rear and only the driver will find reason to complain about lateral support. Another plus: kiss your allergies goodbye! The air conditioning system includes a filter that cuts down on allergens that seep inside the passenger compartment (as long as you remember to change the filter on a regular basis). Another positive note: side-view mirrors are probably three times bigger than those you find on the LeSabre.

Like the Regal, the Century can be equipped with a steering wheel featuring radio controls. But watch out for the buttons, they tend to singe your thumbs, a small detail that needs rethinking.

The Buick division claims that the Century is intended for older drivers and the more miles you spend behind its wheel, the easier that is to believe. Its engine's 160 horses soon begin to huff and puff as they haul the model's 3,300 lbs. The DynaRide suspension is uncomfortable on rough roads, rolls on curves, and dives as soon as you brake with any kind of urgency. And braking power is hard to gauge, thanks largely to a very sensitive pedal. The steering system isolates the driver and provides very little feedback on road conditions, you say? Then again, that's what Buick-type comfort is all about.

Many more negative remarks could be made about the Century, but what's the point? As Buick itself points out, this mid-size model is built to be good company and make your traveling time pleasant, provided your itinerary consists of long, long stretches of ribbon-straight roads. **E.L.**

Specifications of Test Vehicle

Model: Century Custom

Exterior Dimensions	
Wheelbase	109 in.
Overall length	194.6 in.
Overall width	72.7 in.
Overall height	56.6 in.
Curb weight	3,350 lb.
Interior Dimensions	
Seating capacity	6
Head room	F:39.3/R:37.4 in.
Leg room	F:42.4/R:36.9 in.
Cargo volume	16.7 cu. ft.
Engine	
Displacement	V-6 3.1 L.
Horsepower	160 @ 5,200 rpm
Torque, lb-ft.	185 @ 4,000 rpm
Performance	
0-60 mph, acceleration	10.5 sec
60-0 mph, braking	137 ft.
Turning circle	37.4 ft.
EPA city/highway	20/29 mpg
Test mileage	22.6
Fuel tank capacity	17 gal.

Prices

$18,000
$22,000

Custom sedan $19,335

Limited sedan $20,705

Warranty

(years/miles)

Bumper-to-bumper 3/36,000

Powertrain 3/36,000

Rust-through 6/100,000

Other to consider

Ford Taurus

Chrysler Intrepid

Ratings

Category	Rating	Score
Over The Road	Acceleration	6
	Transmission	10
	Braking	4
	Steering	8
	Ride	8
	Handling	7
	Drivability	7
	Fuel Economy	6
Passenger Environment	Comfort/Conven.	8
	Interior Room	8
	Driving Position	8
	Instrumentation	7
	Controls	8
	Visibility	8
	Entry/Exit	8
	Quietness	8
	Cargo Space	8
Workmanship	Interior	8
	Exterior	8
	Value	8

Buick LeSabre

New for 99
More environment-friendly engine
New exterior color

Pros
Powertrain performance
Passenger room
Cargo space

Cons
Rear visibility
Fule economy
Seat comfort

Equipment
Major Standard Equipment: 3.8-liter V-6, automatic transmission, 4-wheel antilock brakes, air conditioning, AM/FM stereo, cruise control, tilt steering wheel, rear defroster, automatic headlamps, automatic power locks, variable-intermittent wipers, theft deterrent system, power windows, stainless-steel exhaust system. **Limited adds:** Auto-matic air conditioning, dual temperature controls, AM/FM/cassette stereo, remote keyless entry, theft alarm system.
Major Options: Satellite communications system, oil level sensor, steering wheel radio and temperature controls, remote keyless entry and traction control.

The final curtain

PRICES
$22,000
$29,000
Custom sedan $23,340
Limited sedan $26,605

WARRANTY (years/miles)
Bumper-to-bumper 3/36,000
Powertrain 3/36,000
Rust-through 6/100,000

OTHER TO CONSIDER
Ford Crown Victoria
Mercury Grand Marquis

The Buick LeSabre always ranks among the most popular full-size cars. Hinting at wealth without ostentation, this mainstream family car offers good value and quality.

The Pontiac Bonneville is mechanical equivalents to the LeSabre. Other competitors in this class are the Chrysler Concorde, Dodge Intrepid, and Mercury Grand Marquis. (The last offers a V-8 and rear-wheel drive.)

Buick's proven 3.8-liter V-6 engine gives the LeSabre good acceleration and capable passing response. The Gran Touring package includes an optional axle ratio to improve acceleration at the expense of highway gas mileage; it helped our test car zip to 60 mph in 8 seconds, but kept our overall fuel economy to about 19 mpg. The engine has ample power over a broad range of speeds, and it always runs smoothly and quietly. The electronically controlled 4-speed automatic shifts with remarkable smoothness.

The sports suspension gives the LeSabre well-controlled handling without sacrificing much ride comfort. It absorbs rough roads and most bumps. Firmer than the base suspension, it provides stability on the highway and extra control on corners. The optional variable-assist power steering never gets especially heavy, and it gives adequate road feedback.

In our tests, the LeSabre stopped in 127 feet from 60 mph — an average distance — with above-average control.

The full-size LeSabre easily accommodates six adults, and all seats offer ample head and leg room. Door-mounted power seat controls are poorly marked and not particularly easy to use. Unfortunately, the bench seats that give 6-passenger seating do so without much support. Entry and exit are easy.

With a low liftover and a wide, flat floor, the LeSabre's trunk gets high ratings.

Visibility suffers because of the moderately wide rear roof pillars. Power mirrors, convenient for a family with several drivers, are available only as an option on the base LeSabre.

The optional instrumentation adds a tachometer and gauges for all important engine functions. Their analog dials are easy to decipher at a glance. Warning lights, however, appear in a band across the top of the dash, out of the driver's main line of sight.

Most of the controls are conveniently located. You'll find a large switch for the headlights on the door panel, away from the more common location on the dash. The climate control system boasts dual temperature controls as a worthwhile option.

A touch of class without flashiness, practicality without starkness — Buick LeSabre continues to send good vibrations. **D.V.S.**

Specifications of Test Vehicle

Model: LeSabre Custom

Exterior Dimensions	
Wheelbase	110.8 in.
Overall length	200.8 in.
Overall width	74.4 in.
Overall height	55.6 in.
Curb weight	3,450 lb.
Interior Dimensions	
Seating capacity	6
Head room	F:38.8/R:37.8 in.
Leg room	F:42.6/R:40.4 in.
Cargo volume	17 cu. ft.
Engine	
Displacement	V-6 3.8 L.
Horsepower	205 @ 5,200 rpm
Torque, lb-ft.	230 @ 4,000 rpm
Performance	
0-60 mph, acceleration	8.2 sec.
60-0 mph, braking	127 ft.
Turning circle	40.7 ft.
EPA city/highway	19/30 mpg
Test mileage	19 mpg
Fuel tank capacity	18 gal.

Ratings 159

Group	Category	Rating
Over The Road	Acceleration	8
	Transmission	10
	Braking	6
	Steering	8
	Ride	8
	Handling	8
	Drivability	9
	Fuel Economy	4
Passenger Environment	Comfort/Conven.	8
	Interior Room	9
	Driving Position	9
	Instrumentation	9
	Controls	7
	Visibility	7
	Entry/Exit	9
	Quietness	8
	Cargo Space	8
Workmanship	Interior	9
	Exterior	7
	Value	8

Buick

Park Avenue

New for 99

Redesigned tail lights
Electrochemical rear-view mirror available
Four new exterior colors

Pros

Roomy interior
Comfortable ride
Powerful supercharged V-6

Cons

Marginal finishing
Size
Major fuel consumption (city driving)

Equipment

Major Standard Equipment: 3.8-liter V-6, automatic transmission, 4-wheel antilock brakes, automatic leveling suspension, power seats, dual control automatic air conditioning, cabin air filter, cruise control, automatic headlamps, automatic power locks, power windows, remote-control decklid release, AM/FM/cassette stereo, tilt steering column. **Ultra adds:** Supercharged 3.8-liter V-6, variable-assist power steering, traction control, tire-pressure monitor, power lumbar-support adjustment, leather upholstery, driver's memory system, heated seats, premium AM/FM/CD stereo, automatic variable-intermittent wipers, automatic dimming mirrors.

You're in for a surprise

Without doubt, the Park Avenue was one of my heartthrobs last year. Surprised? Certainly not as much as I — convinced this immense sedan would drive like a cruise ship steered by the rudder of a leviathan. Let yourself in for a surprise as well behind the wheel of an Ultra, and you will certainly decide, as I did, that many cars at comparable prices do not offer the comfort, space, or smooth ride of the Park Avenue.

The Park Avenue carries five or six passengers, depending on the model. Analog dials, square accessories, a wood strip along the entire dashboard . . . we've seen this dash panel a thousand times among so-called "fancy" American cars. That doesn't change anything (quite the contrary), but seems to give comfort to those who cling to tradition. Rear-seat passengers feel like they're riding in a limousine and baggage has plenty of space in the cavern that serves as a trunk. The only hitch is certain details of the finish lag behind a few rivals better equipped in this area.

Your basic Park Avenue comes with a 3.8-liter V-6 engine, and continues to provide sensible comfort, blending a soft suspension with honest performance. In the Ultra, it's another story. The 3.8-liter supercharged (like that of the Riviera) puts out 240 horsepower, and carries passengers with irresistible force. The Ultra does everything better and quite confidently so. It includes more accessories but fewer occupants (five rather than six passengers). It flies over irregularities in the road surface with ease. Its ability to handle twists and bends is fifty percent better than last year. It tips less on turns and its pick-up guarantees safe passing. It stops on a dime with four discs made bigger last year. And the triple-sealed doors and underchassis afford a ride so quiet, you'll feel like meditating . . .

E.L.

Specifications of Test Vehicle

Model: Park Avenue Ultra

Exterior Dimensions	
Wheelbase	113.8 in.
Overall length	206.8 in.
Overall width	74.7 in.
Overall height	57.4 in.
Curb weight	3,850 lb.
Interior Dimensions	
Seating capacity	6
Head room	F:39.8/R:38 in.
Leg room	F:42.4/R:41.4 in.
Cargo volume	19.1 cu. ft.
Engine	
Displacement	V-6 3.8 L.
Horsepower	240 @ 5,200 rpm
Torque, lb-ft.	280 @ 3,600 rpm
Performance	
0-60 mph, acceleration	8 sec.
60-0 mph, braking	135 ft.
Turning circle	40 ft.
EPA city/highway	18/27 mpg
Test mileage	20 mpg
Fuel tank capacity	18.5 gal.

PRICES
$31,000
$37,000
Sedan
$31,800
Ultra sedan
$36,695

WARRANTY
(years/miles)
Bumper-to-bumper
3/36,000
Powertrain
3/36,000
Rust-through
6/100,000

OTHER TO CONSIDER
Lincoln Continental
Chrysler LHS

Ratings

Group	Category	Rating
Over The Road	Acceleration	8
	Transmission	10
	Braking	5
	Steering	8
	Ride	8
	Handling	8
	Drivability	9
	Fuel Economy	5
Passenger Environment	Comfort/Conven.	8
	Interior Room	9
	Driving Position	9
	Instrumentation	9
	Controls	8
	Visibility	7
	Entry/Exit	9
	Quietness	9
	Cargo Space	9
Workmanship	Interior	9
	Exterior	9
	Value	7

Buick Regal

New for 99

Electrochemically tinted side-view mirrors
Revised ABS system
Improved traction control system

Pros

Strong acceleration
Roomy interior
Good trunk volume

Cons

Hard-to-gauge braking power
Hot steering-wheel mounted controls
Noisy tires

Equipment

Major Standard Equipment: 3.8-liter V-6, automatic transmission, 4-wheel antilock disc brakes, traction control, variable-assist power steering, dual temperature air conditioning, cabin air filter, variable-intermittent wipers, cruise control, power windows, remote keyless entry, power locks, power heated mirrors, AM/FM/cassette stereo, theft-deterrent system, stainless-steel exhaust system. **GS adds:** 3.8-liter supercharged V-6, leather upholstery, tire pressure monitor, sports suspension, power driver's seat, premium stereo, larger aluminum wheels. **Major Options:** AM/FM/CD/cassette stereo, heated seats, integrated child safety seat and power sunroof.

The other Century

PRICES
$21,000
$27,000
LS sedan $22,255
GS sedan $24,955

WARRANTY
Bumper-to-bumper 36,000
Powertrain 3/36,000
Rust-through 6/100,000

OTHER TO CONSIDER
Ford Taurus SHO
Mercury Sable

The big question about the Buick Regal is "Why?" Pontiac has been successful in carving out a niche as the performance division of GM. Now Buick, with its performance-oriented Regal, seems to be competing with Pontiac for the same niche. With the optional 240-horsepower supercharged engine, the Regal brings a little driving excitement to Buick's mainstream lineup.

Available only as a 4-door sedan, the Regal comes in two trim levels—LS and GS. It's built on the same platform as the Buick Century. Like all other Buicks, the Regal now has less powerful air bags to allay consumer concerns about injuries caused by the bags themselves.

On the road, we were surprised at Regal's user-friendly agility without user-abusing ride. Our GS handled several emergency maneuvers without complaint or a hint of misbehavior. Variable-assist power steering, another premium standard feature, improves road feel on the highway. The Regal tracks straight and true, requiring no corrections.

The supercharged 3.8-liter V-6 mirrors the suspension's flexibility. With the 4-speed electronically controlled automatic transmission, it's the very essence of gentility and reasonable fuel consumption, in town or on the interstate. (It needs high-octane gas, though.) Merging onto an expressway, the car has a ready reserve of power even at low engine speeds. The standard, normally aspirated engine is fine, but not a Taurus SHO competitor.

The Regal's standard, 4-wheel antilock disc brakes respond quickly and reassuringly. We easily stopped straight from 60 mph, but stopping distance was only slightly better than average.

The instrument panel has no voltmeter or oil pressure gauge. Even worse, the panel is visually busy: the warning-light symbols remain visible whether the lights are on or off. Otherwise, the interior is handsome and luxurious. All basic controls are logically located and easy to use. The climate control system's buttons could be slightly larger, but the system is intended to function automatically with minimal fiddling. The driver and passenger have separate temperature controls.

Inside, the front seats are particularly comfortable, with visibility so good that a six-foot driver can actually see the front fenders when parking. In the rear, the contoured seats suggest accommodation for two serious passengers, three only on a part-time basis. Splendidly muted, the Regal dismisses most wind and road noise with imperial disdain.

Saying that the Regal seems out of place in Buick's lineup is an understatement. It's nothing more than a Century on steroids, with prices starting $4,000 higher. **D.V.S.**

Specifications of Test Vehicle

Model: Regal GS

Exterior dimensions	
Wheelbase	109 in.
Overall length	196.2 in.
Overall width	72.7 in.
Overall height	56.6 in.
Curb weight	3,500 lb.
Interior dimensions	
Seating capacity	5
Head room	F:39.3/R:37.4 in.
Leg room	F:42.4/R:36.9 in.
Cargo volume	16.7 cu. ft.
Engine	
Displacement	V-6 3.8 L.
Horsepower	240 @ 5,200 rpm
Torque, lb-ft.	280 @ 3,600 rpm
Performance	
0-60 mph, acceleration	7.8 sec.
60-0 mph, braking	131 ft.
Turning circle	37.5 ft.
EPA city/highway	17/27 mpg
Test mileage	26.5 mpg
Fuel tank capacity	17 gal.

Ratings

Category	Rating
Over the Road	
Acceleration	9
Transmission	9
Braking	5
Steering	8
Ride	8
Handling	8
Drivability	8
Fuel Economy	5
Passenger Environment	
Comfort/Conven.	8
Interior Room	7
Driving Position	8
Instrumentation	7
Controls	8
Visibility	8
Entry/Exit	7
Quietness	8
Cargo Space	8
Workmanship	
Interior	8
Exterior	8
Value	8

Ratings 153

Cadillac Catera

New for 99

New fuel tank
Increased radius for remote door lock system

Pros

Attention to finishing details
Quiet ride
Excellent transmission

Cons

A V-6 that lacks power
Limited storage space
Marginal manufacturing quality

Equipment

Major Standard Equipment: 3-liter V-6, traction control, automatic leveling suspension, 4-wheel antilock disc brakes, automatic headlights, wi-per-activated headlights, variable-intermittent wipers, heated windshield washers, remote keyless entry, dual-temperature automatic air conditioning, cabin air filter, rear defroster,AM/FM/cassette stereo, power seats, split-folding rear seat, tilt steering wheel, cruise control, power windows, power heated mirrors, power decklid release, automatic-dimming rear-view mirror.
Major Options: Heated front and rear seats, driver's memory system, power sunroof, leather upholstery, theft-deterrent system.

James Dean

The Catera is the James Dean of the Cadillac family. Born in Europe and reeducated in North America, it has to convince buyers who go for small BMWs and Mercedes to leave their prejudices behind and visit it in a showroom usually reserved for flashy and stodgy boat-like vehicles. In short, no one is beating down the doors, but Cadillac remains hopeful.

If it's been a long time since you've ridden in a Cadillac, this one should come as a pleasant surprise. No danger of being blinded by chrome as you approach the Catera. Touching the materials is enough to see that they are of very good quality and looking at them is enough to see that a lot of thought has gone into matching them with one another. The only slight flaws are a tiny lack of attention to detail and a limited amount of storage space. Still, contrary to Cadillac's claim, the Catera can accommodate not five but four adults because of the transmission tunnel that reduces the amount of usable space in the passenger compartment. Apart from this annoying bump, the Catera is still one of the roomiest cars in its category.

If Catera's early career seems to have been trouble-free, the credit goes to Cadillac, which quickly solved the problems caused by the 3.0-liter V-6. Since reliability was never called into question, now the company has to find a way to give this drivetrain the verve it doesn't always manage to show, particularly in the lower rpm range. Is it the lack of engine speed or the way the vehicle around it has been set up? Regardless, "my" Catera had a hard time getting to within one second of the acceleration times announced by Cadillac. Luckily there's nothing to criticize about the automatic transmission, which shifts smoothly and precisely. Good marks also go to suspension adjustments, a good compromise between the proverbially European firmness and the historic American softness. Other good news: the traction control system, now coupled with a Bosch 5.3 system, no longer limits its intervention to cutting off the motor's energy source and now also calls brakes into action to put pressure on the rear discs. The steering system lacks some precision at the center, but the fact remains that the Catera is an impeccable tourer. Particularly good soundproofing eliminates all noise except for the noise caused by tires traveling on bumpy roads.

Although it needs a tad more balance and consistency to reach the same lofty level as its German-built rivals, the Catera is less pretentious ("Of course! What else can you expect from a Cadillac," its detractors will say) and less expensive to maintain. **E.L.**

Specifications of Test Vehicle

Model: Catera

Exterior Dimensions	
Wheelbase	107.4 in.
Overall length	194 in.
Overall width	70.3 in.
Overall height	56.3 in.
Curb weight	3,750 lb.
Interior Dimensions	
Seating capacity	5
Head room	F:38.7/R:38.4 in.
Leg room	F:42.2/R:37.5 in.
Cargo volume	14.5 cu. ft.
Engine	
Displacement	V-6 3 L.
Horsepower	200 @ 6,000 rpm
Torque, lb-ft.	192 @ 3,600 rpm
Performance	
0-60 mph, acceleration	8.9 sec.
60-0 mph, braking	129 ft.
Turning circle	33.5 ft.
EPA city/highway	18/24 mpg
Test mileage	NA
Fuel tank capacity	18 gal.

Prices
$30,000
$35,000
Sedan $30,635

Warranty
Bumper-to-bumper 4/50,000
Powertrain 4/50,000
Rust-through 6/100,000

Other to Consider
Infiniti I30
Lexus ES300

Group	Category	Rating
Over The Road	Acceleration	8
	Transmission	9
	Braking	5
	Steering	9
	Ride	8
	Handling	9
	Drivability	8
	Fuel Economy	5
Passenger Environment	Comfort/Conven.	8
	Interior Room	8
	Driving Position	8
	Instrumentation	8
	Controls	8
	Visibility	9
	Entry/Exit	8
	Quietness	9
	Cargo Space	8
Workmanship	Interior	9
	Exterior	9
	Value	7

Ratings 160

Cadillac DeVille

New for 99

Standard antitheft system
Electric lumbar support with massage feature
New exterior colors

Pros

Powertrain performance
Passenger/cargo room
Ride comfort

Cons

Handling
Fuel economy
Side-view mirrors

Equipment

Major Standard Equipment: 4.6-liter V-8, traction control, 4-wheel antilock disc brakes, side air bags, power front seat, automatic air conditioning, dual temperature controls, automatic variable-intermittent wipers, cruise control, automatic headlamps, automatic power locks, remote keyless entry, power windows, AM/FM/cassette stereo, tilt steering column, power heated mirrors, theft-deterrent system, stainless-steel exhaust, aluminum wheels. **D'Elegance adds:** Premium memory for driver's preferences, power front seat lumbar adjustment, premium stereo, leather upholstery. **Concours adds:** More powerful engine (300 hp), automatic stability control, individual front seats, fog lamps, power lumbar adjustment.

First class

PRICES
$36,000
$45,000

Sedan
$39,300

D'Elegance sedan
$43,400

Concours sedan
$43,900

WARRANTY
(years/miles)

Bumper-to-bumper
4/50,000

Powertrain
4/50,000

Rust-through
6/100,000

OTHER TO CONSIDER

Lincoln Town Car

With the demise of the rear-wheel-drive Fleetwood, the DeVille takes on added importance in the Cadillac lineup. Now the biggest Cadillac and one of the biggest front-wheel-drive cars on the road, it's a full-size luxury car in the Detroit tradition.

The 4-door DeVille shares many components with the Seville. The new d'Elegance trim level brings a 5-passenger seating package and more luxury cues as an alternative to the sportier, more potent Concours.

The DeVille delivers the ride and handling of a traditional full-size luxury car--that familiar "boulevard ride." A speed-sensitive suspension adjusts automatically to give a softer ride at lower speeds and enhanced control and stability at higher speeds. The car still tends to wallow and roll a bit on undulating pavement, but it absorbs most surface irregularities without complaint. Automatic stability control on the Concours helps drivers recover from minor skids.

The DeVille's speed-sensitive power steering system provides maximum boost when parking, but requires more effort at higher speeds. Much improved from past versions, the steering feels just right under most driving conditions.

The Northstar engine solves any of the DeVille's past performance problems. Just a squeeze of the accelerator summons a surplus of silky smooth, quiet power. The Northstar runs significantly faster than old Cadillac V-8s, and the added muscular sound under the hood adds to the feeling of luxury.

We averaged 16 mpg in our tests. That's far from impressive, but fuel economy may be low on a Cadillac buyer's list of priorities.

The base Deville is one of few sedans that can honestly claim to seat six adults. The cavernous interior has ample head, hip, and leg room for everyone. Thanks to flat cushions, the seats are easy to get in and out of, but they have little lumbar support. On cool mornings, the heated seats remind you just what luxury is.

At 20 cubic feet, trunk space is generous, too. The bumper-level liftover makes loading easy.

Wide rear roof pillars block the driver's over-the-shoulder view. Although the windows are quite large, the outside mirrors are far too small for such a large car. The DeVille's aerodynamic design and ample sound proofing make the interior very quiet at any speed.

If you've owned a Cadillac before, you'll have little trouble feeling at home behind the wheel of a DeVille. The major controls are in familiar locations and are, for the most part, easy to find and operate, day or night. The digital speedometer and fuel gauge, including readouts for instant and average fuel economy, are simple and easy-to-read. If you prefer analog instruments, the Concours trim is your only choice.

With the addition of several new features, the DeVille is setting standards for safety and security among large domestic cars. **D.V.S.**

Specifications of Test Vehicle

Model: DeVille

Exterior Dimensions	
Wheelbase	113.8 in.
Overall length	209.7 in.
Overall width	76.5 in.
Overall height	56.4 in.
Curb weight	4,050 lb.
Interior Dimensions	
Seating capacity	5
Head room	F:38.5/R:38.4 in.
Leg room	F:42.6/R:43.3 in.
Cargo volume	20 cu. ft.
Engine	
Displacement	V-8, 4.6 L.
Horsepower	275 @ 5,600 rpm
Torque, lb-ft.	300 @ 4,000 rpm
Performance	
0-60 mph, acceleration	7.6 sec.
60-0 mph, braking	120 ft.
Turning circle	40.7 ft.
EPA city/highway	17/26 mpg
Test mileage	16 mpg
Fuel tank capacity	20 gal.

Ratings

Group	Category	Rating
Over The Road	Acceleration	9
Over The Road	Transmission	10
Over The Road	Braking	7
Over The Road	Steering	8
Over The Road	Ride	9
Over The Road	Handling	6
Over The Road	Drivability	10
Over The Road	Fuel Economy	3
Passenger Environment	Comfort/Conven.	9
Passenger Environment	Interior Room	10
Passenger Environment	Driving Position	9
Passenger Environment	Instrumentation	7
Passenger Environment	Controls	7
Passenger Environment	Visibility	7
Passenger Environment	Entry/Exit	10
Passenger Environment	Quietness	8
Passenger Environment	Cargo Space	9
Workmanship	Interior	8
Workmanship	Exterior	8
Workmanship	Value	8

Ratings
162

Cadillac

Eldorado

New for 99

Standard antitheft system
Driver's seat with massaging lumbar support
New exterior colors

Pros

Well-balanced chassis
Powerful engine
Original accessories

Cons

Fuel consumption
Model scheduled for withdrawal
Limited head room

Equipment

Major Standard Equipment: 4.6-liter V-8, 4-wheel antilock disc brakes, traction control, automatic shock absorber control, automatic air conditioning, tilt steering wheel, cruise control, rear defroster, automatic headlights, theft-deterrent system, automatic power locks, remote keyless entry, power windows, power seats, digital instruments, AM/FM/cassette stereo, power heated mirrors. **Touring adds:** More powerful engine (300 hp), performance axle ratio, automatic shock absorber control, automatic stability control, dual temperature controls, power lumbar adjustment, leather upholstery, analog instruments, theft alarm.

Dying gracefully

Some of us will doubtless remember 1998 as the year in which European two-door sedans were reborn in North America. We might have expected to attend the Cadillac Eldorado's funeral, especially since, unlike the Seville, it had not been revamped last year. But rumor has it that it will disappear very shortly, only to be resurrected sometime between 2001 and 2002. They say the new Eldorado will have a rear- instead of front-wheel drive and will be based on the Catera, rather than the Seville.

Collectors, you have just a few months to add to your fleet of this majestic two-door sedan, this year notably featuring a vibro-massage seat and three new exterior colors.

The reasoning behind some of the Eldorado's designs wasn't too clear. For example, not only do its huge roof pillars lack finesse, they block the rear corner view. And don't count on the minuscule side-view mirrors to help you out here. The interior tries to seem plush and refined, but the fake wood on the dash and console is in dubious taste. In any case, only four people at a time can inspect such details because space is limited in front and back (once you've managed to crawl in) — particularly in terms of head room. We were comfy in the bucket seats, but at the first turn wished they had offered a bit more support. While it may not be very good at preventing you from being jostled about, the driver's seat does have the advantage of providing the occasional massage, as long as you choose the electric lumbar-support option, which on demand shifts into a sustained up-and-down rolling movement to soothe your aching back. The trunk offers/provides plenty of space for your golf bag to sprawl out in.

No need to put the pedal to the metal to appreciate an Eldorado's performance. The V-8 Northstar that propels it proved powerful, easily manageable, discreet, and a real hog, naturally, with an Eldorado Touring Coupe consuming an average 18 mpg. Nor will you get great savings with the tamer 275-hp model, although it holds the road, handles turns well, and accelerates incredibly fast. The electromagnetic variable-assist speed-sensitive steering (the "Magnasteer") is astoundingly precise and brakes do their fair share to make you feel in complete control of the car, a trait that was lacking in the past. **E.L.**

Specifications of Test Vehicle

Model: Touring Coupe

Exterior Dimensions	
Wheelbase	108 in.
Overall length	200.2 in.
Overall width	75.5 in.
Overall height	53.6 in.
Curb weight	3,850 lb.
Interior Dimensions	
Seating capacity	5
Head room	F:37.8/R:38.3 in.
Leg room	F:42.6/R:36.1 in.
Cargo volume	15.3 cu. ft.
Engine	
Displacement	V-8, 4.6 L.
Horsepower	300 @ 6,000 rpm
Torque, lb-ft.	295 @ 4,400 rpm
Performance	
0-60 mph, acceleration	7.1 sec.
60-0 mph, braking	128 ft.
Turning circle	40.4 ft.
EPA city/highway	17/26 mpg
Test mileage	18 mpg
Fuel tank capacity	20 gal.

Prices

$38,000
$49,000

Coupe
$39,905

Touring coupe
$44,165

Warranty

Bumper-to-bumper
4/50,000

Powertrain
4/50,000

Rust-through
6/100,000

Other to consider

None

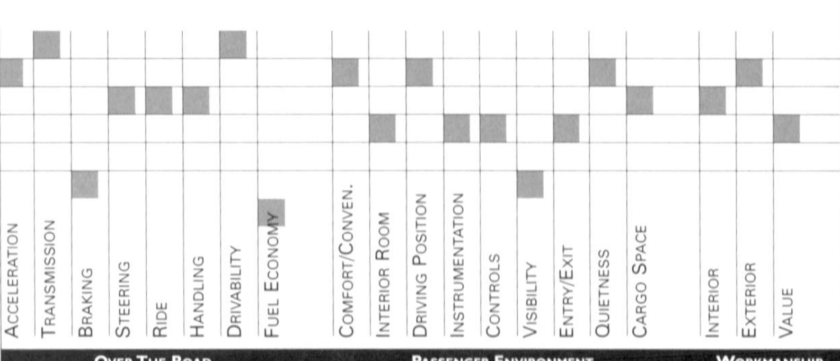

Ratings
154

Cadillac Escalade

new MODEL

New for 99

New model for Cadillac, based on Chevrolet Tahoe and GMC Yukon

Pros

Comfort/convenience
Powertrain
Luxury features

Cons

Handling
Fuel economy
Braking

Equipment

Major Standard Equipment: 5.7 liter V-8 engine, 4-speed automatic transmission, automatic 4-wheel drive, antilock brakes, locking rear differential, towing package, heated 10-way power front seats, heated 60/40 split folding rear seat, programmable remote keyless locking and security, automatic headlights, heated mirrors, air conditioning, Bose AM/FM/cassette/CD changer sound system, power windows and locks, OnStar system.
Major Options: None

Quick damage control

PRICES
$46,500
$50,000

WARRANTY
(years/miles)
Bumper-to-Bumper
4/50,000
Power Train
4/50,000
Rust-through
6/100,000

OTHER TO CONSIDER
Lincoln Navigator

The Escalade is new to the Cadillac lineup of 1999. It is the perfect example of what GM said it was not going to do — and then did it. After watching the dumbfounding success of the Lincoln Navigator and other oversized sport-utility vehicles, Cadillac dealers put the pressure on GM to give them something comparable to sell. Thus the Escalade, a very upscale version of Chevrolet's Tahoe, and the GMC Yukon and Denali.

Front sheetmetal, grill, and body side cladding distinguish Escalade's outward appearance from its corporate cousins. Inside, the shared instrument panel is familiar, but is dressed up with wood trim. The heated power seats are unique to Cadillac. Covered with soft, perforated leather, they offer the ultimate in comfort and support. The rear seat is the split folding design, with space for three adults or for additional cargo. Head, shoulder, and leg room abounds. A fold-down tailgate is just the thing for impromptu social gatherings at the equestrian center.

The Bose Acoustimass sound system features a dual media arrangement. It allows rear-seat passengers to listen to a different audio source, and lets them change volume, stations, and play modes. The standard OnStar communication and GPS-based navigation system is located in the overhead console. The only engine offered is the standard 5.7-liter V-8, capable of 255 hp. Combined with a silky-smooth 4-speed automatic transmission and a fully automatic 4-wheel drive arrangement, this powertrain delivers seamless power under all but the worst driving conditions. However, Escalade's bulk and weight penalize its performance in several important areas. Accelerating its 5600 pounds to 60 mph takes over eleven seconds. Stopping from 60 mph under emergency conditions takes a well-above-average 155 feet. And don't expect fuel economy above the low teens.

With the help of premium shock absorbers and special suspension tweaks, escalade delivers a smooth ride on all but the worst of roads. Like all other tall, heavy SUVs, swaying from side to side on uneven roads spoils the illusion of luxury. Steering and handling on winding roads are anything but quick and agile. The Escalade's size and weight require slowing down on turns that a car could take easily.

The driving position allows a full view of the road ahead and large mirrors help the view to the sides. Roof pillars, headrests, and the vehicle's high stance restrict the view to the rear. Backing up and parking require your full attention, and the large turning radius restricts maneuverability. Entry and exit can only be described as SUV-like, requiring either a climb up or a slide down. Running boards are handy for smaller folks, but only help others get their clothes dirty.

Lincoln succeeded with the Navigator, which is just a gussied-up Expedition. It seems logical to assume Cadillac can do the same with the Escalade. We're betting they sell all they can build. **D.V.S.**

Specifications of Test Vehicle

Model: Escalade

Exterior Dimensions	
Wheelbase	117.5 in.
Overall Length	201.2 In.
Overall Width	77.0 In.
Overall Height	74.3 In.
Curb Weight	5572 lbs.
Interior Dimensions	
Seating Capacity	5
Head Room	F: 39.9/R: 38.9 in.
Leg Room	F: 41.7/R: 36.4 in.
Cargo Room	31 cu.ft.
Engine	
Displacement	5.7 L V-8
Horsepower	255@4600 rpm
Torque, lb-ft.	330@2800 rpm
Performance	
0-60 mph, acceleration	11.5 sec.
60-0 mph, braking	155 ft.
Turning Circle	40.7 ft.
EPA City/Highway	13/16 mpg.
Test Mileage	NA
Fuel Tank Capacity	29.5 gal.

Ratings

Group	Category	Rating
Over The Road	Acceleration	5
	Transmission	9
	Braking	1
	Steering	7
	Ride	8
	Handling	6
	Drivability	8
	Fuel Economy	3
Passenger Environment	Comfort/Conven.	9
	Interior Room	10
	Driving Position	9
	Instrumentation	8
	Controls	9
	Visibility	7
	Entry/Exit	7
	Quietness	8
	Cargo Space	10
Workmanship	Interior	9
	Exterior	9
	Value	6

Ratings
148

Cadillac

Seville

New for 99

Driver's seat with a massage function
Heated seats available
Two new exterior colors

Pros

Acceleration
Handling
Ride

Cons

Fuel economy
Climate controls
Rear visibility

Equipment

Major Standard Equipment: 4.6-liter V-8, ABS, traction control, power seats, tilt steering wheel, AM/FM/cassette stereo, automatic air conditioning, cruise control, remote keyless entry, theft-deterrent system, power locks, power windows, automatic dimming, rear-view mirror, power heated mirrors, **STS adds:** More powerful engine, automatic shock absorber control, dual temperature controls, power lumbar adjustment, leather upholstery, automatic dimming driver-side mirror. **Major Options:** Power moonroof, memory mirrors, antitheft alarm, analog instruments, automatic dimming rear-view mirror, leather upholstery, heated seat.

Ambitions to fulfill

For 1998, Cadillac has redesigned its international-size luxury sedan, the Seville, to make it more competitive in a world market.

The Seville faces a challenge in claiming territory already staked out by the likes of the BMW 5-Series, Lexus GS and LS, and the Mercedes E-Class.

The new, aerodynamic styling still makes the car instantly recognizable as a Seville. It comes in two trims: the luxury SLS and the sporty STS. The SLS has a 275-horsepower V-8, a softer suspension, and less precise steering than the STS, which uses a 300-horsepower version of the same engine.

The Northstar engine continues to deliver smooth response and quick acceleration. As standard equipment, the STS has Cadillac's new "performance algorithm shifting" transmission, which senses your intentions under enthusiastic driving and shifts accordingly. For example, in hard cornering, it will select and hold the appropriate gear, just as an experienced driver would downshift with a manual transmission. Such performance comes at the expense of fuel economy, though; we averaged only 17 mpg.

During normal driving, the steering is quick and precise, with excellent feedback. Unfortunately, the combination of high horsepower and front-wheel drive produces considerable torque steer during hard acceleration. Continuously variable shock absorbers optimize ride and handling on all types of roads. The ride is satisfyingly firm but not harsh; the car exhibits stable, predictable handling. All Sevilles have automatic stability control for better control in bad weather or emergency maneuvers. Driven aggressively, the Seville feels like the luxury sports sedan it strives to be.

Inside, Cadillac has most noticeably improved the seats. They automatically adjust to support you, even when you change positions in the driver's seat. There's generous leg and head room, front and rear. Seat-mounted shoulder belts combine with the multiple seat adjustments to make any driver comfortable behind the wheel. Visibility is good in all directions, and the side-view mirrors are large and well located.

The most frequently used controls are placed closest to the driver. Remote controls for important functions are on the steering wheel, and all other controls are placed logically. The glovebox and center console can hold a variety of commonly carried items, and a pass-through in the rear seatback allows you to carry long items inside the trunk.

Cadillac will also build Sevilles with steering wheels on the right, demonstrating its resolve to take on the world market. With its performance, handling, and comfort, the Seville is a serious contender in its class. **D.V.S.**

Specifications of Test Vehicle

Model: Seville SLS

Exterior Dimensions	
Wheelbase	111 in.
Overall length	204.1 in.
Overall width	74.2 in.
Overall height	54.5 in.
Curb weight	3,900 lb.
Interior Dimensions	
Seating capacity	5
Head room	F:38/R:38.3 in.
Leg room	F:43/R:39.1 in.
Cargo volume	14.4 cu. ft.
Engine	
Displacement	V-8, 4.6 L.
Horsepower	275 @ 5,600 rpm
Torque, lb-ft.	300 @ 4,000 rpm
Performance	
0-60 mph, acceleration	7.1 sec.
60-0 mph, braking	134 ft.
Turning circle	42 ft.
EPA city/highway	17/26 mpg
Test mileage	16 mpg
Fuel tank capacity	20 gal.

Prices

$41,000
$51,000

SLS sedan $44,025

STS sedan $48,520

Warranty

(years/miles)

Bumper-to-bumper 4/50,000

Powertrain 4/50,000

Rust-through 6/100,000

Other to Consider

Lexus GS

Lincoln Continental

Ratings (scale 1–10)

Over the Road: Acceleration, Transmission, Braking, Steering, Ride, Handling, Drivability, Fuel Economy

Passenger Environment: Comfort/Conven., Interior Room, Driving Position, Instrumentation, Controls, Visibility, Entry/Exit, Quietness, Cargo Space

Workmanship: Interior, Exterior, Value

Chevrolet Astro

New for 99

New all-wheel drive system
Redesigned roof console
New exterior colors

Pros

Versatility
Efficient all-wheel drive
Strong engine

Cons

High fuel consumption
Roomy front
Heavy removable bench seat

Equipment

Major Standard Equipment: 4.3-liter V-6, 5-passenger seating, 4-wheel antilock brakes, air conditioning, AM/FM stereo, vinyl upholstery, dual rear panel doors, variable-intermittent wipers. **LS adds:** Cloth upholstery, power locks, tilt steering wheel, cruise control, 8-passenger seating. **LT adds:** Privacy glass, power mirrors, remote keyless entry, power windows. **Major Options:** All-wheel drive, rear air conditioning, 7-passenger seating, 8-passenger seating, rear liftglass, power seats, integrated child-safety seat, AM/FM/cassette stereo, power locks, remote keyless entry, privacy glass, power windows, power mirrors, cruise control, tilt steering wheel, trailer towing package.

Jack of all trades

City or country? Construction sites or farms? On dirt roads or asphalt ribbons? Regardless of the terrain, the Chevrolet Astro is a good road companion. And things are looking even better now, since Ford has interrupted production of its Aerostar, the Astro's biggest rival. For 1999, Chevrolet has eased up and revised the roof console, modernized the all-wheel drive system, and once again improved the capabilities of the four-speed automatic transmission.

By making front seats roomier two years ago, the Astro's designers almost eliminated one of the biggest criticisms heard since this minivan was launched in 1984. As an added bonus, the change came with an all-new dashboard with modern, rounded lines and a passenger air bag. The center console is positioned to provide the driver with easy access to air conditioning and radio controls. Some details are still aggravating, such as the shoddy appearance of certain materials and the positioning of certain accessories (you can't drink and smoke at the same time). Some may say that the seats don't provide enough support, but then again the Astro isn't the type of vehicle to take corners on two wheels.

Despite a number of improvements introduced over the years, the Astro and Safari are still extremely sensitive to crosswinds and the variable-assist steering system does little to correct the problem. These minivans are very well-behaved when winter hits, unless you have the bright idea (and the budget) to check the AWD transmission on the option list. Keep in mind that it does have its faults, reducing handling quality and increasing gas consumption, already high with the 4.3-liter Vortec V-6 engine. As compensation for its penchant for black gold, this engine doesn't have to be coaxed to deliver its power, it really moves. Into the bargain, it has plenty of torque and convincing acceleration power. Lastly, the suspension gobbles up road bumps, though not without some stiffness, but it's better than riding in a school bus, one of my young passengers was heard to comment. On the other hand, brakes tend to fade after a few abrupt stops.

A work vehicle, tool box, or minibus, the Astro can wear a number of different hats. It's up to you to decide which you prefer! **E.L.**

Prices

$18,000
$29,000

3-door van $18,167
LS 3-door van $22,044
LT 3-door van $23,709

Warranty
(years/miles)

Bumper-to-bumper 3/36,000
Powertrain 3/36,000
Rust-through 6/100,000

Other to consider

Volkswagen Eurovan

Specifications of Test Vehicle

Model: Astro

Exterior Dimensions	
Wheelbase	111.2 in.
Overall length	189.8 in.
Overall width	77.5 in.
Overall height	76 in.
Curb weight	4,200 lb.
Interior Dimensions	
Seating capacity	8
Head room	F:39.2/R:37.9/R2:38.7 in.
Leg room	F:41.6/R:36.5/R2:38.5 in.
Cargo volume	41.3 cu. ft.
Engine	
Displacement	V-6 4.3 L.
Horsepower	190 @ 4,400 rpm
Torque, lb-ft.	250 @ 2,800 rpm
Performance	
0-60 mph, acceleration	11.8 sec.
60-0 mph, braking	137 ft.
Turning circle	39.5 ft.
EPA city/highway	16/21 mpg
Test mileage	15 mpg
Fuel tank capacity	25 gal.

Ratings

Group	Category	Rating
Over The Road	Acceleration	5
Over The Road	Transmission	9
Over The Road	Braking	4
Over The Road	Steering	5
Over The Road	Ride	4
Over The Road	Handling	6
Over The Road	Drivability	7
Over The Road	Fuel Economy	3
Passenger Environment	Comfort/Conven.	5
Passenger Environment	Interior Room	8
Passenger Environment	Driving Position	3
Passenger Environment	Instrumentation	8
Passenger Environment	Controls	8
Passenger Environment	Visibility	8
Passenger Environment	Entry/Exit	5
Passenger Environment	Quietness	7
Passenger Environment	Cargo Space	10
Workmanship	Interior	7
Workmanship	Exterior	7
Workmanship	Value	7

Ratings 126

Chevrolet Blazer

New for 99

New TrailBlazer model
Optional Autotrac system

Pros

Efficient powertrain
Good handling
Comfortable ride

Cons

Limited visibility (2 doors)
Marginal braking power
Diffcult rear-seat access

Equipment

Major Standard Equipment: 4.3-liter V-6, automatic transmission, 4-wheel antilock disc brakes, air conditioning, AM/FM stereo, variable-intermittent wipers, split-bench seat, automatic headlamps. **LS adds:** Luggage rack, rear wiper/washer, tilt steering wheel, cruise control, individual front seats, power locks, power windows, power mirrors, power tailgate release, AM/FM/cassette stereo, larger tires, aluminum wheels. **LT adds:** Remote keyless entry, power driver's lumbar adjustment. **Trail Blazer adds:** Leather interior, high intensity headlights

PRICES
$22,000
$30,000

2-door $21,663
4-door $23,188
LS 2-door $24,518
LS 4-door $26,744
LT 2-door $25,153
LT 4-door $28,117

WARRANTY (years/miles)

Bumper-to-bumper 3/36,000
Powertrain 3/36,000
Rust-through 6/100,000

OTHER TO CONSIDER

Ford Explorer
Dodge Durango

A strategic promise

Last year, the Chevrolet Blazer jumped on the sport utility bandwagon with newfound ambition. A new front-end treatment, more aggressively styled wheel covers, more detailed standard equipment and, at long last, a second air bag for the passenger side were a few of its new features. To get us even more excited, some General Motors executives said that they were toying with the possibility of putting an eight-cylinder engine under the hood. The promise wasn't kept, but by way of apology Chevrolet is bringing us the TrailBlazer version and its Autotrac system. Apology accepted!

Heated and leather-covered seats, an electrochemically tinted rear-view mirror, and electronic temperature control are fancy accessories that do nothing to change a driving position made uncomfortable by an overly long steering column that makes you hug your elbows close to your body and stretch your legs as far as they go. Still, seats are comfortable, instrumentation is detailed, and the dashboard looks quite good. On the down side, although they're grouped within easy reach of the driver, the controls are not always positioned where they should be. The radio buttons, for example, are partially hidden behind the shift lever when it's in "D." And the air conditioning controls seem to be placed for the passenger's convenience. On the two-door version, access to the rear calls for acrobatic skills and, in any case, the back bench can take on only two people. The four-door version is roomier (but not as roomy as Ford's Explorer), but the bench seat's cushion is set very low (to get a completely flat surface when it's folded down) and that means that passengers ride with their knees somewhere around their ears, or almost. At least headrests are a nice touch.

On the road, you'll get along well with this utility if you've taken the time to find out all about the four suspension groups available, ranging from "soft" to "sport," not to mention "touring" and "off-road." With the exception of the five-speed manual transmission (available only on the two-door version), the buyer has no other decisions to make as far as the powertrain goes. The 4.3-liter Vortec V-6 is the only engine choice and its performance is beyond reproach, especially when you compare its fuel consumption to some of its rival V-8s. A relatively precise steering system, a turning radius that's tight enough to make city driving pleasant, and a more modern all-wheel drive system are assets that make the Blazer attractive. It's Achilles heel is braking, which offers minimal stopping power and is hard to gauge. **E.L.**

Specifications of Test Vehicle

Model: Blazer LT

Exterior Dimensions	
Wheelbase	107 in.
Overall length	183.3 in.
Overall width	67.8 in.
Overall height	64.2 in.
Curb weight	4,000 lb.
Interior Dimensions	
Seating capacity	5
Head room	F:39.6/R:38.2 in.
Leg room	F:42.4/R:36.3 in.
Cargo volume	16.1 cu. ft.
Engine	
Displacement	V-6 4.3 L.
Horsepower	190 @ 4,400 rpm
Torque, lb-ft.	250 @ 2,800 rpm
Performance	
0-60 mph, acceleration	9.9 sec.
60-0 mph, braking	129 ft.
Turning circle	39.5 ft.
EPA city/highway	16/20 mpg
Test mileage	18 mpg
Fuel tank capacity	18 gal.

10
9
8
7
6
5
4
3
2
1

Over The Road: Acceleration, Transmission, Braking, Steering, Ride, Handling, Drivability, Fuel Economy

Passenger Environment: Comfort/Conven., Interior Room, Driving Position, Instrumentation, Controls, Visibility, Entry/Exit, Quietness, Cargo Space

Workmanship: Interior, Exterior, Value

Ratings
152

Chevrolet Camaro

New for 99
Bigger gas tank
Traction control available with the V-6

Pros
Refinement
Exciting performance capabilities (V-8)
Efficient V-6

Cons
Cramped interior
Very firm suspension
Stiff platform (convertible)

Equipment
Major Standard Equipment: 3.8-liter V-6, manual transmission, 4-wheel antilock disc brakes, air conditioning, tilt steering wheel, variable-intermittent wipers, AM/FM/cassette stereo, folding rear seat, theft-deterrent system, stainless-steel exhaust system. **Z28 adds:** 5.7-liter V-8, automatic transmission, limited-slip differential, sports suspension, larger tires, aluminum wheels.

Prices
$17,000
$29,000

3-door $16,625

3-door open roof $17,620

2-door convertible $22,660

Z28 3-door $20,470

Z28 3-door open roof $21,465

Z28 2-door convertible $28,385

Warranty
(years/miles)

Bumper-to-bumper 3/36,000

Powertrain 3/36,000

Rust-through 6/100,000

Other to Consider
Ford Mustang

The more refined, the less popular...

Why do you like a Mustang better than a Camaro? This is the question facing General Motors, which for the sixth consecutive year is bringing the refinement of these sport coupes one notch higher. For 1999, buyers get a gas tank designed to increase the model's touring range, a traction control system for the V-6, and three new exterior colors.

The wide and heavy doors (be careful not to scrape them on the sidewalk, this car is low) open onto a surprisingly narrow cockpit given the model's exterior dimensions. Into the bargain, the two small bucket seats in the rear are good only for well-behaved children who are old enough not to need a child's seat and who are capable of traveling without their favorite toys. Even the passenger in the front will wonder about the strange bump at his or her feet. (For your information, it's the catalyzer.) Meanwhile, on the opposite side, the driver is most probably regularly cursing the fact that the Camaro's headrests are like cement blocks. And what can we say about the trunk, except that the lid is heavy, the sill is high, and it's barely able to take on three bags of groceries. Let's hope you're on a diet if you take your Camaro out shopping!

When you get behind the wheel, there's some good news and some bad news. Acceleration and pickup are astounding. Tires grip like Velcro and the steering system has all the precision of a heart surgeon. On the other end of the spectrum, the six-speed manual transmission requires a hand and foot of tempered steel and you need healthy kidneys to help you absorb the effects of a bumpy road, especially on sportier versions, where wheel travel is pretty well nonexistent. The automatic transmission works well but the V-8's torque makes shifting a bit brutal. There's no question that the tamer 3.8-liter V-6 is a better idea for anyone looking for a car that makes life as easy as possible. This coupe's tendency to oversteer is spectacular, but it gets tiresome after a while. Lastly, braking efficiency is average in light of the engine's high performance capabilities.

The electrifying performance of this sports coupe should be enough to make the real purist forget about its rough edges. **E.L.**

Specifications of Test Vehicle
Model: Camaro Z28

Exterior Dimensions	
Wheelbase	101.1 in.
Overall length	193.5 in.
Overall width	74.1 in.
Overall height	51.3 in.
Curb weight	3,450 lb.
Interior Dimensions	
Seating capacity	4
Head room	F:37.2/R:35.3 in.
Leg room	F:42.9/R:26.8 in.
Cargo volume	7.6 cu. ft.
Engine	
Displacement	V-8 5.7 L.
Horsepower	305 @ 5,000 rpm
Torque, lb-ft.	335 @ 4,000 rpm
Performance	
0-60 mph, acceleration	NA
60-0 mph, braking	NA
Turning circle	40.1 ft.
EPA city/highway	18/27 mpg
Test mileage	18 mpg
Fuel tank capacity	16.8 gal.

Ratings

Category	Rating	Score
Over The Road	Acceleration	10
	Transmission	7
	Braking	7
	Steering	9
	Ride	5
	Handling	9
	Drivability	7
	Fuel Economy	4
Passenger Environment	Comfort/Conven.	7
	Interior Room	5
	Driving Position	8
	Instrumentation	9
	Controls	9
	Visibility	7
	Entry/Exit	5
	Quietness	6
	Cargo Space	5
Workmanship	Interior	8
	Exterior	7
	Value	8

Chevrolet Cavalier

New for 99

New exterior colors
Improved 2.4 liter

Pros

Passenger/cargo room
Fuel economy
Ride comfort

Cons

Engine noise
Steering/handling
Trunk lid

Equipment

Major Standard Equipment: 2.2-liter I-4 engine, manual transmission, 4-wheel antilock brakes, theft-deterrent system, intermittent wipers. **LS adds:** Automatic transmission, AM/FM stereo, air conditioning, remote control decklid release, tachometer, larger wheels and tires. **Major Options:** 2.4-liter engine, 3-speed automatic transmission, 4-speed automatic transmission, traction control, rear defroster, air conditioning, power locks, power moonroof, power windows, variable-intermittent wipers, tilt steering wheel, cruise control, AM/FM/cassette stereo, AM/FM/CD stereo, larger tires, aluminum wheels.

If it ain't broke...

Chevrolet aims the Cavalier at singles and young married couples. Once the children get older, it becomes a second car or a commuter. Everybody, though, gets a kick out of the Cavalier convertible.

General Motors also markets the Cavalier as the Pontiac Sunfire. GM's Saturn and Chrysler's Neon target the same market.

To keep the advertised base price low, Chevrolet offers a 3-speed automatic transmission only on the base Cavalier. A 4-speed automatic is standard on LS models and optional on all others. A 5-speed manual is available on some sedans. The RS coupe, looks like the sporty Z24 but doesn't have the bigger engine.

The transmissions make a big difference with the 2.2-liter engine. The 3-speed automatic feels all right in everyday driving, but allows considerable engine noise and reduces highway fuel economy. The 4-speed version solves these problems with better response and less engine stress. The 5-speed manual makes the car more fun to drive. With either transmission, the engine always seems to work hard, and not much seems to happen below 3,500 rpm.

The 5-speed gearbox feels a little notchy. Finding the next gear occasionally takes extra effort, even though it requires only short movements of the lever. With the manual, we averaged a respectable 25 mpg.

The Cavalier leans noticeably when cornering. The steering is too light, giving less than ideal road feel. The ride is exceptionally good on most roads. Despite the car's low price, it has standard four-wheel antilock brakes. Traction control, a useful winter feature, is optional; it's not available at all on most larger Chevrolets. Inside, engine noise is always evident, although tire, road, and wind noise is minimal.

The dashboard brings the analog gauges and the center console together in one flowing panel. The stereo is below the climate control knobs, out of the driver's easy reach. In a break with GM tradition, the stalk for the wipers and washers is to the right.

Four adults can travel comfortably in the sedan. Up front, head room is especially generous. Adjustable shoulder belt anchors are available only in the sedan.

Small roof pillars and big windows allow good visibility in all directions. Thanks to big door openings and adequate foot space, stepping into or out of the Cavalier is easy.

For a compact, the Cavalier offers good cargo volume. The liftover is low, but the trunk lid stays unusually low when open.

This is the car that Chevrolet hopes will lure you into the fold for life.

D.V.S.

Specifications of Test Vehicle

Model: Cavalier

Exterior Dimensions	
Wheelbase	104.1 in.
Overall length	180.3 in.
Overall width	67.4 in.
Overall height	54.8 in.
Curb weight	2,700 lb.
Interior Dimensions	
Seating capacity	5
Head room	F:38.9/R:37.2 in.
Leg room	F:42.3/R:34.6 in.
Cargo volume	13.6 cu. ft.
Engine	
Displacement	I-4 2.2 L.
Horsepower	120 @ 5,200 rpm
Torque, lb-ft.	130 @ 4,000 rpm
Performance	
0-60 mph, acceleration	9.6 sec.
60-0 mph, braking	131 ft.
Turning circle	35.6 ft.
EPA city/highway	25/37 mpg
Test mileage	25 mpg
Fuel tank capacity	15.2 gal.

Prices

$13,000
$21,000

Coupe $12,381
Sedan $12,481
RS Coupe $13,641
LS Sedan $14,921
Z24 Coupe $16,481
Z24 2-door convertible $20,081

Warranty

(years/miles)

Bumper-to-bumper 3/36,000
Powertrain 3/36,000
Rust-through 6/100,000

Other to Consider

Dodge Neon
Toyota Corolla

Ratings

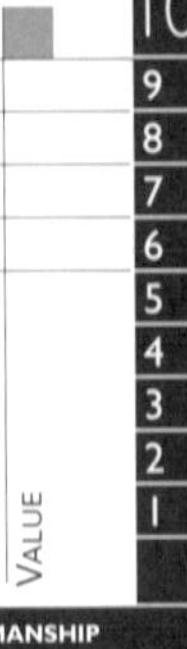

Category	Rating	Score
Over The Road	Acceleration	7
	Transmission	7
	Braking	5
	Steering	7
	Ride	8
	Handling	7
	Drivability	8
	Fuel Economy	6
Passenger Environment	Comfort/Conven.	8
	Interior Room	7
	Driving Position	8
	Instrumentation	7
	Controls	8
	Visibility	8
	Entry/Exit	7
	Quietness	7
	Cargo Space	6
Workmanship	Interior	9
	Exterior	8
	Value	10

Ratings 148

Chevrolet Corvette

New for 99

Telescopic steering wheel available
Newly designed display system
Hard top model

Pros

Performance capabilities
Interior finish
Trunk capacity

Cons

High trunk sill
Awkward removable top
No electric convertible top

Equipment

Major Standard Equipment: 5.7 liter V-8, automatic transmission, 4-wheel antilock disc brakes, air conditioning, intermittent wipers, rear defroster, power windows, power heated mirrors, power locks, remote keyless entry, power driver's seat, leather upholstery, tilt steering wheel, cruise control, AM/FM cassette stereo, heated mirrors, theft alarm system, run-flat tires.

Major Options: 6-speed manual transmission, adjustable shock absorbers, sports suspension, dual-temperature air conditioning, driver's memory system, memory mirrors and seats, AM/FM/CD stereo.

Snobbery

PRICES
$37,000
$50,000

2-door coupe
$39,171

2-door convertible
$45,579

WARRANTY
(year/miles)

Bumper-to-bumper
3/36,000

Powertrain
3/36,000

Rust-through
6/100,000

OTHER TO CONSIDER

BMW M coupe

For automotive snobs, the Corvette will always be the cartoon of sports cars. But what exactly is it that people hate about it? Being what it really is? That it is more affordable, more reliable, better built, and cheaper to maintain than its Italian or English rivals? A few words of advice for its detractors: don't glance at it sideways, take a good, hard look; don't spend foolishly, invest wisely. This fifth-generation Corvette is a true sport model, on a par with the best of its breed and available at a third of the usual price.

Slicker, sleeker, and more aerodynamic, the new Corvette is also sturdier, more functional, and roomier. In this regard we should say that people with overactive imaginations will no longer feel as if they're getting into a coffin as they slide into position aboard a Corvette. Well-designed seats provide comfort and support. The dashboards detailed instrumentation is visually appealing and easy to read, and controls are positioned logically. And the Corvette has quite a trunk, provided you can get past its relatively high sill and, more importantly, provided you can get a good grip on it when you want to open it for loading. Any other defects? Yes, beginning with the coupe's removable roof, which is hard to handle under the hot sun, and the fact that the convertible doesn't come with a power soft top.

Despite the deep-throated exhaust system, this fifth-generation model is by far the most civilized, most pleasant, and easiest to drive (another criticism its detractors can use as a weapon?). Solidly gripped to the road (a traction control system prevents any skating in place), the Corvette gives you a feeling of safety and stability. But you've got to wonder if it's really necessary to offer three kinds of shock absorption given the minimal differences there are between them. And the wind deflector on the front takes quite a beating as soon as roads are even slightly bumpy.

The LS1 all-aluminum 5.7-liter engine is almost as powerful as any of the latest DOHC V-8s. It generates 345 horses and has no trouble showing its strength even in the low-rpm range. The Corvette is also available with a six-speed manual transmission or a four-speed automatic. Traction control, also available, is a feature that will help you save on tire wear. With its huge road-hugging tires, you get from 0 to 60 mph in under 6.0 seconds, with a top speed somewhere around 165 mph. **E.L.**

Specifications of Test Vehicle

Model: Corvette

Exterior Dimensions	
Wheelbase	104.5 in.
Overall length	179.7 in.
Overall width	73.6 in.
Overall height	47.7 in.
Curb weight	3,250 lb.
Interior Dimensions	
Seating capacity	2
Head room	F:37.6 in.
Leg room	F:42.8 in.
Cargo room	11.1 cu. ft.
Engine	
Displacement	V-8 5.7 L.
Horsepower	345 @ 5,600 rpm
Torque, lb-ft.	350 @ 4,400 rpm
Performance	
0-60 mph, acceleration	5.9 sec.
60-0 mph, braking	110 ft.
Turning circle	40 ft.
EPA city/highway	17/25 mpg
Test mileage	22 mpg
Fuel tank capacity	19.1 gal.

Ratings
152

Group	Category	Rating
Over The Road	Acceleration	10
	Transmission	9
	Braking	9
	Steering	8
	Ride	7
	Handling	9
	Drivability	9
	Fuel Economy	5
Passenger Environment	Comfort/Conven.	8
	Interior Room	6
	Driving Position	8
	Instrumentation	9
	Controls	8
	Visibility	4
	Entry/Exit	6
	Quietness	7
	Cargo Space	6
Workmanship	Interior	8
	Exterior	8
	Value	8

Chevrolet Express

New for 99
Superficial changes

Pros
Interior room
Ride comfort
Safety features

Cons
Brake pedal effort
Maneuverability
Entry/exit

Equipment

Major Standard Equipment: 4.3-liter V-6, 4-wheel antilock brakes, air conditioning, variable-intermittent wipers, AM/FM stereo. **LS adds:** Power windows, power locks, tilt steering wheel, cruise control.
Major options: 5-liter V-8, 5.7-liter V-8, 6.5-liter diesel V-8, 7.4-liter V-8, extended wheelbase, sliding side door, 5-passenger seating, 12-passenger seating, 15-passenger seating, rear air conditioning, AM/FM/cassette stereo, AM/FM/CD/cassette stereo, power seats, power windows, power locks, remote keyless entry, privacy glass, cruise control, tilt steering wheel, power heated mirrors, aluminum wheels.

King-size

For large families, the full-size Chevrolet Express van may be the only way for togetherness in travel. Minivans may be trendy and easier to handle, but nothing beats this van for hauling.

For about the same price as a long minivan, the Express offers ample seating for up to eight people, plus a capacious cargo area behind the third seat. We're not talking about cramped accommodations, either; everybody has more than enough head, leg, shoulder, and hip room, regardless of row or seating position.

In a limited market, the Express competes against only three other brands: the Dodge Ram Wagon, the Ford Club Wagon, and the GMC Savana (the Express's General Motors sibling). This is the first GM full-size van with full-frame construction. Although it's not as stylish as the Chevrolet Venture mini- and midivans, the Express is more than just a big breadbox on wheels. In fact, it has more standard safety features than some cars and many trucks have.

The Express is huge. Even the standard-wheelbase model (the only one suitable for family use) measures more than 18 feet long and stands nearly 7 feet tall. Climbing up and into the vehicle is like boarding a small yacht. Inside, the Express is positively cavernous.

Most full-size vans go from the original manufacturer to a secondary one for a "conversion" that adds many comfort and convenience features. The finished product is sold by Chevrolet dealers alongside vans with only factory equipment. Beware of low-quality on some conversions. Problems with them are covered under a warranty separate from GM's.

The standard 4.3-liter V-6 seems barely adequate for the regular eight-passenger van. Towing a trailer, even a small pop-up camper, would be better with one of the V-8s. Our test Express was equipped with the middle-of-the-line 5.7-liter V-8, which delivers 325 lb-ft. of torque. It packed sufficient wallop to pull smartly away from traffic when unladen. The downside is fuel economy; we averaged just 16 mpg without a load.

All that mass contributes to a surprisingly smooth, quiet ride. Its sheer bulk makes the Express difficult to handle and park, but no more so than a full-size extended-cab pickup truck. Even with addition of variable-assist power steering, the Express will never drive like a car, but the feature contributes to better, more enjoyable road feel on the highway. Braking, especially in emergency situations, requires more effort on the pedal than that in other vehicles.

Even though the Express has some drawbacks compared with minivans, they seem rather niggling. For the most haul per dollar, it's tough to beat.
D.V.S.

Specifications of Test Vehicle

Model: Express LS

Exterior Dimensions	
Wheelbase	135 in.
Overall length	218.7 in.
Overall width	79.2 in.
Overall height	79.6 in.
Curb weight	5,100 lb.
Interior Dimensions	
Seating capacity	8
Head room	F:40.6/R1:39/R2:39.1 in.
Leg room	F:41.2/R1:38.5/R2:38.5 in.
Cargo volume	NA
Engine	
Displacement	V-8 5.7 L.
Horsepower	245 @ 4,600 rpm
Torque, lb-ft.	325 @ 2,800 rpm
Performance	
0-60 mph, acceleration	NA
60-0 mph, braking	NA
Turning circle	45.1 ft.
EPA city/highway	14/18 mpg
Test mileage	16 mpg
Fuel tank capacity	31 gal.

Prices
$23,000
$31,000

G1500 3-door van
$22,716

G1500 LS 3-door van
$24,471

Warranty
(years/miles)

Bumper-to-bumper
3/36,000

Powertrain
3/36,000

Rust-through
6/100,000

Other to Consider

Dodge Ram Wagon

Ford Econoline

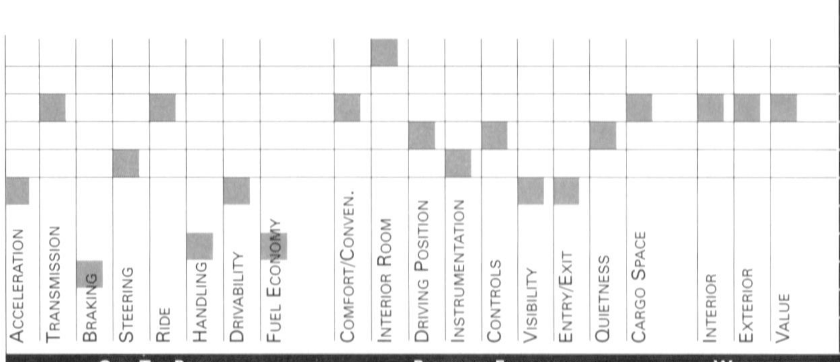

Ratings
127

Chevrolet Lumina

New for 99
200-hp V-6 3800 (LTZ)
New exterior color

Pros
Roomy interior
200-hp V-6
Upcoming bargains

Cons
Model scheduled for withdrawal
Outdated design concept
Dull driving experience

Equipment
Major Standard Equipment: 3.1-liter V-6, automatic transmission, air conditioning, variable-intermittent wipers, automatic headlamps, power locks, tilt steering, theft deterrent system, AM/FM stereo, stainless-steel exhaust system. **LS adds:** 4-wheel antilock brakes, power windows, power mirrors, AM/FM/cassette stereo, larger tires, aluminum wheels. **LTZ adds:** 3.8-liter V-6. Rear spoiler. **Major Options:** 3.8-liter V-6, 4-wheel antilock disc brakes, rear defroster, dual temperature controls, cruise control, integrated child safety seat, power driver's seat, power mirrors, leather upholstery, AM/FM/CD stereo, remote keyless entry, remote-control decklid release.

Rainy day blues

PRICES
$17,000
$23,000
Sedan $17,300
LS sedan $19,300
LTZ sedan $19,800

WARRANTY (years/miles)
Bumper-to-bumper 3/36,000
Powertrain 3/36,000
Rust-through 6/100,000

OTHER TO CONSIDER
Dodge Intrepid
Ford Taurus

The projectors dimmed a long time ago for the Chevrolet Lumina. This mid-size model only emerged in its current form three years ago, which seems like an eternity. It returns to the road one last time this year, to head off to its destination, between light and shadows, and be replaced by the Impala.

Before saying goodbye, however, it will cruise down that final stretch of highway with a 20-hp V-6 purring away under the LTZ's hood.

It is hard to find a passenger compartment as poorly decorated as that of the Lumina. The materials, colors, and entire instrument panel, with its three solitary indicators, may cause you to shed a tear. Fortunately, this imposing glazed panel will soothe your reddened eyes by redirecting them outside. The driving position starts off being fairly comfortable, but becomes exhausting after a mere 60 miles. The driver can still take comfort in the fact that the main commands are close by.

While this mid-size model may not be charming, it is pleasant. There is adequate room in the front and rear for all to be comfortable. And your bags will easily slip into the trunk.

Chevrolet has replaced the 3.4-liter V-6 with the 3.8-liter V-6, renowned for its reliability, endurance, and driveability. But, to enjoy it, you'll have to spring for a few hundred dollars more or settle for the old 3.1-liter V-6, whose sole recommendation way back when was to run reasonably well. This comment also applies to road behavior, which is not particularly exciting unless you search through all the options to get the F41 suspension (which comes with the

sportier model). The steering lacks precision, the brakes fade, and the car handles negotiated turns a bit too quickly.
E.L.

Specifications of Test Vehicle
Model: Lumina

Exterior Dimensions	
Wheelbase	107.5 in.
Overall length	200.9 in.
Overall width	72.5 in.
Overall height	55.2 in.
Curb weight	3,350 lb.
Interior Dimensions	
Seating capacity	6
Head room	F:38.4/R:37.4 in.
Leg room	F:42.4/R:36.6 in.
Cargo volume	15.5 cu. ft.
Engine	
Displacement	V-6 3.1 L.
Horsepower	160 @ 5,200 rpm
Torque, lb-ft	185 @ 4,000 rpm
Performance	
0-60 mph, acceleration	9.4 sec.
60-0 mph, braking	135 ft.
Turning circle	36.7 ft.
EPA city/highway	20/29 mpg
Test mileage	25 mpg
Fuel tank capacity	16.6 gal.

Ratings

Category	Rating
Over The Road	
Acceleration	7
Transmission	8
Braking	5
Steering	7
Ride	7
Handling	7
Drivability	7
Fuel Economy	6
Passenger Environment	
Comfort/Conven.	7
Interior Room	8
Driving Position	7
Instrumentation	6
Controls	7
Visibility	8
Entry/Exit	8
Quietness	8
Cargo Space	7
Workmanship	
Interior	7
Exterior	8
Value	8

Ratings 143

Chevrolet

Malibu

New for 99

Thicker windshield
New exterior colors

Pros

Ride
Steering/handling
Engine/transmission

Cons

Seat lumbar support
Fuel economy

Equipement

Major Standard Equipment: 2.4-liter I-4, automatic transmission, 4-wheel antilock brakes, air conditioning, tilt steering wheel, AM/FM stereo, automatic headlamps, variable-intermittent wipers, theft-deterrent system, stainless-steel exhaust system. **LS adds:** 3.1-liter V-6, power windows, power mirrors, power driver's seat, power locks, cruise control, split-folding rear seat, AM/FM/cassette stereo, remote keyless entry. **Major Options:** 3.1-liter V-6, AM/FM/cassette stereo, AM/FM/CD stereo, AM/FM/CD/cassette stereo, cruise control, power driver's seat, split-folding rear seat, remote keyless entry, power windows, power mirrors, power locks, power moonroof.

A family choice

Thirty-some years ago, the Malibu was a huge success for Chevrolet. This revival aims to repeat that success, and it looks to be right on the money.

The Malibu comes as a base model or a well-equipped LS. Oldsmobile sells the same vehicle as the Cutlass. (The base Cutlass has more standard features than the base Malibu, so take that into consideration when you're comparing prices.) The five-passenger Malibu is close in size to the six-passenger Lumina, but the latter has only 6-cylinder engines.

The Malibu's base engine is a 2.4 liter, twin-cam 4-cylinder, good for 150 horsepower. A 3.1-liter, 150-horsepower V-6 is optional on the base model and standard on the LS. Both engines work through a 4-speed automatic transmission.

Inside, the instrument panel shows attention to detail. High-mounted radio controls and some of the easiest-to-operate ventilation controls in the industry catch your attention immediately. The instruments are ordinary, but easy to read. In a departure from GM convention, the multi-function turn-signal lever with cruise and wiper controls is gone. Lights are on the left stalk, and wipers are on the right, Japanese style; the cruise control is on the steering wheel. The ignition switch is positively radical: it's on the instrument panel, where it's easy to see and reach. High air outlets, an air conditioning vent near the driver's lap, and a nifty cup holder near the driver's left hand are nice touches.

Both front and rear seats are comfortable, but not first-class. Their support wanes on long trips. The fairly low driving position allows a good view of everything. Large side mirrors help rear visibility.

Interior storage space abounds. The base model has a split-folding rear seat to expand the cargo area.

Both engines have more than adequate power for family driving, but the 3.1-liter V-6 is quieter and more enjoyable to drive than the 2.4-liter four. We were a little disappointed with fuel economy. Expect to get about 24 mpg with the V-6. With either engine, the 4-speed automatic transmission always shifts smoothly and predictably.

The independent suspension favors ride comfort without sacrificing too much handling ability. It handled broken pavement easily on our test drives. The steering is precise without the expense of variable power assist. Cornering on winding mountain roads felt secure and stable.

Chevrolet needs more products like the Malibu. Little touches like the location of the ignition switch demonstrate a willingness to do things differently at GM. **D.V.S.**

Specifications of Test Vehicle

Model: Malibu

Exterior Dimensions	
Wheelbase	107 in.
Overall length	190.4 in.
Overall width	69.4 in.
Overall height	56.4 in.
Curb weight	3,100 lb.
Interior Dimensions	
Seating capacity	5
Head room	F:39.4/R:37.6 in.
Leg room	F:41.9/R:38 in.
Cargo volume	16 cu. ft.
Engine	
Displacement	V-6 3.1
Horsepower	155 @ 5,200 rpm
Torque, lb-ft.	185 @ 4,000 rpm
Performance	
0-60 mph, acceleration	8.7 sec.
60-0 mph, braking	127 ft.
Turning circle	36.4 ft.
EPA city/highway	20/29 mpg
Test mileage	NA
Fuel tank capacity	15 gal.

	Rating
Over The Road	
Acceleration	8
Transmission	9
Braking	6
Steering	8
Ride	8
Handling	8
Drivability	9
Fuel Economy	5
Passenger Environment	
Comfort/Conven.	8
Interior Room	8
Driving Position	9
Instrumentation	8
Controls	9
Visibility	8
Entry/Exit	8
Quietness	8
Cargo Space	8
Workmanship	
Interior	8
Exterior	8
Value	8

1999
AAA
TOP CAR

PRICES
$16,000
$19,000
Sedan
$16,485
LS sedan
$18,445

WARRANTY
(years/miles)
Bumper-to-bumper
3/36,000
Powertrain
3/36,000
Rust-through
6/100,000

OTHER TO CONSIDER
Dodge Stratus
Ford Contour

Chevrolet Metro

New for 99

Two new exterior colors

Pros

Fuel economy
Perfect for city driving
Smooth manual transmission

Cons

Disappointing price / equipment ratio
Three-speed automatic transmission only
Lack of interest shown by General Motors

Equipment

Major Standard Equipment: 1-liter I-3, manual transmission, unassisted steering, folding rear seat, stainless-steel exhaust system. **LSi adds:** 1.3-liter I-4, trip odometer, intermittent wipers.
Major Options: 3-speed automatic transmission, 4-wheel antilock brakes, power steering, air conditioning, remote-control mirrors, power locks, AM/FM stereo, AM/FM/cassette stereo, AM/FM/CD/cassette stereo, rear defroster, rear wiper and washer, split-folding rear seat.

Useless

PRICES
$9,000
$11,000

3-door $8,655
LSi 3-door $9,455
LSi sedan $10,055

WARRANTY (years/miles)
Bumper-to-bumper 3/36,000
Powertrain 3/36,000
Rust-through 6/100,000

OTHER TO CONSIDER
Hyundai Accent
Daewoo Lanos

General Motors bills the Metro as the ideal car for a first-time buyer or for families who need an affordable second car. Good arguments, except that given this subcompact's equipment/price ratio it might be a better idea to dig a bit deeper to find the extra cash for a more versatile and comfortable alternative. If you do visit your local GM dealership, don't be surprised if the salesperson gives you the very same arguments I've just mentioned.

Two new color choices have been added to the list for 1999. Four people can pile into this tiny car, which offers just enough room and comfort and not an iota more. Styling isn't particularly exciting and instrumentation is modest, to say the least. Standard equipment isn't very extensive either and several accessories currently on the option list could make life easier, especially on the coupe. An example? How about three: a screen to hide baggage, a rear windshield wiper/washer, and a remote trunk lid release.

From a technical point of view, there are a few innovations. The two-door coupe has the same three-cylinder engine, though it can be replaced by an optional 1.3-liter four-cylinder, which is standard on the sedan. All available powertrains have the same great fuel economy they had in the past. Fun to drive in the city, these subcompacts get boring fast when you take them out on the highway. The steering system is light and imprecise at cruising speeds and heavy when subjected to parking maneuvers (an optional power system is available solely on the sedan). Note also that the three-speed automatic transmission does nothing to make the four-cylinder engine look good. The best bet is the standard manual transmission, which gives the engine enough room to express itself. As for the three-cylinder, which boasts the best fuel economy rating in North America, it moves like a snail. Avoid it if you're the type who's always in a hurry.

When all is said and done, the Metro isn't as attractive as its price first suggests. **E.L.**

Specifications of Test Vehicle

Model: LSi

Exterior Dimensions	
Wheelbase	93.1 in.
Overall length	164 in.
Overall width	62.6 in.
Overall height	55.4 in.
Curb weight	2,000 lb.
Interior Dimensions	
Seating capacity	4
Head room	F:39.3/R:37.3 in.
Leg room	F:42.5/R:32.2 in.
Cargo volume	10.3 cu. ft.
Engine	
Displacement	I-4 1.3 L.
Horsepower	79 @ 6,000 rpm
Torque, lb-ft.	75 @ 3,000 rpm
Performance	
0-60 mph, acceleration	12.3 sec.
60-0 mph, braking	153 ft.
Turning circle	31.5 ft.
EPA city/highway	39/43 mpg
Test mileage	40 mpg
Fuel tank capacity	10.3 gal.

Ratings

Category	Criterion	Rating
Over The Road	Acceleration	4
	Transmission	7
	Braking	2
	Steering	8
	Ride	5
	Handling	5
	Drivability	8
	Fuel Economy	10
Passenger Environment	Comfort/Conven.	6
	Interior Room	6
	Driving Position	7
	Instrumentation	7
	Controls	7
	Visibility	7
	Entry/Exit	7
	Quietness	5
	Cargo Space	5
Workmanship	Interior	8
	Exterior	6
	Value	7

Ratings **127**

Chevrolet Monte Carlo

New for 99

On Star communications system available
Revised accessories list

Pros

Engine power
Instrumentation
Ride comfort

Cons

Engine power
Instrumentation
Ride comfort

Equipment

Major Standard Equipment: 3.1-liter V-6, automatic transmission, 4-wheel antilock brakes, air conditioning, variable-intermittent wipers, power locks, power mirrors, split-folding rear seat, tilt steering column, power windows, AM/FM/cassette stereo, theft deterrent system, stainless steel exhaust system. **Z34 adds:** 3.8-liter V-6 engine, 4-wheel disc brakes, sports suspension, dual temperature controls, individual front seats, cruise control, remote keyless entry, power decklid release, larger tires.
Major Options: 3.8 liter V-6, dual temperature controls, remote keyless entry, cruise control, AM/FM/CD stereo, power moonroof.

The good old days

Chevrolet's Monte Carlo is a 2-door derivative of the Lumina sedan. A Z-number mimics the cachet of the Camaro Z28, but in this case has nothing to do with high performance.

The Monte Carlo comes much better equipped than the Lumina, so take that into account when comparing prices.

This Monte Carlo wasn't meant to be a muscle car like its predecessors, but it's still athletic. The 3.8 engine reduces complexity and cost but actually delivers good performance and fuel economy. There's little reason to choose the standard 3.1-liter engine. With the optional engine, we timed 0-60 mph in under 8.5 seconds and averaged just over 20 mpg in more than 280 miles of combined city and highway driving.

This V-6 is quiet, especially at idle. Some engine vibration comes through to the cabin at higher revs. We also felt torque steer under maximum acceleration from a standstill. General Motors' electronically controlled 4-speed automatic transmission, among the quietest and smoothest on the road, shifts quickly and silently. The gear ratios let the engine perform at its best.

The suspension floats a bit on the highway, but the overall ride is quite comfortable. The Monte Carlo remains likable on long drives. Its steering feels a bit too light for good control during hard cornering, though.

Thanks to large door openings, getting in and out of the roomy front seat presents no problems. Getting past the front safety belts and into the back seat is a gymnastic exercise, however. The back seat can accommodate two large adults comfortably or three average-size people who don't mind sitting shoulder to shoulder. Taller backseat passengers will want more head room, but leg room should be sufficient.

The long, wide, deep trunk affords good space, too; the opening has a reasonable liftover height.

On the flat black instrument panel, the large tachometer and speedometer are easy to read. With the convenient climate control system, individual controls let both the driver and front passenger set the temperature for personal comfort. The radio's large, soft buttons are easy to operate.

The driver has acceptable visibility to the front, but high door sills and wide C-pillars hinder the view to the sides and rear. The side mirrors don't completely overcome those obstacles.

If you think you like the Monte Carlo after a test drive, try the Pontiac Grand Prix. It's a much newer design on the same theme. **D.V.S.**

Specifications of Test Vehicle

Model: Z34

terior Dimensions	
Wheelbase	107.5 in.
Overall length	200.7 in.
Overall width	72.5 in.
Overall height	53.8 in.
Curb weight	3,450 lb.
Interior Dimensions	
Seating capacity	5
Head room	F:37.9/R:36.9 in.
Leg room	F:42.4/R:34.9 in.
Cargo volume	15.5 cu. ft.
Engine	
Displacement	V-6 3.8 L.
Horsepower	200 @ 5,200 rpm
Torque, lb-ft.	225 @ 4,000 rpm
Performance	
0-60 mph, acceleration	8.1 sec.
60-0 mph, braking	131 ft.
Turning circle	39 ft.
EPA city/highway	19/30 mpg
Test mileage	21 mpg
Fuel tank capacity	16.6 ga

Prices

$18,000
$25,000

LS coupe $17,795

Z34 coupe $20,295

Warranty

(years/miles)

Bumper-to-bumper 3/36,000

Powertrain 3/36,000

Rust-through 6/100,000

Other to Consider

Chrysler Sebring

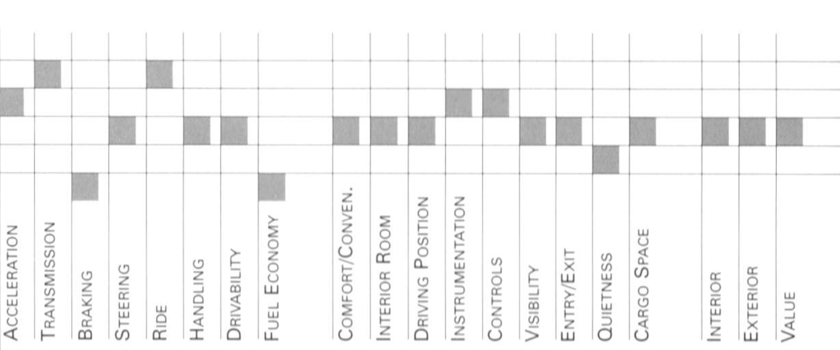

Ratings
142

Chevrolet Prizm

New for 99

New colors

Pros

Ride
Fuel economy
Visibility

Cons

Standard features
Handling
Cargo space

Equipment

Major Standard Equipment: 1.8-liter I-4, manual transmission, variable-intermittent wipers, stainless-steel exhaust system.. **LSi adds:** Power locks, power mirrors, remote keyless entry, split-folding rear seat. **Major Options:** 3-speed automatic transmission, 4-speed automatic transmission, 4-wheel antilock brakes, side air bags, air conditioning, power windows, rear defroster, AM/FM/ cassette stereo, AM/FM/CD stereo, tilt steering column, integrated child safety seat, moonroof, sports suspension, aluminum wheels.

One of the best

PRICES
$14,000
$19,000

Sedan
$13,713

LSi Sedan
$15,269

WARRANTY
(years/miles)

Bumper-to-bumper
3/36,000

Powertrain
3/36,000

Rust-through
6/100,000

OTHER TO CONSIDER

Nissan Sentra

Mazda Protege

Once upon a time, some smart marketing types thought General Motors needed the Geo brand to give its import-based small cars like the Prizm a separate identity. Times and marketing experts change. GM now attaches the Chevy brand to the Prizm.

The Prizm and the Toyota Corolla share the same platform, powertrain, and suspension, but the Prizm gets uniquely styled body panels, both front and rear.

Chevrolet offers the Prizm in two trim levels: a base version with very little standard equipment and the LSi with only a little more. Even a radio must be added as an option, so the price of a Prizm can climb rapidly above the advertised base price.

A 120-horsepower, 1.8-liter 4-cylinder engine is the only choice, but three transmissions are available. A 5-speed manual is standard; 3- and 4-speed automatics are optional.

The 1.8-liter engine performs well and lets the Prizm keep up with most cars its size. It responds well to the throttle and gave us an excellent 32 mpg in our test drives. Engine noise is minimal during normal driving, but can get loud under heavy acceleration. The 4-speed automatic transmission in our test car was commendably smooth and hesitated only slightly during downshifts. It's worth the extra dollars over the 3-speed.

The Prizm's independent suspension provides a controlled, soft ride on the highway and smooths out problems in the road. The car keeps its composure even on rough pavement. However, the soft feel compromises handling, and sharp cornering can cause considerable body roll and tire squealing. The power steering is direct, with a reassuring feel.

For a subcompact, the Prizm feels roomy and open inside. The two front seats and rear bench provide adequate head, shoulder, and hip room for four people. Three in the back is a crowd, but that's not unusual in this class. Leg and knee room in the back seat is tight when the front seats are moved all the way back. Young families will like the built-in child safety seat, and the seats are treated with Scotchgard to make spills easier to clean.

Trunk space is limited, but the optional 60/40 fold-down rear seat adds versatility. The trunk opening is low, wide, and easy to load. A low window sill, large glass areas, and thin roof pillars all combine to make visibility good in all directions.

The Prizm's instruments are basic, but easy to interpret. The radio controls are conveniently high, but the ventilation controls are low and harder to use.

The Prizm, one of the best subcompacts on the market, has always lived in the Corolla's shadow. Perhaps the Chevrolet brand will help get this little gem the attention it deserves. **D.V.S.**

Specifications of Test Vehicle

Model: LSi

Exterior Dimensions	
Wheelbase	97 in.
Overall length	174.2 in.
Overall width	66.7 in.
Overall height	53.7 in.
Curb weight	2,450 lb.
Interior Dimensions	
Seating capacity	5
Head room	F:39.3/R:36.9 in.
Leg room	F:41.7/R:33.2 in.
Cargo room	12.1 cu. ft.
Engine	
Displacement	I-4 1.8 L.
Horsepower	120 @ 5,600 rpm
Torque, lb-ft.	122 @ 4,000 rpm
Performance	
0-60 mph, acceleration	9.6 sec.
60-0 mph, braking	125 ft.
Turning circle	34 ft.
EPA city/highway	28/36 mpg
Test mileage	32 mpg
Fuel Tank Capacity	13.2 gal.

Ratings

Group	Category	Rating
Over The Road	Acceleration	7
Over The Road	Transmission	8
Over The Road	Braking	6
Over The Road	Steering	8
Over The Road	Ride	8
Over The Road	Handling	7
Over The Road	Drivability	9
Over The Road	Fuel Economy	8
Passenger Environment	Comfort/Conven.	8
Passenger Environment	Interior Room	7
Passenger Environment	Driving Position	8
Passenger Environment	Instrumentation	7
Passenger Environment	Controls	8
Passenger Environment	Visibility	9
Passenger Environment	Entry/Exit	7
Passenger Environment	Quietness	7
Passenger Environment	Cargo Space	6
Workmanship	Interior	9
Workmanship	Exterior	8
Workmanship	Value	9

Ratings 154

Chevrolet

S10

New for 99

Better transfer box
New side-view mirrors
New exterior colors

Pros

Good visibility
Energetic V-6
Good transmissions

Cons

Limited choice of models and accessories
No fourth door
Uncomfortable auxiliary seats

Equipment

Major Standard Equipment: 2.2-liter I-4, manual transmission, 4-wheel antilock brakes, automatic headlamps, variable-intermittent wipers, vinyl upholstery, rubber floor covering. **LS adds:** Full carpeting, cloth upholstery, split-bench seat, AM/FM stereo. **Major Options:** 4.3-liter V-6, automatic transmission, part-time 4-wheel drive, electric shift transfer case, rear locking differential, long pickup box, third door, air conditioning, power locks, power windows, power mirrors, remote keyless entry, tilt steering wheel, cruise control, AM/FM/cassette, AM/FM/CD, larger tires, aluminum wheels.

Sonoma or S-10 ?

Do you like GMC Sonoma? If you do, then you like the Chevrolet S-10 since both share the same platform. Like the S-10, the Sonoma has new accessories this year, including a better transfer box, a new family of power heated side-view mirrors and three new exterior colors.

Like the Sonoma, three years ago the S-10 introduced a third door. How about a fourth? Not this year, even if Ford, Mazda, and in the near future, Nissan, will all have one. Is Chevrolet feeling the pressure? You have to wonder. In any event, the S-10 invites you to test its comfortable bucket seats (an option to the standard sliding bench seat), designed to mold and provide support when cornering. The extended cab version includes two minuscule vinyl auxiliary seats, more like ejection seats since no one can sit in them for very long, they're so uncomfortable. To summarize, let's say that the interior is well presented, as long as you have a penchant for the smell and look of plastic.

Chevrolet has eliminated the underhood light, so here's a reminder of what you'll find there: a 2.2-liter four-cylinder engine that's fairly sluggish despite several changes over the years, now resulting in better pickup and better fuel economy. For a bit extra, you can choose the 4x4 version, which is powered by a 4.3-liter Vortec V-6 that is as smooth as it is strong. You don't need to be a pro to make the rear wheels skate — they often lack grip when the truck is traveling unloaded. And this is precisely when road stability is affected by a jerky rear end, which may jeopardize the main mission of the ABS brakes, which is to ensure straight-line stops. When it comes to transmission, the electronically controlled automatic is remarkably smooth, while the manual transmission is impressively easy to use. **E.L.**

Specifications of Test Vehicle

Model: S10 LS

Exterior Dimensions	
Wheelbase	122.9 in.
Overall length	203.7 in.
Overall width	67.9 in.
Overall height	63.3 in.
Curb weight	3,250 lb.
Interior dimensions	
Seating capacity	4
Head room	F:39.5/R:NA in.
Leg room	F:42.4/R:NA in.
Payload capacity	1,150 lb.
Engine	
Displacement	V-6 4.3 L.
Horsepower	180 @ 4,400 rpm
Torque, lb-ft.	245 @ 2,800 rpm
Performance	
0-60 mph, acceleration	9.1 sec.
60-0 mph, braking	138 ft.
Turning circle	43.2 ft.
EPA city/highway	17/22 mpg
Test mileage	15 mpg
Fuel tank capacity	19 gal.

Prices
$12,000
$23,000

Short bed $11,998
LS short bed $13,179
LS extended cab, short bed $15,230

Warranty (years/miles)
Bumper-to-bumper 3/36,000
Powertrain 3/36,000
Rust-through 6/100,000

Other to consider
Ford Ranger
Dodge Dakota

Group	Rating	Score
Over The Road	Acceleration	7
	Transmission	8
	Braking	4
	Steering	6
	Ride	8
	Handling	6
	Drivability	7
	Fuel Economy	3
Passenger Environment	Comfort/Conven.	7
	Interior Room	8
	Driving Position	7
	Instrumentation	9
	Controls	8
	Visibility	9
	Entry/Exit	8
	Quietness	8
	Cargo Space	1
Workmanship	Exterior	7
	Interior	8
	Value	7

Ratings
136

Chevrolet Silverado

New for 99

Totally redesigned with new body
Chassis and powertrain components

Pros

Seat comfort
Quietness
Brakes

Cons

Fuel economy
Door locks

Equipment

Major Standard Equipment: 4.3 liter V-6 engine, 5-speed manual transmission, ABS, AM/FM stereo, vinyl bench seat, automatic headlamps. **LS adds:** Air conditioning, floor and overhead console, cruise control, power locks & windows, AM/FM/CD stereo, cloth seats. **LT adds:** 5.3 liter v-8, automatic transmission, automatic 4-wheel drive, compass, AM/FM/cassette/CD stereo, heated leather power seats, sliding rear window, rear defogger, cast aluminum wheels. **Major Options:** 4.8 liter V-8, 5.3 liter V-8, 6.0 liter V-8, 6.5 liter V-8 diesel, 4-speed automatic transmission, 4-wheel drive, power seats/windows/ door locks, remote locks/security, leather seats.

A big gamble

For Chevrolet, the launch of its new pickup also involves the launch of a new name. The name Silverado identified the top-of-the-line full-size pickups for almost 25 years. Now it identifies the whole line of full-size pickups. Even though the body is completely new, it still looks like a Chevy — just what potential buyers said they wanted.

Within the three Silverado trim levels — base, LS, and LT, there is a range of configurations and options that extends from bare-bones to near-luxury. C/K refers to the 2-wheel drive C-series and the 4-wheel drive K-series. The three truck designations refer to payload capacity: 1500 (1/2 ton), 2500 (3/4 ton), and 3500 (1 ton). Variations include an extended cab with a folding seat that increases inside cargo space by 44 cubic feet. The Silverado offers a third door on the passenger side for easier access to the rear-seat area. Chevy says a 4-door version will be available soon.

There is no lack of choice when it comes to selecting an engine. A 4.3-liter V-6, 4.8-liter V-8, 5.3-liter V-8, 6.0-liter V-8, and a 6.5-liter turbo-diesel make up the list. Our test vehicle had the new 5.3-liter V-8 — expected to be the top-selling Chevy truck engine. With plenty of torque at low speeds, this engine is smooth, quiet, and responsive. It is well-suited to the 4-speed automatic transmission — shifts are so smooth as to be unnoticed. The transmission has a unique feature for those who tow heavy loads. A push button on the shift lever changes the shift pattern to maximize pulling power in each gear. For example, the first-to-second shift occurs at 22 mph in the tow/haul mode, and at 10 mph in normal mode. An automatic 4-wheel drive system called AutoTrac automatically engages the front wheels when the going

gets tough.

Inside, this is one comfortable truck. Whether bench or bucket, the front seats offer good support and comfort. The real news is rear-seat comfort. The rear-seat cushion is larger and more comfortable. The seat back is tilted at a comfortable angle. And extra leg room actually makes it pleasant to ride there. Seat belts incorporated into the front seat backs make rear-seat entry and exit a simple matter.

Whether cruising the interstate or a dirt country road, the Silverado is remarkably composed. Acceleration is smooth and quiet. The much-improved 4-wheel disk brakes deliver substantially shorter stopping distances, with better pedal feel. The conventional recirculating ball steering is tight and accurate, with good on-center feel. The stronger frame makes for a much stiffer structure, and it shows in the way the Silverado rides and handles. The ride is smooth and quiet and it even kept its composure on a section of badly washboarded dirt road.

Chevy truck lovers should be pleased that the Silverado wasn't given a new identity. It is still very much a Chevy, but now it's even better.

D.V.S.

Specifications of Test Vehicle

Model: Silverado 4x4

Exterior Dimensions	
Wheelbase	143.5 in.
Overall Length	227.6 In.
Overall Width	78.5 In.
Overall Height	73.9 In.
Curb Weight	4365 lbs.
Interior Dimensions	
Seating Capacity	5
Head Room	F: 41.0/R: 38.4 in.
Leg Room	F: 41.3/R: 33.7 in.
Payload Capacity	2000 lbs.
Engine	
Displacement	5.3 L V-8
Horsepower	270@5000 rpm
Torque, lb-ft.	315@4000 rpm
Performance	
0-60 mph, acceleration	9.1 sec.
60-0 mph, braking	135 ft.
Turning Circle	43.6 ft.
EPA City/Highway	15/18 mpg.
Test Mileage	17.0
Fuel Tank Capacity	26.0 gal.

Counterpoint

Before the new Silverado and Sierra are comfortably established on the market, GM intends to offer a few new versions of its C (rear-wheel) and K (four whccl on demand) models, especially in the top-of-the-line 2500 and 3500 lineup.

If you don't have a very clear idea of what you're looking for, the C/K pickup is not something that will make it any easier to choose. First of all, there is cab choice: regular or extended? Extended. Okay, with or without a third door? But before deciding on a third door, have you considered a multiseat cab? And the list of possibilities goes on, both inside and under the hood. Mind-boggling! The best advice we can give you is go to a good dealer who will guide you through the maze. Apart from that, as far as the fixed features go, note that some controls are hard to reach, the bench seat offers minimal comfort (choose the bucket seats instead), and rear-seat passengers have limited foot room.

GM has indicated that the 1500 version in this lineup will be withdrawn after December 1998. As for the 2500 and 3500 series, including the new multiseat cab model (Crew Cab) and the short-bodied version of the 4x2 and 4x4, they will be available until December 1999. The base engine will be the 5.0-liter V-8 (there won't be a V-6), followed by the gasoline 5.7- and 7.4-liter; the turbodiesel 6.5-liter will be available throughout the model range, including the 1500 models.

The five-speed manual transmission is ideal for heavy-duty work but for regular daily use, the four-speed automatic transmission is the wisest choice, even if its reliability has been spotty over the years. Note also that a spongy brake pedal manages to destroy some of the confidence you build behind the wheel of this mastodon.

E.L.

PRICES

$16,000
$40,000

1500 4 x 2 Base
$15,995

1500 4 x 4 LS
$23,190

2500 4 x 4 Ext. Cab LT
$32,925

WARRANTY
(years/miles)

Bumper-to- Bumper
3/36,000

Power Train
3/36,000

Rust-through
6/100,000

OTHER TO CONSIDER

Dodge Ram 1500

Ford F150

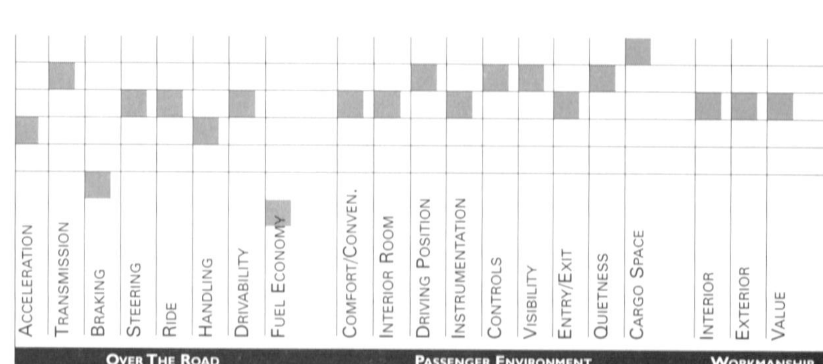

Ratings

158

Chevrolet Suburban

New for 99

Improved automatic transmission
New starter

Pros

Interior room
Engine performance
Versatility
Controls

Cons

Fuel economy
Entry/exit
Rear visibility

Equipment

Major Standard Equipment: 5.7-liter V-8, automatic transmission, 4-wheel antilock brakes, variable-assist power steering, dual rear panel doors, AM/FM stereo, vinyl upholstery, rubber floor covering. **LS adds:** Air conditioning, power mirrors, power windows, power locks, AM/FM/cassette stereo, cruise control, rear defroster, cloth upholstery, carpeting. **LT adds:** Remote keyless entry, leather upholstery.

Profile of a star

PRICES
$25,000
$41,000
1500 4-door truck wagon $25,065
1500 LS 4-door truck wagon $32,483
1500 LT 4-door truck wagon $34,233

WARRANTY
Bumper-to-bumper 3/36,000
Powertrain 3/36,000
Rust-through 6/100,000

There is nothing else out there like the Chevrolet Suburban. For roaming the wide-open spaces, this is the king of sport-utility vehicles. This year, an optional satellite communications system keeps you in touch with emergency help even when you're really far from civilization.

This 4-door SUV is huge: more than 18 feet long with seating for up to nine people and a towing capacity of up to 10,000 pounds. Sometimes called a Cowboy Cadillac, the Suburban would be more appropriately named the Rural. For some upscale families, however, the Suburban (either the Chevy or GMC version) has become the status-symbol station wagon of the '90s. Logically, you can also think of it as a Tahoe Limousine, since its wheelbase is the next step up in the C/K pickup line, the parent for both.

One of the Suburban's strong points is its quiet, smooth highway ride. But the car-like highway ride doesn't translate to car-like handling. It's far from nimble. Its size demands deliberate, planned changes in direction. On the range, you may have room to maneuver this land yacht, but the supermarket parking lots aren't designed for vehicles this long or wide. We needed to make multiple cuts to get in and get out of tight parking spots.

The Suburban's engines are all working-class heroes, with V-8s from 5.7 to 7.4 liters. Chevy offers a turbocharged diesel for good measure. Our truck had the base engine, which was powerful enough for us, though the larger engine would be desirable for towing. The EPA rates the Suburban's fuel economy at a dismal 13 mpg (city) and 18 mpg (highway). We did even worse: 12 mpg. But if you need this vehicle, gas mileage isn't a high priority. The brakes on our test truck did not inspire as much confidence as we would have liked.

Entry and exit are just as difficult as they are in any other full-size truck; you can't climb in and out gracefully. This is a vehicle for blue jeans (with the leather seats, dress jeans). Either way, the optional running boards are a smart buy. Rotary knobs operate the climate controls, and large buttons control the radio. On the instrument panel, the analog gauges are easy to read. While driving, you learn to rely on the large mirrors as well as direct line of sight.

You can easily stow a lot of gear in the massive rear cargo area. The rear opening can be fitted with a traditional tailgate or with panel doors. The latter can be opened while a trailer is attached.

Chevrolet has the most complete range of SUVs under one roof, starting with the mini Tracker and climbing in size and price to the Suburban. If you can't find a suitable SUV there, it doesn't exist. **D.V.S.**

Specifications of Test Vehicle

Model: LT

Exterior Dimensions	
Wheelbase	131.5 in.
Overall length	219.5 in.
Overall width	76.7 in.
Overall height	70.7 in.
Curb weight	4,800 lb.
Interior dimensions	
Seating capacity	9
Head room	F:39.9/R:38.9/R2:37.9 in.
Leg room	F:41.3/R:36.2/R2:37.2 in.
Cargo volume	47.5 cu. ft.
Engine	
Displacement	V-8 5.7 L.
Horsepower	255 @ 4,600 rpm
Torque, lb-ft.	330 @ 2,800 rpm
Performance	
0-60 mph, acceleration	11.5 sec.
60-0 mph, braking	165 ft.
Turning circle	43.7 ft.
EPA city/highway	13/18 mpg
Test mileage	12 mpg
Fuel tank capacity	42 gal.

10
9
8
7
6
5
4
3
2
1
Ratings
144

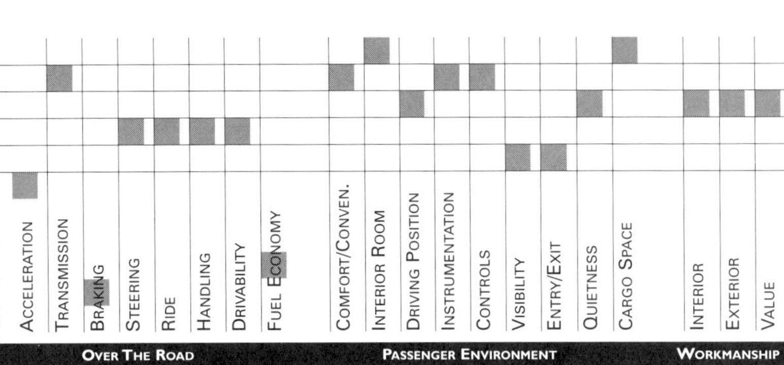

Chevrolet

Tahoe

New for 99

Z72 version available
New starter
Improved automatic transmission

Pros

Interior room
Engine performance
Versatility Controls

Cons

Fuel economy
Entry and exit

Equipment

Major Standard Equipment: 5.7-liter V-8, 4-wheel antilock brakes, AM/FM stereo. **LS adds:** Air conditioning, power mirrors, power windows, power locks, AM/FM/cassette stereo, cruise control, rear defroster. **LT adds:** Remote keyless entry, leather upholstery. **Major Options:** 6.5-liter V-8 turbo-diesel engine, 4-wheel drive, locking rear differential, electric-shift transfer case, air conditioning, AM/FM/cassette stereo, AM/FM/CD/cassette stereo, tilt steering wheel, cruise control, power mirrors, power windows, power locks, rear washer and wiper, remote keyless entry, power driver's seat.

Vacation road

The Chevrolet Tahoe invites comparisons with the Suburban, since both have so much in common, mechanically and functionally. If you look at one, you should look at the other.

As a 4-door, this sport-utility vehicle is nearly 17 feet long—about 20 inches longer than Chevy's Blazer, and 20 inches shorter than the Suburban. Based on General Motors' short-wheelbase C/K pickup truck, the Tahoe seats up to six people, has 30 cubic feet of cargo space, and can tow up to 7,000 pounds. It comes in two trim levels, 2- or 4-door bodies, and 2- or 4-wheel drive. GMC sells the same vehicle under the Yukon name, but only in the more popular 4-door bodystyle. (The Tahoe also offers GM's optional satellite communications system for emergency assistance.) In this size class, the Tahoe competes with the Ford Expedition and Lincoln Navigator; Chrysler offers no comparable-size sport-utility vehicle.

The Tahoe requires a high step-up that makes entry and exit difficult. Because of the height, we recommend the optional running boards for families with small children. Inside, it has the same analog instrument panel as the Suburban and Chevy pickups. Rotary knobs operate the climate system, and the radio has large buttons. The side windows in the rear don't open very far— a minor complaint, now that air conditioning is almost universal.

The base 5.7-liter V-8 engine has power to tow, pass, or accelerate onto highway on-ramps. But even without towing anything, it's difficult to do better than 16 mpg on the highway. Overall, we got a measly 12 mpg, highlighting the penalty you pay every mile in an SUV compared with a car. The Tahoe also offers a 6.5-liter diesel engine that's not available in GMC's Yukon.

Although the roomy, comfortable cabin has car-like amenities, there's no mistaking the fact that the Tahoe is a truck in its handling and ride. Its braking performance doesn't offer a sense of security; deceleration feels more leisurely than it actually is. Compared with the Suburban, the Tahoe's shorter wheelbase reduces ride comfort, but makes more sense in crowded suburban parking lots. The width of both vehicles is the same. Visibility to the rear in the Tahoe is much better than that in the Suburban, but still limited.

The Tahoe's strength is cargo capacity. You can easily stow a lot of gear in the large rear cargo area. For a liftgate, you can choose either a conventional tailgate with a lift-up window or double rear panel doors, which are more practical for short people and for towing.

The Tahoe makes sense for if you need trailer towing capability in a megastation wagon. Its size, however, becomes a disadvantage in the city.

D.V.S.

Specifications of Test Vehicle

Model: Tahoe LS

Exterior Dimensions	
Wheelbase	117.5 in.
Overall length	199.6 in.
Overall width	76.8 in.
Overall height	75 in.
Curb weight	5,350 lb.
Interior dimensions	
Seating capacity	6
Head room	F:39.9/R:38.9 in.
Leg room	F:41.7/R:36.2 in.
Cargo volume	31 cu. ft.
Engine	
Displacement	V-8 5.7 L.
Horsepower	255 @ 4,600 rpm
Torque, lb-ft.	330 @ 2,800 rpm
Performance	
0-60 mph, acceleration	11.5 sec.
60-0 mph, braking	140 ft.
Turning circle	40.7 ft.
EPA city/highway	14/18 mpg
Test mileage	12 mpg
Fuel tank capacity	30 gal.

Prices

$23,000
$35,000

2-door $23,595
LS 2-door $27,954
LS 4-door $29,385
LT 2-door $29,304
LT 4-door $30,735

Warranty

(years/miles)

Bumper-to-bumper 3/36,000
Powertrain 3/36,000
Rust-through 6/100,000

Other to Consider

Ford Expedition

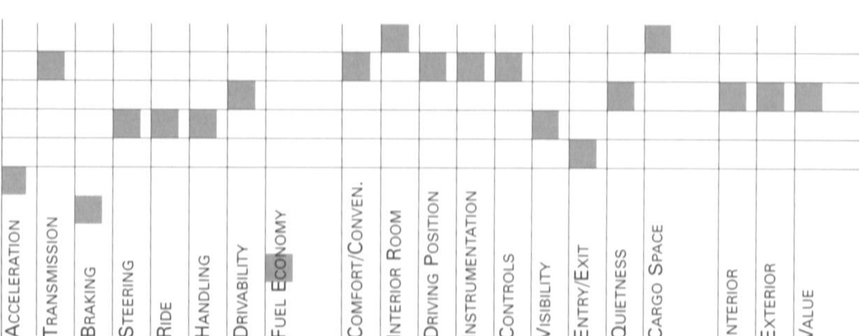

Ratings
150

Chevrolet Tracker

new MODEL

New for 99

Redesigned body
Interior
Suspension and powertrain

Pros

Off-road capabilities
Cargo space

Cons

Radio controls
Rear-seat access

Equipment

Major Standard Equipment: 2-door: 1.6 liter I-4 engine, 5-speed manual transmission, AM/FM radio. 4-door **Adds**: 2.0 liter I-4 engine, split folding rear seat. **Major Options:** 4-speed automatic transmission, 4-wheel drive, antilock brakes, aluminum wheels, upgraded audio systems, skid plates, air conditioning, tilt wheel, cruise control, power windows/locks/mirrors, keyless entry.

Fresh start

PRICES
$13,000
$16,000
4x4 4-door $16,295
2WD 2-door $15,195
2WD 2-door $15,095
4WD conv. $13,995

WARRANTY
Bumper-to-bumper 3/36,000
Powertrain 3/36,000
Rust-through 6/100,000

OTHER TO CONSIDER
Toyota RAV4
Suzuki Vitara

When the Tracker was redesigned for 1999, Chevrolet and its partner Suzuki intentionally rejected the soft look of many of the competing vehicles, and stuck with a traditional tough and rugged appearance. The cute look is gone--now Tracker looks like a real SUV. With an upgraded suspension and more power, the Tracker is well positioned to keep its truck-like image. It's fairly easy to decide on which Tracker to buy. Available in either a 4-door conventional SUV, or the open-air 2-door convertible, the only other major decision is 2-wheel or 4-wheel drive. Beyond that it gets a little more complicated because almost nothing on the Tracker is standard equipment.

The 2-door gets only the 1.6-liter, 4-cylinder engine, good for 90 horsepower. Move up to the 4-door, and you get a 121 horsepower four cylinders. Antilock brakes are optional. Four-wheel drive models have an improved shift-on-the-fly feature, as well as a two-speed transfer case for creeping over obstacles in the back country.

Inside, things are much more comfortable than in the previous model. Overlapping instrument dials add a nice touch. Vent controls are located up high, but the radio is down low, making it difficult to operate without distraction from the real chore of driving. Seat cushions are a little small, but offer just the right firmness. Storage spaces for routine traveling stuff abound.

There's plenty of room up front, but things get cramped in back. Getting into the rear is not easy. Leg room there is minimal and the rear seat is better suited for two adults. The Tracker has huge cargo space behind the rear seat, and if more is needed, the rear seat folds down. Visibility up front and to the sides is fine, and has been improved to the rear by lowering the position of the externally-mounted spare tire.

On the road, Tracker is far better than might be expected. The wider stance improves both ride and handling. The improved steering is light, but satisfactory. The revised suspension makes long trip rides on ordinary roads more than just bearable. The 2.0 liter engine performs adequately under most circumstances, and shifting with the manual transmission is natural and easy. The real advantage for a vehicle like Tracker is its maneuverability. Whether at the mall or on the trail, its short wheelbase makes tight turns, and ease of backing up a real advantage.

Obviously, with its limited interior room, Tracker is not suited for everyone, but if real utility is the objective, Tracker combines a good ride, reasonable handling, 4-wheel drive capability, great cargo capability, and a sort-of fun-to-drive aspect—especially with the 2-door version. **D.V.S.**

Specifications of Test Vehicle

Model: 4-Door 4WD

Exterior Dimensions	
Wheelbase	97.6 in.
Overall Length	159.8 In.
Overall Width	66.7 In.
Overall Height	66.5 In.
Curb Weight	2981 lbs.
Interior Dimensions	
Seating Capacity	5
Head Room	F: 40.7/R: 39.6 in.
Leg Room	F: 41.3/R: 35.9 in.
Cargo Room	27.2 cu.ft.
Engine	
Displacement	2.0L I-4
Horsepower	121@6000 rpm
Torque, lb-ft.	122@3000 rpm
Performance	
0-60 mph, acceleration	10.5 sec.
60-0 mph, braking	135 ft.
Turning Circle	34.8 ft.
EPA City/Highway	NA
Test Mileage	NA
Fuel Tank Capacity	17.4 gal.

Ratings 146

Category	Rating
Over The Road	
Acceleration	6
Transmission	8
Braking	4
Steering	8
Ride	7
Handling	7
Drivability	8
Fuel Economy	6
Passenger Environment	
Comfort/Conven.	7
Interior Room	7
Driving Position	8
Instrumentation	7
Controls	7
Visibility	8
Entry/Exit	8
Quietness	7
Cargo Space	10
Workmanship	
Interior	7
Exterior	8
Value	8

Chevrolet

Venture

New for 99

More powerful 3.4-liter V-6
Extended wheelbase withdrawn on 3-door model
Standard heated side-view mirrors

Pros

Model range
Modular interior
Driveability

Cons

V-6 with marginal power
Mediocre braking system
Inconsistent manufacturing quality

Equipment

Major Standard Equipment: 3.4-liter V-6, automatic transmission, 4-wheel antilock brakes, 7-passenger seating, air conditioning, cabin air filter, theft-alarm system, variable-intermittent wipers, rear washer and wiper, tilt steering wheel, AM/FM stereo, power locks, power mirrors, stainless-steel exhaust system. **LS adds:** Cruise control, AM/FM/cassette stereo, power windows, remote keyless entry. **Major Options:** Traction control, power right-side sliding door, long wheel base, automatic leveling suspension, self-sealing tires, aluminum wheels.

Versatility

The Venture is unquestionably the most versatile model in the trio of small minivans it forms with the Oldsmobile Silhouette and the Pontiac Trans Sport. In fact, it is the only vehicle available in a utility version or outfitted to double as a taxi. But the Venture's primary objective is finding its way to the driveways of young families, who are particularly appreciative of its price-value ratio, an area where the Venture scores precious points in relation to its competition.

A brief word on this Chevrolet's styling: let's just say it loses face in comparison to the Trans Sport, mainly because of its grotesque grille, borrowed from the Caprice. Having said that, like Chrysler's Voyager and Caravan, the Venture comes in standard and extended wheelbase versions, the latter available with a fourth door. And speaking of doors, they open onto a bright, comfortable, and inviting interior. The driving position is good, the view is positively panoramic, equipment is detailed, instrumentation is still minimal, but controls are easy to read and use. A few flaws: speakers that are positioned too low in the trunk, no reachable clothes hooks (three-door version only), and windshield wipers that heap snow, slush, and water a few inches from door pillars. Sadder still is this vehicle's inconsistent manufacturing quality.

Only one engine powers this minivan, a 3.4-liter V-6, which now has an output of 185 horses and 210 pound-feet of torque, but it's still not enough considering the vehicle's weight and purpose in life. However, it does have an interesting amount of pickup power in the lower rpm range.

The four-speed automatic transmission works efficiently and is extremely smooth. As for driveability, the Venture is light-years ahead of its ancestor, the Lumina Van. Easier to handle and more fun to drive, this small minivan has all the assets it takes to compete with the best the industry has. But unlike the competition, the Venture drives and feels more like a truck and is less comfortable when cornering, no doubt because of its width. It's too bad that GM still doesn't offer a four-disc brake system, not even as an option, on the Venture. Like so many other vehicles in the category, it often runs out of steam after a few sudden stops.

True, the powerful General Motors distribution network has a lot to do with the success the Venture is currently enjoying. But it's equally true that the current generation is far ahead of the previous version, even if General Motors can do even better, even faster.
E.L.

Specifications of Test Vehicle

Model: LS

Exterior Dimensions	
Wheelbase	112 in.
Overall length	186.9 in.
Overall width	72 in.
Overall height	67.4 in.
Curb weight	3,650 lb.
Interior Dimensions	
Seating capacity	7
Head room	F:39.9/R1:39.3/R2:38.8 in.
Leg room	F:39.9/R1:36.9/R2:34 in.
Cargo volume	16.3 cu. ft.
Engine	
Displacement	V-6 3.4 L.
Horsepower	185 @ 5,200 rpm
Torque, lb-ft.	210 @ 4,000 rpm
Performance	
0-60 mph, acceleration	10 sec.
60-0 mph, braking	133 ft.
Turning circle	37.4 ft.
EPA city/highway	18/25 mpg
Test mileage	22.5
Fuel tank capacity	20 gal.

Prices

$20,000
$28,000

3-door
$20,249

LS 4-door
$22,079

LS 4-door, ext. length
$22,909

Warranty

Bumper-to-bumper
3/36,000

Powertrain
3/36,000

Rust-through
6/100,000

Other to Consider

Dodge Grand Caravan

Ford Windstar

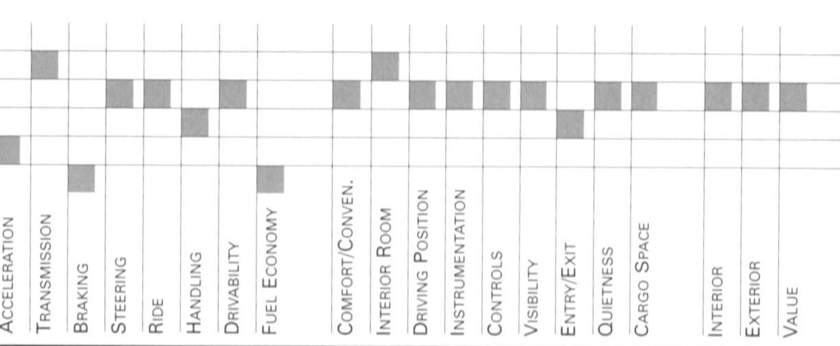

Ratings
152

Chrysler 300M

new MODEL

New for 99
New model for 1999

Pros
Steering/handling
Ride
Powertrain

Cons
Fuel economy
Trunk liftover

Equipment

Major Standard Equipment: 3.5liter V-6 engine, 4-speed automatic transmission, traction control, 4-wheel disc antilock brakes, 17 in. wheels, air conditioning, automatic headlights, power heated memory mirrors, AM/FM/cassette/CD stereo, power/memory/heated leather seats, fold-down split rear seats, security alarm, speed control, tilt wheel, trip computer, power windows and locks, remote entry. **Major Options:** Power moonroof, premium sound system, chrome wheels.

Yearning for the past

The introduction of the 1999 Chrysler 300M brings back one of the best-known performance names of years past. The original Chrysler 300 series, built from 1955 until 1971, were popular for their styling, performance, and luxury. Now, Chrysler offers the new 300M for 1999, aiming it directly at the driver who still wants sport as well as luxury and style in a sedan.

The 300M shares the same platform and powertrain with the Chrysler LHS — many of the specifications are the same. Because the overall length of the 300M is about 10 inches shorter than the LHS, rear-seat leg room is shorter and the trunk is smaller. Both reductions seem to be good trade-offs for the sake of styling.

Only one trim level is offered and there are only two major options, a moonroof and an upscale sound system. Otherwise, the 300M comes loaded with luxury and convenience features such as automatic climate control and 8-way powered heated seats with memory for seat position, mirrors and radio presets. A 253 hp, 3.5 liter V-6, coupled to a 4-speed "AutoStick" automatic transmission is the only powertrain available.

The elegant styling of the exterior carries over into a very roomy interior. Large front and rear doors make entry and exit easy. Plush leather seats have

4-way adjustable head restraints up front and vertically adjustable restraints on the rear seats. The design of the instrument panel is both simple and elegant. Instrument gauges have black letters on white backgrounds that change to a pleasant light green at night. Each gauge is trimmed with a chrome ring for a slightly retro look. A small analog clock is centered above the center console for added effect.

Regardless of the road conditions, the 300M is a joy to drive. Ride and handling are delicately balanced. The ride is on the comfortable side of firm, but never harsh. Handling benefits from using different suspension tuning than that used on the LHS. Winding roads and sharp curves can be taken with a feeling of security and confidence. The non-variable-rate power steering gives good road sensation, but tends to feel heavy at low speeds.

The engine delivers smooth satisfying acceleration — a run from 0 to 60 mph takes 7.5 seconds.The "AutoStick" feature is an interesting novelty at first, but soon becomes a nuisance in ordinary driving. However, we found it useful when driving in hilly country. The brakes felt good during hard braking — we measured a stopping distance of 123 ft. from 60 to 0 mph. Expect fuel economy in the low twenties on mid-grade fuel.

On the practical side, we found the trunk to be better than average size. The rear seats fold down for more capacity, but a high liftover into the trunk area makes loading heavy objects difficult.

The 300M is an enjoyable car to drive. It offers a good blend of performance, driving pleasure, comfort, convenience, and luxury for a reasonable price. **D.V.S.**

Specifications of Test Vehicle

Model: 300M

Exterior Dimensions	
Wheelbase	113.0 in.
Overall Length	197.8 In.
Overall Width	74.4 In.
Overall Height	56.0 In.
Curb Weight	3567 lbs.
Interior Dimensions	
Seating Capacity	5
Head Room	F: 38.3/R: 37.7 in.
Leg Room	F: 42.2/R: 39.1 in.
Cargo Room	16.8 cu.ft.
Engine	
Displacement	3.5 L V-6
Horsepower	253@6400 rpm
Torque, lb-ft.	255@3950 rpm
Performance	
0-60 mph, acceleration	7.5 sec.
60-0 mph, braking	123 ft.
Turning Circle	37.6 ft.
EPA City/Highway	18/27 mpg.
Test Mileage	22.5
Fuel Tank Capacity	17.2 gal.

Counterpoint

Was the Chrysler corporation yearning for the past — like others do for tobacco, alcohol, or love — when some 20 years on it decided to go a little further in the 300 series alphabet? As if a major segment of the population could forget that when the original version was unveiled in 1955 it was a coupe whose rear-drive wheels were powered by a thundering V-8. Can we forgive Chrysler for ruining a name that carries such a rich history with it?

The best we can do is to put our memories aside as we climb aboard this new model.

The 300M is up against sedans that have attracted a lot of attention and that are esteemed. This is where things get a bit touchy, even though Chrysler rightly emphasizes that its 300M is much less expensive than its rivals. There are many reasons for this, first among them the lack of side air bags and a third three-point adjustable seat belt for the rear seat. Sporty character is at a minimum, the speedometer is graduated only to a timid 120 mph, and the emergency brake is foot-operated.

Its mechanical system may not be cutting-edge, but you can't help but admit that the 300M stands up admirably well to comparison with its direct competitors. Now what about handling? Well, it all depends on which options you choose. The base version understeers, slides, and howls as soon as it picks up speed, which makes the drivers feel as if they were aboard a big sedan; on the other hand, the sportier 300M uses hardware usually reserved for drivers who are pros: a firmer suspension, larger tires, and a heavier, more responsive steering system that provides a perfect link between the road surface and the steering wheel. The only problem: a minimally useful traction control system that works only at very low speeds.

In short, the 300M lacks the refinement, the agility, and the personality of its rivals, but its purchase price is a huge advantage.

E.L.

PRICES

$29,000

$32,000

Sedan
$29,295

WARRANTY
(years/miles)

Bumper-to-Bumper
3/36,000

Power Train
3/36,000

Rust-through
7/100,000

OTHER TO CONSIDER

Audi A6 S

Saab 9-5

Group	Category	Rating (1–10)
Over The Road	Acceleration	9
	Transmission	9
	Braking	6
	Steering	8
	Ride	8
	Handling	9
	Drivability	9
	Fuel Economy	5
Passenger Environment	Comfort/Conven.	8
	Interior Room	8
	Driving Position	8
	Instrumentation	9
	Controls	9
	Visibility	8
	Entry/Exit	8
	Quietness	8
	Cargo Space	8
Workmanship	Interior	8
	Exterior	8
	Value	9

Ratings

162

Chrysler LHS

New for '99

Completely restyled exterior and interior
New powertrain and suspension.

Pros

Powertrain
Ride
Comfort/convenience

Cons

Fuel economy
Trunk liftover

Equipment

Major Standard Equipment: 3.5 liter V-6 engine, 4-speed automatic transmission, traction control, 4-wheel disc antilock brakes, 17 in. wheels, air conditioning, automatic headlights, power heated memory mirrors, AM/FM/cassette/CD stereo, power/memory/leather seats, security alarm, speed control, tilt wheel, trip computer, power windows and locks, remote entry. **Major Options:** Power moonroof, premium sound system, chrome wheels.

A pipe-and-slippers model

PRICES
$29,000
$32,000
Sedan
$29,295

WARRANTY
(years/miles)
Bumper-to-Bumper
3/36,000
Power Train
3/36,000
Rust-through
7/100,000

OTHER TO CONSIDER
Buick Park Avenue
Lincoln Continental

After taking a year's hiatus, the Chrysler LHS is back for 1999 with fresh new styling, more power, and better road manners. With its first restyling in five years, it is well-positioned as the company's most elegant sedan. The LHS shares many body, platform, and drivetrain components with its very close cousins the Concorde and Intrepid. But the distinctive front and rear sheetmetal, interior styling and larger engine clearly set it apart from its lower priced relatives.

Available in only one trim level, the LHS comes loaded with a full compliment of comfort, convenience and luxury features. The only major options are a moonroof and a more elaborate sound system. Power is supplied with Chrysler's largest V-6, a 253 hp high-output version, coupled to a conventional 4-speed automatic transmission.

Inside, the LHS provides comfortable accommodations for five adults. Expensive-looking leather seats are comfortable and supportive for all but the most aggressive types of driving. Front seats are heated, 8-way adjustable and have a memory feature that in-cludes outside mirrors and radio presets. Rear seat passengers get 2.5 in. more leg room than in the similar Chrysler 300M. All seats are high off the floor and offer good visibility to the front and sides. Entry and exit, both front and rear are excellent-just step in and sit down.

A full array of white-faced gauges, each surrounded with a chrome bezel give the instrument panel a look of elegance. Electroluminescent lighting is used to illuminate the gauges with a warm green glow at night. An overhead console displays compass, outside temperature and trip computer information. Our only gripe is the location of the audio system below the vent controls.

On the road, the LHS caters to those who prefer comfort over sportiness. The ride is soft, bringing on some body roll during aggressive cornering. But, handling is very good for a car this size. The variable ratio steering has a light touch but still feels precise. The engine and transmission work well together, with a run from 0 to 60 mph taking a very satisfying 8.2 seconds. The brakes performed no better than average in our panic stopping test. Fuel economy should be in the low twenties with mid-grade fuel. However, Chrysler engineers were quick to tell us the engine runs just fine on regular, with little degradation in performance.

The trunk has plenty of space, but its shape and a high lift-over make it difficult to handle large or heavy objects. The rear seat has a center-arm rest pass-through for hauling long objects. A high deck lid makes it difficult to see when backing up.

With its comfortable interior, composed performance, and strikingly good looks, the LHS shines as a near-luxury sedan. And if you want something just a little sportier, a handling package is available. If that's not enough, check out the 300M. **D.V.S.**

Specifications of Test Vehicle

Model: LHS

Exterior Dimensions	
Wheelbase	113.0 in.
Overall Length	207.7 In.
Overall Width	74.5 In.
Overall Height	56.0 In.
Curb Weight	3589 lbs.
Interior Dimensions	
Seating Capacity	5
Head Room	F: 38.3/R:37.2 in.
Leg Room	F: 42.2/R:41.6 in.
Cargo Room	18.6 cu.ft.
Engine	
Displacement	3.5 L V-6
Horsepower	253@6400 rpm
Torque, lb-ft.	255@3950 rpm
Performance	
0-60 mph, acceleration	8.2 sec.
60-0 mph, braking	135 ft.
Turning Circle	37.6 ft.
EPA City/Highway	18/27 mpg.
Test Mileage	23.5 mpg.
Fuel Tank Capacity	17.2 gal.

Ratings

Group	Category	Rating
Over The Road	Acceleration	9
	Transmission	9
	Braking	6
	Steering	9
	Ride	9
	Handling	9
	Drivability	9
	Fuel Economy	6
Passenger Environment	Comfort/Conven.	9
	Interior Room	10
	Driving Position	9
	Instrumentation	10
	Controls	9
	Visibility	9
	Entry/Exit	9
	Quietness	9
	Cargo Space	10
Workmanship	Interior	9
	Exterior	9
	Value	10

158

Chrysler Cirrus

New for 99

Redesigned grille
New hub caps
New exterior colors

Pros

Passenger room
Ride comfort
Handling

Cons

Windshield reflections
Engine torque
Transmission selector

Equipment

Major Standard Equipment: 2.5-liter V-6, automatic transmission, 4-wheel antilock brakes, variable-assist power steering, air conditioning, rear defroster, AM/FM/cassette stereo, power locks, power heated mirrors, remote keyless entry, manual height-adjustable driver's seat, folding rear seat, variable-intermittent wipers, cruise control, tilt steering column, power windows, remote-control decklid release, stainless-steel exhaust system, aluminum wheels. **Major Options:** Sunroof,alloy wheel, theft alarm, AM/FM/cassette stereo, AM/FM/CD/cassette stereo, AM/FM/CD stereo, power driver's seat, leather ulphostory.

A dressed-up compact

The Chrysler Cirrus's modest engine power thwarts its lofty ambitions against strong competition from other compact sedans.

The front-wheel-drive Cirrus aims to be a luxury mid-size car. It competes with the Mercury Mystique, Honda Accord, Oidsmobile Alero, Toyota Camry, and the like. Chrysler has two other versions, the mainstream Dodge Stratus and down-market Plymouth Breeze. Whereas the Stratus offers three engine choices and the Breeze offers two 4-cylinder choices, the Cirrus has only the V-6. It also has only one trim level. All three have the less powerful air bags permitted by new government safety regulations.

In sprints from 0 to 60 mph, we timed the Cirrus LXi around 10 seconds—about average for a mid-size car. The small V-6 does not pull well off the line, making the car feel slower than it actually is. You have to wait for it to get above 4,000 rpm before it starts to show its stuff. It packs good passing power, though; the transmission downshifts to third gear quickly and quietly. Unfortunately, Chrysler omitted a second-gear position on the automatic transmission selector. Without it, driving in slow-moving traffic is inconvenient. We averaged 22 mpg in our test drives.

The Cirrus's long wheelbase eliminates most ride choppiness. The fully independent suspension cushions passengers on poor road surfaces. The steering feels very firm and well balanced for effort and feedback, but its wide turning radius makes parking difficult. The car quickly goes where it's pointed, and the body leans very little during turns. We needed to press the brake pedal hard to get a strong reaction.

The Cirrus has plenty of hip, shoulder, and head room, front and rear. The seats are firm and comfortable. A footrest to the left of the brake pedal helps the driver maintain good posture on long trips. The rear bench seats three people when absolutely necessary— or two comfortably on long drives. The rear seatback folds down almost flat for long cargo.

On the dash, the instruments are commendably large and easy to read. The controls for the radio and climate system are within the driver's reach, but the obviously fake wood grain trim around them looks cheap. Engine, wind, and tire noise is low, but road noise is evident, especially on coarse roads.

Visibility is good to the front and sides. The windshield reflects the dashboard severely on sunny days, however, and thick roof pillars and a tall decklid hinder visibility to the rear.

The upscale Cirrus isn't the value that the mainstream Dodge Stratus is. And, since Chrysler dealers also sell Plymouths, the Cirrus seems like a dressed-up Breeze across the showroom. **D.V.S.**

Specifications of Test Vehicle

Model: Cirrus LXi

Exterior Dimensions	
Wheelbase	108 in.
Overall length	187 in.
Overall width	71.7 in.
Overall height	52.5 in.
Curb weight	3,200 lb.
Interior Dimensions	
Seating capacity	5
Head room	F:38.1/R:36.8 in.
Leg room	F:42.3/R:37.8 in.
Cargo volume	15.7 cu. ft.
Engine	
Displacement	V-6 2.5 L.
Horsepower	168 @ 5,800 rpm
Torque, lb-ft.	170 @ 4,350 rpm
Performance	
0-60 mph, acceleration	9.8 sec.
60-0 mph, braking	122 ft.
Turning circle	37 ft.
EPA city/highway	19/28 mpg
Test mileage	22 mpg
Fuel tank	16 gal.

Prices

$19,000
$23,000

Sedan $19,995

Warranty

(years/miles)

Bumper-to-bumper 3/36,000

Powertrain 3/36,000

Rust-through 7/100,000

Other to Consider

Mercury Mystique

Toyota Camry

Ratings

Group	Category	Rating
Over The Road	Acceleration	7
	Transmission	7
	Braking	6
	Steering	7
	Ride	8
	Handling	8
	Drivability	8
	Fuel Economy	5
Passenger Environment	Comfort/Conven.	8
	Interior Room	8
	Driving Position	8
	Instrumentation	8
	Controls	8
	Visibility	6
	Entry/Exit	8
	Quietness	7
	Cargo Space	7
Workmanship	Interior	8
	Exterior	8
	Value	7

Ratings 147

Chrysler Concorde

New for 99

Comfort-focused suspension
Cargo net in the trunk

Pros

Quietnesss
Ride comfort
Appearance

Cons

Rear visibility
Steering
Trunk shape

Equipment

Major Standard Equipment: 2.7-liter V-6, 4-wheel disc brakes, air conditioning, rear defroster, variable-intermittent wipers, power mirrors, automatic-dimming rear-view mirror, AM/FM/cassette stereo, power driver's seat, tilt steering wheel, power windows, automatic power locks, remote keyless entry, power decklid release, stainless-steel exhaust system. **LXi adds:** 3.2-liter V-6, 4-wheel antilock brakes, automatic temperature control, leather upholstery, full-size spare tire, larger tires. **Major Options:** 4-wheel antilock brakes, traction control, remote keyless entry, split-bench seat, power moonroof.

A solid value

PRICES
$20,000
$30,000
LX sedan $22,060
LXi sedan $22,785

WARRANTY (years/miles)
Bumper-to-bumper 3/36,000
Powertrain 3/36,000
Rust-through 7/100,000

OTHER TO CONSIDER
Mercury Sable
Toyota Avalon

Chrysler didn't wait for the popularity of the Concorde, its upscale family sedan, to decline before redesigning it. New for '98, the Concorde stands out for its design, convenience features, and road manners.

The new Concorde sports a distinctive body that has no obvious front bumper. Although it shares the same platform with the Dodge Intrepid, it has totally different styling.

New engines are part of the package, too, determined by the trim level. The base model comes with a 2.7-liter, 200-horse-power V-6, powerful for its size. The upscale, better-equipped LXi gets a 3.2-liter, 225-horsepower V-6. Both models use the same 4-speed automatic transmission.

The small engine performs adequately for running errands and light duty, but has to work hard when the car is fully loaded. The 3.2-liter engine produces more torque at a lower speed, which is an important difference if you demand more performance.

Inside, the Concorde focuses on practical luxury. It still offers a 50/50 bench seat for those who require seating for six. The rear seat has a pass-through into the trunk for carrying long items, such as skis. There's plenty of storage space; the full front seat includes a wide center compartment with storage slots, coin holder, and fold-out cupholders.

The instrument panel uses a soft-touch covering and features a seamless air bag door, improving the appearance and reducing the potential for theft and tampering. Most controls are well located and easy to use, but the stereo controls would be handier above the vent controls. The plain, basic instrument cluster looks out of place. And the fake wood trim doesn't help coordinate the four other colors in the cabin.

Large doors swing wide for easy entry. Once you're inside, the Concorde feels huge. With either the bench seat or the individual front seats, there is good head, leg, shoulder, and hip room, front and rear. The car's high rear end restricts visibility to the rear, but large side view mirrors help offset this shortcoming.

The large trunk extends far forward, with plenty of room for large objects, but the odd shape of the opening and the high liftover can make loading heavy items difficult.

A fully independent suspension balances a supple ride and crisp handling that is exceptional for a car this size. The car drives like a much smaller one. The steering no longer has variable assist, and the on-center feel is a little vague.

Roomy, comfortable, and enjoyable to drive, the Concorde is a solid value in a family sedan. **D.V.S.**

Ratings

Group	Category	Rating
Over The Road	Acceleration	8
	Transmission	6
	Braking	7
	Steering	8
	Ride	8
	Handling	7
	Drivability	9
	Fuel Economy	7
Passenger Environment	Comfort/Conven.	8
	Interior Room	7
	Driving Position	8
	Instrumentation	8
	Controls	7
	Visibility	7
	Entry/Exit	7
	Quietness	7
	Cargo Space	6
Workmanship	Interior	9
	Exterior	8
	Value	6

Ratings 165

Specifications of Test Vehicle

Model: Concorde LXi

Exterior Dimensions	
Wheelbase	113 in.
Overall length	209.1 in.
Overall width	74.4 in.
Overall height	55.9 in.
Curb weight	3,550 lb.
Interior Dimensions	
Seating capacity	6
Head room	F:38.3/R:37.2 in.
Leg room	F:42.2/R:41.6 in.
Cargo room	18.7 cu. ft.
Engine	
Displacement	V-6 3.2 L.
Horsepower	225 @ 6,300 rpm
Torque, lb-ft.	225 @ 3,800 rpm
Performance	
0-60 mph, acceleration	8.7 sec.
60-0 mph, braking	125 ft.
Turning circle	37.6 ft.
EPA city/highway	19/29 mpg
Test mileage	24 mpg
Fuel tank capacity	17 gal.

Chrysler Sebring

New for 99
Two new exterior colors

Pros
Attractive styling
Cargo capacity
Four-passenger capacity

Cons
Heavy front end
Fading brakes
Rhino agility

Equipment
Major Standard Equipment: 2-liter I-4, manual transmission, air conditioning, AM/FM/cassette stereo, tilt steering wheel, split-folding rear seat, remote-control decklid release, stainless-steel exhaust system. **LXi adds:** 4-wheel antilock disc brakes, power locks, power windows, power mirrors, cruise control, automatic dimming rearview mirror, remote keyless entry, theft-alarm system, AM/FM/CD/cassette stereo, driver's lumbar adjustment, larger tires, aluminum wheels.
Major Options: 2.5-liter V-6, automatic transmission, 4-wheel antilock disc brakes, AM/FM/CD/cassette stereo, leather upholstery.

Beauty's only skin deep

You have to read Chrysler's press releases to appreciate how much importance they attach to the looks of the Avenger and Sebring. All the superlatives in the dictionary are trotted out in praise of the "elegant and dynamic" lines, especially when they come in the latest fashion colors, the more intriguingly named the better. They do look good, no doubt about it, but are looks enough?

With a jutting nose and a tightly clenched jaw, the Sebring is impressive looking, especially when it's equipped with 17-inch wheels. But the wide doors still open onto a very disappointing and almost kitsch interior with its dark-colored fake wood inlays. You don't get into this coupe, you lower yourself into it. The particularly low driving position is not very comfortable (the seatback is stiff and the steering wheel grazes your knees), and rear visibility is hindered by the fact that the trunk lid seems to soar into your field of vision. The "elegant" side-view mirrors provide only a restricted image of what's actually going on around you. On a more positive note, these coupes can accommodate four adults quite comfortably; unfortunately, it has to be said that those who sit in the rear will likely complain that their windows don't roll down. The trunk is convenient with a deep but not too high configuration.

When you drive these coupes your first impression is that they're heavy, and their front-end design makes cornering difficult despite a good steering system. You'll get plenty of feedback on even the smallest of road irregularities so as a driver your full attention is required at all times. Not particularly agile, these two models have a turning radius that will likely require more than one attempt to get them positioned exactly where you want them. With a tendency to understeer, and less exciting than their looks would have you believe, these two starlets will leave you wanting more. The four-speed automatic transmission knocks the wind out of the 2.5-liter V-6 and shifting is erratic. Under such circumstances, braking is adequate, but while they may be able to bite into the road with all their strength, the brakes quickly overheat.

In other words, this model's looks are its biggest asset. **E.L.**

Specifications of Test Vehicle

Model: Sebring LXi

Exterior dimensions	
Wheelbase	106 in.
Length	192.6 in.
Width	70.1 in.
Height	54.8 in.
Curb weight	3,400 lb.
Interior dimensions	
Seating capacity	4
Head room	F:38.7/R:37 in.
Leg room	F:42.4/R:35.2 in.
Cargo Volume	11.3 cu. ft.
Engine	
Displacement	V-6 2.5 L.
Horsepower	168 @ 5,800 rpm
Torque, lb-ft.	170 @ 4,350 rpm
Performance	
0-60 mph, acceleration	10.7 sec.
60-0 mph, braking	137 ft.
Turning circle	40 ft.
EPA city/highway	19/28 mpg
Test mileage	22 mpg
Fuel tank capacity	16 gal.

Prices
$17,000
$22,000

LX 2-doors coupe $24,405

LXi 2-doors coupe $26,720

Warranty
(years/months)

Bumper-to-bumper 3/36,000

Powertrain 3/36,000

Rust-through 7/100,000

Other to consider
Pontiac Grand Am

Toyota Camry Solara

Ratings

Group	Category	Rating
Over The Road	Acceleration	6
	Transmission	7
	Braking	4
	Steering	8
	Ride	8
	Handling	8
	Drivability	8
	Fuel Economy	6
Passenger Environment	Comfort/Conven.	8
	Interior Room	8
	Driving Position	8
	Instrumentation	8
	Controls	8
	Visibility	7
	Entry/Exit	6
	Quietness	8
	Cargo Space	6
Workmanship	Interior	8
	Exterior	8
	Value	7

Ratings 145

Chrysler Sebring Convertible

New for 99

Revised options list
Two new exterior colors

Pros

Family-sized convertible
Attractive styling
Good handling

Cons

Weak brakes
Sluggish engines
Poor rear visibility

Equipment

Major Standard Equipment: 2.4-liter I-4, automatic transmission, air conditioning, AM/FM/cassette stereo, tilt steering wheel, split-folding rear seat, remote-control decklid release, stainless-steel exhaust system. **JXi adds:** 2.5-liter V-6 4-wheel antilock disc brakes, power locks, power windows, power mirrors, cruise control, automatic dimming rear-view mirror, remote keyless entry, theft-alarm system, AM/FM/CD/cassette stereo, driver's lumbar adjustment, larger tires, aluminum wheels. **Major Options:** Semi automatic transmission, manual-automatic transmission, 4-wheel antilock disc brakes, AM/FM/CD/cassette stereo.

PRICES
$17,000
$27,000

JX 2-door convertible
$20,575

JXi 2-door convertible
$25,040

WARRANTY
(years/months)

Bumper-to-bumper
3/36,000

Powertrain
3/36,000

Rust-through
7/100,000

OTHER TO CONSIDER

Ford Mustang Cab

Volkswagen Cabriolet

The wind in your hair

Success took very little time to knock at the door of the Sebring Convertible. In fact, six months after its unveiling, more than 45,000 units had already given a breath of fresh air to their new owners, who just happened to be older than Chrysler had expected. And that's not the only forecast that proved to be off-target: buyers were men more often than women.

With more than $200 million US invested to date, this year the Chrysler corporation has limited its innovation to new colors and to a revised options list, the better to enjoy good profitability levels for as long as possible.

A quick word on the outside, to draw your attention to the Chrysler badge on the redesigned grille and the shining wheel covers that catch your eye without blinding you.

Inside, things look familiar since the Sebring Convertible has copied almost all the features found inside the Cirrus. Almost all: the convertible has built-in seat belts, appreciably more comfortable than the alternative. And for more comfort still, this year Chrysler offers a Limited version, richer-looking and more elegant. This model's most prized attribute is that it can accommodate four people, even if shoulder room is limited. The rear windshield provides minimal visibility, but it does include a defroster for drivers who travel in winter climes. Beware: the wiring tends to get disconnected when you put the top down! Top operation on the Sebring is a marvel and the entire process takes all of 60 seconds, including the time it takes to position the cover. Another comment: since you have to roll down windows to put the soft top back into position, make sure you roll them back up should you take your favorite toy into an automatic carwash. And don't think it can't happen to you!

With a stiffer chassis and more stability, this car has an admirable ride, especially if you choose the reinforced twin suspension and 16-inch wheels. You may lose a bit of comfort, but in exchange you'll get better handling and better roadholding. Unfortunately, these qualities are overshadowed by engines that are more or less anemic. The 2.4-liter four-cylinder is rough, while the 2.5-liter six-cylinder isn't at its best in the lower rpm range. And as soon as you push down hard on the gas pedal, the automatic transmission gets momentarily confused, which doesn't help. Can you trust yourself to avoid such confusion? Then opt for the semi automatic (Autostick) transmission and do the shifting yourself. Braking, another apparent weakness in the Sebring, has received special attention for 1999. The anti lock system is more refined on the JXi (those who choose the JX will have to pay to enjoy it) and two discs take over from the drums that used to be in the back, eliminating problems observed last year. **E.L.**

Specifications of Test Vehicle

Model: Sebring JXi

Exterior dimensions	
Wheelbase	106 in.
Length	192.6 in.
Width	70.1 in.
Height	54.8 in.
Curb weight	3,400 lb.
Interior dimensions	
Seating capacity	4
Head room	F:38.7/R:37 in.
Leg room	F:42.4/R:35.2 in.
Cargo Volume	11.3 cu. ft.
Engine	
Displacement	V-6 2.5 L.
Horsepower	168 @ 5,800 rpm
Torque, lb-ft.	170 @ 4,350 rpm
Performance	
0-60 mph, acceleration	10.7 sec.
60-0 mph, braking	137 ft.
Turning circle	40 ft.
EPA city/highway	19/28 mpg
Test mileage	22 mpg
Fuel tank capacity	16 gal.

Ratings

Group	Category	Rating (1–10)
Over The Road	Acceleration	6
Over The Road	Transmission	8
Over The Road	Braking	4
Over The Road	Steering	6
Over The Road	Ride	8
Over The Road	Handling	8
Over The Road	Drivability	8
Over The Road	Fuel Economy	5
Passenger Environment	Comfort/Conven.	7
Passenger Environment	Interior Room	9
Passenger Environment	Driving Position	8
Passenger Environment	Instrumentation	8
Passenger Environment	Controls	8
Passenger Environment	Visibility	6
Passenger Environment	Entry/Exit	8
Passenger Environment	Quietness	6
Passenger Environment	Cargo Space	5
Workmanship	Interior	8
Workmanship	Exterior	7
Workmanship	Value	9

142

Chrysler

Town & Country

New for 99
Trims and accessories

Pros
Roomy interior
Efficient 3.8-liter V-6
Surprising road stability

Cons
High fuel consumption (AWD)
Hefty price
Weak brakes

Equipment
Major Standard Equipment: 3.3-liter V-6, automatic transmission, 4-wheel antilock brakes, traction control, driver's-side sliding door, 7-passenger seating, dual-temperature air conditioning, rear defroster, windshield wiper de-icer, variable-intermittent wipers, rear wiper and washer, cruise control, tilt steering wheel, AM/FM/cassette stereo, trip computer, power windows, power locks, power heated mirrors, aluminum wheels. **LX adds:** 6-inch-longer wheelbase. **LXi adds:** 3.8-liter V-6 engine, automatic leveling suspension, rear air conditioning, AM/FM/CD/cassette stereo, remote keyless entry, power driver's seat, privacy glass, conventional spare tire, theft-alarm system.

Nice clothes

The Town & Country gives Chrysler a place in the top-of-the-line minivan sector of the automotive industry. But under the glistening chrome and magnificent leather, all we find is a reliable, driveable, and versatile specimen, much like the Dodge Grand Caravan and the Plymouth Grand Voyager. So why pay more?

Assembled in Canada, this minivan boasts a well-finished and richly appointed interior. The inexpensive appearance of certain plastics is jarring, but overall, there's no doubt that this vehicle is the best that Chrysler has to offer. Despite its plunging hood and excellent panoramic vision, the Town & Country is still awkward to park. The passenger compartment is amazingly roomy and baggage space is perfectly acceptable, even appreciable, even when all seats are occupied. Despite the addition of casters, the rear seat is still hard to remove.

Unlike the Grand Caravan and the Grand Voyager, the Town & Country only allows a 3.8-liter V-6 under its hood. All the better, since it is the best at getting this minivan up and about. On the down side, it isn't as powerful as the units made available by the competition, not to mention that it isn't very economical at the gas pumps. These mechanical components are teamed with a four-speed automatic transmission whose reliability record hasn't been exactly spotless in recent years. But Chrysler assures us that all such problems have been resolved.

Road stability is still as astounding as ever, but we expected more in the area of soundproofing. Another disappointment: the noisy and not extremely efficient traction control system. Brakes (discs/drums), even with ABS, have a hard time staving off overheating, although Chrysler has devoted a special effort to correcting this flaw. The AWD version has four discs, lucky duck!

Unless you have money to waste, we suggest you take a look at the Plymouth Grand Voyager and the Dodge Grand Caravan. **E.L.**

Specifications of Test Vehicle

Model: SX

Exterior Dimensions	
Wheelbase	113.3 in.
Overall length	186.4 in.
Overall width	76.8 in.
Overall height	68.7 in.
Curb weight	3,950 lb.
Interior dimensions	
Seating capacity	7
Head room	F:39.8 in./R:40.5/R2:38.1 in.
Leg room	F:40.6 in./R:35/R2:35.2 in.
Cargo volume	12.9 cu. ft.
Engine	
Displacement	V-6 3.8 L.
Horsepower	180 @ 4,400 rpm
Torque, lb-ft.	240 @ 3,200 rpm
Performance	
0-60 mph, acceleration	9.8 sec.
60-0 mph, braking	130 ft.
Turning circle	37.6 ft.
EPA city/highway	17/24 mpg
Test mileage	20 mpg
Fuel tank capacity	20 gal.

Prices
$27,000
$35,000

SX 4-door minivan $26,680

LX 4-door minivan $27,135

LXi 4-door minivan $31,720

Warranty
(years/miles)

Bumper-to-bumper 3/36,000

Powertrain 3/36,000

Rust-through 7/100,000

Other to Consider
Honda Odyssey

Oldsmobile Silhouette

Group	Category	Rating
Over The Road	Acceleration	7
	Transmission	8
	Braking	5
	Steering	7
	Ride	8
	Handling	6
	Drivability	8
	Fuel Economy	5
Passenger Environment	Comfort/Conven.	8
	Interior Room	10
	Driving Position	8
	Instrumentation	8
	Controls	8
	Visibility	8
	Entry/Exit	7
	Quietness	8
	Cargo Space	10
Workmanship	Interior	8
	Exterior	9
	Value	8

Ratings
154

Daewoo Lanos

PRICES
S 3-door $ 8,999
S 4-door $ 9,699
SE 3-door $ 10,600
SE 4-door $10,900
SX 3-door $11,669
SX 4-door $11,969

Equipment

Major Standard Equipment: Dual air bags. **SX adds** : air conditioning.
Major options: Anti lock brakes, automatic transmission

The entry-level model of the Daewoo lineup, the Lanos comes in two versions: a hatchback coupe or a sedan. Developed in Europe and tested on five continents, the Lanos is powered by a 1.6-liter four-cylinder engine (105 horses), available with a manual or automatic transmission.

Specifications of Test Vehicle

Model: Lanos SX (NT)

Exterior Dimensions	
Wheelbase	99.2 in.
Overall lenght	160.4 in.
Overall widht	66.1 in.
Overall height	56.4 in.
Curb weight	2447 lb
Interior dimensions	
Seating capacity	5
Head room	F:39,2/R:37.8 in.
Leg room	F:42/R:34.2 in.
Cargo room	8.8 cu ft
Engine	
Displacement	I-4 1,6 L.
Horsepower	105 @ 5,800
Torque, lb-ft	106 @ 3,400

Performance (NT)

Daewoo Nubira

PRICES
SX 4-door $12,500
SX 5-door $12,500
SX wagon $13,100
CDX 4-door $13,810
CDX 5-door $13,810
CDX wagon $14,410

Equipment

Major Standard Equipment: Air conditioning.
CDX adds: ABS
Major options: Automatic transmission

Daewoo describes the Nubira as a model "for the whole family." Roomier than the Lanos, it is available as a sedan or wagon. In both instances it is powered by a 2.0-liter four-cylinder with a 129-hp output. Standard equipment includes front and rear disc brakes, dual air bag and even heated side view mirrors (quite an asset).

Specifications of Test Vehicle

Model: Nubira Wagon (NT)

Exterior Dimensions	
Wheelbase	101.2 in,
Overall lenght	175.4 in.
Overall widht	66.9 in
Overall height	56.1 in.
Curb weight	2696 lb
Interior dimensions	
Seating capacity	5
Head room	F:38.2/R:38 in.
Leg room	F:41.8/R:34.7 in.
Cargo room	19.4 cu. ft.
Engine	
Displacement	I-4 2,0 L.
Horsepower	129 @ 5,400
Torque, lb-ft	136 @ 4,400

Performance (NT)

Daewoo Leganza

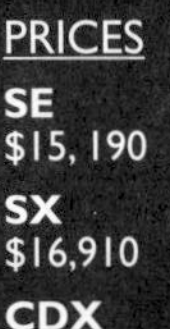

PRICES
SE $15, 190
SX $16,910
CDX $18,910

Equipment

Major Standard Equipment: anti-lock brakes, air conditioning, **SX adds :** automatic transmission.

The top-of-the-line offering in the Daewoo family, the Leganza plans to rub bumpers with compacts like the Hyundai Sonata and Mazda 626. Need convincing? The Leganza has more than enough arguments in its favor: an independent suspension calibrated by the Lotus sports car company, anti lock brakes (standard) and a peppy 2.2-liter four-cylinder engine (131 horses).

Specifications of Test Vehicle

Model: Leganza SE (NT)

Exterior Dimensions	
Wheelbase	105.1 in.
Overall lenght	183,9 in.
Overall wihdt	70 in
Overall height	56.6 in.
Curb weight	3086 lb
Interior dimensions	
Seating capacity	5
Head room	F:39/R:37.4 in.
Leg room	F:42/R:38 in.
Cargo room	14.1 cu ft
Engine	
Displacement	I-4 2,2 L.
Horsepower	131 @ 5,400
Torque, lb-ft	148 @ 4,400

Performance (NT)

Dodge Avenger

New for 99

Two new exterior colors

Pros

Ride
Styling
Passenger room

Cons

Option choices
Engine performance
Engine noise

Equipment

Major Standard Equipment: 2-liter I-4 engine, manual transmission, stainless steel exhaust, rear defroster, variable-intermittent wipers, AM/FM stereo, tilt steering column, split-folding rear seat, remote-control decklid release. **ES adds:** 4-wheel antilock disc brakes, air conditioning, AM/FM/cassette stereo, driver's seat lumbar adjustment, cruise control, aluminum wheels. **Major Options:** 2.5-liter V-6, automatic transmission, 4-wheel antilock disc brakes, power locks, power mirrors, power windows, power seats, AM/FM/CD/cassette stereo, cruise control, power moonroof, leather upholstery, remote keyless entry, theft alarm, aluminum wheels.

Are looks enough?

Looks can be deceiving. With macho styling derived from the Dodge Viper, the Dodge Avenger fools you into thinking it's a performance car. The image falls flat behind the wheel, though. A test drive reveals that the Avenger is all about show and not about go.

Mitsubishi makes the Avenger in Illinois for Chrysler. Chrysler sells the same coupe with minor styling changes as the Chrysler Sebring.

Think of the Avenger as a 2-door Stratus, and you won't be far wrong. There's not much competition for the Avenger from other carmakers. Imports like the Toyota Celica are much smaller; the Chevrolet Monte Carlo is much bigger, and the Ford Mustang is much faster. In our eyes, the Avenger's closest rival is General Motors' compact Pontiac Grand Am and Oldsmobile Alero.

The specs reveal the Avenger's true nature. The more powerful V-6 engine has only an automatic transmission, not a manual. The base engine for both trims is a 2-liter 4-cylinder. Usually an engine from a larger sedan is used in a small coupe to create a performance car. Not in this case.

Our Avenger ES had the 163-horsepower V-6 engine, which moves the car briskly enough but belies the performance promised by the aggressive styling. It proves both harsh and noisy at almost all engine speeds. The lethargic 4-speed automatic transmission further hinders performance. The shifts are smooth enough, but the transmission doesn't get the most out of the engine. Traction control is not offered on Avenger.

Over the road, the Avenger commendably balances a pleasing ride with good handling. The suspension remains composed when pushed hard, yet comfortable on long highway drives. The steering, though communicative, feels artificially heavy at most speeds. The optional 4-wheel disc brakes with antilock control are probably the best technology on the vehicle.

We found the Avenger easy to drive, with logically placed and easily operated controls. It's also very livable, with front seats that offer plenty of room for taller passengers and a back seat that is expansive by small-coupe standards. Grow-ups fit with little complaint. The backseat cushion is higher than the front ones, which gives rear-seat passengers a better view. The trunk provides good cargo capacity.

As a model name, the Avenger evokes memories of real Dodges like the Charger and Challenger. As a car, it inspires a new term: faux fast. Once upon a time, Chrysler thought that vinyl-covered roofs made cars look like real convertibles, and wood-grained plastic looked rich. Similar thinking seems to have spawned the Avenger. **D.V.S.**

Specifications of Test Vehicle

Model: Avenger ES

Exterior Dimensions	
Wheelbase	103.7 in.
Overall length	190.2 in.
Overall width	69.1 in.
Overall height	53.3 in.
Curb weight	3,000 lb.
Interior Dimensions	
Seating capacity	5
Head room	F:37.6/R:36.5 in.
Leg room	F:43.3/R:35 in.
Cargo volume	13.1 cu ft.
Engine	
Displacement	V-6 2.5 L.
Horsepower	163 @ 5,500 rpm
Torque, lb-ft.	170 @ 4,350 rpm
Performance	
0-60 mph, acceleration	10 sec.
60-0 mph, braking	141 ft.
Turning circle	40.7ft.
EPA city/highway	19/28 mpg
Test mileage	24
Fuel tank capacity	16.9 gal.

Prices

$14,000
$22,000

Coupe
$15,905

ES Coupe
$18,180

Warranty

(years/miles)

Bumper-to-bumper
3/36,000

Powertrain
3/36,000

Rust-through
7/100,000

Other to Consider

Oldsmobile Alero

Pontiac Grand Am

Ratings

Group	Category	Rating
Over the Road	Acceleration	6
	Transmission	7
	Braking	4
	Steering	8
	Ride	8
	Handling	8
	Drivability	8
	Fuel Economy	6
Passenger Environment	Comfort/Conven.	8
	Interior Room	8
	Driving Position	8
	Instrumentation	8
	Controls	8
	Visibility	7
	Entry/Exit	6
	Quietness	8
	Cargo Space	6
Workmanship	Interior	8
	Exterior	8
	Value	7

Ratings
145

Dodge Dakota

New for 99

Improved braking system
Steering-mounted radio controls
Stepped up R/T production

Pros

Ideal sizing
R/T version
Astonishing handling

Cons

Brakes: they could be better
Bench sheet or ice floe?
Fuel consumption (V-6 and V-8)

Equipment

Major Standard Equipment: 2.5-liter I-4, manual transmission, rear-wheel antilock brakes, intermittent wipers, AM/FM/cassette stereo, bench seat, vinyl upholstery, vinyl floor covering. **Sport adds:** Split-bench seat, cloth upholstery, carpeting, tachometer, larger tires, aluminum wheels. **SLT Package adds:** Air conditioning, 22-gallon fuel tank. **Major Options:** 3.9-liter V-6, 5.2-liter V-8, automatic transmission, part-time 4-wheel drive, long pick-up bed, 4-wheel antilock brakes, limited-slip differential, air conditioning.

PRICES
$13,000
$25,000

Short bed $12,915
Ext.cab, short bed $16,170
Sport short bed NA
Sport ext. cab, short bed NA
SLT short bed NA
SLT ext. cab, short bed NA

WARRANTY
(years/miles)
Bumper-to-bumper 3/36,000
Powertrain 3/36,000
Rust-through 7/100,000

OTHER TO CONSIDER
Chevrolet S-10
Ford Ranger

Love at first sight

If you're like I used to be and trucks hold absolutely no power of attraction over you, it's because you haven't driven a Dakota yet. What if I told you that it can sweep you off your feet, it can make your heart soar, it can get you to say "I do", would it be enough to spark your curiosity? No? Well then, wait until you drive the R/T version, whose production has been stepped up considerably this year (5,000 units will be available), a model capable of drag racing between two red lights with your brother-in-law's refrigerator safely loaded in the bed! I dare you to try the same exploit with a Viper!

Yes, I love this truck, and Dodge hasn't paid me one cent to say so.

Strongly inspired by the Ram, the Dakota features a very-well-designed interior; it's too bad that some colors (red, for example) are too loud. And it's also unfortunate that such a recently designed vehicle has no second driver's-side door to make it easier to climb into the rear. And while we're on the topic, even if the Dakota claims to be the roomiest choice in its category, it's still true that the rear bench seat (no individual seats are available) is about as comfortable as a slab of ice. Another small observation, from an expert and verified to be true: there isn't enough room between wheel wells to lay the traditional 4'x8' sheet of plywood flat in the truck bed.

Why keep things simple when you can make them complicated? That's the reasoning used by designers active in this market segment, who feel obligated to draw up an options list as long as your arm for every product they concoct. To make a long story short, two words on the 2.5-liter, four-cylinder available as part of standard equipment: avoid it. There, we've said it. As for the 3.9-liter V-6, it's sturdy, sufficiently powerful, and doesn't guzzle too greedily the gas you put in its tank. The same certainly can't be said for the gluttonous 5.2-liter V-8, though it certainly has personality, especially when it's teamed with the manual transmission. But there's something even better: the R/T version, with its 250 horses and 335 pound-feet of torque. Only an automatic transmission can serve as intermediary between the engine and this monster's rear-wheel drive system. (Ladies and gentlemen, restrain yourselves. It's scheduled to arrive next summer.)

The Dakota will leave you with the impression of surprisingly good handling, a remarkably tight turning radius, and braking power that's still hard to gauge and that still tends to fade despite improvements made for this year's offering. With the exception of the last detail, everything is just fine!
E.L.

Specifications of Test Vehicle

Model: Dakota Sport

Exterior Dimensions	
Wheelbase	111.9 in.
Length	195.8 in.
Width	71.5 in.
Height	65.6 in.
Curb weight	3,500 lb.
Interior Dimensions	
Seating Capacity	3
Head room	F:40 in.
Leg room	F:41.9 in.
Payload capacity	1,250 lb.
Engine	
Displacement	V-6 3.9 L.
Horsepower	175 @ 4,800 rpm
Torque, lb-ft.	225 @ 3,200 rpm
Performance	
0-60 mph, acceleration	NA
60-0 mph, braking	NA
Turning circle	36 ft.
EPA city/highway	16/21 mpg
Test mileage	22 mpg
Fuel tank capacity	15 gal.

Ratings

Over The Road		Passenger Environment		Workmanship	
Acceleration	7	Comfort/Conven.	7	Interior	8
Transmission	7	Interior Room	6	Exterior	8
Braking	5	Driving Position	7	Value	8
Steering	7	Instrumentation	7		
Ride	8	Controls	8		
Handling	7	Visibility	7		
Drivability	8	Entry/Exit	6		
Fuel Economy	4	Quietness	7		
		Cargo Space	2		

134

Dodge

Durango

New for 99

3.9-liter V-6 now available
Steering-mounted radio controls (option)
Heated side-view mirrors

Pros

Interesting sizing
Surprisingly good handling
Multiple configurations

Cons

Uncomfortable third seat
Sluggish V-6
Gas-guzzling engines

Equipment

Major Standard Equipment: 3.9-liter V-6, part-time 4-wheel drive, rear-wheel antilock brakes, rear wiper and washer, air conditioning, AM/FM cassette stereo, cruise control, tilt steering wheel, power mirrors, power windows, power locks, remote keyless entry, theft alarm system, luggage rack. **SLT+ adds:** 5.2-liter V-8, AM/FM/CD/cassette stereo, trip computer, automatic-dimming rear-view mirror. **Major Options:** 5.2-liter V-8, 5.9-liter V-8, full-time 4-wheel drive, 4-wheel antilock brakes, third row seat, leather upholstery, AM/FM/CD/cassette stereo, automatic-dimming rear-view mirror, trailer towing package, larger tires, aluminum wheels.

A remarkable start

The sandbox niche where the Blazer, Jimmy, Explorer, and Pathfinder havebeen having fun for the past few years is home to a new playmate: the Dodge Durango, a sport utility that promises to offer more than the competition can deliver, and nothing less. More room, more power, a bigger cargo capacity, all the attributes American buyers go for. It's a compact utility that behaves like a full-size model.

To fool its smaller counterparts and get its bigger ones worrying, the Durango will offer a third bench seat as an option so it can accommodate a total of eight passengers. And speaking of the third seat, potential buyers should note that only children will find it roomy enough, though to its credit it can be tucked away under the floor if needed, as is also the case with the Honda Odyssey. With a completely flat floor, you have a maximum of usable space for cargo. The Chrysler order book proposes several configurations for the buyer to choose from; for example, the choice between a full-size bench seat or bucket seats for the front. The instrument panel is an "old" friend, exactly the same one you'll find in the Dakota truck.

The Durango's designers readily admit that they used the Dakota as their inspiration. As a result, it has the same high-performance engines, namely the 3.9-liter V-6 or one of the two V-8s (5.2 and 5.9). Strangely, accordingly to preliminary information obtained from Chrysler, the standard V-6 will be offered to consumers only several weeks after the model's official launch this fall. In other words, the first customers who decide to buy a Durango will have no other choice but to break into their piggy banks and pay extra for one of the two V8s. Incidentally, we were given a 5.2-liter version for our first test drive and we were not at all impressed by its performance. Under the circumstances, it's hard to believe that the V-6 is a viable choice to power the Durango. The job of transferring power to the four-drive wheels (a rear-wheel drive will be available sometime in the near future) is assigned solely to a four-speed automatic transmission, which proved to be flawless.

On the road, the Durango is astonishingly smooth. Despite its trucky origins, this utility handles surprisingly well and hugs the road reliably given the vehicle's center of gravity. Only one flaw to report: a steering system that's imprecise at center.

Roomier and more powerful than the compact utilities currently on the market, but every bit as practical and more importantly not as clumsy as the category's giants (read: Explorer, Tahoe and company), the Durango is a common-sense choice. **E.L.**

Specifications of Test Vehicle

Model: Durango SLT

Exterior Dimensions	
Wheelbase	115.9 in.
Overall length	193.3 in.
Overall width	71.5 in.
Overall height	72.9 in.
Curb weight	4,750 lb.
Interior Dimensions	
Seating capacity	7
Head room	F:39.8/C:40.6/R:37.9 in.
Leg room	F:41.9/C:35.4/R:30.7 in.
Cargo room	18.8 cu. ft.
Engine	
Displacement	V-8 5.9 L.
Horsepower	245 @ 4,000 rpm
Torque, lb-ft.	335 @ 3,200 rpm
Performance	
0-60 mph, acceleration	9 sec.
60-0 mph, braking	141 ft.
Turning circle	38.9 ft.
EPA city/highway	12/17 mpg
Test mileage	NA
Fuel tank capacity	25 gal.

PRICES
$27,000
$33,000
SLT 4-door $26,910
SLT+ 4-door $28,060

WARRANTY (years/miles)
Bumper-to-bumper 3/36,000
Powertrain 3/36,000
Rust-through 7/100,000

OTHER TO CONSIDER
Chevrolet Blazer
Ford Explorer

Ratings

Group	Category	Rating
Over The Road	Acceleration	7
	Transmission	8
	Braking	4
	Steering	8
	Ride	8
	Handling	7
	Drivability	7
	Fuel Economy	3
Passenger Environment	Comfort/Conven.	8
	Interior Room	8
	Driving Position	8
	Instrumentation	8
	Controls	8
	Visibility	7
	Entry/Exit	6
	Quietness	8
	Cargo Space	9
Workmanship	Interior	8
	Exterior	8
	Value	8

Ratings 146

Dodge — Grand Caravan

New for 99

Standard 17-inch wheels (ES)
Cargo net between front seats
Styling changes

Pros

Roomy interior
Powerful 3.8-liter V-6
Impressive roadholding

Cons

Fuel consumption (AWD)
Disappointing semi-automatic transmission
Limited braking power

Equipment

Major Standard Equipment: 3-liter V-6, 4-speed automatic transmission, 5-passenger seating, AM/FM stereo, variable-intermittent wipers, rear wiper and washer. **SE adds:** 3-liter V-6, 4-wheel antilock brakes, AM/FM/cassette stereo, power heated mirrors, cruise control, tilt steering column, larger tires and wheels. **LE adds:** 3.3-liter V-6 engine, driver's-side sliding door, dual-temperature air conditioning, rear defroster, windshield wiper de-icer, trip computer, remote keyless entry. **ES adds:** 3.8-liter V-6 semi-automatic transmission, larger tires.

PRICES
$18,000
$32,000

3-door $17,415
Grand 3-door $20,125
SE 3-door $21,290
SE Grand 3-door $22,285
LE 4-door $25,030
LE Grand 4-door $26,025

WARRANTY (years/miles)

Bumper-to-bumper 3/36,000
Powertrain 3/36,00
Rust-through 7/100,000

OTHER TO CONSIDER

Pontiac Montana
Toyota Sienna

Up and fighting

Is there any difference between a Caravan and a Grand Caravan? Besides the price, there's weight, all-wheel drive (optional), interior and exterior dimensions. So, yes! For 1999, Dodge has made these two models even more different from each other. Examples? Two good ones come to mind: a four-speed semi-automatic transmission (Autostick) and a sportier appearance.

Assembled in Canada, this small minivan boasts an excellent and carefully thought-out passenger compartment. The inexpensive look of certain plastics does catch your eye and some smaller finishing details need improvement, but overall there's no question that this vehicle is Chrysler's best. With a plunging front end design and the excellent panoramic view it provides, the Grand Caravan fails to inspire the same kind of confidence as the smaller-sized standard version can. On the up side, though, it offers impressive roominess and the space reserved for baggage is completely acceptable and satisfactory, even when all seats are in place. Despite the addition of casters, the rear bench seat is still hard to manoeuvre. When it comes to the second sliding door (on the driver's side), forget the extra expense and go ahead and get it. You'll be glad you did.

If your choice is the ES package, the situation is clear: it houses only the 3.8-liter V-6 engine. And to make matters even better, it is the best pick for powering this minivan, unless fuel economy is your top priority. The LE package features the 3.3-liter as standard equipment and while it's no powerhouse, it gets its job done competently. Note that the semi-automatic transmission is used only in tandem with the ES package. On the LE, the 3.8-liter is teamed with the conventional automatic transmission.

The road stability of this vehicle is still amazing, especially with the 17-inch wheels now available on the ES version. Strangely enough though, only the LE has the advantage of the "Handling" options group. The LE also has an exclusive traction control system, perhaps not one of the most sophisticated, but still a valuable asset on icy roads. As is the case on many other small minivans, brakes (discs/drums), even with an ABS system, show little resistance to overheating — even though Chrysler has devoted extra energy to this problem. The AWD version can count on four discs — how very lucky.

Despite small flaws, the Grand Caravan remains a favorite with consumers, competition be damned. **E.L.**

Specifications of Test Vehicle

Model: Grand Caravan

Exterior Dimensions	
Wheelbase	119.3 in.
Overall length	199.6 in.
Overall width	76.8 in.
Overall height	68.5 in.
Curb weight	3,800 lb.
Interior Dimensions	
Seating capacity	7
Head room	F:39.8/R:40/R2:38.5 in.
Leg room	F:40.6/R:39.6/R2:39.8 in.
Cargo volume	20.3 cu. ft.
Engine	
Displacement	V-6 3.3 L.
Horsepower	158 @ 4,850 rpm
Torque, lb-ft	203 @ 3,250 rpm
Performance	
0-60 mph, acceleration	10.9 sec.
60-0 mph, braking	132 ft.
Turning circle	39.5 ft.
EPA city/highway	18/24 mpg
Test mileage	20 mpg
Fuel tank capacity	20 gal.

Group	Rating category	Score (1–10)
Over The Road	Acceleration	6
	Transmission	6
	Braking	5
	Steering	7
	Ride	7
	Handling	6
	Drivability	7
	Fuel Economy	5
Passenger Environment	Comfort/Conven.	8
	Interior Room	10
	Driving Position	7
	Instrumentation	8
	Controls	8
	Visibility	7
	Entry/Exit	7
	Quietness	7
	Cargo Space	10
Workmanship	Interior	7
	Exterior	7
	Value	8

Ratings
143

Dodge

Intrepid

New for 99

New upholstery (ES)
Cargo net in the trunk
New leather seats

Pros

Exceptionally roomy
Consistent handling
Unbeatable price-useable space ratio

Cons

Awkward size
Disappointing semi-automatic transmission
Uncomfortable bench and bucket seats (base version)

Equipment

Major Standard Equipment: 2.7-liter V-6, automatic transmission, 4-wheel disc brakes, air conditioning, rear defroster, speed-sensitive variable-intermittent wipers, AM/FM/cassette stereo, automatic power locks, individual front seats, tilt steering wheel, cruise control, power windows, stainless-steel exhaust system. **ES adds:** 3.2-liter V-6, semi-automatic transmission, 4-wheel antilock brakes, power driver's seat, remote keyless entry, power decklid release, split-folding rear seat, full-size spare tire, larger tires. **Major Options:** Traction control, 4-wheel antilock brakes, CD changer

A rocky road to the top

The Intrepid hadn't even completed its first official lap around the track before the specialized press was billing it as the revelation of the 1998 model year: a midsize car that just had to be seen to be believed. Paradoxically, since then it has lost its sheen in the media's eyes and with it, its title as "Car of the Year", something it could reasonably have taken for granted given the fanfare. How cruel a disappointment!

Very nicely designed, the Intrepid sports the "advanced cab" style concocted a few years ago by Chrysler to add room to interiors and trunks. On both these points the competition has to bow to Chrysler sedans, which offer much more interior space, enough for five adults. On the down side, to take full advantage of available space, users have to put up with a receding roof line that does nothing to make access easier and that hinders rear visibility into the bargain. Bucket and bench seats on the ES version of the Intrepid are more comfortable than they are on the base version, where they're softer and upholstered with inferior quality material. The dashboard boasts detailed instrumentation, but some controls — like those for the radio and air conditioning — should be repositioned to bring them closer to the driver. In addition, the texture of plastic materials and the color coordination are enough to give you goose bumps in some instances.

Under the hood the choice is the buyer's: one of the two new V6s, a 200-hp 2.7-liter or a 220-hp 3.2-liter. The latter can be coupled with the disappointing four-speed semi-automatic transmission, while the 2.7-litre is teamed up with a standard automatic unit. Having said that, this sedan shows quality assembly and a previously unhoped-for sturdiness, a smoother ride, and engines that offer more refinement. It also handles reliably and has consistent roadholding abilities. Included in the list of disadvantages are a size that some find hard to cope with, a suspension that's stiffer than drivers are used to finding on North American models (then again, is that really a fault?), and braking power that tends to fade.

In short, the Intrepid has a lot of arguments in its favor to convince consumers that it actually is the best midsize American car on today's market. Now all it needs is just a bit more refinement. **E.L.**

Specifications of Test Vehicle

Model: Intrepid ES

Exterior Dimensions	
Wheelbase	113 in.
Overall length	203.7 in.
Overall width	74.7 in.
Overall height	55.9 in.
Curb weight	3,500 lb.
Interior Dimensions	
Seating capacity	5
Head room	F:38.3/R:37.5 in.
Leg room	F:42.2/R:39.1 in.
Cargo room	18.4 cu. ft.
Engine	
Displacement	V-6 3.2 L.
Horsepower	220 @ 6,300 rpm
Torque, lb-ft.	225 @ 3,800 rpm
Performance	
0-60 mph, acceleration	8.6 sec.
60-0 mph, braking	126 ft.
Turning circle	37.6 ft.
EPA city/highway	19/29 mpg
Test mileage	25 mpg
Fuel tank capacity	17 gal.

Prices

$20,000
$27,000

Sedan
$20,440
ES sedan
$23,190

Warranty
(years/miles)

Bumper-to-bumper
3/36,000

Powertrain
3/36,000

Rust-through
7/100,000

Other to consider

Ford Taurus

Toyota Camry

Ratings

Group	Category	Rating
Over The Road	Acceleration	8
	Transmission	9
	Braking	6
	Steering	8
	Ride	9
	Handling	8
	Drivability	9
	Fuel Economy	6
Passenger Environment	Comfort/Conven.	9
	Interior Room	9
	Driving Position	8
	Instrumentation	8
	Controls	8
	Visibility	8
	Entry/Exit	9
	Quietness	8
	Cargo Space	7
Workmanship	Exterior	8
	Interior	7
	Value	9

Dodge Neon

New for 99

A new exterior color

Pros

Interesting price
Roomy interior
Reliability

Cons

Model scheduled for withdrawal
Rough and noisy engines
Oversized dashboard

Equipment

Major Standard Equipment: 2-liter I-4 engine, manual transmission, variable-intermittent wipers, left side-view mirror, stainless-steel exhaust system. Highline adds: Air conditioning, rear defroster, AM/FM stereo, right side-view mirror, remote-control decklid release, split-folding rear seat.
Major Options: More powerful 2-liter I-4 engine, 3-speed automatic transmission, 4-wheel antilock disc brakes, air conditioning, rear defroster, power locks, power mirrors, power windows, cruise control, power moonroof, tilt steering column, split-folding rear seat, remote keyless entry, AM/FM/cassette stereo, AM/FM/CD stereo, aluminum wheels.

PRICES
$10,000
$18,000
Coupe
$12,020
Sedan
$12,220

WARRANTY
(years/miles)
Bumper-to-bumper
3/36,000
Powertrain
3/36,000
Rust-through
7/100,000

OTHER TO CONSIDER
Chevrolet Cavalier
Toyota Corolla

Disconnected

Before the lights go out on it, the Neon plans to make the most of its last year among us. First-time buyers — its avowed target market — failed to show off the same happy grin we've seen on its grille for the past four years.

A new generation is scheduled to appear sometime this year. Very little information has been circulated, but we do know that its platform will also be used in the design of a mini sport ute capable of rivalling the RAV4, CR-V and other Foresters. As soon as Chrysler disconnects the Neon, make sure you connect to our Internet site at www.carsoncd.com for details.

The Neon's passenger compartment is one of the largest of its kind. The finish has also been improved (better late than never!). However, the same cannot be said of its bench seats, which will never win prizes for comfort or support. The massive, engulfing dash panel includes a set of instruments lacking the essential tachometer–just an option for this vehicle. Is assembly quality also an option? Some things, like the powerful jets of water from the automatic washers, accompanied by gusts of wind, slip into the passenger compartment through the side windows, which, we may recall, lack frames.

It's easiest to note competitor progress over the past four years when sitting at the wheel of a Neon. The two standard 2.0-liter four-cylinder engines (one with 8 valves, the other 16) still prove just as powerful as before – but their raw and noisy temperament is less forgivable. They optionally connect to a three-speed automatic transmission that is both rough and clumsy. As for the manual transmission, it's equipped with an imprecise shifter and a clutch that is hardly progressive. Steering assistance is nonetheless ample and substantially contributes to the pleasure of driving. The suspension is reasonably comfortable, while the sporty feel is fundamental in the R/T, which gives it a certain stiffness. Get the anti-lock brake system, which provides better performance this year, and you'll have four disc brakes as a bonus. They are clearly more durable and stable than the classic standard disc-drum brake combination.

While the current Neon is a roughed-out version of an excellent small car, the next generation we shall see in just a few months will be a final copy. Be patient. **E.L.**

Specifications of Test Vehicle

MODEL: DODGE NEON

Exterior Dimensions	
Wheelbase	104 in.
Overall length	171.8 in.
Overall width	67.5 in.
Overall height	54.9 in.
Curb weight	2,500 lb.
Interior Dimensions	
Seating capacity	5
head room	F:39.6/R:36.5 in.
Leg room	F:42.5/R:35.1 in.
Cargo volume	11.7 cu. ft.
Engine	
Displacement	I-4 2 L.
Horsepower	150 @ 6,500 rpm
Torque, lb-ft.	133 @ 5,500 rpm
Performance	
0-60 mph, acceleration	8.1
60-0 mph, braking	142
Turning circle	35.4 ft.
EPA city/highway	29/41mpg
Test mileage	24 mpg
Fuel tank capacity	12.5 gal.

Ratings

147

10
9
8
7
6
5
4
3
2
1

Over The Road: Acceleration, Transmission, Braking, Steering, Ride, Handling, Drivability, Fuel Economy

Passenger Environment: Comfort/Conven., Interior Room, Driving Position, Instrumentation, Controls, Visibility, Entry/Exit, Quietness, Cargo Space

Workmanship: Interior, Exterior, Value

Dodge Ram

New for 99

Standard ABS brakes on the 3500 series
Steering wheel-mounted radio controls
Revamped Sport group styling

Pros

Attractive lines
Quad version
Efficient engines

Cons

Sensitive suspension
Inferior finishing materials
Limited braking power

Equipment

Major Standard Equipment: 3.9-liter V-6, manual transmission, rear-wheel antilock brakes, intermittent wipers, front bumper, vinyl upholstery, vinyl floor covering. **ST adds:** AM/FM/cassette stereo, rear bumper, split-bench seat. **Laramie SLT adds:** Air conditioning, cruise control, tilt wheel, power locks, power mirrors, power windows, chrome wheels. **Major Options:** 5.2-liter V-8, 5.9-liter V-8, 5.9-liter diesel I-6, 8-liter V-10, automatic transmission, part-time 4-wheel drive, 4-wheel antilock brakes, extended cab, long pickup bed, power mirrors, power windows, power locks, remote keyless entry, trailer towing package, chrome wheels, aluminum wheels.

One step behind

Everybody knows it: in terms of sheer numbers, the Dodge Ram will never be able to compete strongly with its GM and Ford rivals. So instead of dazzling them with sales stats, it teaches them a few lessons in creative design and I must say it brings a breath of fresh air to a segment that's often the prisoner of stifling conformity. Is there a backlash in store for 1999? No question: the competition has refined its products considerably and today the Ram comes out the loser in several areas of comparison.

History will remember the Ram as the first standard truck to open its doors to ergonomics, a science which used to frighten some narrow minds who viewed it as a machination likely to emasculate their vehicles' macho looks. Overall design is still as fresh and ingenious as it always was, as witnessed by the multipurpose center armrest, a highly practical touch. In contrast, the quality of materials used in the finishing is questionable and seats offer minimal support. Note that seat belts on extended cab and Quad Cab (for four-door) versions are built into the seat design to make entry and exit easier for rear-seat passengers.

Regardless of which of the five engines Chrysler offers is actually under the hood, the Ram does just fine. But the good news is the availability of the V-10 on Quad Cab models and the short wheelbase 2500 series. Unfortunately, the diesel's power, increased two years ago, comes with a considerable amount of noise. Road stability, which used to be one of the Ram's strong points, isn't as convincing as it once was. The suspension reacts harshly to bumpy roads and provides more than enough feedback to the driver, via the steering system, which is heavy at low speeds. The turning radius is still the Ram's major defect, to the point of compromising certain kinds of maneuvering. Brakes aren't much better and their power is hard to gauge, especially when the vehicle isn't loaded to capacity.

In light of our road test, you have to wonder how the Ram will convince those who swore to be faithful to the F Series and other C/K (now Silverado) models to consider committing adultery. **E.L.**

Specifications of Test Vehicle

Model: Laramie SLT

Exterior Dimensions	
Wheelbase	138.7 in.
Overall length	224.1 in.
Overall width	79.3 in.
Overall height	74.6 in.
Curb weight	4,700 lb.
Interior Dimensions	
Seating Capacity	6
Head room	:40.2/R:39.4 in.
Leg room	F:39.4/R:31.6 in.
Payload capacity	1,700 lb.
Engine	
Displacement	V-8 5.9 L.
Horsepower	245 @ 4,000 rpm
Torque, lb-ft.	335 @ 3,200 rpm
Performance	
0-60 mph, acceleration	9.5 sec.
60-0 mph, braking	145 ft.
Turning circle	46.9 ft.
EPA city/highway	12/18 mpg
Test mileage	NA
Fuel tank capacity	35 gal.

Prices

$14,000
$36,000

Work Special short bed $14,485

SL short bed $16,260

Laramie SLT short bed $19,255

Warranty (years/miles)

Bumper-to-bumper 3/36,000

Powertrain 3/36,000

Rust-through 7/100,000

Other to consider

Chevrolet Silverado

Ford F150

Ratings

Group	Category	Rating
Over The Road	Acceleration	7
	Transmission	8
	Braking	3
	Steering	7
	Ride	7
	Handling	7
	Drivability	8
	Fuel Economy	3
Passenger Environment	Comfort/Conven.	8
	Interior Room	7
	Driving Position	8
	Instrumentation	8
	Controls	8
	Visibility	8
	Entry/Exit	6
	Quietness	8
	Cargo Space	7
Workmanship	Interior	8
	Exterior	8
	Value	8

Ratings 142

Dodge Ram Wagon

New for 99

Redesigned console
Crisper engines

Pros

Interior room
Quietness

Cons

Maneuverability
Rear seat access
Fuel economy
Safety features

Equipment

Major Standard Equipment
3.9-liter V-6, 3-speed automatic transmission, 8-passenger seating, air conditioning, AM/FM/cassette stereo, vinyl upholstery, intermittent wipers. **SLT adds:** Tilt steering column, cruise control, premium AM/FM/cassette stereo, power mirrors, power locks, remote keyless entry, cloth upholstery, chrome wheels. **Major Options:** 5.2-liter V-8, 5.9-liter V-8, 4-speed automatic transmission, 4-wheel antilock brakes, rear air conditioning, power windows, power locks, remote keyless entry, AM/FM/CD stereo, cruise control, tilt steering column, power driver's seat, trailer towing package.

Something old, something new

PRICES
$20,000
$34,000

3-door van
$19,740

WARRANTY
(years/miles)

Bumper-to-bumper
3/36,000

Powertrain
3/36,000

Rust-through
7/100,000

OTHER TO CONSIDER

Chevrolet Express Van

Ford Econoline

Dodge has re-engineered the Ram Wagon in '98, improving it in many ways.

The full-size Dodge Ram Wagon finds a market mainly among commercial operators or nonprofit organizations. Without windows, these vans are still popular with after market companies that install custom interiors and amenities, retailing them through Dodge dealers. The Ram Wagon's only competition comes from the Ford Club Wagon and the General Motors twins, Chevrolet Express and GMC Savana.

With windows and seats, the Ram Wagon comes in only one trim level. Nevertheless, several seating combinations and three engines choices force you to give your selection a lot of thought. The biggest frustration is the lack of standard features. Even power steering is an add-on. So are 4-wheel antilock brakes. The standard rear-wheel-only system doesn't give steering control when the front wheels lock.

The 5.2-liter V-8 has good torque. It's a suitable match with the 4-speed automatic transmission, which delivers smooth, clean shifts even under full throttle. Fuel economy is the pits — about 12 mpg.

Steering feels rather ordinary. When the van is empty, the ride is firm and borders on harsh; it gets much better with a load of people or cargo. The vehicle's height, length, and weight compromise handling ability. Fast cornering is out of the question. The Ram is too tall for many parking facilities and even some home garages. Parallel parking at the curb is much easier with a spotter outside. Maneuvering in parking lots and congested traffic takes patience and caution. The van's larger brakes feel more responsive, but stopping distance is not better than average.

The interior is surprisingly quiet, even at highway speeds. The optional cloth upholstery looks and feels good. The instrument panel has been redesigned to put controls where they belong. Visibility is good to the front and sides, but difficult to the rear, especially with a full load of passengers. The outside mirrors become more important.

The Ram Wagon is all about space. The driver and passengers have plenty of head, shoulder, hip and leg room. In the new design, the engine intrudes less into the passenger compartment, reducing the size of the "dog house" between driver and front passenger. Moving from a front seat to the rear is easier now, too. Cargo space is more than ample. Getting in and out of the Ram requires a climb and can be difficult for short people. Rear-seat passengers have to climb and squirm to get to their seats. The rear seats have comfortable cushions, but the backs are short, forcing passengers to sit in an upright position.

If you can't make do with a minivan, the Ram Wagon gives you comfortable people-hauling capability.

Ratings

Category	Rating
Over The Road	
Acceleration	6
Transmission	7
Braking	4
Steering	6
Ride	7
Handling	5
Drivability	6
Fuel Economy	3
Passenger Environment	
Comfort/Conven.	7
Interior Room	8
Driving Position	7
Instrumentation	7
Controls	8
Visibility	6
Entry/Exit	5
Quietness	7
Cargo Space	8
Workmanship	
Interior	7
Exterior	7
Value	7

Ratings
128

Specifications of Test Vehicle

Model: 1500 SLT

Exterior Dimensions	
Wheelbase	109.6 in.
Overall length	187.2 in.
Overall width	79.8 in.
Overall height	79.5 in.
Curb weight	4,100lb
Interior Dimensions	
Seating capacity	8
Head room	F:39.3/R:37.0/R2:NA in.
Leg room	F:40.5/R:41.6/R2:NA in.
Cargo volume	NA
Engine	
Displacement	V-8 5.2 L.
Horsepower	225 @ 4,400 rpm
Torque, lb-ft.	295 @ 3,200 rpm
Performance	
0-60 mph, acceleration	NA
60-0 mph, braking	NA
Turning circle	40.5 ft.
EPA city/highway	13/17 mpg
Test mileage	NA
Fuel tank capacity	35 gal.

Dodge Stratus

New for 99

Revised suspension
New wheel rims
New exterior colors

Pros

Passenger room
Seat comfort
Entry and exit

Cons

Engine performance
Noise
Visibility

Equipment

Major Standard Equipment: 2-liter I-4 engine, manual transmission, air conditioning, AM/FM/cassette stereo, folding rear seat, cruise control, remote-control decklid release, tilt steering wheel, stainless-steel exhaust system. **ES adds:** 4-wheel antilock brakes, variable-assist power steering, sports suspension, power locks, power heated mirrors. **Major Options:** 2.4-liter I-4 engine, 2.5-liter V-6 engine, automatic transmission, 4-wheel antilock brakes, power locks, power heated mirrors, power windows, integrated child seat, AM/FM/CD stereo, AM/FM/CD/cassette stereo, remote keyless entry, power driver's seat, theft alarm system.

Good consistency

Chrysler offers something for everyone in compact sedans, selling the same car under three different nameplates. The middle-of-the-road Dodge Stratus appeals to the most buyers.

The 4-door Stratus straddles the compact and mid-size markets, where it competes with the Honda Accord, Toyota Camry, Mazda 626, Ford Contour, and Pontiac Grand Am, among others. Within Chrysler, there's also the low-priced Plymouth Breeze and the upscale Chrysler Cirrus. Among these three Chrysler siblings, the Stratus sets itself apart by offering three real engine choices: two 4-cylinder engines (2 and 2.4 liters) and a 2.5-liter V-6. The V-6 offers Chrysler's AutoStick, an automatic transmission that can be operated manually without a clutch. Dodge also sells a 2-door Stratus, called the Avenger.

The 2.4-liter, 4-cylinder engine is a smart choice for the Stratus. It puts out nearly the same torque as the V-6 but costs less, and the two engines get about the same gas mileage. The automatic transmission is frequently indecisive about which gear is best, however. In the absence of the optional traction control system, the AutoStick lets you start in second or third gear for better control. The AutoStick alone is reason enough to choose the V-6 if you prefer an automatic transmission. If you want the V-6 but not AutoStick, you have to choose a Cirrus. This confusing mix of feature availability helps differentiate the nameplates.

The Stratus's fully independent suspension delivers a pleasing ride and above-average handling. If you do a lot of highway driving, move up to the ES trim; its variable-assist power steering gives more road feel, the sports suspension improves handling without penalizing comfort, and the height-adjustable driver's seat helps you get comfortable.

The cabin is unusually noisy at highway speeds, with a mix of wind, engine, and road noise. However, it's roomy and nicely equipped, with one of the freshest designs on the market. Though rear-seat leg room is especially good for a compact, three adults won't find enough space to be comfortable for long in the back seat. The individual front bucket seats are on the firm side, especially by domestic-car standards; on long trips, they hold their comfort well. Entry and exit pose no problems, and there is sufficient trunk space for most families.

In the Stratus, you can't see the rear deck at all through the rear window, so backing up is tricky. Up front, the steep windshield has some bothersome reflections when the light is at 12 o'clock high. You should have fair sailing with the Stratus, Chrysler's least expensive car with the AutoStick transmission. **D.V.S.**

Specifications of Test Vehicle

Model: ES

Exterior Dimensions	
Wheelbase	108 in.
Overall length	186 in.
Overall width	71.7 in.
Overall height	51.9 in.
Curb weight	2,900 lb.
Interior Dimensions	
Seating capacity	5
Head room	F:38.1/R:36.8 in.
Leg room	F:42.3/R:38.1 in.
Cargo volume	15.7 cu. ft.
Engine	
Displacement	I-4 2 L.
Horsepower	132 @ 6,000 rpm
Torque, lb-ft.	129 @ 5,000 rpm
Performance	
0-60 mph, acceleration	10.0 sec.
60-0 mph, braking	155 ft.
Turning circle	37 ft.
EPA city/highway	25/36 mpg
Test mileage	25 mpg
Fuel tank capacity	16 gal.

Prices

$15,000
$20,000

Sedan $15,675

ES sedan $19,495

Warranty (years/miles)

Bumper-to-bumper 3/36,000

Powertrain 3/36,000

Rust-through 7/100,000

Other to consider

Chevrolet Malibu

Ford Contour

Over The Road: Acceleration, Transmission, Braking, Steering, Ride, Handling, Drivability, Fuel Economy

Passenger Environment: Comfort/Conven., Interior Room, Driving Position, Instrumentation, Controls, Visibility, Entry/Exit, Quietness, Cargo Space

Workmanship: Interior, Exterior, Value

10 9 8 7 6 5 4 3 2 1

Ratings
142

Ford

Contour

New for 99

Redesigned bucket seats
Revised instrument cluster
Recalibrated front suspension
Larger gas tank

Pros

European-type roadholding
Perfect finishing
Superb V-6 with manual transmission

Cons

Four-cylinder/automatic duo
Lack of torque at low engine speeds (V-6)
Radio controls

Equipment

Major Standard Equipment: 2-liter I-4, manual transmission, air conditioning, AM/FM stereo, tilt steering column, cabin air filter, intermittent wipers, power mirrors. **SE adds:** Power windows, power locks, cruise control, rear defroster, AM/FM/cassette stereo, larger tires. **SVT adds:** 2.5-liter V-6, 4-wheel antilock disc brakes, sports suspension, power driver's seat, leather upholstery, split-folding rear seat, remote keyless entry, larger tires.
Major Options: 2.5-liter V-6, automatic transmission, 4-wheel antilock brakes, variable-intermittent wipers, rear defroster.

Worth a close look

PRICES
$14,000
$24,000
LX sedan $14,995
SE sedan $16,490
SVT 4-door sedan $22,365

WARRANTY (years/miles)
Bumper-to-bumper 3/36,000
Powertrain 3/36,000
Rust-through 6/100,000

OTHER TO CONSIDER
Honda Accord
Nissan Altima

Of all North American compacts, the Contour is the most consistent in quality, the model that's the most fun to drive and that shows the best finish. Nothing less. The bad publicity it has received is generated mainly from those still miffed over the withdrawal of the Tempo, or gossip mongers who like to point out that its rear seat is cramped. You should know that the Contour runs rings around the late Tempo and that currently, its rear seats provide as much space as you get on rivals that are supposedly roomier. Sceptical? Drop by to look at one. And while you're at it, take the time to say hello to the SVT version of the Contour, the very one that will soon have the rest of the compact category running for cover.

In a nutshell, to some extent the space available to rear-seat passengers is still this compact's Achilles' heel (the same problem many others have, we must say). Ford tried to remedy the situation by cutting down on the thickness of front seatbacks in 1996 and again in 1998 and the same strategy has been adopted for 1999 in the hopes of silencing critics. The outcome? Let's just say that if you assign rear seats to normal-size adults, they'll probably feel cooped up and to get them in the mood, rear doors do nothing to provide easy access. Children, however, won't find anything to complain about. Now, let's get back to the European-type interior and its fine finishing and attractive color schemes. The dashboard is sculpted to surround the driver, front seats are comfortable, and controls are well laid out, all of which makes it easy to drive the Contour over long distances. The only flaw is radio controls that are too small for easy use.

The 2.0-liter four-cylinder found beneath the hood in base versions performs well and is economical provided it's teamed up with the manual transmission, whose shifting is smoother than it used to be. The 2.0-liter's qualities begin to blur when it works with the automatic transmission, which tends to sap its 125-hp output (especially during pickup). My personal preference goes to the 2.5-liter V-6 available as an option (and standard on top-of-the-line models); it's smooth, supple, and powerful. Like me, you'll probably find that it lacks torque in the lower rpm range and on occasion it has its differences with the automatic transmission, ably replaced by the very suave manual. When it comes to road stability this compact outclasses almost all its rivals: steering is precise, the suspension goes the middle road between firmness and comfort (this compact has everything, or almost; you'll notice some roll when cornering and the steering system is too light at higher speeds), braking is good (but much better with the four discs), and the ABS system and traction control are offered as options. **E.L.**

Ratings **141**

Group	Rating item	Score (1–10)
Over The Road	Acceleration	8
	Transmission	6
	Braking	4
	Steering	8
	Ride	8
	Handling	8
	Drivability	7
	Fuel Economy	5
Passenger Environment	Comfort/Conven.	7
	Interior Room	6
	Driving Position	7
	Instrumentation	8
	Controls	8
	Visibility	8
	Entry/Exit	6
	Quietness	7
	Cargo Space	6
Workmanship	Interior	8
	Exterior	9
	Value	7

Specifications of Test Vehicle

Model: Contour SE

Exterior Dimensions	
Wheelbase	106.5 in.
Overall length	185.3 in.
Overall width	69.1 in.
Overall height	54.5 in.
Curb weight	2,750 lb.
Interior Dimensions	
Seating capacity	5
Head room	F:39/R:36.8 in.
Leg room	F:42.4/R:34.4 in.
Cargo volume	13.9 cu. ft.
Engine	
Displacement	V-6 2.5 L.
Horsepower	170 @ 6,250 rpm
Torque, lb-ft.	165 @ 4,250 rpm
Performance	
0-60 mph, acceleration	8.8 sec.
60-0 mph, braking	136 ft.
Turning circle	37.3 ft.
EPA city/highway	21/30 mpg
Test mileage	22 mpg
Fuel tank capacity	15 gal.

Ford

Crown Victoria

New for 99
New exterior colors

Pros
Powertrain performance
Interior room
Trunk space

Cons
Fuel economy
Handling
Trunk access

Equipment
Major Standard Equipment: 4.6-liter V-8, automatic transmission, 4-wheel disc brakes, variable-assist power steering, air conditioning, variable-intermittent wipers, rear defroster, power driver's seat, tilt steering wheel, cruise control, automatic headlamps, theft-deterrent system, power mirrors, power windows, power locks, AM/FM/cassette stereo. **LX adds:** Remote keyless entry, chrome wheels.
Major Options: 4-wheel antilock brakes, traction control, remote keyless entry system, electronic instruments, automatic air conditioning, power passenger's seat, heavy-duty suspension.

A rejuvenated senior

Last year Ford has updated the Crown Victoria—its classic full-size, V-8-powered, rear-wheel-drive sedan—giving it a fresh look and better performance. The Crown Victoria offers excellent ride, comfort, convenience, and value.

The Crown Victoria remains one of very few U.S. rear-wheel-drive sedans. It also retains separate body and frame construction that allows towing heavier trailers. However, Ford no longer offers a towing package.

The big Ford competes with the Pontiac Bonneville as well as with Buicks and Oldsmobiles. The Mercury Grand Marquis is a mechanically identical version of the Crown Victoria with a different appearance.

Emphasizing easier sedan shopping this year, Ford offers only two trim levels (base and LX) and fewer options on the Crown Victoria. A split-bench seat for 6-passenger seating is available.

The 4.6-liter V-8 and the 4-speed automatic combination work well together. Ford has refined the transmission for quicker, smoother downshifts. It still accelerates rather slowly from a stop, but the smooth power train adds to the feeling of luxury. In everyday driving, expect about 20 mpg.

Ford has upgraded the 4-wheel power disc brakes for smoother operation and longer life. Stopping distance should be somewhat longer than average. Antilock brakes continue to be optional; they're still a good idea, though.

Cruising down the highway, the Crown Victoria really excels. The ride is soft and quiet with a touch of luxury. The car's handling is well controlled, but a heavy emphasis on a soft ride compromises handling. Abrupt maneuvers and hard cornering bring on considerable body roll and tire squealing. The optional handling package with a stiffer suspension and better tires helps.

The power steering feels accurate, with good feedback. With rear-wheel drive, there's no torque steer to mar performance. We wouldn't hesitate to drive the Crown Victoria in winter. With optional traction control, you can enjoy the driving pleasure of rear-wheel drive all year round.

The interior is luxuriously quiet, and the seats are exceptionally comfortable. Rear-seat head, leg, and hip room is generous; it takes a car this size for three adults to be comfy in the back seat. Getting in or out of the front or rear seats is as easy as can be. The trunk is larger than average, but impractical in shape. Many people won't be able to reach small items at the bottom.

Rear-wheel-drive cars are a vanishing breed, but they continue to be the platform of choice for large cars worldwide. The Crown Victoria is one good value. **D.V.S.**

Specifications of Test Vehicle

Model: Crown Victoria LX

Exterior Dimensions	
Wheelbase	114.4 in.
Overall length	212 in.
Overall width	77.9 in.
Overall height	56.8 in.
Curb weight	3,900 lb.
Interior Dimensions	
Seating capacity	6
Head room	F:39.4/R:38 in.
Leg room	F:42.5/R:39.6 in.
Cargo volume	20.6 cu. ft.
Engine	
Displacement	V-8 4.6 L.
Horsepower	215 @ 4,500 rpm
Torque, lb-ft	275 @ 3,500 rpm
Performance	
0-60 mph, acceleration	NA
60-0 mph, braking	NA
Turning circle	41.4 ft.
EPA city/highway	17/25 mpg
Test mileage	16 mpg
Fuel tank capacity	19 gal.

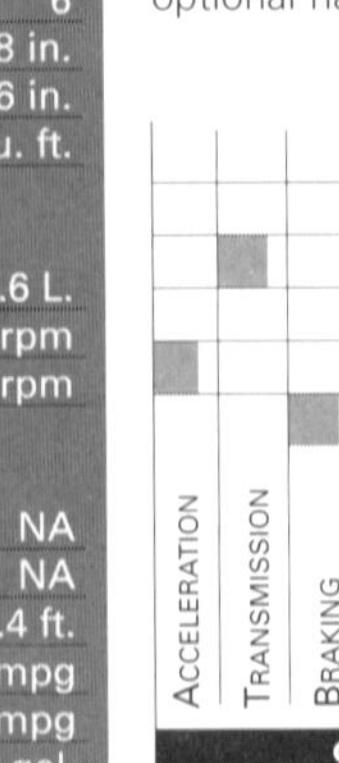

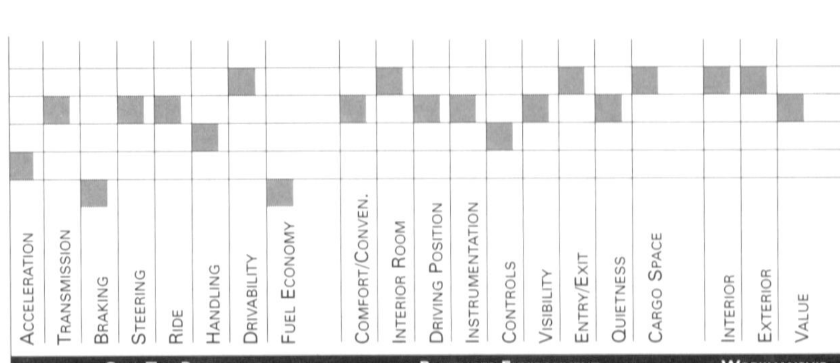

PRICES
$21,000
$28,000
Sedan $22,510
LX sedan $24,530

WARRANTY (years/miles)
Bumper-to-bumper 3/36,000
Powertrain 3/36,000
Rust-through 6/100,000

OTHER TO CONSIDER
Buick Le Sabre

Ratings
156

Ford Econoline

New in 99

No major changes

Pros

Interior room
Ride comfort
Controls

Cons

Overall size
Handling
Fuel economy

Equipment

Major Standard Equipment: 4.2-liter V-6, automatic transmission, 4-wheel antilock brakes, air conditioning, intermittent wipers, AM/FM stereo, vinyl upholstery, painted grille and bumpers.
XLT adds: Power locks, power windows, captain's chairs, cloth upholstery, chrome grille and bumpers.
Major options: 4.6-liter V-8, 5.4-liter V-8, 6.8-liter V-10, 7.3-liter diesel V-8, rear air conditioning, power windows, cruise control, tilt steering wheel, sliding side door, power locks, power mirrors, power driver's seat, captain's chairs, AM/FM/cassette stereo, remote keyless entry, trailer-towing package, larger tires, aluminum wheels.

A bestseller

PRICES
$22,000
$28,000

XL 3-door van
$21,755

XTL 3-door van
$23,706

WARRANTY
(years/miles)

Bumper-to-bumper
3/36,000

Powertrain
3/36,000

Rust-through
6/100,000

OTHER TO CONSIDER

Chevrolet Express Van

Dodge Ram Wagon

Before minivans came on the scene, full size vans like the Ford Econoline were the only choice beyond the station wagon. Even now, some buyers who grew up with these vehicles wouldn't have anything less.

Families usually buy Econolines as conversion vans, vans customized by accessory companies and then sold through Ford dealers. They have features beyond those supplied by Ford, and they're more expensive than the prices shown here. The quality of these modifications varies widely, and they're covered by a warranty separate from Ford's.

Ford's Econoline competes with the Dodge Ram Wagon and General Motors' twins, the Chevrolet Express and GMC Savana. The Econoline is far and away the best-seller in the class.

The Econoline is, in simplest terms, an Econoline cargo van with seats and windows, offering exceptional utility, tremendous cargo space, and a variety of powertrain choices. A serious truck-based vehicle, the Econoline has three chassis weight classes; only the regular Econoline has a likely application as a family vehicle, so it's the only one considered here. It comes in XL and XLT trim levels. At 212 inches, the standard wagon is long, but shorter than the Lincoln Town Car. There are 8- and 12-passenger versions, and the vans have Ford's latest series of truck engines.

Even with the powerful 5.4-liter V-8 engine, carrying six adults in the 8-passenger configuration makes a noticeable performance difference. The automatic transmission upshifts smoothly under normal throttle, but takes a little time to downshift under full throttle. Fuel economy is dismal with these trucks, regardless of the engine specified.

Braking is difficult to modulate with the pedal. Drivers, especially women, must lift their foot from the floor to apply full pressure. The steering transmits little road feel, so highway driving is not especially pleasant.

The long wheelbase and extra mass contribute to a surprisingly well-damped ride, considering the suspension is optimized for hauling loads. Handling requires extra care, particularly when negotiating tight turns and narrow parking spaces, where the long wheelbase is a real disadvantage. This full-size van demands an entirely different driving style than a car does.

The Econoline has head, leg, and hip room to spare. Visibility toward the rear is understandably limited. Most of the major controls are easy to find and operate.

If you need a full-size van, the Econoline should fill your needs. But even loyal Ford buyers should check out the newer designs offered by Chevrolet, Dodge, and GMC. **D.V.S.**

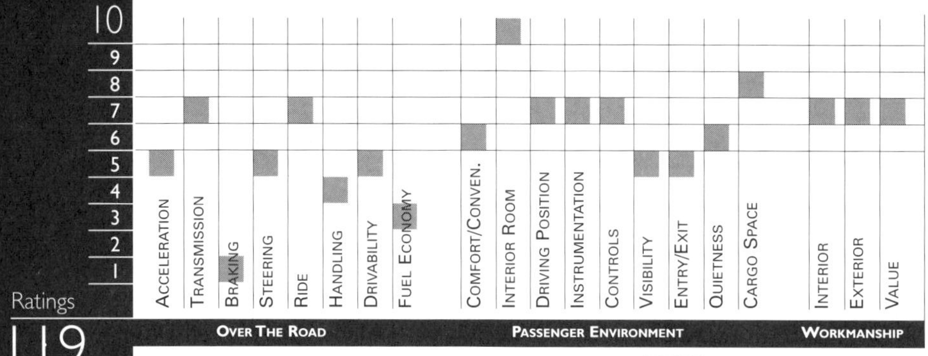

Specifications of Test Vehicle

Model: Econoline XLT

Exterior Dimensions	
Wheelbase	138 in.
Overall length	211.9 in.
Overall width	79.3 in.
Overall height	80.7 in.
Curb weight	5,150 lb.
Interior Dimensions	
Seating capacity	8
Head room	F: 42.5/R:40.2/R2:40.1 in.
Leg room	F:40/R:39.2/R2:41 in.
Cargo volume	16.4 cu. ft.
Engine	
Displacement	V-8 5.4 L.
Horsepower	235 @ 4,250 rpm
Torque, lb-ft.	335 @ 3,000 rpm
Performance	
0-60 mph, acceleration	11.5 sec.
60-0 mph, braking	155 ft.
Turning circle	40.5 ft.
EPA city/highway	12/17 mpg
Test mileage	14 mpg
Fuel tank capacity	35 gal.

Group	Rating category	Rating
Over The Road	Acceleration	5
	Transmission	7
	Braking	1
	Steering	5
	Ride	7
	Handling	4
	Drivability	5
	Fuel Economy	3
Passenger Environment	Comfort/Conven.	6
	Interior Room	10
	Driving Position	7
	Instrumentation	7
	Controls	7
	Visibility	5
	Entry/Exit	5
	Quietness	6
	Cargo Space	8
Workmanship	Interior	7
	Exterior	7
	Value	7

Ratings
119

Ford — Escort

New for 99

New interior color
Revised accessory list

Pros

Proven reliability
Choice of models
Price value ratio

Cons

Model scheduled for withdrawal
Uncomfortable bucket seats
Head room in the rear (sedan)

Equipment

Major Standard Equipment: 2-liter I-4, manual transmission, variable-intermittent wipers, AM/FM stereo, split-folding rear seat. **SE adds:** Air conditioning, power mirrors, driver-side remote keyless entry, rear defroster.
Major Options: Automatic transmission, 4-wheel antilock brakes, air conditioning, rear defroster, driver-side remote keyless entry, remote keyless entry, theft alarm system, power locks, power windows, cruise control, tilt steering column, power mirrors, integrated child-safety seat, AM/FM stereo, AM/FM/cassette stereo, AM/FM/CD/cassette stereo, aluminum wheels.

The last hurrah

Ford owes a lot to the Escort, notably the fact that the model placed the manufacturer at the top of the list for subcompact sales in North America 14 times (in the last 16 years). The Escort also accounts for more than a quarter (27%) of Ford's total sales. Customer loyalty is high; about five million drivers have slipped happily behind its wheel, and 6 out of 10 Escort owners say they'd buy another one.

All of which is to say that the 1999 Escort is exactly the same as last year's model. A very understandable situation since an all-new generation known as the Focus will be introduced early in 1999.

Before we go aboard, a few words about the exterior. The Escort is available as a sedan or station wagon (the ZX2 coupe is another story altogether). Inside, everything was completely and very nicely revamped a little over two years ago. Driving is made very pleasant by the seat position, a fundamental factor that the competition has sadly neglected. The Escort is roomy, except for the head room in the rear of the sedan, proving that Ford has once again chosen style over practicality. One other note: the seats themselves are surprisingly firm, and you may find the services of an orthopedist welcome after a few hundred miles.

Anyone who ever tried to tame the previous generation of Escorts will be delighted to take the wheel now. More stable, more rigid, quieter, and best of all, nicer to handle, this Ford has made visible progress in all areas. The precision steering, with just the right amount of power assistance, even makes the car fun to drive. Better still, the tighter suspension gives a decent ride, and has done away with the marshmallow movements this car used to be known for. The 2.0-liter engine is surprisingly

responsive, providing good acceleration and pickup, and it's matched with good, smooth transmissions, although I prefer the manual unit, less taxing on performance levels.

There's not much else to say about this Escort, other than that it is certainly the most homogenous package built to date, and will be for the next few months. **E.L.**

Specifications of Test Vehicle

Model: Escort SE

Exterior Dimensions	
Wheelbase	98.4 in.
Overall length	174.7 in.
Overall width	67 in.
Overall height	53.3 in.
Curb weight	2,450 lb.
Interior Dimensions	
Seating capacity	5
Head room	F:39/R:36.7 in.
Leg room	F:42.5/R:34 in.
Cargo volume	12.8 cu. ft.
Engine	
Displacement	I-4 2 L.
Horsepower	110 @ 5,000 rpm
Torque, lb-ft.	125 @ 3,750 rpm
Performance	
0-60 mph, acceleration	10.9 sec.
60-0 mph, braking	140 ft.
Turning circle	31.5 ft.
EPA city/highway	26/33 mpg
Test mileage	33 mpg
Fuel tank capacity	12.8 gal.

Prices

$11,000
$17,000

LX sedan $11,870
SE sedan $13,350
SE sedan $14,550

Warranty (years/miles)

Bumper-to-bumper 3/36,000
Powertrain 3/36,000
Rust-through 6/100,000

Other to consider

Dodge Neon
Hyundai Elantra

Over The Road	Rating
Acceleration	6
Transmission	7
Braking	4
Steering	8
Ride	8
Handling	8
Drivability	8
Fuel Economy	8
Passenger Environment	
Comfort/Conven.	7
Interior Room	7
Driving Position	8
Instrumentation	7
Controls	7
Visibility	7
Entry/Exit	7
Quietness	7
Cargo Space	6
Workmanship	
Exterior	8
Interior	7
Value	7

Ratings 142

Ford Expedition

New for 99
More engine power

Pros
Ride
Visibility
Lighting features

Cons
Rear-seat room
Cargo space
Entry/exit

Equipment

Major Standard Equipment: 4.6-liter V-8, automatic transmission, 4-wheel antilock disc brakes, air conditioning, power windows, power locks, power mirrors, rear wiper and washer, AM/FM/cassette stereo, remote keyless entry, theft-alarm system, tilt steering column. **Eddie Bauer adds:** Power quarter windows, automatic headlights, luggage rack, privacy glass, leather upholstery, power captain's chairs, cruise control, aluminum wheels. **Major Options:** 5.4-liter V-8, automatic 4-wheel drive, rear air conditioning, power driver's seat, leather upholstery, cruise control, load-leveling suspension, power quarter windows, power signal mirrors, power moonroof, privacy glass, lighted running boards, AM/FM/CD stereo.

Hard as nails

Ford's biggest sport-utility vehicle, the 4-door Expedition, can tow heavy trailers and provide more comfort than a pickup or van.

The Expedition is Ford's answer to Chevy's popular 4-door Tahoe. Since one version has a gross-weight rating over 8,500 pounds, Ford calls this SUV a heavy-duty wagon but shuns any comparison with the Tahoe's big brother, the Suburban. Like the Suburban, the Expedition offers third-row seats, but they reduce cargo space (12 cubic feet with three rows vs. 32 cubic feet with two). Ironically, the Expedition also competes with the Explorer, which is about the same price in the top trim. Lincoln sells an upscale version, the Navigator.

Based on the big F-150 pickup, the Expedition comes in XLT and Eddie Bauer editions. The full-time 4-wheel drive package is the Explorer's Control Trac automatic 4WD, with driver-selectable 4WD-Hi, 4WD-Lo, and 2WD. Standard 4-wheel antilock disc brakes give this SUV the right stuff. However, Ford hasn't matched Tahoe's optional diesel engine for better fuel economy and torque for heavy pulls.

Under the hood, the Expedition's overhead-cam 4.6- and 5.4-liter V-8s make the Explorer's and Mountaineer's time-honored overhead-valve, 5-liter engine an anachronism. The smooth-running engines bring a new feel to SUV driving. Although giving up some 25 horsepower to Chevrolet's, Ford's 5.4-liter feels peppy and quiet, especially when accelerating. There's not a major power difference between the Expedition's engines.

Variable-assist steering provides good control, ample road feedback, and easy parking. Though longer than the Tahoe, the Expedition can cut 4-feet-sharper turns. Watch its height, though. It's 10 full inches taller than an Explorer, so it won't fit in some parking garages and commercial car washes.

With the optional load-leveling air suspension, our test 4X4 had an exceptionally smooth, comfortable ride. As a plus, the suspension lowers the SUV 1 inch when parked.

We especially liked the optional lighted running boards. Wide rear doors make getting to the back seat easier than expected, but it's still a climb, a crawl, and a clamber into the third-row seats. Kids don't mind, but adults do. A wide, one-piece rear window gives the driver an excellent view, and the sloping hood allows an unobstructed view and easy parking.

The dash layout is similar to the F-150's, but drivers with small feet will find it hard to brake with their heel on the floor. The Expedition's pedal height is better than the F-150's, but not as good as it should be. Otherwise, the cockpit is warm and friendly.

The Expedition answers the question, "What do I buy when there're too many Explorers in my neighborhood?" **D.V.S.**

PRICES
$28,000
$42,000
XLT 4-door truck wagon $28,730
Eddie Bauer 4-door truck wagon $35,105

WARRANTY (years/miles)
Bumper-to-bumper 3/36,000
Powertrain 3/36,000
Rust-through 6/100,000.

OTHER TO CONSIDER
Chevrolet Tahoe
GMC Yukon

Specifications of Test Vehicle

Model: Expedition Eddie Bauer

Exterior Dimensions	
Wheelbase	119.1 in.
Overall length	204.6 in.
Overall width	78.5 in.
Overall height	76.6 in.
Curb weight	4,850 lb.
Interior Dimensions	
Seating capacity	8
Head room	F:39.8/R1:39.8/R2:35.1 in.
Leg room	F:40.9/R1:38.9/R2:28.8 in.
Cargo volume	11.9 cu. ft.
Engine	
Displacement	V-8 5.4 L.
Horsepower	230 @ 4,250 rpm
Torque, lb-ft.	325 @ 3,000 rpm
Performance	
0-60 mph, acceleration	10.7
60-0 mph, braking	147 ft.
Turning circle	40.5 ft.
EPA city/highway	12/16 mpg
Test mileage	12.2 mpg
Fuel tank capacity	30 gal.

Ratings 136

Group	Category	Rating
Over The Road	Acceleration	6
	Transmission	8
	Braking	3
	Steering	6
	Ride	7
	Handling	6
	Drivability	7
	Fuel Economy	2
Passenger Environment	Comfort/Conven.	8
	Interior Room	10
	Driving Position	7
	Instrumentation	7
	Controls	8
	Visibility	8
	Entry/Exit	6
	Quietness	8
	Cargo Space	5
Workmanship	Interior	8
	Exterior	8
	Value	8

Ford Explorer

New for 99

Redesigned front bumper
New XLS version

Pros

Good choice of engines
High-tech transfer box
Very smooth five-speed automatic transmission

Cons

Excessively high fuel consumption (V-8)
Anemic and rough base engine
Price increase

Equipment

Major Standard Equipment: 4-liter V-6 engine, manual transmission, 4-wheel antilock disk brakes, air conditioning, intermittent wipers, AM/FM stereo, split-folding rear seat, vinyl upholstery. **XLS adds:** Power mirrors, power windows, power locks, tilt steering wheel, cruise control, rear defroster, power liftgate release, cloth upholstery, privacy glass, speed-sensitive intermittent wipers, aluminum wheels. **Eddie Bauer adds:** Power driver's seat, AM/FM/CD/ cassette stereo, luggage rack. **Limited adds:** Heated mirrors, remote keyless entry, theft-alarm system, automatic temperature control, memory driver's seat, leather upholstery, running boards.

PRICES
$20,000
$38,000

Sport 2-door $20,065
XL 4-door $21,840
XLT 4-door $26,865
Eddie Bauer 4-door $31,260
Limited 4-door $32,160

WARRANTY (years/miles)

Bumper-to-bumper 3/36,000
Powertrain 3/36,000
Rust-through 6/100,000

OTHER TO CONSIDER

Chevrolet Blazer
Jeep Grand Cherokee

A small disappointment

Everyone was expecting a thoroughly revamped Explorer for the 1999 model year. Imagine our surprise when we realized that changes were pretty well limited to new front bumpers! But since everyone loves the Explorer, Ford can enjoy the luxury of improving it as slowly and surely as it wants. Before we forget, note that a new version is now available, the XLS (a new and improved XL).

The Explorer is available in two- or four-door models. Less popular, the former version can accommodate four occupants, while the latter can take on five, even six, depending on the configuration buyers choose. But keep in mind that rear seats are not necessarily comfortable. In front, congratulations go to the improved bucket seat design which, cross your fingers, lets drivers travel longer distances before they begin to feel the pain. The dashboard is still very appealing, nicely designed, and housing detailed instrumentation. However, the ergonomics of some controls is debatable, among them the flat and undersized air conditioning controls and those used to control the defroster and rear windshield wiper, the latter almost out of reach. Note also that door handles are positioned too close to seat cushions.

In 1999, buyers who opt for this big utility vehicle can still choose between three engines and as many transmissions. The first, a 4.0-liter V-6, has an output of 160 horses. The second, another 4.0-liter V-6, features SOHC technology (only one chain per cylinder bank, two valves per piston) capable of generating 205 horses, although it takes a bit of time for power to kick in. The five-speed automatic transmission does have something to do with this reluctance: the second speed is scrunched in between the first and the former second, which has disappeared. If you plan to haul a trailer or a boat, choose the Mustang's 210-hp 5.0-liter. However, this particular unit comes with permanent all-wheel drive and, consequently, does not benefit from the improved traction control system. But no matter which engine you happen to choose, remember that you'll have to take them into the gas station regularly to satisfy their propensity for gasoline. And as well, keep in mind that despite its luxury tones, the Explorer is still a truck and it behaves like one. Its solid suspension is firm on bumpy roads and it grips surfaces like a truck, what else, although improvements to the rack-and-pinion steering system are a plus. Lastly, brakes are efficient under even the worst of circumstances and the antilock system ensures straight-line stops.

E.L.

Specifications of Test Vehicle

Model: Explorer Limited

Exterior Dimensions	
Wheelbase	111.5 in.
Overall length	188.5 in.
Overall width	70.2 in.
Overall height	67.7 in.
Curb weight	4,150 lb.
Interior dimensions	
Seating capacity	5
Head room	F:39.9 in./R:39.3 in.
Leg room	F:42.4 in./R:37.7 in.
Cargo volume	42.6 cu. ft.
Engine	
Displacement	V-6 4 L.
Horsepower	205 @ 5,000 rpm
Torque, lb-ft.	250 @ 3,000 rpm
Performance	
0-60 mph, acceleration	10.1 sec.
60-0 mph, braking	154 ft.
Turning circle	37.3 ft.
EPA city/highway	15/20 mpg
Test mileage	18 mpg
Fuel tank capacity	21 gal.

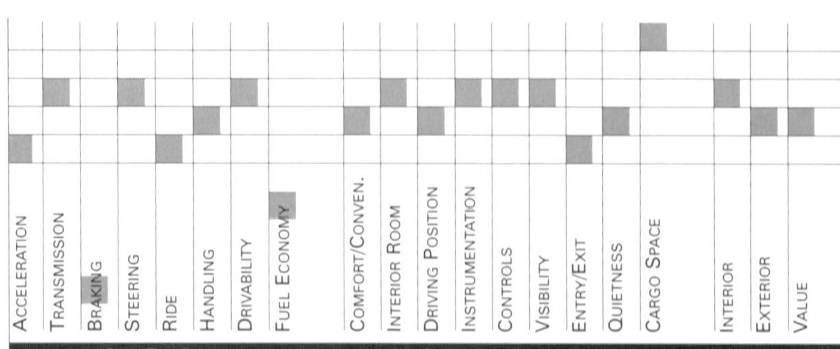

10
9
8
7
6
5
4
3
2
1

Ratings
139

Ford

F-Series Pickup

New for 99

4-door added on Super Cab
Super Duty

Pros

Instruments
Controls
Driveability

Cons

Entry/exit
Braking
Steering
Brake pedal location

Equipment

Major Standard Equipment: 4.2-liter V-6, manual transmission, rear antilock brakes, intermittent wiper, bench seat, vinyl upholstery, vinyl floor covering, AM/FM stereo, painted front bumper, painted grille. **XL adds:** Chrome front bumper, cloth upholstery. **XLT adds:** Rear bumper, variable-intermittent wipers, power windows, power locks, split-bench seat, carpeting. **Lariat adds:** Power mirrors, leather upholstery, aluminum wheels, automatic transmission. **Major Options:** 4.6-liter V-8, 5.4-liter V-8, 5.8-liter V-8, 7.3-liter diesel V-8, 7.5-liter V-8, part-time 4-wheel drive, extended cab, long pickup box, air conditioning, 4-wheel antilock brakes, variable-intermittent wipers, automatic leveling suspension.

PRICES
$14,000
$35,000

F-150 short bed $15,045
F-150 XL short bed $16,015
F-150 XLT short bed $18,770
F-150 Lariat short bed $22,135

WARRANTY
(years/miles)

Bumper-to-bumper 3/36,000
Powertrain 3/36,000
Rust-through 6/100,000

OTHER TO CONSIDER

Chevrolet Silverado
Dodge Ram 1500

A slot machine

The popularity of Ford's F-series pickups —the best-selling vehicle, car or truck, in the U.S.— continues unabated. Those sales statistics include vehicles purchased for commercial use as well as those for purely personal use.

The F-series's overhead-camshaft engines, a rarity in domestic trucks, signal an era of increased refinement in pickups. A completely redesigned front suspension delivers more precise handling and steering than was ever possible with the previous generation of Ford pickups, identified by its boxy styling.

Aggressively and aerodynamically styled, the new generation bears the Ford family look. The equipment, trim, and options remain as complicated as ever. You can choose different cabs, bed lengths, and styles. There are four trim levels, five weight classes, 2- and 4-wheel drive, five engines, and two transmissions. The message is simple: be extra cautious about buying a truck from dealer inventory. Instead, order one speced for your needs.

The rear of the standard cab extends slightly over the box to make room for reclining seats. Extended cabs all have an extra door on the passenger's side to access the rear cab space.

We tested the 4.6-liter V-8 that's one step up from the 4.2 V-6. With the small V-8, the truck accelerates satisfactorily unloaded, but consider the 5.4-liter V-8 if you plan to tow or carry heavy loads. The automatic transmission shifted firmly, both up and down.

On the highway, the F-150 feels soft and comfortable—so soft, in fact, we wonder just how good the base F-150 is for real chores. The soft suspension compromises handling, but trucks typically don't handle as well as real cars. Hard cornering is uncomfortable, and the rear end skips sideways on bumpy curves with a empty pickup box—a common trait among trucks.

Ford has updated the F-150 inside as well as outside. The lower cushion of the rear seat can be folded to create a flat floor for storage. Three-across seating is standard, but a variety of seating options is available. Standard front seats are large and comfortable, but the rear seat is not meant for long-distance travel. No matter how tall you are, you have to hike yourself up to the seat.

Well-designed and -positioned controls distinguish the instrument panel, and larger radio buttons are friendlier to the touch. Visibility benefits from a low hood and large glass area. You need big feet to reach the brake pedal and keep your heel on the floor; Ford still hasn't fixed this problem on the new F-series.

Pickups aren't just for work anymore. They're considered acceptable for almost any transportation need. As a best-seller, expect to see F-150s in shopping malls, school parking lots, suburban driveways, and just about everywhere else. **D.V.S.**

Specifications of Test Vehicle

Model: F-150 XLT

Exterior Dimensions	
Wheelbase	138.5 in.
Overall length	220.8 in.
Overall width	78.4 in.
Overall height	72.8 in.
Curb weight	4,050 lb.
Interior Dimensions	
Seating capacity	6
Head room	F:40.8:/R:37.8 in.
Leg room	F:40.9/R:32.2 in.
Payload capacity	1,950 lb.
Engine	
Displacement	V-8 4.6 L.
Horsepower	220 @ 4,500 rpm
Torque, lb-ft.	290 @ 3,250 rpm
Performance	
0-60 mph, acceleration	9.9 sec.
60-0 mph, braking	147 ft.
Turning circle	40.4 ft.
EPA city/highway	15/20 mpg
Test mileage	15 mpg
Fuel tank capacity	25 gal.

Category	Rating
Over the Road	
Acceleration	7
Transmission	7
Braking	3
Steering	6
Ride	7
Handling	6
Drivability	7
Fuel Economy	3
Passenger Environment	
Comfort/Conven.	8
Interior Room	8
Driving Position	8
Instrumentation	8
Controls	8
Visibility	9
Entry/Exit	6
Quietness	8
Cargo Space	9
Workmanship	
Interior	8
Exterior	8
Value	7

Ratings
141

Ford

Mustang

New for 99

New rear suspension
More power (V-6 and V-8)
New exterior design

Pros

Acceleration
Steering/handling
Braking

Cons

Rear-seat room/comfort
Cargo space
Chassis rigidity (convertible)

Equipment

Major Standard Equipment: 3.8-liter V-6, manual transmission, 4-wheel disc brakes, power mirrors, split-folding rear seat, tilt steering wheel, AM/FM stereo. **GT adds:** 4.6-liter V-8, sports suspension, theft-deterrent system, power windows, power locks, limited-slip differential. **Cobra SVT adds:** More powerful V-8, larger 4-wheel antilock brakes, traction control, larger wheels and tires.
Major Options: Automatic transmission, air conditioning, theft alarm system, 4-wheel antilock brakes, traction control power, driver's seat, power windows, power locks, cruise control, remote keyless entry, AM/FM/cassette stereo, AM/FM/CD stereo.

Ready for a new ride ?

The grand dame of the Pony-cars has been given a facelift that has affected her frame, her engines (more powerful), and her suspension (now independent at the rear). To counter the idea that this is a purely summertime vehicle, you should know that this year, Mustang has traction control to keep the wheels from spinning on icy or snowy surfaces.

The Mustang isn't just a high-performance car with a big V-8 in a small chassis. About 50 percent of all Mustangs have the standard 3.8-liter V-6.

The Mustang V-8 GT's steering, handling, and braking are first-rate, and its ride and handling offset the Camaro's power advantage. The convertible's open-air thrills come at a $6,000 premium; the coupe is a much better value. A limited-edition SVT Cobra version has a more powerful version of the 4.6-liter V-8 (320 hp).

The GT has plenty of spirited performance. Its straight-line acceleration is impressive: a full-throttle run to 60 mph takes a bit over 7 seconds. There's abundant torque for the car's relatively light weight. The 4.6-liter V-8 engine matches the electronic 4-speed automatic transmission nicely: gears shift with a sporty snap but no harshness. Floor the throttle, and the car downshifts almost instantaneously, with plenty of power for passing and expressway merging. The small fuel tank makes for frequent filling station stops with the GT's V-8 engine.

Quick, responsive power steering makes the GT nimble, and body roll is virtually unnoticeable in hard cornering. The stiff chassis improves the convertible markedly, but it's still not as shake-free as the coupe.

Although longer wheelbase, wider track, and the rear suspension improve control and ride comfort compared with earlier generations, the GT's stiff suspension settings and low-profile tires offset parts of those gains; we felt every road irregularity in the seats and large potholes jarred the entire car. The base Mustang, without the GT's tires and performance suspension, makes a more enjoyable commuter car and still delivers a healthy dose of fun.

Inside, the Mustang has two front "pods" — one for the driver and one for the passenger — reminiscent of the original edition 33 years ago. The door panels flow into the instrument panel, which sports a complete set of gauges.

In front, head and leg room are adequate for tall drivers. Rear-seat passengers will feel cramped, especially in the convertible.

The roof pillars and a high parcel shelf limit rearward visibility. The split-folding rear seat adds some storage capacity to the small trunk. Liftover is at bumper level between the tail lights.

In 1964, Mustang defined a whole new automobile class, known as "pony cars." More than 30 years later, buyers continue to prefer the updated original to the competition. Who says sport and refinement can't be combined in an appealing package? **E.L. / D.V.S.**

Specifications of Test Vehicle

Model: Mustang GT

Exterior Dimensions	
Wheelbase	101.3 in.
Overall length	183.2 in.
Overall width	73.1 in.
Overall height	53.3 in.
Curb weight	3,242 lb.
Interior Dimensions	
Seating capacity	4
Head room	F:38.1/R:35.5 in.
Leg room	F:41.8/R:29.9 in.
Cargo volume	10.9 cu. ft.
Engine	
Displacement	V-8 4.6 L.
Horsepower	260 @ 5,250 rpm
Torque	302 @ 4,000 rpm
Performance	
0-60 mph, acceleration	7.2 sec.
60-0 mph, braking	121 ft.
Turning circle	37.11 ft.
EPA city/highway	NA
Test mileage	NA
Fuel tank capacity	15.7 gal.

Prices

$16,995
$32,000
(est.)

Coupe
$16,995

2-door convertible
$21,595

GT coupe
$21,395

GT 2-door convertible
$25,395

Cobra coupe
NA

Cobra 2 door convertible
NA

Warranty

(years/miles)

Bumper-to-bumper
3/36,000

Powertrain
3/36,000

Rust-through
6/100,000

Other to consider

Chevrolet Camaro

Pontiac Firebird

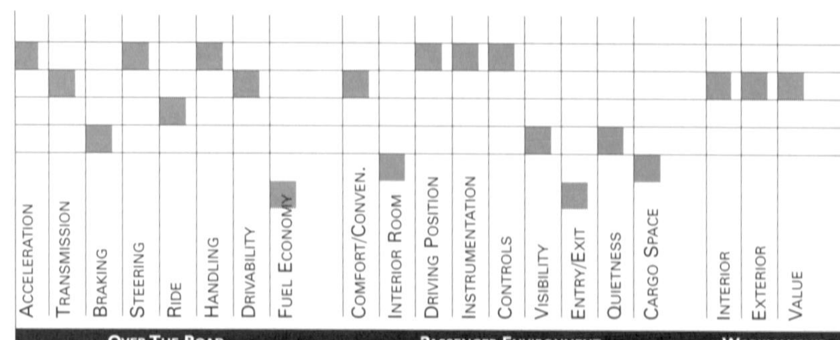

10
9
8
7
6
5
4
3
2
1

Ratings
145

Ford Ranger

New for 99

Four-door model

Pros

Powertrain performance
Interior styling

Cons

Ride comfort
Handling
Rear antilock brakes

Equipment

Major Standard Equipment: 2.5-liter I-4, manual transmission, rear-wheel antilock brakes, intermittent wipers, vinyl upholstery, vinyl floor covering, painted bumpers. **XLT adds:** Cloth upholstering, carpeting, AM/FM stereo, chrome bumpers.
Major Options: 3-liter V-6, 4-liter V-6, automatic transmission, 5-speed automatic transmission, part-time 4-wheel drive, 4-wheel antilock brakes, long bed, extended cab, air conditioning, power windows, power locks, remote keyless entry, AM/FM/cassette stereo, AM/FM/CD/cassette stereo, tilt steering wheel, cruise control, theft alarm system, larger tires, aluminum wheels.

Prescription for success

PRICES
$12,000
$25,000
XL short bed
$11,785
XLT short bed
$13,860

WARRANTY
(years/miles)
Bumper-to-bumper
3/36,000
Powertrain
3/36,000
Rust-through
6/100,000

OTHER TO CONSIDER
Chevrolet S-10
Dodge Dakota

For more than a decade, the Ford Ranger has been the best-selling compact pickup. To stay competitive, Ford has refined, but not radically changed, the Ranger last year.

If you don't like the Ranger's looks, check out a Mazda. The Ranger and Mazda's B-Pickup are produced on the same assembly line and are identical except for styling details. The Ranger competes with compact trucks from Chevrolet, Toyota, and Nissan.

The trim levels ascend from the very basic XL, through the XLT. The standard cab comes with a short or a long box. The standard cab on the new version is 3 inches longer than the one on the old Ranger, for more space inside. You can choose 2- or 4-wheel drive and one of three engines. All of the combinations make it easy to create a truck for your needs, but the cost of the options can add up fast.

In a cost-cutting move, Rangers come standard with rear-wheel-only antilock brakes, which don't give the steering control of a 4-wheel system. All-wheel antilock brakes are an expensive option, but well worth the cost.

The SuperCab Ranger is 16.7 feet long, as long as Ford's smallest full-size F-series pickup. The extended cab, by far the most versatile choice, adds passenger room and interior cargo space at the expense of overall length. The XLT's front bucket seats are as comfortable as those found in most full-size passenger cars. Two small rear seats, useful for only short trips, fold down from the sides. The 4WD version sits a full 3.5 inches higher than a 2WD model, requiring a climb to get in and a jump to get down.

The thoughtfully designed instrument panel has stereo controls properly located above the ventilation controls in a center console. You can turn a knob to select the 4WD mode. The instrument cluster is complete, simple, and easy to interpret at a glance. A key-operated switch disables the passenger-side air bag to allow use of a rear-facing infant seat there.

Ford has replaced the twin I-beam front suspension with a more conventional arrangement. It should make the tires last longer. On the road, we found the improvement in ride and handling slight, so expect a firm, truck-like ride. On bumpy curves, the rear end still tends to skip sideways.

The 4-liter V-6 engine and 5-speed transmission provide lively performance. Getting to 60 mph took us almost 10 seconds. The 4-wheel antilock brakes felt fine, but a simulated panic stop produced disappointing stopping distance in our tests.

Ford knows how to satisfy owners of pickups, big or small. **D.V.S.**

Specifications of Test Vehicle

Model: Ranger XLT

Exterior Dimensions	
Wheelbase	125.7 in.
Overall length	200.7 in.
Overall width	69.3 in.
Overall height	67.5 in.
Curb weight	3,050 lb.
Interior Dimensions	
Seating capacity	5
Head room	F:39.2/R:39.1 in.
Leg room	F:42.2/R:36.2 in.
Payload capacity	1,250 lb.
Engine	
Displacement	V-6 4 L.
Horsepower	158 @ 4,250 rpm
Torque, lb-ft.	223 @ 3,000 rpm
Performance	
0-60 mph, acceleration	9.8 sec.
60-0 mph, braking	147 ft.
Turning circle	41.6 ft.
EPA city/highwa	16/21 mpg
Test mileage	17 mpg
Fuel tank capacity	20 gal.

Ratings 135

Category	Rating
Over The Road	
Acceleration	7
Transmission	8
Braking	3
Steering	7
Ride	7
Handling	7
Drivability	8
Fuel Economy	4
Passenger Environment	
Comfort/Conven.	8
Interior Room	6
Driving Position	7
Instrumentation	8
Controls	8
Visibility	8
Entry/Exit	6
Quietness	7
Cargo Space	2
Workmanship	
Interior	8
Exterior	8
Value	8

Ford

Taurus

New for 99

New exterior colors
Redesigned instrument cluster
Revised suspension

Pros

Good overall balance
Comfort
Wagon version available

Cons

Controversial styling
Access to rear seats
Barely adequate 3.0-liter V-6

Equipment

Major Standard Equipment: 3-liter V-6, automatic transmission, variable-assist power steering, air conditioning, split-bench seat, AM/FM stereo, power windows, power mirrors, rear defroster, tilt steering wheel, variable intermittent wipers. **SE adds:** Cabin air filter, split-folding rear seat, remote-control decklid release, individual front seats, automatic headlamps, AM/FM/cassette stereo, power locks, remote keyless entry, theft alarm system, remote-control decklid release. **SHO adds:** 3.4-liter V-8, 4-wheel antilock disc brakes, power seats, driver's power lumbar adjustment, leather upholstery, chrome wheels.

Take a good, long look!

All those who think that a vehicle's looks don't really count, raise your hands! You have a right to your own opinions, but Ford would still like to present its Taurus, a mid-size model with bold styling. In the hopes of increasing its still fairly lukewarm pool of customers, Ford has changed its range of colors and has redesigned wheel covers to draw attention away from the model's rounded body lines.

A small tip: go beyond appearances, the Taurus deserves a good, long look and it has depth.

Often, it seems that Ford is more concerned with the esthetics and aerodynamics of its products than with their practicality. The Taurus is a good example of this. Access to the inside of this mid-size isn't very easy and if you're a rear-seat passenger, watch that roof line if you don't want to hit your noggin. As you'll soon see, usable space doesn't reflect the car's exterior dimensions. You may not feel cooped up, but this Ford's cockpit isn't spacious, particularly in the back, where the roof slopes down to rob you of a few precious centimeters of head room. Another drawback: storage spaces are lacking in spite of an ingenious multipurpose center armrest (on models with a bench seat), unfortunately not as practical as it looks although it has been revamped for this year. Along the same lines, stylists have redecorated the instrument cluster and the seats and redesigned door panels to include door pockets, at long last.

Debate on this car's styling is endless. But discussions are cut short as soon as the topic of ride comes up. Stable, well-balanced, and comfortable are the three adjectives used most often to describe this particular aspect of the Taurus. And the attributes are even more applicable for 1999 now that 16-inch wheels (formerly exclusive to the SHO) are available as an option. The standard 3.0-liter V-6 on the low-end versions has an output of 145 hp, which is barely enough for a car of this size. More luxurious models have a 3.0-liter V-6 with a 200-hp output, a much better engine choice. In both cases, only a four-speed automatic transmission is used to transfer power to the drive wheels. The perfectly assisted steering system is precise, lets you corner hassle-free, and the suspension is relatively good at keeping roll and sway under control now that shock absorbers and springs have been revised. However, it's too bad that only the wagon gets four disc brakes, which are admirable at staving off overheating, by the way, while the sedan has to make do with the classic disc-drum tandem.

E. L.

Specifications of Test Vehicle

Model: Taurus SE

Exterior Dimensions	
Wheelbase	108.5 in.
Overall length	197.5 in.
Overall width	73 in.
Overall height	55.1 in.
Curb weight	3,350 lb.
Interior dimensions	
Seating capacity	5
Head room	F:39.2/R:36.2 in.
Leg room	F:42.2/R:38.9 in.
Cargo volume	15.8 cu. ft.
Engine	
Displacement	V-6 3 L.
Horsepower	200 @ 5,750 rpm
Torque, lb-ft.	200 @ 4,500 rpm
Performance	
0-60 mph, acceleration	8.7 sec.
60-0 mph, braking	134 ft.
Turning circle	38 ft.
EPA city/highway	18/27 mpg
Test mileage	23 mpg
Fuel tank capacity	16 gal.

Prices

$18,000
$31,000

LX sedan $17,995
SE sedan $18,995
SE 4-door wagon $19,995
SHO 4-door sedan $28,550

Warranty

(years/miles)

Bumper-to-bumper 3/36,000
Powertrain 3/36,000
Rust-through 6/100,000

Other to Consider

Chevrolet Lumina
Dodge Intrepid

Group	Category	Rating
Over The Road	Acceleration	8
	Transmission	7
	Braking	5
	Steering	8
	Ride	8
	Handling	8
	Drivability	8
	Fuel Economy	5
Passenger Environment	Comfort/Conven.	7
	Interior Room	7
	Driving Position	8
	Instrumentation	7
	Controls	8
	Visibility	8
	Entry/Exit	7
	Quietness	8
	Cargo Space	7
Workmanship	Interior	8
	Exterior	9
	Value	7

Ratings 148

Ford Windstar LX

new MODEL

1999

New for 99

Redesigned suspension
Body
Interior and powertrain
Optional side air bags
Back-up warning

Pros

Safety features
Ride
Comfort/convenience

Cons

Handling
Fuel economy
Braking

Equipment

Major Standard Equipment: 3.0 liter V-6 engine, 4-speed automatic transmission, antilock brakes, right-hand sliding door, AM/FM stereo, 7-passenger seating. **LX adds:** 3.8 liter V-6 engine, left-side sliding door, air conditioning, power windows and locks, AM/FM/ cassette player stereo. **SE adds:** Remote heated mirrors, remote entry, 15 in. aluminum wheels, overhead console, power driver seat, tilt wheel. **SEL adds:** Right- and left-hand power sliding doors, automatic headlight control, 16 in. aluminum wheels.
Major Options: Cruise control, traction control, personal audio system, reverse sensing system, quad bucket seats.

AAA **TOP MINIVAN**

PRICES

$19,000
$34,000

Van
$18,995
3.0 L Wagon
$20,800
LX Wagon
$24,240
SE Wagon
$28,075
SE Wagon
$30,995

WARRANTY
(years/miles)

Bumper-to-Bumper
3/36,000
Powertrain
3/36,000
Rust-through
6/100,000

OTHER TO CONSIDER

Honda Odyssey
Toyota Sienna

Yes! A fourth door!

The redesigned 1999 Ford Windstar gets some long-overdue improvements, including an all-new exterior and interior appearance, a driver's-side sliding door, several advanced safety features, and other refinements that finally place it well ahead of the competition.

Inside, the instrument panel has been updated. The instruments are no-nonsense — simple and easy to read. Stereo and ventilation controls are logically placed for easy access. The air conditioning control has finally been updated with a switch that turns the compressor on and off, and the radio has larger buttons for easier operation.

A variety of seating arrangements is available, including second-row captain`s chairs or a two passenger bench seat. The second-row bench seat can be shifted from side to side to accommodate a preferred entrance door. The third-row three-passenger seat can be moved to the second position to maximize seating and cargo capacity. All rear seats are on wheels, but it still takes two people to handle them.

Entry and exit through the two front doors is car-like, but the big news is the addition of a second sliding door on the driver's side. An optional system allows both sliding doors to be opened and closed with electric motors that are activated by a button on the keyless remote fob.

On the road, the Windstar rides and handles like a large station wagon. The ride is soft and comfortable on smooth highways, but uneven pavement causes unpleasant wallowing and swaying. Handling isn't much better — plan ahead for unexpected curves on country roads. The engine and transmission perform well together, and provide reasonably good acceleration. Fuel economy is about average for a van, but the 26-gallon fuel tank makes extended runs possible without stopping. The brakes have been improved, but our panic stop tests still show only average stopping distance.

Cargo capacity with all three seats in place is better than most cars. As in most minivans, visibility from the driver's seat is restricted by rear passengers. A clever, flip-down convex mirror on the overhead console allows the driver to see everything that is going on in the rear seats. And perhaps the most interesting feature is a new safety device, built into the rear bumper, that warns the driver about objects in the vehicle's path when backing up. A series of beeps increases in frequency as an object gets closer to the rear bumper.

Better looks, greater convenience, and improved safety features make the new Windstar a real star in the competitive minivan market. That's why it was chosen as a AAA Top Minivan for 1999. **D.V.S**

Specifications of Test Vehicle

Model: Windstar LX

Exterior Dimensions	
Wheelbase	120.7 in.
Overall length	200.9 In.
Overall width	76.6 In.
Overall height	65.8 In.
Curb weight	NA
Interior Dimensions	
Seating capacity	7
Head room	F: 39.3/S: 41.1/R: 37.9 in.
Leg room	F: 40.7/S: 36.8/R: 35.6 in.
Cargo room	19.5 cu.ft.
Engine	
Displacement	3.8 L V-6
Horsepower	200@4900 rpm
Torque, lb-ft.	240@3600 rpm
Performance	
0-60 mph, acceleration	9.3 sec.
60-0 mph, braking	135 ft.
Turning circle	39.5
EPA city/highway	17/24 mpg.
Test mileage	23
Fuel tank capacity	26 gal.

Group	Rating	Score
Over The Road	Acceleration	7
	Transmission	8
	Braking	5
	Steering	7
	Ride	7
	Handling	6
	Drivability	8
	Fuel Economy	5
Passenger Environment	Comfort/Conven.	8
	Interior Room	10
	Driving Position	8
	Instrumentation	7
	Controls	8
	Visibility	7
	Entry/Exit	8
	Quietness	8
	Cargo Space	9
Workmanship	Interior	8
	Exterior	8
	Value	8

Ratings
150

GMC

Sierra

New for 99

Totally redesigned with new body, chassis, and powertrain components.

Pros

Seat comfort
Quietness
Brakes

Cons

Fuel economy
Door locks

Equipment

Major Standard Equipment: 4.3 liter V-6 engine, 5-speed manual transmission, 4-wheel antilock disc brakes, cloth bench seats, **SLE adds:** Air conditioning, cassette player, remote mirrors, power windows, power locks. **SLT adds:** CD player, remote keyless entry, leather seats, power seats,
Major Options: 4.8 liter V-8, 5.3 liter V-8, 6.0 liter V-8, 6.5 liter V-8 diesel, 4-speed automatic transmission, 4-wheel drive, chrome wheels, towing equipment, front high-back bucket seats, sliding rear window, rear defogger.

A big gamble

The full-size GMC Sierra is all-new for 1999. And by all-new, we mean it is larger, roomier, tougher, and more powerful than ever. In the past, GMC and Chevy pickups have looked pretty much alike, sharing everything but a grill and a few trim pieces. Now, GMC has given the Sierra a distinctive look in an attempt to make it appealing to a more upscale buyer. The sheetmetal parts are unique from the windshield to the front bumper.

Like its rivals, the Sierra comes in dozens of configurations, including 2-door regular cab, 2-door extended cab, and 4-door crew cab; short or long bed; and 2- or 4-wheel drive. There are three trim levels: base SL, mid-level SLE, and top-of-the-line SLT. A three-door extended cab is available now, with a 4-door version planned for the near future.

Choosing an engine requires a little thought. A 4.3-liter V-6, 4.8-liter V-8, 5.3-liter V-8, 6.0-liter V-8, and a 6.5-liter turbo-diesel make up the list of choices. Our test vehicle had the new 5.3-liter V-8 — expected to be the top-selling GMC truck engine. With plenty of torque at low speeds, this engine is smooth, quiet, and responsive. It is well-suited to the 4-speed automatic transmission — shifts are so smooth they go unnoticed. The transmission has a unique feature for those who tow heavy loads. A pushbutton on the shift lever changes the shift pattern to maximize pulling power in each gear. The conventional part-time 4-wheel drive system is engaged with a floor-mounted lever. An automatic 4-wheel drive system called AutoTrac automatically engages the front wheels when necessary.

Both the regular and extended three-door cabs are the roomiest in the segment. Whether bench or bucket, the front seats offer good support and comfort. The rear-seat cushion is larger and more comfortable. The seat back is tilted at a comfortable angle. And extra leg room actually makes it pleasant to ride there. Seat belts incorporated into the front seat backs make rear, seat entry and exit a simple matter.

The controls are located right where they should be. The instrument cluster is simple, easy to read, and has an electronic message center to warn about routine problems — and the not so routine, such as when to change the oil.

Regardless of the road surface, the Sierra is well controlled. Acceleration is smooth and quiet. The much-improved 4-wheel disk brakes deliver substantially shorter stopping distances, with better pedal feel. The new rack and pinion steering, standard on 2-wheel drive models, is precise, with good on-center feel. The stronger frame makes for a much stiffer structure, and it shows in the way the Sierra rides and handles. Our test truck kept its composure, even on a section of badly wash-boarded dirt road.

It's obvious GM has taken the redesign of their new trucks seriously. The new Sierra represents the state in full-size trucks. **D.V.S.**

Specifications of Test Vehicle

Model: Sierra 1500 SLT

Exterior Dimensions	
Wheelbase	143.5 in.
Overall length	227.5 In.
Overall width	78.5 In.
Overall height	73.9 In.
Curb weight	4621 lbs.
Interior Dimensions	
Seating capacity	6
Head room	F: 41.0/R: 38.4 in.
Leg room	F: 41.3/R: 33.7 in.
Cargo capacity	852 lbs
Engine	
Displacement	5.3 L V-8
Horsepower	270@5000 rpm
Torque, lb-ft.	315@4000 rpm
Performance	
0-60 mph, acceleration	8.6 sec.
60-0 mph, braking	135 ft.
Turning circle	47.3 ft.
EPA City/highway	15/18 mpg.
Test mileage	NA
Fuel tank capacity	26.0 gal.

Prices

$16,000
$40,000

C 1500
$15,000

C 1500 SL short bed
$16,335

C 1500 SLE short bed
$18,164

C 1500 SLT short bed
$19,818

Warranty

(years/miles)

Bumper-to-bumper (incl. tires)
3/36,000

Powertrain
3/36,000

Rust-through
6/100,000

Other to Consider

Dodge Ram
Ford F-Series

Group	Category	Rating (1–10)
Over The Road	Acceleration	8
	Transmission	9
	Braking	5
	Steering	8
	Ride	8
	Handling	7
	Drivability	8
	Fuel Economy	3
Passenger Environment	Comfort/Conven.	8
	Interior Room	8
	Driving Position	9
	Instrumentation	8
	Controls	9
	Visibility	9
	Entry/Exit	7
	Quietness	8
	Cargo Space	10
Workmanship	Interior	8
	Exterior	8
	Value	8

Ratings
156

GMC

Jimmy

(see Chevrolet Blazer)

NEW FOR 99

Optional Autotrac system
New exterior colors

PROS

Engine performance
Controls
Maneuverability

CONS

Visibility
Rear-seat access
Fuel economy

PRICE

$22,000 - $30,000

EQUIPMENT

Major Standard Equipment: 4.3-liter V-6, manual transmission, 4-wheel antilock brakes, air conditioning, variable-intermittent wipers, vinyl upholstery. **SLS adds:** AM/FM/cassette stereo, cloth upholstery, split-folding rear seat, tilt steering wheel, cruise control, power windows, power locks, power mirrors, rear defroster, rear washer and wiper, power liftgate release, aluminum wheels. **SLE adds:** Minor trim details. **SLT adds:** Remote keyless entry, power driver's seat. **Envoy adds:** High-intensity head lights, leather ulphostery.

GMC

Safari

(see Chevrolet Astro)

NEW FOR 99

New all-wheel drive system
Redesigned roof console
New exterior colors

PROS

Trailer towing rating
Dutch door option
AWD option

CONS

Front-seat room
Fuel economy; Ride

PRICE

$20,000 - $29,000

EQUIPMENT

Standard: 4.3-liter V-6, automatic transmission, 4-wheel antilock brakes, variable-assist power steering, 5-passenger seating, dual rear panel doors, air conditioning, AM/FM stereo, variable-intermittent wipers. **SLE adds:** 8-passenger seating, front seat lumber adjustment, power locks, tilt steering column, cruise control. **SLT adds:** Privacy glass, power mirrors, power windows, remote keyless entry, aluminum wheels.
Major Options: All-wheel drive, 7-passenger seating, rear air conditioning, rear heater, tilt steering wheel, cruise control, AM/ FM/CD stereo, rear defroster, rear liftglass, power locks, remote keyless entry, privacy glass, power windows, integrated child-safety seat, trailer towing package.

GMC

Savana

(see Chevrolet Express)

NEW FOR 99

Superficial changes

PROS

Interior room
Safety features
Versatility

CONS

Fuel economy
Parking ease
Entry/exit

PRICE

$20,000 - $32,000

EQUIPMENT

Standard: 4.3-liter V-6, automatic transmission, 4-wheel antilock brakes, air conditioning, AM/FM stereo, variable-intermittent wipers, vinyl upholstery, vinyl floor covering. **SLE adds:** Power windows, power locks, tilt steering wheel, carpeting, cloth upholstery, cruise control, chrome bumpers, chrome grille.
Major options: 5-liter V-8, 5.7-liter V-8, 6.5-liter diesel V-8, 7.4-liter V-8, extended wheelbase, sliding side door, 5-passenger seating, 12-passenger seating, 15-passenger seating, rear air conditioning, cruise control, tilt steering wheel, power seats, AM/FM/cassette stereo, AM/FM/CD/cassette stereo, power windows, power locks, remote keyless entry, power heated mirrors, aluminum wheels.

GMC

Sonoma (see Chevrolet S10)

New for 99
Transmission
Styling

Pros
Controls
Transmission
Styling

Cons
Ride comfort
Entry/exit

Price
$12,000 - $23,000

Equipment

Major Standard Equipment:
2.2-liter I-4, manual transmission, 4-wheel antilock brakes, AM/FM stereo, automatic headlamps, vinyl upholstery, variable-intermittent wipers, rubber floor covering. **SLS adds:** Split-bench seat, cloth upholstery, carpeting. **SLE adds:** Aluminum wheels.
Major Options: 4.3-liter V-6, automatic transmission, part-time 4-wheel drive, electric shift transfer case, rear locking differential, long pickup box, third door, air conditioning, remote keyless entry, power windows, power mirrors, tilt steering wheel, cruise control, CD player, off-road suspension, larger tires.

GMC

Suburban (see Chevrolet Suburban)

New for 99
Improved automatic transmission
New starter

Pros
Engine power
Uniqueness
Passenger/cargo room

Cons
Braking
Maneuverability
Fuel economy

Price
$25,000 - $41,000

Equipment

Major Standard Equipment:
5.7-liter V-8, automatic transmission, 4-wheel antilock brakes, variable-assist power steering, AM/FM stereo, variable-intermittent wipers, vinyl upholstery, rubber floor covering. **LS adds:** Air conditioning, rear air conditioning, rear defroster, AM/FM/cassette stereo, power lumbar adjustment, cloth upholstery, carpeting, power mirrors, automatic dimming rear-view mirror, power windows, power locks, tilt steering wheel, cruise control, privacy glass, larger tires, aluminum wheels. **LT adds:** Power driver's seat, leather upholstery, remote keyless entry.

GMC

Yukon (see Chevrolet Tahoe)

New for 99
Autotrac system
Sturdier starter
Improved transmission

Pros
Powertrain
Comfort/convenience
Interior room

Cons
Fuel economy
Maneuverability
Braking

Price
$30,000 - $40,000

Equipment

Major Standard Equipment:
5.7-liter V-8, automatic transmission, 4-wheel antilock brakes, variable-assist power steering, rear panel doors, air conditioning, AM/FM/cassette stereo, variable-intermittent wipers, split-bench seat, power mirrors, rear defroster, power windows, power locks, remote keyless entry, tilt steering wheel, cruise control, aluminum wheels. **SLT adds:** Rear air conditioning, individual front seats, heated seats, power passenger's seat, leather upholstery, heated mirrors, AM/FM/CD/cassette stereo. **Denali adds:** Automatic, 4-wheel drive, trailer towing package, running boards.

Honda Accord

New for 99
Standard antilock brakes on the LX
Standard leather upholstery on the EX

Pros
Roomy interior
Choice of engines
Sure market value

Cons
Conservative styling
Poorly soundproofed passenger compartment
Confused automatic transmission (see article)

Equipment
Major Standard Equipement: 2.3-liter I-4, manual transmission, intermittent wipers, AM/FM/ cassette/stereo, folding rear seat, rear defroster, remote decklid release.
LX adds: More powerful 2.3-liter (150 hp) I-4, air conditioning, cabin air filter, variable-intermittent wipers, cruise control, power mirrors, power windows, power locks, larger tires.
EX adds: 4-wheel antilock brakes, driver's lumbar adjustment, remote keyless entry, power moonroof, aluminum wheels.
Major Options: 3-liter V-6, automatic transmission, automatic air conditioning, leather upholstery, larger tires.

PRICES
$15,000
$25,000
DX sedan $15,690
LX coupe $18,880
LX sedan $18,880
EX coupe $21,390
EX sedan $21,390

WARRANTY
(years/miles)
Bumper-to-bumper 3/36/000
Powertrain 3/36,000
Rust-through 5/unlimited

OTHER TO CONSIDER
Mazda 626
Toyota Camry

Calculated risk

The faster you rise, the harder you fall. Let me reassure you right now, though: no one has taken any risks as they set out to ensure that the Honda Accord, the fifth of the same name, takes the golden path opened up by previous generations. So this is a new Accord, but it feels familiar and it speaks volumes on how much its designers were afraid to stray too far from the old one.

Roomier than its predecessor, the Accord sedan is also more welcoming than a Taurus. Doors open onto the same molded and unexciting interior that Honda seems to hold the secret to designing. The coupe and sedan share the same molded and boring dashboard that Honda seems to hold the secret to using. Under the little awning-type device pointed toward the driver, you'll find clear and easy-to-read instrumentation. The console houses rotary air conditioning controls, supposedly more efficient than the old ones, and larger and easier to use controls for the radio. The rounded bucket seats on the sedan have enough adjustments (including manual height adjustment on less expensive versions) to help you find the ideal driving position. Cargo nets in the trunk (yes, there are more than one) make it easy to load smaller packages; but there's plenty of room for bigger items as well since the trunk is roomier (and there's even more room to spare when the rear seat is folded down) and access is easier on the sedan now that the trunk sill is even with the bumper.

To stay active in the mid-size category, Honda had no other choice but to pay close attention to the V-6 version. The former 2.7-liter has left the building and now it's time for the 3.0-liter (almost identical to the unit you'll find on the Acura CL) to step into the spotlight and take over. Modern, fast, smoother, and quieter than the 2.7-liter it's replacing, this 3.0-liter is just perfect for the new Accord. Careful not to leave the four-cylinder lacking — after all it powers more than three Accords out of four — Honda has revised it as well, bringing it from 2.2 to 2.3 liter. However, only the LX and EX versions have a right to the VTEC version of this four-cylinder; the DX can't have it and as a result it loses the extra 15 horses that the remaining 135 sorely miss. The excellent five-speed manual transmission is efficient at transferring power to the front-wheel drive system and models equipped with the V-6 are coupled solely with an automatic unit, which hesitates between 3rd and 4th gear despite the presence of a mechanism designed to prevent just such an occurrence. Stiffer but not necessarily any lighter (only the EX V-6 is), the new Accord has an updated rear suspension (which rear-seat passengers can thank for their extra leg room), which provides a level of stability and smoothness never reached by the previous model.

Even if over the course of various revampings the Accord's sporty personality has begun to fade, this fifth generation has what it takes to reach the consumer group it needs to regain its title as "bestselling car in the US." **E.L.**

Specifications of Test Vehicle
Model: Accord EX

Exterior Dimensions	
Wheelbase	106.9 in.
Overall length	188.8 in.
Overall width	70.3 in.
Overall height	57.3 in.
Curb weight	3,250 lb.
Interior Dimensions	
Seating capacity	5
Head room	F:40/R:37.6 in.
Leg room	F:42.1/R:37.9 in.
Cargo room	14.1 cu. ft.
Engine	
Displacement	V-6 3 L.
Horsepower	200 @ 5,500 rpm
Torque, lb-ft.	195 @ 4,700 rpm
Performance	
0-60 mph, acceleration	8.2 sec.
60-0 mph, braking	132 ft.
Turning circle	36.4 ft.
EPA city/highway	20/28 mpg
Test mileage	NA
Fuel tank capacity	17.1 gal.

Ratings 150

Group	Category	Rating (1–10)
Over The Road	Acceleration	8
	Transmission	7
	Braking	5
	Steering	8
	Ride	6
	Handling	8
	Drivability	9
	Fuel Economy	6
Passenger Environment	Comfort/Conven.	8
	Interior Room	8
	Driving Position	8
	Instrumentation	9
	Controls	8
	Visibility	8
	Entry/Exit	7
	Quietness	8
	Cargo Space	7
Workmanship	Interior	8
	Exterior	7
	Value	7

Honda

Civic

New for 99

Redesigned air conditioning controls
Revised exterior lines
SiR version (coupe)

Pros

Good choice of models
Agility and driveability
Good visibility

Cons

Difficult access to rear seats
Poor soundproofing
VTEC engine hard to optimize

Equipment

Major Standard Equipment
1.6-liter I-4, manual transmission, intermittent wipers, rear defroster, tilt steering column, split-folding rear seat, AM/FM stereo, remote-control hatch release. **LX adds:** Air conditioning, power mirrors, power windows, power locks, cruise control. **EX adds:** More powerful 1.6-liter I-4, 4-wheel antilock brakes, power moonroof, remote keyless entry. **Major Options:** Automatic transmission, continuously variable transmission, 4-wheel antilock brakes.

Stud value

Although its closest Asian rivals (the Mazda Protege and Toyota Corolla) were recently revamped, the Civic remains the uncontested standard in this category.

Specifications of Test Vehicle

Model: Civic EX

Exterior Dimensions	
Wheelbase	103.2 in.
Overall length	175.1 in.
Overall width	67.1 in.
Overall height	54.7 in.
Curb weight	2,500 lb.
Interior dimensions	
Seating capacity	5
Head room	F:38.2/R:36.2 in.
Leg room	F:42.7/R:34.1 in.
Cargo volume	11.9 cu. ft.
Engine	
Displacement	I-4 1.6 L.
Horsepower	127 @ 6,600 rpm
Torque, lb-ft.	107 @ 5,500 rpm
Performance	
0-60 mph, acceleration	9.1 sec.
60-0 mph, braking	125 ft.
Turning circle	32.8 ft.
EPA city/highway	30/35 mpg
Test mileage	29 mpg
Fuel tank capacity	11.9 gal.

After all, it has established itself as the most versatile model of its group, offering consumers an embarrassment of choices when it comes to equipment and body configurations. In short, Honda's sweep is wide and by redesigning its exterior styling, the builder fully and firmly intends to make consumers forget that the Civic isn't young anymore.

Regardless of the body choice, access to the rear of a Civic is a problem. Once you're inside, though, front and rear (60/40 foldown) reward your efforts with sufficient comfort in front and respectable comfort in the back. The ideal driving position is easy to find (the steering wheel and seat are both height-adjustable) and the Civic's excellent front and rear visibility are reassuring. However, instrumentation is meager and thin soundproofing panels let plenty of noise inside. But still, the Civic has made a significant step forward when it comes to heating and defrosting by offering controls that are even easier to use. Too bad the fan is still so noisy.

This Honda's biggest drawing card is its ride. Stable and easy to maneuver, the Civic has lost none of its proverbial agility and its front end grips the asphalt stubbornly despite its puny tires. To whip up your enthusiasm even more, note that the Civic's brakes are very efficient and good at resisting overheating.

Under the hood, the 1.6-liter four-cylinder leaves us wishing for more. True, the pedal stroke creates the impression that acceleration is a good deal more powerful than it really is; but pickup, notably in the lower rpm range, is capable of no such subterfuge.

To counter this temporary anemia, you'd better learn how to use the gearshift lever, provided, of course, that your model has a manual transmission.

As for the VTEC engine, under normal traffic conditions it's hard to use it to its full potential.

Uncommonly talented, the Civic is a sensible choice in this category. **E.L.**

Prices

$11,000
$18,000

CX 3-door $10,650
DX 3-door $12,100
DX coupe $12,580
DX sedan $12,735
HX coupe $13,400
LX sedan $14,750
EX coupe $15,520
EX sedan $16,480

Warranty

(years/miles)

Bumper-to-Bumper 3/36,000

Powertrain 3/36,000

Rust-through 5/Unlimited

Other to Consider

Mazda Protege

Toyota Corolla

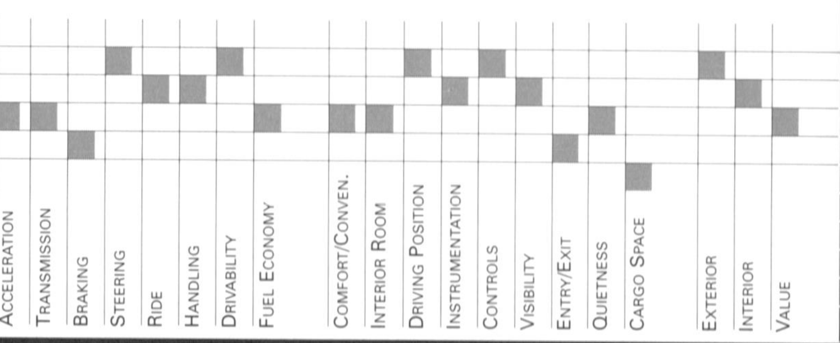

151

Honda

CR-V

New for 99

More engine power

Pros

Engine power
Good cockpit design
Efficient transmissions

Cons

Minimal soundproofing
Limited off-road capabilities
Unresponsive steering system

Equipment

Major Standard Equipment: 2.0 liter 4-cylinder engine, 5-speed manual transmission; 2-wheel drive; air conditioning; AM/FM stereo; power locks, mirrors, and windows; cruise control; rear wiper; tilt wheel; split-folding rear seat; rear defogger. **LX 4WD adds:** 4-wheel drive. **EX 4WD adds:** 4-speed automatic transmission. **Major Options:** Antilock brakes with allow wheels, automatic transmission

In top shape

PRICES
$18,000
$21,000
2wd LX
$18 359
4wd LX
$18 750
4wd EX
$ 20 250

WARRANTY
(years/miles)
Bumper-to-bumper
3/36/000
Powertrain
3/36,000
Rust-through
5/Unlimited

OTHER TO CONSIDER
Subaru Forester
Suzuki Grand Vitara

By all indications you like the Honda CR-V. After all, you've made it the bestselling compact utility vehicle in the country — far ahead of the Jeep Cherokee, which isn't exactly a shabby alternative. Given consumer reaction, Honda has decided to fight to keep its popularity and has addressed the issue of the much-criticized sluggish 2.0-liter four-cylinder engine.

The doors open onto a roomy and bright passenger compartment — it could even be described as clinical. There's plenty of space in the front and the rear (two headrests). However, the air conditioning system isn't very good at getting rid of frost on the windshield and windows fog up, a flaw often found on other products of the same make. Another widespread drawback: lack of soundproofing material, which means plenty of road and tire noise. Honda should also revise its list of accessories and should add a cargo net and a curtain to keep your property safe from prying eyes.

Like Toyota's RAV4, the Honda CR-V rests on an automobile platform (the Civic's, as a matter of fact). With its light and minimally responsive steering system (surprising for a Honda), the CR-V requires a lot of course corrections given its sensitivity to crosswinds. Its suspension is good at swallowing road defects and ABS brakes ensure safe, straight-line stops. With a sporty driver at the wheel, the CR-V understeers very noticeably, but the tendency is nothing to worry about. Its all-wheel drive system consists of a hydraulic torque allocator which, in other words, means that the CR-V is a front-wheel drive as long as its front wheels don't begin to skate. As soon as they begin to slide, part of the power is directed to the rear wheels to rebalance the vehicle. Now more powerful, the 2.0-liter four-cylinder has almost the same weight / power ratio as the category's "heavyweights." And it has more torque as well, which gives it much better pick-up power without the need to keep your hand on the shifter (manual transmission) to keep speeds steady.

The CR-V is an inoffensive utility. Since the vehicle has no transfer box to select a lower gear — a very important possibility on rough terrain — it has limited off-road capabilities. **E.L.**

Specifications of Test Vehicle

Model: CR-V

Exterior Dimensions	
Wheelbase	103.2 in.
Overall length	177.6 In.
Overall width	68.9 In.
Overall height	65.9 In.
Curb weight	3164 lbs.
Interior Dimensions	
Seating capacity	5
Head room	F:40.5/R:39.2in.
Leg room	F:41.5/R:36.7in.
Cargo room	29.6 cu.ft.
Engine	
Displacement	2.0 L
Horsepower	146@5,400 rpm
Torque, lb-ft.	133@4,500 rpm
Performance	
0-60 mph, acceleration	NT
60-0 mph, braking	136 ft.
Turning circle	34.8 ft.
EPA city/highway	22/25 mpg.
Test mileage	23.0 mpg.
Fuel tank capacity	15.3 gal.

Ratings

Category	Rating	Rating
Over The Road	Acceleration	4
	Transmission	7
	Braking	4
	Steering	7
	Ride	7
	Handling	7
	Drivability	8
	Fuel Economy	5
Passenger Environment	Comfort/Conven.	7
	Interior Room	6
	Driving Position	8
	Instrumentation	7
	Controls	8
	Visibility	6
	Entry/Exit	6
	Quietness	5
	Cargo Space	10
Workmanship	Interior	6
	Exterior	8
	Value	6

132

Honda

Odyssey

New for 99

Totally redesigned with two sliding doors
More powerful V-6 engine.

Pros

Room
Entry/exit
Rear seat

Cons

Interior quality
Front seats
Spare tire

Equipment

Major Standard:
Equipment: 3.5-liter V-6 engine, 4-speed automatic transmission, antilock brakes, dual sliding doors, front and rear air conditioning, power windows and locks, AM/FM/cassette audio system, cruise control, **EX adds:** Alloy wheels, power sliding doors, remote entry, automatic headlights, power driver seat, automatic climate control, CD player, steering wheel-mounted audio controls.
Major Options: None

Anything but odd

The name is the same, but that's where the similarity ends. Honda's 1999 Odyssey is larger, more powerful, and loaded with more convenience features than ever. It seems well-positioned to take a larger piece of the minivan market.

First on the list of upgrades is the engine. The in-line four is gone — replaced with a 3.5-liter version of the aluminum SOHC V-6 used in the Accord. Power output is 210 hp, with excellent torque characteristics, thanks to the use of Honda's VTEC system. The 4-speed automatic transmission uses "grade logic" to help it decide which gear to use in hilly terrain.

The body is longer, wider, and taller, addressing the most serious criticism of the previous model — size. Sliding doors on both sides are standard equipment — both are power-operated on the EX.

The bucket seats have firm bottom cushions that might be a little too short for some drivers. The front passenger's leg room is marginal because of restricted travel of the seat. A handy storage tray between the front seats folds down when not needed. Center-row seats can be shifted together to make a bench or separated for a walk-through area. The third-row "magic seat" folds neatly into a floor well when more cargo space is needed. The compact spare has been moved from a rear side wall to a well between the first- and second-row seats. Unfortunately, the well is not big enough to hold a conventional tire.

Entry and exit for the front and center seats is easier than a large car. The sloping hood and large glass area allow a commanding view from the driver's seat. Controls are generally well-placed, but the radio is located below the vent controls, requiring the driver to divert attention from the road. Steering wheel-mounted audio controls in the EX help alleviate this problem. Extensions on sun visors only serve to cover up the rear-view mirror.

Out on the highway, the Odyssey offers no surprises. The ride is firm enough that minor pavement irregularities are felt inside. The trade-off is reasonably good handling — better than most of the competition. Even with the new engine, acceleration is not especially good. Getting Odyssey's 4300 pounds up to 60 mph takes a full 10 seconds. It feels better than it is. The standard antilock brakes have good pedal feel and gave us a panic stopping distance from 60 mph of 135 feet. Fit and finish on our test vehicle's exterior met Honda's high standards. Inside was another story. Several plastic panels had rough edges and were misaligned. And we never found the rattle coming from somewhere in the back.

Is Honda ready to take the minivan crown from Chrysler? Perhaps not yet.
D.V.S.

Specifications of Test Vehicle

Model: Odyssey

Exterior Dimensions	
Wheelbase	118.1 in.
Overall length	201.2 in.
Overall width	75.6 in.
Overall height	69.7 in.
Curb weight	4288 lbs.
Interior Dimensions	
Seating capacity	7
Head room	F: 41.2/C: 40.0/R: 38.9 in.
Leg room	F: 41.0/C: 40.0/R: 38.1 in.
Cargo room	25.1 cu.ft.
Engine	
Displacement	3.5L V-6
Horsepower	210@5200 rpm
Torque, lb-ft.	229@4300 rpm
Performance	
0-60 mph, acceleration	10.0 sec.
60-0 mph, braking	135 ft.
Turning circle	37.7 ft.
EPA city/highway	18/26 mpg.
Test mileage	21.5
Fuel tank capacity	20.0 gal.

Prices

$23,000
$26,000

LX 4-door minivan
$23,810

EX 4-door minivan
$25,800

Warranty

(years/miles)

Bumper-to-bumper
3/36,000

Powertrain
3/36,000

Rust-through
5/Unlimited

Other to Consider

Ford Windstar

Toyota Sienna

Ratings

Group	Category	Rating (1–10)
Over The Road	Acceleration	6
	Transmission	8
	Braking	5
	Steering	9
	Ride	7
	Handling	8
	Drivability	8
	Fuel Economy	5
Passenger Environment	Comfort/Conven.	8
	Interior Room	10
	Driving Position	8
	Instrumentation	8
	Controls	7
	Visibility	8
	Entry/Exit	9
	Quietness	9
	Cargo Space	10
Workmanship	Interior	7
	Exterior	8
	Value	9

Honda Passport

New for 99

No changes

Pros

Cargo space
Room
Comfort

Cons

Fuel economy
Handling
Braking

Equipment

Major Standard Equipment: 3.2-liter V-6, manual transmission, 4-wheel antilock brakes, variable-assist power steering, air conditioning, split-folding rear seat, variable-intermittent wipers, rear wiper and washer, rear defroster, power windows, power locks, power heated mirrors, tilt steering column, cruise control.
EX adds: Power moonroof, remote keyless entry, theft-alarm system, privacy glass, larger tires, aluminum wheels.
Major Options: Automatic transmission, part-time 4-wheel drive, limited-slip differential, larger tires, aluminum wheels.

Is a copy better than the original?

PRICES
$23,000
$30,000
LX 4-door truck wagon
$22,700
EX 4-door truck wagon
$23,850

WARRANTY
(years/miles)
Bumper-to-bumper
3,36,000
Powertrain
3/36,000
Rust-through
5/unlimited

OTHER TO CONSIDER
Nissan Pathfinder
Toyota 4Runner

Not all sport-utility vehicles are what they seem to be. The Honda Passport, for example, is really an Isuzu Rodeo under a different name. True Hondaphiles who trust the Honda name alone should realize that from the very first.

Like many other automakers, Honda bypassed the time-consuming and expensive effort of designing a totally new vehicle for the booming SUV market. Instead, it had Isuzu clone the successful Rodeo and called it Passport.

As an SUV, the Passport comes as a nicely equipped LX and a better-equipped EX. Both can have 2- or 4-wheel drive. An optional shift-on-the-fly arrangement lets you to engage and disengage 4WD while the vehicle is moving, making it easier to drive on all road surfaces and in all weather conditions. All Passports have Isuzu's 3.2-liter, 24-valve, 190-horsepower V-6, even though Honda has a similar engine.

The latest version of the Passport finally has 4-wheel antilock brakes and air conditioning as standard equipment. This non-Honda is also the only vehicle with a Honda nameplate that has true variable-assist power steering.

Inside, the Passport's up-to-date instrument panel greets you when you climb into the driver's seat. The cabin is surprisingly roomy, front and back, but three adults sit shoulder to shoulder in the rear seat. A good view of the road extends ahead, but wide rear roof pillars and the outside rear-mounted spare tire restrict visibility to the back. Getting in means stepping up high, typical of SUVs; a narrow rear door opening further complicates rear-seat entry. For rear loading, the rear window lifts up and the tailgate portion opens like a door.

On the road, the Passport is pleasant but undistinguished. As quiet and smooth as the V-6 is, it nevertheless works hard to move the heavy 4WD Passport. That takes a toll on acceleration and fuel economy. Getting to 60 mph from a standing start took a leisurely 10-plus seconds for us. Don't expect more than about 17 mpg under the best of conditions.

The ride is comfy; this SUV handles most bumps with impressive resilience. Rigid construction makes the Passport feel solid. However, handling is another matter. This is no sports car. The soft suspension allows considerable body roll on turns, and we felt uneasy in tight corners and evasive maneuvers. In our emergency stopping test, the Passport took a disappointing 136 feet to stop from 60 mph.

With Isuzu's excellent reputation for quality trucks, Honda had good reason to choose the Rodeo as the donor from which to clone the Passport. But consider differences in price and warranty before choosing between the two. The Rodeo is not only less expensive, but also has longer powertrain and rust-through coverage.
D.V.S.

Specifications of Test Vehicle

Model: Passport LX

Exterior Dimensions	
Wheelbase	106.4 in.
Overall length	177.4 in.
Overall width	70.4 in.
Overall height	68.5 in.
Curb weight	4,000 lb.
Interior Dimensions	
Seating capacity	5
Head room	F:38.9:/R:38.3 in.
Leg room	F:42.1/R:35 in.
Cargo volume	33 cu. ft.
Engine	
Displacement	V-6 3.2 L.
Horsepower	205 @ 5,400 rpm
Torque, lb-ft.	214 @ 3,000 rpm
Performance	
0-60 mph, acceleration	10.3 sec.
60-0 mph, braking	136 ft.
Turning circle	38.4 ft.
EPA city/highway	16/20 mpg
Test mileage	17 mpg
Fuel tank capacity	21.1 gal.

Ratings
139

Group	Category	Rating
Over The Road	Acceleration	6
	Transmission	7
	Braking	4
	Steering	7
	Ride	7
	Handling	6
	Drivability	8
	Fuel Economy	4
Passenger Environment	Comfort/Conven.	8
	Interior Room	8
	Driving Position	7
	Instrumentation	8
	Controls	7
	Visibility	7
	Entry/Exit	6
	Quietness	7
	Cargo Space	10
Workmanship	Interior	8
	Exterior	8
	Value	6

Honda Prelude

New for 99
No major changes

Pros
Sporty handling
Smooth transmissions
Excellent driving position

Cons
Engine performance in low and average rpm range
Strictly symbolic rear seats
Nonadjustable front seat belts

Equipment
Major Standard Equipment: 2.2-liter I-4, manual transmission, 4-wheel antilock disc brakes, air conditioning, variable-intermittent wipers, rear defroster, theft-deterrent system, AM/FM/CD stereo, power windows, power locks, power mirrors, power moonroof, folding rear seat, cruise control, tilt steering column, remote-control decklid release, aluminum wheels. **Type SH adds:** Automatic understeer compensation system.
Major Options: Semi-automatic transmission.

A shrinking market

Honda's Prelude coupe is back and virtually unchanged for 1999. However, it was entirely revamped only two years ago and its builder managed to keep its sporty characteristics intact without giving it the often excessive comfort of "fat cat" cars. In other words, the Prelude remains a car that's worth driving, although its styling is still rather controversial. Outsized headlamps and a very ordinary rear-end design concept aren't considered as assets by everyone, even some of the make's biggest fans.

Changes aren't very obvious: the Prelude has the same conventional-looking dashboard, of course, but you have to admit that it's well designed. Instrumentation is much easier to read than it was in cars of the previous generation, which seemed to have been designed specifically with Trekkies in mind. Front seats are inviting, but rear passengers will have a hard time climbing aboard; even so, two adults can ride in the back provided the outing isn't for too long a distance. Design oversights include thick roof pillars that do nothing to help visibility and front seat belts that aren't height adjustable.

All Preludes have to make do with the same four-cylinder engine, but it can be paired with one of two transmissions: a five-speed manual or an automatic that's somewhere between a Porsche Tiptronic and a Chrysler Autostick. A small suggestion for Honda: Could you inverse the gear shifting movement so that reversing requires moving the lever backward, not forward? On another note, the engine's 195 horses are noticeable at relatively high rpm levels, which has a negative effect on acceleration and pick-up at lower and average rpm levels.

Two types of suspensions are also available on this automobile, the standard and the hydraulically controlled ATTS, which uses components with more rigidity and is designed to transmit torque to the front wheels in such a way as to keep traction under control. The ATTS's qualities are not as positive if you like a sporty driving style (not to mention that the system can't be deactivated), but it shows off its true worth as soon as you encounter wet or snow-covered road surfaces.

An attractive car with a good engine and remarkable road stability, the Prelude is unfortunately part of a market segment that is less and less popular (the sports coupe category) and its fairly hefty price scares away its potential buyers, the younger crowd. **E.L.**

Specifications of Test Vehicle

Model: Prelude Type SH

Exterior Dimensions	
Wheelbase	101.8 in.
Overall length	178 in.
Overall width	69 in.
Overall height	51.8 in.
Curb weight	3,050 lb.
Interior Dimensions	
Seating capacity	4
Head room	F:37.9/R:35.3 in.
Leg room	F:43/R:28.1 in.
Cargo volume	8.7 cu. ft.
Engine	
Displacement	I-4 2.2 L.
Horsepower	195 @ 7,000 rpm
Torque, lb-ft.	156 @ 5,250 rpm
Performance	
0-60 mph, acceleration	7 sec.
60-0 mph, braking	NA
Turning circle	37.4 ft.
EPA city/highway	23/27 mpg
Test mileage	22 mpg
Fuel tank capacity	15.9 gal.

PRICES
$23,000
$26,000
Coupe
$23,300
Type SH 2-door sport coupe
$25,800

WARRANTY
(years/miles)
Bumper-to-bumper
3/36,000
Powertrain
3/36,000
Rust-through
5/unlimited

OTHER TO CONSIDER
Mercury Cougar
Toyota Celica

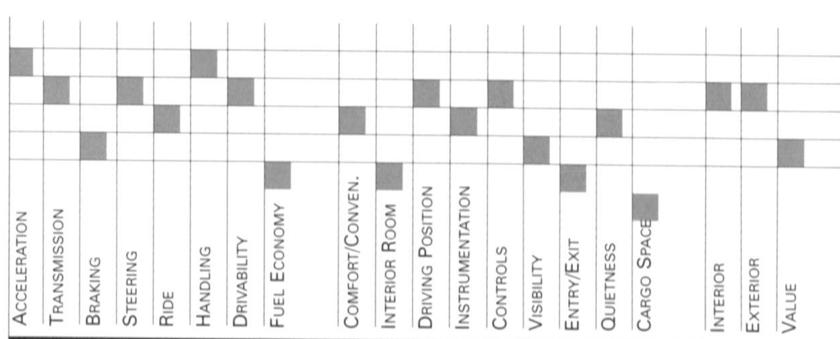

Ratings
139

Hyundai Accent

New for 99

New exterior colors

Pros

Reliability
Fuel economy
Energetic engine

Cons

Long options list
Model scheduled for withdrawal
Balky manual transmission

Equipement

Major Standard Equipment: 1.5-liter I-4, manual transmission, unassisted steering, intermittent wipers, AM/FM/cassette stereo, rear defroster, folding rear seat. **GS adds:** Remote-control hatch release, split-folding rear seat, driver's-seat lumbar adjustment, rear wiper and washer, larger tires. **GSi adds:** AM/FM stereo, power windows, power mirrors, sports suspension, larger tires, aluminum wheels.
Major Options: Automatic transmission, 4-wheel antilock brakes, air conditioning, AM/FM/cassette stereo, AM/FM/CD stereo, moonroof.

PRICES
$9,000
$13,000

L 2-door hatchback
$9,079

GS 2-door hatchback
NA

GL sedan
$10,299

GSi 2-door hatchback
NA

WARRANTY
(years/miles)

Bumper-to-bumper
3/36,000

Powertrain
5/60,000

Rust-through
5/100,000

OTHER TO CONSIDER

Daewoo Lanos

Kia Sephia

A bargain?

If you have approximately $12,000 to spend on a new car, the Hyundai Accent is sure to turn up on your shopping list along with the Chevrolet Metro, Suzuki Swift, and other models of the same ilk.

On the surface, this Hyundai model has a lot going for it (roomy interior, four-cylinder engine). But take a closer look. Ask for power steering, air conditioning or an automatic transmission, none of which is standard on the base version, and you'll pay more, of course. Then again, if you choose the more expensive GL, you'll get all of these goodies as part of standard equipment.

Just to prove that appearances can be deceiving, the sedan and hatchback models have almost identical dimensions and the same wheelbase, so both vehicles have almost the same amount of usable space for passengers. The hatchback version's cargo area is one-third bigger than the sedan's, and the advantage of a wider opening that makes loading easier. Inside, there's plenty of room for such a small car and standard equipment includes a fold-down rear seat, a rear windshield defroster, a center console, and intermittent wipers. But some major accessories, like the radio, power steering system, and air bags, are not available on base models. As for overall interior design, buyers will have to like plastic (and not always the best kind) and the odor that permeates the passenger compartment as a result.

Under the hood of this subcompact is a 1.5-liter four-cylinder engine that has plenty of pep. Its 92 horses never run out of steam and they help the Accent look good when compared to its rivals. Equally surprising is the fact that the engine has more affinity for the automatic transmission than it does for its manual alternative, whose higher gear ratio and deficient synchronization take away from the model's driveability and make the ride far from smooth.

Despite skinny original tires (155/80R-13), the Accent handles well and its independent suspension lets it take tight corners problem-free and gobble up road irregularities with remarkable aplomb. But such tires do have their limitations, so we recommend the 175/70R-13 alternative available as an option on the GL. The manual transmission has a fairly tall gear ratio that takes something away from this model's ride and exposes passengers to a few fits and starts. Note that the ABS system is available only on GL versions.

The Accent is agile, fun to drive, and economical, but beware of its appealing base price, which excludes the possibility of enjoying a number of good features. **E.L.**

Specifications of Test Vehicle

Model: Accent GL

Exterior Dimensions	
Wheelbase	94.5 in.
Overall length	162.1 in.
Overall width	63.8 in.
Overall height	54.9 in.
Curb weight	2,100 lb.
Interior Dimensions	
Seating capacity	4
Head room	F:38.7/R:37.8 in.
Leg room	F:42.6/R:32.7 in.
Cargo volume	10.7 cu. ft.
Engine	
Displacement	I-4 1.5 L.
Horsepower	92 @ 5,500 rpm
Torque, lb-ft.	97 @ 4,000 rpm
Performance	
0-60 mph, acceleration	11.2 sec
60-0 mph, braking	139 ft.
Turning circle	31.8 ft.
EPA city/highway	28/36 mpg
Test mileage	32 mpg
Fuel tank capacity	11.9 gal.

Ratings **135**

Category	Rating	Score (out of 10)
Over The Road	Acceleration	5
	Transmission	7
	Braking	4
	Steering	8
	Ride	7
	Handling	8
	Drivability	8
	Fuel Economy	8
Passenger Environment	Comfort/Conven.	7
	Interior Room	7
	Driving Position	7
	Instrumentation	7
	Controls	5
	Visibility	8
	Entry/Exit	7
	Quietness	6
	Cargo Space	5
Workmanship	Interior	7
	Exterior	6
	Value	8

Hyundai

Elantra

New for 99

2.0-liter engine
Redesigned grille

Pros

Engine performance
Model range
Road stability

Cons

Rough transmissions
Uncomfortable seats
Access to rear

Equipement

Major Standard Equipment: 2.0-liter I-4, manual transmission, variable-assist power steering, variable-intermittent wipers, tilt steering column, rear defroster, AM/FM/cassette stereo, remote-control decklid release.
GLS adds: 4-wheel disk brakes, power locks, tachometer, power mirrors, split-folding rear seat, power windows, larger tires.
Major Options: Automatic transmission, 4-wheel antilock brakes, air conditioning, cruise control, power moonroof, aluminum wheels.

Something to watch

With the Elantra, Hyundai has silenced those who blamed it for building only cheap models. This time out, quality is along for the ride. With better materials and finer finishing, the Elantra is looking good. And into the bargain, its lines are attractive and it comes in two versions: sedan and wagon.

For 1999, the Korean builder has focused its efforts on the passenger compartment, making life aboard the Elantra a more pleasant experience, and has also introduced a 140-hp 2.0-liter four-cylinder engine and a new grille designed to make a statement.

The interior sports a two-tone color scheme and rounded and contemporary styling give the Elantra charm, though it comes with a price tag that's very different from those that Hyundai has attached to its models in the past. Access to front seats poses no problem, but rear-seat passengers have to cope with narrow doors. Once inside everyone has a decent amount of head room and leg room and front seats can be adjusted vertically in addition to offering good lateral support even though their upholstery is particularly stiff, not pleasant to the touch and not very comfortable over long distances. In the wagon the rear seats fold down to create a perfectly flat cargo space, though they don't have headrests. Dual air bags are optional on the GL version.

Reliable road stability, good visibility, energetic engines, a docile steering system and a tight turning radius contribute to the Elantra's driveability. The same goes for the four-speed automatic transmission, which shifts only very reluctantly. The comfortable level once it reaches cruising speed. The 2.0-liter is the best choice for drivers who want the automatic transmission.

The suspension is excellent at compensating for road irregularities and only major potholes can shake its composure. Four disc brakes and an ABS system are available only on the GLS version, which results in safe and straight stopping.

Less expensive than other imports in its category, fun to drive, available in a very practical wagon version — no question: the Elantra has a number of good qualities. **E.L.**

Specifications of Test Vehicle

Model: Elantra

Exterior Dimensions	
Wheelbase	100.4 in.
Overall length	174 in.
Overall width	66.9 in.
Overall height	54.9 in.
Curb weight	2,500 lb.
Interior Dimensions	
Seating capacity	5
Head room	F:38.6/R:37.6 in.
Leg room	F:43.2/R:34.6 in.
Cargo volume	11.9 cu. ft.
Engine	
Displacement	I-4 2.0 L.
Horsepower	140 @ 6,000 rpm
Torque, lb-ft.	133 @ 4,800 rpm
Performance	
0-60 mph, acceleration	10.5 sec.
60-0 mph, braking	146 ft.
Turning circle	32.5 ft.
EPA city/highway	22/30 mpg
Test mileage	25 mpg
Fuel tank capacity	14.5 gal.

PRICES
$11,000
$17,000
Sedan $11,499
4-door wagon NA
GLS sedan $12,549
GLS 4-door wagon $13,399

WARRANTY (years/miles)
Bumper-to-bumper 3/36,000
Powertrain 5/60,000
Rust-through 5/100,000

OTHER TO CONSIDER
Daewo Nubira
Nissan Sentra

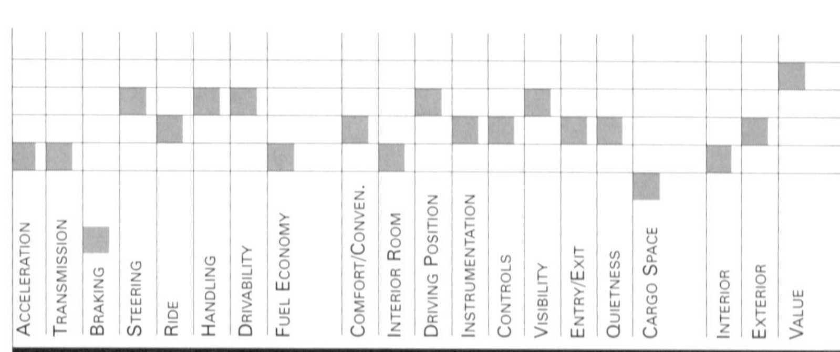

10 9 8 7 6 5 4 3 2 1

Ratings 136

Hyundai Sonata

New for 99

Redesigned body and interior, including side air bags. Two new engines and revised suspension.

Pros

Safety features
Warranty
Ride

Cons

Interior finish
Braking distance

Equipment

Major Standard Equipment: 2.4 liter I-4 engine, 5-speed manual transmission, air conditioning, AM/FM/cassette audio system, power windows/mirrors/locks, side air bags with passenger-presence detector system. **GLS adds:** 2.5 liter V-6, better audio system, cruise control, deluxe cloth interior, 4-wheel disc brakes, better suspension, alloy wheels.
Major Options: 4-speed automatic transmission, leather seats, power driver seat, traction control, antilock brakes, moonroof.

New ambitions

PRICES
$15,000
$19,000
GL sedan
$14,999
GLS sedan
$16,999

WARRANTY
Bumper-to-bumper
5/60,000
Powertrain
10/100,000
Rust-through
5/100,000

OTHER TO CONSIDER
Ford Contour
Oldsmobile Alero

Hyundai's Sonata has been completely redesigned for 1999, to make it a more effective player in the very competitive field of mid-size family sedans.

Sonata is available only as a sedan in two trim levels, base and GLS. The base model is surprisingly well-equipped with comfort and safety features. The main attractions of the GLS are its new V-6 engine, as well as better brakes, suspension, interior, and outside appearance.

Standard on the base model is a 2.4-liter, 149 hp, 4-cylinder engine. The GLS gets a 2.5 liter, 170 hp V-6. A 5-speed manual transmission is standard equipment. Two 4-speed automatics are available — the premium version has adaptive shift control that adjusts shift points to driving style. The GLS gets 4-wheel disc brakes, but ABS and traction control are still options. Gas-pressurized shock absorbers are part of the upgraded suspension on the GLS.

Sonata's interior can best be described as no-nonsense. Even in the GLS, the plastic trim panels don't have a soft touch. The cloth seats and trim are attractive and not overdone, the imitation wood trim on the instrument panel seems unnecessary for a car in this price range. Front seats have adequately large bottom cushions and offer good support and comfort. Leg, head, and shoulder room up front is generous. Rear seats are not as comfortable, and leg room is just adequate. Entry and exit for the front is fine, but rear access is a little restricted by a smaller door opening. Instruments and controls are simple and functional. The audio controls are thoughtfully located above those for ventilation. Visibility is fine in all directions — the standard power side mirrors are sure to be appreciated. Cargo space is just average with a slightly high liftover. The GLS has good highway manners. The ride is not firm, just a little on the soft side to make it more suitable for the U.S. market, according to Hyundai designers. Handling is just what mid-size family sedan owners will expect. Expect some body roll and understeer in tight corners, with no surprises. Steering is light and accurate — just right for the intended market.

The new V-6 gives Sonata a very comfortable feel. There is plenty of power to merge smoothly into freeway traffic. The engine gets a little noisy when pushed to the limit, but under ordinary circumstances, it's smooth and quiet. Hyundai is determined to improve the image of its products, and the new warranty coverage proves the company is serious. However, Hyundai still needs to work on fit and finish, especially inside. Out test car showed several defects in the fit of instrument panel sections. Hyundai continues to improve its products. A test drive will be a convincing experience. If you plan to drive a new Sonata forever, it should be economical family transportation. However, until Hyundai improves its reputation, resale after a few years could be a shocking experience. **D.V.S.**

Specifications of Test Vehicle

Model: Sonata GL

Exterior Dimensions	
Wheelbase	106.3 in.
Overall length	185.4 In.
Overall width	71.6 In.
Overall height	55.5 In.
Curb weight	3100 lbs.
Interior Dimensions	
Seating capacity	
Head room	F: 39.3/R: 37.6 in.
Leg room	F: 43.3/R: 36.2 in.
Cargo room	13.2 cu.ft.
Engine	
Displacement	2.5 L V-6
Horsepower	170@6000 rpm
Torque, lb-ft.	166@4000 rpm
Performance	
0-60 mph, acceleration	8.5 sec.
60-0 mph, braking	135 ft.
Turning circle	NA
EPA city/highway	20/28 mpg.
Test mileage	NA
Fuel tank capacity	17.2 gal.

Ratings 148

Category	Rating (1–10)
Over The Road	
Acceleration	8
Transmission	8
Braking	5
Steering	8
Ride	8
Handling	8
Drivability	8
Fuel Economy	5
Passenger Environment	
Comfort/Conven.	8
Interior Room	8
Driving Position	8
Instrumentation	7
Controls	8
Visibility	8
Entry/Exit	8
Quietness	8
Cargo Space	6
Workmanship	
Interior	6
Exterior	7
Value	8

Hyundai

Tiburon

New for 99

No changes

Pros

Nice lines
Competitive price
Astounding road stability

Cons

Stubborn manual transmission
Limited braking power
Perceived as a "bargain" make

Equipment

Major Standard Equipment: 2-liter I-4, manual transmission, variable-intermittent wipers, rear defroster, power windows, AM/FM/cassette stereo, split-folding rear seat, cargo cover. **FX adds:** 4-wheel disc brakes, rear washer and wiper, power locks, power mirrors, aluminum wheels. **Major Options:** Automatic transmission, 4-wheel antilock brakes, air conditioning, AM/FM/CD/cassette stereo, cruise control, leather upholstery, power moonroof, larger aluminum wheels, remote keyless entry.

Bite me!

It's a well-known fact: success is fleeting in the wonderful world of sports cars. Just ask Hyundai, which only two years ago launched the Tiburon, an affordable and very nice-looking sports model. After coming out with great fanfare, today it's just one of many products, and sports car lovers seem to be looking in rival showrooms. The Tiburon is back for this year with no changes whatsoever, unless you believe the rumor that a convertible is in the offing.

A window on technology and styling, the Tiburon has certainly contributed to overcoming the "cheap" image that has stuck to Hyundai since it first came to North America. Indeed, a passenger compartment embellished with leather seating is a beautiful thing. But it would be even more so if Hyundai had found it in its heart to also offer heated seats. At the same time there's an unfortunate lack of storage space, soundproofing is very limited, and engine noise is a problem in the high-rpm range, and some plastic materials are of very mediocre quality. On the other hand, kudos to the instrumentation and the sensible positioning of main controls in the driver's immediate environment, reminiscent of what could be found on the defunct Talon (Eagle). A brief word about the trunk: except for a high sill, it's capacity is impressive for this category.

Driving under the hood with the Tiburon signature is an Alpha 2.0-liter four-cylinder, an in-house design Hyundai likes to repeat, although it is strongly inspired by a creation from Mitsubishi, which served as a role model for a number of years. Regardless, the 2.0 puts a lot of energy into powering the Tiburon, as witnessed by its loud growl. The same kind of praise isn't earned by the manual transmission, although its ratio is good, shifting takes a firm hand, and the lever lacks precision. On the up side, the Tiburon has a very well-calibrated suspension (Porsche's engineering department got involved) and it keeps roll under tight control. The precise and responsive steering system means that drivers have to be careful where they aim the Tiburon. Brakes resist heating fairly well and braking power is adequate, but nothing more.

E.L.

Specifications of Test Vehicle

Model: Hyundai Tiburon FX

Exterior Dimensions	
Wheelbase	97.4 in.
Overall length	170.9 in.
Overall width	68.1 in.
Overall height	51.3 in.
Curb weight	2,600 lb.
Interior Dimensions	
Seating capacity	4
Head room	F:38/R:34.4 in.
Leg room	F:43.1/R:29.9 in.
Cargo volume	12.8 cu. ft.
Engine	
Displacement	I-4 2 L.
Horsepower	140 @ 6,000 rpm
Torque, lb-ft.	133 @ 4,800 rpm
Performance	
0-60 mph, acceleration	9.1 sec.
60-0 mph, braking	132 ft.
Turning circle	34.1 ft.
EPA city/highway	22/29 mpg
Test mileage	24 mpg
Fuel tank capacity	14.5 gal.

Prices

$14,000
$18,000

3-door
$13,599

FX 3-door
$14,899

Warranty

(years/miles)

Bumper-to-bumper
3/36,000

Powertrain
5/60,000

Rust-through
5/100,000

Other to Consider

Mercury Cougar

Acura Integra

Group	Category	Rating
Over The Road	Acceleration	7
	Transmission	8
	Braking	5
	Steering	8
	Ride	7
	Handling	8
	Drivability	8
	Fuel Economy	6
Passenger Environment	Comfort/Conven.	7
	Interior Room	6
	Driving Position	8
	Instrumentation	7
	Controls	7
	Visibility	6
	Entry/Exit	6
	Quietness	7
	Cargo Space	6
Workmanship	Interior	8
	Exterior	8
	Value	7

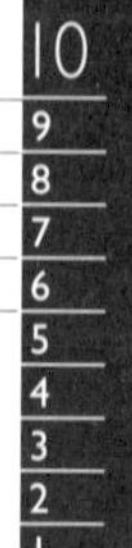

Ratings
140

Infiniti G20

new MODEL

New for 99

New body and interior design
Side air bags.

Pros

Safety features
Sporty personality
Handling

Cons

Ride
Ordinary styling
Engine

Equipment

Major Standard Equipment:
G20: 2.0 liter I-4 engine, 5-speed manual transmission, antilock brakes, air conditioning, cloth interior, split fold-down rear seat, power windows and locks, remote keyless entry, tilt wheel, Bose AM/FM/cassette/CD audio system, cruise control. **Touring Adds:** Low-profile tires, fog lights, automatic climate control, rear spoiler. **Major Options:** 4-speed automatic transmission, leather interior, power sunroof, heated seats.

Unfulfilled expectations

After a three-year hiatus, the Infinity G20 returns to the marketplace with a new body, a freshened interior, a slightly refined powertrain, and a new suspension in the rear. Intended to be a near-luxury sedan, the G20 misses the mark in several important ways.

The standard G20 comes pretty much fully loaded. The sportier G20t has low-profile tires and a viscous limited-slip differential. Both models have only one engine, a 2.0-liter 4-cylinder carryover, tweaked to make it smoother and quieter. You can choose either a 5-speed manual or a 4-speed automatic transmission. The interior is tastefully designed. Materials look upscale, except for the cloth seats. Leather gives the G20 a more appropriate look and feel. Front seats are well-shaped and supportive, with adjustment for lower cushion tilt. The rear seat is firm and capable of hauling three adults — at least for short trips. Entry and exit are reasonably good, even in back. A sloping hood and large glass area make visibility fine in all

Counterpoint

Some expectations go unfulfilled. For example, the first-generation G20 failed to charm the public. At the time, people were quick to say it was too expensive, too small, not powerful enough, or not well-known enough as an excuse to turn a blind eye to its many exciting qualities. Consumers handed down their verdict, but did Infiniti listen? After a three-year absence, Nissan's prestige make has reintroduced the G20 to its showrooms, in a second-generation version that has indeed been improved, but not necessarily where improvements were most urgent.

As soon as you open this model's doors, you're bound to have mixed feelings. On the one hand, you'll immediately appreciate the impeccable manufacturing quality. On the other, you'll immediately notice the inferior quality of some materials and their overly strong resemblance (old-fashioned and drab) to current Nissan products. And this is no haphazard occurrence, since in Europe the G20 goes by its real name: the Nissan Primera.

To spark our imagination, Infiniti readily reminds consumers that the G20 is one of the top cars when it comes to road stability. The G20 handles consistently and predictably and shows good balance. And it's more comfortable as well. But only when you adopt a sporty driving style can you truly appreciate the difference between the base and Touring versions. The base has 15-inch wheels with less gripping power, while the Touring features high-performance tires and a limited slip differential that improves cornering capabilities.

While the chassis quality is unquestionable, this model's powertrain doesn't have the power it needs to capitalize on it, saddled as it is with the 2.0-liter four-cylinder used on the previous version. While it doesn't provide electrifying performance, the 2.0-liter is recognized for its sturdiness and responsiveness, not to mention its willingness to push until it reaches its outer limits. To bring power to the front drive wheels, the G20 uses an imprecise manual transmission or a soporific four-speed automatic. Since it's always wise to choose the lesser of two evils, my preference goes to the manual.

E.L.

directions except to the rear, where the rear spoiler (on the G20t only) blocks the view. Cargo space is just average, but the 60/40 rear seat folds down to make more room there. An especially good safety feature is the center 3-point seat belt in the rear.

The instrument panel has a fresh new design that places everything about an inch closer to the driver than before. Audio and vent controls are within easy reach. Well-proportioned instruments have white-on-black letters for easy reading. Other controls are logically placed and easy to use. However, a drink in the cupholder, just ahead of the shift lever, gets in the way when shifting.

On the road, the G20 is a mixture of fun and disappointment. This car simply needs more power if Nissan ever expects it to be a success. Performance around town is perfectly adequate, but the power to merge into high-speed traffic is lacking. Acceleration to 60 mph takes a full 10 seconds. Either transmission is pleasant to drive, but the manual version seems to get the most out of the engine.

Handling is the G20's strong suit. Even the base model handles tight turns and dips without a sign of stress or strain. The touring suspension in the G20t makes handling even better, if the firmer ride can be tolerated. Steering is light and accurate without a hint of torque steer — perhaps because of the lack of engine power. The brakes have good pedal feel and delivered about average emergency stopping performance.

Not everyone wants a powerhouse under the hood, but the competition has done very well by making performance an important part of their packages. Price-conscious shoppers who find offerings by Audi, BMW, and Mercedes too expensive might want to look at the G20 as an alternative. Then again, they might not.

D.V.S.

Specifications of Test Vehicle

Model: G20 Touring

Exterior Dimensions	
Wheelbase	102.4 in.
Overall length	177.5 in.
Overall width	66.7 in.
Overall height	55.1 in.
Curb weight	2936 lbs.
Interior Dimensions	
Seating capacity	5
Head room	F: 40.0/R:36.8 in.
Leg room	F: 41.5/R:34.6 in.
Cargo room	13.5 cu.ft.
Engine	
Displacement	2.0L I-6
Horsepower	140@6400 rpm
Torque, lb-ft.	132@4800 rpm
Performance	
0-60 mph, acceleration	10.0 sec.
60-0 mph, braking	133 ft.
Turning circle	37.4 ft.
EPA city/highway	23/31 mpg.
Test mileage	24.7
Fuel tank capacity	15.9 gal.

PRICES

$21,000
$28,000

Standard Model 5-Speed Manual
$21,490

Standard Model 4-Speed Automatic
$22,290

Touring Model 5-Speed Manual
$22,990

Touring Model 4-Speed Automatic
$23,790

WARRANTY

Bumper-to-bumper
4/60,000

Powertrain
6/70,000

Rust-through
7/Unlimited

OTHER TO CONSIDER

Audi A4 Turbo

Mazda Millenia

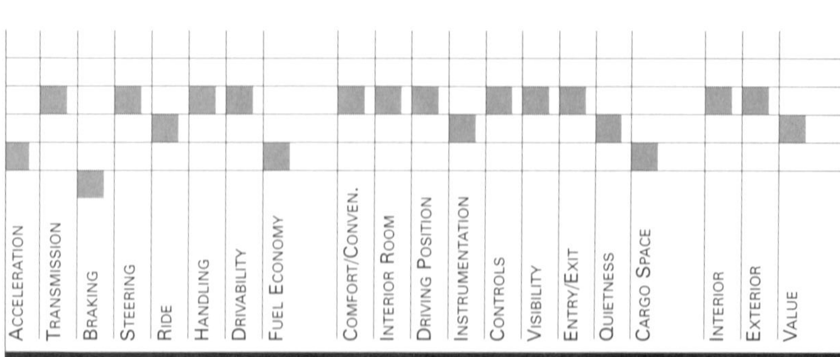

Ratings

147

Infiniti | I30

New for 99

Standard traction control
Standard antitheft system
Front side air bags

Pros

Efficient V-6
Exemplary road stability (Touring)
Finishing and equipment

Cons

A dressed-up Maxima
Light steering system (regular version)
Some controls

Equipment

Major Standard Equipment: 3-liter V-6, 4-wheel antilock disc brakes, air conditioning, automatic temperature control, AM/FM/CD/cassette stereo, power windows, power seats, power locks, power mirrors, rear defroster, cruise control, tilt steering wheel, power decklid release, remote keyless entry, antitheft system. **Touring adds:** Manual transmission, sports suspension, wipers, heated seats, leather upholstery, power moonroof, automatic dimming rear-view mirror, limited slip differential, larger tires. **Major Options:** Automatic transmission, power moonroof, limited slip differential, leather upholstery, heated seats, universal garage door opener.

It's your money...

PRICES
$29,000
$34,000
Sedan $29,395
Sedan $31,695

WARRANTY
Bumper-to-bumper 4/60,000
Powertrain 6/70,000
Rust-through 7/unlimited

OTHER TO CONSIDER
Cadillac Catera
Mazda Millenia

The question I was asking this time last year: "With more detailed finishing, a more elaborate list of accessories and a few additional design details, is the I30 worth a few thousand dollars more compared to Maxima, the model it's derived from?" The answer is no. And the side air bags, traction control, and antitheft systems made available this year won't change my mind.

I've met a number of I30 owners who say that they are very satisfied with their entry-level luxury sedan. First of all, even though it looks like a Maxima, in their hearts they see it as different, with a more classically designed grille and streamlined styling. With its spoiler and magnificent alloy wheels, the Touring has a certain something that grabs and keeps your attention. And high praise goes to the make's dealers, all of whom make a point of pampering their customers. Bring in your I30 for repairs and you'll have access to a courtesy vehicle and when you return to retrieve your car, you'll find it gleamingly clean and the gas tank may have even been filled. Of course, there's a price to pay for all this, as witnessed by the I30's maintenance costs, significantly higher then the Maxima's. I know, I know, it's your money, you can spend it as you see fit.

With exemplary finishing, the I30 features four true places, designed for average-sized adults. Well-designed bucket seats provide ample support and seem to be more comfortable than the Maxima's seats. The dashboard has detailed and easy-to-read instrumentation. Most main controls are within easy reach and equipment is very detailed. Unlike the Maxima, the choice of fabrics and plastics is tasteful. And trims and inlays create a much more appealing effect.

I liked the V-6, which, while not as sophisticated as the competition's engine, is still capable of solid performance and pickup that is surprising for a 3.0-liter. And this unit is known for its sturdiness and reliability as well. Coupled with an efficient four-speed automatic transmission, its shifting is problem-free and it gets its job done smoothly, with no balking. In 1999, note that the traction control system is standard on all models. Road stability is impressive, even though Nissan rejected the idea of complex and costly independent rear suspensions. The twist-beam axle rear suspension is efficient and it's surprising to see that on tight corners on rough roads, the Infiniti stays exactly on course. Handling is sharper on the Touring, which has a firmer suspension and wider tires; a bit stiff on rough surfaces, it takes to winding roads with aplomb and assurance. Slightly light on the regular model, the steering system is firmer on the Touring, probably because of its oversized tires. Lastly, four disc brakes provide plenty of stopping power. A tip: the typical North American driver should opt for the "t-less" I30, which is smoother and more comfortable out on the road. **E.L.**

Specifications of Test Vehicle

Model: Infiniti I30

Exterior Dimensions	
Wheelbase	106.3 in.
Overall length	189.6 in.
Overall width	69.7 in.
Overall height	55.7 in.
Curb weight	3,150 lb.
Interior Dimensions	
Seating capacity	5
Head room:	F:40.1 in./R: 37.4 in.
Leg room:	F:43.9 in./R: 34.3 in.
Cargo volume	14.1 cu. ft
Engine	
Displacement	V-6 3 L.
Horsepower	190 @ 5,600 rpm
Torque, lb-ft.	205 @ 4,000 rpm
Performance	
0-60 mph, acceleration	8.9 sec.
60-0 mph, braking	131 ft.
Turning circle	34.8 ft.
EPA city/highway	21/28 mpg
Test mileage	23 mpg
Fuel tank capacity	18.5 gal.

Ratings 150

Group	Category	Rating
Over the Road	Acceleration	8
	Transmission	9
	Braking	5
	Steering	8
	Ride	9
	Handling	8
	Drivability	8
	Fuel Economy	5
Passenger Environment	Comfort/Conven.	7
	Interior Room	6
	Driving Position	8
	Instrumentation	8
	Controls	8
	Visibility	7
	Entry/Exit	8
	Quietness	9
	Cargo Space	7
Workmanship	Interior	9
	Exterior	8
	Value	5

Infiniti

Q45

New for 99

Electronically controlled suspension
17-inch wheels
Xenon headlights

Pros

Considerable effort to maintain the Q45
Single price
Impeccable manufacturing quality

Cons

Schizophrenic personality
Unexciting handling
Compact-like trunk

Equipment

Major Standard Equipment: 4.1-liter V-8, 4-wheel antilock disc brakes, limited-slip differential, automatic air conditioning, cabin air filter, power heated mirrors, power sunroof, automatic dimming rear-view mirror, leather upholstery, power seats, power lumbar adjustment, driver's memory system, power windows, power locks, cruise control, tilt and steering column, speed-sensitive variable-intermittent wipers, rear defroster, automatic headlamps, AM/FM/CD/ cassette stereo, aluminum wheels. **t adds:** Sports suspension, heated seats. **Major Options:** Heated seats, CD-changer

Supporting role

The first-generation Q45 lacked nothing in style or personality. But it wasn't well-liked. The second generation tries to solve the problem with more subdued styling and handling that's lost its edge. Consumers still don't seem to like it. What's the matter? Infiniti is using solutions, sacrificing the "Luxury" version and concentrating its efforts on the "Touring" edition and showering it with an extensive series of changes, many of them of little impact.

Under the circumstances, it comes as no surprise that despite the efforts made, the Q45 still lags very far behind its predecessor and, worse still, its competitors, especially on the technical level.

The first Q45 was one of the nicest expressions of Japanese automotive know-how. The second generation has lost the way. It may be warmer and more user-friendly, but it doesn't have that "certain something" that made the first Q45 so lovable. And the return of the analog clock high on the console does nothing to change the perception, nor does the glass sunroof (formerly metal) that brightens up an interior that can look dull (depending on the color scheme). The thing is, the Q45 doesn't have all that many faults: the brake pedal makes it impossible to rest your right foot on the dummy pedal and the CD loader is housed in the trunk, which is smaller than any you'll find on the competition's counterparts. On the positive side, the front bucket seats are comfortable, though they offer little support, and the rear bench seat is roomy and generously padded and good for two.

Some 220 lbs lighter, the Q45 now has a less powerful 4.1-liter V-8 (266 horses compared to the 278 provided by the 4.5-liter). But the buyer loses nothing: the weight / power ratio is the same as the previous generation's. The new engine works well with the smooth and precise transmission, which is as everyone would expect. The Q45 is a comfortable and surprisingly agile touring car, even if its steering system provides very little accurate feedback on road conditions. The fly in the ointment is safety and technology: no five-speed automatic transmission and no measures to ensure consistent road stability, two things you find on all models in the same category. This year an electronically controlled suspension is featured, letting drivers choose the ideal degree of shock absorption. Quite an expensive gadget! By contrast, 17-inch wheels are a definite asset and they improve road stability significantly.

Sold at only one price level, the Q45 doesn't have enough talent or presence to play a leading role on the automotive stage, already crowded as it is with luxury models. Too bad. **E.L.**

Specifications of Test Vehicle

Model: Q45

Exterior Dimensions	
Wheelbase	111.4 in.
Overall length	199.6 in.
Overall width	71.7 in.
Overall height	56.9 in.
Curb weight	3,900 lb.
Interior Dimensions	
Seating capacity	5
Head room	F:37.6/R:36.9 in.
Leg room	F:43.6/R:35.9 in.
Cargo volume	12.6 cu. ft.
Engine	
Displacement	V-8 4.1 L.
Horsepower	266 @ 5,500 rpm
Torque, lb-ft.	278 @ 4,000 rpm
Performance	
0-60 mph, acceleration	8.6 sec.
60-0 mph, braking	121 ft.
Turning circle	36.1 ft.
EPA city/highway	18/23 mpg
Test mileage	20 mpg
Fuel tank capacity	21.1 gal.

Prices

$48,000
$50,000

Sedan $48,695

Sedan $50,395

Warranty

Bumper-to-bumper 4/60,000

Powertrain 6/70,000

Rust-through 7/unlimited

Other to Consider

BMW 540 i

Jaguar XJ8

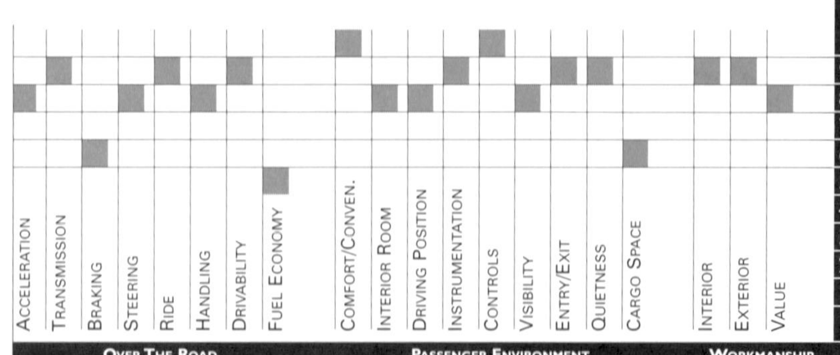

Ratings
165

Infiniti

QX4

New for 99

Restyled
V-6 more powerful

Pros

Sturdiness
Impeccable finishing
Well-designed cockpit

Cons

Marginal braking power
Anemic 3.3-liter engine
Access to rear seats

Equipment

Major Standard Equipment: 3.3-liter V-6, automatic transmission, full-time 4-wheel drive, 4-wheel antilock brakes, variable-assist power steering, variable-intermittent wipers, rear wiper and washer, automatic air conditioning, automatic temperature control, AM/FM/CD/cassette stereo, cruise control, tilt steering column, luggage rack, power seats, leather upholstery, split-folding rear seat, power windows, power heated mirrors, rear defroster, power locks, remote keyless entry, antitheft system, privacy glass, aluminum wheels. **Major Options:** Limited-slip rear differential, power moonroof, heated seats.

A blessing

PRICES
$36,000
$38,000
4-door truck wagon
$35,550

WARRANTY
Bumper-to-bumper
4/60,000
Powertrain
6/70,000
Rust-through
7/unlimited

OTHER TO CONSIDER
GMC Envoy
Toyota 4Runner

Had it not been for the QX4, you have to wonder what would have become of the Infiniti. And justifiably so, since this sport utility accounts for much more than 50 percent of the make's total sales.

Closely related to the popular Pathfinder (Nissan), the QX4 stands out because of its unique body panels, its more elaborate interior design, and its more sophisticated all-wheel drive system. Sprinkle with a few Infiniti logos and there you have it, you've just created a QX4!

For its rich trims, the QX4's interior is still cramped compared to its young competitors. Rear doors are fairly narrow and make access to the rear bench seat difficult. Although covered in leather, it offers only average comfort because of a very straight back. Leg room is limited and some people will have to sit with their knees adjacent to their ears. In front, things are a lot rosier. Controls are well positioned, the quality of materials and finishing attracts only compliments, and an embarrassment of accessories makes riding in the QX4 a lot of fun, if you're assigned to the front.

No, the 3.3-liter V-6 under the QX4's hood isn't very economical when it comes to fuel. And when all is said and done, it isn't very powerful either, since its 168 horses run out of breath very quickly when the passenger compartment is full. On the up side, it's quiet and gets along swimmingly with either of the transmissions that are available. On the road, the suspension is smooth and efficient at countering road defects and the QX4 is predictable under normal conditions. When you decide to pick up the pace, however, body sway becomes noticeable and our test drive model felt even heavier than it really was. To complicate matters, brakes lack bite.

A roomy, luxurious, and very well-assembled sport utility, next spring the QX4 will be replaced by an all-new generation. Let's just hope it will be roomier and more powerful. **E.L.**

Specifications of Test Vehicle

Model: QX4

Exterior Dimensions	
Wheelbase	106.3 in.
Overall length	183.9 in.
Overall width	72.4 in.
Overall height	70.7 in.
Curb weight	4,300 lb.
Interior Dimensions	
Seating capacity	5
Head room	F:38.1/R:37.5 in.
Leg room	F:41.7/R:31.8 in.
Cargo volume	38 cu. ft.
Engine	
Displacement	V-6 3.3 L.
Horsepower	170 @ 4,800 rpm
Torque, lb-ft.	196 @ 2,800 rpm
Performance	
0-60 mph, acceleration	11.2 sec.
60-0 mph, braking	141 ft.
Turning circle	37.4 ft.
EPA city/highway	15/19 mpg
Test mileage	17 mpg
Fuel tank capacity	21.1 gal.

Group	Rating	Score
Over The Road	Acceleration	5
	Transmission	8
	Braking	4
	Steering	7
	Ride	7
	Handling	7
	Drivability	8
	Fuel Economy	4
Passenger Environment	Comfort/Conven.	8
	Interior Room	7
	Driving Position	8
	Instrumentation	7
	Controls	8
	Visibility	7
	Entry/Exit	6
	Quietness	7
	Cargo Space	10
Workmanship	Interior	8
	Exterior	8
	Value	8

Ratings
142

Isuzu

Hombre

New for 99

New streamlined look
Third door available

Pros

Warranty
Safety equipment
Fuel economy

Cons

Few options
Ride

Equipment

Major Standard Equipment: 2.2-liter I-4, manual transmission, 4-wheel antilock brakes, variable-intermittent wipers, bench seat. **XS adds:** Full carpeting, split bench seat. **Major Options:** 4.3-liter V-6, 4-speed automatic transmission, air conditioning, sliding rear window, power windows, power locks, power mirrors, tilt steering wheel, cruise control, heavy-duty suspension, AM/FM/cassette stereo, AM/FM/CD stereo, tachometer.

Asian brothers

Funny thing about Isuzu: it has no exclusive vehicles. It shares everything with another manufacturer. General Motors builds the Hombre pickup, and Isuzu sells it with a few cosmetic changes and fewer choices for buyers.

The Louisiana-built Hombre is a twin of Chevrolet's popular compact S10 pickup and the GMC Sonoma. Under the skin, the three trucks are virtually identical.

Although you can order the Hombre's GM counterparts in literally dozens of powertrain-body-bed combinations, Isuzu restricts your choices. Part-time 4-wheel-drive is available since last year. You can't get the V-6 with the regular cab and 2-wheel drive. You can't get an automatic transmission with the 4-cylinder engine. Finally, you can't customize the cabin with many car-like amenities that domestic-truck owners often take for granted. Perhaps it's related to volume—Chevrolet sells more S10s in a month than Isuzu sells Hombres in a year.

Since Isuzu has already made many of the equipment decisions for you, an Hombre purchase becomes temptingly simple. The regular-cab Hombre comes two trim levels (S and XS); the extended Space Cab comes only as an XS, with a 4.3-liter V-6 and 4-speed automatic transmission as an option.

We tested the base Hombre S, which is fitted with a 118-horsepower, 2.2-liter 4-cylinder engine and a 5-speed manual gearbox. Isuzu offers a 5-year/60,000-mile warranty on the powertrain, compared with GM's 3 years/36,000 miles.

Getting into and out of the Hombre's cabin is something of a climb, but no better or worse than in other compact pickups. Over the road, the base Hombre is a decent entry-level truck. It offers excellent fuel economy; we averaged 25 mpg in our test-drives. With the 4-cylinder engine and 5-speed transmission, it accelerates a bit faster than a couch potato. With the automatic, it will be a step or two slower.

It's a plain-vanilla package, however, up against a lot of spicy competition. Its ride and handling are no better than average for the class. The driver has excellent visibility, another trait typical of pickups. Isuzu doesn't think in terms of cupholders, yet the stick shift's mini-console has a pencil holder.

Like the S10 and the Sonoma, Isuzu's version has standard 4-wheel antilock brakes and daytime running lights—two bright spots in the Hombre safety picture. Another '99 upgrade, lagging behind GM's versions, is a third door.

The warranty is the only reason to choose the Hombre over a Chevy or GMC. We don't expect to see many Hombres in private hands. Commercial fleets appear to be Isuzu's. **D.V.S.**

Specifications of Test Vehicle

Model: Hombre S

Exterior Dimensions	
Wheelbase	108.3 in.
Overall length	189 in.
Overall width	67.9 in.
Overall height	62.1 in.
Curb weight	3,150 lb.
Interior Dimensions	
Seating capacity	3
Head room	F:39.5 in.
Leg room	F:42.4 in.
Payload capacity	1,150 lb.
Engine	
Displacement	I-4 2.2 L.
Horsepower	118 @ 5,200 rpm
Torque, lb-ft.	130 @ 2,800 rpm
Performance	
0-60 mph, acceleration	12.2 sec
60-0 mph, braking	140 ft.
Turning circle	39.6 ft.
EPA city/highway	23/30 mpg
Test mileage	26 mpg
Fuel tank capacity	19 gal.

Prices

$11,000
$16,000

S short bed
$11,449

XS short bed
$11,984

XS extended cab, short bed
$15,165

Warranty

Bumper-to-bumper
3/50,000

Powertrain
5/60,000

Rust-through
6/100,000

Other to Consider

Mazda B-Series

Nissan Frontier

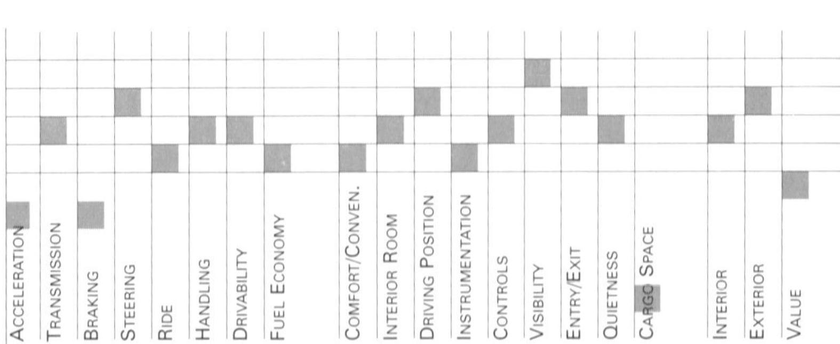

Ratings
128

Isuzu Rodeo

New for 99
LSE version

Pros
Comfortable ride
Powerful V-6
Strong braking

Cons
Step-by-step development
Some design details
Outdated all-wheel drive

Equipment
Major Standard Equipment: 2.2-liter I-4, 4-wheel antilock brakes, variable-assist power steering, split-folding rear seat, rear wiper and washer, stainless-steel exhaust. **LS adds:** 3.2-liter V-6, power locks, power windows, power heated mirrors, luggage rack, AM/FM/cassette stereo, cruise control, tilt steering column, aluminum wheels. **Major Options:** Automatic transmission, part-time 4-wheel drive, limited-slip differential, air conditioning, power moonroof, power windows, power locks, power mirrors, AM/FM/cassette stereo, leather upholstery, tilt steering column, cruise control, remote keyless entry, theft-alarm system, aluminum wheels.

Will the last ever really be first?

PRICES
$18,000
$32,000
S 4-door truck wagon $18,180
LS 4-door truck wagon $23,540
LSE $28,150

WARRANTY
Bumper-to-bumper 3/50,000
Powertrain 5/60,000
Rust-through 6/100,000

OTHER TO CONSIDER
Jeep Cherokee
Nissan Pathfinder

Isuzu took a long time to revamp its Rodeo. Enough, some will say, to analyze where the competition was heading and to get a feel for the market. Too much, others will say, to come up with a new generation positioned somewhere between the CR-V and the Blazer for size, but not for price.

To satisfy the lust for luxury hidden deep within each of our hearts, Isuzu has introduced a new package: the LSE, complete with an interior replete with wood and leather design features, the better to justify its price.

Aerodynamically correct (with a drag coefficient that has shifted from 0.54 to 0.46), a rigid chassis, better soundproofing but a windshield that still comes up short, the Rodeo's features combine to make its interior as intimate as a confessional. In the design department the LS package comes with a number of highly polished wood inlays that alleviate an otherwise depressing look. To distract us a bit Isuzu came up with the good (?) idea of dotting the instrument panel with an array of buttons and controls, not always very wisely positioned in the scheme of things. For example, radio controls are at the foot of the console, which means that the driver has to take his or her eyes off the road to switch stations. Even though front-seat cushions have some drivers leaning far forward to reach pedals, the Rodeo's bucket seats are comfortable enough to make driving long distances problem-free. But the best off are rear-seat passengers (a very rare phenomenon, you have to admit): the fold-down seat fits very well, there is plenty of room for heads and legs and most importantly, adjustable seat belts spell more comfort for passengers who have to sit on either end. The middle passenger may complain about the "stomach belt" and lack of headrest in his or her case.

The new Rodeo has gained in maturity, but it still has the slightly rebellious side that has thrilled and enthraled some 355,000 buyers since 1990. The ball steering system has been traded in for a more precise rack-and-pinion alternative to make life easier for the driver. Brakes have more bite now that they have an efficient and modern antilock system that ensures straight-line stops over surprising shorter distances compared to rival models. The rear suspension is so good at filtering out road defects that the ride could almost be described as less exciting than it used to be. The 3.2-liter V-6 is as strong as ever — no, it's even stronger! In fact, its performance capabilities are so impressive they put to shame most of the V-8 units the competition uses. Pick-up power has increased as well and the Rodeo leaves its counterparts to bask in the red of its tail lights. Some credit goes to the transmissions — manual or automatic. Their gear ratio is perfect and they're as smooth as silk. A drawback: the all-wheel drive selected for the Rodeo has neither the refinement nor the efficiency of similar systems found on today's market.

They say "the last shall be first." Rodeo seems to be the exception that proves the rule. **E.L.**

Specifications of Test Vehicle
Model: Rodeo LS

Exterior Dimensions	
Wheelbase	106.4 in.
Overall length	176.7 in.
Overall width	70.4 in.
Overall height	68.8 in.
Curb weight	3,800 lb.
Interior Dimensions	
Seating capacity	5
Head room	F:37.8/R:37.9 in.
Leg room	F:42.1/R:35 in.
Cargo volume	33 cu. ft.
Engine	
Displacement	V-6 3.2 L.
Horsepower	205 @ 5,400 rpm
Torque, lb-ft	214 @ 3,000 rpm
Performance	
0-60 mph, acceleration	10.3
60-0 mph, braking	136
Turning circle	38.4 ft.
EPA city/highway	16/20 mpg
Test mileage	16 mpg
Fuel tank capacity	21.1 gal.

Ratings

Group	Category	Rating
Over The Road	Acceleration	6
	Transmission	8
	Braking	4
	Steering	8
	Ride	7
	Handling	8
	Drivability	8
	Fuel Economy	4
Passenger Environment	Comfort/Conven.	7
	Interior Room	8
	Driving Position	8
	Instrumentation	8
	Controls	7
	Visibility	6
	Entry/Exit	6
	Quietness	7
	Cargo Space	10
Workmanship	Interior	8
	Exterior	8
	Value	6

142

Isuzu

Trooper

New for 99

Fake wood inlays
Power heated seats (LS)
New exterior color

Pros

Ride
Controls
Interior room

Cons

Entry/exit
Rear-wheel-only antilock brakes Engine performance

Equipment

Major Standard Equipment: 3.2-liter V-6, part-time 4-wheel drive, automatic locking front hubs, 4-wheel disc brakes, variable-assist power steering, rear defroster, rear washer and wiper, tilt steering column, AM/FM/cassette stereo. **LS adds:** Power windows, cruise control, air conditioning, split-folding rear seat, variable-intermittent wipers, theft alarm system. **Limited adds:** 4-wheel disk brakes, auto matic transmission, leather upholstery, heated seats, remote keyless entry,AM/FM/CD stereo, power moonroof. **Major Options:** Air conditioning, 4-wheel antilock brakes, power locks, cruise control, leather upholstery, heated seats, power heated mirrors, CD changer, remote keyless entry, power moonroof.

Living in the shadows

Isuzu has freshened up the appearance and features of the Trooper. The marketing plan is fresh, too—less emphasis on trim levels defined by standard equipment. The Trooper now is all about options.

Honda sells the Trooper as the Acura SLX in the luxury sport-utility vehicle market. To differentiate the two, Isuzu has reduced the number of trim levels on the Trooper from four to one, offering many options. The SLX has one trim level, too, but everything that's optional on a Trooper is standard on the SLX.

For a compact SUV, the Trooper is rather lanky. It stands 6 inches taller than a Ford Explorer on a wheelbase that's 3 inches shorter than the Explorer's. But it has a relatively narrow track (lateral spacing between wheels).

For '99, Isuzu has dropped the rear-wheel-only antilock brakes formerly offered, replacing them with a full 4-wheel antilock system. Only 4-wheel antilock brakes provide steering control in sudden emergency stops.

From a standing start, the 215-horsepower, 3.5-liter V-6 delivers adequate power and acceleration. We reached 60 mph in 10.8 seconds. The automatic transmission downshifts quickly for passing and always shifts smoothly. With the automatic 4-wheel drive system, SUV neophytes don't have to worry about when to shift into 4WD. We averaged an unimpressive 16 mpg, with a lot of highway miles.

The Trooper's highway ride is stable and supple, like a large station wagon's. The suspension's generous travel allows you to tackle rocky trails with confidence. It also allows prominent body lean in turns, so the Trooper feels exceptionally top-heavy. The power steering requires a medium effort and responds well. It self-centers noticeably after turns. We heard some wind noise, but for the most part the Trooper is pleasantly quiet.

The tall cabin ranks among the roomiest in its class—once you get to it. Climbing inside takes real effort. The doors are short from top to bottom. Inside, the cabin has plenty of head room, front and rear; the back seat is wide enough for three adults. Passengers in the rear bench seat will appreciate the reclining backrest. The optional moonroof reduces rear head room by 2 inches. The firm, comfortable front seats are high off the floor, providing excellent visibility to the front and sides. However, thick rear pillars and a full-size spare tire mounted on the outside impair the view out the back. Isuzu's unusual 70/30 rear cargo door opens onto a tall, long cargo deck.

The dashboard is attractive and logically organized. Most of the controls are large enough to use while wearing gloves.

Isuzu offers a better warranty on the Trooper than Acura does on the same basic vehicle. That may be a factor in your buying decision. **D.V.S.**

Prices

$27,000
$34,000
S 4-door truck wagon
$26,550

Warranty
(years/miles)

Bumper-to-bumper
3/50,000

Powertrain
5/60,000

Rust-through
6/100,000

Other to Consider

Infiniti QX4

Mercedes ML320

Specifications of Test Vehicle

Model: Trooper S

Exterior Dimensions	
Wheelbase	108.7 in.
Overall length	185.8 in.
Overall width	69.5 in.
Overall height	72.2 in.
Curb weight	4,550 lb.
Interior Dimensions	
Seating capacity	5
Head room	F:39.8/R:39.8 in.
Leg room	F:40.8/R:39.1 in.
Cargo volume	43.7 cu. ft.
Engine	
Displacement	V-6 3.5 L.
Horsepower	215 @ 5,400 rpm
Torque, lb-ft.	230 @ 3,000 rpm
Performance	
0-60 mph, acceleration	10.8 sec.
60-0 mph, braking	132 ft.
Turning circle	38.1 ft.
EPA city/highway	15/19 mpg
Test mileage	16 mpg
Fuel tank capacity	22.5 gal.

Category	Rating
Over The Road	
Acceleration	7
Transmission	7
Braking	8
Steering	7
Ride	8
Handling	5
Drivability	7
Fuel Economy	4
Passenger Environment	
Comfort/Conven.	8
Interior Room	9
Driving Position	8
Instrumentation	8
Controls	9
Visibility	8
Entry/Exit	5
Quietness	7
Cargo Space	10
Workmanship	
Interior	9
Exterior	8
Value	6

Ratings
148

Jaguar Type-S

New for 99
New model

Pros
NT

Cons
NT

Equipement
Major standard equipement: Anti-lock braking system, automatic transmission, traction control, dual automatic climate control, leather ulphostery, rear defroster, power locks, power moonroof, power driver's seat. **4.0 adds:** a-liter V-8. **Major option:** Heated front seats, rain-sensitive wipers, stability control

The Brit's are back

PRICES
NA

WARRANTY
Bumper-to-bumper 4/50,000
Powertrain 4/50,000
Rust-through 6/unlimited

OTHER TO CONSIDER
Mercedes E 320
BMW 528 i

True, the Type S shares its mechanical platform with the Lincoln LS. So is this a British Lincoln or a true Jaguar? We'll leave it to the purists to decide. However, know that the Type S is intended as a serious contender in the luxury intermediate category. Two models are available: one powered by a 3.0-litre six-cylinder V engine (240 horses) and the other featuring a 4.0-litre V8 (281 horses). Power is transferred to the rear drive wheels via a five-speed automatic transmission, the only unit available. **E.L.**

Specifications of Test Vehicle

Model: V6 (not tested)

Exterior Dimensions	
Wheelbase	114.5 in.
Overall lenght	191.3 in.
Overall widht	71.6 in.
Overall height	55.7 in.
Curb weight	3650 lb.
Interior dimensions	
Seating capacity	5
Head room	F: 38.6/R : 36.4 in.
Leg room	F:43.1/R: 37.7 in.
Cargo room	13.1 cu. ft.
Engine	
Displacement	V6, 3 L.
Horsepower	240 @ 6,800
Torque, lb-ft	221 @ 4,500
Performance	
0-60 mph, acceleration	8 sec
60-0 mph, braking	Not tested
Turning circle	37.7 ft
EPA city/highway	Not tested
Test mileage	Not tested
Fuel tank capacity	18.4

Jaguar

XJ8

New for 99

Engine that complies with environmental standards
Two new exterior colors (Vanden Plas)

Pros

Elegant and distinct styling
Smooth V-8
Significantly improved manufacturing quality

Cons

High fuel consumption
Shallow trunk
Uncomfortable seat cushions

Equipment

Major Standard Equipment: 4-liter V-8, 5-speed automatic transmission, 4-wheel antilock disc brakes, automatic stability control, automatic air conditioning, leather upholstery, power tilt and telescope steering column, AM/FM/cassette stereo, power sunroof, remote keyless entry. **L adds:** Long-wheelbase body **Vanden Plas adds:** Premium leather and wood trim. **XJR adds:** Short-wheelbase body, supercharged 4-liter V-8, traction control, sports suspension, heated seats, larger tires. **Major Options:** Traction control, heated front seats, heated rear seats.

A domesticated feline

The Jaguar camp has lost its sense of tradition and the shift would seem to be for the better. Since the British introduced the 4.0-liter V-8 under the XK8's hood, consumer confidence has been bolstered and sales are increasing at a nice pace. Still, it's true that the engine isn't the only reason the make is on the rise again, Ford, Jaguar's American benefactor, insists on achieving the ultimate objectives of efficiency, profitability, and reliability.

With shinier eyes and a stronger jaw, the XJ series still remains the most classic of all and it hasn't lost any of its shine. Its interior continues to be very comfortable. Ford's influence and expertise have had an effect, among others in door panels molded in a single block to ensure better quality and to reduce manufacturing costs. The same goes for accessories, with a steering wheel (with multiple adjustment possibilities) now sporting the controls for the radio, telephone, and automatic speed system. Unfortunately, the dashboard is still laid out in a very whimsical way. It's high time to clean it up! In addition, bucket seats are short and force the driver to sit on the very edge. Another annoyance is the sound made by indicator lights, something that sounds like two wooden spoons hitting together. The glove box is bigger, but the trunk isn't, and rear seats are no roomier and as cramped as they always have been, unless you opt for the more welcoming extended wheelbase version (Vanden Plas) and its wider doors.

Tradition lovers will soon console themselves after they've spent a few minutes at the wheel of a Jaguar sedan powered by a V-8 engine. Our of respect for the firm's engine experts who worked tirelessly to improve the inline six-cylinder, it should be pointed out that the unit had reached its true peak. Quieter and smoother, the V-8 has no trouble handling this sedan's weight, even if it does exceed two tons. And on a decidedly modernistic note, the engine is teamed up with an excellent five-speed automatic transmission. Divine. As for handling, it has improved significantly since all mechanical features, or almost all, have been reviewed. The steering system is still as precise and the front suspension is all new, in deference to the new engine choice. Not bad to begin with, the brakes now have more power and are helped along by a better ABS system.

According to Jaguar, this series of changes has resulted in a 30 percent decrease in regular maintenance costs. But what Jaguar would also like you to know is that you won't need to visit your local mechanic as often because of malfunctions. And that alone is worth its weight in gold! **E.L.**

Specifications of Test Vehicle

Model: Vanden Plas

Exterior Dimensions	
Wheelbase	117.9 in.
Overall length	202.7 in.
Overall width	70.8 in.
Overall height	53.2 in.
Curb weight	4,050 lb.
Interior Dimensions	
Seating capacity	5
Head room	F:37.8/R:37 in.
Leg room	F:41.2/R:39.2 in.
Cargo volume	12.7 cu. ft.
Engine	
Displacement	V-8 4 L.
Horsepower	290 @ 6,100 rpm
Torque, lb-ft.	290 @ 4,250 rpm
Performance	
0-60 mph, acceleration	7 sec.
60-0 mph, braking	129 ft.
Turning circle	40.7 ft.
EPA city/highway	17/24 mpg
Test mileage	NA
Fuel tank capacity	21.4 gal.

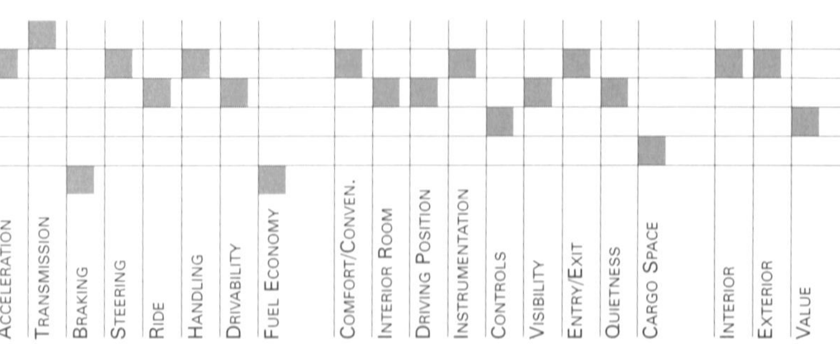

Ratings
160

Prices

$55,000
$71,000

Sedan
$55,780

L sedan
$60,830

Vanden Plas sedan
$64,880

XJR sedan
$69,030

Warranty

Bumper-to-bumper
4/50,000

Powertrain
4/50,000

Rust-through
6/unlimited

Other to Consider

BMW 740 i

Lexus LS400

Jaguar

XK8

New for 99

Minor change
XKR model

Pros

Elegant and distinct styling
Smooth V-8
Significantly improved manufacturing quality

Cons

High fuel consumption
Shallow trunk
Uncomfortable seat cushions

Equipment

Major Standard Equipment: 4-liter V-8, 5-speed automatic transmission, automatic stability control, 4-wheel antilock disc brakes, variable-assist power steering, variable-intermittent wipers, rear defroster, automatic air conditioning, AM/FM/CD/cassette stereo, power heated mirrors, automatic dimming rear-view mirror, power windows,power seats, power driver's lumbar adjustment, power tilt and telescope steering column, cruise control, automatic headlights, power locks, remote keyless entry, theft alarm system, driver's memory system, aluminum wheels. **Major Options:** Traction control, heated seats, headlight washers, chrome wheels.

Second impression

PRICES

$65,000
$76,000

Coupe
$66,330

2-door convertible
$71,330

WARRANTY

Bumper-to-bumper
4/50,000

Powertrain
4/50,000

Rust-through
6/unlimited

OTHER TO CONSIDER

Mercedes SL
Lexus SC400

The Jaguar camp has lost its sense of tradition and the shift would seem to be for the better. Since the British make introduced the 4.0-liter V-8 under the XK8's hood, consumer confidence has been bolstered and sales are increasing at a nice pace. Still, it's true that the engine isn't the only reason the make is on the rise again — Ford, Jaguar's American benefactor, insists on achieving the ultimate objectives of efficiency, profitability and reliability.

With shinier eyes and a stronger jaw, the XJ series still remains the most classic of all and it hasn't lost any of its shine. Its interior continues to be very comfortable. Ford's influence and expertise have had an effect, among others in door panels molded in a single block to ensure better quality and to reduce manufacturing costs. The same goes for accessories, with a steering wheel (with multiple adjustment possibilities) now sporting the controls for the radio, telephone, and automatic speed system. Unfortunately, the dashboard is still laid out in a very whimsical way. It's high time to clean it up! In addition, bucket seats are short and force the driver to sit on the very edge. Another annoyance is the sound made by indicator lights, something that sounds like two wooden spoons hitting together. The glove box is bigger, but the trunk isn't, and rear seats are no roomier and as cramped as they always have been, unless you opt for the more welcoming extended wheelbase version (Vanden Plas) and its wider doors.

Tradition-lovers will soon console themselves after they've spent a few minutes at the wheel of a Jaguar sedan powered by a V-8 engine. Our of respect for the firm's engine experts who worked tirelessly to improve the in-line six-cylinder, it should be pointed out that the unit had reached its true peak. Quieter and smoother, the V-8 has no trouble handling this sedan's weight, even if it does exceed two tons. And on a decidedly modernistic note, the engine is teamed up with an excellent five-speed automatic transmission. Divine. As for handling, it has improved significantly since all mechanical features — or almost all — have been reviewed. The steering system is still as precise and the front suspension is all-new, in deference to the new engine choice. Not bad to begin with, the brakes now have more power and are helped along by a better ABS system.

According to Jaguar, this series of changes has resulted in a 30 percent decrease in regular maintenance costs. But what Jaguar would also like you to know is that you won't need to visit your local mechanic as often because of malfunctions. And that alone is worth its weight in gold! **E.L.**

Specifications of Test Vehicle

Model: XK8

Exterior Dimensions	
Wheelbase	101.9 in.
Overall length	187.4 in.
Overall width	72 in.
Overall height	51 in.
Curb weight	3,650 lb.
Interior dimensions	
Seating capacity	4
Head room	F:37.4/R:33.3 in.
Leg room	F:43/R:NA in.
Cargo volume	11.1 cu. ft.
Engine	
Displacement	V-8 4 L.
Horsepower	290 @ 6,100 rpm
Torque, lb-ft.	284 @ 4,200 rpm
Performance	
0-60 mph, acceleration	6.5 sec.
60-0 mph, braking	125 ft.
Turning circle	36.1 ft.
EPA city/highway	17/24 mpg
Test mileage	18 mpg
Fuel tank capacity	19.9 gal.

Ratings	Rating
Over The Road	
Acceleration	10
Transmission	9
Braking	6
Steering	8
Ride	9
Handling	9
Drivability	9
Fuel Economy	4
Passenger Environment	
Comfort/Conven.	9
Interior Room	4
Driving Position	8
Instrumentation	8
Controls	8
Visibility	7
Entry/Exit	7
Quietness	8
Cargo Space	5
Workmanship	
Interior	8
Exterior	6
Value	8

Ratings 150

Jeep Cherokee

New for 99

Heated front seats (optional on the Limited)
New colors

Pros

Remarkable off-road efficiency
Competitive price
More safety features

Cons

Narrow doors
Outdated handling
Questionable reliability

Equipment

Major Standard Equipment: 2.5-liter I-4, manual transmission, vinyl upholstery, folding rear seat, cruise control, AM/FM stereo, stainless-steel exhaust system. **Sport adds:** 4-liter I-6, cloth upholstery, AM/FM/cassette stereo. **Classic adds:** Air conditioning, power mirrors, tilt steering wheel, aluminum wheels. **Limited adds:** Cruise control, privacy glass, power driver's seat, power windows, remote keyless entry, leather upholstery. **Major Options:** 4-liter I-6, automatic transmission, part-time 4-wheel drive, full-time 4-wheel drive, 4-wheel antilock brakes. Heated front seats.

Prices

$15,000
$28,000

SE 2-door $15,440
SE 4-door $16,480
Sport 2-door $18,055
Sport 4-door $19,090
Classic 4-door $20,480
Limited 4-door $20,480

Warranty

Bumper-to-bumper 3/36,000
Powertrain 3/36,000
Rust-through 7/100,000

Other to consider

Isuzu Rodeo

Redoutable off road

Somewhere between progress and stagnation is the area where Jeep fell when it set out to revamp its Cherokee. Consumers looking to buy a sport-utility vehicle this year could blame the company for its latest move. However, you have to recognize Jeep's integrity, reflected by the fact that it designs its sport utilities with the greatest respect for tradition. Seen from this perspective, the many and profitable changes brought to the dean of the category in recent years are sure to please the make's loyal followers.

Passengers who sit in the rear of the vehicle will have an excellent vantage point on the Cherokee's interior. But not without a bit of a hassle first, since its doors are still narrow, making access difficult; and worse yet, usable space is at a premium once they're inside. Front seats are roomier and give you a front-row view of the instrument panel, now easier to read but still stark and not very refined from the ergonomics standpoint. The ideal driving position is hard to find and seats don't mold very well. On the other hand, headrests featured on the Classic and Limited versions can be locked into position and the Limited's options include heated bucket seats to keep front-seat passengers happy and comfy.

Lift the hood or remove the tires if you like, but you won't find any new mechanical features on the Cherokee. All it is is a utility vehicle that's very comfortable off-road and that shines even in the trenches. However, the situation isn't as good on asphalt, where the Cherokee shows its age. The imprecise steering system makes it hard to stay on course and unlike the Grand Cherokee's system, braking is no model of efficiency. Jeep persists in offering the 2.5-liter four-cylinder, disappointing in several areas

(performance, fuel consumption, lack of smoothness), but is it a better idea to go for the in-line six-cylinder, even if its fuel consumption and reliability has brought many an owner to the edge of tears — I ask you? To give credit where credit is due, though, the Cherokee is redoubtable for off-road adventure.
E.L.

Specifications of Test Vehicle

Model: Sport

Exterior Dimensions	
Wheelbase	101.4 in.
Overall length	167.5 in.
Overall width	69.4 in.
Overall height	64 in.
Curb weight	3,350 lb.
Interior Dimensions	
Seating capacity	5
Head room	F:37.8/R:38 in.
Leg room	F:41.4/R:35 in.
Cargo volume	32.9 cu. ft.
Engine	
Displacement	I-6 4 L.
Horsepower	190 @ 4,600 rpm
Torque, lb-ft.	225 @ 3,000 rpm
Performance	
0-60 mph, acceleration	9 sec.
60-0 mph, braking	134 ft.
Turning circle	35.1 ft.
EPA city/highway	15/21 mpg
Test mileage	18 mpg
Fuel tank capacity	20 gal.

Ratings 136

Category	Item	Rating
Over The Road	Acceleration	7
	Transmission	8
	Braking	5
	Steering	6
	Ride	7
	Handling	7
	Drivability	8
	Fuel Economy	4
Passenger Environment	Comfort/Conven.	7
	Interior Room	6
	Driving Position	7
	Instrumentation	7
	Controls	6
	Visibility	6
	Entry/Exit	7
	Quietness	6
	Cargo Space	10
Workmanship	Interior	7
	Exterior	7
	Value	8

Jeep Grand Cherokee

new MODEL

1999

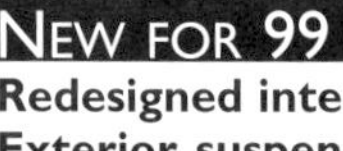

New for 99

Redesigned interior
Exterior, suspension
Engine, transmission, and 4-wheel drive system

Pros

Powertrain
Off-road capability
Seat comfort

Cons

Noise
Fuel economy

Equipment

Major Standard Equipment: 4.0 liter I-6 engine, 4-speed automatic transmission, antilock 4-wheel disc brakes, programmable door locks, cruise control, tilt wheel, manual air conditioning, cloth seats, AM/FM stereo /cassette. **Limited adds:** Heated power mirrors, radio/seat/mirror memory, fog lamps, 4-wheel drive, dual zone automatic air conditioning, overhead console, leather interior, power seats, premium stereo with CD player, security alarm. **Major Options:** Premium 4-wheel drive system, sunroof, full-size spare tire, heated seats, CD changer, off-road suspension.

AAA
TOP SPORT UTILITY

PRICES
$26,000
$35,000
Laredo 2-wheel drive $26,220
Laredo 4-wheel drive $28,190
Limited 2-wheel drive $31,985
Limited 4-wheel drive $34,415

WARRANTY
Bumper-to-bumper 3/36,000
Powertrain 3/36,000
Rust-through 7/100,000

OTHER TO CONSIDER
Ford Explorer
GMC Jimmy

Sport utility: the new leader

Faced with mounting competition from almost every automaker, Jeep has responded with a completely redesigned Grand Cherokee for 1999. Fans of older Cherokees won't be disappointed, however. This new version is better in every way.

The body is all new, but it's instantly recognizable, with a more rounded and stylish appearance. Inside, the instrument panel has a clean, uncluttered design. The instruments are simple and easy to interpret. Audio controls are mounted above the ventilation controls for added safety and convenience.

Large comfortable seat cushions up front contribute to a feel of luxury. Rear seats are not so luxurious and are a little short on leg room. Entry and exit require stepping over a ledge that runs the length of the door openings. This is a carryover from the previous model that should have been eliminated. A change that gets the most attention is relocating the spare tire. Now it's in a compartment under the cargo area floor, freeing up valuable cargo space and improving rear visibility.

Two engines are available for the U.S. market. The 4.0-liter in-line six, rated for 195 hp is the base offering. Even though the new 4.7-liter V-8 is smaller than the 5.2-liter engine it replaces, its 235 hp is a 15 hp increase. The V-8 gets an all-new electronically controlled 4-speed automatic transmission. It is unique in that it has two second-gear ratios. A computer selects the one needed, depending on speed, throttle position, and load.

The new "Quadra-Drive" 4-wheel drive system delivers torque to whichever wheel needs it. There are no levers or switches to operate — hydraulic clutches in the front, center- and rear differentials do the job automatically. The standard 4-wheel drive system with the 6-cylinder engine is Selec-Trac, a selectable rear- or 4-wheel drive arrangement with a lockable center differential.

The Grand Cherokee is a delicate blend of off-road-tough and on-highway manners. Acceleration with the V-8 is surprising. It takes only 7.7 seconds to get from 0 to 60 mph. And the brakes are better too. A panic stop from 60 mph takes 128 ft. That's about average. The highway ride is firm and a little truck-like. While the steering has been upgraded, it still seems slightly vague and disconnected. The new suspension improves handling, but this is still a large sport-utility vehicle and it doesn't corner like a car. Off-road, the Grand Cherokee really shines. The engine has plenty of power and the combination of the new transmission and 4-wheel drive gives it extraordinary capability.

Grand Cherokee fans should be happy Jeep didn't compromise this popular sport utility by making it larger, softer, or less capable off-road. Now it's just better. **D.V.S.**

Specifications of Test Vehicle

Model: Limited

Exterior Dimensions	
Wheelbase	105.9 in
Overall length	181.5 In.
Overall width	72.3 In.
Overall height	69.4 In.
Curb weight	3969 lbs.
Interior Dimensions	
Seating capacity	5
Head room	F:39.7 /R:39.5 in.
Leg room	F:41.4 /R:35.3 in.
Cargo room	39.0 cu.ft.
Engine	
Displacement	4.7 L V-8
Horsepower	235@4800 rpm
Torque, lb-ft.	295@3200 rpm
Performance	
0-60 mph, acceleration	7.7 sec.
60-0 mph, braking	128 ft.
Turning circle	36.5 ft.
EPA city/highway	15/20 mpg.
Test Mileage	NA
Fuel tank capacity	20.5 gal.

Ratings

Group	Category	Rating
Over The Road	Acceleration	9
	Transmission	8
	Braking	5
	Steering	8
	Ride	8
	Handling	7
	Drivability	8
	Fuel Economy	4
Passenger Environment	Comfort/Conven.	8
	Interior Room	9
	Driving Position	8
	Instrumentation	8
	Controls	8
	Visibility	7
	Entry/Exit	7
	Quietness	7
	Cargo Space	10
Workmanship	Interior	8
	Exterior	8
	Value	7

Jeep Wrangler

New for 99

Stronger manual transmission (4.0-liter L-6)
Switch for front passenger's air bag
New colors

Pros

Exceptional off-road capabilities
More modern interior
Better stability on paved surfaces

Cons

Skittish suspension
Rough four-cylinder
Long options list

Equipment

Major Standard Equipment: 2.5 liter I-4, part-time 4-wheel drive, unassisted steering, vinyl upholstery, front bumper, **Sport adds:** 4-liter I-6, power steering, AM/FM radio, rear seat, rear bumper. **Sahara adds:** Cloth upholstery, side steps, heavy-duty battery, larger fuel tank, intermittent wipers, AM/FM cassette radio, full-size spare tire, aluminum wheels. **Major Options:** 3-speed automatic transmission, air conditioning, limited-slip rear differential, power steering, 4-wheel antilock brakes, AM/FM stereo,AM/FM/cassette stereo, tilt steering column, larger fuel tank, cloth upholstery, heavy-duty charging system, hard top, tow hooks, off-road suspension, tires, and wheels.

Mud slinging!

Here's a statistic that speaks volumes: half of all Jeep Wrangler buyers venture off-road, where none of the model's supposed rivals — the Rav4, Sidekick, and Tracker — can keep up with it, even with a head start! Domination is also evident when it comes to sales, where the Wrangler enjoys a comfortable lead since it holds 37 percent of its market segment.

Fans won't find it unusual that almost all of the Wrangler's accessories appear on the option list. The list is long, so the price for the base version quickly climbs to several thousands more when you set out to dress it up properly before taking it out of the showroom. Examples? Here are two: the mechanism used to tip over the front seat and the rear bench seat. And on the latter subject, we should mention that it can accommodate two passengers over short distances, unless it's folded down to increase cargo space, which is otherwise ridiculous. In the front, you'll be comfortable if you can ignore that the seat cushion provides minimal support, which almost has you sitting on the edge of your seat as you drive the vehicle.

Formerly too spread-out to be easily read, instrumentation is now positioned within a cluster, which is easier to move to the right when the Wrangler is exported to Asia. The soft top features an efficient design, though it takes a while to get the knack of handling it.

Before you get behind the Wrangler's wheel, leave your prejudices behind and give even the tiniest bit of credibility to the designers' claim to have made it more "civilized." If you need convincing, consider that the suspension now has coil springs, significantly more comfortable then the old leaf springs that used to keep the vehicle above the road surface. This sport utility has more stability and, more importantly, it's more comfortable on paved roads even though it can provide plenty of feedback as it negotiates holes and bumps on unbeaten tracks. A good thing, we must say, since braking isn't a standard of efficiency, especially without ABS (yes, that's another option).

To power this "dual purpose" utility, two engines are available for work. The 2.5-liter is a big and rough four-cylinder, and with power and torque re-energized two years ago, it's well-suited to the job, especially when it's teamed with a manual transmission. The 4.0-liter in-line six-cylinder is quieter provided you avoid the three-speed automatic transmission, which adds a few decibels to the noise level. Among other things this engine requires a 70-liter gas tank (another option) if you want reasonable range.

The off-road exploits that you can manage on a Wrangler leave the competition far behind. But unless you're a diehard all-terrain fan, can you really turn a blind eye to asphalted roads and practicality, two areas where, despite remarkable improvements, the Wrangler demands a lot of extra thought? In short, are you sure you can spend 12 happy months behind this model's wheel? **E.L.**

Specifications of Test Vehicle

Model: Wrangler SE

Exterior Dimensions	
Wheelbase	93.4 in.
Overall length	151.8 in.
Overall width	66.7 in.
Overall height	70.2 in.
Curb weight	3,100 lb.
Interior Dimensions	
Seating capacity	4
Head room	F:42.3/R:40.6 in.
Leg room	F:41.1/R:34.9 in.
Cargo volume	11.3 cu. ft.
Engine	
Displacement	I-4 2.5 L.
Horsepower	120 @ 5,400 rpm
Torque, lb-ft.	140 @ 3,500 rpm
Performance	
0-60 mph, acceleration	10.5 sec.
60-0 mph, braking	164 ft.
Turning circle	33.6 ft.
EPA city/highway	19/21 mpg
Test mileage	16 mpg
Fuel tank capacity	15 gal.

Prices

$14,000
$23,000

SE 2-door convertible
$14,090

Sport 2-door convertible
$17,505

Sahara 2-door convertible
$19,615

Warranty

Bumper-to-bumper
3/36,000

Powertrain
3/36,000

Rust-through
7/100,000

Other to Consider

Suzuki Vitara
Toyota Rav4

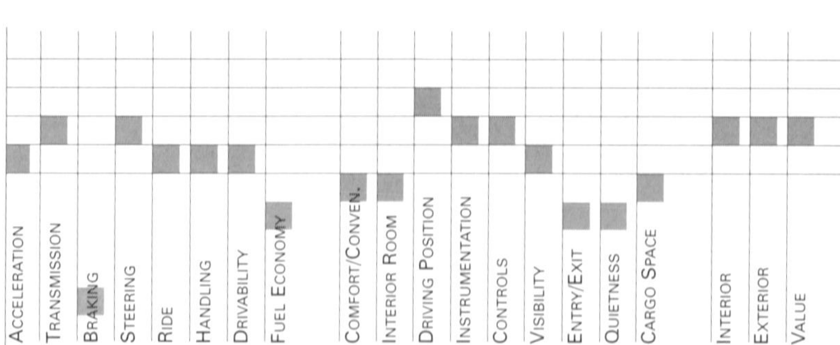

10
9
8
7
6
5
4
3
2
1

Kia Sephia

New for 99
Carryover

Pros
Better aerodynamics
Quiet ride
Roominess

Cons
Stripped-down base version
Unproven reliability
Minimal instrumentation

Equipment

Major Standard Equipment: Dual air bags, manual transmission, tinted glass, remote trunk release, front 3-point seat belts with adjustable anchors, rear window defroster. **LS adds :** Engine-speed sensitive power steering, variable intermittent wipers, tilt steering. **Major options:** Air conditioning alloy wheels, AM/FM/cassette, antilock brakes, automatic transmission, cruise control, power windows, power door locks.

The $10,000 question

PRICE
$9,000
$11,000
4-door
$9,995
4-door LS
$10,995

WARRANTY
(years/miles)
Bumper-to-bumper
3/36,000
Powertrain
5/60,000
Rust-through
5/100,000

OTHER TO CONSIDER
Hyundai Accent
Daewoo Lanos

Not familiar with the Kia Sephia? Good! Those who did encounter the first-generation Sephia know that it was a rough draft compared to the category's success stories. For its entry on the Canadian market, Kia is offering (oh, joy!) the final and perfected version of its model, much more inspired and much more original that we could have expected based on the initial effort. And the Sephia is a real Kia now, since the builder is using its very own mechanical components instead of merely borrowing them from Mazda, its partner corporation.

To rival the current Civic and Corolla, Kia got rid of the old Mazda Protegé platform in favor of an all-new, longer and wider alternative. Then the car builder added a more aerodynamic body. Doors open onto a completely revamped interior, much more inviting for rear-seat passengers than it was before. It's too bad Kia didn't add a few more instruments while it was at it, but at least those it does offer are easy to read and consult. Critics will be less indulgent as they contemplate the very short list of accessories that come with the base version. More stripped down than this, and you're stark naked! At the very least, buyers have to spend over $3,000 to own a properly equipped Sephia.

The 1.8-liter four-cylinder under the Sephia's hood is billed as the first engine built entirely by the Korean manufacturer. It is slightly more powerful than the Mazda engine used on the previous Sephia, but a significant drop in torque is its most worrisome characteristic. Regardless, this powertrain is a good match for either one of the two available transmissions.

With a relatively precise steering system and a well-calibrated suspension, the Sephia is a good choice as a day-to-day vehicle. Potential buyers will be particulary happy with the model's much improved soundproofing. Some of the progress can be attributed to better aerodynamics, but attention to detail and better quality soundproofing materials also have something to do with it.

More consistent, more refined, and roomier than its predecessor, in many ways the new Sephia still lags behind the category's leaders — except when it comes to price. **E.L.**

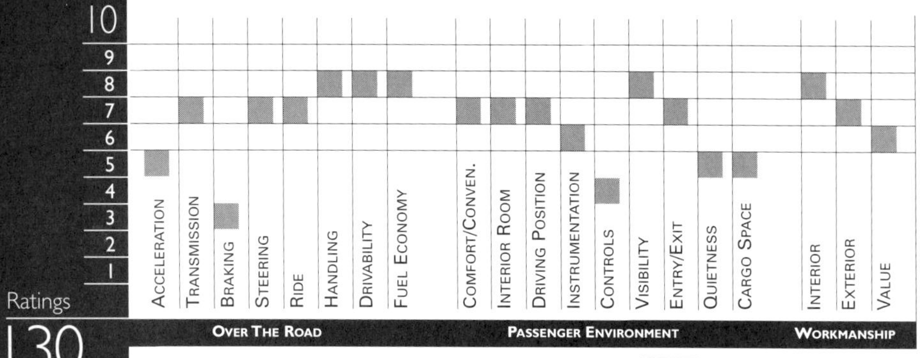
10
9
8
7
6
5
4
3
2
1
Ratings
Acceleration
Transmission
Braking
Steering
Ride
Handling
Drivability
Fuel Economy
Comfort/Conven.
Interior Room
Driving Position
Instrumentation
Controls
Visibility
Entry/Exit
Quietness
Cargo Space
Interior
Exterior
Value
Over The Road
Passenger Environment
Workmanship

Specifications of Test Vehicle

Model: Kia Sephia LS

Exterior Dimensions	
Wheelbase	100.8 in.
Overall lenght	174.4 in.
Overall widht	66.9 in.
Overall height	55.5 in.
Curb weight	2, 551 lb
Interior dimensions	
Seating capacity	4
Head room	F:39.6/R: 37.7 in.
Leg room	F:43.3/R: 34.4 in.
Cargo room	10.4 cu ft
Engine	
Displacement I-4 1,8 L.	
Horsepower	125 @ 6,000
Torque, lb-ft	108 @ 4,500
Performance	
0-60 mph, acceleration	NA
60-0 mph, braking	NA
Turning circle	32.1 ft
EPA city/highway	24/31
Test mileage	NA
Fuel tank capacity	13.2 gal.

Sportage

KIA

New for 99

New convertible

Pros

Increased safety
Convertible version
Manual transmission

Cons

Unsure balance
Stiff automatic transmission
Minimal comfort

Equipment

Major Standard Equipment: 2-liter I-4, manual transmission, intermittent wipers, power mirrors, rear defroster, split-folding rear seat, power windows, power locks, tilt steering wheel, theft-deterrent system. **EX adds:** Cruise control, rear wiper, luggage rack. **Major Options:** Automatic transmission, part-time 4-wheel drive, limited-slip differential, 4-wheel antilock brakes, air conditioning, cruise control, antilock brakes, automatic transmission, leather upholstery, AM/FM/CD stereo, luggage rack.

And now, introducing...

Kia, which means "blossom of the Orient" in Korean, says that the financial problems it has experienced in the recent past will have no effect on the marketing of the firm's products in North America or on the development of new products aimed at North American consumers.

Along with the Sephia, Kia plans to introduce the Sportage, a sport utility that resembles the Vitara, CR-V, and Forester. After my test drive done, my message would be: good luck!

Two years ago, the Sportage made headlines by offering the first air bag for knees, although the front-seat passenger was still riding without benefit of extra protection. The injustice was rectified on 1998 models, and a second air bag is on the list of passive safety features. As a premium, before adding the new feature, Kia has redesigned the dashboard and the center console (now equipped with an armrest) and proposes a height-adjustable steering column to make it easier to find the ideal driving position.

The Korean firm maintains that five people can ride in the Sportage. What the manufacturer doesn't mention is that the rear-seat occupants will have to jostle for elbow room and deal with a rather straight seat back, which doesn't make riding very comfortable. Things are better in the front, and bucket seats offer satisfactory comfort, but nothing extra. Lastly, it's too bad that the rear windshield wiper still isn't part of the base versions (2- or 4-wheel drive), which hurts visibility when weather conditions are poor.

Face to face with the RAV4, CR-V, Forester, and others, the Sportage can't withstand comparison and the 130 horses generated by its Mazda 2.0-liter four-cylinder engine are more convincing on paper than they are on the road. A gruff engine and stubborn automatic transmission also take away from the fun of driving this utility. The best idea is to make your choice the five-speed manual transmission designed by Getrag; it's a more efficient and less expensive alternative.

It should also be said that the Sportage's hefty weight cancels out any goodwill the engine tries to show. This Kia's suspension was designed with the help of Lotus Engineering, but the process hasn't led to as drastic and positive a change as it has on the Sephia. Still, thanks to its modest size, the Sportage is a fun all-terrain that handles well even if at times it seems to be on the point of losing its balance (in the rear-wheel drive mode), especially on roads that provide minimal tire-grip potential, and even if it feels like the defunct Suzuki X-90. Lastly, braking hasn't improved any and only rear wheels are equipped with ABS.

In light of this first test drive, by all indications Kia will have a very hard time lifting the Sportage to the top of the automotive industry's ranks. **E.L.**

Specifications of Test Vehicle

Model: Sportage

Exterior Dimensions	
Wheelbase	104.3 in.
Overall length	170.3 in.
Overall width	68.1 in.
Overall height	65 in.
Curb weight	3,300 lb.
Interior Dimensions	
Seating capacity	5
Head room	F:39.6/R:37.8 in.
Leg room	F:44.5/R:31.1 in.
Cargo room	25.8 cu. ft.
Engine	
Displacement	I-4 2 L.
Horsepower	130 @ 5,500 rpm
Torque, lb-ft.	127 @ 4,000 rpm
Performance	
0-60 mph, acceleration	11 sec.
60-0 mph, braking	164 ft.
Turning circle	34.8 ft.
EPA city/highway	19/23 mpg
Test mileage	18 mpg
Fuel tank capacity	15.8 gal.

Prices

$14,000
$19,000

4x2 $14,795
4x4 $16,295
EX 4x2 $17,395
EX 4x4 $18,595

Warranty

Bumper-to-bumper 3/36,000
Powertrain 5/60,000
Rust-through 5/100,000

Other to Consider

Chevrolet Tracker
Suzuki Vitara

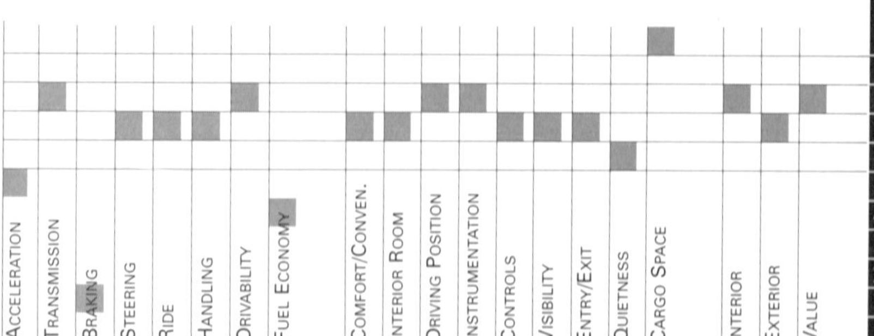

Ratings

Land Rover Discovery

New for 99
Revamped body
New transmission

Pros
New-found reliability
Off-road capabilities
Extraordinary visibility

Cons
Difficult access to the rear
Marginal engine power
High fuel consumption

Equipment

Major Standard Equipment: 4-liter V-8, all-wheel drive, 2-speed transfer case, 4-wheel antilock disc brakes, dual-temperature air conditioning, variable-intermittent wipers, power heated mirrors, automatic dimming rear-view mirror, rear washer and wiper, cruise control, power windows, power locks, remote keyless entry, power heated seats, leather upholstery, split-folding rear seat, dual power moonroofs, AM/FM/cassette stereo, trailer towing package, aluminum wheels. **LSE adds:** Chrome bumpers, body-colored grille, premium stereo. **Major Options:** Rear air conditioning, leather upholstery, double jump seats, power seats, hydraulic rear step, chrome bumpers.

Prestige and performance

PRICES
$35,000
$40,000
LE 4-door
$34,500
LSE 4-door
$38,000

WARRANTY
(years/miles)
Bumper-to-bumper
3/42,000
Powertrain
3/42,000
Rust-through
6/unlimited

OTHER TO CONSIDER
Infiniti QX4
Mercedes ML 320

With the Discovery series, introduced in 1989, the renowned British sport-utility expert, now part of the BMW fold, enjoyed a great deal of success on the European market. Updated regularly over the years, the vehicle made its North American debut in 1994 and since then has been the object of much admiration, especially from a well-off clientele base sensitive to the prestige attached to the make, whose Range Rover model is the uncontested aristocrat of its niche.

Land Rover is launching the second-generation Discovery, baptized the Series II, with added enthusiasm generated by the fact that in the most serious and well-respected automotive industry surveys, the model is moving toward the top of reliability and customer satisfaction ratings by leaps and bounds.

The Discovery has been revamped almost completely, but it looks so much like the previous model that you'll have a hard time telling the two apart. Inside, the all-new dashboard looks like the old one as well. The same goes for seats, which are very comfortable despite an oversized center console. As for the slightly elevated rear bench seat, it is very comfortable and provides an excellent view of the outside, whether you're on safari at your local wildlife park or on an excursion in the back of beyond. However, access is somewhat difficult because doors are too short and positioned directly over the wheel wells, which restricts footwork to a minimum.

The Series II is 6.6 inches longer, mainly to increase cargo space and to accommodate the optional third seat, which folds to the sides in a split configuration. The front and rear tracks are 2.2 and 3 inches wider, respectively, resulting in more stability and less sway.

Rear overhang is a bit longer, but the Discovery is still an exceptional off-road vehicle. It has a new all-wheel traction control system that makes the ride smoother. A feature unique to Land Rover is the Hill Descent Control system that monitors wheel speed and applies brakes to help maintain proper speed when descending steep slopes. The two systems make optimum use of the four-circuit antilock system, which is standard on this vehicle, of course. And to minimize sway, Land Rover has equipped the Discovery with an Active Cornering Enhancement system that measures lateral acceleration during cornering and uses a hydraulic system to apply torque to the body via two piston/lever configurations (to replace conventional anti-roll bars).

The 4.0-liter engine, with an aluminum block and a center camshaft, has been revised and refined and is coupled with a new, electronically controlled four-speed automatic transmission. It's smooth and cooperative and it always sounds good, but its 188-hp output is barely enough under usual driving conditions, especially compared to the power generated by similar type engines used on rival models. When can consumers expect a rugged version of BMW's superb 4.4-liter V-8? Soon, let's hope. **M.L.**

Specifications of Test Vehicle

Model: Discovery LSE

Exterior Dimensions	
Wheelbase	100 in.
Overall length	178.7 in.
Overall width	70.6 in.
Overall height	77.4 in.
Curb weight	4,450 lb.
Interior Dimensions	
Seating capacity	5
Head room	F:37.4/R:39.2 in.
Leg room	F:38.5/R:36.3 in.
Cargo volume	45.8 cu. ft.
Engine	
Displacement	V-8 4 L.
Horsepower	182 @ 4,750 rpm
Torque, lb-ft.	233 @ 3,000 rpm
Performance	
0-60 mph, acceleration	10.9 sec
60-0 mph, braking	139 ft.
Turning circle	39.4 ft.
EPA city/highway	14/17 mpg
Test mileage	14 mpg
Fuel tank capacity	23.1 gal.

Ratings

Category	Rating
Over the Road	
Acceleration	6
Transmission	8
Braking	4
Steering	7
Ride	7
Handling	6
Drivability	8
Fuel Economy	3
Passenger Environment	
Comfort/Conven.	7
Interior Room	8
Driving Position	9
Instrumentation	7
Controls	6
Visibility	6
Entry/Exit	6
Quietness	8
Cargo Space	10
Workmanship	
Interior	9
Exterior	9
Value	7

Ratings 141

Land Rover

Range Rover

New for 99

Side air bags
Electronic traction control system
New exterior colors

Pros

Off-road capabilities
Astonishing acceleration power
Comfortable and quiet ride

Cons

High fuel consumption
Large size
Reliability problems

Equipment

Major Standard Equipment: 4-liter V-8, all-wheel drive, 4-wheel antilock disc brakes, air suspension, dual-temperature automatic air conditioning, cabin air filter, heated windshield washers, rear washer and wiper, headlamp wipers and heated washers, heated windshield, power moonroof, tilt and telescoping steering column, power windows, power locks, remote keyless entry, memory seats, AM/FM/CD/cassette stereo, automatic dimming rear-view mirror, theft alarm system, trailer towing package. **4.6 HSE adds:** 4.6-liter V-8, larger tires, mud flaps. **Major Options:** Extra-cost paint colors.

Big and pretentious

Modesty will never overwhelm the Land Rover team when it starts to sing the praises of the Range! While it has a sure talent for negotiating the obstacles Mother Nature throws its way, a passenger compartment that could almost double as a Victorian living room, and a price that makes it exclusive, it has a long way to go before becoming the king of luxury utilities it's claimed to be. First of all, it needs closer attention to manufacturing quality and, above all, reliability. And side air bags are certainly not enough to make us change our verdict.

Birds of a feather flock together, the saying goes. BMW (which now owns the British firm) and Land Rover were made to get along. For proof, read the owner's manual from cover to cover to understand how the Range's accessories work. Front seats, power adjustable in all possible directions, take orthopedic care of the back, kidneys, and neck rather than subjecting them to overly soft padding. As for the bench seat, it's even firmer and it has a wider base; the seatback folds down in two (60/40) sections, but it's unlikely you'll need more space than the very roomy trunk already provides.

When you're behind the wheel of a Range Rover, it's hard not to feel superior to the motorists around you. Set high, the Range looks invincible. And it almost is, particularly when weather conditions make road surfaces slippery, in which case it's unflappable. General comments: the ride is as quiet as can be, may have slightly "military" reactions that reflect road conditions, and cornering unpredictability is due to the fact that the Range brings driving sensations that few have ever experienced. Lastly, the responsive steering system makes up for the horrendous turning radius and phenomenal torque manages to shatter the inertia of this massive vehicle, giving it astonishing acceleration. In this regard, potential buyers should note that the SE is powered by a 188-hp 4.0-liter V-8, and the HSE is equipped with a 222-hp 4.6-liter. Muscle-bound powertrains, yes, but according to owners they suffer from a series of minor flaws that no one should have to put up with on a vehicle sold at this price. **E.L.**

Prices

$56,000
$64,000

4.0 SE 4-door
$56,000

4.6 HSE 4-door
$63,500

Warranty

(years/miles)

Bumper-to-bumper
3/42,000

Powertrain
3/42,000

Rust-through
6/unlimited

Other to consider

Lexus LX 470

Lincoln Navigator

Specifications of Test Vehicle

Model: 4.0 SE

Exterior Dimensions	
Wheelbase	108.1 in.
Overall length	185.5 in.
Overall width	74.4 in.
Overall height	71.6 in.
Curb weight	4,950 lb.
Interior Dimensions	
Seating capacity	5
Head room	F:38.1/R:38.2 in.
Leg room	F:42.6/R:36.5 in.
Cargo volume	31 cu. ft.
Engine	
Displacement	V-8 4 L.
Horsepower	190 @ 4,750 rpm
Torque, lb-ft.	236 @ 3,000 rpm
Performance	
0-60 mph, acceleration	11.9 sec.
60-0 mph, braking	140 ft.
Turning circle	39 ft.
EPA city/highway	13/17 mpg
Test mileage	16 mpg
Fuel tank capacity	24.6 gal.

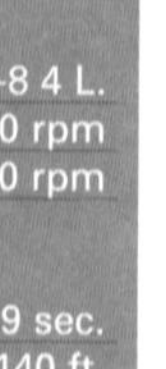

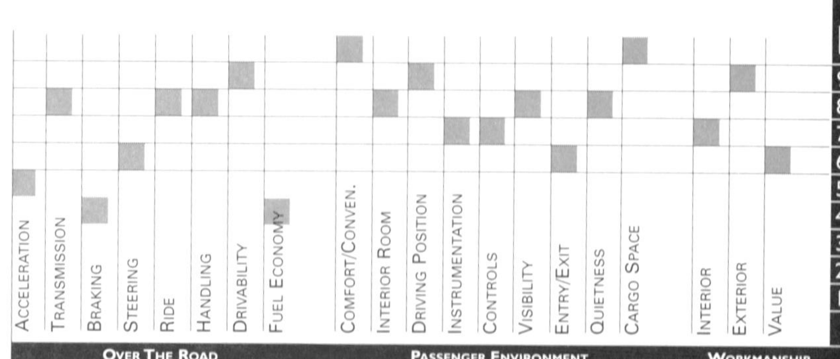

Ratings
147

Lexus

ES 300

New for 99

Variable Valve Timing intelligence (VVT-i) system

Pros

Level of sophistication
Quality after-sales service
Exemplary finishing

Cons

Unexciting lines
Comfort-focused ride
Unresponsive steering system

Equipment

Major Standard Equipment: 3-liter V-6, automatic transmission, 4-wheel antilock disc brakes, variable-assist power steering, stainless-steel exhaust system, automatic air conditioning, variable-intermittent wipers, tilt steering column, cruise control, automatic headlamps, AM/FM/cassette stereo, power heated mirrors, rear defroster, power windows, power locks, power seats, power driver's lumbar adjustment, power decklid release, remote keyless entry, theft alarm system, full-size spare tire, aluminum wheels.
Major Options: Automatic shock-absorber control, traction control, leather upholstery, memory driver's seat, AM/FM/CD/cassette stereo, heated seats, power moonroof, chrome wheels, all-season tires.

Ornate

PRICES
$31,000
$35,000
Sedan
$31,400

WARRANTY
(years/miles)
Bumper-to-bumper
4/50,000
Powertrain
6/70,000
Rust-through
6/unlimited

OTHER TO CONSIDER
Infiniti I30
Mazda Millenia

It's no secret: under the gilt and the leather of a Lexus ES300 is a Toyota Camry. When the ES300 was revamped (coincidentally, at the same time as the Camry), the kinship between the two models became less obvious, but remained discernible: a single platform, the same engines (but with less horsepower for the ES300), and similar sizing. To ward off any possible criticism, Lexus decked out the ES300 in a series of innovative touches including the VVT-i (for Variable Valve Timing intelligence) to give the 3.0-liter V-6 better pick-up ability. However, it's a shame that the Vehicle Skid Control system — which prevents understeering and oversteering by electronically modulating braking power and by shutting off the fuel supply — is available as an option.

Longer, wider, and more aerodynamic than the previous generation, this Lexus opens wide onto a richly equipped and carefully assembled passenger compartment. With clear and bright instruments and well-designed controls that are easy to reach, it's hard to criticize the ES300. But as is the case with its closest rivals, its rear bench seat can only fit two adults if you want them to be comfortable.

At the risk of angering Lexus, I must say that the ES300 handles very much like a Camry XLE V6. There's no doubt that it has better soundproofing than its sister model, but the character traits that are supposed to set it apart aren't as major as Lexus would have us believe. The result: a light steering system, efficient brakes, excellent traction control, and a transmission willing to comply with the driver's every whim. The degree of shock absorption provided by the suspension can be adjusted, but some possibilities have little or no effect on the vehicle's ride while the mechanism itself is very expensive to repair or replace. In short, we would surely rate the ES300 as a much better car if we weren't already familiar with the Camry XLE V-6 or the roomier Avalon. **E.L.**

Over the Road	Rating
Acceleration	10
Transmission	10
Braking	7
Steering	9
Ride	10
Handling	9
Drivability	9
Fuel Economy	7

Passenger Environment	Rating
Comfort/Conven.	10
Interior Room	8
Driving Position	9
Instrumentation	10
Controls	10
Visibility	9
Entry/Exit	10
Quietness	10
Cargo Space	7

Workmanship	Rating
Interior	10
Exterior	10
Value	9

Ratings
165

Specifications of Test Vehicle

Model: ES 300

Exterior Dimensions	
Wheelbase	105.1 in.
Overall length	190.2 in.
Overall width	70.5 in.
Overall height	54.9 in.
Curb weight	3,300 lb.
Interior dimensions	
Seating capacity	5
Head room	F:36.8/R:36 in.
Leg room	F:43.5/R:34.4 in.
Cargo volume	13 cu. ft.
Engine	
Displacement	V-6 3 L.
Horsepower	200 @ 5,200 rpm
Torque, lb-ft.	214 @ 4,400 rpm
Performance	
0-60 mph, acceleration	7.2sec.
60-0 mph, braking	125 ft.
Turning circle	36.7 ft
EPA city/highway	19/27 mpg
Test mileage	24 mpg
Fuel tank capacity	18.5 gal.

Lexus

GS

New for 99

No changes

Pros

Sporty handling
Excellent transmission
Impeccable manufacturing quality

Cons

Controversial styling
Minimal trunk volume
Rear seats

Equipment

Major Standard Equipment: 3-liter I-6, 5-speed automatic transmission, traction control, 4-wheel antilock disc brakes, automatic stability control, variable-assist power steering, dual-temperature air conditioning, cabin air filter, variable-intermittent wipers, rear defroster, power tilt and telescope steering wheel, cruise control, power windows, power locks, remote keyless entry, power decklid release, auto-dimming rear-view mirror, AM/FM/cassette stereo, automatic headlights, theft-deterrent system, aluminum wheels. **GS 400 adds:** 4-liter V-8, semi-automatic transmission, automatic dimming side mirrors, leather upholstery, driver's memory system.

1999 AAA TOP CAR

A pleasant encounter

Even if it did look superb, the first GS was mediocre at best. This time out, Yasushi Nakagawa, the project's head engineer, has come up with a second generation with plenty to see and admire.

For those automotive journalists who want to pad their articles, the GS's interior has plenty to talk about. Leather and wood combine to create a warm, comfortable, tasteful, and refined ambience. However, the dashboard breaks the spell with a design that looks as if it belongs in a spaceship. The Opti-tron lighting developed by Lexus neutralizes any annoying reflections and makes it easy to read the dials, tucked back in cylinders. Lastly, on the right the oversized console, unable to accommodate the hand brake, is home for the radio, air conditioning, and navigation system controls.

The three headrests mounted on the rear bench seat leave no doubt that it is meant for three passengers. The only problem: the third person will have to deal with a fairly uncomfortable multi-function seatback (it hides a large armrest and a pair of cupholders) and a massive bump (remember, the GS is loyal to rear-wheel drive).

Technically speaking, the new GS models bring us back to square one and quickly make potential owners forget about the pitiful performance levels seen in the previous generation. With leading-edge driveability, powerful acceleration, and impressive pickup, the two GS models also demonstrate that Lexus is capable of building something other than boring automobiles. While the GS approaches and in some areas even surpasses the 5-Series, some critics will no doubt point out that its performance levels are artificially achieved. The GS's excellent road stability is due to its VSC (Vehicle Skid Control), similar to the ESP system made available by Mercedes, which prevents understeering and oversteering by electronically modulating brakes and by shutting off the fuel supply. The VVT-i (for Variable Valve Timing intelligence) system lets the six- and eight-cylinders in the GS supply 80 % of their torque at 1,800 rpm. The engines are coupled with a five-speed automatic transmission and aboard the GS400, speeds can be selected manually using buttons mounted on the horizontal branches of the steering wheel. However, note that unlike almost all other systems of the same type, this system is fun to use and amazingly efficient. Unfortunately, Lexus hasn't decided to mimic BMW by offering a five- or six-speed transmission, claiming that consumers looking for cars in this particular price range don't want that alternative.

With the GS300 and the GS400, Lexus makes liars out of some observers who predicted that the Japanese automobile industry was incapable of reacting effectively to the strong comeback staged by German builders. **E.L.**

Specifications of Test Vehicle

Model: GS 400

Exterior Dimensions	
Wheelbase	110.2 in.
Overall length	189 in.
Overall width	70.9 in.
Overall height	56.7 in.
Curb weight	3,700 lb.
Interior Dimensions	
Seating capacity	5
Head room	F:39.2/R:37 in.
Leg room	F:44.5/R:34.3 in.
Cargo room	14.8 cu. ft.
Engine	
Displacement	V-8 4 L.
Horsepower	300 @ 6,000 rpm
Torque, lb-ft.	310 @ 4,000 rpm
Performance	
0-60 mph, acceleration	6.6 sec.
60-0 mph, braking	120 ft.
Turning circle	36.1 ft.
EPA city/highway	17/23 mpg
Test mileage	NA
Fuel tank capacity	19.8 gal.

Prices
$37,000
$50,000
GS 300 sedan $37,800
GS 400 sedan $46,000

Warranty
Bumper-to-bumper 4/50,000
Powertrain 6/70,000
Rust-through 6/unlimited

Other to consider
BMW 540 i
Mercedes E 430

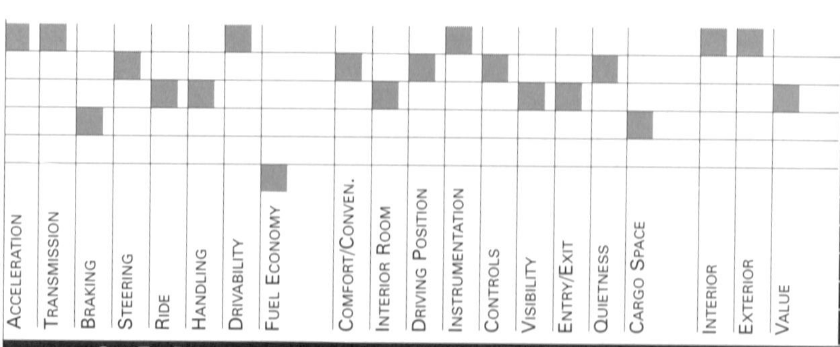

Ratings
172

Lexus LS 400

New for 99

Leather- and wood-wrapped steering wheel

Pros

Unparalleled refinement
Total reliability
Good after-sales service

Cons

Trunk volume
Uninspired lines
Virtually no driveability

Equipment

Major Standard Equipment: 4-liter V-8, variable-assist power steering, 4-wheel antilock disc brakes, dual-temperature automatic air conditioning, cabin air filter, speed-sensing wipers, leather upholstery, power seats, power windows, cruise control, power tilt and telescope steering wheel, tilt-away steering column, AM/FM /cassette stereo, rear defroster, power heated mirrors, automatic dimming mirrors, remote keyless entry, theft alarm system. **Major Options:** Power moonroof, driver's memory system, air suspension, high-intensity headlamps, AM/FM/CD/cassette stereo, heated seats, navigation system, chrome wheels.

Perfect, but boring

PRICES
$53,000
$62,000
Sedan
$54,100

WARRANTY
Bumper-to-Bumper
4/50,000
Power Train
6/70,000
Rust-through
6/Unlimited

OTHER TO CONSIDER
BMW 540i
Jaguar XJ8

The LS 400 has one ambition: perfection. That's why each year, its designers make changes so that it can look its very best and offer us details we may not even have known existed.

But the obsession to be even more than perfect is pursued to the detriment of its personality. Cold and austere, the LS 400 has no discernible soul. For 1999, its stylists have made a special small effort and wrapped the steering wheel in leather and wood, while also launching a new color: Mystical Gold.

On the outside, the LS 400 is still devoid of any warmth, even if its wheel covers, hood, grille, and headlights were all redesigned last year. Inside, however, the ambiance is warmer, thanks to the magnificent wood inlays on the dashboard, the console, the shift lever, and even the steering wheel. A nice touch. Besides redecorating, Lexus also came up with a more efficient air conditioning system and a new onboard computer. Who could ask for more! Or more accurately, we would have asked for something different, like a heated rear bench seat (Jaguar has one) or a see-through shade for the rear window (a feature on the Audi A8). On the other hand, the LS 400 is roomier than it used to be and offers power height-adjustable seat belts that its German rival doesn't have.

Any other criticism? Trunk volume is a disappointment given the size of this car.

Whether it's at rest or moving, this Lexus is a heavyweight, on a par with its rival and role-model, the Mercedes S-Class. Its 32-valve V8 is incontestably the quietest engine in the entire automotive industry and the five-speed automatic transmission it's paired with shifts effortlessly and completely unnoticed by driver and passengers. In short, you hear nothing and you feel nothing when you drive or ride in this car, all the more so since the steering system insulates and provides little or no information on road conditions. And maybe that's for the better, since the LS 400 is not a great touring car. Its weight, its size, and its soft ride rob it of a great deal of agility, not to mention that the brakes could bite a lot more in emergency situations.

The LS 400's designers have a way to go yet before they attain perfection. But we have to admit that in several areas (reliability, service, finish, quality), the LS 400 has already reached its objective. **E.L.**

Specifications of Test Vehicle

Model: LS 400

Exterior Dimensions	
Wheelbase	112.2 in.
Overall length	196.7 in.
Overall width	72 in.
Overall height	56.5 in.
Curb weight	3,900 lb.
Interior Dimensions	
Seating capacity	5
Head room	F:37.9/R:35.7 in.
Leg room	F:43.7/R:36.9 in.
Cargo volume	13.9 cu. ft.
Engine	
Displacement	V-8 4 L.
Horsepower	290 @ 6,000 rpm
Torque, lb-ft.	300 @ 4,000 rpm
Performance	
0-60 mph, acceleration	7.1 sec.
60-0 mph, braking	123 ft.
Turning circle	34.8 ft.
EPA city/highway	19/25 mpg
Test mileage	20 mpg
Fuel tank capacity	22.5 gal.

Ratings

Group	Category	Rating
Over The Road	Acceleration	9
Over The Road	Transmission	9
Over The Road	Braking	6
Over The Road	Steering	8
Over The Road	Ride	10
Over The Road	Handling	7
Over The Road	Drivability	8
Over The Road	Fuel Economy	4
Passenger Environment	Comfort/Conven.	10
Passenger Environment	Interior Room	9
Passenger Environment	Driving Position	8
Passenger Environment	Instrumentation	10
Passenger Environment	Controls	9
Passenger Environment	Visibility	8
Passenger Environment	Entry/Exit	9
Passenger Environment	Quietness	9
Passenger Environment	Cargo Space	6
Workmanship	Interior	10
Workmanship	Exterior	10
Workmanship	Value	7

Ratings 166

Lexus

LX 470

New for 99

Introduced in mid-'99 with new interior, exterior, and powertrain.

Pros

Comfort/convenience
Powertrain performance
Fit & finish

Cons

Fuel economy
Rear seats
Handling

Equipment

Major Standard Equipment: 4.7 liter V-8 engine, 4-speed automatic transmission, adjustable height control, locking center differential, rear limited slip differential, antilock brakes, power folding heated side mirrors, eletrochromic mirrors, automatic headlights, automatic climate control, rear climate control, leather seat trim, foldable and reclining split second-row seat, foldable and removable third-row seat, heated power front seats, power windows and locks, power tilt and telescope steering wheel, AM/FM/cassette/CD changer audio system, keyless remote entry, security system. **Major Options:** Moonroof, premium audio system.

The lure of profit

The new Lexus LX 470 is the upscale version of Toyota's also-new Land Cruiser. It's aimed squarely at those who want the biggest and best and probably don't know, or even care, what the term "fuel economy" means. The LX 470 is big, luxurious, and dominates the rest of the market when it comes to standard features. Being big does not necessarily tell the whole story, so read on.

In addition to the features common to the Land Cruiser, the LX 470 offers several exclusive variations. Adjustable Height Control or AHC uses pressurized shock absorbers to change the body height — high, normal, and low. The Adaptive Variable Suspension or AVS continuously changes shock absorber valving at each wheel. A computer system selects from a range of different settings, depending on feedback from various road sensors.The system senses irregularities, steering activity, and other factors to adjust shocks to a stiffer value as needed for a more stable ride or soften to absorb a bump.

Inside, expect nothing but the best: soft leather seats, thick carpet, and gadgets everywhere. One-touch up and down power windows are provided for all seats. Standard is a single-feed six CD changer. Lexus trademark electroluminescent gauges highlight the instrument panel. Wood veneer trims the doors and the center console. Front seats are fully supportive and comfortable. The center row can accommodate three adults comfortably. Now for the bad news. Don't even think of asking adults to sit in the third row. It's there only for emergencies. Entry and exit are typical of every large sport utility vehicle. It's a climb up and/or a slide down. Running boards seem to help only in getting clothes dirty. The high seating position guarantees a good view of the road ahead. Large side-view mirrors help with the view to the sides. But visibility to the rear is hampered by the general configuration of the vehicle. Use caution when maneuvering in parking lots.

On the road, the LX 470 is comfortable, even luxurious, when cruising the interstates. Acceleration from a stop to cruising speed is a seamless experience smooth, quiet, and uneventful.Console buttons can select a power shift mode for a more thrilling experience, or a second-gear start for better traction on slippery roads. However, country roads bring out the weaknesses in such a heavy, ponderous vehicle. Uneven pavement brings on swaying from side to side, and curvy roads remind the driver that this is no sports car. The vehicle that seemed so stable and predictable on the highway is suddenly a handful when turns and hills are encountered. Brake pedal feel is quite good, and the stopping distance from 60 mph was above average for a vehicle this heavy.

The LX 470 is a perfectly capable vehicle, whether on- or off-road. The real mystique is knowing that it can handle practically any situation, while dropping off guests at the country club. **D.V.S.**

Specifications of Test Vehicle

Model: 4-wheel-drive

Exterior Dimensions	
Wheelbase	112.2 in.
Overall Length	192.5 In.
Overall Width	76.4 In.
Overall Height	72.8 In.
Curb Weight	5401 lbs.
Interior Dimensions	
Seating Capacity	8
Head Room	F: 40.0/C: 39.4/R: 36.3 in.
Leg Room	F: 42.3/C: 34.3/R: 27.3 in.
Cargo Room	19.1 cu.ft.
Engine	
Displacement	4.7L V-8
Horsepower	230@4800 rpm
Torque, lb-ft.	320@3400 rpm
Performance	
0-60 mph, acceleration	9.9 sec.
60-0 mph, braking	135 ft.
Turning Circle	39.7 ft.
EPA City/Highway	13/16 mpg.
Test Mileage	10.8
Fuel Tank Capacity	25.4 gal.

Prices

$56,500
$60,000

LX 470
4-door
sport utility
4-wheel drive
$56,400

Warranty

Bumper-to-Bumper
4/50,000

Power Train
6/70,000

Rust-through
6/Unlimited

Other to Consider

Land Rover Range SE

Lincoln Navigator

Ratings

Category	Rating
Over The Road	
Acceleration	7
Transmission	9
Braking	5
Steering	7
Ride	8
Handling	7
Drivability	8
Fuel Economy	1
Passenger Environment	
Comfort/Conven.	8
Interior Room	9
Driving Position	8
Instrumentation	9
Controls	8
Visibility	7
Entry/Exit	7
Quietness	9
Cargo Space	9
Workmanship	
Interior	9
Exterior	9
Value	6

Ratings
150

Lexus RX300

new MODEL

New for 99

Totally new vehicle, based on Lexus ES300 platform.

Pros

Ride
Handling
Versatility

Cons

Off road capability
Fuel economy
Styling

Equipment

Major Standard Equipment: 3.0 liter V-6 engine, 4-speed automatic transmission, 2-wheel drive, antilock brakes, side air bags, automatic headlights, sliding rear seat with 60/40 split seat back, automatic climate control, trip computer, premium sound system.

Major Options: Leather seating, power moonroof, heated front memory seats, CD changer, traction control.

PRICES
$32,000
$39,000

WARRANTY
Bumper-to-Bumper 4/50,000
Power Train 6/70,000
Rust-through 6/Unlimited

OTHER TO CONSIDER
Infiniti QX4
Mercedes ML320

First in a dynasty

The 1999 Lexus RX300, along with several competitors, represents a new breed of sport-utility vehicles. All-weather capability, style, comfort, and luxury all combine to give the SUV buyer something other than a truck derivative to consider.

The RX300 is derived from the Lexus ES300 platform, but the similarity ends there. The body, suspension, and many of the powertrain components are unique. Power is supplied by a 3.0-liter V-6, using Toyota's VVT-i system. It produces 220 hp, with a full 80 % of its torque available at only 1600 rpm. Practically all engine vibration is neutralized by active engine mounts that create pulses of force, opposite to the engine movements. A 4-speed automatic transmission incorporates a transfer case with a viscous coupling to the rear wheels. It is a full-time arrangement with no intervention possible by the driver.

Inside, the RX300 is pure Lexus. The instrument panel uses the well-known Lexus Optitron backlighting, making it easy to read under any condition. The console is two separate units. The upper console is U-shaped and contains most of the controls, including an LCD screen for operating the air conditioning, sound system, and the trip computer. Intended to be trendy and compact, it requires the driver to look at the display (instead of the road) to make the slightest change in any setting. The upper part of the console also houses the unconventional shift lever, leaving room for storage in the lower console.

Interior fit and finish are what you might expect upscale materials and real wood trim are standard. The firm, supportive front bucket seats recline almost completely. The rear seat is cleverly designed to recline, fold nearly flat, and has about four inches of travel to maximize either leg room or cargo capacity.

On the road, the RX300 is refined. The ride is Lexus-smooth and the drivetrain is Lexus-quiet. Acceleration is satisfying getting, from 0 to 60 mph takes only 8.9 seconds. The brakes have good pedal feel and can stop the RX from 60 mph in only 126 feet. Handling is luxury-car-like. Expect some body roll and mild understeer in tight corners. Entry and exit are car-like, with no climbing required. Even so, the driver sits fairly high, for good visibility in all directions. The large rear opening and low liftover make loading heavy objects a simple matter.

On slippery surfaces, the all-wheel drive works invisibly. We drove on a slippery dirt road without hesitation. However, this is no off-road vehicle. Ground clearance and the lack of a 2-speed transfer case limit the kind of terrain one can reasonably expect to travel.

Lexus has targeted the RX300 at a different kind of SUV buyer. Off-road performance is of no concern. Comfort, luxury, security, and a generous measure of utility are what the RX300 is all about. **D.V.S.**

Specifications of Test Vehicle

Model: 4-Wheel Drive

Exterior Dimensions	
Wheelbase	103.1 in.
Overall Length	180.1 In.
Overall Width	71.5 In.
Overall Height	65.7 In.
Curb Weight	3900 lbs.
Interior Dimensions	
Seating Capacity	
Head Room	F: 39.5/R: 39.2 in.
Leg Room	F: 40.7/R: 36.4 in.
Cargo Room	30.4 cu.ft.
Engine	
Displacement	3.0 L V-6
Horsepower	220@5800 rpm
Torque, lb-ft.	222@4400 rpm
Performance	
0-60 mph, acceleration	8.9 sec.
60-0 mph, braking	126 ft.
Turning Circle	41.3 ft.
EPA City/Highway	17/21 mpg.
Test Mileage	18.8
Fuel Tank Capacity	17.2 gal

Ratings

Group	Category	Rating
Over The Road	Acceleration	8
	Transmission	9
	Braking	6
	Steering	8
	Ride	8
	Handling	7
	Drivability	8
	Fuel Economy	4
Passenger Environment	Comfort/Conven.	8
	Interior Room	7
	Driving Position	9
	Instrumentation	9
	Controls	8
	Visibility	8
	Entry/Exit	8
	Quietness	9
	Cargo Space	10
Workmanship	Interior	8
	Exterior	9
	Value	6

157

Lexus SC

New for 99

No changes

Pros

Braking
Handling
Acceleration

Cons

Fuel economy
Rear-seat room
Cargo space

Equipment

Major Standard Equipment: 3-liter I-6, automatic transmission, 4-wheel antilock disc brakes, variable-assist power steering, stainless-steel exhaust system, automatic air conditioning, rear defroster, power heated mirrors, automatic dimming mirrors, variable-intermittent wipers, automatic headlamps, tilt and telescoping steering wheel, theft-deterrent system, power seats, power windows, power locks, remote keyless entry, power decklid release, limited driver's memory, trip computer, AM/FM/cassette stereo, full-size spare tire, aluminum wheels. **SC 400 adds:** 4-liter V-8, leather upholstery, power tilt steering column, automatic tilt-away steering column.

Still a great coupe

For a luxury sports coupe, the Lexus SC looks the part. Only about 5,000 are sold each year. If you buy one, you'll be in select company.

Like European luxury carmakers, Lexus uses letters to designate models (in this case, SC, for "sports coupe") followed by the engine displacement, in deciliters. The SC's standard engine is the 225-horsepower, 6-cylinder used in the GS 300. A step up to the SC 400 brings the 4-liter V-8 with the automatic transmission found in the LS 400 and GS 400.

With a wide power band and response, the 4-liter engine offers better performance in the SC 400 than it does in the LS 400, because the latter is 300 pounds heavier. The V-8 works well with the 5-speed automatic transmission, giving us a 0-60 mph time of only 6.5 seconds. On our test drives, we averaged just under 17 mpg on high-octane gas.

The independent suspension has a sporty, firm feel, but provides a comfortably cushioned ride without sacrificing handling. On the highway, the SC rides with supple smoothness. And on a twisting road or in an emergency lane change, it responds reassuringly. The car's braking performance was among the best we tested. The 4-wheel antilock disc brakes stopped it from 60 mph in 112 feet.

Although the front-seat comfort earns high marks, taller occupants will find tight clearance overhead. In the back, the sloping rear glass pinches head room. Leg and foot room there ranges from little to none. Lexus doesn't even pretend that the SC will seat three people in back. And, at 9.3 cubic feet, the trunk is just plain small, and the rear seatback doesn't fold down to expand capacity.

The steering wheel tilts up automatically when you turn off the ignition, making exit and entry easier. Special hinges push the doors forward as they swing out for better access. Tall windows, large rear-view mirrors, and moderately narrow roof pillars help visibility.

On the dash, the SC sticks to basics. The instruments are limited to speedometer, tachometer, and coolant temperature and fuel gauges. The large knob for temperature control is too easily confused with the volume knob on the radio. Other controls are perfectly positioned and easy to use.

Although not as silent as the vault-like LS 400, the SC coupe is pleasantly hushed. Only the V-8's throaty rumble and an appropriate feedback of road noise punctuate the silence in the cabin.

The SC is a true Lexus and shares few parts with Toyota products. With the 6-cylinder engine, the SC 300 isn't as quick as the 400, but offers a better value. **D.V.S.**

Prices

$44,000
$59,000

SC 300 coupe $43,400

SC 400 coupe $55,700

Warranty

(years/miles)

Bumper-to-bumper 4/50,000

Powertrain 6/70,000

Rust-through 6/unlimited

Other to Consider

Volvo C70

Mercedes CLK

Specifications of Test Vehicle

Model: SC 400

Exterior Dimensions	
Wheelbase	105.9 in.
Overall length	192.5 in.
Overall width	70.9 in.
Overall height	53.2 in.
Curb weight	3,550 lb.
Interior Dimensions	
Seating capacity	4
Head room	F:36.7/R:36.1 in.
Leg room	F:44.1/R:27.2 in.
Cargo volume	9.3 cu. ft.
Engine	
Displacement	V-8 4 L.
Horsepower	290 @ 6,000 rpm
Torque, lb-ft.	300 @ 4,000 rpm
Performance	
0-60 mph, acceleration	6.5 sec.
60-0 mph, braking	112 ft.
Turning circle	36.1 ft.
EPA city/highway	19/25 mpg
Test mileage	17 mpg
Fuel tank capacity	20.6 gal.

Ratings (scale 1–10)

Over The Road: Acceleration, Transmission, Braking, Steering, Ride, Handling, Drivability, Fuel Economy

Passenger Environment: Comfort/Conven., Interior Room, Driving Position, Instrumentation, Controls, Visibility, Entry/Exit, Quietness, Cargo Space

Workmanship: Interior, Exterior, Value

Ratings 157

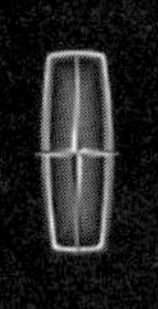

Lincoln LS

new MODEL

New for 99

New model

Pros

Not tested

Cons

Not tested

Equipement

Not available

A new Lincoln era

For the past few months, Lincoln has been busy preparing the world for an international-caliber luxury sedan capable of standing up to the very best on the planet's roads: the LS. The new model will be available in two versions, one powered by a six-cylinder (LS6) and the other by an eight-cylinder (LS8). It will even be available with a five-speed manual transmission, a first for Lincoln. Other surprises include a battery positioned in the trunk for optimal weight distribution and a list of standard accessories as long as your arm.

PRICE

Not available

WARRANTY
(years/miles)

Bumper-to-bumper
4/50,000

Powertrain
4/50,000

Rust-through
6/100,000

OTHER TO CONSIDER

Cadillac Catera

Jaguar S-Type

Specifications of Test Vehicle

Model: LS 6

Exterior Dimensions	
Wheelbase	NA
Overall lenght	NA
Overall widht	NA
Overall height	NA
Curb weight	NA
Interior dimensions	
Seating capacity	5
Head room	NA
Leg room	NA
Cargo room	NA
Engine	
Displacement	V6 3.0 L
Horsepower	210 @ 6.,500
Torque, lb-ft	205 @ 4,750
Performance	
0-60 mph, acceleration	Not tested
60-0 mph, braking	Not tested
Turning circle	NA
EPA city/highway	Not tested
Test mileage	Not tested
Fuel tank capacity	NA

Lincoln

Continental

New for 99

Side air bags
New audio system
New exterior colors

Pros

Technical innovations
Smooth and strong engine
Comfortable ride

Cons

Marshmallow suspension
Long turning radius
Limited space in the rear

Equipment

Major Standard Equipment: 4.6-liter V-8, 4-wheel antilock disc brakes, traction control, driver-controlled variable-assist power steering, automatic air conditioning, cabin air filter, power seats, leather upholstery, tilt steering wheel, cruise control, automatic headlamps, remote keyless entry, theft-deterrent system, power heated mirrors, power windows, automatic power locks, AM/FM/cassette stereo. **Major Options:** Power moonroof, heated seats, split-bench seat, driver's memory system, adjustable shock absorbers, run-flat tires, tire pressure monitor, emergency satellite communications system, chrome wheels.

Back to square one

Had they lived in the 18th century, the stylists responsible for the 1995 edition of the Lincoln Continental would have been hung, drawn, and quartered for giving the sedan such dull and lifeless lines! But not only are we not living in the 18th century, Lincoln had a chance to go back to the drawing board. In the meantime, though, a very costly error has given its arch rival, the Cadillac Seville, time to leap ahead in the sales books.

Be this as it may, it is back to square one in 1999 since the two protagonists have both taken on a whole new look to lure consumers to their respective showrooms. Once again, the Continental comes out second.

When you take a close look at the Continental, last year's design revisions haven't changed this model's appearance as much as Lincoln would seem to want consumers to believe. There's no question that the rear is the best part of this model, mainly because of the tail light design, very evocative of what you see on models manufactured by Jaguar, currently owned by Ford. After a while it's equally obvious that while it's easier to load baggage into the trunk (although the ingenious storage drawer has been eliminated), the extra space comes at a cost to rear-seat passengers, who have a few inches less for their knees. On the other hand, front-seat passengers will appreciate extra head room and side air bags. The interior design has changed and ergonomics have improved, but the steering wheel is in the same sightline as several instruments, including the speedometer, and the gearshift lever is anything but smooth (a word of advice to the design team: take a look at the Jaguar's).

While shorter than it once was, the Continental's hood still covers the Intech V-8, which notably has a major amount of extra torque thanks to changes made to its camshafts. The four-speed automatic transmission transfers the engine's 260 horses to the front wheels and shaves a few tenths of a second off the previous model's acceleration time. Unfortunately, the same can't be said of the turning radius, which is longer on the new version. After Lincoln made a few changes to front-end design without making it any sturdier, the adjustable suspension is part of the options list. As a result the Continental still has a more than cushy ride and the chassis sways on curves as the car understeers with not the smallest sign of shame. Thank goodness drivers can count on four disc brakes and an antilock system.

Esthetically more refined, the Continental is capitalizing on its regal image. It's too bad that efforts to improve technological features are somewhat ruined by the use of a few ridiculous gadgets. **E.L.**

Specifications of Test Vehicle

Model: Continental

Exterior Dimensions	
Wheelbase	109 in.
Overall length	207 in.
Overall width	73.6 in.
Overall height	56 in.
Curb weight	3,850 lb.
Interior Dimensions	
Seating capacity	5
Head room	F:39.2/R:38 in.
Leg room	F:41.9/R:38 in.
Cargo volume	18.9 cu. ft.
Engine	
Displacement	V-8 4.6 L.
Horsepower	260 @ 5,750 rpm
Torque, lb-ft	270 @ 3,000 rpm
Performance	
0-60 mph, acceleration	8.1 sec
60-0 mph, braking	128 ft.
Turning circle	41.1 ft.
EPA city/highway	17/24 mpg
Test mileage	18 mpg
Fuel tank capacity	20 gal.

PRICES
$38,000
$45,000

4-door sedan
$38,995

WARRANTY
(years/miles)

Bumper-to-bumper
4/50,000

Powertrain
4/50,000

Rust-through
6/100,000

OTHER TO CONSIDER

Cadillac Seville

Chrysler LHS

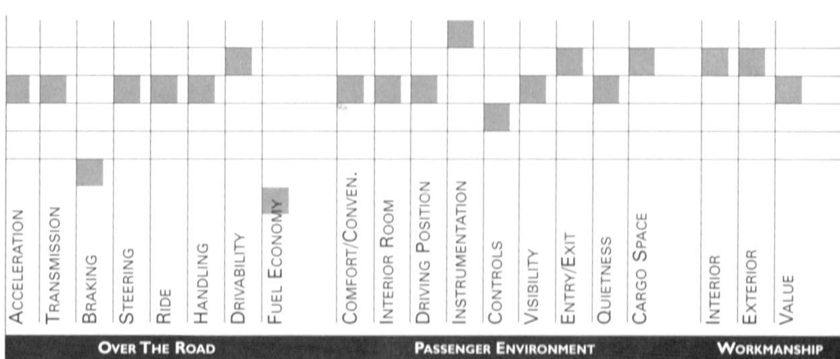

Ratings

Lincoln

Navigator

New for 99

300-hp 5.4-liter V-8 (lae availabilty
Adjustable pedals

Pros

Higher performance capabilities
Detailed equipment
Easier access to rear seats

Cons

Spectacular size
Outrageous fuel consumption
Skittish rear suspension

Equipment

Major Standard Equipment:
5.4-liter V-8, automatic transmission, 4-wheel antilock brakes, automatic leveling suspension, air conditioning, automatic temperature control, speed-sensitive variable-intermittent wipers, rear defroster, power heated mirrors, automatic headlights, power windows, power locks, remote keyless entry, AM/FM/cassette stereo, cruise control, tilt steering wheel, power captain's chairs, leather upholstery, driver's memory feature, privacy glass, trailer towing package, aluminum wheels. **Major Options:** Automatic 4-wheel drive, rear air conditioning, automatic-dimming rear-view mirror, power moonroof, split-bench second-row seat.

Rebirth

Lincoln has taught good manners to the rough-and-ready Ford Expedition, decking it out in regal style and giving it a fancy new name, the Navigator. An old familiar recipe, you say? No question, but it works! Proof: 60 % of Navigator buyers are people who had never gone to a Lincoln dealership in the past. But the make's executives have another reason to be proud: over a period of several months, the advent of the Navigator made it possible for Lincoln to unseat its eternal rival, Cadillac, in the sales race.

Well aware that a counteroffensive is being planned (GMC Yukon Denali and Cadillac Escalade), Lincoln has added a host of innovations to its Navigator, including adjustable pedals (an option) designed to make it easy for drivers to find the ideal driving position, be they short or tall.

One thing is sure, the Navigator doesn't fail to make a strong visual impression. To get to its throne (sorry, I mean passenger compartment), just hop onto the lighted step. Magnificent leather seats await you in a warm ambiance created by an 18-inch carpet and polished inlays. Lincoln invites up to eight passengers into the Navigator's decor; but let's be honest, access to the rear seat (don't forget there's another one in the middle) takes the talent of a skilled contortionist, not to mention the fact that the seatback is perfectly vertical and absolutely uncomfortable. It's easy to sacrifice this seat (especially now that it features smaller casters) to add to the vehicle's very limited cargo space.

Intent on avoiding the embarrassment of being left in the competition's dust at traffic lights, the Navigator teams its 5.4-liter V-8 with 32 valves and a DOHC, bringing the power level to 300 horses (40 more than last year's model had) and 360 pound-feet of torque (a gain of 15 pound-feet). This is the only powertrain allowed aboard the Navigator this year. Given the vehicle's weight, the power increase is an excellent move. Acceleration and pickup are now well within the acceptable range. Another strong point is the perfect work accomplished by the automatic transmission. Choices? Buyers have one and only one decision to make: two-wheel or four-wheel drive. The latter option is the most popular, not so much because of its off-road capabilities (an area where the expensive Land Rover is king), but because of its stability on slippery roads. Points to remember when it comes to the Navigator: high gas consumption, a rear suspension that has trouble handling bumpy roads, and a size that makes you think twice before taking it out on the town.

At the risk of breaking a few sensitive hearts, the Navigator is a much better choice than the Land Rover and the LX470. This Lincoln is more reliable than the former and less pretentious than the latter. We can at least agree on that, can't we? **E.L.**

PRICES
$39,000
$50,000

4-door truck wagon
$39,310

WARRANTY
(years/miles)

Bumper-to-bumper
4/50,000

Powertrain
4/50,000

Rust-through
6/100,000

OTHER TO CONSIDER

Cadillac Escalade
GMC Denali

Specifications of Test Vehicle

Model: Navigator

Exterior Dimensions	
Wheelbase	119 in.
Overall length	204.8 in.
Overall width	79.9 in.
Overall height	79.9 in.
Curb weight	5150 lb.
Interior Dimensions	
Seating capacity	7
Head room	F:39.8/R1:39.8/R2:35.1 in.
Leg room	F:41/R1:39.7/R2:28.8 in.
Cargo room	12 cu. ft.
Engine	
Displacement	V-8 5.4 L.
Horsepower	260 @ 4,500 rpm
Torque, lb-ft.	345 @ 3,000 rpm
Performance	
0-60 mph, acceleration	12.5 sec.
60-0 mph, braking	154 ft.
Turning circle	40.5 ft.
EPA city/highway	12/16 mpg
Test mileage	11 mpg
Fuel tank capacity	30 gal.

Ratings
134

Over The Road		Passenger Environment		Workmanship	
Acceleration	4	Comfort/Conven.	9	Interior	8
Transmission	8	Interior Room	10	Exterior	9
Braking	1	Driving Position	7	Value	6
Steering	7	Instrumentation	7		
Ride	8	Controls	8		
Handling	6	Visibility	7		
Drivability	7	Entry/Exit	6		
Fuel Economy	2	Quietness	8		
		Cargo Space	6		

Lincoln

Town Car

New for 99

Side air bags
Two-toned colors

Pros

Entry/exit
Passenger/cargo room
Ride

Cons

Rear visibility
Braking

Equipment

Major Standard Equipment
4.6-liter V-8, automatic transmission, 4-wheel antilock disc brakes, traction control, variable-assist power steering, automatic air conditioning, variable-intermittent wipers, rear defroster, power seats, leather upholstery, tilt steering wheel, automatic headlamps, cruise control, remote keyless entry, theft-deterrent system, power heated mirrors, power windows, power locks, remote keyless entry, AM/FM/cassette stereo, aluminum wheels. **Signature adds:** Driver's memory system, steering wheel stereo and climate controls. **Cartier adds:** Heated seats. **Major Options:** Power moonroof.

250

A matter of conscience

As the last full-size, rear-wheel-drive U.S. luxury sedan, the Lincoln Town Car has a class to itself. In redesigning its most popular model, Lincoln aims to attract younger buyers without alienating loyal owners.

The new Town Car retains the old one's body-on-frame construction, but it's 31/2 inches shorter and wears more modern, rounded-corner styling. A special package with less chrome and a stiffer suspension aims at those younger buyers, creating what will be seen as a Lexusesque Lincoln.

The Town Car comes in the Executive, Signature, and Cartier trim levels. The Cartier gets 20 more horsepower than the first two. But at only 220 horsepower, it falls far short of the top Cadillac, which has 300. Lincoln uses the Mercury Grand Marquis's engine in the heavier Town Car, diminishing luxury performance.

Chassis improvements transform the Town Car's feel. It still has a soft, luxurious ride but no longer bobs or weaves like a punch-drunk heavyweight. Body lean is controlled, and this big sedan grips well on twisting, hilly roads. The steering is still too light and lacks road feel; it centers quickly after a turn, though. Larger brakes provide better feel and durability, but stopping distance is still excessive.

With the Touring Sedan Package, the ride is slightly firmer, the steering a little tighter, and the grip even more secure, making the Town Car feel more athletic without sacrificing comfort. All models have a new traction control system that operates at all speeds instead of at low speeds only.

The car accelerates adequately from a stop, and the smooth, refined V-8 delivers sufficient passing power for most situations. Luxury, however, is about excess. With four adults aboard, more power would be appreciated. You can expect fuel economy in the low 20s.

Lincoln persists in calling the Town Car a 6-passenger sedan, but the front-center position is suitable for kids only. The rear-center position seat is similarly cramped, and in both places the passenger straddles the driveline tunnel. Other occupants get ample room to relax in comfortable leather seats. Getting in and out is easy in a car this size.

Large dials for the speedometer and fuel and temperature gauges mark the instrument cluster. Everything else is handled by tiny green warning lights that disappear in daylight. New styling hasn't changed the wide rear roof pillars and a skimpy back window that make parking and lane changes more difficult.

The Continental's trunk volume has shrunk 9 percent, but Ford claims the usable space is the same. A deep, wide center well holds large items, but small things fall out of easy reach.

Without competitive pressure from a rear-wheel-drive Cadillac, this Lincoln Town Car has changed, but not always for the better. **D.V.S.**

Specifications of Test Vehicle

Model: Signature Series

Exterior Dimensions	
Wheelbase	117.7 in.
Overall length	215.3 in.
Overall width	78.2 in.
Overall height	58 in.
Curb weight	4,000 lb.
Interior Dimensions	
Seating capacity	6
Head room	F:39.2/R:37.5 in.
Leg room	F:42.6/R:41.1 in.
Cargo volume	20.6 cu. ft.
Engine	
Displacement	V-8 4.6 L.
Horsepower	200 @ 4,500 rpm
Torque, lb-ft	265 @ 3,500 rpm
Performance	
0-60 mph, acceleration	9.9 sec
60-0 mph, braking	141 ft.
Turning circle	42.2 ft.
EPA city/highway	17/25 mpg
Test mileage	22 mpg
Fuel tank capacity	19 gal.

Prices

$38,000
$48,000

Executive sedan
$38,995

Signature sedan
$40,995

Cartier sedan
$43,495

Warranty

(years/miles)

Bumper-to-bumper
4/50,000

Powertrain
4/50,000

Rust-through
6/100,000

Other to Consider

Cadillac De Ville

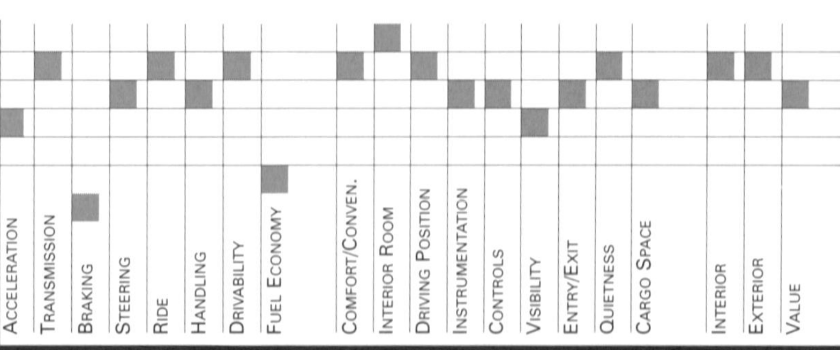

Ratings 161

Mazda 626

New for 99

Longer list of standard accessories

Pros

Reliability
Comfortable ride
Good handling

Cons

Step-by-step changes
Pickup at lower engine speeds (V-6)
ABS brakes available only on the ES

Equipment

Major Standard Equipment: 2-liter I-4, manual transmission, variable-assist power steering, intermittent wipers, rear defroster, tilt steering column, split-folding rear seat. **LX adds:** Air conditioning, cruise control, oscillating air vents, power locks, power windows, power side mirrors, power decklid release, AM/FM/CD stereo. **ES adds:** 2.5-liter V-6, 4-wheel antilock disk brakes, traction control, power moonroof, theft-deterrent system, remote keyless entry, power driver's seat, leather upholstery, larger tires, aluminum wheels. **Major Options:** 2.5-liter V-6, automatic transmission, 4-wheel antilock brakes, air conditioning, AM/FM/CD stereo, remote keyless entry, power driver's seat, power moonroof, aluminum wheels.

A well-kept secret

PRICES
$16,000
$25,000

DX sedan $15,695
LX sedan $18,115
ES sedan $19,995

WARRANTY (years/miles)

Bumper-to-bumper 3/50,000
Powertrain 3/50,000
Rust-through 5/unlimited

OTHER TO CONSIDER

Ford Contour
Nissan Altima

Mazda completely redesigned its mid-size 626 last year. Now, this sporty family sedan might get the attention it deserves.

With its new body, the 626 strongly resembles the Millenia. Designed exclusively for the North American market, the 626 is built in Michigan at a plant owned jointly by Ford and Mazda. Its main competitors include the Honda Accord, Toyota Camry, and Nissan Altima, as well as the Ford Contour and Dodge Stratus.

The 626 is available in DX, LX, or ES trim. With some trim levels, you can choose either a 2-liter 4-cylinder engine or a 2.5-liter V-6. Either a 4-speed manual or 5-speed automatic round out the powertrain choices.

If you like to drive, you'll feel at home in the 626. The firm seats provide good support for long trips, and leg room is ample in front. Despite the car's larger interior, three passengers still aren't comfortable in back; rear leg room has actually decreased slightly in the new design. The rear seatback splits to fold down, and the trunk has a wide opening with a low liftover.

The exceptionally clean instrument panel has a contemporary look, with traditional analog gauges. Unfortunately, the stereo controls are small and mounted low in a center console, where they're hard to read and operate. The new design still has the popular, functional motorized air vents that swing in the center of the dash.

The 626 really excels on the road. It feels like a sports sedan. The V-6 feels powerful, responsive, and yet remarkably smooth from idle all the way up to the red line. With the 5-speed manual transmission, the 626 consistently sprinted to 60 mph in 7.5 seconds without much fuss or bother. The clutch, gear shift, and engine harmonize to make driving very pleasant. Even though Mazda has improved the automatic transmission, it still lacks the sophistication of its competitors'. Upshifts are smooth and well-timed, but downshifts are unpredictable.

Although not state-of-the-art, the steering and handling are still impressive. The 626 is more agile than many of its competitors. The variable-assist power steering is quick and precise at higher speeds, yet light when parking. The ride has a firmness that makes the car handle well, adding to the sports sedan feel. Some may not appreciate the firm ride on rough pavement, but others will appre-ciate the control and fun on twisting mountain roads. The 4-wheel antilock brakes provide stopping power and control appropriate for a sports sedan.

Mazda's 626 offers a sporty alternative to the blandness of many other mid-size sedans. If Camry and Accord shoppers aren't willing to look at something more exciting, perhaps the 626 will continue to be one of Mazda's best-kept secrets. **D.V.S.**

Specifications of Test Vehicle

Model: 626 ES

Exterior Dimensions	
Wheelbase	105.1 in.
Overall length	186.8 in.
Overall width	69.3 in.
Overall height	55.1 in.
Curb weight	2,800 lb.
Interior Dimensions	
Seating capacity	5
Head room	F:39.2/R:37 in.
Leg room	F:43.6/R:34.6 in.
Cargo room	14.2 cu. ft.
Engine	
Displacement	V-6 2.5 L
Horsepower	170 @ 6,000 rpm
Torque, lb-ft	163 @ 5,000 rpm
Performance	
0-60 mph, acceleration	7.5 sec.
60-0 mph, braking	120 ft.
Turning circle	36.1 ft.
EPA city/highway	20/26 mpg
Test mileage	25 mpg
Fuel tank capacity	16.9 gal.

Ratings

Group	Category	Rating (1–10)
Over The Road	Acceleration	9
	Transmission	9
	Braking	7
	Steering	9
	Ride	7
	Handling	9
	Drivability	9
	Fuel Economy	6
Passenger Environment	Comfort/Conven.	8
	Interior Room	7
	Driving Position	8
	Instrumentation	8
	Controls	7
	Visibility	8
	Entry/Exit	8
	Quietness	8
	Cargo Space	7
Workmanship	Interior	8
	Exterior	8
	Value	9

Mazda

B-Series

New for 99

Fourth door available

Pros

Ride
Visibility
Styling

Cons

Acceleration
Braking
Handling

Equipment

Major Standard Equipment: 2.5-liter I-4, manual transmission, rear-wheel antilock brakes, vinyl floor covering, intermittent wipers, AM/FM radio, painted bumpers. **SE adds:** AM/FM stereo, cloth upholstery, carpeting, chrome bumpers. **Major Options:** 3-liter V-6, 4-liter V-6, 4-speed automatic transmission, 5-speed automatic transmission, part-time 4-wheel drive, 4-wheel antilock brakes, air conditioning, power mirrors, power windows, tilt steering column, cruise control, power locks, remote keyless entry, individual front seats, AM/FM/cassette stereo, AM/FM/CD stereo, trailer towing package, larger tires, aluminum wheels.

A Kissing cousins

The Mazda B-Series and the Ford Ranger pickups are built at the same New Jersey plant. Mazda designers made their pickup look sportier to distinguish it from the Ranger. Despite their identical mechanical components, Mazda B Series pickups don't sell as well as Ford Rangers.

On Mazda trucks, the engine size becomes part of the model designation. The base B2500 has a 119-horsepower, 2.5-liter 4-cylinder engine. The B3000 has an optional 150-horsepower, 3-liter V-6, and the B4000, an optional 160-horsepower, 4-liter V-6. Manual 5-speed transmissions are standard. A 4-speed automatic is available on the B2500 and B3000, with a 5-speed automatic available on the B4000. With the regular cab, you can choose SX or SE trim levels; extended cabs all are SEs.

The new B-Series has conventional suspension arms. A fully boxed frame adds rigidity for better ride and handling. On the 4X4, a new automatic system with a dash-mounted switch allows you engage or disengage the 4-wheel drive at virtually any speed.

Interior refinements include a deactivation switch for the passenger air bag, storage trays, and cupholders. On the dash, the stereo controls are thoughtfully placed above the ventilation controls in a center console. The instrument cluster is complete, with simple, easy-to-read gauges.

We found the optional individual seats comfortable, with plenty of support for traveling rough roads. The extended cab has two side-mounted fold-down seats that look usable, but they're small and hard. Entry and exit involve a high step in 4X4 models. Even with seats that tip forward, getting to the back seat is less than graceful, except if you choose the Cab Plus 4.

Despite, last yea rmajor suspension changes, the B4000 has a firm, truck-like ride. Driving on bad pavement with no load in the bed makes for a rough ride. As in most other pickups, bumpy turns cause the rear end to jump around. The steering is tight and accurate. The B-Series handles like a truck; it's nothing special. An emergency stop from 60 mph took a disappointing 139 feet with the 4-wheel antilock brakes.

The 4-liter engine provides plenty of torque for normal situations; nevertheless, reaching 60 mph took over 10 seconds on our test runs. The 5-speed transmission offers more flexibility for pulling, but doesn't seem to improve acceleration. The engine remains reasonably quiet under most conditions.

If you want a Ford pickup that doesn't look like a Ford pickup, then the Mazda B is for you. All the good mechanical stuff is there under the skin.

D.V.S.

Specifications of Test Vehicle

Model: B4000 SE

Exterior Dimensions	
Wheelbase	125.7 in.
Overall length	202.9 in.
Overall width	69.4 in.
Overall height	64.7 in.
Curb weight	3,650 lb.
Interior Dimensions	
Seating capacity	5
Head room	F:39.2/R:35.6 in.
Leg room	F:42.2/R:40.3 in.
Payload capacity	1,250 lb.
Engine	
Displacement	V-6 4 L.
Horsepower	158 @ 4,250 rpm
Torque, lb-ft.	223 @ 3,000 rpm
Performance	
0-60 mph, acceleration	10.3 sec.
60-0 mph, braking	139 ft.
Turning circle	41.6 ft.
EPA city/highway	16/21 mpg
Test mileage	17 mpg
Fuel tank capacity	17 gal.

Prices

$11,000
$23,000

SX short bed
$11,385

SE short bed
$13,205

SE extended cab, short bed
$15,345

Warranty

Bumper-to-bumper
3/50,000

Powertrain
3/50,000

Rust-through
5/unlimited

Other to Consider

Izuzu Hombre

Nissan Frontier

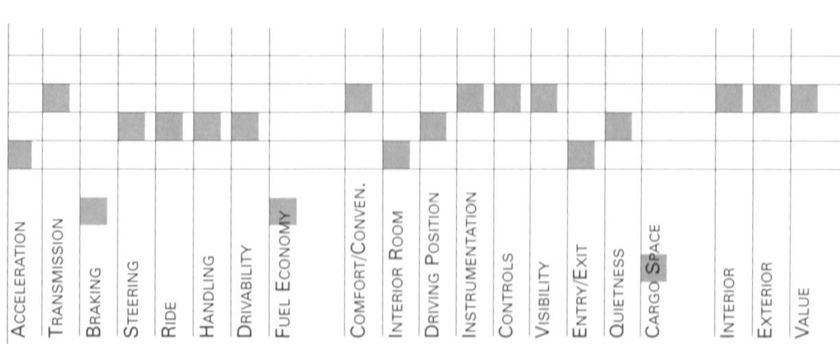

Ratings
134

Mazda Miata

new MODEL

New for 99

Restyled body and interior, more engine power, minor suspension improvements.

Pros

Powertrain performance
Steering/handling
Driving fun

Cons

Cargo spac
Interior room
Convertible top boot

Equipment

Major Standard Equipment: 1.8 liter I-4 engine, 5-speed manual transmission, AM/FM/cassette radio, 4-wheel disc brakes. **Major Options:** Automatic transmission, air conditioning, removable hard top, antilock brakes, power steering, leather upholstery, power windows, cruise control, limited-slip differential, cast wheels.

Riding the wave

When Mazda's Miata was first introduced in 1993, it reignited interest in roadsters. Now Mercedes, BMW, and Porsche offer roadsters, and soon Honda and Toyota plan to get in on the act. Mazda responded with a new and improved version for 1999 – it isn't totally different, just a much better Miata.

Still instantly recognizable, the body has had a total makeover. The shape is pretty much the same, but exposed oblong headlights replace the familiar pop-ups. The rear end is freshened to give it a more muscular look.

All new Miatas are powered by the same 1.8-liter in-line DOHC four. A new camshaft and a variable intake control system boost horsepower from 133 to 140. The manual transmission has been reworked for even easier shifting. The automatic remains pretty much the same. Numerous suspension revisions and a stiffer chassis complete the list of changes under the skin.

The interior has been redone – it has a fresh new look, with added comfort features. The instrument panel has a new center cluster that contains the vent and audio controls, along with a key-operated switch for the passenger-side airbag. Doors have convenient map pockets, but otherwise, storage space is hard to find. Cargo space is larger and more usable, thanks to the relocation of the spare tire under the

trunk floor.

The Miata has always been fun to drive; the newly refined engine makes it even better. It still responds best at high revs and can reach 60 mph in about 8 seconds. The revised transmission has even shorter throws for almost effortless shifting. The clutch, engine, and transmission are perfectly harmonized for a great driving experience. Running through the gears is the best part of driving in hilly or twisty terrain. Mazda has clearly emphasized steering and handling at the expense of a soft ride. A firm suspension and short wheelbase combine to give it a choppy feel on the highway. But, with plenty of grip in the corners, minimal body lean, and appropriate feedback through the steering wheel, the Miata is a joy on country roads. Rear – wheel drive just enhances the driving experience. The optional 4-wheel antilock disc brakes are outstanding. Two can remove or install the optional hardtop easily. It improves security, but precludes a spontaneous conversion to open motoring. The manual convertible top lowers effortlessly, even from the driver's seat. The boot needs a lot of fussing to get it right. No need to worry about scratching the rear window, though – it's glass, with a built-in defogger. With the top up, road noise is muted, but when down, things can get noisy. As in all convertibles, visibility is great with the top down, but very restricted when up.

Several 500-mile stints behind the wheel of the new Miata convinced us this is a car you can learn to love. We never tired of its responsive character and its endearing looks. This car is just pure fun. Some of the competition is twice the price – that just makes the Miata an even better value. **D.V.S.**

Specifications of Test Vehicle

Model: Miata

Exterior Dimensions	
Wheelbase	89.2 in.
Overall Length	155.3 in.
Overall Width	66.0 in.
Overall Height	48.3 in.
Curb Weight	2470 lbs.
Interior Dimensions	
Seating Capacity	2
Head Room	F: 36.5 in.
Leg Room	F: 42.0 in.
Cargo Room	6.1 cu.ft.
Engine	
Displacement	1.8L I-4
Horsepower	140@6500 rpm
Torque, lb-ft.	119@5500 rpm
Performance	
0-60 mph, acceleration	8.5 sec.
60-0 mph, braking	110 ft.
Turning Circle	30.2 ft.
EPA City/Highway	25/29 mpg.
Test Mileage	NA
Fuel Tank Capacity	12.7 gal.

Counterpoint

Tom Matano, director of Mazda's California design studio, lights another cigarette, flicks his graying hair out of his eyes, and provides a straightforward explanation for the blending of styles: "If nobody could identify the Miata from 65 yards away, then we'd know we'd gone too far." That's why, seen straight on, the little Japanese model still has the same smiling face as it had in 1989, the primary attraction for more than 450,000 consumers worldwide. Its eyelids don't close anymore though, but as compensation, its headlights seem to glow happily, much like the eyes of the owners who enjoy driving it in the heat of heady summer nights.

It's too bad that the steering wheel doesn't tilt, seats come with a minimum of adjustment possibilities, cupholders are positioned very oddly on the center console and you have to raise the armrest to use them, and the soft-top housing seems to be quite fragile, besides calling for relatively skilled handling if you have big hands. When the top is up, side supports hinder visibility and force drivers to be extra careful when overtaking other vehicles and the A-Pillar may provide sturdiness, but it restricts the field of vision on tight corners.

Peppy and agile, the Miata has no qualms about behaving like exactly what it is: a toy. The quick, direct, and responsive steering system lets you correct rear-end slippage effectively and spells precision on tight corners. On the base version the driver gets less feedback on road conditions, mainly because of smaller tires (14-inch instead of 15) and the lack of a limited slip differential. The only way to make this convertible lose its cool is to take corners at high speeds and even then, it does better than the previous version.

Beautiful in its simplicity, fun to drive, capable of exciting performance levels, the second-generation Miata is a perfect choice for anyone who wants to enjoy the thrill of riding in the wind without the hassle of begging for a banker's indulgence.

É.L.

PRICES

$20,000

$28,000

WARRANTY

Bumper-to-Bumper
3/50,000

Power Train
3/50,000

Rust-through
5/Unlimited

OTHER TO CONSIDER

None

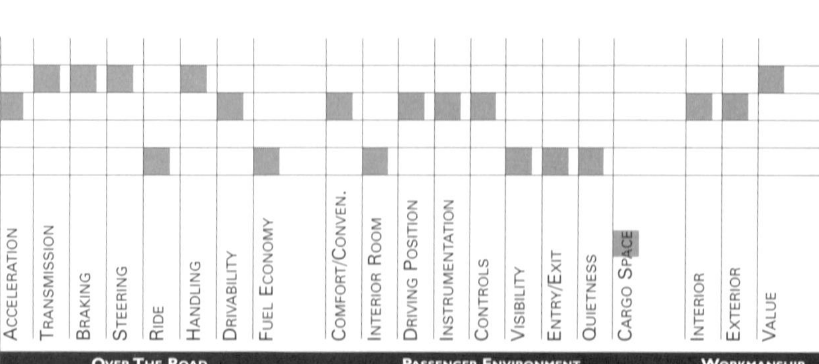

Ratings

148

Mazda

Millenia

New for 99

Bigger wheels
Redesigned grille
Passenger compartment design details

Pros

Appealing lines
Powerful Miller-cycle engine
Attention to detail

Cons

Lack of prestige
Cramped interior
Sluggish base engine

Equipment

Major Standard Equipment: 2.5-liter V-6, automatic transmission, 4-wheel antilock disc brakes, variable-assist power steering, automatic air conditioning, variable-intermittent wipers, rear defroster, cruise control, power tilt wheel, power mirrors, power windows, power locks, power decklid release, power driver's seat, AM/FM/CD/cassette stereo, theft-deterrent system, power moonroof, aluminum wheels. **S adds:** 2.3-liter V-6 Miller cycle, traction control, leather upholstery, power passenger's seat, remote keyless entry, power moonroof, larger tires. **Major Options:** Traction control, heated front seats, heated mirrors, leather upholstery, remote keyless entry.

A second coming

PRICES
$29,000
$38,000

4-door sedan
$26,995

S 4-door sedan
$31,495

WARRANTY
(years/miles)

Bumper-to-bumper
3/50,000

Powertrain
3/50,000

Rust-through
5/unlimited

OTHER TO CONSIDER

Acura 3.2 TL

Lexus ES300

If you can believe the statements made by Mazda executives, the Millenia's sluggish sales are due to the fact that its long-term leasing plans aren't competitive, a plausible claim when you know that consumers interested in luxury cars tend to lease rather than buy. If it becomes more affordable, it will attract new fans more easily because when it comes to looks, the Mazda is a bombshell, even with its redesigned grille.

Narrow door openings made it hard to climb aboard and a low roof line will have your rubbing you head in exasperation more than once. Rear-seat passengers feel a bit cramped, unlike those assigned to the front, where seats mold well. While the interior design used to be quite dull, Mazda lets the sun shine in this year. Wood-grain trims and chrome design details make for an attractive overall look. Owners will appreciate the second cupholder and the high-tech ashtray. And our hats are off to the quality of manufacturing found on this model and to its intelligently positioned controls as well.

The Millenia rides a lot like the 626, the model it was derived from. This is a stable and quiet car but it's weak when powered by the 2.5-liter V-6, paired with a transmission that's slow to respond to the demand for more acceleration power. The Miller cycle 210-hp 2.3-liter V-6, the alternative engine, saves the day and delivers more convincing acceleration and pickup, but it hardly makes the car fly. And that's a good thing, because the brakes aren't the best.

Solid and refined, the Millenia is less expensive than its competition and often more appealing and capable of better performance levels. **E.L.**

Ratings	Rating (1–10)
Over The Road	
Acceleration	8
Transmission	9
Braking	8
Steering	8
Ride	8
Handling	7
Drivability	8
Fuel Economy	5
Passenger Environment	
Comfort/Conven.	8
Interior Room	7
Driving Position	8
Instrumentation	8
Controls	8
Visibility	8
Entry/Exit	7
Quietness	8
Cargo Space	6
Workmanship	
Interior	9
Exterior	9
Value	6

Ratings
153

Specifications of Test Vehicle

Model: Millenia S

Exterior Dimensions	
Wheelbase	108.3 in.
Overall length	189.8 in.
Overall width	69.7 in.
Overall height	54.9 in.
Curb weight	3,400 lb.
Interior Dimensions	
Seating capacity	5
Head room	F:37.9/R:36.5 in.
Leg room	F:43.3/R:34.1 in.
Cargo volume	13.3 cu. ft.
Engine	
Displacement	V-6 2.3 L.
Horsepower	210 @ 5,300 rpm
Torque, lb-ft.	210 @ 3,500 rpm
Performance	
0-60 mph, acceleration	8.3 sec.
60-0 mph, braking	114 ft.
Turning circle	37.4 ft.
EPA city/highway	20/28 mpg
Test mileage	21 mpg
Fuel tank capacity	18 gal.

Mazda

Protegé

New for 99

New model

Pros

Ride
Driveability
Value

Cons

Center console
Rear seat room

Equipment

Major Standard Equipment: 1.6 L 4-cylinder engine, 5-speed manual transmission, 60/40 split rear seat back. **LX Adds:** Adjustable seats, power windows & locks, keyless entry. **ES Adds:** 1.8L 4-cylinder engine, air conditioning, 15-inch wheels, **Major Options:** 4-speed automatic transmission, antilock brakes, power moonroof.

Serious contender

Mazda has totally revised its entry-level sedan for 1999. The new Protege features new styling and structure, along with upggraded powertrain and suspension components. Only 10% of its parts are carried over from last year's model. Priced in the mid-teens, it competes head-on with the Honda Civic and Toyota Corolla.

The Protege is still offered in three trim levels. The top-of-the-line ES comes with a 1.8-liter, 122 hp engine, and other amenities like air conditioning and power windows . The base DX and better equipped LX use a 1.6-liter, 105 hp engine. All three models are available with either a 5-speed manual or 4-speed automatic transmission. Antilock brakes are optional on the LX and ES.

Although the interior dimensions are about the same as last year's model, there seems to be more room inside. In fact, the well-trimmed cabin is almost the roomiest found in a small sedan. The front seats are generally comfortable, but the small cushions might not provide enough thigh support for larger people. LX and ES models have manual adjusters for cushion height and tilt on the front seats. Both driver and passenger have plenty of leg room and the center console does not rub the driver's leg. Things get a little tighter in the back seat, but the rear doors allow easy access. The rear seat is supposed to be big enough for three adults, but two will get along much better. Trunk space is about average, with a low liftover.

Instruments and controls are well laid out and easy to use. The radio is thoughtfully located high in the center of the dash. However, a drink in one of the cupholders is right where the shift lever and your hand want to be at times. A sloping hood and deck lid, combined with large side-view mirrors allow a good view in all directions.

Even though 60% of Protege buyers will opt for the LX with an automatic transmission, the ES might be a better overall choice. The 1.6-liter engine in the DX and LX is a marginal performer. Even the ES, with its 1.8-liter engine runs out of breath when pushed hard to merge with freeway traffic. Accelerating from 0 to 60 mph takes almost ten seconds. However, for those still concerned about such things, fuel economy in the high twenties is possible.

Over the road, the Protege's above average ride quality is impressive. Steering is not as sharp and precise as some of the competition, and steering effort is a little high. Handling is good enough to encourage spirited driving. Understeer is minimal— the ES's 15-inch tires hang on well in turns. Mazda did away with 4-wheel disc brakes on this new model, but brake performance has actually improved. Stopping from 60 mph took 133 feet.

Overall, the Protege is a good example of doing things right. With reasonable power, excellent ergonomics, good road manners and up-to-date styling, it deserves serious consideration by Civic and Corolla shoppers. **D.V.S.**

Specifications of Test Vehicle

Model: Protege ES

Exterior Dimensions	
Wheelbase	102.8 in.
Overall Length	174.0 In.
Overall Width	67.1 In.
Overall Height	55.5 In.
Curb Weight	2537 lbs.
Interior Dimensions	
Seating Capacity	5
Head Room	F: 39.3/R: 37.4 in.
Leg Room	F: 42.2/R: 35.4 in.
Cargo Room	12.9 cu.ft.
Engine	
Displacement	1.8 L 4-cylinder
Horsepower	122@6000 rpm
Torque, lb-ft.	120@4000 rpm
Performance	
0-60 mph, acceleration	9.9 sec.
60-0 mph, braking	133 ft.
Turning Circle	34.1 ft.
EPA City/Highway	26/30 mpg.
Test Mileage	28.1
Fuel Tank Capacity	13.2 gal.

Prices

$12,500
$19,000

DX sedan
$12,420
LX sedan
$13,580
ES sedan
$15,375

Warranty

(years/miles)

Bumper-to-bumper
3/50,000

Powertrain
3/50,000

Rust-through
5/unlimited

Other to Consider

Honda Civic

Toyota Corolla

Over The Road	Rating
Acceleration	7
Transmission	8
Braking	5
Steering	7
Ride	8
Handling	8
Drivability	8
Fuel Economy	7
Passenger Environment	
Comfort/Conven.	7
Interior Room	7
Driving Position	8
Instrumentation	7
Controls	8
Visibility	8
Entry/Exit	7
Quietness	8
Cargo Space	6
Workmanship	
Interior	8
Exterior	8
Value	9

Ratings
149

Mercedes-Benz C-Class

New for 99

Supercharged engine
New name

Pros

Higher performance levels
Manufacturing quality
Attractive price

Cons

Sensitivity to crosswinds
Loud engine

Equipment

Major Standard Equipment: 2.3-liter I-4 supercharged, 5-speed automatic transmission, 4-wheel antilock disc brakes, smart passenger-side air bag, automatic air conditioning, rear defroster, power windows, power driver's seat, vinyl upholstery, automatic dimming mirrors, power locks, remote keyless entry, cruise control,AM/FM/WB/cassette stereo, aluminum wheels. **C280 adds:** 2.8-liter V-6, traction control, power passenger's seat. **Major Options:**Automatic stability control, traction control, headlight washers, telescoping steering column, high-intensity headlights.

Transplant time

PRICES
$30,000
$41,000

C230 sedan
$31,795

C280 sedan
$36,195

WARRANTY
(years/miles)

Bumper-to-bumper (incl. tires)
4/50,000

Powertrain
4/50,000

Rust-through
4/50,000

OTHER TO CONSIDER

BMW 528i
Audi A4 S

For the third year in a row, the most affordable Mercedes on the North American market has undergone a name change. After the C220 and the C230 we now have the C230 Kompressor (German for "compressor" or "supercharger"), here with Ñ as you've no doubt already guessed Ñ a heart artificially pumped by a volumetric compressor, just like the SLK's unit. The C230 has a lot of performance potential, no question. But a strong heart is not worth much without strong legs, and the C-Class is getting shaky on its pins.

Even if the C-Class is rated as having slightly more useable space than its German-built rivals such as the Audi A4, it has to bow to some of the Swedes (Saab 9-3 and Volvo S70) and Japanese (notably the Infiniti I30), which provide more room for bench seat passengers and a roomier trunk. The front seats have a very German firmness about them and while the dashboard is designed to provide additional protection in case of impact, it makes it hard to find the ideal driving position.

The C230 boasts a 2.3-liter four-cylinder featuring an Eaton compressor. Like magic, its power has gone from 148 to 185 horses and torque has leapt from 162 to 200 pound-feet. From lamentable, its performance levels have moved to honorable and according to Mercedes, the C230 now takes two seconds less to get from a standing start to 60 mph. While quicker and more energetic than the normally-aspirated 2.3-liter it is replacing, the new engine is noisy when pressed to work hard.

The C230 Kompressor offers consistent and reassuring handling, but despite a traction control system, driving on wet or snow-covered roads is touch and go. And unlike the C280, the C230 Kompressor has no ESP road stability system. For its part, the steering system provides good feedback on road conditions, but it is still relatively heavy at center. Lastly, note that the C-Class is sensitive to crosswinds.

With its supercharged engine, the C230 is back in the spotlight. However, some of its rivals don't even need technical magic to shine and stand out from the crowd. **E.L.**

Specifications of Test Vehicle

Model: C230

Exterior Dimensions	
Wheelbase	105.9 in.
Overall length	177.4 in.
Overall width	67.7 in.
Overall height	56.1 in.
Curb weight	3,250 lb.
Interior Dimensions	
Seating capacity	5
Head room	F:37.2/R:37 in.
Leg room	F:41.5/R:32.8 in.
Cargo volume	12.9 cu. ft.
Engine	
Displacement	I-4 2.3 L.
Horsepower	185 @ 5,300 rpm
Torque, lb-ft.	200 @ 2,500 rpm
Performance	
0-60 rpm, acceleration	9.2 sec.
60-0 rpm, braking	110 ft.
Turning circle	35.2 ft.
EPA city/highway	23/30 mpg
Test mileage	25 mpq
Fuel tank capacity	16.4 gal.

Ratings
162

Group	Category	Rating
Over The Road	Acceleration	7
	Transmission	9
	Braking	9
	Steering	9
	Ride	8
	Handling	8
	Drivability	9
	Fuel Economy	6
Passenger Environment	Comfort/Conven.	8
	Interior Room	7
	Driving Position	9
	Instrumentation	8
	Controls	8
	Visibility	7
	Entry/Exit	8
	Quietness	9
	Cargo Space	6
Workmanship	Interior	9
	Exterior	9
	Value	9

Mercedes-Benz C43

New for 99
New model

Pros
Impeccable road stability
Fabulous engine
Definite exclusivity

Cons
Some control designs
No height-adjustable steering column
Ageing chassis

Equipment
Major Standard Equipment: 4.3-liter, V8, automatic transmission, air conditioning, anti-lock braking system, cruise control, headlamps wipers and washer, leather ulphostery, power windows, speed control, split folding rearseat, sport seats, traction control, antiskid control. **Major options :** High intensity headlights.

new MODEL

A valiant heart

To date, the C43 is the most powerful and sportiest of the C-Class sedans. It was developed by the AMG expert, today part of the German firm and responsible, among other things, for the extraordinary CLK-GTR, the uncontested champion of the FIA's GT series. These people know what real performance is. And the C43 is the latest in a long line of super-sedans to proudly carry the Mercedes-Benz name. The C43 is powered by a unique version of the Mercedes' new "modular" 4.3-liter V-8. The C43's engine is the most powerful by far, with 302 horses (available at 5,850 rpm) that can rely on a maximum torque level of 302 pound-feet between 3,250 and 5,000 rpm.

AMG has modified this model by using a different rear bumper and more eye-catching fenders and rocker panels. However, the inside of the C43 is where its sporty personality shines brightest, with three large dials, fully adjustable leather-covered seats that provide excellent support, and a superb sports-style steering wheel, though it is a bit too thick where the spokes meet the rim. Front and side air bags provide good passive safety. From the luxury standpoint, the C43 has beautiful wood inlays, a transparent sunroof, cruise control and a split rear seat that folds down to increase the already roomy trunk's usable space. Mercedes went all out! And it's a shame that the steering column isn't adjustable. These may seem to be minor details and small inconveniences, but then again they're hard to take on a car that goes for more than $50,000. It's high time for a new-generation C-Class — the current generation is showing its age, especially when it pulls up alongside the competition!

I have to say this first: the C43 has a heart of steel and its gorgeous sound goes from a purr to a growl at the slightest touch of the gas pedal. This engine is available exclusively with a five-speed automatic transmission identical to the unit featured on the 500SL convertible and it offers exemplary precision and responsiveness, perfectly in keeping with the performance levels this model is capable of reaching. Acceleration and pickup are equally impressive; the C43 goes from 0 to 60 mph in 6.35 seconds and does the 1/4 mile in 14.61 seconds at 98 mph!

AMG has modified the suspension and mounted tires of different sizes on the front and rear, on alloy wheels, if you please. Thanks to an anti-lock system and bigger ventilated discs, braking is very efficient. The C43 also has traction control and ESP (electronic stability program). This car clings to the road, even on the tightest corners, and its sway is negligible. However, it lacks the ultimate refinement, precision and agility you find behind the wheel of a BMW M3. **M.L.**

Specifications of Test Vehicle

Model: Mercedes C43

Exterior Dimensions	
Wheelbase	105.9 in.
Overall lenght	177.4 in.
Overall wihdt	67.7 in
Overall height	56.1 in.
Curb weight	3380 lb.
Interior dimensions	
Seating capacity	5
Head room	F:38/R:36 in.
Leg room	F:41.5/R:32.8 in.
Cargo room	16.5 cu. ft.
Engine	
Displacement	V-8, 4.3 L.
Horsepower	302 @ 5,850
Torque, lb-ft	302 @ 3,250
Performance	
0-60 mph, acceleration	6.0
60-0 mph, braking	125 ft
Turning circle	35.2 ft
EPA city/highway	17/22
Test mileage	20.2
Fuel tank capacity	16.4

Prices
$50,000
$60,000
C43
$52,750

Warranty
(years/miles)

Bumper-to-bumper (incl. tires)
4/50,000

Powertrain
4/50,000

Rust-through
4/50,000

Other to consider
Jaguar XJR
BMW M3

Ratings

Group	Category	Rating
Over The Road	Acceleration	10
	Transmission	9
	Braking	10
	Steering	10
	Ride	7
	Handling	9
	Drivability	9
	Fuel Economy	4
Passenger Environment	Comfort/Conven.	7
	Interior Room	7
	Driving Position	9
	Instrumentation	8
	Controls	7
	Visibility	7
	Entry/Exit	8
	Quietness	8
	Cargo Space	6
Workmanship	Interior	9
	Exterior	9
	Value	8

Mercedes-Benz CLK

New for 99

Revised accessory list
Convertible model
V-8 4.3 liter

Pros

Exceptional manufacturing quality
Proven capabilities
Impressive handling

Cons

No fully adjustable seat belts
Heavy feel
No manual transmission

Equipment

Major Standard Equipment: 3.2-liter V-6, 5-speed automatic transmission, 4-wheel antilock disc brakes, traction control, side air bags, rear fog light, dual-temperature automatic air conditioning, rear defroster, leather upholstery, power seats, driver's memory system, power locks, remote keyless entry, theft-deterrent system, AM/FM/cassette stereo, power decklid release, telescoping steering column, cruise control, aluminum wheels.
Major Options: Automatic stability control, high-intensity headlights, automatic windshield wipers.

Charming and efficient

PRICES
$40,000
$45,000
CLK 320
2-door coupe
$41,195

WARRANTY
(years/miles)
Bumper-to-bumper (incl. tires)
4/50,000
Powertrain
4/50,000
Rust-through
4/50,000

OTHER TO CONSIDER
BMW M3
Volvo C70

In the past, Mercedes has never shown a particularly talented hand when it comes to designing coupes. While this body type is usually associated with strong emotions and extra creativity, Mercedes coupe models look more like sedans, minus two doors. Having said that, the renowned European manufacturer's new coupe, the CLK, makes a welcome break with tradition in the form of an appealing blend between the E-Class E (with E for esthetics) and the C-Class C (with C for chassis).

Doors open onto a bright and attractive interior. Tasteful wood inlays share space with the luxurious leather on the console and doors. The list of accessories and innovations is every bit as impressive as the remote control electronic key that lets you roll down windows and open the sunroof automatically so the car will be nice and cool by the time you get inside. Wonderful! Bucket seats may seem a bit firm at first but as the miles fly by, they prove to be extremely comfortable, with just the right amount of support. It's too bad that to add to comfort, Mercedes set aside the idea of offering fully adjustable seat belts for front-seat passengers and decided on a steering column that's depth, but not height, adjustable. Given the limited head room and leg room, rear seats are best suited to children, all the more so since rear visibility is barely adequate for certain specific types of manoeuvers. Luckily, rear seats fold down to provide more room than the small trunk can provide on its own.

Besides distinctive styling, a coupe should offer performance levels that are more electrifying than anything you can find in a sedan. Although it's lighter than the C280, the CLK coupe offers respectable capabilities on the road, and in comparison it gets along better than the Volvo C70. In its defence, buyers should note that Mercedes uses a fairly sluggish automatic transmission in tandem with its 3.2-liter six-cylinder engine. On the other hand, the CLK makes up for its faults by providing good road stability and plenty of sturdiness. This Mercedes is particularly fond of wide-open curves, where it can really show its mettle. The suspension is stiff on bumpy roads, but never to the point of making passengers uncomfortable. Lastly, a short turning radius contributes to the CLK's good handling.

With a personality more remarkable for its classiness than its sportiness, the CLK coupe still has a number of qualities, most notably more refinement and smoothness than many of its rivals.
E.L.

Specifications of Test Vehicle

Model: CLK320

Exterior Dimensions	
Wheelbase	105.9 in.
Overall length	180.2 in.
Overall width	67.8 in.
Overall height	53 in.
Curb weight	3,250 lb.
Interior Dimensions	
Seating capacity	4
Head room	F:36.9/R:35.6 in.
Leg room	F:41.9/R:31.1 in.
Cargo room	11 cu. ft.
Engine	
Displacement	V-6 3.2 L.
Horsepower	215 @ 5,700 rpm
Torque, lb-ft.	229 @ 3,000 rpm
Performance	
0-60 mph, acceleration	7.2 sec.
60-0 mph, braking	117 ft.
Turning circle	35.1 ft.
EPA city/highway	21/29 mpg
Test mileage	NA
Fuel tank capacity	16.4 gal.

Ratings

Category	Rating
Over The Road	
Acceleration	9
Transmission	9
Braking	7
Steering	9
Ride	8
Handling	8
Drivability	8
Fuel Economy	6
Passenger Environment	
Comfort/Conven.	8
Interior Room	6
Driving Position	9
Instrumentation	8
Controls	8
Visibility	7
Entry/Exit	6
Quietness	9
Cargo Space	5
Workmanship	
Interior	9
Exterior	8
Value	7

Mercedes-Benz E-Class

New for 99

Inflatable curtain for head protection
Optional electronic stabilizer
Side curtain airbag

Pros

Good handling
Powerful engine
Built to be solid and safe

Cons

Gas pedal
Trunk volume
Long list of expensive accessories

Equipment

Major Standard Equipment: 3-liter I-6 diesel, 5-speed automatic transmission, 4-wheel antilock brakes, smart passenger's air bag, side air bags, traction control, dual-temperature automatic air conditioning, cabin air filter, AM/FM/WB/cassette stereo, automatic dimming rear-view mirror, memory tilt and telescoping steering column, cruise control, automatic dimming mirrors, vinyl upholstery, power locks, remote keyless entry, power windows, power mirrors, theft-deterrent system, aluminum wheels. **E320 adds:** 3.2-liter gasoline V-6, leather upholstery. **E430 adds:** 4.3 liter V-8, electronic stability program (ESP).

Faster, further, higher

The market niche occupied by the Mercedes E-Class is by far one of the busiest and most exciting in the entire automotive industry and to keep its place in the sun, the model range is back with a host of innovations. We already knew that the in-line six-cylinder would be replaced by a V-6 with three valves per cylinder and we had already heard that a wagon version would join the line-up. But what we weren't expecting was a turbo to supercharge the diesel in-line six-cylinder, not to mention the commercialization of an AWD version, designed to enter the fray that previously involved only Audi and Volvo.

It doesn't take much time to take to an E. An ideal driving position, detailed instrumentation, a high number of practical accessories (provided your budget can stretch that far), what is there to criticize? Well, a few things: the shift lever is as ugly as it is oversized; the trunk is only average-sized and shamefully deprived of a cargo net (unless you choose it as an option); visibility to the side isn't excellent either, and it can make changing lanes a tricky business. Furthermore, when it's raining hard the single windshield wiper has its work cut out for it. A brief comment on the number and cost of options: astronomical, headlamp washers at $415, orthopedic seats at $605 each, reading lights for rear-seat passengers at $195. Reach for the stars, and your wallet!

With almost perfect weight distribution, the E achieves a nice equilibrium. Even the recirculating ball steering system is extremely precise and the tight turning radius makes for very easy manoeuvering in the city. The 4.3-liter V 8 is clearly more effective than the former 4.2-liter even though some critics are unhappy with its lack of technical daring. This eight-cylinder has only one overhead cam (instead of the former engine's dual overhead cam) and it has three valves per cylinder instead of four. A jarring factor: the five-speed automatic transmission that backs the engine suffers from a gas pedal that isn't at all progressive (a phenomenon not found on the E320), and when pressed hard, the result is very confused and hesitant shifting.

All things considered, there can be no doubt that the improvements brought to the E-Class make it even more attractive. **E.L.**

Specifications of Test Vehicle

Model: E320

Exterior Dimensions	
Wheelbase	111.5 in.
Overall length	189.4 in.
Overall width	70.8 in.
Overall height	56.7 in.
Curb weight	3,600 lb.
Interior Dimensions	
Seating capacity	5
Head room	F:37.6/R:37.2 in.
Leg room	F:41.3/R:36.1 in.
Cargo volume	15.3 cu. ft.
Engine	
Displacement	V-6 3.2 L.
Horsepower	221 @ 5,500 rpm
Torque, lb-ft.	232 @ 3,000 rpm
Performance	
0-60 mph, acceleration	8 sec.
60-0 mph, braking	114 ft.
Turning circle	37.1 ft.
EPA city/highway	21/29 mpg
Test mileage	23 mpg
Fuel tank capacity	21.1 gal.

PRICES
$40,000
$54,000
E300 sedan $42,995
E320 sedan $46,795
E320 wagon $47,795
E430 $51,895

WARRANTY (years/miles)
Bumper-to-bumper (incl. tires) 4/50,000
Powertrain 4/50,000
Rust-through 4/50,000

OTHER TO CONSIDER
BMW 528 i
Volvo S80

Category	Rating
Over The Road	
Acceleration	8
Transmission	10
Braking	8
Steering	9
Ride	9
Handling	9
Drivability	9
Fuel Economy	5
Passenger Environment	
Comfort/Conven.	9
Interior Room	8
Driving Position	9
Instrumentation	8
Controls	9
Visibility	8
Entry/Exit	8
Quietness	9
Cargo Space	7
Workmanship	
Interior	10
Exterior	10
Value	9

Ratings **171**

Mercedes-Benz M-Class

New for 99

V-8 engine (ML430)

Pros

Off-road capabilities
Towing capacity
Short turning radius

Cons

Some inferior quality materials
Forest of levers on the steering column
Limited availability

Equipment

Major Standard Equipment: 3.2-liter V-6, 5-speed automatic transmission, full-time 4-wheel drive, 4-wheel antilock disc brakes, air conditioning, cabin air filter, intermittent wipers, rear defroster, rear wiper, split-folding rear seat, power windows, power locks, remote keyless entry, cruise control, tilt steering column, AM/FM/WB/cassette stereo, antitheft system, cargo cover, aluminum wheels. **ML430 adds:** 4.3 liter V-8. **Major Options:** Power moonroof, leather upholstery, power heated seats, automatic-dimming rear-view mirror, privacy glass, trip computer,AM/FM/WB/CD stereo.

The lesson Mercedes teaches

PRICES

$34,000
$40,000

ML320
$35,345

ML430
$44,345

WARRANTY
(years/miles)

Bumper-to-bumper (incl. tires)
4/50,000

Powertrain
4/50,000

Rust-through
4/50,000

OTHER TO CONSIDER

Land Rover Discovery

Infiniti QX4

Mercedes came late to the sport-utility vehicle party, but certainly brought something extra. Sensibly sized and reasonably priced, the ML320 offers features, comfort, and status that most other manufacturers simply can't.

The ML320 competes with the Ford Explorer and Expedition, GMC Denali, Jeep Grand Cherokee, Oldsmobile Bravada, and other upscale SUVs from mainsteam manufacturers. Offered in only one model and bodystyle, it has a state-of-the-art 3.2-liter V-6 and a 5-speed automatic transmission.

All ML320s come with a unique all-wheel drive arrangement that senses when a wheel is spinning, applies the brakes to it, and diverts power to the wheels with traction. Think of it as all-wheel traction control. Unlike other AWD systems, the ML has a 2-speed transfer case for better-than-average off-road capability

Stepping into the ML is easy, both front and back. The key word here is "stepping." Unlike every other vehicle in this class, it doesn't require a climb. Once inside, you'll feel right at home if you're familiar with Mercedes cars. The steering wheel tilts, and even the manually adjustable seats adjust six ways. The driving position is almost perfect, making visibility good in all directions. The seats are firm and supportive—great for long trips, where the support of softer seats wanes. The instrument panel and controls have that familiar look and solid feel. We liked the look and feel of the materials used to finish the interior.

The driving experience is also typically Mercedes—rock solid and predictable. Even though the new V-6 engine performs well, the extra weight of the large body and AWD equipment keeps it from being great. In our tests, acceleration to 60 mph took slightly over 9 seconds—not bad for an SUV. At best, fuel economy will be in the low 20s.

The ride is on the firm side, but certainly not harsh. The M-Class handles as well as an SUV can. Although that's good, Mercedes cars are better. The body rolls a bit during high-speed turns, but not to an uncomfortable degree. Although the steering is precise, it doesn't return to center willingly after a tight low-speed turn. The brakes engage quickly, but stopping from 60 mph took a disappointing 140 feet.

For a vehicle built on a car platform, the ML320 shows amazing off-road capability. The 4-wheel independent suspension provides an acceptable ride on even the worst roads. The best part is the AWD system. We tried it on a mud-slick course with one front wheel and the rear wheel on the opposite side in holes, so the two remaining wheels were off the ground. It was unstoppable.

Solid, luxurious, and capable, the ML320 is much more affordable than you might expect for something with a three-pointed star. **D.V.S.**

Specifications of Test Vehicle

Model: ML320

Exterior Dimensions	
Wheelbase	111 in.
Overall length	180.6 in.
Overall width	72.2 in.
Overall height	69.9 in.
Curb weight	4,200 lb.
Interior Dimensions	
Seating capacity	5
Head room	F:39.8/R:39.7 in.
Leg room	F:40.3/R:38 in.
Cargo room	44.7 cu. ft.
Engine	
Displacement	V-6 3.2 L.
Horsepower	215 @ 5,500 rpm
Torque, lb-ft.	233 @ 3,000 rpm
Performance	
0-60 mph, acceleration	9.2 sec.
60-0 mph, braking	140 ft.
Turning circle	37 ft.
EPA city/highway	17/21 mpg
Test mileage	18 mpg
Fuel tank capacity	19.2 gal.

Ratings

Group	Category	Rating
Over The Road	Acceleration	8
	Transmission	9
	Braking	4
	Steering	7
	Ride	8
	Handling	8
	Drivability	8
	Fuel Economy	4
Passenger Environment	Comfort/Conven.	8
	Interior Room	9
	Driving Position	9
	Instrumentation	8
	Controls	8
	Visibility	7
	Entry/Exit	8
	Quietness	8
	Cargo Space	10
Workmanship	Interior	8
	Exterior	9
	Value	10

158

Mercedes-Benz

S-Class

New for 99

Totally redesigned exterior and interior, air suspension, powertrain refinements, standard navigation and location system, advanced side impact protection, adaptive cruise control.

Pros

Ride/handling powertrain performance controls, safety features.

Cons

None

Equipment

Major Standard Equipment: 5.0 liter V-8, 5-speed automatic transmission, four door – mounted airbags, two side-curtain airbags, antilock brakes, traction control, electronic stability control, turn-signal indicators in side-view mirrors, air suspension, navigation system, emergency aid system, steering wheel control for nav, audio and phone, automatic climate control, power front seats. **Major Options:** Comfort seats with active ventilation and pulsating massage, heated power rear seats, individual rear seats, adaptive speed control (mid '99).

The top car

Stung by criticizm from abroad, Mercedes has redesigned its new S Class sedans to be more environmentally correct, while enhan-cing comfort, convenience, and safety. The S sedan has shed over 600 pounds, taken on a sleek, aerodynamic look, and added features such as on-board navigation as standard equipment.

While available in a number of variations around the world, the only model on sale in the U.S. is the long-wheelbase version with either of two V-8s. The 4.3-liter engine is good for 275 hp, while the 5.0-liter upgrade cranks out 302 hp.

Safety features abound. Front airbags are two-stage, adjusting their deployment force to crash severity. Side airbags are installed in all four doors. And the two front doors have side air curtains that lower instantaneously during a side impact to protect the driver or front passenger's head.

The standard on-board navigation system has steering wheel controls and a turn instruction display below the speedometer, to minimize driver distraction. A satellite location feature allows the driver to summon help with the push of a button. Heated, ventilated, massaging seats with adjustable-length bottom cushions ensure driving comfort. Entry and exit, both front and rear, are luxury-excellent. Remotely controlled fold-down rear head restraints improve visibility to the rear, but pop up when a rear seat belt is fastened. Cargo space is just average for a car this size.

The instrument panel is not "Mercedes" at all. It is cleaned up and puts controls where they belong. Window switches are in the armrests (although a little low), vent controls are simplified, and the shifter no longer has the miserable pattern of the past. Now there's only park, reverse, neutral, and drive, in a straight pattern. If the driver wishes to downshift a gear or two, a tap on the lever to the left does the job. Manual upshifts need only a tap to the right.

On the road, the S500 is pure delight. The ride control system adapts to road conditions, for a consistently good ride. The air suspension improves handling. Fast, sweeping curves create little body roll, since the shock absorbers change their characteristics to suit. Steering is precise, with good on-center feel. However, recovery from sharp turns isn't quite quick enough. Brakes are sensitive and effective. The adaptive speed control, called Distronic, uses radar signals to maintain a safe distance from the car ahead, even as its speed changes. Acceleration is quick, smooth, and quiet. Fuel economy is said to have improved by up to 17%, so average consumption in the low twenties is likely.

Mercedes designers obviously paid close attention to market needs and wants. They fixed many of the things that needed improvement. So, the new S Class has successfully leap-frogged the competition – at least for now. **D.V.S.**

Specifications of Test Vehicle

Model: S500

Exterior Dimensions	
Wheelbase	121.5 in.Overall
Length	203.1 In.
Overall Width	70.3 In.
Overall Height	56.9 In.
Curb Weight	4139 lbs.
Interior Dimensions	
Seating Capacity	5
Head Room	F: 39.3/R: 38.8 in.
Leg Room	F: 41.3/R: 39.6 in.
Cargo Room	17.7 cu.ft.
Engine	
Displacement	5.0 L
Horsepower	302@5600 rpm
Torque, lb-ft.	339@2700 rpm
Performance	
0-60 mph, acceleration	6.09 sec.
60-0 mph, braking	128 ft.
Turning Circle	38.4 ft.
EPA City/Highway	12/24 mpg.
Test Mileage	NA
Fuel Tank Capacity	26.2 gal.

1999

AAA
TOP CAR

PRICES
NA

WARRANTY
Bumper-to-Bumper 4/50,000
Power Train **4/50,000**
Rust-through 4/50,000

OTHER TO CONSIDER
BMW 740 il
Lexus LS400

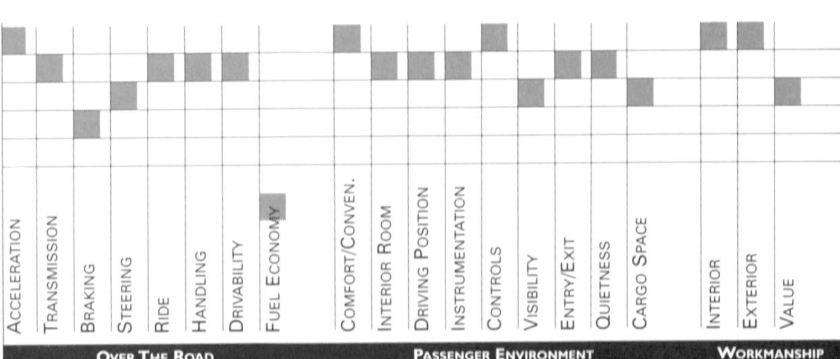

Ratings
174

Mercedes-Benz SL

New for 99

Three valves per cylinder (SL500)
New design details

Pros

Smoother V8 on the SL500
Wide range of accessories
Constant technological advances

Cons

Thirsty V12
No glass rear windshield
Unexciting driving experience

Equipment

Major Standard Equipment: 5-liter V-8, 5-speed automatic transmission, 4-wheel antilock disc brakes, traction control, smart passenger-side air bag, automatic air conditioning, automatic variable-intermittent wipers, headlight washers, remote keyless entry, power tilt and telescoping steering column, AM/FM/WB/cassette stereo, theft alarm system, automatic rollbar, removable hardtop, aluminum wheels. **SL600 adds:** 6-liter V-12, automatic stability control, automatic shock absorber control, high-intensity headlamps. **Major Options:** Automatic stability control, automatic shock absorber control, high-intensity headlights, glass-roofed removable hardtop, heated seats, orthopedic seats.

Last call

PRICES
$80,000
$134,000
SL500
$81,695
SL600
$127,495

WARRANTY
(years/miles)
Bumper-to-bumper (incl. tires)
4/50,000
Powertrain
4/50,000
Rust-through
4/50,000

OTHER TO CONSIDER
Jaguar XK8 Cabriolet

The Mercedes-Benz SL has power, grace, and head-turning looks. Its style, quality, and engineering put it in a class by itself.

The SL's engine choices let you reduce your acceleration time while you reduce your bank account. The cylinder count jumps from a V-8 to a V-12. Like other Mercedes, the SL has automatic stability control, which senses directional changes and impending loss of control and selectively applies just one wheel's brake to help avoid skids. A pop-up roll bar automatically deploys if sensors predict a rollover, and side air bags offer additional crash protection. For winter driving, there's traction control plus a low-ratio reverse gear to reduce wheel spinning.

Excellent structural rigidity is one of the first attributes you'll notice about the SL. The chassis shows little flexing over rough pavement.

The 315-horsepower V-8 makes the SL both quick and fast. Under heavy acceleration, it's strong at any speed. It cruises and passes on the highway effortlessly. You can feel the 5-speed automatic transmission downshift, although most other shifts go unnoticed. The engine requires high-octane gas—not much of a consideration in this price class.

The rear-wheel-drive SL's wide stance, high-performance tires, and sophisticated suspension give a secure, predictable feel on twisty roads. We felt no undue body lean or sway, and steering is precise and responsive. The brakes are exceedingly powerful, with a stopping distance of 104 feet from 60 mph.

The SL's safety belts are incorporated into the seat frame; the shoulder belts adjust electrically with the head restraint. Initially, the seats feel too hard, but they prove very supportive and comfortable during long drives. Most drivers can easily find a safe, comfortable driving position, although tall people may find insufficient leg and head room. The trunk is small but usable.

On the instrument panel, Mercedes's traditional analog gauges are easy to read. The switches and dials are large and easy to operate. You can lower the fully automatic convertible top, store it, and lock it under a hard cover, all by pushing one button. The top latches to the windshield electrically. A see-through wind deflector attaches to the raised roll bar, greatly reducing turbulence in the open cockpit.

With the top up, wind noise is minimal, but there are large blind spots to the rear, and the rear window is clear plastic rather than glass. A detachable hardtop is standard equipment; a more exotic and expensive version has a full glass roof.

The SL is the world's best convertible. **D.V.S.**

Specifications of Test Vehicle

Model: SL500

Exterior Dimensions	
Wheelbase	99 in.
Overall length	177.1 in.
Overall width	71.3 in.
Overall height	51.3 in.
Curb weight	4,150 lb.
Interior Dimensions	
Seating capacity	2
Head room	F:37.1 in.
Leg room	F:42.4 in.
Cargo volume	7.9 cu. ft.
Engine	
Displacement	V-8 5 L.
Horsepower	302 @ 5,600 rpm
Torque, lb-ft.	339 @ 3,900 rpm
Performance	
0-60 mph, acceleration	6.7 sec.
60-0 mph, braking	104 ft.
Turning circle	35.4 ft.
EPA city/highway	16/23 mpg
Test mileage	18 mpg
Fuel tank capacity	21.1 gal.

Ratings

Category	Rating
Over The Road	
Acceleration	10
Transmission	9
Braking	10
Steering	10
Ride	8
Handling	9
Drivability	9
Fuel Economy	4
Passenger Environment	
Comfort/Conven.	9
Interior Room	7
Driving Position	9
Instrumentation	9
Controls	8
Visibility	5
Entry/Exit	8
Quietness	8
Cargo Space	3
Workmanship	
Interior	10
Exterior	10
Value	4

159

Mercedes-Benz

SLK

New for 99

Manual transmission

Pros

Unique roof mechanism
Beautiful styling
At last, a manual transmission

Cons

Rough engine
Minuscule trunk
Long waiting list

Equipment

Major Standard Equipment: 2.3-liter I-4, 5-speed automatic transmission, traction control, 4-wheel antilock disk brakes, power retractable hardtop, dual roll bars, dual-temperature air conditioning, rear defroster, headlight washers, power heated mirrors, leather upholstery, AM/FM/WB/cassette stereo, telescoping steering column, power windows, power locks, remote keyless entry, cruise control, aluminum wheels. **Major Options:** Heated seats, manual transmission (no charge).

Clearing a path to the top

Imagine the sheer joy a builder (and its dealerships) would feel if the worldwide order book for one of its products was completely filled and if consumers were lined up to the other side of the new millennium as they awaited their very own unit. A fantasy? No, Mercedes is in this very position since it introduced the SLK. And the honeymoon should get even more intense now that Mercedes is offering a manual transmission, an alternative reserved exclusively for the European marketplace until now.

With the SLK, Mercedes has recreated the ambience that surrounded the roadsters of the 1950s. But did it really have to use fake inlays and a very fragile cupholder (perched atop the console)? And while we're looking at the dashboard, let's do an inventory just to prove that nothing is missing. On a down note, however, it's a shame that Mercedes persists in using the same scrawny lever (over here, to the left of the steering wheel) to change speeds and that it charges for leather seats heated electrically, even if they are comfortable! Look under the carpet if you want, peek under the seats if you must, there can be no doubt what soever that this Mercedes offers impeccable finishing. With the roof folded down onto itself in the back, you can drive to the golf course with the wind in your hair, but without your clubs, unless you have a caddy traveling in a separate car.

There are two ways to gauge the SLK. The first consists of a direct confrontation with the Z3 and other Boxsters, from the standpoint of pure performance. In this regard, the SLK is outdistanced fast. Not only does its supercharged 2.3-liter four-cylinder sound rough, it is. And when teamed with the standard automatic transmission, it challenges the driver even further, with balky shifting. The manual transmission comes free of charge.

The second way to gauge the SLK is to look at it like the most civilized and cooperative (in other words: well-behaved) of all roadsters and the most attractive because of the way it sheds its roof (an asset no one ever tires of), not to mention the sturdiest chassis ever seen. The SLK hugs the road, brakes efficiently (better than a 2.3-liter Z3 but not as well as a Boxster), and is a whole lot of fun to drive, winter or summer. **E.L.**

Specifications of Test Vehicle

Model: SLK230

Exterior Dimensions	
Wheelbase	94.5 in.
Overall length	157.3 in.
Overall width	67.5 in.
Overall height	50.7 in.
Curb weight	3,050 lb.
Interior Dimensions	
Seating capacity	2
Head room	F:37.4 in.
Leg room	F:42.7 in.
Cargo room	3.6 cu. ft.
Engine	
Displacement	I-4 2.3 L.
Horsepower	185 @ 5,300 rpm
Torque, lb-ft.	200 @ 2,500 rpm

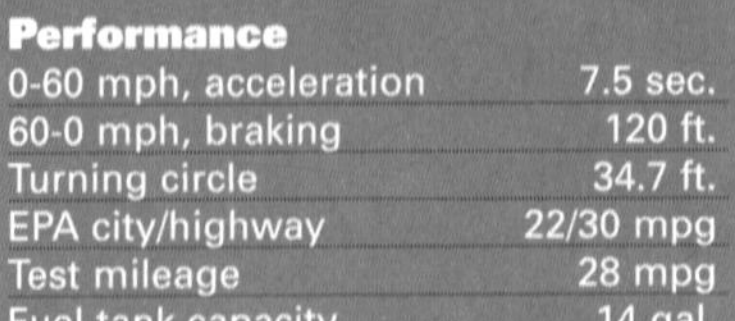

Performance	
0-60 mph, acceleration	7.5 sec.
60-0 mph, braking	120 ft.
Turning circle	34.7 ft.
EPA city/highway	22/30 mpg
Test mileage	28 mpg
Fuel tank capacity	14 gal.

PRICES
$40,000
$43,000
SLK230
$40,595

WARRANTY
(years/miles)
Bumper-to-bumper (incl. tires)
4/50,000
Powertrain
4/50,000
Rust-through
4/50,000

OTHER TO CONSIDER
BMW Z3
Porsche Boxster

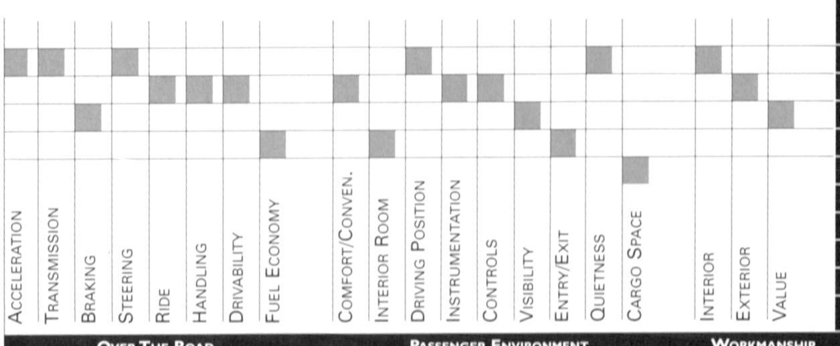

149

Mercury Cougar

new MODEL

New for 99

Totally redesigned with no resemblance to previous model.

Pros

Steering
Handling
Driveability

Cons

Automatic
Fuel economy
Cargo space

Equipment

Major Standard Equipment: 2.0-liter 4-cylinder engine, 5-speed manual transmission, air conditioning, power locks and windows, trip computer, tilt wheel, cloth seats, split-fold rear seat, AM/FM/cassette stereo. **Major Options:** 2.5-liter V-6 engine, 4-speed automatic transmission, traction control, ABS, cruise control, side air bags, premium/leather seats, power moonroof, premium sound systems, aluminum wheels.

Generation gap

After a year's hibernation from the marketplace, the Mercury Cougar has re-emerged as a lean, mean competitor that bears no resemblance to its former self. Gone is the padded vinyl-top sedan image of a Cougar in favor of a sleek coupe with "new-edge" styling. Gone are the older buyers, too. Now the focus is on young buyers with offerings of "fun, flair, and flexibility."

The Cougar comes only as a coupe. Even though it doesn't look the part, it's a hatchback, complete with fold-down rear seats. The standard spoiler is a delete option. The new Cougar benefits from using much of the Contour/Mystique platform and powertrain. Two engines are available, a 2.0-liter 125 hp version and a 2.5-liter V-6 rated at 170 hp. Either engine can be mated with a 5-speed manual or 4-speed automatic transmission. Traction control and antilock brakes are available as options.

Inside is an entirely new instrument panel with bulging round vent registers above the center console. Contrary to conventional wisdom, the vent controls are located up high, with the radio controls located so low the driver has to look down to operate them. The instruments are simple and easy to read. Space for storing travel items is limited and the single flimsy cupholder in the center console is almost useless.

The molded front seats are form-fitting and feature optional side airbags that extend upward to protect the driver and front passenger's heads. The front seatbelts are height-adjustable, something not usually found in coupes. Entry and exit up front requires a few gyrations to settle down into the seats. Even though the front seats tilt and slide forward, getting into the rear seats is still a chore. Once there, the seats are comfortable – but only on short trips.

The steering is sharp and precise. Combine that with excellent handling characteristics and real drivers will be looking for the long way home. The ride is on the satisfactory side of firm, but some might find it too harsh. The 4-cylinder engine is adequate, but the V-6 is much more satisfying. But, that's only if equipped with the manual transmission. Our experience with the automatic was disappointing. Upshifts were just OK — downshifts were sluggish and poorly timed. Acceleration from 0 to 60 mph took 9.6 seconds with the automatic, while the manual transmission delivers times closer to 7 seconds. Measured fuel economy was only in the low twenties. We thought it would be better.

Visibility is good up front and to the sides, thanks to the low hood and doors. However, tiny side-view mirrors, a high tail, and the spoiler all combine to limit visibility to the rear. Cargo space is adequate with the rear seats up, but is compromised by a high liftover.The new Cougar is certainly a better car than its predecessor. Fun, flare, flexibility? Yes! Properly equipped, it's agile and fun to drive. It's styling certainly gives it flare. We're just not so sure about flexibility. **D.V.S.**

Specifications of Test Vehicle

Model: Cougar V-6

Exterior Dimensions	
Wheelbase	106.5 in:
Overall Length	185.0 In:
Overall Width	69.6 In.
Overall Height	52.2 In.
Curb Weight	3020 lbs.
Interior Dimensions	
Seating Capacity	4
Head Room	F:37.8 /R:34.6 in.
Leg Room	F:42.6 /R:33.2 in.
Cargo Room	12.4 cu.ft.
Engine	
Displacement	2.5 L V-6
Horsepower	170@6250 rpm
Torque, lb-ft.	165@4250 rpm
Performance	
0-60 mph, acceleration	9.6 sec.
60-0 mph, braking	133 ft.
Turning Circle	35.8 ft.
EPA City/Highway	19/28 mpg.
Test Mileage	21.3 mpg.
Fuel Tank Capacity	15.6 gal.

Counterpoint

To rejuvenate its image, and as an added bonus its clientele base, Mercury has set out to convince the 25-to-39 crowd to leave their prejudices behind for a while, just long enough to drop by one of the company's dealeships. The challenge is no small task considering that the average age of motorists who drive the most popular of all Mercury models, the Grand Marquis, is a venerable 68!

Getting into the Cougar is a simple and smooth operation. Its seats are so cushy, heavyweights will feel the need to go on a diet to avoid sinking down too deeply into them. On the other hand, taller passengers will appreciate the comfort of the V-6 version's bucket seats, the only ones offering adjustable headrests. A few flaws do detract from the otherwise perfect picture: the tachometer has no red zone; the steering wheel hides a critical portion of the speedometer; and on the automatic version, there's no indicator to tell you what gear you've last shifted into.

Lastly, although visibility is positively panoramic, when the weather is poor the base version Cougar has you longing for a rear windshield wiper. Sideview mirrors are barely adequate in size, but at least they're heated.

No need to go into a detailed technical analysis: the Cougar borrows 72% of its mechanical components from the same platform used for the Mystique (Mercury).

Remarkably well-balanced, this Mercury is smooth and precise, thanks to a firm steering system that adds to the sense of security the driver feels as soon as he or she gets behind the wheel. The Cougar handles corners wonderfully well and only sharp curves taken at high speeds lead to the slightest trace of understeering.

The Cougar has all the assets it takes to fulfill its mission: attracting a younger clientele to Mercury showrooms. Now it's up to the make's dealers to capitalize on the influx, and most importantly, to demonstrate that they've dropped the "who cares" attitude they showed when they were sent to the rescue of Merkur products. ***E.L.***

PRICES

$16,500

$23,000

2-door I-4
$16,595

2-door V-6
$17,095

WARRANTY

Bumper-to-Bumper
3/36,000

Power Train
3/36,000

Rust-through
6/100,000

OTHER TO CONSIDER

Acura Integra

Honda Accord Coupe

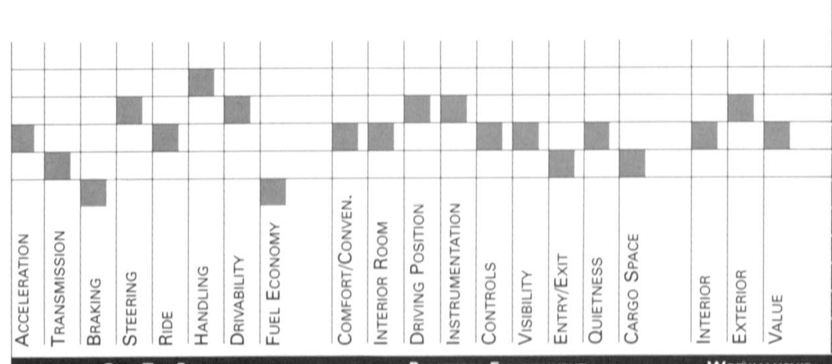

Ratings
140

Mercury

Grand Marquis

New for 99

New exterior colors

Pros

Entry/exit
Passenger/cargo room
Engine performance

Cons

Fuel economy
Handling
Braking

Equipment

Major Standard Equipment: 4.6-liter V-8, automatic transmission, 4-wheel disc brakes, variable-assist power steering, air conditioning, variable-intermittent wipers, rear defroster, power driver's seat, tilt steering wheel, automatic headlamps, cruise control, theft-deterrent system, power mirrors, power windows, power locks, AM/FM/cassette stereo. **LS adds:** Remote keyless entry, chrome wheels. **Major Options:** 4-wheel antilock brakes, traction control, remote keyless entry system, electronic instruments, automatic air conditioning, power front passenger's seat, heavy-duty suspension.

A rejuvenated senior

PRICES
$22,000
$31,000
GS sedan
$22,825
LS sedan
$24,725

WARRANTY
(years/miles)
Bumper-to-bumper
3/36,000
Powertrain
3/36,000
Rust-through
6/100,000

OTHER TO CONSIDER
Buick Le Sabre

Last year, Mercury has freshened up and powered up the Grand Marquis, helping this full-size family sedan stay competitive with the completely redesigned Chrysler Concorde.

The Grand Marquis shares its rear-wheel-drive platform with the Lincoln Town Car, which was more extensively restyled this year. The Mercury underwent mostly mechanical changes, ones that it shares with the Ford Crown Victoria.

The base GS and more-expensive LS models have a standard 200-horsepower, 4.6-liter V-8, an increase of 10 horsepower over last year. Both models now have power locks and cruise control as standard features. All-speed traction control, grouped with antilock brakes as an option, has replaced the system that operated at low speeds only.

The ride is stable and comfortable, but definitely on the soft side. The car bounces slightly over uneven surfaces, but the suspension readily absorbs bumps and potholes. Handling is slightly improved over last year's model, but cornering is always accompanied by considerable body roll. The heavy-duty suspension with its air springs and better tires helps slightly. Steering requires light effort at all speeds, but is accurate and has good on-center feel.

The Grand Marquis accelerates briskly and delivers reassuring passing power. This V-8 runs smoothly and quietly. The transmission downshifts promptly when more power is needed for passing. We averaged 16 mpg in mostly highway driving.

Although the Marquis is rated as a 6-passenger sedan, an adult in the center front seat will crowd the driver. The situation is no worse than that in other large cars, and some people prefer the more open feeling of a split-bench front seat. Other occupants get ample space. In back, there is enough leg room to accommodate 6-footers with space for their feet under the front seats.

The dashboard has large analog gauges and three rotary knobs for the climate system that are easy to use while driving. When you use the slide-out cupholders, they block the climate controls. The stereo is at top center of the dash, but it's tilted away from the driver, so you have to lean forward to reach it.

Despite wide rear roof pillars, you get a clear view through the tall side windows. You can even see the trunk if you stretch your neck.

A deep well in the trunk provides ample but impractical cargo room. Lifting heavy things in or out will stress your back. Small items at the front are just out of reach.

Ford has made its big Mercury rear-wheel-drive family sedan more modern and capable. But, without exclusive features, it's still a dressed-up Ford Crown Victoria. **D.V.S.**

Specifications of Test Vehicle

Model: Grand Marquis LS

Exterior Dimensions	
Wheelbase	114.4 in.
Overall length	212 in.
Overall width	77.9 in.
Overall height	56.8 in.
Curb weight	3,900 lb.
Interior Dimensions	
Seating capacity	6
Head room	F:39.4/R:38 in.
Leg room	F:42.5/R:39.6 in.
Cargo volume	20.6 cu. ft.
Engine	
Displacement	V-8 4.6 L.
Horsepower	215 @ 4,500 rpm
Torque, lb-ft	275 @ 3,500 rpm
Performance	
0-60 mph, acceleration	NA
60-0 mph, braking	NA
Turning circle	41.4 ft.
EPA city/highway	17/25 mpg
Test mileage	16 mpg
Fuel tank capacity	19 gal.

Ratings

Group	Category	Rating (1–10)
Over The Road	Acceleration	6
	Transmission	8
	Braking	5
	Steering	8
	Ride	8
	Handling	7
	Drivability	9
	Fuel Economy	5
Passenger Environment	Comfort/Conven.	8
	Interior Room	9
	Driving Position	8
	Instrumentation	8
	Controls	7
	Visibility	8
	Entry/Exit	9
	Quietness	8
	Cargo Space	9
Workmanship	Interior	9
	Exterior	9
	Value	8

Mercury

Mountaineer

New for 99

New seats design
Reverse park aid (opt.)
Rearload leveling (opt.)

Pros

Interior room
Visibility
Utility

Cons

Ride
Handling
Fuel economy

Equipment

Major Standard Equipment: 4-liter V-6, 4-wheel antilock disc brakes, air conditioning, power windows, power locks, power mirrors, AM/FM/cassette stereo, split-folding rear seat, cruise control, tilt steering wheel, power liftgate release, rear defroster, rear wiper and washer, privacy glass, aluminum wheels. **Major Options:** 5-liter V-8, automatic 4-wheel-drive, AM/FM/CD stereo, AM/FM/CD/cassette stereo, power seats, leather upholstery, integrated child-safety seat, automatic dimming rear-view mirror, automatic door locks, power driver's seat, keyless entry, remote keyless entry, theft-alarm system, power moonroof, luggage rack, running boards, chrome wheels.

Another rebadged Ford

Like many a Mercury, the Mountaineer is just a Ford (Explorer, in this case) with more chrome and a different marketing plan.

Nowadays, when every manufacturer thinks it needs a sport-utility vehicle, Lincoln-Mercury dealers have not only the Mountaineer, but also the Lincoln Navigator, a derivative of the Ford Expedition. The Mountaineer competes with the Jeep Grand Cherokee, Mercedes-Benz M-Class, Toyota 4Runner, Oldsmobile Bravada, Nissan Path-finder, Mitsubishi Montero, Isuzu Trooper, and, of course, Explorer.

Buying a Mountaineer requires some thought. The type of 4-wheel drive system you get depends on the engine you choose. V-6s get an automatic system, and the V-8 has 2WD or optional all-wheel drive.

The Mountaineer's interior shows its upscale appeal. Adjustable leather seats, thick carpeting, a killer sound system, and other creature comforts make you forget this is really a truck. Automatic air conditioning (a must, we think, in an upscale SUV) isn't available in Mountaineer. The high driving position gives you a great view of the road ahead, and rear-seat passengers have a panoramic view. The instruments and controls are well positioned and easy to read and operate.

Traveling down the highway brings you back to the reality that this is a truck. The ride is gentle on only the smoothest of pavement and gets downright rough on typical city streets. Country roads become tolerable when everyone on board gets accustomed to the rocking body motion. Even though the firm suspension takes its toll on the ride, it doesn't improve handling that much. The body still heels over in tight corners. The steering is predictable, but not particularly responsive. The brakes are disappointing. After several attempts, our best stopping distance from 60 mph was 167 feet.

The 5-liter V-8 that had plenty of punch in the Mustang has to work much harder in the 4,200-pound Mountaineer. The transmission performs admirably under light load, with transparent, well-timed shifts. Under full load, upshifts are very firm, and downshifts are annoyingly delayed. Full-throttle acceleration also brings out a rumble in the engine. For some it may be the sound of power. To us, it detracts from the Mercury image. Fuel economy is dismal; we averaged only 15 mpg.

The optional running boards collect grime in bad weather, which inevitably transfers to your legs, and going out in bad weather was why you bought an SUV in the first place.

Why people would think of going to a Mercury dealer to buy a truck escapes us. But if you insist, check out the Sable station wagon. It has more comfort, better gas mileage, and easier access.

D.V.S.

Specifications of Test Vehicle

Model: Mountaineer

Exterior Dimensions	
Wheelbase	111.5 in.
Overall length	188.5 in.
Overall width	70.2 in.
Overall height	67.6 in.
Curb weight	4,400 lb.
Interior Dimensions	
Seating capacity	5
Head room	F:39.9/R:39.3 in.
Leg room	F:42.4/R:37.7 in.
Cargo volume	42.6 cu. ft.
Engine	
Displacement	V-8 5 L.
Horsepower	215 @ 4,200 rpm
Torque, lb-ft.	288 @ 3,300 rpm
Performance	
0-60 mph, acceleration	9.3 sec.
60-0 mph, braking	167 ft.
Turning circle	37.3 ft.
EPA city/highway	14/18 mpg
Test mileage	15 mpg
Fuel tank capacity	21 gal.

PRICES
$27,000
$35,000
4-door truck wagon
$26,680

WARRANTY
(years/miles)
Bumper-to-bumper
3/36,000
Powertrain
3/36,000
Rust-through
6/100,000

OTHER TO CONSIDER
Oldsmobile Bravada
Jeep Grand Cherokee

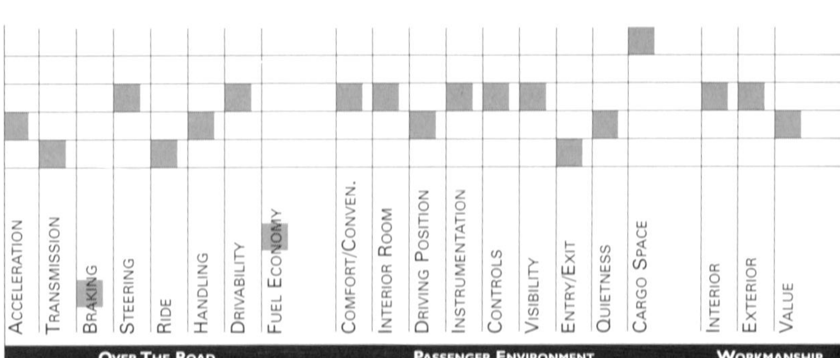

Ratings 139

Mercury Mystique

New for 99

Larger fuel tank
Improved front suspension
Redesigned front seats

Pros

Handling
Fuel economy
Engine performance

Cons

Rear-seat room
Entry/exit
Radio controls

Equipment

Major Standard Equipment: 2-liter I-4, manual transmission, air conditioning, cabin air filter, AM/FM/cassette stereo, cruise control, tilt steering wheel, intermittent wipers, remote-control decklid release, power locks, power windows, power mirrors, split-folding rear seat. **LS adds:** Remote keyless entry, leather upholstery, power driver's seat, variable-intermittent wipers, larger tires, aluminum wheels. **Major Options:** 2.5-liter V-6, automatic transmission, 4-wheel antilock brakes, AM/FM/cassette stereo, remote keyless entry, integrated child-safety seat, power driver's seat, aluminum wheels.

PRICES
$16,000
$23,000
GS sedan $16,925
LS sedan $18,280

WARRANTY (years/miles)
Bumper-to-bumper 3/36,000
Powertrain 3/36,000
Rust-through 6/100,000

OTHER TO CONSIDER
Chrysler Cirrus
Nissan Altima

Last chance

Many buyers may mistakenly assume that the Mystique, like other Mercurys, is more expensive than the equivalent Ford model. Although the Ford Contour outsells the Mystique 3 to 1, the Mercury is just as good.

The Mystique is only superficially different from the Contour. The two cars are built from the same chassis design, and both offer the same options. The differences lie only in standard equipment and option packaging. Both have two trim levels (GS and LS for the Mystique). Cars like the Chrysler Cirrus, Mazda 626, and Nissan Altima will also interest Mystique shoppers.

The Mystique with the 4-cylinder engine might be considered the "sleeper" of the line. This powertrain—the 2-liter engine and 5-speed manual transmission—is truly remarkable. The engine is well-matched to the manual gearbox. With a lusty 125 horsepower, the car packs plenty of zip for passing or merging into fast-moving freeway traffic. As a bonus, gas mileage is terrific. We averaged nearly 30 mpg in mixed driving, with a high percentage on the highway.

The Mystique performs solidly and dependably. Its controlled, predicable handling is European-inspired. (Ford of Europe handled much of the initial development for this design.) Its steering is quick and precise, and the ride is firm without feeling coarse. The steering effort, however, is much lower than we expected.

Inside, the instrument panel (revised this year) is sculpted around the driver, and all the controls have a soft, yet high-quality feel. Their location and operation follow the European pattern, however, so they may seem strange to U.S. drivers. On the whole, the cabin feels secure and looks stylish. The front seats provide decent lateral support and feel quite comfortable even on longer trips. The rear seat remains a bit cramped, however, despite Ford's efforts to squeeze more room from the cushions. Narrow doors make entry to the rear seat difficult, and you have to grope blindly to find the inside door release, which is buried next to the seat cushion.Visibility is good in all directions, thanks to the generous use of glass and the vehicle's rounded shape. However, the rear deck falls away quickly from the rear window, so you can't see it when you're backing up. The complex controls on the stereo system take a long time to master. We heard a bit of wind and road noise above 60 miles an hour, but at idle the cockpit seems remarkably quiet.

Mercury dealers would be very happy to put you in a Mystique. In fact, they'd be happy to put you in any of their versions of a Ford. In the 4-cylinder Mystique, you'll get a good driving bargain among small cars.
D.V.S.

Specifications of Test Vehicle

Model: Mystique GS

Exterior Dimensions	
Wheelbase	106.5 in.
Overall length	184.8 in.
Overall width	69.1 in.
Overall height	54.5 in.
Curb weight	2,800 lb.
Interior Dimensions	
Seating capacity	5
Head room	F:39/R:36.8 in.
Leg room	F:42.4/R:34.4 in.
Cargo volume	13.9 cu. ft.
Engine	
Displacement	I-4 2 L.
Horsepower	125 @ 5,500 rpm
Torque, lb-ft.	130 @ 4,000 rpm
Performance	
0-60 mph, acceleration	9 sec
60-0 mph, braking	130 ft.
Turning circle	36.5 ft.
EPA city/highway	24/35 mpg
Test mileage	30 mpg
Fuel tank capacity	15 gal.

Ratings
145

	Over The Road							Passenger Environment										Workmanship		
	Acceleration	Transmission	Braking	Steering	Ride	Handling	Drivability	Fuel Economy	Comfort/Conven.	Interior Room	Driving Position	Instrumentation	Controls	Visibility	Entry/Exit	Quietness	Cargo Space	Interior	Exterior	Value
Rating (1–10)	7	7	5	8	8	8	8	7	7	6	7	8	8	8	6	7	6	8	8	8

Mercury Sable

New for 99
Improved ride quality
New mini-center console
Revised gauge cluster

Pros
Handling
Driveability
Bodystyle choice

Cons
Entry/exit
Engine performance
Interior room

Equipment
Major Standard Equipment: 3-liter V-6, automatic transmission, variable assist power steering, air conditioning, split-bench seat, AM/FM/cassette stereo, cruise control, power windows, power mirrors, rear defroster, tilt steering wheel, variable-intermittent wipers, split folding rear seat. **LS adds:** Cabin air filter, individual front seats, power driver's seat, theft alarm system, power locks, remote keyless entry, aluminum wheels. **Major Options:** More powerful 3-liter V-6, automatic temperature control, 4-wheel antilock brakes, AM/FM/CD stereo, power locks.

Not a looker

You can tell a Sable from a Taurus by the Mercury's chrome grille. Other than the grille and a few other details, there's little difference between the two cars. Since the Taurus outsells the Sable 3 to 1, the Mercury version gives you a less common look in the same basic shape.

Although a few options are still available "a la carte" on the Sable, Mercury now groups most of the popular options in packages. The Sable's trim levels follow the familiar Mercury designations, GS and LS.

With the base 3-liter V-6, the Sable seems underpowered, particularly with four adults on board. Compared with the optional 200-horsepower V-6, the standard engine makes the Sable feel like a couch potato. (Since it costs only $550 more, the bigger engine is a better bet. Both engines can go 100,000 miles before requiring new spark plugs, and both get the same gas mileage.) With the small V-6, the 4-speed automatic transmission shifts very smoothly in ordinary driving and responds quickly when full performance is demanded.

This third-generation Sable retains some driving characteristics familiar from the first generation over a decade ago—a controlled amount of body roll, for example. If you own an older one, you'll feel right at home in a new one after the first hard turn. That response has always been one of the Sable's defining elements. The Sable's precise handling and crisp steering mimic that of European cars and appeals to many people who would otherwise consider imports. The ride itself is a bit harsh, but not objectionably so. The car is quite easy to maneuver and park in tight quarters. We noticed little nose-diving under hard braking.

In the Sable, Ford has always devoted attention to small, thoughtful details, and this one is no exception. The dashboard is user-friendly, and the firmer seats hold their comfort well on all-day trips. On the downside, rear-seat head room is tight.

The interior has a lot of volume, but feels smaller than you would expect from the specs. And watch out if you're much over 5 foot 5 and try to clamber into the back seat; the curve of the door opening is waiting for your head. The steeply sloping windshield has some unpleasant reflections in certain light.

The trunk has ample space, and the low liftover height makes loading and unloading easy. The fold-down rear seatbacks in the sedan increase cargo-carrying options. As a station wagon, the Sable really shines as a minivan alternative. Chrysler and General Motors have no station wagons in this size.

The Mercury Sable has few peers in the mainstream family car class—unless, of course, you consider the Ford Taurus. **D.V.S.**

Specifications of Test Vehicle
Model: Sable GS

Exterior Dimensions	
Wheelbase	108.5 in.
Overall length	199.1 in.
Overall width	73 in.
Overall height	57.6 in.
Curb weight	3,600 lb.
Interior Dimensions	
Seating capacity	6
Head room	F:39.3/R:38.9 in.
Leg room	F:42.2/R:38.5 in.
Cargo volume	38.4 cu. ft.
Engine	
Displacement	V-6 3 L.
Horsepower	145 @ 5,250 rpm
Torque, lb-ft.	170 @ 3,250 rpm
Performance	
0-60 mph, acceleration	9.6 sec.
60-0 mph, braking	135 ft.
Turning circle	38 ft
EPA city/highway	18/26 mpg
Test mileage	22 mpg
Fuel tank capacity	16 gal.

Prices
$19,000
$28,000

GS sedan $18,995
LS sedan $20,095
LS 4-door wagon $21,195

Warranty
(years/miles)

Bumper-to-bumper 3/36,000
Powertrain 3/36,000
Rust-through 6/100,000

Other to Consider
Buick Regal
Chrysler Concorde

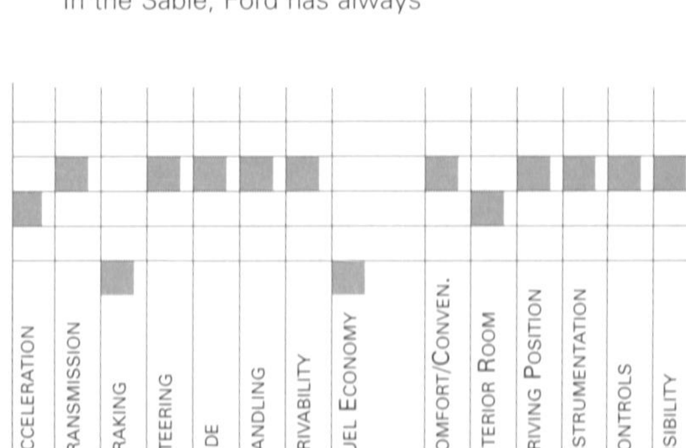

Ratings

Mercury Villager

New for 99

Redesigned interior and exterior with dual sliding doors and more powerful engine.

Pros

Comfort/convenience
Ride/handling
Entry/exit

Cons

Acceleration

Equipment

Major Standard Equipment: 3.3 liter V-6 engine, 4-speed automatic transmission, antilock brakes, cruise control, power windows and locks, air conditioning, security system, AM/FM/cassette audio system, luggage rack. **Estate Adds:** Second-row quad bucket seats. **Sport Adds:** Performance tires, 16 in. alloy wheels, handling suspension, black-on-white instruments, second-row captain's chairs. **Major Options:** Power sunroof, premium sound system, towing package, power seats, leather seats, memory seats, rear air conditioning, rear audio controls, remote keyless entry, trip computer.

A nice alternative

PRICES
$23.000
$26,000

Base
$22,995

Estate
$25,595

Sport
$25,595

WARRANTY

Bumper to Bumper
3/36,00

Power Train
3/36,00

Rust-through
6/100,000

OTHER TO CONSIDER

Nissan Quest

Mercury's Villager minivan is a pleasant alternative for those who don't want or need a full-size minivan. Completely redesigned for 1999, the new Villager is slightly longer, with more engine power and more comfort and convenience features than before.

Mercury offers the Villager in three trim levels – base, Sport, and Estate. The body is completely restyled to accommodate dual sliding doors. The new engine is a 3.3-liter V-6, capable of 170 horsepower – 20 more than last year.

The interior is restyled, but carries over many features from the previous model. The instrument panel is closer to the driver for easier reach of controls. Instruments have black faces with small white lettering. Controls are located in familiar places. The dash-mounted rotary headlight switch is especially convenient. Audio controls are thoughtfully located above the lesser-used vent controls, for better visibility. Cruise controls remain on the steering wheel.

Storage spaces abound. A large storage bin below the center console, a new overhead console, side pockets in the doors and a storage drawer under the front passenger's seat provide plenty of space for everyone's "stuff". A personal audio system allows front passengers to listen to one medium, while rear passengers can listen to a different medium through headsets.

Villager's "in-track" seating system is said to allow up to 52 different seating configurations when equipped with quad seats. Seats have been redesigned to offer better long-trip comfort. Large seat cushions are soft, but offer good support. A tip/slide system allows reasonably easy access to the third row. The third seat can slide back and forth to allow either more leg room in front, or more cargo space behind.

Villager sits low like a car, so entry and exit through any of the doors is easy. A rear swing-up tailgate provides access to the rather limited storage area. A convenient adjustable tray makes the rear cargo area more useful. Visibility is good to the front and sides, but as in most minivans, passengers and head restraints block the view to the rear.

Ride and handling seem better than most minivans. The ride is slightly firm, but not harsh. Handling is adequate for all but the worst of situations. Steering effort is light, making Villager easy to maneuver and park. Even though the engine has been upgraded for '99, its performance is still marginal. Acceleration from a stop to 60 mph takes over 12 seconds, so plan ahead before merging with fast traffic. The new antilock brake system performs without much fuss. We recorded a full-effort stopping distance from 60 mph of 137 feet – about average. Villager's size and maneuverability make it easier to drive than most of its competitors. Perhaps the improvements for '99 will give it the kind of attention it deserves from the marketplace. **D.V.S.**

Specifications of Test Vehicle	
Model: Villager GS	
Exterior Dimensions	
Wheelbase	112.2 in.
Overall Length	194.7 in.
Overall Width	74.9 in.
Overall Height	70.1 in.
Curb Weight	lbs.
Interior Dimensions	
Seating Capacity	7
Head Room	F: 39.7/C: 39.9/R: 38.0 in.
Leg Room	F: 39.9/C: 36.4/R: 36.3 in.
Cargo Room	NA
Engine	
Displacement	3.3L V-6
Horsepower	170@4800 rpm
Torque, lb-ft.	200@2800 rpm
Performance	
0-60 mph, acceleration	12.5 sec.
60-0 mph, braking	137 ft.
Turning Circle	39.9 ft.
EPA City/Highway	17/24 mpg.
Test Mileage	20.3
Fuel Tank Capacity	20 gal.

Ratings 145

Group	Category	Rating
Over The Road	Acceleration	4
	Transmission	8
	Braking	4
	Steering	8
	Ride	8
	Handling	8
	Drivability	8
	Fuel Economy	5
Passenger Environment	Comfort/Conven.	8
	Interior Room	8
	Driving Position	8
	Instrumentation	7
	Controls	8
	Visibility	7
	Entry/Exit	8
	Quietness	8
	Cargo Space	6
Workmanship	Interior	8
	Exterior	8
	Value	8

Mitsubishi 3000GT

New for 99

No changes

Pros

Advanced technology
Impressive styling
Convincing performance levels

Cons

Very stiff suspension
High weight
Cramped interior

Equipment

Major Standard Equipment: 3-liter V-6, manual transmission, 4-wheel disc brakes, air conditioning, power windows, power locks, remote keyless entry, theft alarm system, power mirrors, tilt steering column, cruise control, remote-control hatch release, cargo cover, AM/FM/ cassette stereo. **SL adds:** More powerful 3-liter V-6, power sunroof, AM/FM/CD/cassette stereo, steering wheel stereo controls, larger tires. **VR-4 adds:** Turbocharged 3-liter V-6, all-wheel drive, 6-speed manual transmission, limited-slip differential, 4-wheel steering. **Major Options:** 4-wheel antilock brakes, AM/FM/CD/cassette stereo, power sunroof.

A paunchy missile

Behind the sleek silhouette of the 3000 GT lies all of Mitsubishi's expertise. This model is a mobile showcase that the Japanese firm has proudly paraded past consumers for eight years now, still motivated by the conviction that it incarnates the epitome of high-performance capabilities, refinement, and sophistication. But both literally and figuratively, the ambition is a lofty one and it proves to us how much the 3000 GT is exactly the opposite of what a sports model should be: agile, light, and simple.

The wide (and heavy) doors open onto an interior that is cluttered and distracting. Cluttered because the dashboard is so overwhelming you'll wonder how you'll find enough room for your posterior (especially if it's well-padded). Distracting because it features a very unusual design, so much so you'll wonder if you haven't climbed into the cockpit of a bomber plane as you contemplate row upon row of instruments. Impressive maybe, but when it comes to reading them — forget it! The same goes for the controls and other buttons staring at you from all sides, creating the distinct feeling that you just aren't skilled enough to drive so complex a vehicle. Luckily the bucket seats (the rear bench seat is included for the sake of appearances only) are comfortable and help you regain your composure. However, the respite will be only temporary since the next obstacle will be coping with less-than-perfect visibility, calling for extreme caution when parking or overtaking other cars on the road.

To reach the largest possible range of buyers, the 3000 GT is available in three versions, offering three very different kinds of performance. The base model, with its ridiculous 161 horses, isn't even a match for an Integra Type R or a GTi VR6. To save face you'd best consider the SL, whose engine has a second camshaft and more importantly, a precious 57 more horses, with power still directed to the front wheels. To make driving a pleasant experience, an attribute of the VR-4 version, you'll have to lay out several thousand dollars more. With its 320-hp supercharged engine and its all wheel drive, the 3000 GT VR-4 proves to be quite an automobile, even on roads with minimal tire-grip potential. This being said, acceleration and pickup shove you well back into your seat when driving in the first four gears (the fifth and sixth have a very high ratio). Speaking of the transmission, it still isn't perfectly synchronized and shifting gears calls for a firm hand. A precise steering system, impressive stability, and powerful braking are all on hand when you get behind the wheel of a 3000 GT VR-4. On the down side: suspensions are horrendously stiff and throw the car off course as soon as road surfaces show signs of wear and tear. Backache sufferers be warned!

The 3000 GT in a nutshell: heavy, complex and cumbersome. On the other hand, less-than-expert hands will find it reassuring. **E.L.**

Specifications of Test Vehicle

Model: 3000GT VR-4

Exterior Dimensions	
Wheelbase	97.2 in.
Overall length	180.3 in.
Overall width	72.4 in.
Overall height	49.3 in.
Curb weight	3,750 lb.
Interior Dimensions	
Seating capacity	4
Head room	F:36.1/R:34.1 in.
Leg room	F:44.2/R:28.5 in.
Cargo volume	11.1 cu. ft.
Engine	
Displacement	V-6 3 L.
Horsepower	320 @ 6,000 rpm
Torque, lb-ft.	315 @ 2,500 rpm
Performance	
0-60 mph, acceleration	5.7 sec.
60-0 mph, braking	115 ft.
Turning circle	38.7 ft.
EPA city/highway	18/24 mpg
Test mileage	20 mpg
Fuel tank capacity	19.8 gal.

Prices

$28,000
$48,000

3-door $27,770

SL 3-door $35,190

VR-4 3-door $46,230

Warranty

(years/miles)

Bumper-to-bumper 3/36,000

Powertrain 5/60,000

Rust-through 7/100,000

Other to Consider

Chevrolet Corvette

Category	Rating
Over The Road	
Acceleration	10
Transmission	7
Braking	8
Steering	8
Ride	5
Handling	9
Drivability	7
Fuel Economy	5
Passenger Environment	
Comfort/Conven.	7
Interior Room	5
Driving Position	8
Instrumentation	8
Controls	7
Visibility	5
Entry/Exit	6
Quietness	7
Cargo Space	5
Workmanship	
Interior	7
Exterior	7
Value	5

Ratings 136

Mitsubishi Diamante

New for 99

No changes

Pros

Styling
Quietness
Ride comfort

Cons

Interior room
Poor ergonomics
Lacks equipment for the category

Equipment

Major Standard Equipment: 3.5-liter V-6, 4-wheel antilock disc brakes, air conditioning, power windows, power locks, remote keyless entry, remote-control decklid release, tilt steering column, cruise control, theft- alarm system, power mirrors, AM/FM/cassette stereo, full-size spare tire. **LS adds:** AM/FM/CD stereo, heated mirrors, power driver's seat, leather upholstery, limited driver's memory, power moonroof, larger tires. **Major Options:** Integrated child-safety seat, automatic dimming rear-view mirror, power moonroof, AM/FM/CD/cassette stereo, steering-wheel stereo controls, power seats, larger tires.

A diamond in the rough

PRICES
$28,000
$35,000

GS sedan
$27,650

LS sedan
$33,050

WARRANTY
(years/miles)

Bumper-to-bumper
3/36,000

Powertrain
5/60,000

Rust-through
7/100,000

OTHER TO CONSIDER

Acura 3.2 TL
Infiniti I30

Contrary to what its name implies, the sparkle off the Mitsubishi Diamante doesn't outshine others in the category of luxury sedans selling for under $30,000. In fact, even if Mitsubishi gave it a new polish last year, the Diamante still isn't pure crystallized carbon, it's more of a zircon — a stone that may be transparent, but that comes with a number of flaws.

Compared to the frigidly stark interiors of some of its rivals, the Diamante's is more exciting and instruments and controls are positioned here, there, and everywhere, giving the eye something to feast on wherever it may fall. But you do get tired of trying to master the air conditioning controls and fiddling with the radio calls for the skill of a surgeon. And if you're behind the wheel, that's not all you have to worry about: you'll have to find some way to relieve the pain in your right leg, jammed up against the oversized center console. Luckily, other passengers will find plenty of room aboard the Diamante. And there's space enough for a good bit of baggage as well.

Lighter and more powerful as a result of its revamping one year ago, the Diamante has a very positive weight/power ratio. Its 3.5-liter V-6 never runs out of energy and the four-speed automatic transmission it's teamed up with is so precise, you'll forget it's even there. Only one sour note in this song of praise: the Diamante still doesn't have a traction control system to rein in the engine's 210 horses when they decide to kick out when road conditions aren't the best for tire grip.

Unlike other Mitsubishi sedans, there's no question that the Diamante is the only model to offer a suspension carefully calibrated to offer a good compromise between comfort and road stability. And to add to driveability, a smooth and precise steering system lets you take corners with assurance.

On the negative side, Mitsubishi should really reconsider its list of accessories and should add an ABS system (standard only on the LS) to help its disc brakes along.

In its current form, the Diamante doesn't shine enough to distract consumers from its competitors, which often offer more consistent quality and more detailed equipment. **E.L.**

Specifications of Test Vehicle

Model: Diamante LS

Exterior Dimensions	
Wheelbase	107.1 in.
Overall length	194.1 in.
Overall width	70.3 in.
Overall height	53.9 in.
Curb weight	3,500 lb.
Interior Dimensions	
Seating capacity	5
Head room	F:39.4/R:37.5 in.
Leg room	F:43.6/R:36.6 in.
Cargo volume	14.2 cu. ft.
Engine	
Displacement	V-6 3.5 L.
Horsepower	210 @ 5,000 rpm
Torque, lb-ft.	231 @ 4,000 rpm
Performance	
0-60 mph, acceleration	8.4 sec.
60-0 mph, braking	127 ft.
Turning circle	36.7 ft.
EPA city/highway	18/24 mpg
Test mileage	22 mpg
Fuel tank capacity	19 gal.

Ratings

Category	Rating	Score (1–10)
Over The Road	Acceleration	8
	Transmission	7
	Braking	6
	Steering	8
	Ride	8
	Handling	8
	Drivability	9
	Fuel Economy	5
Passenger Environment	Comfort/Conven.	7
	Interior Room	6
	Driving Position	6
	Instrumentation	7
	Controls	7
	Visibility	8
	Entry/Exit	8
	Quietness	9
	Cargo Space	7
Workmanship	Interior	8
	Exterior	9
	Value	7

Mitsubishi Eclipse

New for 99

No changes

Pros

Performance (turbo)
Choice of models
Handling (AWD)

Cons

Entry/Exit
Last year in this actual form
Cargo space (convertible and AWD)

Equipment

Major Standard Equipment: 2-liter I-4, manual transmission, variable-assist power steering, tilt steering column, AM/FM/cassette stereo, remote-control hatch release, rear defroster, stainless-steel exhaust system. **GS adds:** 4-wheel disc brakes, split-folding rear seat, power mirrors, rear wiper and washer, larger tires. **GS-T adds:** More powerful 2-liter I-4, cruise control, power windows, power locks, AM/FM/CD/cassette stereo, air conditioning, sports suspension, aluminum wheels. **GSX adds:** All-wheel drive, larger brakes, leather upholstery, remote keyless entry, theft-alarm system, larger tires.

Streets on fire

Behind the wheel of the Eclipse, the expression "becoming one with your vehicle" takes on all of its meaning. Particularly narrow, the cockpit limits the movements of its driver, strapped up tight in his or her seat, facing detailed and easy-to-read instrumentation. The right hand falls directly on the shift lever and in the background are the radio's very small controls. Storage spaces are scarce and this model's trunk volume is an excellent incentive to traveling "light." To gain a few precious inches, designers showed no qualms about scrimping on the rear seat, suitable only for very small children.

The Eclipse's main attraction is that it can give you a taste of what a high performance vehicle feels like without leaving you penniless. The ultimate version, the GSX AWD, behaves so consistently and hugs the road so hard you'll be surprised to find yourself asking the supercharged four-cylinder for more power. You can even pretend you're Jeff Gordon with no risk of a premature visit to the local morgue. On the other hand, fun comes at a cost: the suspension shakes you like an apple tree and the noise from the all-wheel drive is hardly music to the ears. Add to this a body that doesn't always seem to be rigid enough and a braking system that lacks the bite to match such high-powered perfomances. The regular version, with less muscle, has none of the faults the GSX AWD shows, but at the same time it's not as exciting either.

The all-wheel drive Eclipse has another fine quality for a sport model: the ability to "play" in the snow while its rivals are mounted on blocks waiting for the good weather to come back. **E.L.**

Specifications of Test Vehicle

Model: Eclipse GS

Exterior Dimensions	
Wheelbase	98.8 in.
Overall length	172.4 in.
Overall width	68.3 in.
Overall height	49.8 in.
Curb weight	2,850 lb.

Interior Dimensions	
Seating capacity	4
Head room	F:37.9/R:34.3 in.
Leg room	F:43.3/R:28.4 in.
Cargo volume	16.6 cu. ft.

Engine	
Displacement	I-4 2 L.
Horsepower	140 @ 6,000 rpm
Torque, lb-ft.	130 @ 4,800 rpm

Performance	
0-60 mph, acceleration	10.2 sec.
60-0 mph, braking	124 ft.
Turning circle	38.1 ft.
EPA city/highway	23/33 mpg
Test mileage	26 mpg
Fuel tank capacity	16.9 gal.

Prices
$16,000
$28,000

RS 3-door $16,180
GS 3-door $18,340
GS 2-door convertible $22,140
GS-T 3-door $23,640
GS-T 2-door convertible $27,390
GSX 3-door $26,980

Warranty (years/miles)

Bumper-to-bumper 3/36,000
Powertrain 5/60,000
Rust-through 7/100,000

Other to consider

Mercury Cougar
Honda Prelude

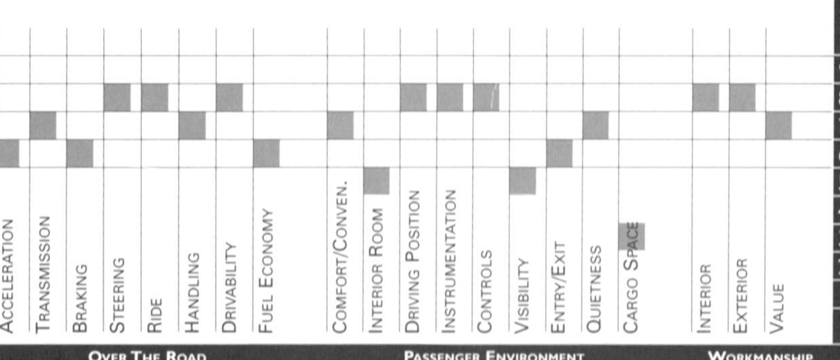

Ratings
136

Mitsubishi Galant

new MODEL

New for 99

Interior and exterior styling
New V-6 engine
Revised suspension

Pros

Room/comfort
Ride
Cargo space

Cons

Fuel economy
Transmission availability

Equipment

Major Standard Equipment: 2.4 liter 4-cylinder engine, 4-speed cloth upholstery, air conditioning, power windows and locks, tilt wheel, rear defogger, AM/FM/cassette stereo. ES Adds: Better cloth upholstery, split folding rear seat, power side-view mirror, 5-speed manual transmission. ES V-6 Adds: 3.0 liter V-6 engine, antilock 4-wheel disc brakes, larger tires. LS V-6 Adds: Leather seats, premium sound system, aluminum alloy wheels, security system, side airbags. GTZ Adds: Custom exterior, spoiler, sport-tuned suspension, full instrumentation, leather side trim. **Major Options:** Sunroof, side airbags, CD changer.

A promising 4th generation

PRICES
$17,500
$26,000
DE sedan $17,410
ES sedan $18,410
LS sedan $24,670

WARRANTY
Bumper-to-Bumper 3/36,000
Power Train 5/60,000
Rust-through 7/100,000

OTHER TO CONSIDER
Honda Accord
Toyota Camry

The 1999 Mitsubishi Galant is the fourth generation for this mid-size sedan. This year, it sports new aggressive styling, a more responsive suspension, and for the first time, a V-6 engine. Galant competes in the crowded segment, dominated by Camry and Accord. Mitsubishi is counting on the Galant's success to start rebuilding the company's reputation. It seems they're off to a good start.

The 2.4-liter, 4-cylinder, 145 hp engine is a refined carryover from past years. An all-new 3.0-liter V-6 delivers 195 hp. A 4-speed automatic transmission is standard equipment on both engines, but a 5-speed manual will be available only for the 4-cylinder engine sometime during the 1999 model year. Galant features 4-wheel independent suspension. The rear suspension is improved and now resembles the design in Mitsubishi's larger sedan, the Diamante.

The interior of the Galant is fairly typical for a mid-size sedan. Basic instruments are combined in a single pod. The radio is thoughtfully mounted above the vent controls for easy viewing. Controls for both are large, easy-to-operate knobs. Large cupholders are built into the center console. The seats are comfortable and supportive. Rear-seat head and legroom are adequate. Entry to the front is easy — getting into the back seat requires just a little bending. Visibility from the driver's seat is good in all directions. The trunk is average size, with a low lift over for easy access.

On the road, the Galant is very pleasant to drive. The V-6 engine is smooth and quiet, with a nice, powerful feeling. Acceleration from 0 to 60 mph takes about 8.7 seconds. Average fuel economy in the low 20s can be expected. The 4-cylinder engine is almost as smooth, with enough power to do most highway chores adequately. It just has to work a little harder. The automatic transmission has the ability to adapt to the driver's style. It worked well most of the time, but seemed sluggish when downshifting in light traffic. Ride and handling are a well-balanced combination. The suspension works well on all but the roughest roads. Steering is quick and accurate, with predictable understeer and moderate body roll when cornering aggressively. Brake pedal feel is good, but panic stopping distance from 60 mph was a longer-than-average 141 feet in our tests.

Obviously, Toyota and Honda dominate the segment where Mitsubishi hopes to grow the Galant. With its sharp looks, refined drive train, and good manners, Galant is a sensible alternative for those buyers who don't want what everyone else is driving.
D.V.S.

Specifications of Test Vehicle

Model: Galant ES V-6

Exterior Dimensions	
Wheelbase	103.7 in.
Overall Length	187.8 In.
Overall Width	68.5 In.
Overall Height	55.7 In.
Curb Weight	3140 lbs.
Interior Dimensions	
Seating Capacity	5
Head Room	F:39.9 /R:37.7 in.
Leg Room	F: 43.5/R: 36.3 in.
Cargo Room	14.0 cu.ft.
Engine	
Displacement	3.0 L V-6
Horsepower	195@5500 rpm
Torque, lb-ft.	205@4500 rpm
Performance	
0-60 mph, acceleration	8.7 sec.
60-0 mph, braking	141 ft.
Turning Circle	38.7 ft.
EPA City/Highway	20/27 mpg.
Test Mileage	22.0
Fuel Tank Capacity	16.3 gal.

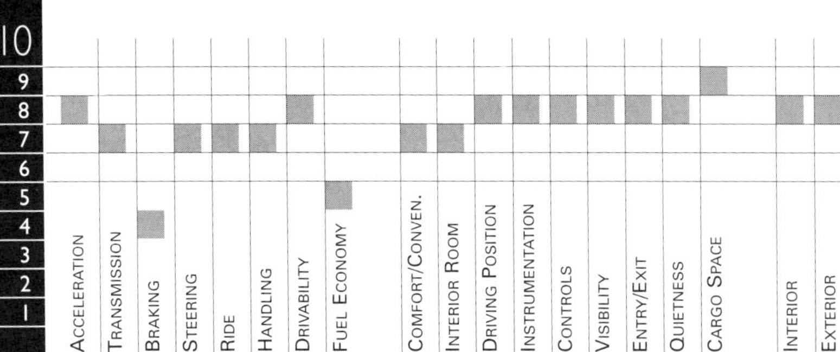

Mitsubishi

Mirage

New for 99

No changes

Pros

Attractive looks
Peppy 1.8-liter engine
Consistent road stability

Cons

Manufacturing quality
Manual transmission
Limited instrumentation

Equipment

Major Standard Equipment: 1.5-liter I-4, manual transmission, remote-control decklid release. **LS adds:** 1.8-liter I-4, air conditioning, height-adjustable driver's seat, split-folding rear seat, intermittent wipers, tilt steering column, AM/FM/CD stereo, larger tires, aluminum wheels. **Major Options:** Automatic transmission, 4-wheel antilock brakes, air conditioning, tilt steering column, height-adjustable driver's seat, variable-intermittent wipers, power windows, power locks, power mirrors, cruise control, AM/FM/cassette stereo, power moonroof, larger tires, aluminum wheels.

Down to earth

In a Mitsubishi showroom, you soon come back down to earth as you contemplate the Mirage side-by-side with Eclipse, Diamante, and 3000 GT models. But while it may not be anything dazzling, the Mirage does have a number of other talents, including the fact that since its revamping in 1997, this is a modern and perfectly well-balanced subcompact.

While the coupe and the sedan don't feature exactly the same platform, both models are equivalent when it comes to presentation — and of course, presentation improves as your budget outlay climbs higher. The base version (DE) is so dull it can make you cry. Which leads to an unhealthy rush to spiff it up with all manner of accessories, while another version, the LS, comes with a better powertrain right off the bat (1.8 liter instead of 1.5 liter). To convince you to untie your purse springs, the DE's seats provide a comfort level and driving position that are immeasurably inferior to what you find on the LS, equipped with bucket seats that fit well and a few additional adjustments (including a tilt steering wheel). Once seated, you're looking at an instrument cluster reduced to its simplest form. To counterbalance, main controls are within easy reach for the driver, even though some (radio and air conditioning controls) go against the principles of ergonomics.

The version you decide on (DE or LS) and even the model (two- or four-door) have enough bearing on the ride to make it worthwhile to keep a few important points in mind. First of all, the DE, which as we've said is powered by a 1.5-litre four-cylinder (92-hp) engine, is known to be sturdy and is capable of reaching adequate performance levels, but nothing beyond. For more fun at the wheel and to compare more favorably to the competition, the LS uses a 1.8-liter four-cylinder (113-hp) that's hard to ignore. Faster, this engine (surprise!) is as noisy or noisier than the 1.5-liter once it goes beyond the 3,500-rpm point. But any advantage the 1.8-liter brings with it vanishes into thin air because of the five-speed manual transmission, Mitsubishi's recurrent fly in the ointment; slow to respond and poorly synchronized, it puts a definite end to any possible pleasure behind the wheel of this model. The only solution is to dig into your savings and spring for an automatic, which (you just can't win) increases acceleration and pick up times!

The suspension minimizes roll when cornering and provides good feedback on road defects. Tires do what they can to hug the road, which is hard for them to do when surfaces are wet. Power steering makes maneuvering easier, but robs the driver of any feel for the road and is too light at cruising speed.

Good-looking and intelligently designed, the Mirage has more personality than many of its direct competitors. Now's the time to improve the quality of its finishing, often cited by this model's detractors. **E.L.**

Specifications of Test Vehicle

Model: Mirage LS

Exterior Dimensions	
Wheelbase	95.1 in.
Overall length	168.1 in.
Overall width	66.5 in.
Overall height	52.4 in.
Curb weight	2,250 lb.
Interior Dimensions	
Seating capacity	5
Head room	F:38.6/R:35.8 in.
Leg room	F:43/R:31.1 in.
Cargo volume	11.5 cu. ft.
Engine	
Displacement	I-4 1.8 L.
Horsepower	113 @ 5,500 rpm
Torque, lb-ft.	116 @ 4,500 rpm
Performance	
0-60 mph, acceleration	8.2 sec.
60-0 mph, braking	115 ft.
Turning circle	32.8 ft.
EPA city/highway	29/36 mpg
Test mileage	31 mpg
Fuel tank capacity	13.2 gal.

Prices
$11,000
$16,000

DE coupe $11,580
DE sedan $12,880
LS coupe $15,030
LS sedan $13,830

Warranty (years/miles)
Bumper-to-bumper 3/36,000
Powertrain 5/60,000
Rust-through 7/100,000

Other to Consider
Honda Civic
Nissan Sentra

Group	Category	Rating
Over The Road	Acceleration	8
	Transmission	7
	Braking	8
	Steering	7
	Ride	6
	Handling	7
	Drivability	7
	Fuel Economy	7
Passenger Environment	Comfort/Conven.	7
	Interior Room	6
	Driving Position	7
	Instrumentation	6
	Controls	7
	Visibility	6
	Entry/Exit	6
	Quietness	6
	Cargo Space	5
Workmanship	Interior	8
	Exterior	8
	Value	7

Ratings
136

Mitsubishi Montero

New for 99

No changes

Pros

Engine performance
Comfort/convenience
Roomy

Cons

Entry/Exit
Fuel economy
Handling

Equipment

Major Standard Equipment: 3.5-liter V-6, automatic transmission, automatic 4-wheel drive, 2-speed transfer case, 4-wheel antilock disc brakes, air conditioning, 7-passenger seating, split-folding second-row seat, folding third-row seat, AM/FM/cassette stereo, tilt power windows, power locks, steering column, cruise control, power mirrors, rear defroster, variable-intermittent wipers, rear wiper and washer, privacy glass, power moonroof, stainless-steel exhaust system, aluminum wheels. **Major Options:** Locking rear differential, power driver's seat, heated seats, power sunroof, heated mirrors, remote keyless entry, theft alarm system, adjustable shock absorbers.

Win on sunday, sell on monday

PRICES
$34,000
$41,000
4-door wagon
$33,530

WARRANTY
(years/miles)
Bumper-to-bumper
3/36,000
Powertrain
5/60,000
Rust-through
7/100,000

OTHER TO CONSIDER
Isuzu Trooper
Acura SLX

It isn't every year that a manufacturer takes all three top spots in the Dakar-Paris rally. Mitsubishi knows that, and it intends to capitalize on the remarkable success of its Montero to win over those who like to defy the laws of nature without sacrificing a smidgen of comfort. It's called combining business with pleasure.

Much like the others in its lineup, for some people getting into the Montero calls for solid mountain-climbing skills. This is especially true for rear-seat passengers, since they have to manage with fairly narrow doors and a bench seat (the third row seat) that isn't very inviting if you're over 12 years old. However, no criticism can be aimed at the front bucket seats or the second bench seat, where five people can travel comfortably. Visibility is excellent, except towards the back, where large headrests and an emergency wheel mounted on the hatchback make driving in reverse a potentially hazardous idea.

The Montero likes to play at being macho, but does it do as well in the urban jungle? Well, it has a pleasant surprise in store for you: this car is surprisingly agile given its overall size. The credit goes to its responsive and precise steering system, which prevents it from ever looking foolish and out of place in the city. The suspension has enough travel to make driving on the highway extraordinarily comfortable and only tight corners show up its softness, producing a noticeable amount of roll. On the other hand, the Montero's braking is as good as it gets and stopping is perfectly safe over reasonable distances. This utility features a 200-hp 3.5-liter V6 that may not be thundering, but certainly measures up to the best power trains in the category when it comes to performance levels, pick-up power and fuel economy.

Will winning the 1997 Dakar rally was enough to rob the spotlight from the category's new stars, all fresher and more modern looking? The answer will be clear a few months from now. **E.L.**

Specifications of Test Vehicle

Model: Montero SR

Exterior Dimensions	
Wheelbase	107.3 in.
Overall length	186.6 in.
Overall width	69.9 in.
Overall height	74.8 in.
Curb weight	4,450 lb.
Interior Dimensions	
Seating capacity	7
Head room	F:40.9/R:40/R2:34.8 in.
Leg room	F:40.3/R:37.6/R2:19.4 in.
Cargo volume	8.8 cu. ft.
Engine	
Displacement	V-6 3.5 L.
Horsepower	200 @ 5,000 rpm
Torque, lb-ft.	228 @ 3,500 rpm
Performance	
0-60 mph, acceleration	9.7 sec.
60-0 mph, braking	120 ft.
Turning circle	38.7 ft.
EPA city/highway	16/19 mpg
Test mileage	15 mpg
Fuel tank capacity	24.3 gal.

Ratings

Category	Rating	Score
Over The Road	Acceleration	7
	Transmission	8
	Braking	7
	Steering	8
	Ride	7
	Handling	6
	Drivability	8
	Fuel Economy	3
Passenger Environment	Comfort/Conven.	9
	Interior Room	8
	Driving Position	8
	Instrumentation	8
	Controls	8
	Visibility	7
	Entry/Exit	5
	Quietness	8
	Cargo Space	4
Workmanship	Interior	9
	Exterior	8
	Value	6

Mitsubishi

Montero Sport

New for 99

No changes

Pros

Cargo room
Visibility
Ride

Cons

Interior storage space
Fuel consomption
Engine performance

Equipment

Major Standard Equipment: 2.4-liter I-4, manual transmission, AM/FM stereo, tilt steering column, folding rear seat, stainless-steel exhaust system. **LS adds:** 3-liter V-6, AM/FM/cassette stereo, privacy glass. **XLS adds:** Air conditioning, 4-wheel antilock brakes, rear heater, power moonroof, cruise control, power windows, power locks, power mirrors. **Major Options:** Part-time 4-wheel drive, limited-slip rear differential, locking rear differential, air conditioning, 4-wheel antilock disc brakes, remote keyless entry, theft-deterrent system, power moonroof, power windows, power locks, power mirrors, cruise control.

A useless fad diet

To put an end to the rising fortunes of the Pathfinder, 4Runner, Rodeo and other utilities, Mitsubishi decided to use every possible means at its disposal, including putting the Montero on a starvation diet. The operation may have appeared simple, but judging by the unhappy results, it also involved some danger.

Like many other utility vehicles in the same category, climbing into the Montero is a problem and very near an impossibility given that its high-perched floor is a bit too close for comfort to a roof whose lines are not designed to be accommodating. Those who want to ride in the rear seat had better be contortionists of considerable talent since doors don't open very wide. And if it's not one thing, it's another: if they do manage to get inside, they'll be pitted against a cramped and uncomfortable bench seat. Front seat occupants fare much better, enjoying bucket seats offering decent comfort and support. Owners can rejoice in excellent visibility from all angles, a number of storage spaces and a detailed and easy-to-read instrument panel.

To melt down the Montero's price, Mitsubishi had no other choice but to go ahead with a few select organ transplants. Exit the 2.7-liter V6; say hello to a 2.4-liter four-cylinder or a 3.0-liter V6, depending on the version of your choice. Neither power train can get this utility's (considerable) back side moving with perceptible energy. For some reason the Montero Sport has a different suspension and it has a negative effect on its performance on the road: it's stiff when it has to cope with road defects and produces a considerable amount of roll on tight corners. Oddly, the steering system seems less responsive than the regular Montero's and brakes seem to lack bite.

The Montero Sport is a strange exercise in marketing. Two years after its launch, it's already the last in its class! **E.L.**

Specifications of Test Vehicle

Model: LS

Exterior Dimensions	
Wheelbase	107.3 in.
Overall length	178.3 in.
Overall width	66.7 in.
Overall height	65.6 in.
Curb weight	4,000 lb.
Interior Dimensions	
Seating capacity	5
Head room	F:38.9/R:37.3 in.
Leg room	F:42.8/R:33.5 in.
Cargo volume	34.3 cu. ft.
Engine	
Displacement	V-6 3 L.
Horsepower	173 @ 5,250 rpm
Torque, lb-ft	188 @ 4,000 rpm
Performance	
0-60 mph, acceleration	NA
60-0 mph, braking	NA
Turning circle	38.7 ft.
EPA city/highway	18/21 mpg
Test mileage	15 mpg
Fuel tank capacity	19.5 gal.

Prices

$18,000
$32,000

ES 4-door truck wagon $18,030
LS 4-door truck wagon $22,260
XLS 4-door truck wagon $28,360

Warranty

(years/miles)

Bumper-to-bumper 3/36,000
Powertrain 5/60,000
Rust-through 7/100,000

Other to consider

Nissan Pathfinder
Isuzu Rodeo

Category	Rating
Over the Road	
Acceleration	6
Transmission	6
Braking	5
Steering	7
Ride	8
Handling	7
Drivability	7
Fuel Economy	3
Passenger Environment	
Comfort/Conven.	7
Interior Room	8
Driving Position	8
Instrumentation	8
Controls	6
Visibility	8
Entry/Exit	6
Quietness	7
Cargo Space	10
Workmanship	
Interior	8
Exterior	8
Value	7

Ratings
140

Nissan Altima

New for 99

Revised list of accessories

Pros

Extensive and competitive model range
Proven reliability
Attractive price

Cons

Cramped interior
Long turning radius
Poor ergonomics

Equipment

Major Standard Equipment: 2.4-liter I-4, manual transmission, intermittent wipers, rear defroster, power mirrors, power windows, tilt steering column, remote decklid release. **GXE adds:** Air conditioning, split-folding rear seat, power locks, cruise control, AM/FM/CD/cassette stereo. **SE adds:** Remote keyless entry, theft-alarm system, sports suspension, aluminum wheels. **GLE adds:** Automatic transmission, variable-intermittent wipers, power seats. leather upholstery. **Major Options:** Automatic transmission, 4-wheel antilock brakes, power seats, leather upholstery, remote keyless entry, theft-alarm system, power moonroof, aluminum wheels.

Prudently bold

PRICES
$15,000
$24,000

XE sedan $15,480
GXE sedan $17,680
SE sedan $18,980
GLE sedan $20,480

WARRANTY (years/miles)
Bumper-to-bumper 3/36,000
Powertrain 3/36,000
Rust-through 5/60,000

OTHER TO CONSIDER
Mazda 626
Mercury Mystique

One third of Nissan's North American sales are Altimas, so you can imagine the fears and doubts that must have bedeviled the men and women assigned to come up with this second generation. As we might have expected, Nissan demonstrated good sense in reformu-lating its economy model. It is clearly more spacious, but what else? In fact, only the design of the rear portion, visibly inspired by the now-defunct J30, reveals a real originality that Nissan has filled in with earthy hues.

Ergonomics experts will tell you drivers spend more time fooling around with radio controls than those for air conditioning or heating. With this in mind and for obvious safety reasons, such controls have been moved and replaced to make sure we don't take our eyes off the road.

Nissan does things its own way and, contrary to all expectations, left the radio under the lower portion of the dash, beneath the aircon console. The latter, incidentally, is a slap in the face of ergonomic rules, forcing us to set the interior temperature with a sloppy cursor. Another minor detail is the interior, and simulated wood (only available on more costly models) hues give the cab a cozy feel like none of its Japanese rivals. The bucket seats are comfortable enough and the rear bench seat holds two people without complaints. A third? He or she would be more comfortable on board a standard XE or GXE, neither of which has a central armrest. A gentle hint: why deprive the XE of the invaluable device that reminds you that your key is in the starter when you leave the car?

The Altima has remained impervious to the gripes of critics who swooped down on it for refusing to offer a six-cylinder version. The second generation will also have to batten down its hatches because Nissan has done the same thing all over again (it must protect its Maxima!) and is using the same 2.4-liter four-cylinder engine. Wider and longer, the Altima is also heavier than its predecessor, which costs it in terms of the power-weight ratio. It particularly compensates for this loss by releasing its 154 lbs-ft of torque sooner, giving it performance very close to that of the prior generation. Moreover, the motor is subtler, which helps establish the Altima's aura of overall solidity. However, the greater stability of its chassis does not result in a sportier compact. In fact, only the SE and its attractions (thicker stabilizer bars, stiffer springs, and tires with better grip) make Altima really nice to drive. The others (XE, GXE, and GLE) have too much roll in the turns, require more pumping when you brake and understeer sooner.

Nicely finished, sturdy, spacious, reliable, and competitively priced, the Altima is one of a long list of colorless, odorless, tasteless compacts that are congesting the market. But, don't despair, because Jerry Hirshberg, director of the Nissan design studios in California, has been heard to say: "In 2001, the third generation of Altima will be exciting." If the good Lord lets us see the day, we shall be there to witness it. **E.L.**

Specifications of Test Vehicle

Model: Altima GLE

Exterior Dimensions	
Wheelbase	103.1 in.
Overall length	183.1 in.
Overall width	69.1 in.
Overall height	55.9 in.
Curb weight	3,000 lb.
Interior Dimensions	
Seating capacity	5
Head room	F:39.4/R:37.7 in.
Leg room	F:42/R:33.9 in.
Cargo room	14 cu. ft.
Engine	
Displacement	I-4 2.4 L.
Horsepower	150 @ 5,600 rpm
Torque, lb-ft.	154 @ 4,400 rpm
Performance	
0-60 mph, acceleration	9.1 sec.
60-0 mph, braking	121 ft.
Turning circle	37.4 ft.
EPA city/highway	22/30 mpg
Test mileage	27 mpg
Fuel tank capacity	15.9 gal.

Ratings **149**

Category	Rating
Over The Road	
Acceleration	7
Transmission	7
Braking	6
Steering	8
Ride	8
Handling	8
Drivability	8
Fuel Economy	6
Passenger Environment	
Comfort/Conven.	8
Interior Room	7
Driving Position	7
Instrumentation	9
Controls	7
Visibility	8
Entry/Exit	7
Quietness	7
Cargo Space	6
Workmanship	
Interior	8
Exterior	9
Value	8

Nissan

Frontier

New for 99

V-6 engine
Four-wheel drive
Four-door model in the coming year

Pros

Sturdy and reliable
Quality assembly
Precise manual transmission

Cons

Rough V-6
Uncomfortable auxiliary seats
Slightly soft suspension

Equipment

Major Standard Equipment: 2.4-liter I-4, manual transmission, rear-wheel antilock brakes, unassisted steering, bench seat, driver-side mirror, vinyl upholstery, vinyl floor covering, painted front bumper. **XE adds:** Air conditioning, power steering, passenger-side mirror, rear bumper, chrome bumpers, cloth upholstery, carpeting. **SE adds:** Individual front seats, cruise control, tilt steering column, variable-intermittent wipers, privacy glass, moonroof, AM/FM/CD/cassette stereo, aluminum wheels. **Major Options:** Automatic transmission, part-time 4-wheel drive, 4-wheel antilock brakes, air conditioning.

Reinforcements

It was last year that Nissan unveiled the replacement for its venerable Hardbody, which was beginning to run out of steam. The Frontier name was all new, but at the time only one engine was available, a 2.4-liter four-cylinder designed to meet new fuel consumption and pollution standards. A few months after the Frontier's launch, consumers were given access to an all-wheel drive version and in 1999, a 3.3-liter V-6 has appeared, just before Nissan begins commercializing a four-door Frontier.

While the Frontier's platform is nothing but a modified version of the Hardbody's, this model's interior has been entirely revamped. The dashboard boasts fairly detailed instrumentation, easier to read now that most reflection-related problems have been eliminated. At last, the clock has been positioned adjacent to the radio and all heating and air conditioning controls are within easy reach and simple to use. Two air bags provide optimal protection, and the passenger's can be deactivated at the flick of a switch. The Frontier is available with a regular or extended cab, the latter capable of accommodating two more occupants in the rear, but in limited comfort, in sharp contrast to the front bucket seats. Incidently, the automatic transmission lever is now mounted on the steering column.

Notwithstanding the promise to provide more power, the four-cylinder is a tad short-winded, and going from a standing start to 60 mph takes approximately 12 seconds. However, to its credit it's quiet on the highway and its manual transmission is impressively precise. The V-6 engine is quiet as well, but clearly lacks power in the lower rpm range. Braking is efficient thanks to the standard ABS system on rear wheels and, in fact, the Frontier's brakes show the best results recorded for trucks. The suspension on the base model with extended cab is very smooth; the vehicle's front end does nose dive on sharp corners, just like big American cars used to, but the vehicle still rides smoothly and comfortably. **E.L.**

Prices

$12,000
$21,000

Short bed
$11,990

XE short bed
$13,190

XE ext. cab, short bed
$14,640

SE ext. cab, short bed
$17,990

Warranty

(years/miles)

Bumper-to-bumper
3/36,000

Powertrain
5/60,000

Rust-through
5/60,000

Other to consider

Mazda B-Series

Isuzu Hombre

Specifications of Test Vehicle

Model: Frontier SE

Exterior Dimensions	
Wheelbase	116.1 in.
Overall length	196.1 in.
Overall width	71.9 in.
Overall height	65.9 in.
Curb weight	3,700 lb.
Interior Dimensions	
Seating capacity	4
Head room	F:39.3/R:NA in.
Leg room	F:40.8/R:NA in.
Payload capacity	NA
Engine	
Displacement	I-4 2.4 L.
Horsepower	143 @ 5,200 rpm
Torque, lb-ft.	154 @ 4,000 rpm
Performance	
0-60 mph, acceleration	10 sec.
60-0 mph, braking	143 ft.
Turning circle	39 ft.
EPA city/highway	18/21 mpg
Test mileage	NA
Fuel tank capacity	15.9 gal.

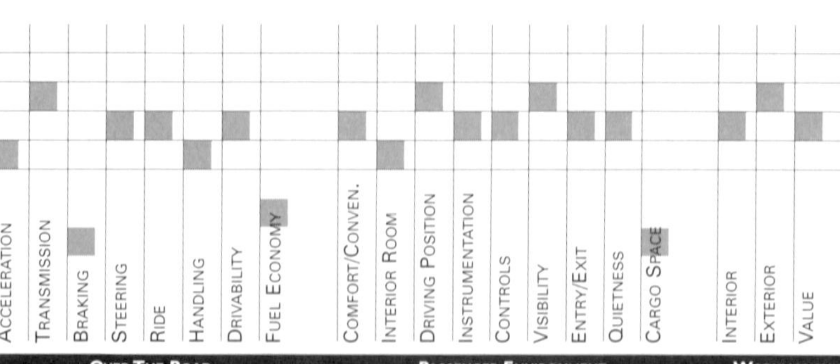

Ratings
130

Nissan Maxima

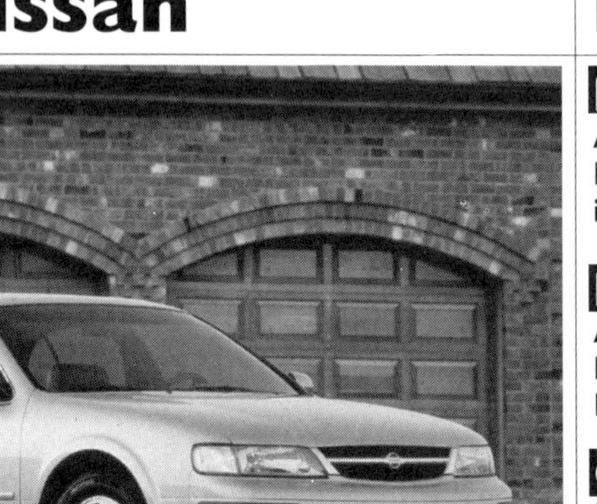

New for 99

Anti-theft Engine immobilizer

Pros

Acceleration
Ride
Handling

Cons

Features
Option packages
Leg room

Equipment

Major Standard Equipment: 3-liter V-6, manual transmission, 4-power mirrors, air conditioning, power windows, power locks, cruise control, tilt steering column, AM/FM/cassette stereo. **SE adds:** AM/FM/CD/cassette stereo, sports suspension. **GLE adds:** Automatic transmission, automatic temperature control, variable-intermittent wipers, power seats, leather upholstery, remote keyless entry, antitheft system. **Major Options:** Automatic temperature control, side air bags, power moonroof, 4-wheel antilock brakes, power seats, heated front seats, heated mirrors, leather upholstery, remote keyless entry, antitheft system.

What's in a name ?

PRICES
$21,000
$29,000
GXE sedan $21,989
SE sedan $23,989
GLE sedan $26,389

WARRANTY (years/miles)
Bumper-to-bumper 3/36,000
Powertrain 5/60,000
Rust-through 5/60,000

OTHER TO CONSIDER
Oldsmobile Intrigue

The Nissan Maxima is just another nice car. That may seem like faint praise for Nissan's flagship sedan. But in fact the Maxima is very close in size to Nissan's much less expensive, redesigned Altima and lacks many of the luxury features that mean good value.

The division of features among various Maxima trim levels poses some problems. For example, you must pay extra or go to the most expensive trim level, the GLE, to get variable-intermittent windshield wipers—a feature that's commonly standard equipment on cars in this price class. Just as significant are the features that aren't included. Antilock brakes are extra-cost options on all trim levels. Traction control isn't available at all; its absence is conspicuous, since Nissan markets the Maxima as a low-level luxury model. Side air bags are a new option, but not by themselves. You have to buy heated seats and heated outside mirrors, too.

The V-6 engine is peppy and responsive, especially from 30 to 60 mph, where it generates much of its torque. The 3-liter engine is especially strong in such workaday maneuvers as entering busy freeways and passing slower traffic on two-lane roads. The automatic transmission shifts smoothly and precisely, and its gear ratios are neatly matched to the engine's power curve. From a standing stop, we reached 60 mph in 8.8 seconds. We averaged 24 mpg on high-octane gas.

The power disc brakes give the car an average stopping distance with the optional antilock brakes. The variable-effort power steering sends enough feedback through the wheel to keep the driver well-connected to the road and provides enough assist at low speeds. The suspension absorbs most surface imperfections without compromising control. Overall, the car rides comfortably and handles nearly as well as a sports sedan.

Wind, road, and engine noise is minimal inside the cockpit. A good, long drive in the Maxima won't leave you tired and anxious to get out.

Inside, the Maxima boasts acceptable front leg room, although the center console restricts the lateral space. There's ample front and rear head room, thanks to a new, thinner sunroof design. The front seats are comfortable, especially on long trips, and easy to adjust. Three adults will still find it difficult to squeeze together into the rear bench seat, but there's adequate room for two. On the dash, the analog gauges are easy to read, and the major controls are within easy reach.

Unfortunately, the Maxima does not live up to the promise of its name. It's too basic for a sporty sedan aimed at upscale buyers. If the car appeals to you and more luxury features are on your must-have list, take a look at the Infiniti I30. **D.V.S.**

Ratings

148

Group	Category	Rating
Over The Road	Acceleration	8
	Transmission	9
	Braking	5
	Steering	8
	Ride	8
	Handling	8
	Drivability	8
	Fuel Economy	6
Passenger Environment	Comfort/Conven.	7
	Interior Room	6
	Driving Position	8
	Instrumentation	8
	Controls	8
	Visibility	7
	Entry/Exit	8
	Quietness	8
	Cargo Space	7
Workmanship	Interior	8
	Exterior	8
	Value	5

Specifications of Test Vehicle

Model: Maxima GLE

Exterior Dimensions	
Wheelbase	106.3 in.
Overall length	189.4 in.
Overall width	69.7 in.
Overall height	55.7 in.
Curb weight	3,050 lb.
Interior Dimensions	
Seating capacity	5
Head room	F:40.1/R:37.4 in.
Leg room	F:43.9/R:34.3 in.
Cargo volume	14.5 cu. ft.
Engine	
Displacement	V-6 3 L.
Horsepower	190 @ 5,600 rpm
Torque, lb-ft.	205 @ 4,000 rpm
Performance	
0-60 mph, acceleration	8.8 sec.
60-0 mph, braking	131 ft.
Turning circle	34.8 ft.
EPA city/highway	21/28 mpg
Test mileage	24 mpg
Fuel tank capacity	18.5 gal.

Nissan Pathfinder

New for 99

Restyle
More horsepower

Pros

Sturdiness
Impeccable finishing
Well-designed cockpit

Cons

Marginal braking power
Anemic 3.3-liter engine
Access to rear seats

Equipment

Major Standard Equipment: 3.3-liter V-6, manual transmission, 4-wheel antilock brakes, split-folding rear seat, tilt steering wheel, variable-intermittent wipers, AM/FM/CD stereo. **SE adds:** 4-wheel drive, automatic temperature control, power heated mirrors, power windows, power locks, cruise control, remote keyless entry, luggage rack, cargo cover, privacy glass. **LE adds:** Automatic transmission, limited-slip differential, running boards. **Major Options:** Automatic transmission, part-time 4-wheel drive, remote keyless entry, power heated mirrors, cruise control, power seats, heated seats, power moonroof.

Not as much fun

As much as I was charmed by the first-generation Pathfinder, so much of a disappointment is the second one to me. Was I expecting too much? I'm not sure. But what I do know is that the first generation was downright exciting. Energetic and fun to drive, the original Pathfinder has an appealing personality, diametrically opposed to its replacement's, a model that plays at being aristocratic with its chrome grille and wheel covers so shiny and flashy you'll think twice before daring to drive this model through mud puddles.

The Pathfinder was made bigger two years ago, at the same time as it was given a restyling and more extensive equipment. The bright, well-finished, and carefully designed interior is definitely attractive. The dashboard houses detailed equipment, controls are positioned logically, and an additional air bag has been added to protect the front-seat passenger. But rear-seat passengers are those who benefit most from the revamping, although narrow doors make getting in and out slightly difficult.

No, the 3.3-liter V-6 under the Pathfinder's hood isn't very economical when it comes to fuel. And when all is said and done, it isn't very powerful either, since its 168 horses run out of breath very quickly when the passenger compartment is full. On the up side, it's fairly quiet and gets along swimmingly with either of the transmissions that are available. On the road, the suspension is efficient at countering road defects and the Pathfinder is predictable under normal conditions. When you decide to pick up the pace, however, body sway becomes noticeable and the Pathfinder feels even heavier than it really is. To complicate matters, brakes lack bite.

Those familiar with the first-generation Pathfinder will no doubt mourn its agility and driveability. As for other potential owners, they'll find this second generation to be a roomy, luxurious, and very well-assembled sport utility.

E.L.

Specifications of Test Vehicle

Model: Pathfinder LE

Exterior Dimensions	
Wheelbase	106.3 in.
Overall length	188.2 in.
Overall width	68.7 in.
Overall height	67.1 in.
Curb weight	4,000 lb.
Interior Dimensions	
Seating capacity	5
Head room	F:39.5/R:37.5 in.
Leg room	F:41.7/R:31.8 in.
Cargo volume	38 cu. ft.
Engine	
Displacement	V-6 3.3 L.
Horsepower	170 @ 4,800 rpm
Torque, lb-ft.	196 @ 2,800 rpm
Performance	
0-60 mph, acceleration	11.5 sec.
60-0 mph, braking	140 ft.
Turning circle	35.4 ft.
EPA city/highway	15/19 mpg
Test mileage	17 mpg
Fuel tank capacity	21.1 gal.

Prices

$24,000
$36,000

XE 4-door truck wagon $23,999

SE 4-door truck wagon $29,099

LE 4-door truck wagon $30,449

Warranty

(years/miles)

Bumper-to-bumper 3/36,000

Powertrain 5/60,000

Rust-through 5/60,000

Other to Consider

Chevrolet Blazer

Isuzu Rodeo

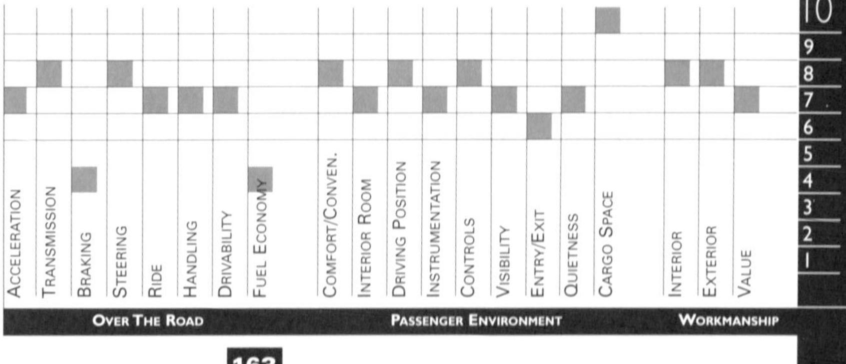

Ratings

Category	Criterion	Rating
Over The Road	Acceleration	7
	Transmission	8
	Braking	4
	Steering	8
	Ride	7
	Handling	7
	Drivability	7
	Fuel Economy	4
Passenger Environment	Comfort/Conven.	8
	Interior Room	7
	Driving Position	8
	Instrumentation	7
	Controls	8
	Visibility	7
	Entry/Exit	6
	Quietness	7
	Cargo Space	10
Workmanship	Interior	8
	Exterior	8
	Value	7

Ratings **143**

Nissan Quest GXE

NEW MODEL

NEW FOR 99

New model

PROS

Four doors, at last
Smooth ride
Modular passenger compartment

CONS

Lazy engine
Major turning radius
Rough transmission

EQUIPMENT

Major Standard Equipment:
GXE: 3.3 liter V-6 engine, 4-speed automatic transmission, antilock brakes, cruise control, power windows and locks, air conditioning, remote keyless entry, security system, AM/FM/cassette audio system, luggage rack. **GLE Adds:** Leather seats, power front seats, memory driver's seat, automatic climate control, alloy wheels, CD changer, rear air conditioning, rear audio controls. **SE Adds:** Performance tires, 16 in. alloy wheels, handling suspension, black-on-white instruments, second-row captain's chairs, front and rear air conditioning, rear audio controls. **Major Options:** Power sunroof, premium sound system, towing package.

Not Alone

PRICES
$23,000
$29,000

XE 3-door minivan
$23,099

GXE 3-door minivan
$26,049

GLE 3-door minivan
$28,597

WARRANTY

Bumper-to-bumper
3/36,00

Power Train
5/60,000

Rust-through
5/60,000

OTHER TO CONSIDER

Honda Odyssey

Toyota Sienna

Nissan no doubt sighed with relief when it learned that Mercury would not be bringing its revamped Villager to the Canadian market. Unfortunately for Nissan, the Villager is still part of Mercury's team in the US for '99.

Regardless of the Villager, Nissan can begin dreaming of a second-generation Quest capable of stealing a few sales from the category's leading models as well.

For 1999, Nissan has revised its models' names. The XE becomes the GXE, which now answers to the letters SE, and the GLE is the model at the top of the lineup.

Open your eyes: if the Quest has a definite family likeness linking it to its predecessor, note that it's longer and has a driver's side sliding door to provide easier access to the vehicle. The biggest beneficiaries of this change are baggage and cargo, now that there's more room for both.

The Quest's interior is as appealing as always. Stylists have redone the dashboard, now more functional and, more importantly, now featuring a center portion with better ergonomics, pointed towards the driver. Bucket and bench seats, a strong point in the Quest's favor, have stayed in their original positions and are still molded very well. The hatchback is easier to open and close and the cargo area has a very practical shelf for transporting groceries.

History tells us that owners of the previous generation Quest wanted more power. And their wish has come true, since the Quest has shed the 3.0-liter V6 in favor of a 3.3-liter (the same unit used to power the Pathfinder, QX4 and Frontier). Although it does have more power, the new V6 seems to be rougher and listless. Worse still, the four-speed automatic transmission, the only one available, is not as precise or as smooth as its rivals. Changes made to the suspension have a positive effect on comfort without jeopardizing the very nice balance achieved by the Quest. The steering system is fairly precise, but oddly, the turning radius is long (longer than on Chrysler's extended versions), which penalizes the Quest when it takes to city streets. Featuring the classic disc/drum duo, brakes ensure stable stopping. Still, when will we see four discs, always a good idea, after all? **E.L.**

SPECIFICATIONS OF TEST VEHICLE

MODEL: QUEST GXE

Exterior Dimensions	
Wheelbase	112.2 in.
Overall Length	194.8 in.
Overall Width	74.9 in.
Overall Height	67.3 in.
Curb Weight	3986 lbs.
Interior Dimensions	
Seating Capacity	7
Head Room	F: 39.7/C: 39.9/R: 37.6 in.
Leg Room	F: 39.9/C: 36.4/R: 36.3 in.
Cargo Room	NA
Engine	
Displacement	3.3L V-6
Horsepower	170@4800 rpm
Torque, lb-ft.	200@2800 rpm
Performance	
0-60 mph, acceleration	12.7 sec.
60-0 mph, braking	138 ft.
Turning Circle	39.9 ft.
EPA City/Highway	17/24 mpg.
Test Mileage	NA
Fuel Tank Capacity	20 gal.

Ratings 145

Group	Rating	Score
Over The Road	Acceleration	4
	Transmission	8
	Braking	4
	Steering	8
	Ride	8
	Handling	8
	Drivability	8
	Fuel Economy	5
Passenger Environment	Comfort/Conven.	8
	Interior Room	8
	Driving Position	8
	Instrumentation	7
	Controls	8
	Visibility	7
	Entry/Exit	8
	Quietness	8
	Cargo Space	6
Workmanship	Interior	8
	Exterior	8
	Value	8

Nissan

Sentra

New for 99

New front-end design

Pros

Sturdy and reliable
Good fuel economy
Good handling

Cons

Minimal driveability
Annoying automatic transmission
Poor choice of tires

Equipment

Major Standard Equipment: 1.6-liter I-4, manual transmission, unassisted steering, tilt steering wheel, driver-side mirror, vinyl upholstery, rear defroster. **XE adds:** Power steering, air conditioning, passenger-side mirror, cloth upholstery, AM/FM/cassette stereo, intermittent wipers, remote-control decklid release. **GXE adds:** Split-folding rear seat, power mirrors, power windows, power locks. SE adds: 2-liter I-4, remote keyless entry, aluminum wheels. **SE adds:** 2.0-liter I-4.
Major Options: Automatic transmission, 4-wheel antilock disc brakes, power moonroof.

Drab and dreary

Jerry Hirshberg, head stylist at Nissan's California design studios, promised the future Sentra will have a more assertive personality. We can certainly believe him because the current version doesn't give us much reason to stare in the meantime. Quite frankly, looking at a Sentra is about as exciting as looking at a toaster — even though it has the advantage of a transplanted face, extracted from the defunct 200 SX! Too bad, because for anyone who gets the chance to drive it, the Sentra will prove a steadfast traveling companion.

The Sentra's drab and dreary passenger compartment can hold four. Seats provide decent support and the rear bench seat can yield in whole or in part to increase the size of the trunk. Easy-to-read instrumentation fits into the conservatively styled, nicely molded dash. But it is incomplete, lacking a tachometer as a standard item. On the other hand, all Sentras have tilt steering wheels and the usual ubiquitous cup holders.

On the road, the 1.6-liter four-cylinder engine is reasonably driveable, but whines when too much is asked of it. Poorly suited to the automatic transmission, its performance levels are ever so slightly higher with the manual alternative. Shifting with the manual transmission is smooth, but the way gears are staggered saves on fuel rather than boosting performance. That's all for the best as the disc-drum braking system is no model of efficiency and the brake pedal makes it hard to gauge stopping power. Narrow tires with little grip may also explain relatively long stopping distances. Outside the flexibility of the suspension — which produces a marked roll on corners — the narrowness of the tires (except on the GXE, now better equipped in this area) detracts from the Sentra's true potential. Not a real joy to drive, the Sentra is, however, entertaining to park, because of its manoeuvrability.
E.L.

Specifications of Test Vehicle

Model: Sentra GLE

Exterior Dimensions	
Wheelbase	99.8 in.
Overall length	171.1 in.
Overall width	66.6 in.
Overall height	54.5 in.
Curb weight	2,450 lb.
Interior dimensions	
Seating capacity	5
Head room	F:39.1/R:36.5 in.
Leg room	F:42.3/R:32.4 in.
Cargo volume	10.7 cu. ft.
Engine	
Displacement	I-4 1.6 L.
Horsepower	115 @ 6,000 rpm
Torque, lb-ft.	108 @ 4,000 rpm
Performance	
0-60 mph, acceleration	9.7 sec.
60-0 mph, braking	147 ft.
Turning circle	34.1 ft.
EPA city/highway	27/36 mpg
Test mileage	31 mpg
Fuel tank capacity	13.2 gal.

PRICES
$11,000
$18,000

Sedan $11,989
XE sedan $14,189
GXE sedan $15,389
SE sedan $17,239
GLE sedan $16,239

WARRANTY (years/miles)

Bumper-to-bumper 3/36,000
Powertrain 5/60,000
Rust-through 5/60,000

OTHER TO CONSIDER

Mazda Protegé
Saturn SL

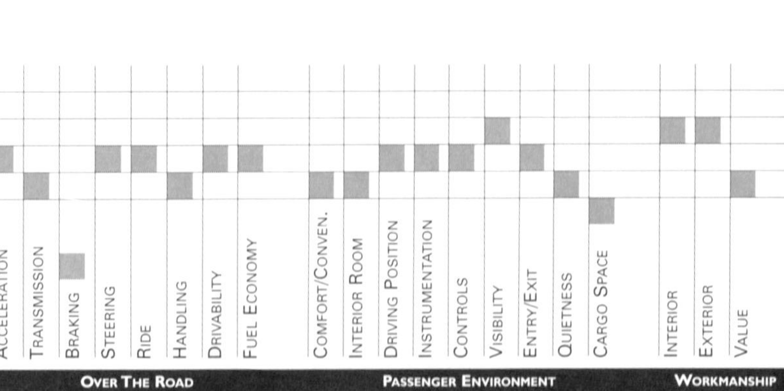

Ratings
131

Oldsmobile Alero

New for 99

New model

Pros

Detailed equipment
Smooth and efficient transmission
Rigid chassis

Cons

Slightly light steering system
Some materials of inferior quality
Turning radius

Equipment

Major Standard Equipment: 2.4-liter I-4, automatic transmission, traction control, 4-wheel antilock brakes, air conditioning, tilt steering wheel, split-folding rear seat, AM/FM stereo, automatic power door locks, variable-intermittent wipers, rear defroster. **GL adds:** Variable-assist power steering, power windows, power mirrors, AM/FM/cassette stereo, tire pressure monitoring system. **GLS adds:** 3.4-liter V-6, power driver's seat, AM/FM/ CD/cassette stereo, larger tires. **Major Options:** 3.4-liter V-6, leather upholstery, power moonroof, sports suspension.

PRICES
$17,000
$23,000

GX coupe $16,850
GX sedan $16,850
GL coupe $19,180
GL sedan $18,745
GLS coupe $21,400
GLS sedan $21,400

WARRANTY (years/miles)

Bumper-to-bumper (incl. tires) 3/36,000
Powertrain 3/36,000
Rust-through 6/100,000

OTHER TO CONSIDER

Nissan Altima
Mazda 626

A promise kept

If Oldsmobile is serious about rejuvenating its image and attracting a younger and more discriminating clientele, the new Alero lineup is the best card the company has dealt itself in a long time.

The smooth grille on these new compacts clearly demonstrates their relationship to the Intrigue sedan and their sibling, the Aurora. In the rear, the huge taillights are the Alero's alone, however. Sedan or coupe, the overall effect is quite good, including the passenger compartment design. Seats mold well and in general they offer very satisfactory support. However, seat padding on the GL, the most affordable version, provides slightly less support for thighs than do the leather seats on the GLS, a cut above.

The dashboard design is thoroughly classic and modern, dominated by large and perfectly clear dials. All in all, controls are very well positioned and show good ergonomics. Assembly and finishing are well within the acceptable average, although some gray plastic buttons and switches are there to remind us that this is a car produced by the GM empire. Standard equipment is very detailed and the rear seat folds down in a 60/40 configuration. This adds space to the fairly roomy trunk, though loading it is made difficult by a narrow opening, courtesy of the long and angled rear windshield, a modern-day classic in this category.

While they aren't as spectacular as their relatives, the Alero models manage to be very nice-looking, especially inside. But most surprising is that their mechanical components are identical! Whatever Oldsmobile has done to refine and hone engineering skills, the Alero's overall handling is a pleasant surprise. These cars capitalize fully on their solid body and structure. They feature an independent suspension, equipped with four struts. The steering system is slightly overassisted and slightly light, but reasonably precise and excellent at taking corners. Without comparing them directly, on winding roads the agility and aplomb of these models is impressive enough to remind drivers of some of the products turned out by a prestigious Bavarian builder.

The less elaborate GL models are as well-balanced as their GLS counterparts; they're just lower-key automobiles. An optional Sport package should enhance overall handling on both, although we haven't had a chance to test it yet. Manoeuvering is somewhat difficult as a result of the long turning radius (especially excessive given the size of these models). On the other hand, in general braking is powerful and efficient, among other reasons because the Aleros are equipped with four disc brakes, reserved solely for the GT in the Grand Am series. Two powertrains are available. A 170-hp 3.4-liter V-6 is optional on the GL and standard on the GLS. It proves to be smooth, efficient, and fun to listen to. The other alternative is a 150-hp 2.4-liter DOHC four-cylinder whose performance and smoothness are completely satisfactory. Both are teamed up with flawless four-speed automatic transmissions.

While not perfect, there can be no doubt that these are the best compacts that GM's five makes have produced to date. **M.L.**

Specifications of Test Vehicle

Model: Alero GL

Exterior Dimensions	
Wheelbase	107 in.
Overall length	186.7 in.
Overall width	70.1 in.
Overall height	54.5 in.
Curb weight	3,000 lb.
Interior Dimensions	
Seating capacity	5
Head room	F:38.4/R:37 in.
Leg room	F:42.2/R:35.5 in.
Cargo room	15.3 cu. ft.
Engine	
Displacement	V-6 3.4 L.
Horsepower	170 @ 4,800 rpm
Torque, lb-ft.	200 @ 4,000 rpm
Performance	
0-60 mph, acceleration	8.5 sec.
60-0 mph, braking	NA
Turning circle	35.1 ft.
EPA city/highway	20/29 mpg
Test mileage	NA
Fuel tank capacity	15 gal.

Ratings

Group	Category	Rating (1–10)
Over The Road	Acceleration	8
	Transmission	9
	Braking	5
	Steering	8
	Ride	8
	Handling	8
	Drivability	8
	Fuel Economy	6
Passenger Environment	Comfort/Conven.	8
	Interior Room	8
	Driving Position	8
	Instrumentation	8
	Controls	9
	Visibility	8
	Entry/Exit	8
	Quietness	7
	Cargo Space	7
Workmanship	Interior	8
	Exterior	9
	Value	9

157

Oldsmobile

Aurora

New for 99

New engine supports
Three new exterior colors

Pros

Solid chassis
Excellent visibility
Roomy trunk

Cons

Disappointing fuel economy
Front seat belts not height adjustable
Limited braking power

Equipment

Major Standard Equipment: 4-liter V-8, 4-wheel antilock disc brakes, traction control, dual-temperature automatic air conditioning, variable-intermittent wipers, AM/FM/CD/ cassette stereo, power seats, leather upholstery, tilt steering wheel, cruise control, power windows, automatic headlamps, power locks, remote keyless entry, power heated mirrors, automatic dimming rear-view mirror, theft-deterrent system, stainless-steel exhaust system, aluminum wheels. **Major Options:** Performance axle ratio, high-speed tires, satellite communications option, power moonroof, heated front seats, chrome wheels.

A pioneer

With the Aurora, Oldsmobile never hid its intention to do battle with the most talented and the most prestigious imported automobiles. Consequently, you can just imagine Oldsmobile's satisfaction when the company learned that the Aurora is short-listed fairly regularly by consumers who buy an Acura, a Lexus, or other Infiniti models.

There may not be an Aurora in every driveway, but what's important is that it is beginning to restore the prestige of a century-old make.

Doors open wide onto an inviting and warm interior. The nicely designed dashboard features a host of instruments and controls, all easy to consult and use. Five people can travel aboard the Aurora, but the fifth person may have something to say about the marginal comfort of the middle space in the rear seat. In front, the bucket seats provide good support and are adjustable to offer a variety of driving positions. The only fault we detected: seat belts are not height adjustable. Apart from that one small oversight, we should say that visibility is good and the trunk has the volume you would expect in a car this size.

The Aurora has the advantage of resting on one of the most rigid platforms ever developed by General Motors. When you drive it, you get a very real sense of security, sturdiness, and durability. But unlike the Riviera, which shares its chassis, the Aurora can rely on a tamer version of the Northstar V-8 developed by Cadillac. This powertrain lacks nothing in heart or panache, and its only weakness is its fuel consumption, which will do nothing to attract the environmentally conscious. Despite its size and weight, the Aurora takes well to winding roads. It has nice aplomb when cornering, good motor functions and the ability to stay precisely on course no matter what. Brakes are respectable but tend to fade rather quickly.

Is the Aurora a good car? Yes, but before you rate it you have to be willing to set aside your prejudices concerning American-built automobiles. **E.L.**

Specifications of Test Vehicle

Model: Aurora

Exterior Dimensions	
Wheelbase	113.8 in.
Overall length	205.4 in.
Overall width	74.4 in.
Overall height	55.4 in.
Curb weight	4,000 lb.
Interior Dimensions	
Seating capacity	5
Head room	F:38.4/R:36.9 in.
Leg room	F:42.6/R:38.4 in.
Cargo volume	16.1 cu. ft.
Engine	
Displacement	V-8 4 L.
Horsepower	250 @ 5,600 rpm
Torque, lb-ft.	260 @ 4,400 rpm
Performance	
0-60 mph, acceleration	7.9 sec.
60-0 mph, braking	119 ft.
Turning circle	41.9 ft.
EPA city/highway	17/26 mpg
Test mileage	19 mpg
Fuel tank capacity	20 ga

Prices

$36,000
$38,000

Sedan
$36,900

Warranty

(years/miles)

Bumper-to-bumper (incl. tires)
3/36,000

Powertrain
3/36,000

Rust-through
6/100,000

Other to Consider

Lexus ES300
Infiniti I30

Ratings

Group	Category	Rating
Over The Road	Acceleration	9
	Transmission	10
	Braking	7
	Steering	8
	Ride	8
	Handling	8
	Drivability	9
	Fuel Economy	4
Passenger Environment	Comfort/Conven.	8
	Interior Room	8
	Driving Position	8
	Instrumentation	8
	Controls	9
	Visibility	8
	Entry/Exit	9
	Quietness	9
	Cargo Space	8
Workmanship	Interior	8
	Exterior	8
	Value	9

Ratings **163**

Oldsmobile Bravada

New for 99
New option package

Pros
Engine performace
4WD operation
Seat comfort

Cons
Fuel economy
Entry/exit
Luxury features

Equipment
Major Standard Equipment: 4.3-liter V-6, automatic transmission, automatic 4-wheel drive, locking rear differential, 4-wheel antilock disc brakes, automatic air conditioning, cruise control, tilt steering wheel, variable-intermittent wipers, rear defroster, rear wiper and washer, AM/FM/CD stereo, remote keyless entry, theft alarm system, power locks, power heated mirrors, power windows, power seats, split-folding rear seat, luggage rack, privacy glass, leather upholstery, power liftgate release, aluminum wheels. **Major Options:** Power moonroof, AM/FM/CD/cassette stereo, cloth upholstery, heated seats, trailer towing package.

Aristocrat

PRICES
$31,000
$33,000
4-door truck wagon
$30,645

WARRANTY
(years/miles)

Bumper-to-bumper (incl. tires)
3/36,000

Powertrain
3/36,000

Rust-through
6/100,000

OTHER TO CONSIDER
Mercury Mountaineer

Think of the Oldsmobile Bravada as a trendy version of the Chevrolet Blazer or GMC Jimmy. It has few options, so it's an easy-order route to uptown transporation.

This upscale sport-utility vehicle gives Oldsmobile dealers a chance to sell a popular vehicle without having to become truck experts for just one product. Aimed at first-time buyers, every Bravada has automatic 4-wheel drive to eliminate fiddling with levers and selectors. The system, called SmartTrak, is exclusive for Oldsmobile and requires no driver intervention to work. It also comes with 4-wheel antilock disc brakes.

The Bravada has no engine choices. It comes with General Motors' 190-horsepower, 4.3-liter V-6, a rugged and responsive engine that provides a lot of low-speed torque. One downside to the powerful engine and heavy weight: fuel economy is typical for its class. With a lot of highway driving, we were lucky to average 20 mpg.

The Bravada's steering is quick and precise, feeding plenty of information from the road back to the driver. It's easy to park, even without the benefit of variable power assist. The vehicle feels quite stable when cornering or executing lane changes. The ride is comfortable because the suspension has been optimized for highway use. The controlled ride soaks up most surface imperfections and irregularities. Its ride won't be confused with that of the Oldsmobile Regency, though. Tire and road noise remains muted.

The Bravada stands at a comfortable height compared with other SUVs. Even so, its rear doors don't open quite far enough to permit larger-than-average people to enter and exit easily. The two leather seats in front give reasonable hip and head room. Considering its compact dimensions, the Bravada offers decent rear-seat room and comfort, but only if you're trying to accommodate fewer than three people. The cargo space is typical of compact SUVs.

Inside, the Bravada boasts some of the equipment and comfort of more-expensive imports—leather upholstery and subtle applications of wood-grain trim, for example. The instrumentation is fairly complete, and the major controls have a soft-touch feel. The switches and knobs are located right where you'd expect them. Visibility is good in all directions.The Bravada presents a stylish package, but it needs more luxury features to be a real Oldsmobile. **D.V.S.**

Specifications of Test Vehicle

Model: Bravada

Exterior Dimensions	
Wheelbase	107 in.
Overall length	183.7 in.
Overall width	67.6 in.
Overall height	63.2 in.
Curb weight	4,050 lb.
Interior Dimensions	
Seating capacity	5
Head room	F:39.6/R:38.2 in.
Leg room	F:42.4/R:36.3 in.
Cargo volume	37.3 cu. ft.
Engine	
Displacement	V-6 4.3 L.
Horsepower	190 @ 4,400 rpm
Torque, lb-ft.	250 @ 2,800 rpm
Performance	
0-60 mph, acceleration	9.9 sec.
60-0 mph, braking	127 ft.
Turning circle	39.5 ft.
EPA city/highway	16/20 mpg
Test mileage	19 mpg
Fuel tank capacity	18 gal.

Group	Rating	Score
Over The Road	Acceleration	7
	Transmission	9
	Braking	6
	Steering	8
	Ride	7
	Handling	7
	Drivability	9
	Fuel Economy	4
Passenger Environment	Comfort/Conven.	9
	Interior Room	8
	Driving Position	8
	Instrumentation	8
	Controls	8
	Visibility	7
	Entry/Exit	7
	Quietness	8
	Cargo Space	10
Workmanship	Interior	8
	Exterior	8
	Value	8

Ratings
154

Oldsmobile Intrigue

New for 99
New 3.5-liter engine
Standard traction control with the 3.5-liter
Autobahn options package available on all models

Pros
Roomy interior
Rigid chassis
Most consistent of all GM midsize models

Cons
Lack of agility
Gear ratio
Steering-wheel torque effect

Equipment
Major Standard Equipment: 3.8-liter V-6, 4-wheel antilock brakes, traction control, air conditioning, AM/FM/ cassette stereo, power mirrors, power windows, automatic power locks, cruise control, tilt steering wheel, aluminum wheels. **GL Adds:** Dual-temporature automatic air conditioning, remote keyless entry, heated mirrors, driver's power seat. **GLS Adds:** Leather interior, power passenger seat, CD player. **Major Options:** Driver's power seat, split-folding rear seat, remote keyless entry, AM/FM/CD/cassette stereo, steering wheel-mounted stereo controls, power moonroof, chrome wheels.

1999

AAA
TOP CAR

An Oldsmobile with new-found pride

This year, the Intrigue is the older sibling of the all-new Alero models. Their respective lines are strikingly similar, recalling the powerful rounded Aurora, the flagship model of the Oldsmobile lineup.

In its second year, this midsize sedan has a long-awaited new DOHC V6. The engine was developed by the same team that came up with the Northstar and Aurora V8, under the watchful eye of engineer Max Freeman. It's a full 50 lbs lighter than the venerable 3.8-liter, which it will replace across the board by the end of this model year. The Shortstar, as it is affectionately known, will first be offered on GLS versions and will later be found on every model in the entire range.

The Intrigue hasn't changed much since it was launched last year. Its new engine is a definite improvement, making this model smoother and adding to its refinement, as planned. But the agile and energetic Alero makes the Intrigue look like a dullard when it comes to road stability. However, consumers should keep in mind that it was intended not as a sports car, but a good-sized American-style intermediary with a European look and a European-type passenger compartment. In short, the Intrigue is solid, comfortable, roomy, practical and fairly well-equipped.

The Intrigue is powered by a DOHC 3.5-liter V6 with an output of 215 horses. This 90-degree V6 engine isn't as naturally smooth as the more common 60-degree V6 and the reason is that it comes from the V8, which must be 90 degrees for maximum balance. To counter the problem, the engine has a counter-rotating shaft driven by the primary timing drive at crankshaft speed.

The new engine gives the Intrigue the added refinement it was lacking until now, but this model still isn't a powerhouse. During acceleration, we noticed a major gap between the automatic transmission's first two speeds, which tends to hold back the Intrigue's initial drive. In addition, shifting is far from perfectly smooth. This is surprising for a car from GM, whose subsidiaries are known for their technical prowess in this particular area. And when setting out from a standing start, the steering wheel feeds back a strong torque effect.

The dean of GM's divisions undoubtedly thinks that the Intrigue is a work of art completed — after all, it has finally added the name to the model's rounded flank. **M.L.**

Specifications of Test Vehicle

Model: Intrigue GL

Exterior Dimensions	
Wheelbase	109 in.
Overall length	195.9 in.
Overall width	73.6 in.
Overall height	56.6 in.
Curb weight	3,450 lb.
Interior Dimensions	
Seating capacity	5
Head room	F:39.3/R:37.4 in.
Leg room	F:42.4/R:36.9 in.
Cargo room	16 cu. ft.
Engine	
Displacement	V-6 3.8 L.
Horsepower	195 @ 5,200 rpm
Torque, lb-ft.	220 @ 4,000 rpm
Performance	
0-60 mph, acceleration	8.5 sec.
60-0 mph, braking	135 ft.
Turning circle	36.6 ft.
EPA city/highway	19/30 mpg
Test mileage	24 mpg
Fuel tank capacity	18 gal.

PRICES
$21,000
$27,000
GX $21,735
GL $23,135
GLS $25,505

WARRANTY
(years/miles)
Bumper-to-bumper 3/36,000
Powertrain 3/36,000
Rust-through 6/100,000

OTHER TO CONSIDER
Nissan Maxima
Toyota Camry

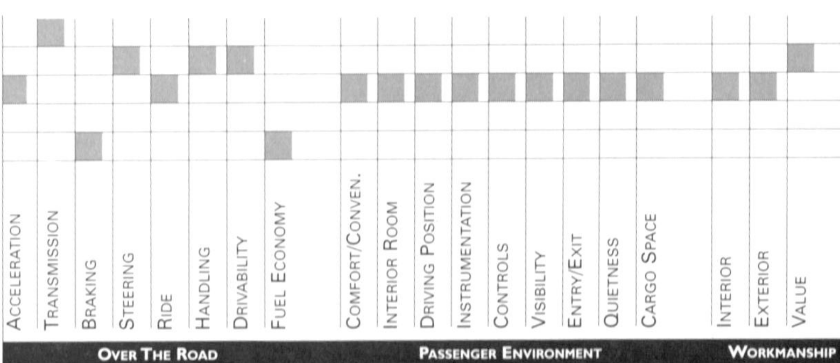

10
9
8
7
6
5
4
3
2
1

Ratings
162

Oldsmobile Silhouette

New for 99

With Premiere Edition Factory-installed video system

Pros

Ride
Convenience features
Door options

Cons

Engine power
Handling

Equipment

Major Standard Equipment: 3.4-liter V-6, automatic transmission, 4-wheel antilock brakes, 7-passenger seating, split-folding rear seats, AM/FM/cassette stereo, air conditioning, cabin air filter, tilt steering wheel, cruise control, automatic power locks, power mirrors, luggage rack, remote keyless entry, theft-deterrent system, power sliding door, power seats, privacy glass. **GLS adds:** Automatic leveling suspension, traction control, second-row captain's chairs, steering wheel-mounted stereo controls, larger tires, aluminum wheels.

PRICES
$24,000
$26,000

GL 4-door
$24,990

GS 4-door
$25,370

GLS 4-door
$28,020

WARRANTY
(years/miles)

Bumper-to-bumper (incl. tires)
3/36,000

Power train
3/36,000

Rust-through
6/100,000

OTHER TO CONSIDER

Honda Odyssey

Chrysler Town-Country

Upscale buyers wanted

The Pontiac Montana minivan goes after the sporty crowd; the Chevrolet Venture targets the value-conscious. The Silhouette, Oldsmobile's version, shares its design with those two General Motors minivans. It seems to aim at upscale buyers, but doesn't distinguish itself.

In redesigning its minivans, GM replaced the friendly, dent-resistant plastic fenders with solid steel. The current Silhouettes have gentler air bags permitted by new safety regulations. The safety belts now have pretensioners to remove slack in a crash. GM has the first minivans with side air bags.

The Silhouette's drivetrain is smooth and quiet. But the serious horsepower found in upscale Oldsmobiles is missing; engine performance is far from luxurious. Even if this engine gets five more horses this year. The Silhouette is as heavy as an Aurora, with only 70 percent of the latter's power. The engine and transmission work well together but leave you wishing for more oomph. We averaged about 20 mpg.

On the road, the Silhouette rides comfortably—much like an Olds Eighty Eight. Forward visibility in this minivan is much better than that in the old one; large side mirrors help, too. The GLS's firmer suspen-sion don't make the ride harsher with the van lightly loaded. No one will accuse the Silhouette of sporty handling, though.

Entry and exit are easy, because the Silhouette feels to be the right height for a minivan. There's also an optional power sliding door on the passenger's side. It saves the driver a long reach or a long walk around the van to open the door, but it may startle unsuspecting bystanders.

For the rear, you can order a 60/40 split-bench seat, with or without built-in child safety seats, for the second row. Captain's chairs, like the standard front seats, are also available for the second row. Either seat arrangement has a 2-2-3 setup. You can tilt the driver's seatback forward to allow access to the area behind the seat without opening the sliding door. It's handy for stashing briefcases and coats.

The front seats have large, comfortable cushions. Even the manually adjusted seats remained comfortable on long drives. The split bench seats are something else, however; they're too low for adult comfort. Head room is fine in the rear.

The instruments are white-on-black, with no glitzy electronics. You won't break a fingernail working the soft-touch controls. Power controls operate the windows, including the swing-out side ones in the rear.

GM's minivans are every bit as good as Chrysler's and Ford's. Personal brand preference is the only compelling reason to choose the Olds over its other GM versions. **D.V.S.**

Specifications of Test Vehicle	
Model: Silhouette GLS	
Exterior Dimensions	
Wheelbase	120 in.
Overall length	201.4 in.
Overall width	72.2 in.
Overall height	68.1 in.
Curb weight	3,950 lb.
Interior Dimensions	
Seating capacity	7
Head room	F:39.9/R1:39.3/R2:38.8 in.
Leg room	F:39.9/R1:39/R2:36.7 in.
Cargo volume	24.2 cu. ft.
Engine	
Displacement	V-6 3.4 L.
Horsepower	185 @ 5,200 rpm
Torque, lb-ft.	210 @ 4,000 rpm
Performance	
0-60 mph, acceleration	10.6 sec.
60-0 mph, braking	135 ft.
Turning circle	39.7 ft.
EPA city/highway	18/25 mpg
Test mileage	20 mpg
Fuel tank capacity	25 gal.

Group	Category	Rating
Over the Road	Acceleration	6
	Transmission	9
	Braking	5
	Steering	8
	Ride	8
	Handling	7
	Drivability	8
	Fuel Economy	5
Passenger Environment	Comfort/Conven.	8
	Interior Room	9
	Driving Position	8
	Instrumentation	8
	Controls	8
	Visibility	8
	Entry/Exit	7
	Quietness	8
	Cargo Space	10
Workmanship	Interior	8
	Exterior	8
	Value	7

Ratings
153

Plymouth

Breeze

New for 99

New wheel rims
New exterior colors

Pros

Interior room
Limited options
Trunk size

Cons

Engine performance
Manual windows
Noise

Equipement

Major Standard Equipment: 2-liter I-4, manual transmission, air conditioning, variable-intermittent wipers, rear defroster, AM/FM stereo, tilt steering wheel, remote-control decklid release, stainless-steel exhaust system. **Major Options:** 2.4-liter I-4, automatic transmission, 4-wheel antilock brakes, power windows, power locks, power heated mirrors, AM/FM/CD stereo, AM/FM/CD/cassette stereo, height-adjustable driver's seat, integrated child safety seat, cruise control, remote keyless entry, power moonroof, full-size spare tire.

As thrifty as thrifty can be

The Plymouth Breeze is an honest, no-frills car. With few options and choices available, buying one is a breeze.

The Breeze is the low-priced companion to the Dodge Stratus and Chrysler Cirrus. The Cirrus is sold from the same showrooms as the Breeze. Both the Cirrus and Breeze have one trim level, so think of the Cirrus as the upscale version of the Breeze.

The Breeze has two 4-cylinder engines, a 2-liter or 2.4-liter. A 5-speed manual transmission is standard, and a 4-speed automatic is optional. (The Cirrus offers a V-6.) With the automatic transmission, acceleration is far from quick, clearly making the bigger engine the better choice in the Breeze. Under acceleration, the engine becomes noisy, as 4-cylinder engines tend to do. Nevertheless, the Breeze has ample power around town, with enough in reserve for comfortable highway passing. The small engine helps gas mileage. With the automatic, we averaged 26 mpg, with just over 30 mpg on the highway.

The Breeze is nimble enough and handles competently, but lacks the sportier, fun-to-drive feel of the Stratus ES. Its motions are always well controlled, and it doesn't float on the road. We were impressed by the car's structural integrity; we heard no squeaks or shudders, even when we drove over severely broken pavement. The Breeze's braking performance is undistinguished. We recommend the optional antilock brake system to enhance safety.

The Breeze's interior room embarrasses the Honda Accord and Ford Contour. Five adults can travel easily with reasonable comfort. On the highway, though, interior noise is higher than that in other cars.

The seats are comfortable, especially for a low-end sedan, but not as supportive as those in the Stratus and Cirrus. Attractive fabrics and the addition of a center-mounted console with cubby space and rear cupholders gives the Breeze an inviting interior. The trunk has nearly 16 cubic feet of space.

The controls are easy to reach without taking your eyes off the road. Although the Breeze comes with an AM/FM radio as standard equipment, a cassette player is optional. So are power locks and windows. (In fact, all power accessories are options on the Breeze. With just a single trim level, there's no way to opt for a fancier package that includes more amenities.) Power windows may be a good idea if you're short; when you wind the manual windows up or down, your forearm will hit the front edge of the seat.

Plymouth makes buying a Breeze almost as simple as buying a cantaloupe: you don't have face agonizing decisions over minor differences in trim levels. **D.V.S.**

Specifications of Test Vehicle

Model: Breeze

Exterior Dimensions	
Wheelbase	108 in.
Length	186.7 in.
Width	71.7 in.
Height	51.9 in.
Curb weight	2,900 lb.
Interior Dimensions	
Seating capacity	5
Head room	F:38.1/R:36.8 in.
Leg room	F:42.3/R:37.8 in.
Cargo volume	15.7 cu. ft.
Engine	
Displacement	I-4 2 L.
Horsepower	132 @ 6,000 rpm
Torque, lb-ft.	129 @ 5,000 rpm
Performance	
0-60 mph, acceleration	11.1 sec
60-0 mph, braking	135 ft.
Turning circle	37 ft.
EPA city/highway	3/33 mpg
Test mileage	26 mpg
Fuel tank capacity	16 gal.

Prices

$14,000
$18,000

Sedan
$15,510

Warranty
(years/months)

Bumper-to-bumper
3/36,000

Powertrain
3/36,000

Rust-through
7/100,000

Other to Consider

Chevrolet Malibu

Nissan Altima

Ratings

Over The Road		Passenger Environment		Workmanship	
Acceleration	5	Comfort/Conven.	7	Interior	7
Transmission	6	Interior Room	8	Exterior	7
Braking	5	Driving Position	8	Value	7
Steering	7	Instrumentation	7		
Ride	7	Controls	8		
Handling	7	Visibility	6		
Drivability	8	Entry/Exit	8		
Fuel Economy	6	Quietness	6		
		Cargo Space	7		

Ratings
137

Plymouth

Prowler

New for 99

More engine power
Passenger air bag deactivation
Three new exterior colors

Pros

Collector's item
Proven mechanics
Careful construction

Cons

Disappointing transmission
Exhausting to drive
Poor visibility

Equipment

Major Standard Equipment: 3.5-liter V-6, semi-automatic transmission, air conditioning, AM/FM/CD/cassette stereo, cruise control, tilt steering wheel, manual folding top, power locks, remote keyless entry, power windows, power mirrors, leather upholstery, stainless-steel exhaust system, extended mobility tires, aluminum wheels. **Major Options:** Cargo trailer.

PRICES

$38,000
$44,000

2-door convertible
$38,300

WARRANTY
(years/miles)

Bumper-to-bumper
3/36,000

Powertrain
3/36,000

Rust-through
7/100,000

OTHER TO CONSIDER

None

Nostalgia *is* what it used tobe

After the Viper, Chrysler decided to play the nostalgia card once again with the Prowler. Black, purple, yellow, or red (the four colors available this year), this delightful hot rod is the pride and joy of Plymouth dealers, who are relying on it to revitalize the make's image, until recently threatened with total annihilation. So even if all of this year's Prowlers have already been sold, drop by your local Plymouth dealership to give the manager and staff a bit of reassurance.

With the exception of contortionists working with the Cirque du Soleil, very few acrobats have enough talent to slide effortlessly behind the Prowler's wheel. The first obstacle is a narrow door opening that forces you to hold your breath and hurtle yourself into the bucket seat. An extra effort and you'll manage to sink your derrière and shoulders tightly into the leather box that doubles as a seat. While your right foot travels between the gas and brake pedals, your left foot wonders where it could possibly rest comfortably. Dials are aligned in rows right in front of your eyes, with the exception of the tachometer, perched on the steering column in the purest of hot rod traditions. Look toward the horizon and your vision is immediately limited by a minuscule windshield that makes you feel as if you're wearing bifocals.

Start the engine. The 3.5-liter V-6 has a more metallic, deeper, and more consistently impressive sound, thanks to its 253 horses, 39 more than it had last year. To deliver the engine's power to the rear wheels, Plymouth uses the services of the Autostick four-speed automatic, something drivers get tired of using fairly fast. Another disappointment is overall performance. The Prowler doesn't get out of the starting blocks with the same kind of enthusiasm as a Viper even though its instrument panel and steering column are very good at simulating the symptoms of Parkinson's disease under strong acceleration. With tires this big and suspension components borrowed from the Viper (in the front only), the Prowler isn't very comfortable. But its roadholding is amazing — so much so that you'll find it hard to get rear tires to leave the road even momentarily. As a consolation, it has no trouble understeering. **E.L.**

Specifications of Test Vehicle	
Model: Prowler	
Exterior Dimensions	
Wheelbase	113.3 in.
Overall length	165.3 in.
Overall width	76.5 in.
Overall height	50.9 in.
Curb weight	2,850 lb.
Interior Dimensions	
Seating capacity	2
Head room	F:37.4 in.
Leg room	F:42.9 in.
Cargo room	1.8 cu.ft.
Engine	
Displacement	V-6 3.5 L.
Horsepower	253 @ 6,400 rpm
Torque, lb-ft.	255 @ 3,950 rpm
Performance	
0-60 mph, acceleration	6.1 sec.
60-0 mph, braking	119 ft.
Turning circle	38.5 ft.
EPA city/highway	NA
Test mileage	19.2 mpg
Fuel tank capacity	12 gal.

10 9 8 7 6 5 4 3 2 1

Ratings
138

Over The Road: Acceleration, Transmission, Braking, Steering, Ride, Handling, Drivability, Fuel Economy

Passenger Environment: Comfort/Conven., Interior Room, Driving Position, Instrumentation, Controls, Visibility, Entry/Exit, Quietness, Cargo Space

Workmanship: Interior, Exterior, Value

Plymouth

New for 99

Cargo net between front seats
Headrests mounted on the middle and rear seats

Pros

Excellent visibility
Attractive price
Proven reliability

Cons

Limited choice of accessories
Anemic four-cylinder
Limited cargo capacity

Equipment

Major Standard Equipment: 2.4-liter I-4, 4-speed automatic transmission, 4-wheel antilock brakes, 5-passenger seating, AM/FM stereo, variable-intermittent wipers, rear wiper and washer. **SE adds:** 3-liter V-6, 4-speed automatic transmission, 4-wheel antilock brakes, 7-passenger seating, power heated mirrors, cruise control, AM/FM/cassette stereo, tilt steering column, larger tires. **Major Options:** 3-liter V-6, 3.3-liter V-6, driver's side sliding door, dual-temperature air conditioning, rear air conditioning, remote keyless entry, integrated child safety seat, power windows, automatic leveling suspension, heavy-duty suspension.

Economy class

While the Town & Country is aimed at older families who are relatively well-off, the Plymouth Voyager does its recruiting among young families who want to travel in comfort with the kids along for the ride, all at the best possible price. Keeping this in mind, are you surprised to learn that improvements for 1999 are few and far between, precisely with a view to keeping production costs steady?

Assembled in Canada, this minivan has a very nice passenger compartment that shows attention to detail. The bargain-basement look of certain plastics creates a jarring effect, as do some finishing details, but overall, this vehicle is undoubtedly one of the best Chrysler has to offer. With its plunging hood and the resultant excellent and panoramic vision, this vehicle inspires the type of confidence that the extended wheelbase version (the Grand Voyager) can't. On the other hand, there's not as much usable space aboard the Voyager, especially when it comes to cargo space when all seats are in use. Despite its new wheels, the rear bench seat is still hard to remove. And when it comes to the second sliding door (standard on the SE version), never mind the expense — go for it.

Of all the engines invited on-board, the 3.3-liter V-6 is best at getting its job done. For their part, the 3.0-liter V-6 and the 2.4-liter four-cylinder have a hard time, especially the latter of the two. Road stability remains as astounding as it always was, but it's still too bad that unlike the Caravan, the Voyager doesn't feature
16-inch wheels and doesn't have a traction control system, always an invaluable asset on slippery roads.
As is the case with many other small minivans, even with ABS, brakes (discs/drums) tend to overheat fairly quickly, no matter how much special effort Chrysler has devoted to fixing this particular problem.

Despite a few flaws, the Voyager remains a serious candidate in the eyes of young families who know how to add. **E.L.**

Specifications of Test Vehicle

Model: Voyager SE

Exterior Dimensions	
Wheelbase	113.3 in.
Overall length	186.3 in.
Overall width	76.8 in.
Overall height	68.5 in.
Curb weight	3,700 lb.
Interior Dimensions	
Seating capacity	7
Head room	F:39.8/R:40.1/R2:38.1 in.
Leg room	F:40.6/R:36.6/R2:35.8 in.
Cargo volume	13.6 cu. ft.
Engine	
Displacement	V-6 3.3 L.
Horsepower	158 @ 4,850 rpm
Torque, lb-ft.	203 @ 3,250 rpm
Performance	
0-60 mph, acceleration	9.8 sec.
60-0 mph, braking	118 ft.
Turning circle	37.6 ft.
EPA city/highway	18/24 mpg
Test mileage	19 mpg
Fuel tank capacity	20 gal.

Prices
$17,000
$30,000

3-door minivan $17,415
Grand 3-door minivan $20,125
SE 3-door minivan $21,290
SE Grand 3-door minivan $22,285

Warranty (years/miles)

Bumper-to-bumper 3/36,000
Powertrain 3/36,000
Rust-through 7/100,000

Other to consider

Chevrolet Venture
Ford Windstar

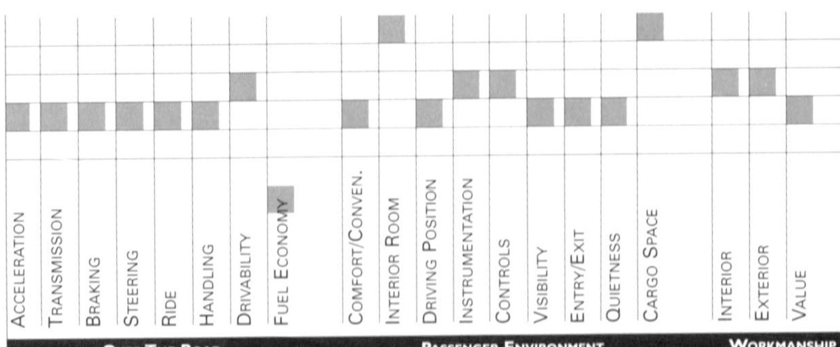

Ratings
148

Pontiac Bonneville

New for 99

Three new body colors, Three others withdrawn

Pros

Roomy interior
Proven reliability
SSEi version

Cons

Model scheduled for withdrawal
Outdated styling
Mediocre brakes

Equipment

Major Standard Equipment: 3.8-liter V-6, 4-wheel antilock brakes, air conditioning, automatic power locks, automatic headlamps, power windows, AM/FM stereo, cruise control, tilt steering wheel, theft-deterrent system. **SSE adds:** Traction control, automatic air conditioning, variable-assist power steering, power driver's seat, leather upholstery, automatic leveling suspension, AM/FM/cassette stereo, power heated mirrors, automatic dimming rear-view mirror, remote keyless entry, aluminum wheels. **Major Options:** Supercharged 3.8-liter V-6, head-up instrument display, AM/FM/CD stereo, power moonroof, automatic shock absorber control, automatic leveling suspension.

Still just a kid

PRICES
$22,495
$33,495
SE sedan
$23,495
SSE sedan
$30,495

WARRANTY
(years/miles)

Bumper-to-bumper
3/36,000

Powertrain
3/36,000

Rust-through
6/100,000

OTHER TO CONSIDER
Ford Taurus

It's a well-known fact: children never grow old in the eyes of their parents! They're always as well-behaved, as good-looking, as talented. Need evidence? Then read what Pontiac has to say to buyers who choose the 1999 Bonneville: this car is designed for a clientele that views an automobile's esthetics as extremely important. Is the makeup on this mid-size model thick enough to make Pontiac forget that the Bonneville has reached the age when the first pension check usually comes in the mail?

Is Pontiac styling extravagant? No question, but boy! do they ever age badly! And the Bonneville is no exception to the rule, even though the "metallic galaxy gray" available this year has given it more panache. And so from exciting, this model has drifted to grotesque. And the passenger compartment fares no better: futuristic at one point in time, today it is clearly outmoded despite its orange instrumentation. Although roomy in the front and rear, this model lacks storage spaces. Another drawback: side-view mirrors are so small, they make some manoeuvers hazardous.

The Bonneville is no easy car to buy. A good understanding of its catalog of options is vital, unless you don't mind ending up behind the wheel of a car that's not much fun to drive. Be warned: handling and ride are closely linked to your choice of suspension and tires. Very aseptic on the base (SE) version, road stability is reassuring when you opt for the SSE package, featuring a firmer suspension that keeps body sway under better control.

The standard V-6 3800 is efficient and a very good match for the four-speed automatic transmission. The supercharged version (SSEi) of the Bonneville is capable of strong acceleration, but its capability in this area is hard to optimize because of mediocre brakes (a mix of discs and drums). And making the traction control system optional does nothing to give the Bonneville credibility — especially since it's part of standard equipment on the Sunfire. **E.L.**

Specifications of Test Vehicle

Model: Bonneville SSE

Exterior Dimensions	
Wheelbase	110.8 in.
Overall length	202.1 in.
Overall width	74.5 in.
Overall height	55.7 in.
Curb weight	3,600 lb.
Interior Dimensions	
Seating capacity	5
Head room	F:39.2/R:38.3 in.
Leg room	F:42.6/R:38 in.
Cargo volume	18 cu. ft.
Engine	
Displacement	V-6 3.8 L.
Horsepower	240 @ 5,200 rpm
Torque, lb-ft.	280 @ 3,200 rpm
Performance	
0-60 mph, acceleration	7.9 sec.
60-0 mph, braking	135 ft.
Turning circle	40.5 ft.
EPA city/highway	17/27 mpg
Test mileage	21 mpg
Fuel tank capacity	18 gal.

Ratings
157

Over The Road		Passenger Environment		Workmanship	
Acceleration	9	Comfort/Conven.	9	Interior	8
Transmission	9	Interior Room	9	Exterior	8
Braking	5	Driving Position	10	Value	7
Steering	8	Instrumentation	8		
Ride	7	Controls	6		
Handling	9	Visibility	8		
Drivability	8	Entry/Exit	9		
Fuel Economy	5	Quietness	6		
		Cargo Space	9		

Pontiac

Firebird

New for 99

Bigger fuel tank
Traction control system on the V6
30th anniversary edition of the Trans Am

Pros

Styling
Handling

Cons

Ride comfort
Rear seat room
Parking ease

Equipment

Major Standard Equipment: 3.8-liter V-6, manual transmission, 4-wheel antilock disc brakes, air conditioning, rear defroster, folding rear seat, theft-deterrent system, stainless-steel exhaust, aluminum wheels. **Formula adds:** 5.7-liter V-8, automatic transmission, limited-slip differential, power mirrors, premium stereo, power mirrors, automatic power locks, power windows, sports suspension. **Trans Am adds:** Leather upholstery, power driver's seat, theft alarm system.

The Macho car

With its updated styling, improved high-performance powertrain, and more refined yet still muscular sound, the Pontiac Firebird appeals to those who won't be satisfied with an ordinary coupe or convertible.

The Firebird offers more variations than its cousin, the Chevrolet Camaro. The coupe is available in base, Formula, or Trans Am trim levels; the convertible comes only as a base model or Trans Am.

Since last year, a 5.7-liter engine delivering 305 horsepower in standard dress or 320 horsepower with the Ram Air option is available on the Formula or Trans Am models. If you need a little relief on your insurance rates, the base Firebird has a 3.8-liter V-6, good for 200 horsepower. If you don't need the ultimate in V-8 power, the V-6 still offers decent performance.

The 3.8-liter engine can be coupled with either a 5-speed manual or 4-speed automatic transmission. The 5.7-liter engines use either a 6-speed manual or 4-speed automatic transmission.

We tested a Trans Am with the Ram Air option and a 6-speed transmission. The powertrain performed flawlessly on the highway. But in slow city traffic, the transmission forces a shift from first to fourth gear under light acceleration. Designed to improve emission control, the feature quickly becomes irritating. We averaged a surprising 25 mpg, but the V-8 engine requires high-octane gas.

Pontiac retuned the Firebird's suspension last year, improving the ride quality without sacrificing steering or handling. The ride is still firm, but gets harsh on only the worst roads. Good handling, one of the Firebird's major virtues, made our test drive through the mountains a real joy.

Larger 4-wheel disc brakes give excellent stopping ability.

Entry and exit for the convertible with the top down are no problem. However, getting in and out of the coupe requires some bending and twisting, and access to the back seat requires major contortions.

The rear seat is not meant for adults of any size. It's suitable only for small children or packages. The seating in front is comfortable, but the seats are set too low for long-distance comfort. A large bump intrudes on the floor on the passenger's side.

The Firebird is a driver's car, so the instrument panel has been redesigned to tilt the center section toward the driver. The controls for the stereo are up high and easy to see. Simple ventilation controls are also easy to see and use. The full instrumentation includes Pontiac's warm red lighting.

The Firebird is still a macho car—but one that appeals to women drivers, too. **D.V.S.**

Specifications of Test Vehicle

Model: Firebird Formula

Exterior Dimensions	
Wheelbase	101.1 in.
Overall length	193.4 in.
Overall width	74.5 in.
Overall height	52 in.
Curb weight	3,450 lb.
Interior Dimensions	
Seating capacity	4
Head room	F:37.2/R:35.3 in.
Leg room	F:43/R:28.9 in.
Cargo volume	12.9 cu. ft.
Engine	
Displacement	V-8 5.7 L.
Horsepower	305 @ 5,200 rpm
Torque, lb-ft.	335 @ 4,000 rpm
Performance	
0-60 mph, acceleration	6.7 sec.
60-0 mph, braking	117 ft.
Turning circle	40.1 ft.
EPA city/highway	17/26 mpg
Test mileage	25 mpg
Fuel tank capacity	16.8 gal.

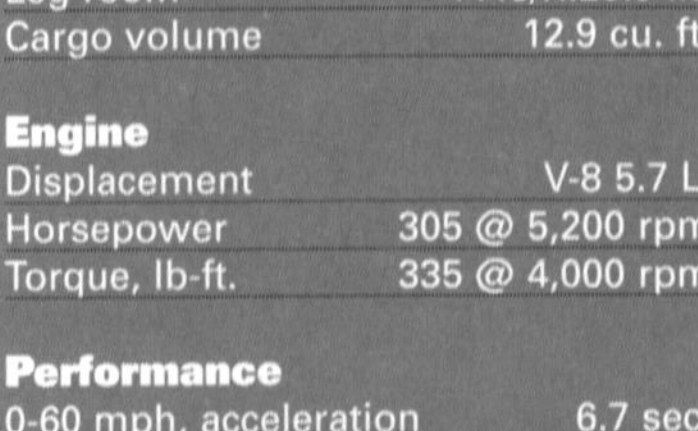

Prices

$16,000
$32,000

Base
$18,700

Convertible
$25,320

Formula
$23,600

Trans Am convertible
$30,780

Warranty

(years/miles)

Bumper-to-bumper
3/36,000

Powertrain
3/36,000

Rust-through
6/100,000

Other to Consider

Ford Mustang

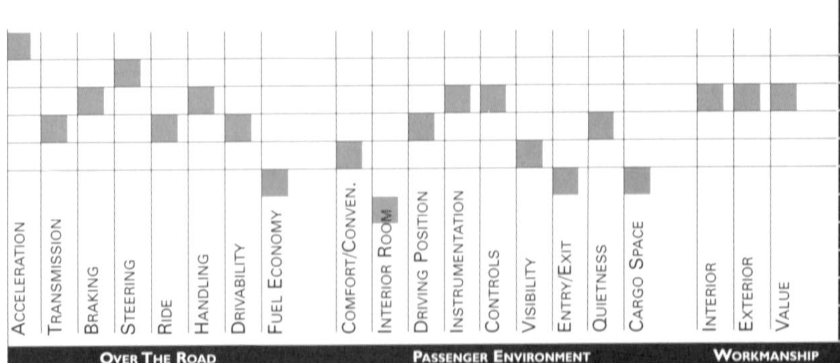

Pontiac Grand Am

new MODEL

New for 99

Completely new, based on Oldsmobile Alero design

Pros

Powertrain
Ride/handling
Comfort

Cons

Quietness
Fuel economy

Equipment

Major Standard Equipment: 2.4 liter 4-cylinder engine, automatic transmission, traction control, ABS, air conditioning, rear defogger, power door locks, automatic light control, AM/FM stereo, split folding rear seat, tilt wheel. **SE1 Adds:** Remote mirrors, aluminum wheels, cruise control, power windows, AM/FM cassette stereo, height adjustable driver seat. **SE2 Adds:** Larger tires, premium cloth/leather interior, remote keyless entry, CD player, V-6 engine, premium aluminum wheels. **Major Options:** Rear spoiler, ash tray, leather seats, premium sound system, sunroof.

Love or hate ?

Introduced mid-year as a '99, Pontiac's best seller, the Grand Am, has been totally redesigned. It uses the same platform and much of the same running gear as the new Oldsmobile Alero. However, with its aggressive styling and raked body cladding, it looks nothing like its corporate cousin.

Aiming to please just about anyone who likes its appearance, the Grand AM comes in ten combinations of body style and trim level — five coupes and five sedans. The base SE is no-frills basic transportation, followed by a better-equipped SE1 and top-of-the-line SE2. Then there's the boy-racer GT version with a ram-air package and other goodies.

Two engines are available. A 2.4-liter Twin Cam 4-cylinder produces 150 hp. Replacing the prior 3.1-liter V-6, the new 3.4-liter V-6 delivers 170 hp. Only a 4-speed automatic is offered — a different version for each engine.

The interior can only be described as cockpit-like. Instruments are recessed in pods and the center of the dash is tilted toward the driver. The large speedometer and tach are easy to read — all instruments glow with Pontiac's trademark warm-red illumination at night. Audio controls are thoughtfully located high for easy viewing. Vent controls are just below. All controls are easy to find and operate.

Front occupants enjoy plenty of head room. Leg room is a little skimpy for the front passenger. Recesses in the doors increase elbow room up front. Excellent seats offer firm cushions, and good back and thigh support. Rear leg room is fine, but some might find their heads touching the rear glass. Rear seatbacks seem to tilt too far back. The rear seat is rated for three, but the unlucky center occupant has to sit on an uncomfortable hump. Trunk space is about average, but the liftover is somewhat high and the opening is restricted — a concession to styling. Folding seat backs add to cargo space.

Ride comfort is quite good for a car in this class. The new suspension is well tuned and absorbs most bumps gracefully. Handling doesn't seem to suffer at all from the good ride characteristics. It handles surprisingly well, with little body roll on fast turns. Brake pedal feel and emergency stopping distance are about average.

Performance with the 4-cylinder engine is just so-so. It gets the job done around town, but gets noisy and rough when pushed hard. The real gem is the V-6. It responds instantly with real guts and revs willingly. The automatic transmission is well matched to the engine. It shifts seamlessly at just the right times for a very enjoyable driving experience. The Ram Ar variant of the V-6 adds 5 hp,but is "more for show than go".

Whether you love or hate the new Grand Am, you can't argue with its success. **D.V.S**

PRICES
$17,000
$23,000

SE coupe $16,595
SE sedan $16,995
GT coupe $19,595
GT sedan $19,995

WARRANTY (years/miles)

Bumper-to-bumper 3/36,000
Powertrain 3/36,000
Rust-through 6/100,000

OTHER TO CONSIDER

Dodge Stratus
Ford Contour

Specifications of Test Vehicle

Model: Grand Am SE

Exterior Dimensions	
Wheelbase	107.0 in.
Overall length	186.3 In.
Overall width	70.4 In.
Overall height	55.1 In.
Curb weight	3116 lbs.
Interior Dimensions	
Seating capacity	
Head room	F:38.3/R:37.2 in.
Leg room	F:42.1/R:35.5 in.
Cargo room	14.3 cu.ft.
Engine	
Displacement	3.4 L V-6
Horsepower	170@5200 rpm
Torque, lb-ft.	195@4000 rpm
Performance	
0-60 mph, acceleration	7.7 sec.
60-0 mph, braking	140 ft.
Turning circle	37.7 ft.
EPA city/highway	20/28 mpg.
Test mileage	20.1
Fuel tank capacity	15.2 gal.

Ratings 157

Group	Category	Rating
Over The Road	Acceleration	9
	Transmission	9
	Braking	5
	Steering	8
	Ride	8
	Handling	8
	Drivability	8
	Fuel Economy	5
Passenger Environment	Comfort/Conven.	8
	Interior Room	8
	Driving Position	8
	Instrumentation	8
	Controls	9
	Visibility	8
	Entry/Exit	8
	Quietness	7
	Cargo Space	7
Workmanship	Interior	8
	Exterior	9
	Value	9

Pontiac

Grand Prix

New for 99

New exterior colors
Two-zone air conditioning (GTP)

Pros

Attractive lines
Detailed instrumentation
Model range

Cons

Oversized dashboard
Marginal manufacturing quality
Stiff suspension (GTP)

Equipment

Major Standard Equipment: 3.1-liter V-6, automatic transmission, 4-wheel antilock disc brakes, traction control, variable-intermittent wipers, power mirrors, automatic headlamps, power windows, automatic power locks, theft-deterrent system, AM/FM stereo, tilt steering wheel. **GT adds:** 3.8-liter V-6, AM/FM/cassette stereo, cruise control, remote-control decklid release, aluminum wheels.
Major Options: Supercharged 3.8-liter V-6, more powerful 3.8-liter V-6, head-up instrument display, dual temperature air conditioning, split-bench seat, integrated child-safety seat, remote keyless entry, AM/FM/CD stereo.

Annoying

You have to be strong to resist the temptation the Pontiac Grand Prix brings your way. Sleek lines, an impressive cockpit, supercharged mechanics — this Pontiac has major assets to console new fathers who've had to give up a Firebird in favor of a family-oriented vehicle. All this to say that the Grand Prix promises a lot, but in the end, it doesn't deliver much.

The strong and silent type, this model looks rock solid. Shorter than its predecessor, the Grand Prix is still as roomy as a Taurus, for example. Pontiac refers to it as a five-passenger vehicle, on condition that the fifth person agrees to put up with a hard seatback that doubles as a housing for a plastic shelf with cupholders. The frontseat passengers don't have much to complain about. Bucket seats are inviting, but they offer minimal support for thighs. The cumbersome dashboard groups together detailed instrumentation that's easy to read and the console is oriented toward the driver to make it easy to use various controls. Now comes the criticism: the vehicle we test drove was very poorly assembled and the passenger compartment was filled with the kind of noise you really shouldn't have to endure at this price level. Among other things, the trunk's narrow opening makes it awkward to load heavy or large items.

To keep its sporty image intact, the cornerstone to its success, Pontiac had to give the Grand Prix the means to fulfill its ambitions and pretensions. Despite the fact that a supercharged engine is available, statistics show that most buyers choose the standard Series II 3800 V-6. For cooling reasons, caution has led engineers to shave 10 horses off the unit, which usually has a total of 205. Not the best of situations! However, the four-speed automatic transmission helps it achieve acceptable performance levels while keeping fuel consumption reasonable, unless you drive in the city, where the Grand Prix develops a powerful thirst.

There's good reason to question the suspension's efficiency. It's harsh and it shakes up the Grand Prix at the slightest bump or irregularity in the road surface. The power steering system is heavy and rarely lets you negotiate a corner without having to correct the initial trajectory. Wide tires delay the car's tendency to oversteer and provide optimal adherence when roads are dry. Although we didn't have the chance to test them thoroughly, the brakes seemed to be efficient, but nothing special.

There isn't much else to say, except that this model's assembly quality should be reconsidered seriously. And soon! **E.L.**

Specifications of Test Vehicle

Model: Grand Prix SE

Exterior Dimensions	
Wheelbase	110.5 in.
Overall length	196.5 in.
Overall width	72.7 in.
Overall height	54.7 in.
Curb weight	3,400 lb.
Interior Dimensions	
Seating capacity	5
Head room	F:38.3/R:36.7 in.
Leg room	F:42.4/R:35.8 in.
Cargo volume	16 cu. ft.
Engine	
Displacement	V-6 3.8 L.
Horsepower	195 @ 5,200 rpm
Torque, lb-ft.	230 @ 4,000 rpm
Performance	
0-60 mph, acceleration	8.5 sec.
60-0 mph, braking	134 ft.
Turning circle	36.9 ft.
EPA city/highway	19/30 mpg
Test mileage	21 mpg
Fuel tank capacity	18 gal.

Prices

$19,000
$25,000

SE sedan
$19,975

GT coupe
$21,555

GT sedan
$21,705

Warranty
(years/miles)

Bumper-to-bumper
3/36,000

Powertrain
3/36,000

Rust-through
6/100,000

Other to Consider

Ford Taurus

Nissan Maxima

Category	Item	Rating
Over The Road	Acceleration	8
	Transmission	10
	Braking	5
	Steering	9
	Ride	7
	Handling	9
	Drivability	8
	Fuel Economy	5
Passenger Environment	Comfort/Conven.	8
	Interior Room	7
	Driving Position	8
	Instrumentation	8
	Controls	8
	Visibility	8
	Entry/Exit	8
	Quietness	8
	Cargo Space	8
Workmanship	Interior	8
	Exterior	8
	Value	8

Ratings
156

Pontiac Sunfire

New for 99
New colors

Pros
Fuel economy
Engine/transmission
Interior room

Cons
Seat comfort
Instrumentation
Entry/exit

Equipment
Major Standard Equipment: Manual transmission, 4-wheel anti-lock brakes, AM/FM stereo, automatic headlamps, folding rear seat, intermittent wipers, theft-deterrent system, stainless-steel exhaust system. **GT adds:** Air conditioning, rear defroster, tilt steering wheel, larger tires, aluminum wheels. **Major Options:** 2.4-liter I-4 engine, 3-speed automatic transmission, 4-speed automatic transmission, traction control, remote keyless entry, air conditioning, power mirrors, power windows, cruise control, rear defroster, AM/FM/CD stereo, power moonroof.

Off to the races

Small, affordable, slightly dashing—that's the Pontiac Sunfire. And it comes as an inexpensive convertible to boot.

As a coupe, convertible, or sedan, Pontiac's small car shares all of its chassis components with the Chevrolet Cavalier. The Honda Civic, Nissan Sentra, Mazda Protege, Ford Escort, and Saturn compete with the Sunfire. None comes as a convertible, however.

Part of the Sunfire's low base price is low-tech hardware, such as a 3-speed automatic transmission. The more costly 4-speed automatic includes traction control to eliminate the drive wheels spinning during acceleration on slick surfaces.

The base 2.2-liter engine with the 3-speed automatic performs much better than expected. The engine has been retuned for more power at city driving speeds with either the manual or the automatic trans-mission. The automatic lets the engine speed up instantly, and it's a good package in town. But without overdrive, the 3-speed automatic is noisier on the highway.

To give you the illusion of good performance, the accelerator pedal has a short travel from idle to wide open, so it doesn't take much pedal movement to get more action from the engine. That's fine in good weather, but makes the Sunfire trickier to handle in snow. The ride is characteristic of Pontiacs: firm but not too stiff. We thought the steering effort was too light and slow to respond.

Inside, the Sunfire is attractive. The front seats could use denser foam in the driver's seat cushion; a long drive proved uncomfortable. However, our rear-seat passengers reported the back seat comfortable on short jaunts. The coupe is noticeably lower, with less head and leg room in the rear seat. Entry and exit to the front seat are more difficult in the coupe, too.

The trunk lid doesn't swing up high enough, so you can bump your head if you're not careful. The trunk has sufficient space, but the opening is small.

On the instrument panel, a few elements need refining. The directional controls for the vents, for example, are too small to grip easily. And, at night, the windshield reflects light from the instruments. The light on the odometer isn't bright enough, so following mileage directions at night isn't much fun.

D.V.S.

PRICES
$12,000
$22,000

SE coupe
$13,255

SE sedan
$13,255

SE 2-door convertible
$19,495

GT coupe
$16,255

WARRANTY
(years/miles)

Bumper-to-bumper
3/36,000

Powertrain
3/36,000

Rust-through
6/100,000

OTHER TO CONSIDER

Dodge Neon

Nissan Sentra

Specifications of Test Vehicle

Model: Sunfire SE

Exterior Dimensions	
Wheelbase	104.1 in.
Overall length	181.9 in.
Overall width	67.4 in.
Overall height	53 in.
Curb weight	2,650 lb.
Interior dimensions	
Seating capacity	5
Head room	F:37.6/R:36.6 in.
Leg room	F:42.1/R:32.6 in.
Cargo volume	12.4 cu. ft.
Engine	
Displacement	I-4 2.2 L.
Horsepower	115 @ 4,800 rpm
Torque, lb-ft.	135 @ 3,600 rpm
Performance	
0-60 mph, acceleration	10.2 sec.
60-0 mph, braking	132 ft.
Turning circle	37.2 ft.
EPA city/highway	23/29 mpg
Test mileage	25 mpg
Fuel tank capacity	15.2 gal.

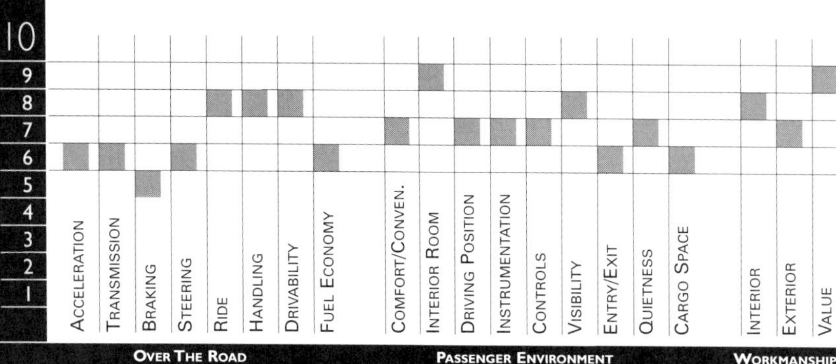

Ratings
141

Pontiac Montana

New for 99

More horsepower
Power hated mirrors
New colors

Pros

Ride
Versatility
8-passenger seating

Cons

Handling
Engine performance

Equipment

Major Standard Equipment: 3.4-liter V-6, automatic transmission, 4-wheel antilock brakes, automatic headlamps, tilt steering wheel, 7-passenger seating, AM/FM stereo, air conditioning, cabin air filter, variable-intermittent wipers, rear washer and wiper, automatic power locks, power mirrors, stainless-steel exhaust system. **Major Options:** 8-passenger seating, traction control, left-side sliding door, power right-side sliding door, dual integrated child safety seat, self-sealing tires.
Leather ulphosrery

Nice, but not perfect

Forget the Trans Sport, this Pontiac minivan is now known as the Montana, which, until last summer, until last year, was a special option package

The Montana aims for the look of a sport-utility vehicle and the versatility of a minivan. Built on the same platform as the Chevrolet Venture and Oldsmobile Silhouette, the Montana now has short and long versions. Either length seats up to eight people; Chevy and Olds versions seat only seven.
An optional left-side sliding door complements the slick power sliding door on the right. There is only one trim level.

With giant side-view mirrors and "halo" head restraints, this Montana is easy to drive. The modular seats can be flipped and flopped into lots of configurations, including some you never thought of. Removing the back seats makes the cargo area 4 full feet wide.

The Montana's seats feel unlike those in the Venture or Silhouette. The front captain's chairs have large cushions and a manually adjustable lumbar support. Even the manually adjusted seats were very comfortable on long drives. The center-row captain's chairs are more comfortable than the modular seats. Adults won't like the middle row bench seat, which is too low. Children might like it better, at least until they become teenagers.

The comprehensive instruments have Pontiac's signature warm-red back-lighting. The driver has a clear line of sight to all the controls and can operate them even with long fingernails or gloved hands. The controls are simple and easy to use, except for the high-end audio system, which is difficult to decipher.

On the road, the Montana is relaxing and rather car-like. But minivans were never intended to be sports cars, and this one is no exception. It leans and plows through hard turns. The standard antilock brakes and optional traction control help in bad weather.

Although the 3.4-liter V-6 does a suitable job, the Montana really deserves the Bonneville's 3.8-liter V-6. The minivan is 200 pounds heavier than the Bonneville and has a larger cargo volume to boot. The responsive 4-speed automatic makes the most of the power available.

With new safety features, the Montana and other GM minivans have taken a step ahead of Chrysler and Ford. **D.V.S.**

Specifications of Test Vehicle

Model: Trans Sport

Exterior Dimensions	
Wheelbase	120 in.
Overall length	201.3 in.
Overall width	72.7 in.
Overall height	68.1 in.
Curb weight	3,950 lb.
Interior Dimensions	
Seating capacity	8
Head room	F:39.9/R1:39.3/R2:38.9 in.
Leg room	F:39.9/R1:39/R2:36.7 in.
Cargo volume	24.2 cu. ft.
Engine	
Displacement	V-6 3.4 L.
Horsepower	185 @ 5,200 rpm
Torque, lb-ft.	210 @ 4,000 rpm
Performance	
0-60 mph, acceleration	10.5 sec.
60-0 mph, braking	134 ft.
Turning circle	39.7 ft.
EPA city/highway	18/25 mpg
Test mileage	22.6
Fuel tank capacity	25 gal.

PRICES
$21,000
$26,000
3-door minivan $20,840
4-door minivan $22,380
4-door minivan, extended length $23,090

WARRANTY (years/miles)
Bumper-to-bumper 3/36,000
Powertrain 3/36,000
Rust-through 6/100,000

OTHER TO CONSIDER
Dodge Grand Caravan
Ford Windstar

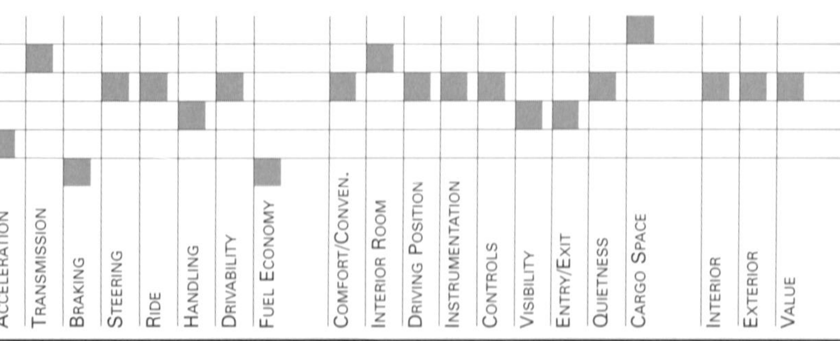

Ratings
153

Porsche | 911

New for 99

All new body, interior and suspension design with new liquid-cooled engine.

Pros

Powertrain
Performance
Steering/handling
Driving fun

Cons

Interior room
Entry/exit (top up)
Price

Equipment

Major Standard Equipment: 3.4 liter H-6 engine, 6-speed manual transmission, antilock brakes, traction control, 17 in. alloy wheels, AM/FM/ cassette audio system, automatic climate control, leather seats. **Major Options:** Tiptronic 5-speed semi-automatic transmission, navigation system, CD changer, premium sound system, premium leather seats, motor sound package.

The reincarnation of a myth

PRICES
$78,000
$88,000
Carrera S coupe $65,815
Carrera Cabriolet 2-door convertible Est. $73,000

WARRANTY
Bumper-to-Bumper 4/50,000
Power Train 4/50,000
Rust-through 10/unlimited

OTHER TO CONSIDER
Acura NSX-t

The all-new 911, introduced earlier this year, is the second example from Porsche about how to survive in an upscale, low-volume market. First came the Boxster, with its clever engineering for efficient manufacturing. Now, the new 911 shares that technology to make it more competitive. Even though the 911 shares more than a few parts with the Boxster, it's still unique, with a character all its own.

The coupe and cabriolet are mechanically identical. The new 3.4-liter, DOHC, liquid-cooled, horizontally opposed six is smaller and lighter than the old air-cooled version, but at 296 hp, it is more powerful and more fuel efficient. The new Carrera can be equipped with either a 6-speed manual or 5-speed semi-automatic 181transmission. (Tiptronic) Who offers drivers the choice of shifting manually, or letting the transmission shift for itself. Steering wheel-mounted buttons control shifting in the manual mode. Both transmissions have closer gear ratio spacing to take advantage of the engine's torque and power characteristics. Also new is the suspension, more refined force-sensitive steering, and better brakes. Advanced safety features include pop-up roll bars and side airbags that protect the head, as well as the torso.

Inside there are no surprises. The instrument panel is similar to the Boxster's, with overlapping gauges to conserve space. Suspended pedals replace the previous model's floor-mounted design. Front seats are firm, supportive, and totally comfortable. No one would choose to ride in the rear seat unless it was a dire emergency. The convertible is worse than the coupe — top storage uses valuable space behind the seat back.

There's a distinct lack of places to put things inside, and cargo space is divided between front and back. Don't expect to haul anything large. The electrohydraulic top requires only the touch of a button to open or close in less than 20 seconds. Entry and exit with the top down is no problem, but with the top up,considerable bending and twisting is needed. As in any convertible, visibility to the rear is restricted by the small rear window. To make matters worse, the window is a view-distorting flexible plastic.

Driving is what the 911 is all about. On the road, the powertrain performs flawlessly. Acceleration with either transmission is stunning, but the manual is more fun. Getting to 60 mph takes about 5 seconds. The engine is smooth and quiet – the exhaust sound is almost musical. Steering is light and totally linear, with great on-center feel. Handling is just what should be expected – no body roll, with a slight tendency toward understeer when pushed hard in a corner. Brakes have a good feel, but our panic stop test gave us only average results.

Those who liked the previous 911 should be happy with the new one. This new version has more power, better safety features, more room and comfort, and still has much of the same character as the old one. **D.V.S.**

Specifications of Test Vehicle

Model: 911 Cabriolet

Exterior Dimensions	
Wheelbase	92.6 in.
Overall Length	174.5 in.
Overall Width	69.5 in.
Overall Height	51.8 in.
Curb Weight	2910 lbs.
Interior Dimensions	
Seating Capacity	2+2
Head Room	F: 37.0/R: 31.5 in.
Leg Room	F: 44.5/R: 15.5 in.
Cargo Room	5.2 + 9.5 cu.ft.
Engine	
Displacement	3.4 L
Horsepower	296 @ 6800 rpm
Torque, lb-ft.	258 @ 4600 rpm
Performance	
0-60 mph, acceleration	5.1 sec.
60-0 mph, braking	121 ft.
Turning Circle	34.8 ft.
EPA City/Highway	17/25 mpg.
Test Mileage	NA
Fuel Tank Capacity	17 gal.

Ratings

Group	Category	Rating
Over The Road	Acceleration	10
	Transmission	9
	Braking	7
	Steering	9
	Ride	6
	Handling	10
	Drivability	9
	Fuel Economy	5
Passenger Environment	Comfort/Conven.	7
	Interior Room	6
	Driving Position	8
	Instrumentation	8
	Controls	8
	Visibility	6
	Entry/Exit	6
	Quietness	7
	Cargo Space	6
Workmanship	Interior	8
	Exterior	10
	Value	5

Ratings
150

Porsche

Boxster

New for 99

S version possibly available this year

Pros

A real Porsche
Powerful brakes
Two trunks

Cons

Expensive accessories
Inferior quality of some materials
Pickup at low and average engine speeds

Equipment

Major Standard Equipment: 2.5-liter HO-6, manual transmission, 4-wheel antilock disc brakes, roll bars, air conditioning, cabin air filter, power windows, power folding top, leather upholstery, AM/FM/cassette stereo, rear foglight, theft-deterrent system, aluminum wheels. **Major Options:** Semi- automatic transmission, traction control, removable hardtop, wind baffle, AM/FM/CD stereo, trip computer, cruise control remote keyless entry, theft alarm system, power heated seats, larger tires.

Not a real bargain

There are three young men at your door, cameras slung over your shoulder, asking if they can have their pictures taken next to your Porsche Boxster. This is one of the many experiences I have had in the past few days while driving this Porsche.

But, beyond the power of fascination the Boxster commands in passing, it is certainly the interminable, costly list of manufacturer options that draws our attention.

Esthetically, the Boxster hails from a line of glorious ancestors, one of which was lamentably made infamous as James Dean drove it into a tragic accident.

Faithful to its tradition, Porsche decorates the Boxster's passenger compartment minimally. It is properly finished, but is it ever sad! The bucket seats, partially covered in leather, offer a multitude of adjustments so you can find a good position in which to drive. Unfortunately, the tilt and telescopic steering wheel is hard on your legs. Worse still are the smooth, bright controls for a radio with very mediocre reception and the dubious ergonomic air conditioning. On the other hand, in contrast with its rivals, this Porsche, with its two baggage compartments, gives you no excuse to do your shopping alone.

Seventeen minutes is all the time it takes to pull the motor, housed between the passenger compartment and the rear axle. Porsche reassures your banker by saying no routine maintenance is needed on it for the first 60,000 miles. For most mortals, whose chances of setting their eyes on this 2.5-liter flat six-cylinder engine are almost nil, here is a brief summary of its specifications. First of all, it's closely derived from the good old 911 Boxster engine, except it's water-cooled. It puts out 201 horses, and if you've never heard them, Porsche makes them sound just right. Along with this motor, Porsche offers the ultimate five-speed semi-automatic, an amazing Tiptronic S. Whatever your choice (manual or automatic), the Boxster promises you can break the 60-mph barrier in a bit less than six seconds, then watch the speedometer climb into totally forbidden zones. Less amazing is pickup at low and moderate speeds, where the Boxster seems to be panting. This hardly diminishes the pleasure of being at its wheel, however. Stable and balanced, it forgives both inexperience and audacity. And if things get bad, you can always count on the super-powerful brakes.

With the Boxster, Porsche introduces a new era for modern sports cars that are pleasant to spend time in. Too bad the German maker didn't take the opportunity to reduce the number and price of its accessories. **E.L.**

Specifications of Test Vehicle

Model: Boxster

Exterior Dimensions	
Wheelbase	95.2 in.
Overall length	171 in.
Overall width	70.1 in.
Overall height	50.8 in.
Curb weight	2,800 lb.
Interior Dimensions	
Seating capacity	2
Head room	F:38 in.
Leg room	F:41.6 in.
Cargo room	9.2 cu. ft.
Engine	
Displacement	HO-6 2.5 L.
Horsepower	201 @ 6,000 rpm
Torque, lb-ft.	181 @ 4,500 rpm
Performance	
0-60 mph, acceleration	6.7 sec.
60-0 mph, braking	120 ft.
Turning circle	35.8 ft.
EPA city/highway	19/26 mpg
Test mileage	22 mpg
Fuel tank capacity	15.3 gal.

PRICES
$41,000
$49,000
convertible
$41,785

WARRANTY
(years/miles)
Bumper-to-bumper
2/unlimited
Powertrain
2/unlimited
Rust-through
10/unlimited

OTHER TO CONSIDER
BMW Z3 2.8
Mercedes SLK

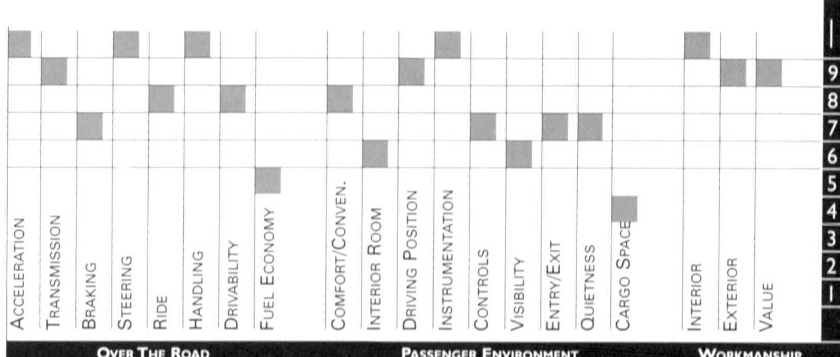

Ratings
159

Saab 9-3

new MODEL

NEW FOR 99

New model

PROS

Handling
Super comfortable seats
Powerful Turbo engine

CONS

Less than perfect finish
Lack of torque at low-end
No traction control system

EQUIPMENT

Major Standard Equipment: Turbocharged 2.0-liter I-4, manual transmission, 4-wheel antilock disk brakes, air conditioning, cabin air filter, rear defroster, rear washer and wiper, telescoping steering wheel, AM/FM/WB/cassette stereo, remote keyless entry, power locks, power windows, cruise control, power heated mirrors, heated seats, folding rear seat, aluminum wheels. **SE adds:** automatic air conditioning, power seats, driver's memory system, leather upholstery, power moonroof, trip computer, sports suspension, larger tires. **HO adds:** Turbocharged 2-liter I-4 (200 hp).

PRICES

$25,000
$44,000

9-3 3-door $26,225
9-3 5-door $26,725
9-3 2-door convertible $38,725
9-3 3-door $30,995
9-3 5-door $33,275
9-3SE 2-door convertible $44,570

WARRANTY (years/miles)

Bumper-to-bumper 4/50,000
Powertrain 4/50,000
Rust-through 6/unlimited

OTHER TO CONSIDER

Audi A4S
BMW 323 i

Worth the trip

Introduced last April as a 1999 model, the Saab 9-3 takes over where the 900 left off. Although it has the same lines, the 9-3 was the object of a detailed makeover and its designers will tell you that more than 1,000 components (no, I didn't count them) bear the stamp of innovation. On the outside, the 9-3 is easy to recognize because of its more stylized grille and its redesigned headlights. Inside, bucket seats hide side air bags and are topped with a headrest, all the better to avoid whiplash should you be rear-ended.

When trying to describe the 9-3's passenger compartment, the term "cockpit" seems to be more appropriate. Seats are extremely comfortable, instruments are easy to read (including the Night Panel system designed to display a more limited range of information), controls are positioned perfectly logically, visibility is impeccable (except on the convertible, given the narrow rear windshield and wide pillars). As for the trunk (with the exception of the convertible model, all the 9-3s have a rear hatch), it easily swallows anything you want to transport — no need to limit the amount of baggage you can take with you. Criticisms include less than perfect finishing (but no suspicious rattling), rear windows (on the coupe) that still roll down only half-way, and the inability to equip the model with both a cassette player and a CD player — it's one or the other.

Forget the convertible: even with a sturdier chassis it still falls short. On the other hand, three- and five-door models are just rigid enough and a lot of fun to drive. The turbocharged 2.0-liter four-cylinder engine's 185 horses take a bit of time to spring into action, but once they do, the mechanical system shines, with plenty of energy in the mid-and high-rpm range, excellent fuel consumption with an average of 24 mpg (although it uses only Super), and a low noise level. Given the fact that the 9-3 has no traction control system, on slippery road surfaces almost inevitably leads to a loss of power in front wheels. The engine is teamed with a somewhat rubbery manual transmission and a hydraulic clutch that proves to be very balky, at times making you look like a beginner behind the wheel in city traffic. Saab claims to have eliminated the problem on the models slated for sale this fall. Buyers can always opt for the automatic transmission.With a better-calibrated suspension, less roll when taking corners, but the same significant tendency to understeer (after all, this is a front-wheel drive), the 9-3 isn't as sporty as Audi's A4 Quattro can be, not even as sporty as the BMW's 3-Series, and you'll have to sweat bullets to keep the pace set by its two German rivals. On the other hand, a more precise steering system makes it easier to take corners with this Saab and a short turning radius makes it very easy to handle when driving in the city. Composed of four discs, the braking system, (with ABS) features an electronic power adjustment system that can bring the car to a full stop over short distances. **E.L.**

SPECIFICATIONS OF TEST VEHICLE

MODEL: SAAB 9-3

Exterior Dimensions	
Wheelbase	102.4 in.
Overall length	182.6 in.
Overall width	67.4 in.
Overall height	56.6 in.
Curb weight	3,000 lb.
Interior Dimensions	
Seating capacity	5
Head room	F:39.3/R:37.8 in.
Leg room	F:42.3/R:34.1 in.
Cargo room	24 cu. ft.
Engine	
Displacement	I-4 2 L.
Horsepower	185 @ 5,500 rpm
Torque, lb-ft.	194 @ 2,100 rpm
Performance	
0-60 mph, acceleration	7.1 sec.
60-0 mph, braking	120 ft.
Turning circle	34.4 ft.
EPA city/highway	21/27 mpg
Test mileage	24 mpg
Fuel tank capacity	18 gal.

Ratings 160

Group	Category	Rating
Over The Road	Acceleration	9
	Transmission	7
	Braking	7
	Steering	9
	Ride	8
	Handling	8
	Drivability	7
	Fuel Economy	6
Passenger Environment	Comfort/Conven.	8
	Interior Room	8
	Driving Position	8
	Instrumentation	9
	Controls	7
	Visibility	8
	Entry/Exit	7
	Quietness	9
	Cargo Space	10
Workmanship	Interior	9
	Exterior	9
	Value	7

Saab

9-5

New for 99

9-5 Wagon is new model, based on 9-5 sedan.

Pros

Powertrain
Performance
Interior room
Ride & handling
Safety features

Cons

None

Equipment

Major Standard Equipment: 2.3 liter I-4 turbo engine, 5-speed manual transmission, antilock brakes, traction control, dual-zone air conditioning, tilt and telescope wheel, cruise control, power windows/seats/locks/mirrors, AM/FM/WB/CD/cassette audio system with steering wheel controls, remote keyless entry, alloy wheels, velour seats, trip computer, sunroof.
Major options: 3.0 liter V-6, automatic transmission, leather upholstery, ventilated seats, heated seats.

1999

AAA
TOP WAGON

Mission accomplished

The Saab 9-5 sedan was introduced early in the 1999 model year. Expanding its 1999 model line, Saab introduces its sporty, aerodynamic 9-5 station wagon. Available this spring, the 9-5 Wagon will compete with offerings from Audi, BMW, Mercedes, and Volvo in the premium wagon segment.

The 9-5 Wagon comes loaded with standard luxury features. The only choices for top-of-the-line V-6 buyers are leather, heated, or ventilated seats. All 9-5 models offer a choice of two engines and either a manual or automatic transmission. The base engine is a 2.3-liter 4-cylinder that uses a light-pressure turbocharger to boost horsepower to 170. The other offering is an asymmetrically turbocharged, 3-liter V-6 that produces 200 horsepower.

The standard traction antilock brakes include a feature for electronic brake force distribution. Called EBD, it automatically maximizes the grip for each wheel independently to reduce stopping distances. The V-6 engine includes an integrated electronic traction control system.

From the driver's perspective, the interior has a cockpit-inspired look. The gray instrument panel is slightly curbed around the driver with black controls and buttons logically grouped by function.

The driver and passengers are treated to seats that offer good, firm support. A novel option cools the front seats by circulating air through perforations in the leather seat cushions. A good seating position and tall windows give the driver good visibility in all directions. Either side of the rear seat-back can be folded or removed to expand the Wagon's already generous cargo space. Loading cargo is made easier with the optional sliding floor that can be rolled out almost 20 inches. The tailgate opens high enough for most adults to stand under it. The cargo area features an innovation from the aircraft industry called CargoTracks – a system of rails with one-grip locks and special belts to keep cargo from shifting during hard braking or a crash.

The V-6 is smooth and quiet, even under full power. Shifts with the automatic transmission are well-timed and smooth. Saab has finally fixed the manual transmission shifter. Now it feels well-connected and precise. The sensitive, capable brakes delivered better-than-average stopping distance in our simulated panic stops. Even though the Wagon is a fairly large car, it rides and handles like a premium sports sedan. The ride is firm, but not harsh. Steering is precise with just a hint of torque steer under hard acceleration.

With its full compliment of safety features, respectable performance, and a very user-friendly interior, Saab seems to have found the right combination for competing in the luxury wagon segment. **D.V.S.**

Specifications of Test Vehicle

Model: 9-5 Wagon

Exterior Dimensions	
Wheelbase	106.4 in.
Overall length	189.3 in.
Overall width	70.5 in.
Overall height	61.1 in.
Curb weight	3810
Interior Dimensions	
Seating capacity	5
Head room	F: 38.7/R:37.6 in.
Leg room	F: 42.2/R:36.6 in.
Cargo room	37 cu.ft.
Engine	
Displacement	3.0L V-6
Horsepower	200@5000 rpm
Torque, lb-ft.	229@2500 rpm
Performance	
0-60 mph, acceleration	8.5 sec.
60-0 mph, braking	125 ft.
Turning circle	35.4 ft.
EPA city/highway	18/26 mpg.
Test mileage	NA
Fuel tank capacity	18.5 gal.

Prices
$35,000
$40,000
sedan 30,570
SE sedan 34,070

Warranty
Bumper-to-bumper 4/50,000
Powertrain 4/50,000
Rust-through 6/Unlimited

Other to Consider
Audi A6 Avant
BMW 528iT

Category	Rating
Over The Road	
Acceleration	8
Transmission	8
Braking	6
Steering	8
Ride	8
Handling	9
Drivability	9
Fuel Economy	5
Passenger Environment	
Comfort/Conven.	9
Interior Room	10
Driving Position	8
Instrumentation	8
Controls	7
Visibility	8
Entry/Exit	9
Quietness	9
Cargo Space	10
Workmanship	
Interior	9
Exterior	9
Value	8

Ratings
165

Saturn SC

NEW FOR 99
Third door
Reduce NVH

PROS
Handling
Fuel economy
Ride comfort

CONS
Controls
Engine noise
Four-passenger seating

EQUIPMENT

Major Standard Equipment: 1.9-liter I-4, manual transmission, AM/FM stereo, split-folding rear seat, intermittent wipers, rear defroster, tilt steering column. **SC2 adds:** More powerful 1.9-liter I-4, air conditioning, sports suspension, variable-assist power steering. **Major Options:** Automatic transmission, 4-wheel antilock brakes, traction control, air conditioning, cruise control, AM/FM/cassette stereo, AM/FM/CD stereo, CD changer, power moonroof, power passenger-side mirror, power windows, leather upholstery, remote keyless entry, antitheft system, power locks, aluminum wheels.

PRICES
$13,000
$20,000

SC1 coupe
$12,385

SC2 coupe
$14,945

WARRANTY
(years/miles)

Bumper-to-bumper
3/36,000

Powertrain
3/36,000

Rust-through
6/100,000

OTHER TO CONSIDER

Ford Escort ZX2

Hyundai Tiburon

Original, isn't it ?

With a back seat designed for merely occasional use, Saturn's little SC coupe is not as practical as the SL sedan, but it's more fun.

Redesigned in '97, the latest version is quieter, roomier, smoother riding, and more comfortable than the previous one. The roofline now provides more headroom, front and rear, and the rear seat gains nearly 5 inches of leg room. Saturn gives us further proof that it's from another planet this year by adding a third door to its coupe. This third door on the passenger side, like some pickup trucks, make it easier for backseat passengers to climb in and out.

The base SC1 that we drove had the 1.9-liter, 100-horsepower, 4-cylinder engine. It doesn't provide stirring performance for a sporty coupe, especially with the automatic. Saturn claims the engine is much quieter than before, but we couldn't tell the difference—it's still noisy. (The optional engine easily remedies that; it also delivers 24 percent more power, making it the sportier choice.) The automatic transmission performed extremely well. Highway fuel economy with the base engine surprised us; we easily got 37 mpg on the interstate. Around town, gas mileage is less, of course, but still very good.

The Saturn coupe exhibits good ride and handling. If you drove the original Saturn coupe, you might fear that the new, longer wheelbase sacrifices some nimbleness. If so, it's too little to detect. The body leans just a bit on corners, keeping the SC one of the better-driving small cars. Antilock brakes, standard on other small GM cars, continue to be optional on Saturns, but traction control is standard now.

A full 11⁄2 inches lower than the sedan, the coupe make entry and exit more difficult. In back, a console separating the two seats has replaced the center-position safety belt, even though the sedan will seat three children in the same space. Sacrificing such simple utility for young families strikes us as a strange decision in a car that wants to be appreciated for its practical touches. Saturns still feature dent-resistant body panels.

The dash and center console still have easy-to-read gauges, but the controls need improvement. The turn signal lever is farther than usual from the steering wheel; if you have small hands, it's hard to flick it on without taking your hand off the steering wheel. And the traction control system still has its annoying warning light. It stays on when the system is on, the opposite of every other vehicle's. The light is distracting in night driving. The horn control is also poorly located—two tiny buttons low on the steering wheel. It's hard to find in emergencies.

Don't buy a Saturn just because it's American. Buy it because it's still one of the better values in small cars. **D.V.S.**

Ratings 144

Group	Category	Rating (1–10)
Over The Road	Acceleration	5
	Transmission	8
	Braking	5
	Steering	8
	Ride	8
	Handling	8
	Drivability	9
	Fuel Economy	7
Passenger Environment	Comfort/Conven.	8
	Interior Room	7
	Driving Position	8
	Instrumentation	7
	Controls	5
	Visibility	7
	Entry/Exit	8
	Quietness	6
	Cargo Space	5
Workmanship	Interior	8
	Exterior	8
	Value	9

SPECIFICATIONS OF TEST VEHICLE

MODEL: SATURN SC1

Exterior Dimensions	
Wheelbase	102.4 in.
Overall length	180 in.
Overall width	67.3 in.
Overall height	53 in.
Curb weight	2,350 lb.
Interior dimensions	
Seating capacity	4
Head room	F:38.5/R:35.7 in.
Leg room	F:42.6/R:31 in.
Cargo volume	11.4 cu. ft.
Engine	
Displacement	I-4 1.9 L.
Horsepower	100 @ 5,000 rpm
Torque, lb-ft.	114 @ 2,400 rpm
Performance	
0-60 mph, acceleration	11.5 sec.
60-0 mph, braking	130 ft.
Turning circle	37.1 ft
EPA city/highway	27/37 mpg
Test mileage	29.2 mpg
Fuel tank capacity	12.1 gal.

Saturn SL / SW

New for 99
Additional soundproofing

Pros
Visibility
Braking
Driving position
Fuel economy

Cons
Engine noise
Rear-seat room
Controls

Equipment

Major Standard Equipment: 1.9-liter I-4,unassisted steering, driver-side mirror, AM/FM stereo, tilt steering column, rear defroster, intermittent wipers, split-folding rear seat, remote-control decklid release, stainless steel exhaust. **SL1 adds:** Power steering, passenger-side mirror. **SL2 adds:** More powerful 1.9-liter I-4, variable-assist power steering, sports suspension, air conditioning, power mirrors, tachometer, driver's lumbar adjustment. **Major Options:** Automatic transmission, 4-wheel antilock brakes, traction control, air conditioning, cruise control, AM/FM/CD stereo, power moonroof, power windows.

When does the reinventing process begin?

If you're shopping for compacts, you have to test drive a Saturn SL. Its appeal ranges from friendly dealerships to friendly, dent-resistant fenders.

Saturn offers three body styles in its line: the 2-door coupe (SC), the 4-door sedan (SL), and the station wagon (SW). Numbers after the letters designate trim levels and their accompanying engines. Sedans also come in a low-priced, minimally equipped version solely for advertising purposes; they don't even have power steering.

The SL2's 124-horsepower engine is noisy, especially at higher speeds. Road noise is also prominent. Noise aside, the engine is lively and responsive and delivers good fuel economy, even with the automatic transmission. We averaged 27 mpg in a mix of suburban commuting and highway driving.

The automatic transmission decisively chooses the best gear for a situation. It still shifts into overdrive very quickly with a light load; you can override that with the overdrive lockout. The transmission shifts smoothly during normal driving but more noticeably under hard throttle.

The SL steers and handles well. The quick, responsive steering and good-size tires improve control. Cornering is surprisingly flat for an economy car. The all-independent suspension is compliant enough to smooth out most ripples in the road surface, yet stiff enough to maintain handling control. It fails to absorb only the sharpest bumps. The antilock disc brakes provide powerful stopping power. From 60 mph, the SL2 stopped in 124 feet in our tests.

Inside, the sedan is functional and simple. The controls are sensibly positioned, with two exceptions. The turn signal lever is farther than usual from the steering wheel, making it less convenient for drivers with small hands. Also, the small horn buttons are near the bottom of the steering wheel rim, far from the driver's hands. You won't find them in a hurry.

The front seats are comfortable. The back seat has a bit more head room than the original Saturn had, but you'll still find leg and hip room cramped back there. Nevertheless, the sedan is roomier than the coupe. Families with children will appreciate the sedan's third safety belt in the back seat. A bumper-high liftover aids access to the trunk, and the rear seats fold down for more room.

Visibility is unobstructed in all directions. Dent-resistant plastic body panels help protect against inevitable dings in parking lots, but the paint is as easily scratched as that on other cars.

Saturn owners like their cars and the low-key, no-pressure sales approach. You might, too. **D.V.S.**

Specifications of Test Vehicle

Model: SL2

Exterior Dimensions	
Wheelbase	102.4 in.
Overall length	176.9 in.
Overall width	66.7 in.
Overall height	55 in.
Curb weight	2,400 lb.
Interior Dimensions	
Seating capacity	5
Head room	F:39.3/R:38 in.
Leg room	F:42.5/R:32.8 in.
Cargo volume	12.1 cu. ft.
Engine	
Displacement	I-4 1.9 L.
Horsepower	124 @ 5,600 rpm
Torque, lb-ft.	122 @ 4,800 rpm
Performance	
0-60 mph, acceleration	8.5 sec.
60-0 mph, braking	124 ft.
Turning circle	37.1 ft.
EPA city/highway	26/36 mpg
Test mileage	27 mpg
Fuel tank capacity	12.1 gal.

Prices

$11,000
$19,000

SL sedan $11,035

SL1 sedan $11,735

SW1 4-door wagon $12,735

SL2 sedan $13,195

SW2 4-door wagon $14,695

Warranty
(years/miles)

Bumper-to-bumper 3/36,000

Powertrain 3/36,000

Rust-through 6/100,000

Other to Consider

Ford Escort

Nissan Sentra

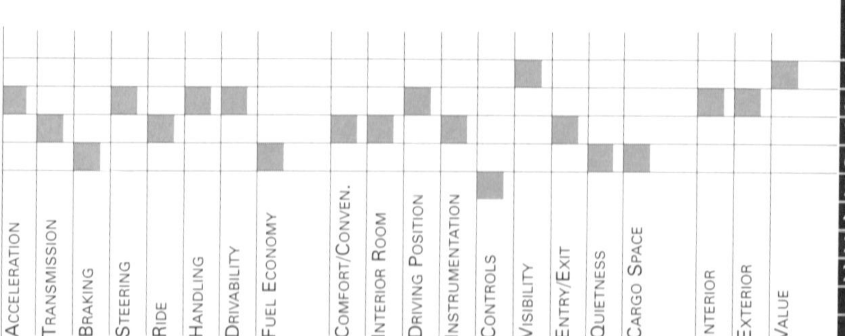

Ratings

145

Subaru Forester

1999

AAA **TOP SPORT UTILITY**

PRICES
$19,000
$24,000
L 4-door $19,995
S 4-door $22,195

WARRANTY (years/miles)
Bumper-to-bumper 3/36,000
Powertrain 3/36,000
Rust-through 5/unlimited

OTHER TO CONSIDER
Honda CR-V
Suzuki Grand Vitara

New for 99

"Limited" version available

Pros

Driveability
Clever storage spaces
Excellent automatic transmission

Cons

Uncomfortable back seat
Layout details (see article)
Some fragile-looking accessories

Equipment

Major Standard Equipment: 2.5-liter HO-4, manual transmission, all-wheel drive, variable-assist power steering, air conditioning, intermittent wipers, rear wiper and washer, rear defroster, power windows, AM/FM/cassette stereo, tilt steering column. **L adds:** 4-wheel antilock brakes, power locks, remote keyless entry. **S adds:** Four-wheel disc brakes, power mirrors, cruise control, larger tires, aluminum wheels. **Major Options:** Automatic transmission, cruise control, cargo cover.

Well done, indeed!

Subaru has been billing itself as the king of all-wheel drive for a long time now. So naturally, it has decided to offer its own particular answer to the CR-V (Honda) and other RAV4 lookalikes by introducing the Forester, a hybrid utility vehicle that has its own way of venturing off the usual course. Sport/utility.

You don't just get into a Forester, you slide into it. No doubt its low ground clearance limits off-road possibilities (beware of rocks — protection plates are not part of standard equipment), but makes life easier when you want to load its noisy baggage rack (standard) with a luge, snowboard, or other bulky sports equipment without giving an impromptu ballet performance. The passenger compartment isn't as modular as it is on the CR-V, for example, especially when it comes to access to the rear seats, with a bench seat about as comfortable as an ironing board. Its only original feature, it folds down at an angle that's perfect if the little ones onboard decide to take a nap. And if sleep time is out of the question, you can keep the kids busy looking for hidden treasures in the 20 or so storage spaces tucked away here and there in the passenger compartment. Subaru has paid attention to detail, but the rear side window needs a defroster and doors are an annoyance because they open off-center. Add to this a few ergonomic details (a radio positioned under the air conditioning block) and a few accessories that are fairly fragile (cupholders, for example) and you get a pretty good idea of what's in store.

Impeccable all-wheel drive, an almost perfect weight distribution (49/51), a sturdy engine, powerful brakes, a tight turning radius, a surprising towing capacity — the Forester casts a shadow on its closest rivals. Another strong point: an easily accessible drivetrain, making it very easy to check fluid levels and replace key parts. A tip of the hat to the five-speed manual transmission, which this time out shows definite improvement; the gearshift lever has gained in precision, but the smoother automatic is still the better choice. Aggressive 16-inch tires go all-out to counter the vehicle's tendency to oversteer or understeer under certain circumstances. All in all, the Forester is a lot of fun.

No Adonis, perhaps, but the Forester has what it takes to light up a constellation of stars — the make's symbol — in a market that is due to reach some kind of saturation point soon. **E.L.**

Specifications of Test Vehicle

Model: Forester S

Exterior Dimensions	
Wheelbase	99.4 in.
Overall length	175.2 in.
Overall width	68.3 in.
Overall height	65 in.
Curb weight	3,100 lb.
Interior Dimensions	
Seating capacity	5
Head room	F:40.6/R:39.6 in.
Leg room	F:43/R:33.4 in.
Cargo room	33.2 cu. ft.
Engine	
Displacement	HO-4 2.5 L.
Horsepower	165 @ 5,600 rpm
Torque, lb-ft.	162 @ 4,000 rpm
Performance	
0-60 mph, acceleration	9.9 sec.
60-0 mph, braking	127 ft.
Turning circle	38.3 ft.
EPA city/highway	21/26 mpg
Test mileage	24 mpg
Fuel tank capacity	15.9 gal.

Ratings 148

Over The Road		Passenger Environment		Workmanship	
Acceleration	7	Comfort/Conven.	8	Interior	7
Transmission	8	Interior Room	7	Exterior	7
Braking	6	Driving Position	8	Value	8
Steering	7	Instrumentation	7		
Ride	7	Controls	7		
Handling	7	Visibility	8		
Drivability	8	Entry/Exit	8		
Fuel Economy	6	Quietness	7		
		Cargo Space	10		

Subaru

New for 99

TS version (sedan)
Revised 2.2-liter engine

Pros

All-wheel drive
Solid and precise steering
Peppier 2.2-liter engine

Cons

High price
Unframed side windows

Equipment

Major Standard Equipment: 2.2-liter HO-4, manual transmission, all-wheel drive, variable-assist power steering, tilt steering column, air conditioning, cruise control,AM/FM/ cassette stereo, rear defroster, intermittent wipers, power locks, power windows, remote-control decklid release. **Outback Sport adds:**4-wheel antilock brakes, raised sports suspension. 2.5 **RS adds:** 2.5-liter HO-4, 4-wheel disc brakes, sunroof, sports suspension, larger wheels and tires. **Major Options:** Automatic transmission, cruise control, CD player.

Odd man in?

Perhaps Subaru is enjoying a modest little victory. During 1997 alone, sales of the Impreza sedan, coupe, and wagon models soared dramatically. And in 1998?

A bit less spectacular, naturally, but still almost as good. No doubt the addition of the Outback Sport wagon model and the 2.5 RS coupe over the last few years has put Impreza in the limelight. And the winning trend continues — this year it also comes in a new sedan version: the TS. Lights, camera, action!

A hearty round of applause to Subaru stylists, who so neatly concealed the Impreza's unimpressive lines — although in the case of the 2.5 RS, they got carried away with a fin that seems to reach up to the sky. Too bad, though, that the wraparound bucket seats of the 2.5 RS weren't placed on board standard Imprezas or the Outback Sport and the TS. Also a shame that the dash is so dismal you could cry, and you have to keep your head down in back. In contrast with the wagon model — where the wheel wells take up useful space — the rear bench of the coupes and sedans doesn't fold back to increase luggage space. Another weakness, common to all Imprezas: the wind whistles through side windows.

To fully appreciate a Subaru, you have to take it out on a stormy day. It can't get enough of bad weather.

Where your usual car would zigzag, slip, and skid, Subaru's all-wheel drive gives the Impreza superb control. It's a real joy to encounter those tough situations where you can fully exploit the handling, agility, sturdiness, and stability of this Subaru. Still, the 2.5 RS's 2.5-liter engine ensures excellent performance (but that goes without saying!). This year's good news is a more level power curve at reduced engine speeds. And the 2.2-liter engine is full of get-up-and-go. Also a nice surprise: the manual shift is much better, and shifts gears more smoothly. But watch out. The 2.5 RS's particularly narrow gearshift grid could lead to mistakes. However, should this occur, Subaru provides two pairs of discs to brake excessively enthusiastic driving styles.

The Outback Sport, 2.5 RS, and TS versions herald previously unknown Impreza talents. To judge by the reaction of young Honda and Volkswagen owners, right now the Impreza is the hot car in its class. **E.L.**

Specifications of Test Vehicle

Model: 2.5 RS

Exterior Dimensions	
Wheelbase	99.2 in.
Overall length	172.2 in.
Overall width	67.1 in.
Overall height	60 in.
Curb weight	2,900 lb.
Interior Dimensions	
Seating capacity	5
Head room	F:39.2/R:37.4 in.
Leg room	F:43.1/R:32.4 in.
Cargo volume	25 cu. ft.
Engine	
Displacement	HO-4 2.5 L.
Horsepower	165 @ 5,600 rpm
Torque, lb-ft.	162 @ 4,000 rpm
Performance	
0-60 mph, acceleration	8.7 sec.
60-0 mph, braking	127 ft.
Turning circle	33.5 ft
EPA city/highway	23/30 mpg
Test mileage	25 mpg
Fuel tank capacity	13.2 gal.

Prices

$16,000
$20,000

L coupe $16,390
L sedan $16,390
L 4-door wagon $16,790
Outback Sport 4-door wagon $18,490
2.5 RS coupe $19,690

Warranty

(years/miles)

Bumper-to-bumper 3/36,000
Powertrain 3/36,000
Rust-through 5/unlimited

Other to consider

Honda Civic
Saturn SL

Group	Category	Rating
Over The Road	Acceleration	7
	Transmission	7
	Braking	6
	Steering	8
	Ride	8
	Handling	7
	Drivability	7
	Fuel Economy	6
Passenger Environment	Comfort/Conven.	7
	Interior Room	7
	Driving Position	8
	Instrumentation	8
	Controls	7
	Visibility	8
	Entry/Exit	6
	Quietness	7
	Cargo Space	10
Workmanship	Interior	8
	Exterior	8
	Value	7

Ratings
147

Subaru Legacy GT

New for 99

Revised 2.2L

Pros

All-wheel drive
Proven reliability
Improved manual transmission

Cons

Model scheduled for withdrawal
Fuel consumption
Balky gear shifting

Equipment

Major Standard Equipment: 2.2-liter HO-4, manual transmission, all-wheel drive, variable-assist power steering, air conditioning, rear defroster, AM/FM/cassette stereo, driver-side mirror, tilt steering column. **L adds:** 4-wheel antilock disc brakes, power windows, power locks, cruise control, power mirrors. **Outback adds:** 2.5-liter engine. **GT adds:** Sports suspension, power moonroof. **Outback Limited adds:** Heated seats, heated mirrors, windshield wiper deicer, AM/FM/WB/CD/cassette stereo.

PRICES
$17,000
$27,000

Brighton
$17,390

L sedan
$19,690

L wagon
$20,390

Outback wagon
$22,990

GT sedan
$23,290

GT wagon
$23,990

Outback Limited wagon
$25,090

GT Limited sedan
$24,590

WARRANTY
(years/miles)

Bumper-to-bumper
3/36,000

Powertrain
3/36,000

Rust-through
5/unlimited

OTHER TO CONSIDER

Ford Taurus
Volvo V70

GT: two letters too many?

To boost sales recorded by its Legacy sedans (the company currently sells four times as many wagons, Outback included), some time ago Subaru decided to concoct a GT version. The recipe? It's disarmingly simple: a rear spoiler, a sculpted hood, alloy wheels and tires with enough traction, and performance capabilities to keep up with the other steroid-pumped compacts out there.

When you open the doors you're faced with a somber interior, dark even with the addition of minuscule wood inlays (fake, of course). As for accessories, Subaru spoils its Legacy without falling into wretched excess, which no one would have complained about in any case given the asking price involved here. An ingenious detail: cupholders open and slide toward the passenger to keep from hiding radio and air conditioning controls (hard to adjust because the cursor lacks precision). Four passengers can travel the Legacy with no complaints, but those in the rear will find the angle of seatbacks (folddown) uncomfortable and not too generous on the padding.

The Legacy is powered by a flat 2.5-liter engine that gives up its 155 horses only reluctantly. Its 16 valves are loud and clear only when you climb into the tachometer's red zone (in fifth gear, particularly short, the sound level inside the passenger compartment increases by several decibels). And it isn't much fun to wrestle with the manual transmission, quite capable of giving back as good as it gets. Keeping on course isn't that easy and shifting gears on this model will make you look like a beginner through no fault of your own. Never mind what your banker says: invest the extra it takes to get the excellent automatic transmission. The GT is excellent in curves thanks to its steering system, and regardless of weather conditions, Subaru's all-wheel drive creates a reassuring sense of trust. Quality tires and a suspension that has undergone a few revisions (firmer, but with no negative effect on comfort) are two big pluses for better roadholding. And braking is strong and effective into the bargain.

It used to take more than a spoiler and alloy wheels to earn the GT label. Oh, how times have changed! **E.L.**

Ratings	Group	Score (1–10)
Acceleration	Over The Road	7
Transmission	Over The Road	8
Braking	Over The Road	6
Steering	Over The Road	8
Ride	Over The Road	8
Handling	Over The Road	7
Drivability	Over The Road	8
Fuel Economy	Over The Road	6
Comfort/Conven.	Passenger Environment	7
Interior Room	Passenger Environment	8
Driving Position	Passenger Environment	7
Instrumentation	Passenger Environment	8
Controls	Passenger Environment	8
Visibility	Passenger Environment	8
Entry/Exit	Passenger Environment	7
Quietness	Passenger Environment	7
Cargo Space	Passenger Environment	6
Interior	Workmanship	8
Exterior	Workmanship	8
Value	Workmanship	8

Ratings
148

Specifications of Test Vehicle

Model: Legacy GT

Exterior Dimensions	
Wheelbase	103.5 in.
Overall length	181.5 in.
Overall width	67.5 in.
Overall height	55.7 in.
Curb weight	3,150 lb.
Interior Dimensions	
Seating capacity	5
Head room	F:37.2/R:36.5 in.
Leg room	F:43.3/R:34.6 in.
Cargo volume	12.6 cu. ft.
Engine	
Displacement	HO-4 2.5 L.
Horsepower	165 @ 5,600 rpm
Torque, lb-ft.	162 @ 4,000 rpm
Performance	
0-60 mph, acceleration	9.6 sec
60-0 mph, braking	126 ft.
Turning circle	34.8 ft.
EPA city/highway	21/26 mpg
Test mileage	26 mpg
Fuel tank capacity	15.9 gal.

Suzuki

Esteem

New for 99

Restyled front
More powerful engine (late availability)

Pros

Rear seat room
Fuel economy

Cons

Ride comfort
Engine performance
Noise
Personality

Equipment

Major Standard Equipment: 1.6-liter I-4, manual transmission, air conditioning, intermittent wipers, rear defroster, AM/FM/cassette stereo, remote-control decklid release, stainless-steel exhaust system.
GLX adds: Power mirrors, power windows, power locks, remote keyless entry, split-folding rear seat, larger tires.
Major Options: Automatic transmission, 4-wheel antilock brakes, cruise control, power sunroof.

Looking for recognition

In its top-of-the-line GLX trim, the Suzuki Esteem offers good value. And, unlike most its competitors, the Esteem offers a station wagon.

With the Esteem, Suzuki faces a formidable struggle for acceptance against such better-known subcompacts. To achieve its objective, Suzuki restyled the Esteem's front end this year, giving it a bolder and modern appearance. Sometime this year the Esteem should get a more powerful engine (1.8 liter). The front-wheel-drive, 4-door Esteem comes in two trim levels: GL and top-of-the-line GLX. The latter has a long list of standard equipment, including power windows, power door locks, and power mirrors. The only option available on the GL trim is an automatic transmission. Suzuki dealers, however, offer many dealer-installed options, at prices set by the local dealer.

The 1.6-liter, 4-cylinder engine produces a modest 95 horsepower—no match for the class leaders and woefully inadequate if you're hauling more than one or two people. The 5-speed transmission, geared to take best advantage of the engine's limited power, shifts smoothly and cleanly. The Esteem's fuel economy is noteworthy; we averaged 31 mpg in a mix of city, suburban, and highway driving.

Engine noise becomes a problem at highway speeds, as does wind, road, and tire noise.

Although the ride quality is a little coarse, the Esteem's all-independent suspension maintains its poise under most circumstances. The power steering doesn't furnish enough feedback to the driver, but otherwise the car seems fairly responsive. Although the Esteem GLX feels nimble, the larger tires and wheels are reason enough to choose it over the GL.

The cabin is pretty roomy, with a surprising amount of head, hip, and shoulder room, both front and rear. Rear leg room especially surprised us, considering the Esteem's modest exterior dimensions. Suzuki calls the Esteem a five-passenger car, but in truth only two adults can fit comfortably in the rear. Rear-seat passengers will find entry and exit a bit difficult because the rear doors are too narrow. At 12 cubic feet, the sedan's trunk space is better than most in its class. Visibility is quite good in all directions.

The cockpit, while fairly modern, is very generic. A pod in front of the steering wheel houses the analog gauges, while audio and climate controls are in an oval center console. In keeping with typical Japanese practice, most major controls are on steering column stalks.

The Suzuki Esteem offers an appealing value among small economy cars. However, only about 8,000 are sold annually. Buying one will make you a member of a very small club.
D.V.S.

Specifications of Test Vehicle

Model: Esteem GLX

Exterior Dimensions	
Wheelbase	97.6 in.
Overall length	171.2 in.
Overall width	66.5 in.
Overall height	55.9 in.
Curb weight	2,400 lb.
Interior Dimensions	
Seating capacity	5
Head room	F:38.8/R:38 in.
Leg room	F:42.3/R:34.1 in.
Cargo volume	24 cu. ft.
Engine	
Displacement	I-4 1.6 L.
Horsepower	95 @ 6,000 rpm
Torque, lb-ft.	98 @ 3,000 rpm
Performance	
0-60 mph, acceleration	9.8 sec.
60-0 mph, braking	150 ft.
Turning circle	32.2 ft.
EPA city/highway	30/37 mpg
Test mileage	31 mpg
Fuel tank capacity	13.5 gal.

Prices
$12,000
$16,000
GL sedan $12,629
GL 4-door wagon $13,129
GLX sedan $13,729
GLX 4-door wagon $14,229

Warranty (years/miles)
Bumper-to-bumper 3/36,000
Powertrain 3/36,000
Rust-through 3/unlimited

Other to Consider
Hyundai Accent

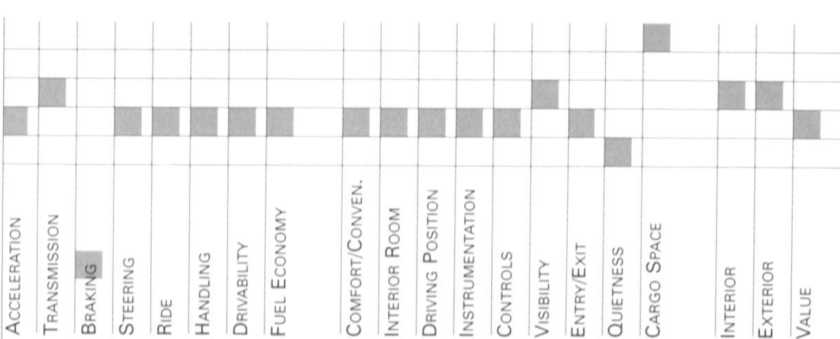

10
9
8
7
6
5
4
3
2
1

Ratings
141

Suzuki

Grand Vitara

new MODEL

New for 99

Redesigned body and interior new V-6 engine

Pros

Driveability
Off-road capability
Cargo space

Cons

Radio controls
Rear door access

Equipment

Major Standard Equipment: 2.0 liter I-4 engine, 5-speed manual transmission, tilt wheel, AM/FM cassette stereo, cloth seats, split folding rear seatbacks, rear wiper/defogger. **JX Adds:** 4-wheel drive. **Grand Vitara Adds:** 2.5 liter V-6 engine, cruise control, air conditioning, power windows, remote mirrors, remote keyless entry, roof rails. **JS+ and JLX + Adds:** antilock brakes. JLX & JLX+ Adds 4-wheel drive. **Major Options:** 4-speed automatic transmission.

Strange name, but a great little suv

Introducing the Suzuki Grand Vitara. It's a substantial little sport utility vehicle that replaces the well-known Sidekick sport. Apparently there was a good reason to change the name. This is a totally new vehicle, part of a strategy to change the image of Suzuki. It's longer, wider, and taller than the Sidekick sport. It has a new chassis, new body, and most important, a new V-6 engine–first and only in the small SUV category. The Grand Vitara is available only as a 4-door, in JS, JS+, JLX, and JLX+. Basically, any model that includes the letter "S" is 2-wheel drive, and "X" is 4-wheel drive. The symbol "+" means antilock brakes are included, and all Grand Vitaras get the new V-6.Unlike the competition, the Vitara uses body-on-frame construction. The rear suspension has been redesigned for a better ride. A 2.0-liter, 4-cylinder engine is available in base 4-door models of Vitara — the 2-door version gets either a 1.6- or 2.0-liter four. The Grand Vitata's 2.5-liter V-6 is a DOHC design, good for 155 hp.

Any engine can connect to one of two new transmissions – a 5-speed manual with short, tight throws, or a 4-speed automatic with significantly smoother shift feel. All 4-wheel drive versions use a lever-actuated transfer case to connect the front wheels. A new pneumatic hub locking system allows shift-on-the-fly operation.

Inside, the Grand Vitara has a whole new personality. Overlapping instrument dials add a nice touch. Vent controls are located up high, with the radio down low. Radio controls are so small they are almost invisible. Seat cushions are a little small, but offer just the right firmness. There's plenty of room up front, but things get cramped in back. Leg room is minimal and the seat is better suited for two adults.

On or off road, the Grand Vitara is tight and quiet. The suspension works well on rough terrain, absorbing most bumps gracefully. Maneuvering in tight spaces is easy. Out on smooth roads, the steering feels light. The high stance allows considerable body roll, but we always felt in control.

The V-6, coupled to the manual transmission, is fun to drive. It revs up willingly, without a lot of noise or vibration. Even the automatic is a good alternative. Shifts are smooth and well-timed.

During our test drive, we were constantly reminded that this is one tough little SUV. And the availability of a 2-speed transfer case makes it possible to go just about anywhere. Good looks, a great powertrain, comfortable interior, and fun to drive should help Suzuki put a sizable dent in the competition. **D.V.S.**

Specifications of Test Vehicle

MODEL: GRAND VITARA JLX+

Exterior Dimensions	
Wheelbase	97.6 in:
Overall length	164.6 In:
Overall width	70.0 In.
Overall height	68.5 In.
Curb weight	3197 lbs.
Interior Dimensions	
Seating capacity	5
Head room	F: 39.9/R: 39.6 in.
Leg room	F: 41.4/R: 35.9 in.
Cargo room	22.5 cu.ft.
Engine	
Displacement	2.5 L V-6
Horsepower	155@6500 rpm
Torque, lb-ft.	160@4000 rpm
Performance	
0-60 mph, acceleration	9.2 sec.
60-0 mph, braking	143 ft.
Turning circle	34.0 ft.
EPA city/highway	19/21 mpg.
Test mileage	NA
Fuel tank capacity	17.4 gal.

Counterpoint

Suzuki has been cultivating the small sport-utility niche for almost two decades. But, lacking (major) resources, a richer and more ambitious competition has harvested the fruits of this crop. This is a quick appraisal of the situation in 1999, a year in which Suzuki aims to reassert itself as leader of the pack, relying on its V-6's off-road abilities to help it climb to the top.The Grand Vitara comes here straight from Japan. While it still looks a lot like its predecessor, the Sidekick Sport, the Grand Vitara wears an entirely remodeled body, with unsealed ribbed paneling that may encourage corrosion over time.Users can wear skirts or kilts when they set out in the Grand Vitara, thanks to the easy-access front bucket seats, an advantage found in most rival models as well. However, they cut into the space of rear-seat passengers, who have to cope with narrow doors and intrusive wheel housing. Another drawback is the relatively small cargo space offered by the Grand Vitara, a disadvantage that competitive models do not share. The Grand Vitara comes with a 2.5-liter V-6 engine.that is powerful, compared to its two best-known rivals, the CRV and the RAV4, but barely any better that the Forester's engine.The Grand Vitara proved very agile on rough roads where its rivals wouldn't dare to tread for fear of leaving their innards behind. However, the Grand Vitara still isn't invincible, with minimal exhaust system protection underneath. And, while the off-road qualities of Suzuki utility vehicles have never been questioned, their abilities on paved roads have. Long outings in their noisy cabs set on wooden suspensions may have once proved real torture for some. However, with the new Grand Vitara this kind of experience is a thing of the past. As proof, now you can have a conversation with fellow occupants without shouting. The smoother suspension is a good compromise between roadholding characteristics and comfort. There's a bit of roll, but nothing to get excited about.

E. L.

PRICES

JS
17,999

JS+
18,999

JLX
18,999

JLX+
19,999

WARRANTY

Bumper-to-bumper
3/36,000

Powertrain
3/36,000

Rust-through
3/Unlimited

OTHER TO CONSIDER

Honda CR-V

Subaru Forester

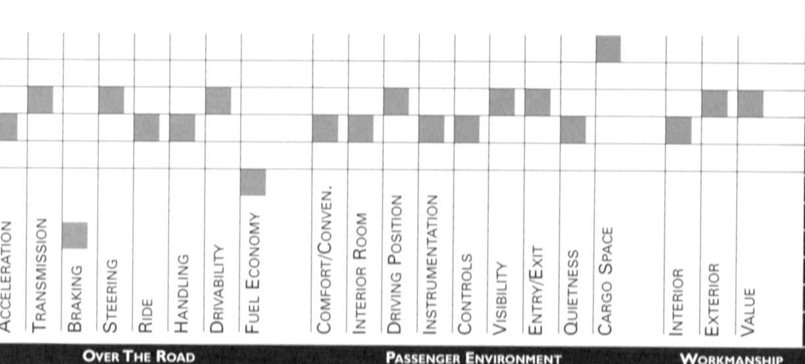

Ratings

144

Suzuki Swift

New for 99

Two new exterior colors

Pros

Fuel consumption
Perfect for city driving
Good manual transmission

Cons

Disappointing price equipment ratio
Automatic transmission with three speeds only
Heavy steering system

Equipment

Major Standard Equipment: 1.3-liter I-4, manual transmission, unassisted steering, intermittent wipers, rear defroster, fold-down rear seat, cargo cover, stainless-steel exhaust system. **Major Options:** 3-speed automatic transmission, 4-wheel antilock brakes.

PRICES
$9,000
$11,000
4-door
$9,479

WARRANTY
(years/miles)
Bumper-to-bumper
3/36,000
Powertrain
3/36,000
Rust-through
3/unlimited

OTHER TO CONSIDER
Chevrolet Metro Coupe
Hyundai Accent Coupe

City slicker

Suzuki bills the Swift as "an ideal vehicle for first-time buyers or for families who need an affordable second car." These are two valid arguments, but given this mini subcompact's equipment price ratio, you'll have to loosen your purse strings if you want a more versatile and more comfortable vehicle. And chances are that your Suzuki dealer will use the very same arguments to steer you toward the Esteem.

Two new colors are available in 1999. Four people can cram into this tiny car, which offers a barely adequate amount of room and marginal comfort. The presentation is nothing particularly exciting and to say the least, instrumentation is modest. Standard equipment isn't extensive, and several accessories that are currently optional could definitely make life easier. Examples? How about three: a curtain to keep baggage hidden from prying eyes, a wiper/washer for the rear windshield, and an automatic trunk release for the hatchback.

Unlike the Metro (Chevrolet), the Swift houses only a 1.3-liter four-cylinder under its hood, a choice that remains very economical when it comes to fuel consumption. Fun to drive in the city, this mini isn't as good out on the highway. Its steering system is imprecise and very light at cruising speeds, and heavy during parking maneuvers. Note also that the three-speed automatic transmission compromises the capabilities of the four-cylinder. Buyers would be well-advised to stay with the standard manual transmission, which gives the engine free rein to show what it can do. All in all, the Swift isn't as attractive as its price would have you believe. **E.L.**

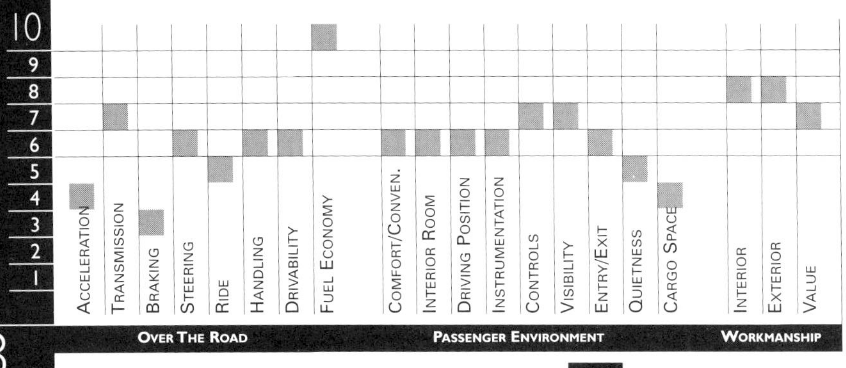

Specifications of Test Vehicle

Model: Swift

Exterior Dimensions	
Wheelbase	93.1 in.
Overall length	149.4 in.
Overall width	62.6 in.
Overall height	54.7 in.
Curb weight	1,900 lb.
Interior Dimensions	
Seating capacity	4
Head room	F:39.1/R:36 in.
Leg room	F:42.5/R:32.2 in.
Cargo volume	8.4 cu. ft.
Engine	
Displacement	I-4 1.3 L.
Horsepower	79 @ 6,000 rpm
Torque, lb-ft.	75 @ 3,000 rpm
Performance	
0-60 mph, acceleration	12.3 sec.
60-0 mph, braking	147 ft.
Turning circle	31.5 ft.
EPA city/highway	39/43 mpg
Test mileage	41 mpg
Fuel tank capacity	10.3 gal.

Ratings 123

Group	Category	Rating
Over The Road	Acceleration	4
	Transmission	7
	Braking	3
	Steering	6
	Ride	5
	Handling	6
	Drivability	6
	Fuel Economy	10
Passenger Environment	Comfort/Conven.	6
	Interior Room	6
	Driving Position	6
	Instrumentation	6
	Controls	7
	Visibility	7
	Entry/Exit	6
	Quietness	5
	Cargo Space	4
Workmanship	Interior	8
	Exterior	8
	Value	7

Toyota

4Runner

New for 99

Design revisions (interior and exterior)
Accessory list revision

Pros

Comfort
Renowned sturdiness
Resale value

Cons

Too bourgeois
Wind noise
Aging chassis

Equipment

Major Standard Equipment: 2.7-liter I-4, manual transmission, AM/FM stereo, intermittent wipers, power rear window. **SR5 adds:** 3.4-liter V-6, 4-wheel antilock brakes, tilt steering column, AM/FM/cassette stereo, rear wiper and washer. **Limited adds:** Air conditioning, larger front brakes, leather upholstery, power seats, AM/FM/CD stereo, power windows, power locks, cruise control, aluminum wheels. **Major Options:** Automatic transmission, part-time 4-wheel drive, locking differential, 4-wheel antilock brakes, larger front brakes, air conditioning, rear heater, rear wiper and washer, power moonroof, tilt steering column, off-road suspension.

A stay-at-home

Like its compatriot and rival, the Pathfinder (Nissan), Toyota's 4Runner is getting more and more "middle class," and that's a real shame. Previous generations were so lively, so much fun, and so much more approachable. Toyota's retort? "But it's consumers who want it to be more sedate, more luxurious, and roomier — as long as it looks rugged." Well, it may look as rough and ready as always, but looks can be deceiving. Unlike the previous generation and contrary to the impression many people are still under, the current generation does not have the same stiff chassis found on the 4Runner's older cousin, the truck (now known as the Tacoma).

You have to step high to get into a 4Runner. But once you've overcome that initial trial, things are cushy: a bright passenger compartment, generously padded bucket and bench seats, careful finishing, a nice dashboard, very detailed instrumentation (but where's the oil pressure gauge?), and controls that are placed mostly within close reach of the driver. In fact, only the tiny radio controls are a hassle, unless you want to include the small air nozzles and rear doors that don't open very wide.

Toyota persists in making two engines available to potential buyers: a 2.7-liter four-cylinder and a 3.4-liter V-6. Need we point out that the second is best suited to this particular vehicle? On hills, however, whether you're accelerating or slowing down, the V-6 is loud enough to drown out any conversation. As speeds increase, you begin to hear the wind whistling as you streak along.

A transfer box lets the driver select rear- or 4-wheel drive. The Limited also has a button to activate the 4x4 system on the fly, so the transfer switch can be put to more use than going from "4H" to "4L". The rack-and-pinion steering system is light and precise, while brakes are efficient.

Toyota has come up with a 4Runner that's less punishing on the road, easier to keep under control, and more comfortable for cockpit occupants.
E.L.

Specifications of Test Vehicle

Model: 4Runner SR5

Exterior Dimensions	
Wheelbase	105.3 in.
Overall length	178.7 in.
Overall width	66.5 in.
Overall height	67.5 in.
Curb weight	3,900 lb.
Interior Dimensions	
Seating capacity	5
Head room	F:39.2/R:38.7 in.
Leg room	F:43.1/R:34.9 in.
Cargo volume	44.6 cu. ft.
Engine	
Displacement	V-6 3.4 L.
Horsepower	183 @ 4,800 rpm
Torque, lb-ft.	217 @ 3,600 rpm
Performance	
0-60 mph, acceleration	9.7 sec.
60-0 mph, braking	139 ft.
Turning circle	37.4 ft.
EPA city/highway	17/20 mpg
Test mileage	18 mpg
Fuel tank capacity	18.5 gal.

Price

$21,000
$36,000

4-door truck wagon $20,558

SR5 4-door truck wagon $25,118

Limited 4-door truck wagon $32,248

Warranty
(years/miles)

Bumper-to-bumper 3/36,000

Powertrain 5/60,000

Rust-through 5/unlimited

Other to Consider

Isuzu Rodeo

Nissan Pathfinder

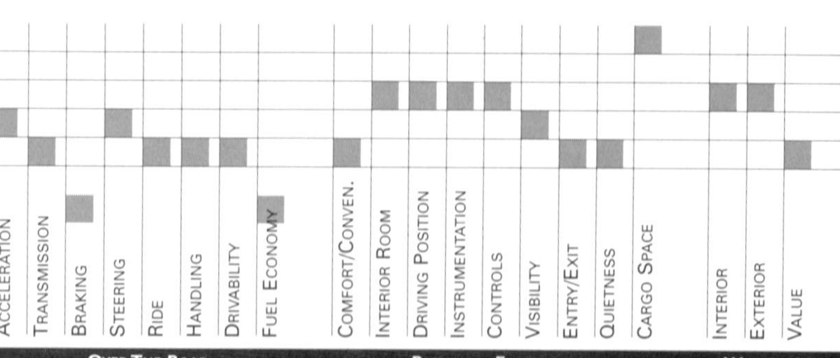

Ratings

Toyota | Avalon

New for 99

Anti-theft engine immobilizer

Strong Pros

Entry/exit
Room/comfort
Quietness

Cons

Controls
Fuel economy
Engine performance

Equipment

Major Standard Equipment: 3-liter V-6, automatic transmission, 4-wheel antilock disc brakes, variable-intermittent wipers, rear defroster, individual front seats, tilt steering column, cruise control, power windows, power locks, AM/FM/cassette stereo, remote-control decklid release. **XLS adds:** Power seats, automatic air conditioning, automatic headlamps, remote keyless entry, theft alarm system, aluminum wheels. **Major Options:** Traction control, power moonroof, front bench seat, power seats, leather upholstery, individual front seats, theft alarm system, AM/FM/CD cassette stereo, aluminum wheels.

PRICES
$24,000
$31,000
XL sedan $24,998
XLS sedan $28,998

WARRANTY
(years/miles)
Bumper-to-bumper 3/36,000
Powertrain 5/60,000
Rust-through 5/unlimited

OTHER TO CONSIDER
Buick Le Sabre
Mercury Grand Marquis

Does size matter ?

The Avalon is the unknown Toyota. In sales and promotion, it's overshadowed by the Camry. But, for many shoppers, the base Avalon could be a better value than an option-loaded Camry.

Built in the U.S., the Avalon is based on the same mechanical components as the Camry, but its wheelbase is about 4 inches longer. It's the first, and still only, car from a Japanese automaker to offer a front bench seat.

Toyota equips the Avalon comfortably. The top-of-the-line XLS offers only a few options. You don't have to get the front bench seat if you don't want it; individual front seats are a no-cost option on the XLS, but not on the XL.

The Avalon's 3-liter V-6 is the same one that's optional in the Camry, but with a bit more power and torque. The engine still needs too many rpms for good acceleration feel. At idle, it runs so smoothly and quietly that you barely hear it. In normal driving, it never rises above a hum. We averaged 22 mpg. In highway passing, the engine responds with reassuring power. The transmission downshifts quickly and engine speed rises immediately to a noisy 4,000 rpm. All shifts are smooth and virtually unnoticeable.

The Avalon's independent suspension soaks up most inconsistencies in the road while the body remains unbothered. The ride tends to be firmer than the soft, floating ride typical of six-passenger American cars. We noticed some body lean in hard cornering, but traction remains good. We also noticed some torque steer during full-throttle acceleration from a standing start.

The Avalon stands tall at the curb, which gives it good head room. The front bench seat can indeed accommodate three, but not comfortably. It does, however, make the interior feel more spacious. If the front middle position is vacant, the seatback can be folded down as an armrest and storage compartment. Leg room also is impressive, especially in the back seat. Getting in and out is quite easy, thanks to large door openings.

The wide, long trunk has a low liftover. With the latest restyling, the opening is less restricted than it was. The wheel wells intrude some into the trunk, and the rear seatback doesn't fold down.

For the driver, visibility is good in all directions. Although most controls are large and easy to reach, the sound system has 19 buttons, and the climate control system has a lot, too—pretty intimidating for a just-plain-folks family car. Don't try to operate them while you're driving.

For some buyers, the Avalon may seem to be too little of a step up from the Camry. Thinking of the Avalon as a low-level Lexus would be closer to the mark. **D.V.S.**

Specifications of Test Vehicle

Model: Avalon XLS

Exterior Dimensions	
Wheelbase	107.1 in.
Overall length	191.9 in.
Overall width	70.5 in.
Overall height	56.7 in.
Curb weight	3,350 lb.

Interior Dimensions	
Seating capacity	6
Head room	F:39.1/R:37.8 in.
Leg room	F:44.1/R:38.3 in.
Cargo volume	15.4 cu. ft.

Engine	
Displacement	V-6, 3 L.
Horsepower	200 @ 5,200 rpm
Torque, lb-ft.	214 @ 4,400 rpm

Performance	
0-60 mph, acceleration	7.9 sec.
60-0 mph, braking	131 ft.
Turning circle	37.6 ft.
EPA city/highway	21/30 mpg
Test mileage	22 mpg
Fuel tank capacity	18.5 gal.

Ratings

161

Group	Category	Rating
Over The Road	Acceleration	9
	Transmission	9
	Braking	5
	Steering	8
	Ride	8
	Handling	8
	Drivability	8
	Fuel Economy	5
Passenger Environment	Comfort/Conven.	9
	Interior Room	9
	Driving Position	8
	Instrumentation	9
	Controls	6
	Visibility	8
	Entry/Exit	10
	Quietness	9
	Cargo Space	7
Workmanship	Interior	10
	Exterior	8
	Value	8

Toyota

Camry

New for 99

Adjustable front headrests
New upholstery
Revised accessory list

Pros

Refined drivetrains
Reliability
Powerful V-6

Cons

Mininal visual appeal
Cramped rear
Mushy tires

Equipment

Major Standard Equipment: 2.2-liter I-4, manual transmission, AM/FM stereo. **LE adds:** 4-wheel antilock brakes, air conditioning, cruise control, power windows, power locks, power mirrors, AM/FM/cassette stereo. **XLE adds:** Heated mirrors, AM/FM/CD stereo, remote keyless entry, power passenger's seat, theft alarm system. **Major Options:** 3-liter V-6, automatic transmission, side air bags, air conditioning, traction control, AM/FM/CD stereo, AM/FM/ CD/cassette stereo, power moonroof, power driver's seat, integrated child safety seat, power windows, power locks, remote keyless entry, power mirrors.

The title holder

Toyota hit a home run two years ago when it came out with an entirely revamped Camry. Roomier and, more importantly, more fun to drive, the current generation sparked a great deal of interest, to the point of grabbing the title of bestselling car in North America from the Taurus (Ford) and Accord (Honda). For 1999, Toyota is giving the model an even bigger edge, among other things by making the CE (four-cylinder V6) more elaborate.

Longer, wider, more aerodynamic, the Camry boasts a passenger compartment with an obviously careful finishing. A small visor overhangs the T-shaped instrument cluster to ward off reflections. That's good, but what about the steering wheel spokes that hide part of the tachometer and the speedometer — in the critical zone (50 to 70 mph)? The center console has been playing musical chairs: now the radio is in the upper portion and the rotary controls for the air conditioning are underneath. Another observation: the parking brake is positioned between the two front seats instead of on the floor. Practical. However, not so handy are the rear seats, which seem to be even more cramped when compared to what the competition offers.

Formerly unexciting and nonchalant, now the Camry offers an exhilarating driving experience. Its revitalized 2.2-liter four-cylinder (standard) has muscle, but it still sings loudly when asked to accelerate strongly. It is coupled with a standard automatic transmission whose best quality is going unnoticed.
My personal preference is the 3.0-liter V-6, which is responsive, powerful, quiet, and refined. This model's major drawback is its braking, which is so unstable it's sure to worry the driver. The ABS system can remedy the situation, but remember that it is no longer available on the four-cylinder CE. Too bad. Lastly, to make the situation a bit worse, tires are of very marginal quality. **E.L.**

Specifications of Test Vehicle

Model: Camry LE

Exterior Dimensions	
Wheelbase	105.2 in.
Overall length	188.5 in.
Overall width	70.1 in.
Overall height	55.4 in.
Curb weight	3,250 lb.
Interior Dimensions	
Seating capacity	5
Head room	F:38.6/R:37.6 in.
Leg room	F:43.5/R:35.5 in.
Cargo volume	14.1 cu. ft.
Engine	
Displacement	V-6 3 L.
Horsepower	194 @ 5,200 rpm
Torque, lb-ft.	209 @ 4,400 rpm
Performance	
0-60 mph, acceleration	8.8 sec.
60-0 mph, braking	129 ft.
Turning circle	35.4 ft.
EPA city/highway	19/27 mpg
Test mileage	20 mpg
Fuel tank capacity	18.5 gal.

Price

$17,000
$32,000

CE sedan
$17,458

LE 4-door Sedan
$20,218

XLE sedan
$23,178

Warranty
(years/miles)

Bumper-to-bumper
3/36,000

Powertrain
5/60,000

Rust-through
5/unlimited

Other to Consider

Honda Accord

Volkswagen Passat

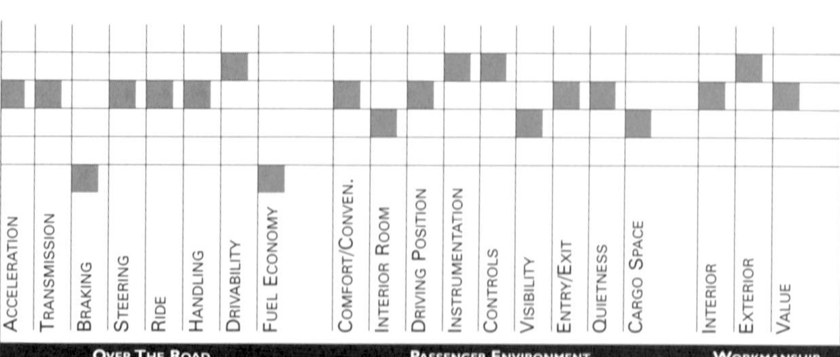

Ratings
155

Toyota

Celica

New for 99

ST discountinued

Pros

Driving position
Engine response
Gear shifting

Cons

Hatch liftover
Entry/exit

Equipment

Major Standard Equipment: 2.2-liter I-4, manual transmission, variable-assist power steering, tilt steering column, rear defroster, remote-control decklid release, power mirrors, AM/FM stereo, 4-wheel antilock disc brakes, AM/FM/ cassette stereo, power windows, power locks. **Major Options:** Automatic transmission, AM/FM/cassette stereo, AM/FM/ CD/cassette stereo, power moonroof, aluminum wheels, fog lamp.

PRICES
$18,000
$28,000
GT Liftback $20,238
GT conv. $24,438

WARRANTY (years/miles)
Bumper-to-bumper 3/36,000
Powertrain 5/60,000
Rust-through 5/unlimited

OTHER TO CONSIDER
Honda Prelude

Assisted suicide?

This time last year, no one knew if Toyota was willing to commute the Celica's death sentence. The current generation, the sixth since the 1970s, isn't a top seller and according to one of the make's executives, it's bound to die a natural death.

But all is not lost since a seventh generation will be lauched in the coming months (prototypes are already on our roads). You don't want to wait? Well, if you can't, note that the current Celica comes only in two bodystyles: hatchback and convertible and one trim level: GT.

Over the years, this coupe has become more and more inoffensive. What a shame the 2.2-liter engine isn't as efficient as it is noisy. With a power level as modest as this, it's hard to make the most of the Celica's very rigid chassis.

The light clutch and short shifting movements of the 5-speed manual transmission add to the driving fun. The manual shift lever is perfectly positioned for easy operation.

Although we would prefer lighter steering for parking lot maneuvers, the Celica's steering is perfectly suited the road: precise and responsive, with the right amount of feedback in cornering. Unlike many other front-wheel-drive cars, the ST doesn't suffer from torque steer when accelerating.

Toyota has aimed for a better ride and increased stability in the Celica, and it shows. Although the ride is still stiff, the suspension absorbs bumps sufficiently. The Celica corners flatly and securely. The GT has a stiffer suspension and corners even more confidently and athletically, but it doesn't ride as comfortably.

Like other sporty cars, the Celica gives front-seat occupants more room and comfort than it gives rear-seat passengers. The comfortable seats have a manual height adjustment that helps you find a good driving position easily. After a difficult crawl into the back seat, adults will find their heads rubbing the roof lining and their knees touching the front seatbacks. In back, there are only two safety belts for the deeply contoured seats. A third would be appreciated for car-pooling children, even though three adults would never consider riding back there. The high liftover to the cargo hatch makes loading and unloading cargo clumsy.

Controls are well marked and easy to operate. The instruments are large and legible, but an oil pressure gauge and voltmeter are missing.

We heard a moderate amount of road noise. Toyota has made the car so quiet in other respects, however, the road noise and transmission whine become more noticeable.

Celicas used to be everywhere, but small coupes like this have fallen out of favor with consumers. If you still count yourself a sporty-coupe fan, the Celica may be your car. **D.V.S. / E.L.**

Specifications of Test Vehicle

Model: Celica GT

Exterior Dimensions	
Wheelbase	99.9 in.
Overall length	174.2 in.
Overall width	68.9 in.
Overall height	50.8 in.
Curb weight	2,755 lb.
Interior Dimensions	
Seating capacity	4
Head room	F:38.5/R:33.2 in.
Leg room	F:43.1/R:29.2 in.
Cargo volume	16.2 cu. ft.
Engine	
Displacement	I-4 2.2 L.
Horsepower	130 @ 5,400 rpm
Torque, lb-ft.	145 @ 4,400 rpm
Performance	
0-60 mph, acceleration	9,7 sec.
60-0 mph, braking	120 ft.
Turning circle	34.2 ft.
EPA city/highway	29/35 mpg
Test mileage	30 mpg
Fuel tank capacity	15.9 gal.

Ratings

Group	Category	Rating (1–10)
Over The Road	Acceleration	6
Over The Road	Transmission	9
Over The Road	Braking	7
Over The Road	Steering	9
Over The Road	Ride	7
Over The Road	Handling	8
Over The Road	Drivability	8
Over The Road	Fuel Economy	7
Passenger Environment	Comfort/Conven.	8
Passenger Environment	Interior Room	3
Passenger Environment	Driving Position	5
Passenger Environment	Instrumentation	8
Passenger Environment	Controls	9
Passenger Environment	Visibility	7
Passenger Environment	Entry/Exit	6
Passenger Environment	Quietness	7
Passenger Environment	Cargo Space	8
Workmanship	Interior	9
Workmanship	Exterior	9
Workmanship	Value	5

Ratings
145

Toyota Corolla

New for 99

3-speed automatic transmission withdrawn
Standard air conditioning on the LE version
New colors

Pros

Proven reliability
Good manufacturing quality
Energetic engine

Cons

Expensive options packages
Minimal driveability
Dull-looking interior

Equipment

Major Standard Equipment: 1.8-liter I-4, manual transmission. **CE adds:** Air conditioning, rear defroster, AM/FM stereo. **LE adds:** Power locks, power mirrors, power windows.
Major Options: 4-speed automatic transmission, 4-wheel antilock brakes, side air bags, integrated child safety seat, tilt steering column, moonroof, aluminum wheels.

1999

AAA **TOP CAR**

Proven value

The revamping of the Corolla product range proves that Toyota has the means to achieve its ambitions. This time out Japan's No. 1 builder came out with an eccentric version to spark new interest in the Old World and then introduced another, more classic livery for Japan and North America, where it wants to build on success. In all, 22 plants assemble one or another of the versions proposed to meet demand more effectively.

Oddly, when Australians took a look at Corolla destined for the North American market they preferred the European version and its bolder design. No wonder! From the rear, the sedan in store for us looks a whole lot like the Chevrolet Malibu. Coincidence or a lack of inspiration? Who knows! What's important is that it has a better drag coefficient than its ancestor and is easier (and less expensive) to assemble and repair. At a glance, yet again the Corolla's passenger compartment seems dull. The instrument panel is boring (no tachometer on the base model) and only the CE and LE versions can escape criticism. Some accessories and controls have been subjected to a round of musical chairs, notably the radio controls, now easier to reach because of a change instigated. Also the Corolla is an inch or so wider, but in this case his wish didn't come true. Given the imperatives of product-line hierarchy, the current Corolla has the same inside measurements and relatively cramped rear seats. On the up side, the trunk lid dips into the bumper to provide easy access and two ingenious pulls make it easy to fold down the rear seat when you're loading it. Kids will love to volunteer for this chore!

Technically speaking, the new Corolla is powered by a 1.8-liter four-cylinder that's been revamped from cylinder head to housing. With more energy and more torque, this engine is surprisingly smooth and amazingly quiet. And this is all the more true in 1999, now that Toyota has very wisely decided to stop using its outdated three-speed automatic transmission that we all viewed as the major culprit for increasing the noise level when the Corolla was out on the highway. The four-speed automatic and five-speed manual are almost perfect. Road stability is consistent, but driveability is marginal despite praiseworthy efforts to improve it. A wider stabilizer bar has had almost no net effect and in our opinion the suspension seems to be even smoother. Soft, lazy, and other similar epithets are usually used to describe the ride you get when driving this model. Poor tire performance also tends to worsen the Corolla's tendency to understeer.

The seventh-generation Corolla doesn't generate any kind of strong emotion and it's the type of car that doesn't need a strong commitment from its driver. Toyota knows we have other things to worry about. **E.L.**

Specifications of Test Vehicle

Model: Corolla LE

Exterior Dimensions	
Wheelbase	97 in.
Overall length	174 in.
Overall width	66.7 in.
Overall height	54.5 in.
Curb weight	2,550 lb.
Interior Dimensions	
Seating capacity	5
Head room	F:39.3/R:36.9 in.
Leg room	F:42.5/R:33.2 in.
Cargo room	12.1 cu. ft.
Engine	
Displacement	I-4 1.8 L.
Horsepower	120 @ 5,600 rpm
Torque, lb-ft.	122 @ 4,400 rpm
Performance	
0-60 mph, acceleration	9.6 sec.
60-0 mph, braking	125 ft.
Turning circle	32.2 ft.
EPA city/highway	28/36 mpg
Test mileage	NA
Fuel tank capacity	13.2 gal.

PRICES
$12,000
$22,000
VE: $12,638
CE: $13,328
LE: $15,288

WARRANTY (years/miles)
Bumper-to-bumper 3/36,000
Powertrain 5/60,000
Rust-through 5/unlimited

OTHER TO CONSIDER
Honda Civic
Mazda Protegé

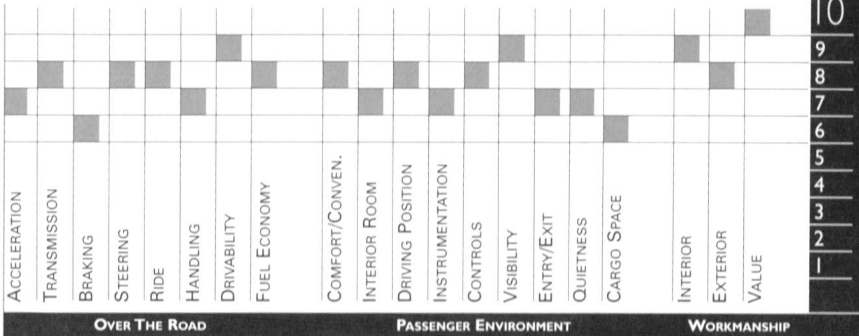

Group	Category	Rating (1–10)
Over The Road	Acceleration	7
	Transmission	8
	Braking	6
	Steering	8
	Ride	8
	Handling	7
	Drivability	9
	Fuel Economy	8
Passenger Environment	Comfort/Conven.	8
	Interior Room	7
	Driving Position	8
	Instrumentation	7
	Controls	8
	Visibility	9
	Entry/Exit	7
	Quietness	7
	Cargo Space	6
Workmanship	Interior	9
	Exterior	8
	Value	10

Ratings 155

Toyota

Land Cruiser

New for 99

Introduced in mid-'98 with New interior, exterior and powertrain.

Pros

Comfort/convenience
Powertrain performance
Fit & finish

Cons

Fuel economy
Rear seats
Handling

Equipment

Major Standard Equipment: 4.7 liter V-8 engine, 4-speed automatic transmission, antilock brakes, 4-wheel drive, heated power front seats, reclining split-folding rear seats, automatic climate control, AM/FM/CD audio system, cruise control, automatic headlights. **Major options:** Rear air conditioning, sunroof, locking rear differential, leather seats, third seat.

PRICES
$46,000
$52,000
Base
$46,898

WARRANTY
Bumper-to-Bumper
3/36,000
Power Train
5/60,000
Rust-through
5/Unlimited

OTHER TO CONSIDER
Chevrolet Tahoe
Ford Expedition

A Toyota with a Lexus heart

The fifth-generation Toyota Land Cruiser was introduced in mid-1998. It's all new from the ground up, but the big news is V-8 power for the first time ever in a Toyota product sold in the U.S. Choosing a Land Cruiser is simple. Toyota offers only one body style and one powertrain. Few options are available.

The engine is 4.7 liters with double overhead cams and variable valve timing – a variation of the very successful Lexus LS400's V-8. It makes 230 horsepower and an even more impressive 320 pound-feet of torque. Power goes to all four wheels by way of a 4-speed automatic transmission and a full-time 4-wheel drive arrangement. The solid front axle has been replaced by a new independent setup, and the front differential lock is no longer available.

Inside, comfort and convenience features abound. Seats are large and comfortable, with plenty of leg and head room in the front and center positions. New analog gauges are easy to read, while the audio and vent controls have been repositioned to be more user-friendly. Door openings have been enlarged but entry/exit still requires a bit of a climb. Getting to the third seat takes more effort than it's worth. After getting there, no one will want to stay for long. Even when folded, it takes up valuable cargo space. Getting items in and out of the rear cargo space requires a difficult reach or an ungraceful climb.

On- or off-road, the new powertrain performs flawlessly. The new V-8 is silky-smooth and quiet, yet feels strong and capable. But, it feels better than it is. Even with the added power, getting the Land Cruiser's 5000+ bulk to 60 mph takes almost 10 seconds. Expect fuel economy to be dismal – in the low teens, at best. The transmission shifts are almost imperceptible under normal driving conditions.

Land Cruiser weight also extracts a penalty when it comes to handling. Hard turns and evasive maneuvers produce considerable body roll and a general feeling of insecurity. However, the ride is soft and almost luxurious. The steering is light and provides adequate road feedback. Off-road, the light steering, good ride, and capable 4-wheel drive system combine for a satisfying experience, even over the roughest terrain.

From the driver's seat, the view of the road ahead and to the side is commanding. However, manuevering in parking lots and tight spaces is complicated by an obstructed view to the rear and a wide turning radius.

If off-roading is important, and if you can afford the price and the frequent feedings, few sport utilities compare to the Land Cruiser in comfort and luxury. **D.V.S.**

Specifications of Test Vehicle

Model: Land Cruiser

Exterior Dimensions	
Wheelbase	112.2 in.
Overall Length	192.5 in.
Overall Width	76.4 in.
Overall Height	73.2 in.
Curb Weight	5115 lbs.
Interior Dimensions	
Seating Capacity	NA
Head Room	F: 40.6/C: 39.8/R:36.8 in.
Leg Room	F: 42.3/C: 34.3/R:27.3 in.
Cargo Room	20.8 cu.ft.
Engine	
Displacement	4.7L V-8
Horsepower	230@4800 rpm
Torque, lb-ft.	320@3400 rpm
Performance	
0-60 mph, acceleration	9.8 sec.
60-0 mph, braking	133 ft.
Turning Circle	39.7 ft.
EPA City/Highway	13/16 mpg.
Test Mileage	13.9
Fuel Tank Capacity	25.4 gal.

Ratings

Over The Road		Passenger Environment		Workmanship	
Acceleration	7	Comfort/Conven.	8	Interior	9
Transmission	9	Interior Room	9	Exterior	9
Braking	5	Driving Position	8	Value	6
Steering	8	Instrumentation	9		
Ride	8	Controls	8		
Handling	6	Visibility	8		
Drivability	8	Entry/Exit	6		
Fuel Economy	2	Quietness	8		
		Cargo Space	9		

150

Toyota

Prius

New for 99
New model

Equipment
Not available

Pros
Economical and environment-friendly
Realistic technology
Several proven mechanical components

Cons
Some fine-tuning still required
Questionable acceleration
How custumers will respond?

The year 2000 is upon us!

Like other builders, Toyota has made environmental issues its top priority. The crucial difference is that Toyota is intent on breaking new ground in this area and, fortunately for consumers who live and drive in northern regions, one project focuses specifically on winter driving conditions.

Toyota has a lot of work to do between now and then. First, the Prius has to meet the legal and commercial requirements of the various markets it will enter. Even more importantly, it must ensure that these same markets are ready for it — after all, this is the car of the future.

The Prius project saw the light of day. After six months, the design team had put down on paper its vision of the vehicle of the future. Senior management took note, but sent the engineers back to the drawing board. Cutting fuel economy by half wasn't enough. The standard was set at 100%. In a heartbeat, all technologies then under development at Toyota went out the window. Were there any other options? Apparently the one and only answer was hybrid technology. Furthermore, it looked like a realistic solution. Compared with a completely electrical car, hybrid technology requires no new infrastructures (charging stations, etc.), nor does it involve any problems related to vehicle range or to winter conditions.

The system developed by Toyota combines a 1.5-liter gasoline engine and an electric engine. The latter is powered by a battery that draws its power from either the gasoline engine, the braking system (which recovers energy while stopping the vehicle), or both.

Here's how it works. The car starts off using the electric engine. The gasoline engine kicks in to assist as you accelerate. During braking, inertia from the wheels activates the electric engine, which then acts as an alternator. The resultant electricity is stored in the battery. And when you stop (in a traffic jam, for example), the gasoline engine turns off automatically.

In contrast to the EV1 from General Motors, whose tapered line forewarns consumers that they are about to be exposed to a different kind of driving experience, the body of the Prius belies the technology that underlies it. "This was precisely our intention.

I can tell you right off, even the Japanese version of the Prius handles like a . . . Corolla. Criticism? Overly sensitive brakes, a soft suspension and undersized tires. But wait to see the American version before making your final judgement. The same applies to the engine. It may be a bit anemic right now but Toyota promises changes in this area as well.

The Prius sells for some 2.5 million yen in Japan, or about US $16,500 (approx.). This is much less than the product actually costs, claims the Japanese press. Toyota is mum on the subject. Although Toyota is not making any profit on this model for the moment, it is making huge strides in increasing its visibility on the market and in wooing "green" consumers and onlookers — two very wise moves. **E.L.**

Specifications of Test Vehicle

Model: Prius

Exterior Dimensions	
Wheelbase	100.4 in.
Overall lenght	168.3 in.
Overall width	66.7 in.
Overall height	58.7 in.
Curb weight	2,728 lb
Interior dimensions	
Seating capacity	5
Head room	na
Leg room	na
Cargo room	na
Engine	
Displacement	1.5L I-4
Horsepower	58 @ 4, 000
Torque, lb-ft	75 @ 4, 000
Performance	
0-60 mph, acceleration	na
60-0 mph, braking	na
Turning circle	na
EPA city/highway	na
Test mileage	66 mpg (Japanese)
Fuel tank capacity	13.2

PRICE
$16,500 (est)

WARRANTY
(years/miles)
Bumper-to-bumper
3/36,000
Powertrain
3/36,000
Rust-through
5/unlimited

OTHER TO CONSIDER
None

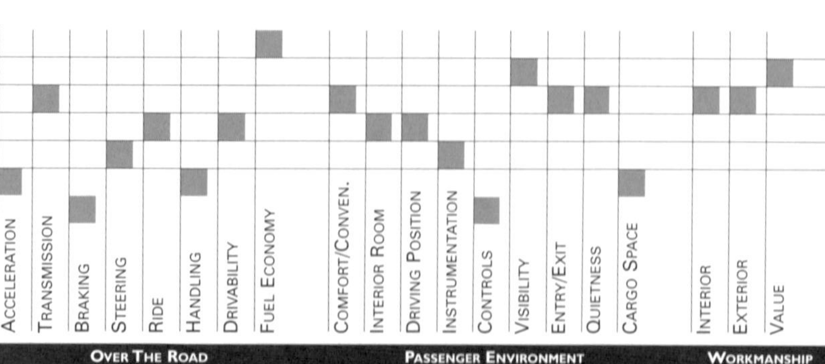

Ratings
139

Toyota RAV4

New for 99

Power
Noise
Sport leather interior
2-door hardtop replace by soft top

Pros

Drivetrain
Cargo room
Utility

Cons

Power
Noise
Ride
Handling

Equipment

Major Standard Equipment: 2-liter I-4, manual transmission, all-wheel drive, center differential lock, intermittent wipers, rear wiper and washer, rear defroster. **Major Options:** Automatic transmission, 4-wheel antilock brakes, limited-slip differential, air conditioning, AM/FM stereo, AM/FM/cassette stereo, cruise control, power windows, power moonroof, power locks, power mirrors, tilt steering column, leather interior, limited slip differential.

Variation on a familiar theme

PRICE
$15,000
$23,000
2-door $15,388
4-door $16,248

WARRANTY (years/miles)
Bumper-to-bumper 3/36,000
Powertrain 3/36,000
Rust-through 5/unlimited

OTHER TO CONSIDER
Honda CR-V
Suzuki Vitara

A pocket-size sport-utility vehicle, the Toyota RAV4 is fun to drive if you can live with its strange handling, choppy ride, and noisy interior.

Toyota created the RAV4 (Recreational Active Vehicle with 4-wheel drive) by raiding various corporate parts bins, combining some passenger car elements with those of a light, off-road vehicle.

As 2- and 4-door wagons with unibody construction and 4-wheel independent suspension, all RAV4s have a wide track, short overhangs, and a high ground clearance for good stability, maneuverability, and utility off-road. Originally intended to compete with the Honda CR-V, Chevrolet Tracker, Suzuki Vitara, and Kia Sportage, the RAV4's high price forces it to compete with larger, more powerful, and more versatile SUVs.

Showing the RAV4's car-like nature, the 2-wheel drive RAV4 has front-wheel drive instead of rear-wheel drive, which is more common on 2WD SUVs. And, unlike most other SUVs, the 4WD RAV4 has permanently engaged all-wheel drive, using the All-Trac system once found on Celicas, Tercels, and Corollas.

The 2-liter, 127-horsepower 4-cylinder engine provides leisurely acceleration and gets noisy when you push it hard. The automatic transmission on our test vehicle worked so well with AWD that a late spring snow presented no traction worries, even under bad conditions.

A simple interior spotlights a well-laid-out, uncluttered instrument panel. The controls are easy to find and operate. High seats give everyone a great view to the front, but the headrests and spare tire block vision to the rear. The RAV4's small, firm seats are fine for short trips, but larger people will find them uncomfortable on longer ones. Although the rear seat is intended for three, two adults will take up the available space.

The RAV4 has more storage space behind its rear seat than any full-size passenger car. Because it's shorter, the 2-door version has less than half of the 4-door's cargo space.

A short wheelbase combined with stiff suspension causes aggravating hops over large bumps. Cornering at any speed produces body roll, almost excessively with a fully loaded vehicle. Toyota wants you to consider the RAV4 car-like. For us, that's asking too much.

The RAV4 is anything but quiet. You hear wind, road, engine, and tire noise at all but the slowest speeds. With little insulation between the roof and the headliner, the RAV4 becomes almost deafening in a rainstorm. To make matters worse, the wind whistles around the luggage rack.

Though well-built, the RAV4 is nothing to rave about. Its price makes a Jeep Cherokee look like a better value. **D.V.S.**

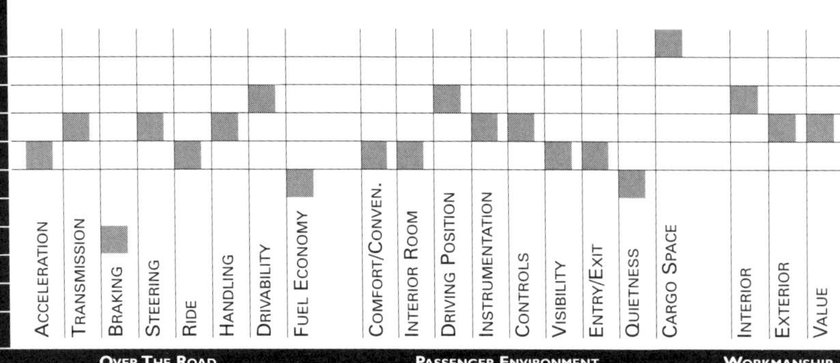

Specifications of Test Vehicle

Model: RAV4

Exterior Dimensions	
Wheelbase	94.9 in.
Overall length	163.8 in.
Overall width	66.7 in.
Overall height	65.4 in.
Curb weight	2,900 lb.
Interior Dimensions	
Seating capacity	5
Head room	F:40.3/R:39 in.
Leg room	F:39.5/R:33.9 in.
Cargo volume	26.8 cu. ft.
Engine	
Displacement	I-4 2 L.
Horsepower	127 @ 5,400 rpm
Torque, lb-ft.	132 @ 4,600 rpm
Performance	
0-60 mph, acceleration	10.5 sec.
60-0 mph, braking	145 ft.
Turning circle	36.1 ft.
EPA city/highway	22/26 mpg
Test mileage	22 mpg
Fuel tank capacity	15.3 gal.

Toyota Sienna

New for 99

3-door version withdrawn
Antitheft system and electric sliding door (XLE)
Standard roof rack on LE models

Pros

Smooth powertrain
Well-balanced chassis
Reliability

Cons

Rattling noises
Dubious ergonomics
Uncomfortable benchseats

Equipment

Major Standard Equipment: 3-liter V-6, automatic transmission, 4-wheel antilock brakes, AM/FM/cassette stereo. **LE adds:** Front and rear air conditioning, rear defroster, cruise control, power windows, power mirrors, power locks, privacy glass. **XLE adds:** Power driver's seat, second-row captain's chairs, heated mirrors, automatic headlights, remote keyless entry, theft alarm system. **Major Options:** Third-row seat, power passenger-side sliding door, front and rear air conditioning, power driver's seat, leather upholstery, power windows, power mirrors, power locks, remote keyless entry, theft alarm system, power moonroof.

Second opinion

With the Sienna, Toyota is legitimately vying for more than a supporting role in the small minivan market segment.Although more conventional and more affordable, this model will never be a superstar. In comparison to the Camry and the Avalon, the production capacity assigned to the Sienna isn't enough to bring it into the lead in its category. And that's a good "excuse" for rectifying some of the drawbacks identified to date.

Doors (four in number) open onto a carefully presented and designed interior. When you take a closer look, however, you'll see that ergonomically the Sienna has given up some ground. First of all, the radio is positioned too low, forcing drivers to take their eyes off the road to tune a station in. Secondly, a mass of levers juts out from the left side of the steering column like so many unwanted weeds. Other flaws include a heavy rear hatch and rear speakers that are too low to allow for good sound circulation. The excessively wide center pillar makes it difficult for passengers in the middle benchseat (or comfortable bucket seats, depending on the choice) to exit the vehicle. Another drawback: rear-seat belts can't be adjusted, and rear seats are usually where children travel. And while the windshield angle is similar (with a two-degree difference) to the angle on a Caravan, it's still hard to gauge exactly where the front ends stops. So be careful when you park. Lastly, manufacturing quality is definitely up to the standards Toyota has accustomed consumers to expect from it. The various models we test drove all presented annoying rattles and other suspicious noises.

The Sienna handles smoothly. Resting on an extended Camry platform, the Sienna even goes so far as to borrow its drivetrain. So under the hood you'll see a 3.0-liter V-6 that's easier to reach and therefore less expensive to maintain. This engine has very reasonable acceleration power, but it tends to run out of breath when solicited repeatedly. The automatic transmission, the only one available, has the best imaginable quality: it shifts gears so smoothly you'll forget it's even there. Although its steering system is slightly imprecise at center, the Sienna still has a turning radius that puts it on the same level as its direct competitors. Carefully calibrated, the suspension keeps roll to a minimum when cornering. The braking system raises no criticism and under normal use, it won't fade. But given total weight when loaded and the inestimable value of its occupants (our children), all minivans should be equipped with four disc brakes, a "luxury" even the LE version fails to offer. Too bad!

A number of small defects hurt the Sienna's overall rating, but its reliability and the value associated with the Toyota name makes it well worth considering. **E.L.**

Specifications of Test Vehicle

Model: Sienna LE

Exterior Dimensions	
Wheelbase	114.2 in.
Overall length	193.5 in.
Overall width	73.4 in.
Overall height	67.3 in.
Curb weight	3,900 lb.
Interior Dimensions	
Seating capacity	7
Head room	F:40.6/R1:39.9/R2:37.7 in.
Leg room	F:41.9/R1:36.6/R2:34 in.
Cargo room	18 cu. ft.
Engine	
Displacement	V-6 3 L.
Horsepower	194 @ 5,200 rpm
Torque, lb-ft.	209 @ 4,400 rpm
Performance	
0-60 mph, acceleration	10.2 sec.
60-0 mph, braking	139 ft.
Turning circle	40 ft.
EPA city/highway	18/24 mpg
Test mileage	NA
Fuel tank capacity	21 gal.

Prices

$21,000
$40,000

CE $21,140
LE $23,500
XLE $27,100

Warranty

(years/miles)

Bumper-to-bumper 3/36,000
Powertrain 5/60,000
Rust-through 5/unlimited

Other to Consider

Dodge Grand Caravan
Ford Windstar

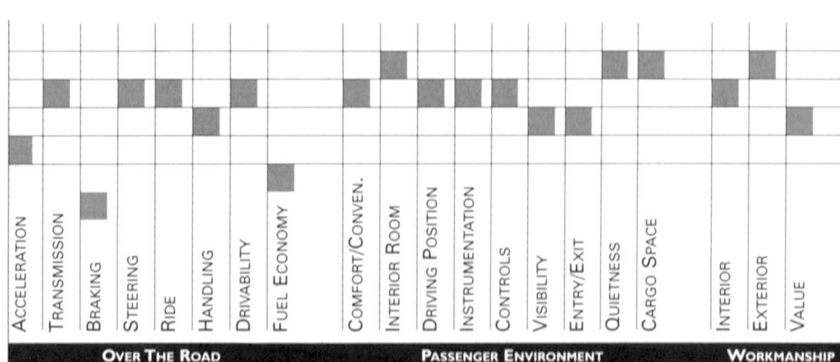

Ratings

151

TOYOTA Solara

new MODEL

New for 99

New model

Pros

Proven reliability
Roomy interior
Efficient engines

Cons

Unexciting lines
Seat belts not fully adjustable
Lack of attention to detail

Equipment

SE: 2,2 I-4, manual transmission, tilt steering. **SLE adds:** 3,0 L V6, AM/FM stereo/ cassette/ CD, antilock braking system, anti-theft system, keyless entry. **Major options:** 3,0 L V6, automatic transmission, moonroof, traction control, side-impact airbags, power driver's seat, leather ulphostery

WARRANTY (years/miles)

Bumper-to-bumper 3/36,000

Powertrain 5/60,000

Rust-through 5/unlimited

OTHER TO CONSIDER

Acura CL

Honda Accord Coupe

Timid

Yuichiro Obu, the head engineer for the Camry Solara project, admits that as we approach the new millennium, launching a sport coupe is a major challenge. And as a matter of fact, many automotive industry analysts are quick to point out that it is very unlikely that baby boomers will tire of utility vehicles any time soon, so they won't be flocking in to buy coupes.

Elegant, no doubt, but somewhat unexciting at the same time, the Camry Solara's rear-end design reminds onlookers of the Lexus SC coupe. Long doors open onto an interior that exudes quality at first glance, and a closer look reveals a finishing obviously based on attention to detail, all too rare on today's market. However, the same attention wasn't brought to other areas of the Camry Solara. Front seats are not fully adjustable, rear windows don't open, the steering wheel hides some instruments on the dashboard and some controls are hard to decipher, those used to adjust the side-view mirrors, for example. Other points of contention — and they are numerous — include a glove box that bangs your knees when you open it, the fact that the passenger seat in the front has no pullrod to let the driver move it forward without moving from the driver's seat should someone need access to the vehicle's rear (more elaborate versions feature a mechanism that slides the seat forward), assist grips that are positioned too low to be truly useful, and the fact that there is no way to heat the optional leather seats in the front. That's a long list of faults, true, but keep in mind that most of this car's rivals have just as many.

There's no need to go into detail on the technical aspects of this coupe, which shares the Camry's platform and with few exceptions, most of the same mechanical features as well. When you think of it, there are a lot of similarities in the approach taken by Honda and Toyota when they developed their respective coupe models. The 2.2-liter four-cylinder is surprisingly smooth, quiet (except when accelerating) and moderate at the gas tank. Another observation: at cruising speed (60 mph), the four-cylinder turns at exactly the same speed as the V6, specifically 2,200 rpm.

As surprising as it may seem, when it comes to smoothness and performance the four-cylinder can't compete with the V-6, but I've seen more energetic 200-hp units than those generated by this engine. Automatic or manual? Both are remarkably smooth, but keep in mind that the manual transmission shaves off only a few tenths of a second from the acceleration time recorded with the automatic.

The Camry Solara's temperament depends on the version you choose. The base version, with 15-inch tires, tends to understeer, loses some traction when cornering and is less stable when braking (disc/drum combination) than more elaborate versions. True, the latter do have bigger tires (16 inches) and four disc brakes, which eliminates the unsteadiness felt in the base model's steering system while also minimizing understeering and ensuring shorter stopping distances (with the standard anti-lock system in this instance). **E.L.**

Specifications of Test Vehicle

Model: Camry Solara

Exterior Dimensions	
Wheelbase	105.1 in.
Overall lenght	190 in.
Overall widht	71.1 in.
Overall height	55.1 in.
Curb weight	3120 lb
Interior dimensions	
Seating capacity	4
Head room	F:38.3/R: 36.3 in.
Leg room	F:43.3/R: 35.2
Cargo room	14.1 cu. ft.
Engine	
Displacement	I-4 2,2 L.
Horsepower	135 @ 5,200
Torque, lb-ft	147 @ 4,400
Performance	
0-60 mph, acceleration	NA
60-0 mph, braking	NA
Turning circle	38.1 ft
EPA city/highway	NA
Test mileage	NA
Fuel tank capacity	18.5

Ratings 150

Category	Rating
Over The Road	
Acceleration	8
Transmission	8
Braking	5
Steering	8
Ride	8
Handling	8
Drivability	9
Fuel Economy	6
Passenger Environment	
Comfort/Conven.	7
Interior Room	7
Driving Position	8
Instrumentation	8
Controls	8
Visibility	6
Entry/Exit	6
Quietness	8
Cargo Space	7
Workmanship	
Interior	8
Exterior	10
Value	9

Toyota

Tacoma

New for 99

Front seatbelt pretensioners
New colors

Pros

Engine performance
Fit and finish

Cons

Safety features
Standard features
Entry/exit height (4WD)
Noise

Equipment

Major Standard Equipment: 2.4-liter I-4, manual transmission, unassisted steering, bench seat, vinyl upholstery. Limited adds: Power steering, sliding rear window, individual front seats, cloth upholstery, cruise control, tilt steering column, power locks, power windows, AM/FM/cassette stereo, larger tires. **Prerunner adds:** 3.4-liter V-6. **Major Options:** 3.4-liter V-6, automatic transmission, power steering, part-time 4-wheel drive, shift-on-fly 4WD, 4-wheel antilock brakes, air conditioning, power windows, cruise control, sliding rear window, AM/FM/cassette stereo, moonroof, off-road suspension.

Price factor

When you add up the cost of options, the Toyota Tacoma becomes a pretty pricey pickup.

Although it looks contemporary on the outside, the Tacoma has the most traditional, truck-like cabin among compact pickups, including its chief competitors, the Ford Ranger and the Chevrolet S-10/GMC Sonoma. It doesn't offer the long-bed/short-bed choice of small domestic pickups.

In safety features, the Tacoma has a passenger-side air bag, available 4-wheel antilock brakes, and adjustable shoulder belts, making it fully competitive with other pickups. In fact, the Tacoma has more safety features than Toyota's more mature T100. In other respects, the Tacoma lags behind the small-truck leaders, Ford and General Motors. Where the Ranger and the S-10 feature in-dash switching between 2- and 4-wheel drive, the Tacoma still has a second shift lever on the floor. (You can get a One-Touch Hi-4 button on the shift lever for easier 4WD engagement.) Only the top-of-the-line Limited 4WD has a trip odometer! Options easily can double the cost of a Tacoma.

The optional 3.4-liter V-6 and automatic transmission offer a good combination of power and economy. We averaged nearly 19 mpg, a reasonable return for such a package. There's always ample power for passing on two-lane highways. The wheels spin easily when you try to accelerate too fast with an empty pickup box.

The Tacoma's variable-assist power steering makes maneuvering at highway speeds easy, and parking isn't difficult. Off the pavement, it negotiates rugged terrain and narrow trails in the woods with equal aplomb. The ride is definitely bouncy on the highway, but well-damped for off-highway excursions.

The Tacoma's cabin has that spartan, utilitarian feel of pickups from the 1970s, despite lots of optional features and power accessories. There's plenty of room in front, but the rear bench seat in the Xtracab is another story. Because it faces front (rather than side to side, as in most traditional extended-cabs), leg room is limited.

It's difficult to hoist yourself into the cab, let alone into the rear, because of the Tacoma's height. The 4WD and off-road suspension make the truck 6 inches higher. Noise from the road and the drivetrain is bothersome inside at highway speeds. Toyota's workmanship is superb, as expected.

While Toyota rides on its reputation, the Tacoma is left trying to follow the ruts left by Ford and Chevy. **D.V.S.**

Specifications of Test Vehicle

Model: Tacoma

Exterior Dimensions	
Wheelbase	121.9 in.
Overall length	203.1 in.
Overall width	66.5 in.
Overall height	66.9 in.
Curb weight	3,400 lb.
Interior Dimensions	
Seating capacity	5
Head room	F:38.4/R:35.5 in.
Leg room	F:42.8/R:27.2 in.
Payload capacity	1,650 lb.
Engine	
Displacement	V-6 3.4 L.
Horsepower	190 @ 4,800 rpm
Torque, lb-ft.	220 @ 3,600 rpm
Performance	
0-60 mph, acceleration	8.9 sec
60-0 mph, braking	130 ft.
Turning circle	40 ft.
EPA city/highway	16/19 mpg
Test mileage	18 mpg
Fuel tank capacity	18 gal.

Price

$13,000
$27,000

Standard cab, short bed $12,538
Extended cab, short bed $14,708
Limited extended cab, short bed $16,048

Warranty

(years/miles)

Bumper-to-bumper 3/36,000

Powertrain 5/60,000

Rust-through 5/unlimited

Other to Consider

Chevrolet S-10

Ford Ranger

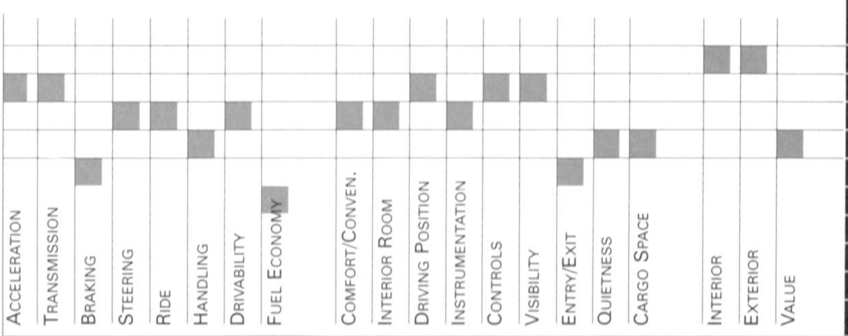

Ratings
138

Volkswagen

Eurovan

new
MODEL

NEW FOR 99

V-6 for all versions
Longer list of accessories

PROS

Superb handling
Superior V-6
Versatility

CONS

Utilitarian styling
Austere interior
Price

EQUIPMENT

Major Standard Equipment:
GLS: Automatic transmission, air conditioning, AM/FM/cassette, anti-lock braking system, cruise control, power lock, rear defroster, rear window/wiper washer, speed control, telecopic steering wheel.
MV adds: snap-on curtains for side windows. **Major options:** AM/FM/CD player, heated front seats, leather interior, metallic paint, sunroof.

Distinct and proud of it!

PRICES

GLS
$29,900

MV
$31,400

WARRANTY

Bumper-to-Bumper
2/24,000

Power Train
10/100,000

Rust-through
12/Unlimited

OTHER TO CONSIDER

Chevrolet Astro

GMC Safari

The Eurovan is the latest descendant of the famous VW minibus of the 1960s. Like many of its buyers, it has matured and changed considerably over the years, but it still wants to be different. Its power now comes from the fabulous VR6 and its body comes in a multitude of configurations that can turn it into a minivan for seven, a lean and mean utility vehicle or a cute camping van, the most popular (and most expensive) alternative in the lineup.

German by nature, the Eurovan has a sober but functional design, obvious in everything from the instrument panel to the rear door design. There's nothing frivolous to be found; instead, expect the calculated usability of a craftsman's workshop and the feeling of durable sturdiness. Each part is designed and installed to withstand decades of use.

For 1999, the list of accessories is considerably longer, meaning that if you want to spend extra money, your only choices are basically heated bucket seats, a sliding roof and metallic paint.

The amount of space in the passenger compartment says a lot. Its 1,900 cubic feet provide plenty of room for elbows, heads and bulky baggage. The Transporter version even has a steel partition separating the front of the vehicle from the rest of it and a large double door in the rear. The camper van is fitted out at Winnebago's U.S. plant (which took over from Westphalia on the North American market) and it provides the model's sliding roof and other accessories as well.

In the end, the Eurovan isn't all that different from its predecessors. It still doesn't like crosswinds and despite its more powerful engine, at best, performance levels are acceptable. But they're still much better than what the diesel engine used to offer: acceleration times that could be measured using a calendar! With better soundproofing, the Eurovan is pleasant to drive. Its well-calibrated suspension, precise steering system and short turning radius are assets drivers will appreciate as the miles fly by. In short, if integrity and durability easily come before power and cargo capacity on your list of priorities, it could well be that one or another of the Eurovan metamorphoses will meet your needs.

Like the hippies of the '60s, the Eurovan is an eccentric in the minivan clan. It does show some strokes of genius, but it has major drawbacks at the same time. **E.L.**

SPECIFICATIONS OF TEST VEHICLE

MODEL: EUROVAN MV

Exterior Dimensions	
Wheelbase	115 in.
Overall lenght	188.5 in.
Overall width	72.4 in
Overall height	76.4 in.
Curb weight	4220 lb.
Interior dimensions	
Seating capacity	7
Head room	F:39.3/R:43.1 in.
Leg room	F:37.8/R:28.3 in.
Cargo room	21.7 cu. ft.
Engine	
Displacement	V-6, 2,8 L.
Horsepower	140 @ 4,500
Torque, lb-ft	177 @ 3,000
Performance	
0-60 mph, acceleration:	12.9 sec.
60-0 mph, braking:	na
Turning circle	38.4 ft
EPA city/highway	15/20
Test mileage	17.1
Fuel tank capacity	21.1 ga.

Ratings

Over The Road		Passenger Environment		Workmanship	
Acceleration	4	Comfort/Conven.	6	Interior	8
Transmission	7	Interior Room	10	Exterior	8
Braking	6	Driving Position	4	Value	5
Steering	7	Instrumentation	6		
Ride	7	Controls	6		
Handling	7	Visibility	8		
Drivability	7	Entry/Exit	8		
Fuel Economy	3	Quietness	6		
		Cargo Space	10		

Ratings
133

Volkswagen

Golf

New for 99

Totally redesigned exterior
Interior
Suspension and powertrain.

Pros

Acceleration
Handling
Safety features
Driving fun

Cons

Rear seat comfort
Interior room

Equipment

Major Standard Equipment:
GL: 2.0L. I-4 engine, 5-speed manual transmission, traction control, antilock brakes, air conditioning, remote side mirrors, remote locking system,AM/FM/ cassette audio system, adjustable height and angle seats, split folding rear seat, cloth seats **GLS Adds:** Power windows, heated power side mirrors, cruise control, upgraded audio system, center arm rest, velour seats. **GLX Adds:** 2.8L. V-6 engine, sunroof, alloy wheels, rain sensor. **GTI Adds:** 16" tires, automatic climate control, trip computer, heated leather sport seats with adjustable lumbar support. **Major Options:** Automatic transmission, leather upholstery, CD changer.

A new image

The fourth-generation Volkswagen Golf is completely redesigned and has grown slightly for '99, but it retains the classic hatchback design of its predecessors. A refined suspension and powertrain are complimented with a full array of safety features.

Choosing a new Golf is a bit of a challenge, because it comes in confusing array of models, body styles and trim levels. The basic Golf is available as a 2-door GL or 4-door GLS. Both are powered by a 2.0-liter SOHC 4-cylinder engine, good for 115 horsepower. Later in the '99 model year, the clean, fun-to-drive, and remarkably frugal TDI diesel will also be available. The sporty GTI comes only as a 2-door. The GTI GLS uses the same 4-cylinder engine as the Golf, but the GTI GLX is powered by a 174-horsepower VR-6. Mated to both the VR-6 and 2.0-liter engines is a standard 5-speed manual with a hydraulic clutch. The 2.0-liter can be ordered with an optional 4-speed automatic transmission. Traction control and antilock brakes are standard on all models.

Even the entry-level Golf GL is well-equipped, with standard features such as air conditioning, side airbags, antilock brakes, remote locking and a premium audio system. The GLS adds a few comfort and convenience features, while the GTI GLX is loaded with extras like automatic climate control and rain-sensing wipers, and a premium interior.

Inside, both the Golf and GTI feature a completely redesigned high-quality environment. Full instrumentation uses two large, easy-to-read dials that are backlit with a distinctive glowing blue. Bright red needles stand out from the background. All plastic surfaces have a soft touch.

As in all VWs, the seats are well bolstered and firm for comfort during long drives. Finding the right driving position is made easier with the pump action height adjustment, as well as the tile & telescoping steering wheel. Up front there is plenty of head, shoulder and leg room. Integrated into the front seats is an "easy entry" mechanism to allow the seat to move forward and up for easier access to the rear seating area. Even so, getting in and out of the rear seat still requires some bending and twisting. Once there, space is limited—don't even think of traveling far with more than two small adults in the rear. Cargo space is hugh, compared with most other compacts, and it can be made even bigger by folding down the rear seat back.

On the road is where the GTI shines. The VR6 is a total blast to drive. It gets to 60 mph in an effortless 7 seconds, and has the steering and handling capability to match. Working through the gears on twisty, hilly terrain demonstrates why driving enthusiasts really like this car.

The new GTI is a fine example of how VW has changed its image. This loveable little car might not suit everyone, but it's a solid performer. Its no-nonsense ability to deliver on performance and fun is sure to attract more than a few serious drivers. **D.V.S.**

Specifications of Test Vehicle

Model: Golf GTI

Exterior Dimensions	
Wheelbase	98.9 in.
Overall Length	163.3 In.
Overall Width	68.3 In.
Overall Height	56.7 In.
Curb Weight	2980 lbs.
Interior Dimensions	
Seating Capacity	
Head Room	F: 37.1/R: 36.5 in.
Leg Room	F: 41.3/R: 33.3 in.
Cargo Room	18 cu.ft.
Engine	
Displacement	2.8L VR-6
Horsepower	174@5800rpm
Torque, lb-ft.	181@3200 rpm
Performance	
0-60 mph, acceleration	7.0 sec.
60-0 mph, braking	120 ft.
Turning Circle	35.1 ft.
EPA City/Highway	20/28 mpg.
Test Mileage	NA
Fuel Tank Capacity	14.5 gal.

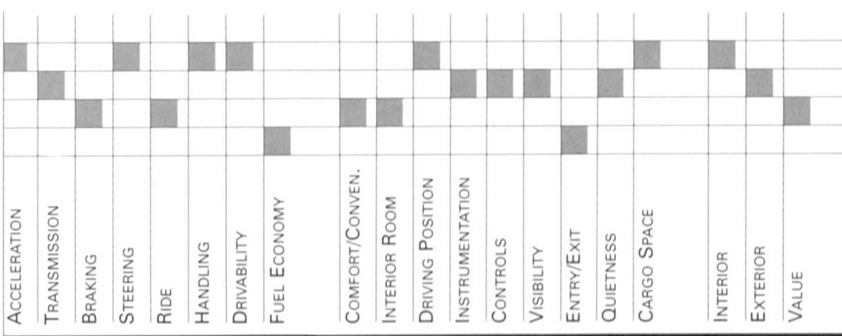

10
9
8
7
6
5
4
3
2
1

Ratings
155

PRICES
$15,500
$24,000

Golf GL
$15,425

Golf GL 2-door TDI
$16,720

Golf GLS 4-door
$16,575

Golf GLS 4-door TDI
$17,925

GTI 2.0L 2-door
$18,025

GTI VR6 2-door
$22,675

WARRANTY

Bumper-to-Bumper
2/24,000

Power Train
10/100,000

Rust-through
12/Unlimited

OTHER TO CONSIDER

Acura Integra Type R

Subaru 2.5RS

Volkswagen Jetta

New for 99

Completely redesigned exterior, interior, suspension and powertrain.

Pros

Steering
Handling
Engine performance
Safety features

Cons

Rear headroom
Rear entry/exit

Equipment

Major Standard Equipment:
GL: 2.0 I-4 engine, 5-speed manual transmission, traction control, antilock brakes, air conditioning, remote side mirrors, remote locking system, AM/FM/ cassette audio system, adjustable height and angle seats, split folding rear seat, cloth seats. **GLS Adds:** Power windows, heated power side mirrors, cruise control, upgraded audio system, center arm rest, velour seats. **GLX Adds:** V-6 engine, sunroof, alloy wheels, automatic climate control, trip computer, heated power seats with adjustable lumbar support, rain sensor.
Major Options: Automatic transmission, leather upholstery, CD changer, sport seats.

PRICES

$17,500
$25,000

Jetta GL 4-door
$17,225

Jetta GL 4-door TDI
$18,520

Jetta GLS 4-door
$18,205

Jetta GLS TDI
$19,225

Jetta GLS VR6
$20,475

Jetta GLX
$24,025

WARRANTY

Bumper-to-Bumper
2/24,000

Power Train
10/100,000

Rust-through
12/Unlimited

OTHER TO CONSIDER

Nissan Altima

Ford Contour

"Wunderbar"

Last year it was the stylish new Passat, then the new Beetle, and now the Volkswagen lineup is totally up to date with an all new Jetta. Even with its new headlights, the Jetta is still instantly recognizable from the front. However, from the rear, it looks like a scaled-down Passat.

The 4-door Jetta comes in three trim levels, the GL, GLS and top-of-the-line GLX. Even the entry-level GL is well-equipped, with standard features such as air conditioning, side airbags, antilock brakes, tilt/telescope wheel, remote locking and a premium audio system. The GLS adds a few comfort and convenience features, while the GLX is loaded with extras like automatic climate control and rain-sensing wipers.

The base engine in the GL and GLS is a refined version of VW's 2.0-liter four, capable of 155 horsepower. Optional on the GLS and standard for the GLX is an upgraded 174-horsepower VR-6. The standard transmission is a 5-speed manual– a 4-speed automatic is optional. Traction control and antilock brakes are also standard equipment.

Inside, the Jetta doesn't feel like a compact sedan. Up front there is plenty of head, shoulder and leg room. The interior is finished with a nicely chosen combination of matching fabrics and quality trim materials. All plastic surfaces have a soft touch that makes them feel–well, almost luxurious. The instrument cluster houses four circular dials, with illuminated red needles and bright blue backlighting.

Front seats are firm and well bolstered for support. A unique handle beside each seat adjust height. Bottom seat cushions are on the short side and will not please larger occupants. A tilt/telescope steering wheel allows a precise driving position. Even though all seating positions in the rear have head restraints and full 3-point belts, conditions back there are somewhat cramped. Knee room is barely adequate for adults, and the sunroof uses up valuable head room. Two adults use up most of the space, but three children can travel comfortably there. Entry and exit for the rear is less than easy or graceful. A small door opening and a high step-over make entry and exit to the rear less than easy or graceful. The just-average trunk space can be increased with the split folding rear seat back.

The Jetta is a driver's car. Ride and handling are nicely balanced–the ride just on the firm side and handling that can satisfy most enthusiasts. Steering is light and accurate. The 4-cylinder engine is fine around town, but runs out of breath in hill country or trying to merge at full speed. However, the VR-6 seems to do everything well. Matched to a 5-speed manual transmission, we recorded sprints to 60 mph in just over 7 seconds. The 4-wheel disk brakes performed well and stopped the Jetta from 60 mph in a better-than-average 122 feet.

Jetta is a solid performer, a car with good styling, great driveability and a full compliment of safety features. VW seems to be on a roll–no wonder, with cars like the Jetta. **D.V.S.**

Specifications of Test Vehicle

Model: Jetta GLX

Exterior Dimensions	
Wheelbase	98.9 in.
Overall Length	172.3 In.
Overall Width	68.3 In.
Overall Height	56.9 In.
Curb Weight	3019 lbs.
Interior Dimensions	
Seating Capacity	5
Head Room	F: 37.9/R: 36.5 in.
Leg Room	F: 41.3/R: 33.3 in.
Cargo Room	13.2 cu.ft.
Engine	
Displacement	2.8 V-6
Horsepower	174@5800 rpm
Torque, lb-Full-Time.	181@3200 rpm
Performance	
0-60 mph, acceleration	7.2 sec.
60-0 mph, braking	122 ft.
Turning Circle	35.8 ft.
EPA City/Highway	19/28 mpg.
Test Mileage	NA
Fuel Tank Capacity	14.5 gal.

Group	Category	Rating
Over The Road	Acceleration	9
	Transmission	8
	Braking	6
	Steering	9
	Ride	8
	Handling	9
	Drivability	9
	Fuel Economy	6
Passenger Environment	Comfort/Conven.	8
	Interior Room	7
	Driving Position	9
	Instrumentation	8
	Controls	8
	Visibility	8
	Entry/Exit	6
	Quietness	7
	Cargo Space	6
Workmanship	Interior	8
	Exterior	8
	Value	8

Ratings
155

Volkswagen Passat

New for 99
V-6 engine
Wagon

Pros
Roomy interior and trunk
Excellent handling
Choice of powertrains

Cons
Small right-hand side-view mirror
Unproven reliability
Disappointing semi-automatic transmission

Equipment

Major Standard Equipment: 1.8-liter I-4, manual transmission, traction control, 4-wheel antilock brakes, side air bags, air conditioning, theft alarm, cruise control, trip computer, AM/FM/cassette stereo, rear defogger, power windows, central locking system, fully adjustable front seats, split-folding rear seat, tilt and telescope wheel. **GLS V-6 adds:** 2.8-Liter V-6, traction control. **Major Options:** 5-speed semi-automatic transmission, all-wheel drive, sunroof, leather upholstery, heated seats.

A Volkswagen by Audi?

Where did Ferdinand Piech intend to take Volkswagen? A glance at the specs shows just how closely the Passat is based on the Audi, Piech's former employer. Not only does the Passat use the Audi's platform, it adopts the latter's entire suspension, 1.8 supercharged engine, and semiautomatic transmission as well. While it doesn't feature the Audi's Quattro system, it does offer its own all-wheel drive (Synchro) mechanism, its standard V-6 engine, and a wagon version.

At first glance you may wonder: is this an A4 Audi or a Passat? The question comes as a shock and the German builder is doing all it can to bring even the most vehement critics on side. "The rounded roof and puffed out fenders evoke the Beetle," it claims. Maybe. But whatever the source of its inspiration, one factor is particularly worthy of note—the Passat's aerodynamics, a remarkable Cd of 0.27 on the European model. Again, the interior looks like an Audi's interior. While the quality of materials is certainly a notch below what you'll find on the A4 and while its appearance is a bit austere by contrast, the Passat outclasses the A4 — at least in terms of passenger and cargo space.

In short, the ambience on board a Passat is a bit chilly, but it does create a strong impression. You come away noticing the quality of its finishing, its roomy interior, and what appears to be an almost unlimited number of accessories. One minor flaw: a small right-hand side-view mirror (Audi solved the same problem on its A4 this year), making certain maneuvers a challenge.

Driving enthusiasts, get ready. Consistent and reassuring, the Passat accelerates, corners, and brakes better than any of its rivals. However, these qualities are not as remarkable in the semiautomatic version. It's tough for this transmission to select the right shifting alternative from the 244 possibilities available to it. In turn, this results in dead air time during acceleration or pickup.

Would you be surprised if I told you the Passat rides like the A4 Turbo? The only difference is that when we test drove it, the Passat seemed slightly more stable in the fast lane. Like the A4, the Passat sits on a slightly soft suspension that has a negative effect on braking (drivers have to pump brakes) and when cornering (noticeable sway). A precise and responsive steering system and a tight turning radius make this vehicle more agile than its size would suggest. As a bonus, its tough and sturdy disc brakes are powerful and resistant.

The Passat is far and away the best-equipped and safest model in its category — and the most expensive as well. Also keep in mind that the Passat runs solely on super fuel and comes with a fairly stingy warranty. A small consolation: maintenance is free during the warranty period. Why exactly choose it? Let's just say that the Passat has a lot of sins that need forgiving.
E.L.

Specifications of Test Vehicle

Model: Passat GLS

Exterior Dimensions	
Wheelbase	106.4 in.
Overall length	184.1 in.
Overall width	68.5 in.
Overall height	57.4 in.
Curb weight	3,250 lb.
Interior Dimensions	
Seating capacity	5
Head room	F:39.7/R:37.8 in.
Leg room	F:41.5/R:35.3 in.
Cargo room	15 cu. ft.
Engine	
Displacement	I-4 1.8 L.
Horsepower	150 @ 5,700 rpm
Torque, lb-ft.	155 @ 4,600 rpm
Performance	
0-60 mph, acceleration	8.2 sec.
60-0 mph, braking	120 ft.
Turning circle	37.4 ft.
EPA city/highway	21/31 mpg
Test mileage	NA
Fuel tank capacity	18.5 gal.

Prices
$21,000
$26,000
GLS 4-door sedan
$21,700

Warranty
(years/miles)

Bumper-to-bumper
2/24,000

Powertrain
10/100,000

Rust-through
11/unlimited

Other to Consider
Honda Accord
Toyota Camry

Group	Category	Rating
Over The Road	Acceleration	8
	Transmission	9
	Braking	7
	Steering	9
	Ride	7
	Handling	9
	Drivability	9
	Fuel Economy	6
Passenger Environment	Comfort/Conven.	8
	Interior Room	7
	Driving Position	8
	Instrumentation	8
	Controls	8
	Visibility	8
	Entry/Exit	8
	Quietness	9
	Cargo Space	7
Workmanship	Interior	9
	Exterior	9
	Value	8

Ratings
161

Volkswagen New Beetle

new MODEL

New for 99

Totally new car, derived from the new Golf platform.

Pros

Appearance
Ride/handling
Driving fun

Cons

Rear seat room
Braking distance

Equipment

Major Standard Equipment: 2.0 liter 4-cylinder engine, 5-speed manual transmission, air conditioning, side airbags, AM/FM/cassette stereo, central locking, security alarm, heated power outside mirrors, bud vase. **Major Options:** Turbo-diesel engine, 4-speed automatic transmission, antilock brakes, sport package, cruise control, power windows, sunroof, leather seats, heated seats.

Dream weaver

If it's smiles you want, smiles you'll get while driving Volkswagen's New Beetle. Practically everyone over 40 remembers the original Beetle. For many it's still a love affair that just goes on for no particular reason. So now they smile when they see a new one.

Although the New Beetle bears some resemblance to the original, nothing is the same. It's cleverly designed body is made of laser-welded galvanized steel, with plastic fenders. Under that lovable body is a thoroughly up-to-date VW Golf platform and powertrain. That means the engine is transversely mounted up front to drive the front wheels. And yes, the trunk is in the back now.

Three engines are available. The most popular is expected to be a 2.0-liter, 115 hp in-line four. For about $800, those who still care about fuel economy can opt for a 1.9-liter, 90 hp turbo diesel. New to the engine lineup is a 1.8-liter turbo-charged four, the same one available in the Passat and Audi A4. A 5-speed manual and 4-speed automatic are offered on all engines.

Wide doors make access to the front seats remarkably easy. Upfront

head, leg, and shoulder room are generous. The front buckets have large, firm cushions, with a clever mechanism for adjusting the seats up and down. The view from the front seats is somewhat radical. The entire theme is a blend of retro accents and modern materials. The windshield is beyond reach, and the top of the dash is large enough to be minivan-like. Instruments are located in one large pod. A large speedometer is flanked by a tiny fuel gauge and tachometer. Front seats slide and tilt for access to the rear. However, getting to the back seat is coupe-like difficult. Once there, most will find head and leg room skimpy at best. The cargo space is also small, but can be more than doubled by folding down the rear seatback.

The New Beetle is a delight to drive. Acceleration is better (and more fun) with the manual transmission, but even with the automatic, it feels better than it really is. Although the gasoline engine is a better performer, the diesel does a credible job. Its torque at low engine speed helps compensate for less power. Steering is quick and light. Driven hard, the Beetle feels like a Golf – and that's not a bad thing. Quick turns bring on a bit of body roll, but things are never out of control. Considering the good handling manners, the ride is surprisingly good.

Brake performance is somewhat disappointing. The 4-wheel discs took 145 feet to stop from 60 mph using full braking effort. The large glass area makes visibility good in all directions. Wind and road noise are minimal, but the engine is a steady drone at highway speeds.

The New Beetle may be a little radical, but this affordable little sweetheart has done more to improve Volkswagen's corporate image than anything in recent memory. The folks at VW are smiling too. **D.V.S.**

Specifications of Test Vehicle

Model: New Beetle

Exterior Dimensions	
Wheelbase	98.9 in.
Overall Length	161.1 in.
Overall Width	67.9 in.
Overall Height	59.5 in.
Curb Weight	2800 lbs.
Interior Dimensions	
Seating Capacity	4
Head Room	F: 42.0/R: 34.0 in.
Leg Room	F: 45.5/R: 23.0 in.
Cargo Room	10.3 cu.ft.
Engine	
Displacement	2.0L I-4
Horsepower	115@5200 rpm
Torque, lb-ft.	122@2600 rpm
Performance	
0-60 mph, acceleration	10.1 sec.
60-0 mph, braking	145 ft.
Turning Circle	35.4 ft.
EPA City/Highway	23/29 mpg.
Test Mileage	25.3
Fuel Tank Capacity	14.5 gal.

Counterpoint

Curvy flanks, arched roof, giant wheels: it's hard to resist the bait thrown out by this young German. And how can you not smile when you see Volkswagen's range of colors, rivaled only by a pack of Smarties? The enchantment continues once you open the doors to contemplate an imaginative, sunny, and flowery (each New Beetle has a flower vase in it) interior.

Three dashboard indicators vie for space in a cluster festooned with warning lights. Of course the speedometer takes precedence over the tachometer and gas gauge, positioned at the bottom but nevertheless perfectly visible. The same thing can't be said for the front-end of the vehicle, however, mostly because of the instrument panel's astonishing depth. While this does makes some kinds of maneuvers harder, it would be unfair to peg it as a major drawback since the driver eventually ends up getting his or her proper bearings.

The New Beetle is no lightweight model. So despite a manual transmission, it takes a little more than 10 seconds to get from 0 to 60 mph, not to mention the fact that fuel consumption is not very convincing either. Volkswagen suggests that owners quench the engine's thirst with Super gasoline, which may provide better combustion but also costs more.

Well perched on huge 16-inch wheels, the New Beetle takes corners well and handles very predictably. In addition, its short turning radius makes it nice and agile, a quality that is enhanced by the excellently gauged steering system. But don't judge a book by its cover: the New Beetle balks at being treated like a toy and it signals its disapproval with a perceptible reluctance to change courses quickly. But the biggest source of concern is the new-age Bug's low ground clearance (identical to the Miata's), enough to make drivers afraid of getting stuck when roads are snow-covered.

In short, the New Beetle can't claim to be completely functional. But then again, does it have to be?

E.L.

PRICES

$15,000

$20,000

Volkswagen New Beetle
$15,700

WARRANTY

Bumper-to-bumper
2/24,000

Power Train
2/24,000

Rust-through
12/Unlimited

OTHER TO CONSIDER

None

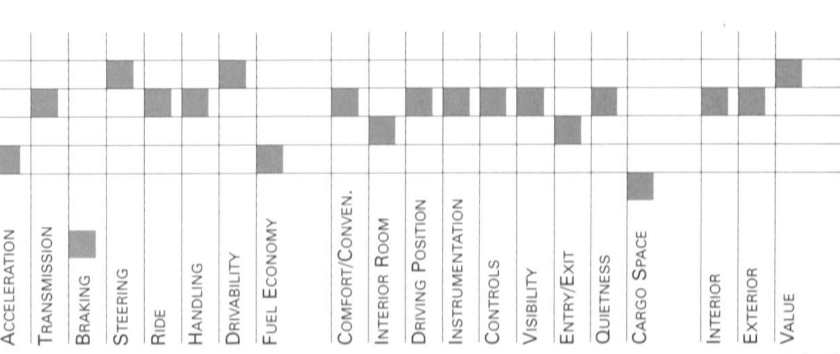

Volvo S80

New for 99

New model replaces the 90 series

Pros

Powertrain performance
Ride/handling
Comfort/convenience
Safety features

Cons

None

Equipment

Major Standard Equipment: 2.9 liter I-6 engine, 4-speed automatic transmission, antilock brakes, traction control, side-impact head protection curtain, dual-zone climate control, AM/FM/CD audio system, power seats/windows/locks/mirrors, memory seats, cruise control, trip computer, tilt/telescope wheel, alloy wheels. **T6 Adds:** 2.8 liter I-6 twin turbo engine, Geartronic automatic transmission, fog lights, walnut inlays, premium audio system. **Major options:** Sunroof, security system, in-dash CD changer, navigation system, 17 in. alloy wheels, leather interior,

PRICES
$40,000
$45,000
S80 4-door
$35,820
S80 T6 4-door
$40,385

WARRANTY
Bumper-to-bumper
4/50,000
Power Train
4/50,000
Rust-through
8/Unlimited

OTHER TO CONSIDER
Audi A6 S
BMW 528 i

The new image leader

The folks at Volvo are determined to change their stodgy image. First it was the C70 that looked nothing like anything Volvo ever built before. Now it's the S80, with dramatic new styling, impressive performance, the largest interior of any Volvo, and an industry-leading array of safety features. Although not promoted as a direct replacement, the S90 and V90 will disappear from Volvo's lineup as the S80 is introduced.

The S80 comes in two variations – a well-equipped base model with a normally aspirated in-line six-cylinder engine, and the slightly upscale T6 with its twin-turbo six. A conventional 4-speed automatic transmission is standard equipment on the base S80, while the T6 gets what Volvo calls Geartronic – a 4-speed automatic with a feature for manually changing gears if desired. A manual transmission is not offered. Both models feature antilock brakes and traction control.

In addition to the standard array of front and side airbags, the S80 has an inflatable side curtain that pops into place at the onset of a side collision to protect the door-side occupants, both front and rear. A new whiplash protection system in the front seats uses a mechanism that permits the back to slide rearward and then downward on impact. The idea is to limit the forces on the body and minimize the catapulting motion that causes whiplash.

Inside, driver and passengers are treated to firm, supportive seats with plenty of leg and head room. Even the rear seat has room to stretch out. The instrument cluster features easy-to-read gauges and two windows that display trip computer and other often-used information. The flat center console has rather unconventional audio and vent controls. Even so, the controls are intuitive and easy to operate. A surprising number of cupholders are built into the lower part of the center console and the door panels. Trunk space is large and well-shaped, with a low liftover for easy loading. The rear seatback folds down to make additional space for long items like skies.

On the road, the S80 feels strong and solid. The twin-turbo-equipped T6 is a delight to drive. The engine is smooth, quiet, and responds almost instantly to a touch of the accelerator. Turbo lag is minimal, and can be noticed only during all-out acceleration from a stop. Full torque is on hand at only 2000 rpm, and sprints to 60 mph can be done in less than 7 seconds. The brakes felt better than they really were – measured stopping distances were just average. Steering is light and accurate, but as in most high-horsepower front wheel drives, hard acceleration is accompanied by torquesteer. The ride is just a little on the firm side, but never harsh. Quick turns offer no handling surprises. In fact, spirited driving on twisty, hilly roads brings out the best in the S80.

With its up-to-date looks, impressive performance, and luxury features, the new S80 is going to give the folks at Acura, BMW, and Lexus something to worry about. **D.V.S.**

Specifications of Test Vehicle

Model: S80 T6

Exterior Dimensions	
Wheelbase	109.9 in.
Overall Length	189.8 in.
Overall Width	72.1 in.
Overall Height	57.2 in.
Curb Weight	3600 lbs.
Interior Dimensions	
Seating Capacity	5
Head Room	F: 39.0/R:37.5 in.
Leg Room	F: 44.5/R:27.5 in.
Cargo Room	21 cu.ft.
Engine	
Displacement	2.8L I-6 Twin turbo
Horsepower	268@5800 rpm
Torque, lb-ft.	280@2000 rpm
Performance	
0-60 mph, acceleration	6.8 sec.
60-0 mph, braking	127 ft.
Turning Circle	38.1 ft.
EPA City/Highway	18/26 mpg.
Test Mileage	22.5
Fuel Tank Capacity	21.1 gal.

Ratings

Group	Category	Rating
Over The Road	Acceleration	10
	Transmission	9
	Braking	6
	Steering	8
	Ride	8
	Handling	9
	Drivability	9
	Fuel Economy	5
Passenger Environment	Comfort/Conven.	9
	Interior Room	8
	Driving Position	9
	Instrumentation	8
	Controls	9
	Visibility	8
	Entry/Exit	9
	Quietness	9
	Cargo Space	9
Workmanship	Interior	9
	Exterior	9
	Value	8

168

Volvo

C70

New for 99

Convertible version

Pros

Irresistible performance capabilities
Elegant looks
Manufacturing quality

Cons

Seat belts not height adjustable
Poorly matched automatic transmission
Heavy steering system at low speeds

Equipment

Major Standard Equipment: 2.4-liter I-5, manual transmission, 4-wheel antilock disc brakes, automatic air conditioning, rear defroster, headlight washers, rear fog light, cruise control, tilt steering wheel, power seats, leather upholstery, AM/FM/cassette stereo, power windows, power locks, remote keyless entry, power heated mirrors, power moonroof, aluminum wheels. **Major Options:** Automatic transmission, traction control, heated seats, larger tires.

This, a Volvo?!

A bit as if the annulment of its marriage with Renault had given it the urge to flirt, Europe's largest builder of mid-size wagons is introducing a new look that's a welcome change from the "Scandinavian cupboard" style featured for too long on its products. Before the astonishing S80, Volvo brought us the C70, a coupe intended to spark emotion and sheer pleasure, but without breaking with the make's tradition of safety and practicality.

Doors open onto a massive instrument panel that weighs down the passenger compartment. However, some

controls feature an appealing design and incorporate some of the latest concepts in ergonomics. The two sculpted bucket seats provide a delightful driving position; unfortunately seat belts are not height adjustable and the right-hand windshield wiper produces a blind spot that can be a considerable hindrance in bad weather. Rear seats can accommodate two adults, but head room is at a premium. The trunk is amazingly deep, but the tail light design makes its opening smaller. Lastly, a word on the sound system: the C70 is the first standard model to offer Dolby Surround Sound (versions with the new feature can be recognized by the loudspeaker positioned high on the instrument panel and a compact disc changer built into the radio space).

The underbelly of this Swedish beauty could give you goose bumps: a turbocharged five-cylinder (236-hp), a manual transmission (the automatic alternative is not as good a match for the engine and Volvo has already indicated that it will be replaced with a semiautomatic), a Sport chassis, and low-profile tires. Most impressive on the first tryout are this model's surprising progressiveness and the drivetrain's energetic acceleration. The next surprise is a steering system that can be heavy at low speeds, calling for more muscle power on winding roads. The huge tires (18 in. rims are even available as an option) postpone the drive system's tendency to understeer and have very little effect on comfort. However, the C70 really shines at high speeds on straight stretches. Wheels with well-distanced spokes let brakes breathe easy, but the pedal on the test drive model called for a foot of steel.

The C70 lends itself well to just about every excess that's part of passionate automobile driving. And coming from a Nordic manufacturer, that's quite a feat. **E.L.**

Prices

$39,000
$45,000

2-door coupe
$38,995

Coupe LPT
$37,570

Coupe HPT
$40,945

Convertible
$43,970

Warranty

(years/miles)

Bumper-to-bumper
4/50,000

Powertrain
4/50,000

Rust-through
8/unlimited

Other to Consider

BMW 323 is

Mercedes CLK

Specifications of Test Vehicle

Model: C70 HPT

Exterior Dimensions	
Wheelbase	104.9 in.
Overall length	185.7 in.
Overall width	71.5 in.
Overall height	55.7 in.
Curb weight	3,350 lb.
Interior Dimensions	
Seating capacity	4
Head room	F:37.4/R:36.6 in.
Leg room	F:41.3/R:34.6 in.
Cargo room	13.1 cu. ft.
Engine	
Displacement	I-5 2.4 L.
Horsepower	236 @ 5,100 rpm
Torque, lb-ft.	243 @ 2,700 rpm
Performance	
0-60 mph, acceleration	6.9 sec.
60-0 mph, braking	115 ft.
Turning circle	38.4 ft.
EPA city/highway	19/25 mpg
Test mileage	NA
Fuel tank capacity	18.5 gal.

Group	Category	Rating (1–10)
Over The Road	Acceleration	10
	Transmission	9
	Braking	8
	Steering	8
	Ride	8
	Handling	9
	Drivability	9
	Fuel Economy	5
Passenger Environment	Comfort/Conven.	9
	Interior Room	7
	Driving Position	9
	Instrumentation	8
	Controls	7
	Visibility	7
	Entry/Exit	6
	Quietness	9
	Cargo Space	6
Workmanship	Interior	9
	Exterior	9
	Value	6

Ratings **158**

Volvo S70 / V70

New for 99

No changes

Pros

Roominess
Choice of models
Sturdy body

Cons

Marginal 2.4-liter engine
Sensitive rear suspension (wagon)
Disappointing automatic transmission

Equipment

Major Standard Equipment
2.4-liter I-5, manual transmission, 4-wheel antilock disc brakes, dual-temperature air conditioning, tilt and telescope steering wheel, power locks, remote keyless entry, power windows, power heated mirrors. **GT adds:** Power moonroof, power driver's seat. **GLT adds:** More powerful 2.4-liter I-5, automatic air conditioning. **T5 adds:** Even more powerful 2.3-liter I-5, power passenger's seat. **AWD adds:** Heated front seats and al wheel drive. **XC adds:** CD charger, raised suspension.

PRICES
$27,000
$42,000

S70 4-door $26,985
V70 4-door $28,285
S70 GT $29,540
V70 GT $30,840
S70 GLT $32,440
V70 GLT $33,740
S70 T5 $34,010
V70 T5 $35,310
V70 AWD $34,420
V70 XC AWD $37,385
V70 R AWD $40,995

WARRANTY (years/miles)
Bumper-to-bumper 4/50,000
Powertrain 4/50,000
Rust-through 8/unlimited

OTHER TO CONSIDER
Acura 3.2 TL
Saab 9-5

A trip to the Fountain of Youth

New names (S70, V70), a more carefully sculptured look and interiors that have been revamped almost entirely are the ingredients that spell a longer career for the famous Scandinavian car builder's most popular sedans and wagons. Last year the 850 underwent a total of 1,800 modifications (and no, we didn't count them one by one) before it earned its new numeric moniker.

Volvo deigners have finally designed to put away their T-squares for a while. Now the instrument panel blends into door panels; the still oversized controls are more comfortable to the touch, and wood inlays are more common and warmer looking (except for the pale birch, which is just as ugly as it's always been). This interior has an intimate and very well-finished environment. Bucket seats, another new feature, are exquisitely comfortable and lateral support has improved. Front and rear seats are roomy and the wagon version's trunk (now known under the letter V) is big and easy to access.

Regardless of the packaging, all models come with the same transverse 2.4-liter five-cylinder. Just peppy enough in the normally aspirated version, the engine gets a swift kick in the right place when it's teamed up with a turbocharger. This accessory's magic brings total horsepower up to 240 in the extreme T packaging, which translates into astonishing acceleration power and sure head-turning capacity since, in white, black, or red, a Volvo wagon that can swallow the asphalt effortlessly is something that won't go unnoticed. But like the AWD, the T is an exceptional vehicle and realistically, the success of this series depends on the base and GLT models, both of which have reliable and neutral roadholding ability. The wagon's rear suspension is jumpy when the trunk is empty and, overall, the 70 Series doesn't take to winding roads very well. Even though it got a bit more horsepower last year, the base engine is very low-key and the GLT's unit (coupled with a 190-hp low-pressure turbo) is better and offers more convincing acceleration and pickup. The automatic transmission is very good at its job and the five-speed is the best choice.

The versatility of Volvo's 70 Series is still its best quality and it certainly has a lot to do with this wagon's popularity

E.L.

Specifications of Test Vehicle

Model: Volvo V70

Exterior Dimensions	
Wheelbase	104.3 in.
Overall length	185.9 in.
Overall width	69.3 in.
Overall height	56.2 in.
Curb weight	3,750 lb.
Interior Dimensions	
Seating capacity	5
Head room	F:39.1/R:37.9 in.
Leg room	F:41.4/R:35.2 in.
Cargo room	37.1 cu.ft.
Engine	
Displacement	I-5 2.4 L.
Horsepower	190 @ 5,200 rpm
Torque, lb-ft.	199 @ 1,800 rpm
Performance	
0-60 mph, acceleration	8.3 sec.
60-0 mph, braking	123 ft.
Turning circle	37.7 ft.
EPA city/highway	20/28 mpg
Test mileage	25 mpg
Fuel tank capacity	18.5 gal

Ratings

Category	Rating
Over The Road	
Acceleration	8
Transmission	9
Braking	6
Steering	8
Ride	7
Handling	8
Drivability	9
Fuel Economy	6
Passenger Environment	
Comfort/Conven.	9
Interior Room	9
Driving Position	9
Instrumentation	8
Controls	7
Visibility	7
Entry/Exit	9
Quietness	9
Cargo Space	10
Workmanship	
Interior	9
Exterior	9
Value	9

Ratings 165

Autograph®

Performance
Specifications
Passenger comfort
New for 99
Pros and Cons
Equipment
Engine
Ratings

Acura
Aston Martin
Dodge
Ferrari
Lamborghini
Lotus

Road test review

Acura

NSX-T

NEW FOR 99

No changes

PROS

Surprisingly docile
Admirably well-designed interior
Exotic and reliable

CONS

Sometimes tricky handling
Front-end lifting at high speeds
Prestige attached to the make

Showing its age

PRICES

NSX
$85,000 (est)

NSX-T
$89,00 (est)

Ten years ago, the future looked very rosy: Honda was chalking up Formula I wins and championships galore and the Japanese builder was dreaming of triumph on more ordinary roads with its NSX, later nicknamed the "Japanese Ferrari". Like the Lexus LS 400 before it, the general opinion was that the NSX would make major European car builders eat humble pie. And to the NSX's credit, we must say that the Porsche 911, its main rival, is the guilty party in making this model look a tad outdated.

The NSX has two seats in the purest sense of the term and its satin soft cockpit barely offers more head or leg room than that of small and medium-sized cars. Its low-set seats, gracefully sculpted in the ergonomic tradition of true sports cars, are designed to facilitate good support-while still allowing the slightly stocky to feel completely at ease. Visibility isn't perfect, but in what sports car is it? Plus the air-conditioning has to be on high to clear out the stifling heat of the interior. Finally, as space is limited, there are just two small baggage compartments, one in front, the other behind.

Someone once said: "real sports cars should accelerate as fast as they brake." Acura must have been listening, because last year, it not only boosted the NSX-T's displacement to 3.0 liter from 3.2, it also changed the braking system. People say the NSX-T is docile, which is true. This sports car is quite civilized next to many of its more physically demanding rivals. And, while it is docile, drivers will quickly reach their limits not necessarily the same as those of the car. At this point, things could go haywire, because a mid-engine car like this is not very forgiving of a beginner's mistakes. If you take your foot off the pedal during a hard turn, you may feel like the brake lights are spinning toward you. The NSX-T quickly becomes lighter and less stable at higher speeds. Faster than 120 mph, the front end loses its balance and requires constant vigilance. The six gears are properly staggered, while the automatic SportShift transmission makes it easy getting around town, like offering you manual control when you want it. **E.L.**

SPECIFICATIONS OF TEST VEHICLE	
MODEL: NSX-T	
Exterior dimensions	
Wheelbase	99,6 in.
Overall lenght	174.2 in.
Overall width	71.3 in.
Overall height	46.1 in.
Curb weight	3066 lb
Engine	
Displacement	V6 3,2 L.
Horsepower	290 @ 7,100
Torque	224 @ 5,500
Weight/power ratio	10.5
Performance	
0-60 mph, acceleration	5.4 sec.
60-0 mph, braking	NT

Aston Martin

DB7

New for 99

No changes

Pros

Powerful braking
Prestige make
Electrifying performance

Cons

Cramped rear seats
Limited distribution
Hefty price tag

Letter and word games

After changing hands time and time again over a period of decades, Aston Martin seems to have found the dream partner in Ford and the happy outcome of this union couldn't be better reflected than it is in the DB7.

Its resemblance with the XK8 is annoying to a lot of people, all the more since the Coventry feline costs half the price of its illustrious compatriot from Newport-Pagnell. But that hasn't stopped Aston Martin from selling 700 units in 1997 (a record), including one now owned by none other than Prince Charles.

Both versions of this model are 2+2 models, although rear-seat passengers would be best advised to keep their knees curled close to their bodies. Front power seats are low, provide good support, and feature buttery Connoly-hide leather. They are positioned between large side windows and a high center console that can easily accommodate either the automatic transmission gear box or the five-speed manual transmission's lever. Thick carpets and walnut inlays are proof of the traditional luxury finish and comfort so dear to the British. Instruments are classic, with the tachometer surrounded by only four secondary gauges. The steering wheel is wide and holds well and the view from behind it, along the long and sleek hood, is positively inebriating. The two-tone color schemes may be a bit excessive, but that's a matter of taste. In short, this kind of vehicle is perfect as long as you don't want to go unnoticed.

The DB7 (DB are the initials of David Brown, who owned the make from 1947 to 1972) is still powered by an in-line six-cylinder engine. The unit is a 24-valve, 3.2-liter (developed by Jaguar... well, well!), supercharged to produce 325 horses. Its strong torque and above-average flexibility provide a cushiony ride that's best in the city and when needed, spell strong acceleration as well. The low-profile Bridgestone tires and independent front and rear suspensions provide reassuring roadholding capabilities and the huge disc brakes and ABS system have no trouble at all bringing this vehicle to a full stop.

The DB7's electrifying performance levels are equalled only by its exclusiveness. Think about it: fewer than 2,000 Aston Martins have been sold in North America since 1950. **E.L.**

PRICE
$130,000

Specifications of Test Vehicle

Model: DB7

Exterior dimensions	
Wheelbase	102 in.
Overall lenght	182.9 in.
Overall width	72 in.
Overall height	48.7 in.
Curb weight	3890 lb.
Engine	
Displacement	I-6 3,2 L.
Horsepower	335 @ 6,000
Torque	361 @ 3,000
Power/weight ratio	11.61
Performance	
0-60 mph, acceleration	6.3 sec.
60-0 mph, braking	NT

Dodge

Viper

New for 99
Leather option available
18-inch wheels
Standard electric side view mirrors

Pros
Electrifying performance
Price/performance ratio
Consistent coupe version

Cons
For strong-armed drivers only
Complicated roof (RT/10)
Acrobatic driving position

An irresistible temptation

PRICE (1998)
GTS
$66,000
RT/10
$64,000

Young drivers slaver over the Viper, but more often than not its buyers belong to the male, gray-haired crowd (only 6% of buyers are women). Those nostalgic for American-style sporty driving find some comfort behind the wheel of this model, a veritable caricature of the glory days of sports cars. The feeling is easy to understand: according to the USAC, the Viper is fastest at getting to 100 mph (14.78 seconds) and the loan you'll need to get it will look like an automobile loan, not a mortgage.

If you're a contortionist, getting into a roadster is a good way to keep your skills sharp. And finding the ideal driving position is an equally efficient way to stay flexible. Pedals positioned off-center and towards the left (now adjustable), a limited number of seat adjustment possibilities and the fact that the driver has no footrest are all factors that add to general discomfort. However, in other respects the roadster has made significant progress since it first appeared. To optimize economy and versatility (the roadster and the coupe share the same assembly line), the RT/10 uses the GTS coupe's door panels, which already include door handles worthy of the name and electric windshield wiper controls. On the other hand, we're still waiting on improvements to the horrendous soft top and its maddeningly complicated design. Happy are those who can't stand looking tousled: the GTS coupe and its ample headroom is available. As a premium the coupe even comes with a storage space behind the two front seats, likely big enough to handle a briefcase or two. In 1999, the RT/10 and GTS have a lot of good news for consumers. First of all, if buyers are willing to pay, extra bucket seats can be enveloped in rich leather by Conolly (official supplier of Jaguar), and the dashboard features brushed aluminium appliqués.

Under an exterior that indicates that this automobile's technology may be outdated, the Viper has evolved further than you might think. Its insides are technologically advanced and don't forget that its big truck-size V-10 was developed by the designers responsible for the unit that powers the Lamborghini. The small and winding test track in Chelsea, Michigan is the perfect testing ground to show off all of the Viper's dynamic qualities. However, it does give drivers a good idea of the V10's potential. Its fabulous torque catapults the Viper out of the track's tight hairpin turns, provided you can gauge the gas pedal properly (especially if the road surface is wet). Failing to do so could well put you into a tailspin. Acceleration power is impressive, even a bit on the violent side. Using the clutch and manual six-speed transmission requires a strong hand — for those who are interested the lever now features better ergonomics — and drivers would be well advised to avoid traffic jams. Lastly, the steering system and suspension combine to provide very accurate feedback on even the smallest of road defects.

Is this model an instrument of torture or a mean and lean sports car? Well, the Viper is a bit of both. But it's hard not to like this beast. Just ask Eve! **E.L.**

Specifications of Test Vehicle

Model: Viper RT/10

Exterior dimensions	
Wheelbase	96.2 in.
Overall lenght	176.7 in.
Overall width	75.7 in.
Overall height	47 in.
Curb weight	3319 lb.
Engine	
Displacement	V10 8 L
Horsepower	450 @ 5.200
Torque	490 @ 3,700
Power/weight ratio	7.37
Performance	
0-60 mph, acceleration	5.0 sec.
60-0 mph, braking	NT

Ferrari

F355

New for 99

F1 model

Pros

Good semi-automatic transmission
Docile handling
Impressive refinement level

Cons

Model scheduled for replacement
Cramped interior
Noisy and slow reverse (F1)

Italian rumors

The most attractive and least expensive of the Ferrari models is back on the road for one last time, since its replacement (code name: 131) will be launched in the fall of 1999. In the meantime, the rumor mill is running furiously: a six-speed sequential transmission, an aluminum body, a 400-hp engine, no more hidden headlights. Only one thing is sure: the new model will be signed Pininfarina.

For its farewell tour, the F355 is available in four models. The Berlinetta, GTS and Spider are already familiar to us, the newcomer being the little F1, so named because it features an exclusive semi-automatic transmission inspired by the unit that Schumacher and Irvine use on their F1 race cars. Gears are shifted via steering wheel-mounted controls, just like they are on Grand Prix racers, so as a result there is no clutch pedal; drivers use only two aluminum pedals. Shifting into reverse is (too) slow and is done using a minuscule lever positioned exactly where the gear shift lever is usually found.

Now let's take a look at less technical features. When you look at the F355's two bucket seats, unless you're anorexic, you wonder how you're ever going to fit into them. Clearly, their narrowness and design is intended for skinny people only. Luckily, conscientious importers will ask for your measurements before ordering your Berlinetta or GTS, the only versions available with "oversized" seats. If you fit in the "out of the ordinary" category, you'll have to forego the pleasures of driving a Spider, reserved for the slim and slender only.

Heavier, the Spider is still every bit as rigid as the GTS (removable roof) version and has the exact same exquisite handling as the Berlinetta. All three models share the same 3.5-liter V-8 with five valves per cylinder, eager to leave it up to the driver to decide how to use the 375-hp output. Power is transferred to rear wheels via an astonishingly civilized six-speed manual gearbox. On the other hand, besides the anti-lock brakes mounted on all four models - with an ABS system that can be deactivated much to the pleasure of F1 driving purists - potential buyers should note that the standard steering system on the F355 is overly assisted and not direct enough.

And the F1? Sheer magic. At the wheel of this version drivers need never take their foot off the gas pedal, gears shift as quickly as they do with a conventional manual transmission. However, to keep jostling to a minimum we suggest that you do ease up on the accelerator as you shift. The only flaw: shifting into reverse is slow as slow can be and accompanied by a quite worrisome grinding noise - proof that there's always room for improvement no matter how good it gets. **E.L.**

PRICE
$131,325

Specifications of Test Vehicle

Model: F355

Exterior dimensions	
Wheelbase	96,5 in.
Overall lenght	167,3 in.
Overall width	74,8 in.
Overall height	46,1 in.
Curb weight	3290 lb
Engine	
Displacement	V8 3.5 L.
Horsepower	375 @ 8,250
Torque	268 @ 6,000
Weight/power ratio	8.77
Performance	
0-60 mph, acceleration	5.2 sec.
60-0 mph, braking	NT

Ferrari

550 Maranello

NEW FOR 99

No changes

PROS

Staggering performance
Easy to drive
Constantly improved finishing

CONS

Astronomical price
Balky transmission
No semi-automatic transmission

PRICE
$201,600

Regressing?

The Ferrari 550 Maranello's arrival on the market has a great deal of ink and saliva flowing. With this new model, Ferrari has set aside the spectacular mid-engine technology borrowed from the racing world and has decided on a more conventional front-engine configuration. The Ferrari 550 Maranello still boasts a very refined design concept, but the purists among the make's fans invariably see this model as a regression.

There's no question that before the 550, Maranello Ferrari had already demonstrated its expertise in front-engine architecture with the superb 456 GT, now known as the 456 M. But since it was a true 2+2, the need to provide enough room for passengers made it impossible to use a mid-engine solution. In contrast, the 550 Maranello is a two-seater in the strictest sense of the word. If you compare the two models, you'll see that in general they have the same features, with the exception of the Maranello's 485-hp 65 degree V-12, as compared to the 456 M's 442-hp unit. Both models have a six-speed transmission (unlike the 550 Maranello, the 456 M also comes with an automatic transmission) located over rear wheels to provide better weight distribution.

The 550 Maranello has a shorter wheelbase, but its passenger compartment is remarkable, mainly due to excellent ergonomics. Its wide and deep seats are exceptionally comfortable and, generally speaking, progress has been made in the area of construction quality and finishing. The first things you'll notice about the 550 Maranello are its easy access, good visibility and extremely good instrumentation. Just close the door and you're ready to go to the ends of the earth with this new Ferrari!

The first impression when you test drive this model is shaped by smooth controls, a smooth clutch and smooth shifting. This Ferrari is a modern automobile on a par with the automotive industry's best references, whether from BMW or Mercedes, not to mention all the distinction and raw power that comes with Cavillino drivetrain technology. The V-12 purrs in the lower rpms and growls affectionately as it climbs higher. On board, indicator needles gyrate at the least provocation, but the 550 Maranello offers such consistent handling that domesticating its power is never a problem. However, the six-speed transmission is harder to tame and calls for a hand of steel to guide the lever through the nickel-covered gear box. As docile as it is feline and racy, the Ferrari 550 Maranello has absolutely staggering efficiency on the road and is unquestionably one of Ferrari's most impressive accomplishments. All it needs is the superb F1 semi-automatic! Wonder when we can expect it? **E.L.**

SPECIFICATIONS OF TEST VEHICLE

MODEL: 550 MARANELLO

Exterior dimensions	
Wheelbase	98.4 in.
Overall lenght	179.1 in.
Overall width	76.2 in.
Overall height	50.3 in.
Curb weight	3725 lb.
Engine	
Displacement	V12 5,5 L.
Horsepower	485 @ 5,000
Torque	419 @ 5,000
Power/weight ratio	7,68
Performance	
0-60 mph, acceleration	4.6 sec.
60-0 mph, braking	NT

Ferrari 456M

New for 99
M version
New V-12 ignition sequence

Pros
Exquisite styling
Consistently better finishing
Civilized ride

Cons
Automatic transmission limitations
Astronomical price
Incredible repair costs

A salute to artistry

If they could come back, do you think that Da Vinci, Picasso and Gaugin would redo their works of art? Never, you might say, and no doubt you're right. You never rework a masterpiece for fear of robbing it of its magic. Yet the Pininfarina team, which gave shape and color to several generations of Ferrari models, has been successful in revising one of its many milestone accomplishments: the 456. The operation began by dropping the GT suffix and replacing it with the letter M (for Modificata) and continued with the removal of the vents that used to mark the hood (now made of carbon fiber) and the addition of two fog lamps to the grille. And the 456's insides are equally attractive, believe me.

Pininfarina, Ferrari's official styling genius, deserves a monument for his 456M. A sublime work of art on four wheels catches attention from all sides even before it has the chance to show its real prowess out on the road. All those who dare to claim that the 456M doesn't send shivers up their spines, raise your hands! And this model is just as magnificent on the inside, although it seems to bask in the nostalgia reminiscent of the 1960s, as witnessed by its circular air vents.

This 2+2 coupe has four leather bucket seats; in the front, they have been redesigned to offer more comfort, but traveling in the rear isn't a very pleasant prospect. To maintain the proper weight distribution on the 456M with automatic transmission (weight distribution has gone from 51/49 to 49/51), Ferrari has mounted the gearbox/differential duo on the rear end. However wise this decision may have been, it cuts down on trunk volume.

Ferrari freaks will be outraged by the decision to match the 456's V-12 with an automatic transmission, but the truth is that 90% of the 456s sold in North America have one. All we can do is deplore the fact that it doesn't show as much refinement as everything else on this car does. First of all, it has only four speeds - but much worse, it blocks the engine at 6,750 rpm, while the manual transmission gives it free rein up to 7,200 rpm. In contrast, it's best appreciated in bottleneck traffic and is much better than the six-speed transmission, whose clutch is a real challenge if you don't have a foot and leg of steel.

Still, remember that the 456M is not for homebodies. Its acceleration power can rip your heart, its pickup is terrifying and its top speed will leave you gasping for breath. However, it still has a friendly personality and, unlike other products of the same make, you can take it on long outings without the fear that driving it will wear you down and out. This is true because of an even more effective suspension, with variable-travel shock absorbers that offer more adjustment possibilities. Automatic level control also ensures that your (small) rear-seat passenger won't throw off the car's balance. Lastly, and this is good news, the 456M has inherited the traction control system that used to be available exclusively on the 550 Maranello.

Obedient and well-mannered, the 456M can be driven with the latest high-tech athletic footwear or comfy Gucci loafers - it all depends on your mood!

E.L.

PRICE (1998)
$219,400

Specifications of Test Vehicle

Model: F456M

Exterior dimensions	
Wheelbase	102.4 in.
Overall lenght	186.2 in.
Overall width	75.6 in.
Overall height	51.2 in.
Curb weight	3900 lb
Engine	
Displacement	V12 5.5 L.
Horsepower	436 @ 6,250
Torque	398 @ 4,500
Weight/power ratio :	
Performance	
0-60 mph, acceleration	5,1 sec.
60-0 mph, braking	NT

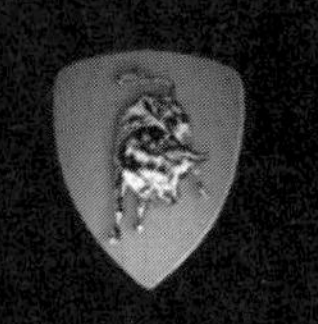

Lamborghini

Diablo

NEW FOR 99

SV version

PROS

Exceptional performance capabilities
Ability to fascinate
Exoticism

CONS

Overpowering transmission
Reliability record
Astronomical price

A German toreador enters the ring

PRICE
$279,400

Ciao to Burma, Lamborghini has changed hands - again. From now on, the famous "furious bull" from San Agatha will have Audi as its toreador. From wherever he may be and with the Ingolstadath firm now at the helm of his empire, Ferrucio Lamborghini must rejoice at the battle that looms between the Volkswagen group (which owns Audi) and the Fiat kingdom (which owns Ferrari). This is a battle that couldn't be played out when Lamborghini was alive, not because of a lack of ideas but because of a lack of financial means.

According to rumors, Audi is on the verge of giving the go-ahead to the L140 (known as the P140 in Chrysler's time), a Lambo available at less than $200,000 and designed with the F355 as its target. On the other hand, the future of the firm's projected utility vehicle (LM03) is in some doubt. And what about the Diablo? A new SV version (with rear-wheel drive) has joined the Roadster (with all-wheel drive) and both are awaiting a restyling that should come some time soon.

Three times in its history (1965, 1968 and 1980), Lamborghini tested public opinion by launching convertible prototypes. But despite the positive reaction they elicited, none reached the standard production stage - except, that is, for the Diablo Roadster, unveiled in 1991. In the past five years, several changes have been made to its original design, one being the addition of a removable roof that can be stored under the engine's redesigned hood since the 140-liter trunk is too small. To its credit the roof is easy to remove, but given its relatively large size two people should tackle it. With the exception of a radio with more power, the Roadster has the very same passenger compartment as the SV. The driving position is satisfactory even though the steering wheel and pedals are off center. Some controls meet the highest of industry standards, but others seem to be last-minute choices.

To make the most of the resources and potential available to the driver, the Diablo is energy focused. The V-12's angry growl goes straight to your heart and acceleration and pick-up will pin you well back into your seat. The crescendo of power is interrupted only when you shift gears - and when you do, you'll need a hand of iron in a glove of steel. Besides which, you'll need good muscle tone to use the clutch. It follows that bottlenecks and Sunday-driver outings are to be avoided, especially since visibility aboard this car is virtually nonexistent. The steering system loyally feeds back every bump to the driver and the suspension jostles passengers about as soon as the asphalt is less than absolutely perfect. Luckily the Diablo has a hydraulic system to hoist ground clearance to 1.5 inches.

To appreciate the Diablo, you really have to have the money and the will to dominate it. If you don't, then don't expect to have much fun. **E.L.**

SPECIFICATIONS OF TEST VEHICLE

MODEL: DIABLO ROADSTER

Exterior dimensions	
Wheelbase	104.3 in.
Overall lenght	175.9 in.
Overall width	80.2 in.
Overall height	43.8 in.
Curb weight	3584.4 lb.
Engine	
Displacement	V12 5.7 L.
Horsepower	530 @ 7,100
Torque	445 @ 5,500
Weight/power ratio	6.76
Performance	
0-60 mph, acceleration	4,7 sec.
60-0 mph, braking	NT

Lotus

Esprit V8

NEW FOR 99

No changes

PROS

Exoticism
Thundering performance levels

CONS

Extremely limited distribution
Renault transmission
Precarious visibility

Timeless

For those who have a passion for automobiles, the Lotus Esprit is an old acquaintance. Introduced in 1975, the British beauty still has the chiselled lines originally conferred upon it by "automobile couturier" Guiorgio. However, it has strayed somewhat from the concept developed by its creator, Colin Chapman, who wanted it to be simple, light and powered by a thundering four-cylinder. Today, tired of being criticized for its rudimentary powertrain — a supercharged four-cylinder — the Esprit now boasts a Lotus designed V-8. So the scene is set for car-lovers to meet up again with an old acquaintance that really isn't one at all.

If it's been a long time since you've sat in a Lotus, you should be pleasantly surprised. Doors open wider for easier access to the inside. However, the driving position isn't any more comfortable than it was — regardless of how luxurious the passenger compartment looks — because the huge tunnel housing the transmission and doubling as an armrest takes up a lot of vital space and forces the driver to lift his or her elbow to shift gears. In addition to the general discomfort — if not to a downright sense of insecurity — visibility to the side and rear is virtually nil, which makes some maneuvers risky at the very least.

I should tell you right now, the Esprit doesn't look its 23 years. The steering system is incredibly quick and precise. The suspension is good at handling road irregularities, but remember that this Lotus should always, always be driven with care and concentration, especially since its V-8 pushes it to the very limit. It may not sound very exciting, but this V-8 pushes you back into your seat with every change of speed. The transmission still comes from Renault and it's a major handicap for driveability. Fortunately, the ABS brakes are problem-free and ensure sure, straight-line stops.

Its very limited distribution and sparse dealership network doesn't provide the Lotus with much media visibility. Too bad! **E.L.**

PRICE
$86,000
(estimated)

SPECIFICATIONS OF TEST VEHICLE

MODEL: ESPRIT V8

Exterior dimensions	
Wheelbase	96 in.
Overall lenght	172 in.
Overall width	73.5 in,
Overall height	45.3 in.
Curb weight	3043 lb.
Engine	
Displacement	V8 3.5 L.
Horsepower :	350 @ 6,500
Torque :	400 @ 4,250
Power/weight ratio : 8.69	
Performance	
0-60 mph, acceleration	4.9 sec.
60-0 mph, braking	NT

Glossary of automotive terms

adjustable suspension control: A system that lets the driver choose the degree of firmness for the shock absorbers, from soft (to cushion bumps) to firm (to eliminate body lean on curves and corners).

all-wheel drive (AWD): A drivetrain that powers all four wheels continuously. It cannot be switched to two-wheel drive. (Compare with "four-wheel drive.")

automatic dimming mirror: A light-sensitive mirror that detects bright lights from a trailing vehicle and darkens to reduce glare.

automatic leveling suspension: A system that adjusts the pressure of air springs as necessary to compensate for sagging caused by heavy loads.

body lean: Tendency of a vehicle to heave to one side on a turn.

curb weight: A vehicle's weight ready to go, including gasoline and other fluids but not including occupants.

daytime running lights (DRLs): Front lights (usually headlights) that operate at reduced power whenever the engine is on, making the vehicle more conspicuous to other drivers and helping to prevent collisions.

disc brakes: Devices in which calipers squeeze brake pads against both sides of a disc attached to the wheel to stop a vehicle. Disc brakes are superior to drum brakes, in which curved shoes press against the inside of cup-shaped cylinder.

driver preferences: Seat position, mirror angles, radio stations, and other adjustments favored by a driver. Based on an electronic memory in some cars, the seat and other features are readjusted on command to "fit" a particular driver.

drivetrain: The engine, transmission, clutch, drive shaft, differential, and U-joints, which together generate and transfer power to the drive wheels.

dual-shift mode automatic trans- mission: A transmission that allows the driver to choose the basis for determining shift points. In a "sport" or "power" mode, for example, the transmission will upshift later (at a higher engine speed) and downshift sooner (with less accelerator pedal movement) to improve performance; in a "normal" or "economy" mode, it will upshift sooner and downshift later to improve fuel economy.

dual-temperature air conditioning: Separate controls allowing the driver and passenger to adjust air flow temperature independently for their own comfort.

fold-away mirrors: Side mirrors that swing on hinges, flexing with minor impacts from garages or other cars without breaking off.

four-wheel drive (4WD): A drivetrain that sometimes sends power to all four wheels. Part-time 4WD cannot be engaged on dry pavement or other surfaces with good traction without damaging the tires and drivetrain. Full-time 4WD can safely be engaged anytime, anywhere, either when the driver wants it or when sensors detect wheel slippage. (Compare with "all-wheel drive.")

fuel injection: A system that mixes gasoline under pressure with air before the mixture enters an engine's combustion chambers. Compared to a carburetor, it allows more precise control of the fuel-air mixture, and therefore better gas mileage and power management. Multipoint injection (MPI) has an injector for each cylinder.

gear ratio: The number of revolutions a transmission gear must make to turn a different-size gear one revolution, which affects a vehicle's acceleration and other performance characteristics.

head room: Distance from the seat to the headliner.

horizontally opposed (HO) engine: Also called a "pancake" or "boxer," a design in which pistons on one side of the engine are in the same horizontal plane as those on the other side. This design reduces engine height and lowers the center of gravity compared with other designs. (Compare "in-line" and "V.")

in-line (I) engine: A simple design in which the cylinders line up in a single, straight row. (Compare "horizontally opposed" and "V.")

integrated child safety seat: A restraint built into the rear seatback to secure and protect small children in a crash. It eliminates the need to fit a store-bought safety seat.

intermittent wipers: Windshield wipers that include an extremely low-frequency setting in which the blades pause several seconds between wipes during very light rain or mist. "Variable-intermittent wipers" allow the driver to adjust the length of the pause. "Speed-sensitive variable-intermittent wipers" wipe faster at higher vehicle speeds and more slowly at lower vehicle speeds. "Automatic variable-intermittent wipers" activate automatically in rain and adjust for the intensity of the rain.

keyless entry: A feature that operates the door locks by a sequence of numbered buttons rather than a key for added security and convenience. A "remote keyless entry" system uses an infrared signal from a key fob.

leg room: Distance from the hip joint to the ankle joint, when seated, plus 10 inches.

liftover: Distance from the ground to the lower edge of the trunk or hatch opening. The lower the liftover, the easier it is to load heavy objects.

limited-slip differential: Directs power to the drive wheel with the best traction, compared with an open differential, which sends power to the wheel with the worst traction.

locking center differential: A feature on four-wheel-drive vehicles that eliminates slippage between the front and rear wheels to improve hill climbing. It is used primarily off-road or on extremely slippery pavement.

manual-automatic transmission: A transmission that allows the driver to choose between shifting gears by hand (without a clutch pedal) or allowing the transmission to shift automatically.

minivan: A minivan with a wheelbase over 114 inches, allowing more interior room but restricting maneuverability.

naturally aspirated: An engine without a turbocharger or supercharger.

overdrive: An additional gear in most transmissions for highway cruising. It reduces engine speed below that of normal high gear for better fuel economy and less engine noise, but reduced acceleration and hill-climbing ability.

overhead cam: An engine design in which the camshaft (which opens and closes the valves in a specific sequence) is in the cylinder head, directly over the valves. It allows higher engine speeds for more power at higher engine speeds than an overhead valve engine, which has only the valves in the cylinder heads. A double-overhead cam (DOHC) has two camshafts (one for the intake valves, the other for the exhaust valves), allowing designers more freedom with other engine details, compared with a single-overhead cam (SOHC).

oversteer: A vehicle's tendency to turn more sharply than intended, causing the tail to swing wide in a rear-wheel skid. (Compare "understeer.")

pillar: Roof and windshield support. "A" pillars are in the front, between the windshield and driver/passenger window; "B" pillars are in the middle, between the driver/passenger window and the backseat windows; and "C" pillars are behind the back seat. Station wagons have "D" pillars in the rear of the cargo area.

powertrain: Engine-transmission combination.

red line: Tachometer reading showing the maximum safe engine speed.

reduced-force air bags: Air bags introduced in some '98 models, which inflate 20 to 35 percent more gently than formerly required by government rules. The air bags are intended to protect people in a crash while minimizing the possibility of injury from the explosive thrust of the air bag itself. They are sometimes referred to as "depowered," "second-generation," "next-generation," or "less forceful" air bags.

shift-on-the-fly 4WD: The ability to switch from two-wheel drive to four-wheel drive without the driver stopping the vehicle.

signal mirrors: Side mirrors that, for greater safety when changing lanes, make a car's turn signal visible to a motorist who might be in the car's left or right blind spot.

stability control: A system that applies the brake on a single wheel, as necessary, to help a driver regain control in a skid caused by oversteering or understeering on a curve.

supercharger: An air pump driven directly by the engine to force more air into the cylinders, increasing the engine's power. (Compare "turbocharger.")

theft alarm system: Security measure that includes a honking horn, flashing lights, or other audible or visual warnings of a theft or break-in.

theft deterrent system: A security measure that makes a car more difficult to steal (such as a computer chip embedded in the ignition key). It may or may not include an visual or audible alarm.

throw: Distance the gearshift lever must move to reach the next gear.

torque: An engine's turning force, measured in pounds-feet (lb-ft.), which indicates acceleration and hill-climbing ability.

torque converter: Device for multiplying the engine's torque and transmitting it to the automatic transmission, improving initial acceleration.

torque steer: The tendency of front-wheel-drive cars to pull to one side during sudden, hard acceleration.

traction control: A system that applies the brakes or reduces engine power to control wheel slippage on wet, icy, or slick surfaces.

transaxle: A single unit combining the transmission and differential, usually found in front-wheel-drive vehicles or rear-engine, rear-wheel-drive ones.

transfer case: An extra transmission on four-wheel-drive systems, which directs power to the front and rear axles and contains the gears for low-range 4WD.

trip computer: An electronic instrument that automatically calculates and displays fuel consumption, miles to travel on gas remaining in the tank, and other measurements.

truck wagon: A vehicle with the chassis of a truck and an enclosed, station-wagon-like body with a rear liftgate or tailgate.

turbocharger: An air pump driven by exhaust gas that forces more air into the cylinders, increasing the engine's power. (Compare "supercharger.")

turbo lag: The delay between the driver steeping on the accelerator and the turbocharger boosting power.

turning circle: As used in this book, the width of a street on which a car can make a U-turn without the tires touching the curb. This "curb-to-curb" turning circle differs from a "wall-to-wall" turning circle, which measures the width of a street on which a car can make a U-turn without its body touching objects along the side.

unassisted steering: A steering system in which the driver provides all the power, without any power assist.

understeer: A vehicle's tendency to resist turning and continue straight ahead in a front-wheel skid. (Compare "oversteer.")

V: An engine design in which the cylinders are arranged in two slanted rows, forming a "V"—a more compact shape than an in-line. (Compare "horizontally opposed" and "in-line.")

variable-assist power steering: A hydraulic system that changes the effort the driver must use to turn the steering wheel, depending on the speed of the engine or the speed of the vehicle. The wheel is easy to turn during parking and other low-speed maneuvers; it's more difficult to turn at highway speeds, giving the driver a better feel for the road when only slight course corrections are required.

wheelbase: The distance from the center line of the front wheels to the center line of the rear ones; the wheelbase length affects a vehicle's ride and maneuverability.

Index by make and model